NEW
DIRECTIONS
IN AMERICAN
RELIGIOUS HISTORY

EDITED BY

Harry S. Stout

D. G. Hart

NEW YORK   OXFORD   •   OXFORD UNIVERSITY PRESS   1997

Oxford University Press

Oxford   New York

Athens   Auckland   Bangkok   Bogota   Bombay   Buenos Aires
Calcutta   Cape Town   Dar es Salaam   Delhi   Florence   Hong Kong
Istanbul   Karachi   Kuala Lumpur   Madras   Madrid   Melbourne
Mexico City   Nairobi   Paris   Singapore   Taipei   Tokyo   Toronto   Warsaw

and associated companies in
Berlin   Ibadan

Published by Oxford University Press, Inc.
198 Madison Avenue, New York, New York 10016

Library of Congress Cataloging-in-Publication Data
New directions in American religious history / edited by
Harry S. Stout and D. G. Hart.
p.   cm.
Proceedings of a conference held Oct. 21–23, 1993 in Racine, Wis.
Includes bibliographical references.
ISBN 0-19-510413-7; 0-19-511213-x (pbk)
1. United States—Church history—Congresses.
2. Christianity—United States—Congresses.   I. Stout, Harry S.
II. Hart, D. G. (Darryl G.)
BR515.N47   1997
277.3—dc20   96-10983

1 3 5 7 9 8 6 4 2
Printed in the United States of America
on acid-free paper

PREFACE

⬚ ⬚ ⬚

16.81

THIS BOOK OF ESSAYS proceeds from a conference on "New Directions in American Religious History," held at the Wingspread Conference Center in Racine, Wisconsin, October 21–23, 1993. In organization and format the conference was modeled on a similar one held at Wingspread in 1977 and the book which stemmed from it, entitled *New Directions in American Intellectual History.* In both conferences, leading scholars were invited to reflect on their specialties in, respectively, American intellectual and American religious history in ways that summarized both where the field is and where it ought to move in the decades to come. Like that work, this conference was intended to tap the energies at work in a new generation of religious historians alongside the old. Four members of the 1993 seminar were present in 1977, evidencing the close connection between intellectual and religious history. But seventeen members were new, reflecting both differences in the field that have become pronounced over the past two decades and the coming of age of new scholars whose work was just beginning or not even begun in 1977.

We would like to acknowledge the valuable contributions made by the other participants at the Wingspread Conference: Paul Carter, Nathan

93694

O. Hatch, Bruce Kuklick, Mark A. Noll, George M. Marsden, Grant L. Wacker, and William R. Hutchison. We would also like to acknowledge the help of James Lewis and John M. Mulder of the Louisville Institute for the Study of Protestantism and American Culture at Louisville Presbyterian Theological Seminary for providing the funding for and offering wise counsel about this project, and Edith Blumhofer and Larry Eskridge of the Institute for the Study of American Evangelicals, which cosponsored the conference and facilitated conference arrangements. Finally, a special word of thanks to Susan J. Poulsen and M. Jon Vonracek of the Johnson Foundation, our experienced and gracious hosts, for three days of incomparable conversations in the midst of unsurpassed beauty.

New Haven, Connecticut   H. S. S.
Philadelphia, Pennsylvania   D. G. H.
October 1996

CONTENTS

NEW
DIRECTIONS
IN AMERICAN
RELIGIOUS HISTORY

INTRODUCTION

IN 1977, RELIGIOUS HISTORY was largely identified as a subfield of American intellectual history. When Henry May described the "recovery" of religious history, his subject matter was dominated by Perry Miller and the "Puritan synthesis" that ran from John Winthrop and Jonathan Edwards through Ralph Waldo Emerson and the American Renaissance up to Reinhold Niebuhr and neo-orthodoxy. Yet as substantial as the recovery was, it was under siege from almost the time May wrote his article. In fact, both intellectual history and religious history were already challenged in 1977, by the "New Social History," and the tone of the conference at Wingspread that year reflected this beleaguered status. The mood of intellectual (and religious) history in 1977 was defensive. The New Social History had begun its invasion of all fields in American history and threatened to turn the mainline of intellectual history as it had evolved since the 1950s into a sideline. In religion, the threat was doubly severe. Mainline Protestant denominations, which had inspired much of the canon until then, were themselves "declining" at a precipitous rate.

The wariness of the 1977 participants, confronting a field in eclipse, was reflected both in the essays themselves and in the book's introduction. Conference planner and volume coeditor John Higham announced a "loss of momentum" in intellectual history and went on to note: "It was now the social historians' turn to bask in the limelight, rallying throngs of students, mounting lavishly funded projects, and issuing brave pronouncements on their generalizing mission" (xiii).

Sixteen years later, in 1993, both fields had changed dramatically. Intellectual history has survived the challenge of the New Social History, though not without altering its focus from "elite" systems of formal thought to "popular culture" and "mentalité." And religious history has thrived as never before. If intellectual history has experienced a rise and decline and resurrection, religious history's rise is novel and still peaking. Never before have so many religious studies appeared on so many groups in so many books, journals, and dissertations as at the present.

With this unprecedented expansion in mind, the conference planners for the 1993 meeting invited twenty of the nation's most distinguished historians to address aspects of religion in American history. Not all of these historians (and one sociologist) were trained in religion; indeed, a majority were trained outside of religion and do not identify themselves as religious historians. But all are now confronting religion as a main theme in American history. In contrast to 1977, the mood at Wingspread was expansive. For better and for worse, religion is at center stage, and the question is where will it all lead.

One major theme in virtually all religious histories of the past two decades has been the discovery of religious "outsiders." Even as evangelicals, Roman Catholics, Mormons, and charismatics have displaced the mainline as the vital center of religious growth and enthusiasm in contemporary American society, so have they assumed primary interest in the field of history and the social sciences. Indeed the language of outsiders-become-insiders, and peripheries-become-centers, is now a commonplace in the literature on religion in America.

In this period of growth and transition, it is appropriate to ask what subjects, styles, and methodologies might prove the most useful for ongoing appreciations of religion's place in American history. The answers, as they unfolded in three days of conference discussions, grouped themselves into four discrete areas: regions, themes, events, and "outsiders." Among other things, religious history is the study of places and regions, of themes that permeate all times and places, of transformative "events" that reconfigure social and religious institutions, and of ethnocultural "outsiders" whose presence is so compelling that they obliterate their status as peripheral and dominate attention.

Given the decisive shifts in historiography from mainline to sideline in the past twenty years, the conference planners asked the participants to think of the new groups they are studying and the histories they yield in dialectical tension with the old Protestant mainline histories, thus bringing the old "Church History"—Protestant centered and intellectually based—into dialogue with the new, non-mainline-centered and socially based "religious history."

Though by no means exhaustive, the essays that follow provide strategic glimpses into all of these dimensions of religious history. They reveal as well a field in agitation and motion, with few common destinations. Collectively, they confirm a field exploding its confines and spilling out into all of American history.

In the opening essay by Harry S. Stout and Robert M. Taylor, Jr., the field of American religious history and the sociology of religion is traced over the past two decades. Based on careful surveys of the literature, together with two formal surveys sent to religious scholars in 1973 and 1993, they document the revolutions that have taken place in the field both in numbers and content. In 1973, American religious history was still written largely within divinity schools by scholars preoccupied with the Protestant mainline. The tools were largely the tools of intellectual history. Conversely, in 1993, American religious history has come to be written in university departments of history, religious studies, and American studies. The central preoccupations have been with the "marginal" groups from "Fundamentalists" to charismatics, to Mormons, to women, to African American Christians, and to Roman Catholics. And the methods have been the methods of social and cultural history. Like virtually all fields of American history, religious history is simultaneously rich in its diversity of interests and methods and rudderless in its overall direction or sense of professional priorities.

From the opening overview, we turn to essays dealing with three key regions: Puritan New England, the South, and Canada. Clearly, the coverage is not inclusive, but collectively, they do suggest themes and questions that can be applied to other regions in comparative contexts. We begin with Puritan New England. At the 1977 conference, David D. Hall suggested that Puritanism could be fruitfully studied in terms of the cultural and ideological connections binding "elites" and ordinary men and women. Yet those connections should not be construed as a complete identification of the Puritan rank and file with the official theology of the clergy. In his 1993 essay, he calls for a more "multilayered" understanding of Puritanism that recognizes ambiguities in the movement, particularly as they involve the mentalities of clergy and laity. In fact, he suggests, Puritanism contained considerably more ambiguities and crossed signals that transcended official theologies and platforms, and that were expressed outside of church settings. He singles out the family as a "religious" institution as persuasive and authoritative as the one defined by the clergy. And while overlapping in religious concerns, there were also clear differences in style and understanding.

Studies of religion in the antebellum South, black and white, have exploded since 1977, and no one has done more to stimulate their growth than Donald G. Mathews. Like Hall, Mathews calls for a more complex model of "Christianization" in the South that encompasses the experiences of white and African American Christians in the cultural contexts of conversion, guilt, violence, gender, and war. Far more than a survey of the literature, Mathews's bringing together of diverse groups and themes represents the sketch of a new synthesis on the still misunderstood process of Christianizing the South.

If Puritans and antebellum Southerners are familiar to all students of American religious history, Canadian religious history is not. Too often, "American" is taken to mean the United States, with scant attention to nations north and south. In Phyllis Airhart's essay, Canadian religious historiography is examined in contrast to the United States. Lacking galvanic events like the American Revolution or ensuing imperialistic missions of "Manifest Destiny," where does Canadian religion derive its mythic stories, its sense of magnitude and relevance? Before the rise of the New Social History, Airhart suggests, these were difficult questions. But through the methodologies of the *Annales* school, introduced by "Francophone historians," religious history has been recast as the history of ordinary people, and in that recasting, found a narrative voice rendering it distinct. These differences, Airhart points out, are clearly manifest in popular religions. In particular, she looks at the contrasting styles of "radical evangelicalism" in the United States and Canada for clues to Canada's religious life. She also sketches out a program of research for previously neglected groups, including the numerically dominant, but largely invisible, United Church of Canada.

Events, no less than regions, have characterized much scholarship in American religious history. And no events have received more attention, both singly and in relationship to one another, than the "Great Awakening" of mid-eighteenth-century colonial America, and the American Revolution. Ever since Alan Heimert's seminal masterpiece on *Religion and the American Mind,* scholars of ideas and politics have had to confront the connections between religious awakenings and the social and political restructurings wrought by the American Revolution. In practice, this has led to imaginative reconstruction of social meanings in religious revivals and religious meanings in political revolutions.

For all of the attention paid to the eighteenth-century Great Awakening in American historiography, there has been no synthetic history since Joseph Tracy's nineteenth-century classic. But there are classic debates arguing diametrically opposed theses. On the one hand, scholars following Perry Miller's and Alan Heimert's lead have sought to examine the Great Awakening as the first stage of the American Revolution. Others, most notably Jon Butler, have argued that the "Great Awakening" is a nonevent, a historians' fiction. In his essay, Allen Guelzo carefully reviews the literature on the Great Awakening down to the present, and suggests an interpretive context in which a new synthesis might be written. Rather than examining the Awakening as primarily a social or political event, he suggests it be viewed as a religious event. In the context of religious meanings, he suggests, the Great Awakening was not causally connected to the Revolution, as Perry Miller and Alan Heimert first suggested, but neither was it a historians' fiction. It was rather a movement offering a religious redefinition of faith that paved the way for modern evangelicalism.

Clearly, there was more to eighteenth-century religion than religious revivals. For the majority of ordinary men and women in colonial America, religion constituted the single most powerful cultural system of the era and supplied ultimate explanations for life that could not be found anywhere else. With this broader understanding of religion in mind, Gordon Wood probes the social world of the eighteenth-century American colonists/patriots for clues to the relation of religion to the Revolution. Few, if any, of these Founding Fathers were enthusiastic about religion, and fewer still understood their actions as religiously grounded; some were outright deists. Where then is the connection? The answer, Wood suggests, lies less in political treatises and constitutional debates than in the categories of social and cultural history. When the focus shifts from enlightened "elites" to "ordinary people," a fundamental question appears: "Was popular religion like a raging river that suddenly went underground [during Revolution] only to reemerge downstream with more force and vigor than ever?" This is certainly the conventional wisdom on the part of historians, but Wood argues, it is a flawed wisdom. Religious beliefs did not simply disappear during the Revolution; historians just do not know where to look. The place to look is not in mutually exclusive political dichotomies between "liberal" Loyalists and "evangelical" patriots but in more deeply rooted demographic and economic determinants that helped to prepare American society for revolution.

Running through all the regions and events that identify primary markers in American religious history are underlying themes that reappear in every place and every generation. In turning to the question of revivals and the definition of the self in antebellum America, Daniel Walker Howe covers the broad period from the Revolution to the Civil War, a subject that has enjoyed the most creative growth in the past decade. With all that research behind him, Howe suggests a new interpretation that would look at religion less on its own terms than for its interaction with politics, moral philosophy, and "polite culture." Where earlier portraits of antebellum religion tended to ignore individuals and instead referred to movements as aspects of social control, Howe urges new studies of individuals that will be sensitive to the ways in which they sought to reform or reshape themselves as much as their society. Alongside individual studies, Howe outlines a strategy for examining religious organizations that would focus as much on institutional forces and organizational theory as on revivals or episodic awakenings. These institutional forces, he suggests, grew nationwide by 1850, but then split over the "gigantic problem of slavery."

Race was not the only issue Americans faced in organizing religious institutions. Ethnicity was another. John Higham, who more than any other scholar has plumbed the depths of immigrant experiences, and whose presence at the conference served as a symbolic bridge between this and the earlier Wingspread conference, explores the issue of ethnicity and religion against two contrasting models of interaction. All too often, "ethnic history" or the "history of immigration" is identified with "new" Roman Catholic or Jewish immigrants whose identity derived from their status as immigrants. But what do ethnicity and immigration have to do with the construction of a "mainstream" Protestant identity? Quite a bit, Higham persuasively argues. As early as the disestablishment of religion in the early Republic, Protestants began pursuing a generalized Protestant communal identity, interdenominational in scope and at least implicitly cooperative. Beneath all the divisions and contentions, broader social and cultural boundaries were being drawn, creating a shared ethnic identity. Negatively, this broader ethnic and national identification was fueled by a common anti-Catholicism activated by the onset of mass immigration from Europe. More positively, it was promoted by the onset of romanticism in letters and religion. Together, they created a Protestant cultural identity and ongoing ethnocultural conflicts that would engage evangelical Protestants and nativists long after the Civil War.

Unlike race, ethnicity, and gender, which are relative newcomers to studies of religion, economics enjoys a long-standing relationship going back to the founding works of Max Weber and Karl Marx. In recent years, however, with the collapse of communism in Eastern Europe, systematic attention to religion and economics has lacked a context. In an attempt to rekindle interest in the field and establish its importance both to studies of religious history and sociology, Robert Wuthnow and Tracy L. Scott engaged in a broad-gauge survey of literature treating economics and religion from community economic studies in the colonial era through the twentieth century. When all of this literature is pulled together, fundamental questions emerge which point the way to future research. The essay makes a powerful case for religion's central importance to economic life in American society and then goes on to chart some of the issues surrounding this topic in terms of the intersection of changing religious organizing and changing religious life, the parallel or contradictory religious motivations of working-class Americans and industrialists, and the impact of a religious "industrial work ethic" on such empirically measurable factors as frugality, diligence, and temperance. Wuthnow's and Scott's dual grounding in history and sociology is important both for their substantive findings and as a model of interdisciplinary research bringing together the fields of history and sociology.

Urban religion and community studies are beginning to attract renewed attention. In contrast to earlier scholarship that examined Protestantism's encounter with the city largely in tragic terms of failed missions and rampant secularism, several contributors to this volume present revisionist models with more balanced conclusions. Based on his ongoing study of religion in New York City, Jon Butler challenges historiographical stereotypes about a failed Protestant encounter with the city. In contrast to European cities in the period between 1870 and 1920, when a pervasive and measurable secularism prevailed at the institutional level, American cities were more notable for their ongoing religious vitality. From a set of complete and previously neglected religious surveys undertaken in 1896 by the Federation of Churches and Christian Workers of New York City, Butler traces "a remarkable urban Protestant resilience" that suggests new models for understanding how Protestant churches expanded in urban America even as they declined in Europe.

Of all the cross-fertilizations of religious history with other fields, none have been more productive in the recent literature than studies of religion and gender. Wherever historians look in religion, they find women playing a disproportionate role both in membership and in voluntary leadership. In her essay, Susan Juster recognizes this phenomenon, and then goes on to ask how it affected rhetorical discourse. From a diverse sampling of religious records, including Puritans, Quakers, spiritualists, and mystics, and diverse periods stretching from the colonial era where oral discourse dominated to the nineteenth century where print culture increasingly held sway, Juster traces shifting conceptions of gender and discourse reflecting the shift from oral culture to print culture, and from agriculture to commerce. Central to this shift, she argues, is an altered conception of gender itself, from a discrete role that men and women could both take up, to a psychosexual identity forever segmenting and defining male and female "spheres" and states of being. By looking at religion and gender in the context of language and rhetoric, she provides a compelling explanatory context for the transformation of "woman's role" in nineteenth-century America.

One field largely neglected in the new religious history has been missions. As Dana Robert's essay makes clear, this omission is unfortunate because much creative work has appeared in the period since World War II. By borrowing models from cultural anthropology and linguistics, contemporary missiologists are producing a new generation of scholarship that walks the line between praising missionaries uncritically as disinterested servants of God, or condemning them in equally uncritical prose as the witting or unwitting tools of western imperialism. By transcending political categories and examining missions anthropologically, it is possible to reconceive the field in ways that fit well with much of the newest work in American religious history.

"Culture" has become the favorite catchword in recent literature on religion, yet until recently it has not informed much scholarship in twentieth-century religion. Richard Fox recognizes this void and proposes a new, "cultural" context for explaining twentieth-century American religious history. Recognizing that all church history in the Protestant liberal tradition is at least implicitly apologetic and sectarian, Fox proposes an alternative methodology anchored in a new "essentialist" cultural history, which would render religion meaningful to "secularists" who feel no personal or spiritual affinity to the religious groups they study. By way of illustration, he analyzes Robert Orsi's *Madonna of 115th Street,* showing how that approach can be expropriated by scholars whose primary interest in religion is more secularly grounded in the pursuit of American culture rather than the understanding of American religion qua religion. He then goes on to suggest a similar framework for his own study of liberal Protestant culture in the nineteenth and twentieth centuries and the rise of evangelicalism. The approach promises a new understanding not only of the "decline" of Protestant liberalism, but also of the rise of evangelicalism as a "mass faith."

A fourth group of essays deals with religious "outsiders" in mainline "Protestant America." To the familiar themes of Puritans and evangelicals, this section also explores the history and historiography of groups that were both outside of, yet constantly interacting with, white Protestants. African American religion has existed from the start in such an ambiguous position. Judith Weisenfeld explores the complexities of African American religious experience in a comprehensive framework embracing male and female, North and South, rich and poor. She contextualizes the complexity around two distinct but paradoxically interlocking themes: marginality and centrality. As never before, scholars are aware that African American religious history is central to American religious history. Free black and slave religion has stood throughout American history as the "shadow" of white Christianity. Yet at the same time, African Americans have been so distanced from equality and empowerment that their marginality conjures the image more of an American Egypt than of an American Israel. In their own margin, African Americans found a space and a voice to create their own meaning. And in interdenominational agencies like the YWCA, they found bridges to white American Protestants. The goal, Weisenfeld argues, is to project both these poles in methodological tension.

American Catholics, since the 1840s America's largest denomination, have been largely ignored in historical scholarship outside of Catholic institutions. Even when American intellectual historians "recovered" religion in the 1960s, they recovered white Protestant religion. Consequently, American Catholic thought has never been explored within the academic categories of American intellectual history. Non-Catholic historians are pursuing Catholicism now, to be sure, but it is within the terms and context of social history. Unlike Protestant history, there is no prior tradition of intellectual history that "new" historians need to revise. The need, Patrick Carey urges, is therefore to open up Catholicism to intellectual history, both for the sake of American intellectual history generally, where a substantial gap in coverage appears, and for Catholic historians in particular, who need to reconnect with the normative centers of their tradition, largely ignored in the pursuits of social history.

A major theme in recent historiography has been the secularization of the university. In a provocative reexamination of this issue, David A. Hollinger challenges the secularization model, and instead proposes the term "de-Christianization" to describe what happened to the modern university and, more generally, to "public culture" in the twentieth century. Central to this cultural transformation, Hollinger shows, was the massive infusion of Jewish intellectuals (many of them nonobservant or "free-thinking") into American universities and public life. Working in the European tradition of Marx, Freud, and Durkheim, these intellectuals sought a "universal language" of culture that inevitably transcended religious particularities, and replaced an implicit Christian consensus with a vibrant cultural pluralism. One part of this pluralistic mosaic—and a large part at that—is Christianity, which, Hollinger argues, has hardly disappeared from American public life. Like Butler, Hollinger reverses earlier jeremiads positing a decline of "true Christianity," and asks instead: "Why is there so much Christianity in the United States in the twentieth century?" In fact, Christianity is still shaping society to a surprising degree, and models of secularization may be simply one more variant on the old Protestant myth of declension.

Fueling much of the growth of American religious history is the contemporary "Religious Right," and new global upsurges of "fundamentalism" in all faith traditions. In a concluding essay that confronts the American present, Anne Loveland brings the story full-circle by exploring recent literature on religion and modern American politics and society. By focusing on the "public realm," Loveland shows how religious history has moved in new directions that promote the history of African American religious history and women's religious history. Alongside these recent interests, Loveland traces the emergence of a public evangelical Christianity in the 1970s and its impact on contemporary American politics.

Collectively, these essays show how scholarship in regions, themes, events, and ethnocultural outsiders is being transformed by a "new religious history." If the destination is not always clear, the energy is at hand and the questions posed. Less a summation of work in progress than an agenda of uncompleted research, these essays show the promise and the pitfalls awaiting those who till the rich and variegated fields of American religion.

PART I

AMERICAN
RELIGION
AND SOCIETY

I

STUDIES OF RELIGION IN AMERICAN SOCIETY

The State of the Art

◼ ◼ ◼

Harry S. Stout
Robert M. Taylor, Jr.

A MINIHISTORIOGRAPHICAL REVOLUTION has occurred in studies of American religion over the past 20 years as they have proliferated at the epicenter of the historical and sociological enterprises. Religious history has entered the mainstream of historical research, no longer confined to the American Society of Church History and its sponsoring divinity schools. Likewise, the sociology of religion, once marginalized in its discipline, has become a leading edge in sociological research through its base in the Society for the Scientific Study of Religion. Spurred by the creation of new departments of religion, by increasing numbers of faculty and graduate students, by the addition of American religious history to history and American studies programs, and, not least, by unprecedented levels of funding by private foundations, the field has exhibited more growth than any other save women's studies. Yet while historians and sociologists bask in the glow of energized disciplines, their common institutional goals remain unexplored. What would the future hold if the two fields resumed the short-lived conversations of the late 1970s? This question we try to answer in the context of our commenting on the character of contemporary American religion research.

To an extent, our assessment of religious studies today is subjectively grounded in our two decades of work in the field. Apart from the impressions, however, our analysis relies on two questionnaires mailed in the summers of 1974 and 1993.[1] In scope and compass, the questionnaires differed. The 1974 questionnaire focused on the "stars" of American religious history, while in 1993 we spread a broader net and included scholars from religion and sociology departments. Where the earlier questionnaire invited qualitative and discursive answers, the more recent one's format allowed for quantitative inquiry. The differences in scale and format make systematic comparisons of the two instruments impossible. Yet, as discrete "soundings," the questionnaires represent an experimental merging of "narrative" and "quantitative" information which, we hope, can model the integrative scholarship we advocate for the larger field.

The 1974 questionnaire went to 75 elite historians (and a handful of sociologists of religion) at a time when the American history profession was never livelier or more focused around its professional and national responsibilities.[2] Debates on the profession's and the nation's identity and direction occurred against a backdrop of profound social unrest that directed a rethinking of the "uses of history" alongside standards of objectivity and detachment.[3] Social scientific approaches to history, assisted by new technological possibilities, gave rise to challenges in articulating theory and practicing quantitative methods. Traditional fields of study vied for status with popular specialties on women, blacks, labor, religion, business, culture, immigration, family, and demography.[4] It seemed, at the time, that debates *mattered,* that the profession *mattered,* that the "facts" *mattered.* The serious young scholars with the weight of the world and of their profession on their shoulders appear to some 1990s standards as naive "moderns" unaware of the postmodern freeze to come and its indictment of all science and theory. But then the future was theirs to mold in reasonable and responsible ways. That they failed to accurately predict the future reminds us that historians are better chronicling the past than forecasting what is to come, even of their own fields.

As a group, the 1974 shapers of the church history field represented a generation reared in the triumph of World War II: drawn heavily from, and engrossed in the study of, the Protestant mainline; based in divinity school programs at elite universities; members of the American Society of Church History (ASCH); contributors and readers of the ASCH journal, *Church History.*[5] They did not figure prominently in major historical organizations nor in university faculties of arts and sciences. Their relative isolation worked well as long as intellectual and doctrinal history prevailed in the larger historical community, because historians would still rely on them to cover religious ideas. However, the introduction of a "New Social History" directed to "ordinary people" would require a "New Religious History"—one central to our 1974 questionnaire.

Perry Miller guided that 1970s generation of American religious scholars as well as intellectual history generally. He rehabilitated the Puritans, put colonial New England on the historiographical map, and offered a model of research that placed religious history within American intellectual history.[6] As a result, church history expanded from divinity schools into history and English departments. To Henry F. May, in 1964, Miller's achievement meant nothing less than "The Recovery of American Religious History."[7] But Miller posited a model of secularization "from Puritan to Yankee" that also circumscribed religion's importance to the larger historical enterprise within a colonial and early national setting. Ironically, then, as religious scholarship widened, its study became identified solely with Puritanism and New England.[8]

Meanwhile in the divinity schools religious history thrived. New intellectual and cultural histories transcended the old "denominational synthesis" and carried the weight of post-Revolutionary religious history in the divinity schools. Membership in the ASCH increased, as did subscriptions to *Church History*. The future looked bright.[9] Two giants of the discipline, Sydney Ahlstrom and Sidney Mead, wrote religious history as intellectual history, but, while representing the culmination of a tradition inspired by Perry Miller, they also signaled newly emerging intellectual and cultural themes: post-Puritan religion, secularization, civil religion, and pluralism.[10]

The drawback for many divinity-based scholars in dealing with new realities was their own institutional commitments. These scholars could be critical of, but could not ignore, the traditions that fed them. Reflecting the conservatism of the profession, the 1974 questionnaire respondents did not perceive any discontinuous or institutional changes on the horizon; the essential institutional setting and culture of religious history would remain continuous with its past.[11]

The major threat to the continuation of established patterns of thought came from the New Social History beginning in 1970.[12] The application of theory and method from the social sciences to bodies of historical data dealing with ordinary people created a seismic shaking of historical and sociological studies. Suddenly (if briefly) historians began consulting sociology for theory and methods, and sociologists began reading historians for social context. From this fruitful interplay emerged the vision of a new synthesis or paradigm in American history where historians and sociologists working with common theoretical contexts and methodologies could outline the structural and functional dynamics of social change from "traditional" to "early modern" to "modern."[13]

From today's vantage, it is clear how the New Social History heralded (or threatened) discontinuous change—an entirely new agenda for religious research and an entirely new place for religion in the larger historical enterprise. Once social and cultural history recovered religion and displaced intellectual history as the subject of choice for aspiring young graduate students, religion would be at the heart of the American history enterprise. Religious history as social and cultural history, with no spatial or chronological bounds, represented a route for religious history's escape from the iron cage of Puritanism. More ominously, it represented a methodological route for religious history's institutional escape from divinity-based programs into the university and mainstream historical research.[14]

In 1974, the implications of a new social scientific orientation including quantitative methods went largely unforeseen by historians of American religion. No one except for William McLoughlin, from his footing in American studies, predicted sweeping changes for religious studies. Although most looked upon the New Social History merely as another tool rather than a transformer of disciplines and institutions, reservations were not lacking. Ahlstrom thought the biggest barrier to the emergence of a "New Religious History" would be "the low quality and truistic 'findings' of many social and sociological studies. . . . Subtract human intentionality and institutions are mute." William Clebsch feared quantitative methods for their tendency "to yield results that are questionable because the phenomenon being delineated and described consists entirely of [numerical] variables." Timothy Smith saw in social science methodology a "narrowness of perspective which preoccupation with statistics seems to inflict upon scholars." The reductionist tendencies inherent in new scientific approaches bothered many respondents. George Marsden noted that when social scientific approaches are viewed as a New Religious History "the implication seems to be that most things should be reduced to their social scientific dimensions. Such reductionism would throw many questions about religion out of balance." Some divinity-based historians feared theological problems and a marginalization of the theologian's task. Clarence Goen thought the primary barrier to a New Religious History to be "the inescapable necessity for adequate theological interpretation, which social scientists often ignore." Likewise, Nelson Burr exclaimed his belief "in the Biblical philosophy of history, the theological approach; for otherwise I feel that history doesn't make sense to most people."[15]

All university-based social and religious historians agreed that a New Religious History would find its way into history departments. Cedric Cowling observed that the New Religious History "should bring religious history more fully into the mainstream, increasing respect for it among social scientists and all specialists in the study of America." Similarly, Robert Berkhofer advocated the application of social theory and history to the religious record in a pattern whereby "American religious history incorporates some of the more advanced trends occurring in social history and in intellectual history."

The ethnocultural political historian Richard Jensen saw a New Religious History creating a "much broader based social history" with less emphasis on class and more on ethnoreligious groupings. John M. Murrin commented that one consequence of the behavioral approach "will be to generate a compelling need to reexamine what people thought and wrote about their religious experience, if only because it will force us to place old ideas in a strikingly new context." Ideally, thought Michael Zuckerman, "a new Religious History would force a reintegration of American History generally. A new wholism of temporal and regional and ethnic cultures that would acknowledge wider unities and deeper diversities than are now admitted."

Among the handful of sociologists who responded, Benton Johnson cautioned against using quantitative methods with no grounding in social theory. And Sister Marie Augusta Neal believed a New Religious History would lead to "the discovery of the historical dynamic of religious experience as variables more independent than recently assumed." Significantly, virtually every historian polled in 1974 was reading some sociology alongside their primary research interests, and all recognized the need to embed their research in broader theoretical contexts. The three most cited theorists were Max Weber, Erik Erickson, and Peter Berger, with mention also given to Durkheim, Freud, and the anthropologist Anthony F. C. Wallace.

I

While the bulk of our historians willingly made concessions to social scientific theory and "other" religious traditions, none really envisioned a different discipline. It would remain, in their view, predominantly a divinity-based enterprise. In retrospect, the historians could not have been more wrong. We have witnessed in 20 years as sharp a break with the continuity of church history as the field has experienced since becoming "professionalized" in the early twentieth century. It is nothing short of a revolution contributed to by a nation moving simultaneously in conservative, fundamentalist, and multicultural directions. In the same way that religious revivals in the 1950s and theological "neo-orthodoxy" promoted a recovery of scholarly interest in "mainline" religion in the 1960s, so new religious revivals in the 1970s together with a revitalized Roman Catholicism and an evangelical "moral majority" sparked a recovery of scholarly interest in religion in the 1980s. Such is the power of the "religious factor," particularly the "evangelical" factor in current historiography that historian Jon Butler recently described an "evangelical paradigm" as "the *single* most powerful explanatory device adopted by academic historians to account for the distinctive features of American society, culture, and identity."[16]

Other unforeseen trends evolved on an institutional plane, all to the detriment of divinity-based church history. The creation of religion departments in faculties of arts and sciences opened up new vistas of research and writing not bound by confessional boundaries or denominational ties.[17] The decline in numbers within mainline Protestantism has been paralleled by a movement within the academy to study those groups leading the 1980s "revival"—Roman Catholics, Mormons, evangelicals, and Pentecostalists (black and white, North and South), and turn attention from the colonial era to the early republic and beyond when many of the evangelical denominations began.[18] All the while in divinity-based domains, history faculties continue to decline, and Ph.D. programs increasingly compete with university history and religion departments. Reformation studies, the divinity-based compliment to Puritan and mainline studies, has also fallen on hard times. The ASCH now competes with fragmentary subfields, each with its own newsletters and programs. *Church History* experiences fewer submissions annually, and its relevance to American history has clearly diminished.[19]

Meanwhile, sociologists no less than historians have benefited from the 1970s revivals. Suddenly, it is no longer anachronistic to explore the "religion variable" in sociological analysis.[20] The secularization paradigm has come in for sustained scrutiny, and the jury is still out.[21] Students of the nonprofit sector are coming to grips with the dominant place religious organizations occupy in the American philanthropic picture. And organizational theorists are beginning to see the roots of modern organizations in religious agencies.[22]

With these developments in mind, we returned to "the state of the art" in another questionnaire in the summer of 1993, one much more extensive and one that required a more quantifiable format to assist in the interpretation.[23]

The academic respondents—the 495 respondents earmarked for analysis in this essay—turned out to be remarkably white, male, and middle-aged, having been born in the baby boom period between 1946 and 1964. When asked "from where did you receive your highest degree," a bewildering number of public and private universities were named. Obviously, some time has passed when a cadre of "key" institutions, such as Yale, Harvard, and Chicago, turned out most of the students.

Most striking, since 1974, is the number of historians who have migrated out of divinity schools and into newly formed departments of religious studies in colleges and universities. In all, 82% of our respondents are college- or university-based, compared to only 5.3% in divinity schools.

Less than 10% of the historians surveyed indicated membership in professional organizations outside of history. This insularity extended to subspecialty organizations in the field. In fact, only three organizations held anything remotely like a quorum of religious historians: the ASCH, still respectable at 42%, the Organization of American Historians at 53%, and the American Historical Association at 61%. Less than 2% of sociologists surveyed belonged to any of these three organizations. Even the Social Science History Organization attracts only slightly more than 5%. Conversely, the sociologists tend to a larger degree than historians to hold memberships in their own organizations, such as the American Academy of Religion, to which 66% of sociologists belong.

The 1993 respondents moved sharply from the mainline Protestant orientation of the 1960s and 1970s to one more evangelical and Roman Catholic. Thirty-two percent of the respondents identified themselves as "evangelical Protestant," 18% as "liberal Protestant," and 9% as "other Protestant" (for a total of 59% Protestant). Roman Catholics numbered 26%, and Jews 4%—a rough microcosm of the American population.[24] Those claiming no religious community numbered 6.5%. Islamic, Eastern Orthodox, Native American, African American Christian denominational, Buddhist, and Hindu scholars collectively numbered less than 1%. When broken down by discipline, the proportions vary in some significant ways. Sociologists by a 28% to 17% margin prefer liberal Protestantism, while historians prefer evangelicalism by a striking 37% to 13% margin.

In contrast to academics generally, the religion scholars registered a strong religious faith. For example, 78% classified themselves as either "very religious" (47%) or "quite religious" (31%). Only 6% ($n = 9$) classified themselves as "not very religious." In addition, the largest number (41%) chose the field because of a "lifelong interest in religion," thus reinforcing the pattern of religiosity. In sum, this community of scholars is primarily Protestants, Catholics, and Jews "preaching to the converted" in their own constituencies.

Within the large umbrella of religious faiths, the most studied topics are in Catholicism and Protestant evangelicalism. We found nearly 200 of our respondents studying topics in Roman Catholicism ($n = 88$) or "evangelicalism"—including fundamentalism, revivalism, and missions ($n = 100$). The signs of growth in these two areas are everywhere from journals and books to institutes, such as the Institute for the Study of American Evangelicals, the Cushwa Center, or the Overseas Ministries Study Center, to new academic appointments in "Roman Catholic History" at non-Catholic institutions. Once the "religious outsiders," taking a back seat to mainline Protestant studies, the 1990s generation is now on the inside.

Studies responsible for feeding the new "evangelical paradigm" are often produced by secular university historians who tend to treat evangelicalism as an aspect of what to them are the "broader" demographic, ideological, or cultural themes. If not quite epiphenomenal, religion is often used in these studies as a tool to understand something other— something presumably more "basic" and intrinsic to the discipline.[25] While not prominent in our survey (because they tend not to join religious organizations), they exert a powerful influence on the field. For our purposes, we wanted to see how the scholars singled out in our survey perceived religion's explanatory value vis-á-vis race, class, and ethnicity.[26] Not surprisingly, our respondents differed from scholars-at-large in according religion a coequal status. Historians generally allotted religion more importance than ethnicity and social class, but hedged on race.

The weighing of religion as a causal force in historical change rests on continued blossoming of scholarship. In the wake of church history's displacement from the divinity schools has come new research into formerly "marginalized" movements along with researchers from diverse religious backgrounds. Related to this is an apparent decrease in academics who profess a "liberal Protestant" faith. Contemporary scholars pursue subjects that speak to their own beliefs, interests, and preoccupations. Thus, by the fact of rising numbers of Roman Catholic and evangelical scholars, we should expect a corresponding increase in research devoted to those faith traditions. There are other reasons for the rise in religious studies. Our Roman Catholic and evangelical respondents emphasized a greater interest in religion among the public at large, while liberal Protestants stressed a burgeoning awareness of religious pluralism in society-as-a-whole. Interestingly, the "emergence of a religious right" and "increased availability of funding" were considered much less important.

The importance of funding, we think, may be underestimated. Fifty-two percent of our respondents received significant financial support from outside agencies or from their home institutions. Leading in external funding research were the Lilly Endowment, The Pew Charitable Trusts, and Henry Luce Foundations (in that order), foundations virtually unheard of in historical research in 1974 (funding from home institutions remained constant). In 1974, prominent scholars of American religion, like American history scholars generally, largely depended on public support through the National Endowment for the Humanities, the National Science Foundation, American Council of Learned Societies, or Guggenheim, agencies whose support for religion was (and remains) disproportionately small.[27] Federal scholarship programs have shied away from religious topics in both history and sociology. Against this backdrop, the investments of, first, Lilly under Robert Lynn, and then Pew, Luce, and programs established by particular faith communities such as the Billy Graham Center, the Cushwa Center, or the Southern Baptist Archives, are of undeniable importance. The appearance of massive funds for conferences, research projects, and fellowships has opened opportunities for scholars who otherwise might be left out or channeled into other research areas.

The increase in foundation support has also affected the type of research projects undertaken, particularly in sociology, where large surveys conducted by teams of scholars have become more the norm. With no funds for travel, data collection, research assistants, and computer analysis, research tends to turn inward on its own assumptions and preexistent paradigms. Studies tend to be more "clever" than the pioneering that comes with amassing large bodies of data.[28] History, too, has been profoundly influenced by foundations. Although a more individually based discipline, historians in the 1980s began assembling "teams" and conferences tackling large projects.[29] In our estimation, foundations have in some measure stepped into the void of the older divinity-engaged history to promote history with "mission" applications in the mainline, evangelical, and Roman Catholic communities. The gains are obvious, as are the losses. Traditions outside these major faiths are often ignored in scholarship. The overwhelming preponderance of scholars from Christian (and secondarily Jewish) communities is in part the product of these institutional forces.

Besides discovering the institutional forces behind the efflorescence of religious scholarship and what topics are being explored, we wanted to know which scholars—old and new—are read for content and methodology? What do our respondents identify as the highest achievements in their field? To what extent do historians read sociologists and vice versa? In 1974, American historians generally and religious historians in particular read sociologists. What about 1993?

American religious historians mostly appear to read deeply within their own *recent* historiography, a striking reversal of 1974 trends. When asked to identify scholars "very important" to their work, no one name emerged. No individual scholar was cited by more than half of our historian respondents. Martin Marty led with 42%, followed closely by Sydney Ahlstrom (40%), Perry Miller (39%), and Edmund Morgan (38%). Interestingly, two of these four persons never identified themselves as religious historians, a third wrote a Puritan synthesis, and the fourth is still very much alive and more current than "classic." Significantly, 34% of historian respondents listed William Warren Sweet as "not important." No early divinity-based historians received a nod, which suggests that today's religious history is lacking in enduring authoritative sources actively read by the profession. The discipline has no "founding fathers." With the exception of H. Richard Niebuhr, no other figure in the social sciences attracted more than 20%. Ironically, American religious history is among the most history-*less* disciplines.

In contrast, sociologists are more apt to read the old sociology classics alongside the new. Max Weber ranked "very important" with virtually every sociologist of religion—a figure without parallel among historians. Robert Bellah and Peter Berger followed close behind. Also, sociologists apparently read (and find very important) H. Richard Niebuhr and Martin Marty. While far from agreement on what the work of these sociological classics mean, they are read by the field as a whole. American religious history has no comparable classics.[30]

Classics aside, religious historians do read each other along with some current sociologists. When asked whether each increasingly consulted the other, almost three-fourths (72%) answered yes, an affirmation also indicated in the tally for the "three most important recent books or articles." Scholars whose work received more than 10 votes include: Robert Bellah, Jon Butler, Jay Dolan, Roger Finke and Rodney Stark, Nathan Hatch, James Hunter, George Marsden, Martin Marty, Mark Noll, Clark Roof,

Stephen Warner, Harry Stout, and Robert Wuthnow. Wuthnow and Hatch received over 50 citations. Their path-breaking works on *The Restructuring of American Religion* and *The Democratization of American Christianity*, respectively, are read by both camps. Twenty-six of Robert Wuthnow's 86 votes came from sociologists, with historians and religious studies scholars voting the rest.

In asking who among present religion scholars are viewed as most important to the field, four rose to the top: Martin Marty, Jon Butler, Nathan Hatch, and George Marsden (with the largest number going to Hatch). Marty clearly enjoys the greatest longevity. The other three scholars have produced major defining works within the past decade. The two most recent—Butler and Hatch—evidence clearly the methodologies and priorities of the New Social History. Both examine religion as a "popular culture" with an emphasis on the laity. Their work represents the most obvious of lay-centered, interdisciplinary studies by such other scholars as David Hall, Marilyn Westercamp, and Leigh Schmidt. Marsden's study of fundamentalism is a transitional work concerned with a "popular" religious culture, yet written within the Milleresque religious-history-as-intellectual-history framework.

Sociologists also identified a handful of most widely read scholars, including Wuthnow, Hunter, Bellah, and Greeley, with Wuthnow dominating. Today's foundation-supported sociologists of religion have moved decisively in empirical directions sustained by the acquisition of rich new bodies of survey data. The great scope of this team-oriented research may require a generation to sort out.

What frameworks of methodology and theory, if any, do our respondents utilize? When asked if they agree that the "basic methods of scholarship on religion in my field have changed very little over the past twenty years," a startling 69% of our respondents agreed. However, many of these were historians. Here, as elsewhere, emerges a pattern of cognitive dissonance whereby the historians see little change, having so thoroughly absorbed the tenets and methodologies of the New Social History, a clear reversal from 1974 when they saw major changes ahead in scholarship. The older denominational and divinity-based traditions are barely a memory. On the other hand, sociologists see change, with 53% disagreeing.

The 1974 respondents had much to say, pro and con, about the then-novel application of the computer and quantitative methods of sampling and statistical analysis. In 1993 the matter raises far less passion. When asked whether "studies of religion would stand to benefit greatly from the increased use of quantitative data and analysis," 55% agreed and 45% disagreed. In neither case did the question seem to arouse much excitement. No commentary accompanied the question, except one: "Those who answer 'Strongly Disagree' may not return this questionnaire!"

To what degree were our respondents theory-driven, and which theories, if any, did they find useful in their work? Relatedly, we wanted to know whether religion represented peculiar methodological and theoretical problems uncommon to, say, race, gender, or class. When asked whether "religion is such a singular phenomenon that it should be studied in its own terms rather than from the perspective of broader social science paradigms," 75% disagreed. Both historians and sociologists disagreed, but the latter more so. When sorted by faith communities, among the minority who agreed the strongest concentration was in the evangelical Protestant camp, while liberal Protestants, Catholics, and Jews most strongly disagreed.

Here was one of the few times where evangelical and Catholic answers varied significantly. Clearly, for many of the affirmatives, the suspicion of social science is grounded in religious reservations. One respondent commented that "social science is narrower than religion. We should rather study social science from broader religious perspectives."

Secularization is the most persistent of all theories involving religion and American society. Fifty-five percent of the respondents agreed that "secularization remains the dominant trend concerning religion in western societies." Sociologists and historians divided on this question in similar proportions though the former were less likely to agree by a 48% to 58% margin. The disagreement about the reality and explanatory power of secularization often boils down to differences about method and definition that have mired the field as did definitions of "church," "sect," and "cult" in the 1960s. One respondent felt that secularization is less the trend than a "wider and more unprecedented accommodation" of different groups and traditions. Another added: "the answer totally depends on one's definitional scheme for religion and secularization." One who strongly disagreed observed: "secularization has always been overrated, [it is] more true of the academy than anywhere else."

One thing is clear. The concept (and perhaps the reality) of secularization has turned historians away from the study of twentieth-century religion, unlike sociologists who pursue the topic as a live issue. For historians, as far back as the 1960s, secularization is an accepted reality for the twentieth century, which means that their research centers on earlier periods. As a consequence, nearly all creative methodology and influential writing in American religious history has concentrated on premodern topics and methodologies appropriate to premodern cultures. Influential historians such as Hall, Orsi, Shipps, Butler, Albanese, Mathews, Hatch, Johnson, or Ryan all (thus far) established their reputations with pre-twentieth-century topics. Even the prominent exceptions—Hutchison, Marsden, and Marty—confine their twentieth century emphases to Protestant institutional and intellectual history.[31]

Although historians and sociologists have little direct contact, the responses of the two groups were remarkably similar on many of the evaluative questions. Both camps are exceptionally religious, conservative, and persistent in their assumptions and methodologies. Sixty-five percent of the respondents said they had not undergone a major shift in their overall scholarly outlook and analytical perspective as a result of recent developments in the religion field.

Though slow to incorporate outside theory into their research or consult "classics," today's religious historians do read widely outside their specialty in the broader historical literature, as do sociologists. When asked whether "my most important new ideas concerning religion come not from reading about religion itself but from reading more widely in my broader scholarly discipline," over 60% of both disciplines agreed. Clearly historians and sociologists have loyalties to their respective disciplines and consult their respective leading lights.

In the 1970s, many divinity-based scholars of religion felt ignored by their professional colleagues. Yet, in 1993, when asked whether their interest in religion made them feel slighted and underappreciated by colleagues, a majority (58%) disagreed.

Flipping the question over to record agreement showed slight differences between historians and sociologists (37% and 44% respectively.) A more significant differentiation occurred where 43% of evangelicals agreed with the statement in contrast to 30% of liberal Protestants—a divergence that possibly reflects the more liberal posture of academia.

When asked whether "the study of religious organizations needs to move beyond some of its older rubrics (for example, church versus sect) and seek out new models and insights from the study of secular organizations," a stunning 81% basically agreed. Marginal comments reinforced agreement. One respondent wrote: "In my view this is the key." Another added assent, with the qualification that the field "needs to seek out new models and insights without repudiating old ones." While differences between historians and sociologists were often slight, as in the case above where sociologists agreed by a ratio of nine to one and historians by eight to one, there occurred differences, which tended to be consistent in the directions they moved. Given their moorings in social theory, sociologists to a greater extent than historians are willing to consult theory, move outside of religious literature, and define religion as a category of culture. When asked whether "scholarship on religion would be enhanced if we defined 'religion' in such a way that it could be seen as an analytic dimension of all social phenomena and processes," the differences between historians and sociologists agreeing (45% and 56%, respectively) are evident but not momentous.

In looking to the future, our respondents emphasized the need to investigate relatively unexplored topics. As with questions of theory, it appears they are content to continue what they're doing, but believe that somebody *(else)* needs to be working on other areas. At least satisfied, some perhaps satiated, with the present glut of studies on evangelicalism and Roman Catholicism, those questioned in 1993 singled out new op-

portunities in the study of "popular religions" and the "unchurched."
Sociologists, principally, singled out theory and methods. Other topics
clustered around social issues, particularly subjects relevant to women
and the family. Over the past two decades, the rise of major scholarship
in women's history has been as spectacular if not more so than religious
studies.[32] Our responses clearly indicate that studies of women and religion—religion of all denominations and movements—is high on the list
of priorities. Women's history and feminist theory will play a major role
in attuning religious history to the larger narrative of American history.
Today's leading women's scholars—Nancy Cott, Mary Ryan, Catherine
Albanese, Rosemary Reuther—will be tomorrow's "classics." While respondents expressed surprise that no women appeared on our list of possible classics in the field, this omission was less a deliberate oversight
than a reflection of who our respondents read while pursuing degrees in
graduate schools. At that time, influential women historians and sociologists of religion were themselves in graduate school.

Given our own disciplinary moorings in history, our questions betrayed a bias toward historians and the worlds they inhabit. But in one
battery of questions we enlisted the advice of sociologists and asked the
respondents to think in theoretical terms about the areas in which religious studies have succeeded or failed. We asked them to rank the relative success of "religion as a cultural or symbolic system" (the anthropological approach), "religion at the individual or social psychological
level," "religious organizations" (the sociological approach), "religion as
an aspect of the community," "religion within processes of social
change," "religious movement," and "comparative and non-Western religions."

Two major patterns emerged. First, the historians were not used to
thinking in broad systems-based theoretical terms. In fact, 165 of our
sampling did not even respond to these questions—a majority of them
historians. Second, where historians ranked the questions a prominent
divergence from sociologists appeared in areas the historians identified as
most successful. For example, where historians think the field has done
well on religious organizations, sociologists point to religion at the individual or social psychological level as our most knowledgeable dimension. Sociologists and historians join hands in ranking as number two
"religious movements" from Mormonism to New Age, and all agreed
that we know least about comparative and nonwestern religions. Given
the ethnic and religious backgrounds of our scholars and their focus on
American subjects, the isolation of American religion and its interpretation within the categories of Judaism and Christianity is truly striking.
What little comparative work exists in "transatlantic" eighteenth-century
studies and Anglo-American nineteenth-century religious studies has, by
the twentieth century, virtually disappeared. Of twentieth century religious historians, only Martin Marty has embarked on a large-scale comparative "Fundamentalisms" project.[33]

The high rankings that scholars gave to our understanding of religious organizations and movements suggests that in these areas will occur theoretical breakthroughs. Sociology and history together have enjoyed their greatest strengths in understanding religious movements along a continuum from the dual vantage of Weberian models of charisma in the formation of religious movements and neoinstitutional organization theory in the bureaucratization and perpetuation of religious institutions. The influence of Anthony Wallace, Victor Turner, Mary Douglas, and Clifford Geertz and the anthropological school, meanwhile, insures that the institutional analysis is not so much in the functional models where "culture" and ideas are ignored or epiphenomenal, but in integrative approaches that examine the culture——the symbolic core of organizations as much as their structural and institutional fields. At the same time, neoinstitutional theory accounts for the routinization of charisma in irrational ways that neither Weber nor Parsons perceived within their rationalistic and evolutionary models of social change.[34]

2

What conclusions can be taken from our two soundings of historians and our single sounding of sociologists? In regard to history, there can be no doubt that a revolution has occurred over the past 20 years, producing a New Religious History. This revolution is complete, encompassing who is conducting the leading research; what is being studied; how it is being studied; and, perhaps most momentously, where it is being studied. Crucial to this New Religious History is its location at the center of the American history enterprise. No longer marginalized as "church history," today's New Religious History, as Jon Butler points out, offers the promise (and pitfalls) of a new historiographical paradigm. Sociology has also moved dramatically in terms of theory and methodology, though not to the same institutional extent as history. Quite simply, there never was a tradition of divinity-based professional sociology with anything like the influence divinity schools exerted on earlier church history.

The revolution in American religious history has yielded a startling range of "gains" in terms of new and exciting research projects. We are surely the richer for the explosion of knowledge on previously neglected groups whether they be Mormon, Roman Catholic, evangelical, or charismatic; on previously neglected cultures and races, be they slaves, Native Americans, or Asian Americans; and on previously neglected women generally. And when we look at the ongoing work on the mainline traditions sponsored by the Lilly Endowment, we see that that field has never been more widely peopled.

Advances also have been made on the theoretical and interdisciplinary levels. Most notable has been work in the premodern periods. Jon Butler's and David Hall's comparative perspectives; Mark Noll's and George Rawlyk's transatlantic and Canadian essays; Jan Shipps's and Catherine

Albanese's comparative religions approach to, respectively, Mormonism and Native American traditions; Nathan Hatch's, Daniel Walker Howe's, and Patricia Bonomi's exploration of democratization and Christianity; Donald Mathews's and Rhys Isaac's work on the South; David Nord's and David Harrel's explorations of religion and media; David Brion Davis's, Albert Rabateau's, and Eugene Genovese's studies of slavery and slave religion; Jay Dolan's microcosmic institutional approach to the Catholic parish; Robert Orsi's anthropological approach to Catholic culture; R. Lawrence Moore, Ann Braude, and Steven Stein on "religious outsiders"; George Marsden and Joel Carpenter on fundamentalism; or Grant Wacker and Edith Blumhofer on Pentecostalism, all represent stellar achievements.[35] In addition, steady movement has occurred in quantitative studies of religion and congregations summarized in Robert P. Swierenga's and Philip VanderMeer's recently edited *Belief and Behavior*.[36] With few exceptions, these studies embrace the nineteenth century; the once-dominant place of colonial America—and the Puritans—has clearly passed, and the twentieth century has yet to receive its due.

Likewise, the sociology of religion is alive and doing well. If sociologists have not produced grand theory as once promised, they have, in our view, done something even grander: abandoned the search. Pursuing only modern societies and concentrating on empirical data rather than universal paradigms, sociologists have conducted many elegant local, micro case studies. The heyday of functionalism with its megatheories and megaclaims has receded sharply in favor of more modest, and more successful, efforts to establish theoretical constructs with no broader application than the particular societies—or groups—examined. Microcosmic studies with limited generalizations now appear to be de rigueur in institutional studies. And rich survey studies now tell us in unmatched detail individual and group preferences, behavioral patterns, and symbolic yearnings.[37]

Nevertheless, despite the obvious gains made over the past decades, they must also be judged years of lost opportunities and even, in the case of history, a regression. To a much greater extent than in 1974, historians and sociologists do not talk outside their disciplines except in rare instances of foundation-supported conferences and consultations. This appears to be especially true of historians, some of whom registered strong criticisms of sociology with little positive ballast. Complaints that sociology was "lifeless," that it was "unreadable" or "too theoretical and bland," appeared in the margins. One respondent opined: "I have just spent a year with a bunch of sociologists—never again!" Yet another wrote: "I'm not very 'theory-driven,' and see too much of American religious history as 'theory-laden,' too willing to import theoretical explanatory devices rather than taking phenomena 'on their own terms.' "

The last comment is particularly curious because if our soundings reveal anything it is that history is neither theory-laden nor even very historical. The reverse appears more accurate. Our sample historians do not seem particularly interested in theory, or in the twentieth century, or even in their own "classics." Earlier religious history—the history of the divinity-based mainline—does not appear to orient this generation of historians in their work. What counts most is what has been written in the past 10 years. Ironically, it is the historians and not the sociologists who are most presentist and lacking in any "history."

In seeking to account for the ahistorical presentism of American religious historiography, two explanations come to mind. First is the fact that religious history is hardly alone in its myopia. American history writing generally appears uniquely fragmented and incoherent. Debate, confrontation, and disagreement, to say nothing of the principle of cultural and epistemological relativism have always been integral to the historical profession. But now the fragmentation has itself fragmented; the vital centers represented by such traditions as scientific history, Progressivism, the New Left, or the New Social History have disappeared. In the past one read a common body of classical literature either to support, to revise, or to demolish; now there are no classics. Nor is there any pressing theory or methodology to be pursued other than the postmodern suppression of all theory as "logocentric" and "hegemonic." The combined forces of postmodern criticism and the collapse of communism in central Europe have so thoroughly deconstructed the enterprise that no clear markers remain.[38]

The New Social History, once the beacon for common consumption and debate, has itself moved decisively from sociology and social structure to cultural studies and ethnography. And with this shift the "New" history—including religious history—has moved much closer to the humanities and culture studies than to the social sciences.[39] Constructive conversation with sociology, so conspicuous in 1974 when we took our first sounding, has largely stopped. With the new "literary turn" has come new preoccupations with the local and idiosyncratic.[40] Insofar as postmodern criticism has influenced history writing and American Studies, it has come at the expense of the New Social History's initial preoccupation with theory, empiricism, and model-building.

In place of modernization theory, Marxist analysis, and functionalism, we are now inundated with texts. Cultural history, as Gordon Wood has recently pointed out, "has seized the day during the past generation."[41] Clifford Geertz first popularized this notion for historians (and not a few anthropologists) by viewing culture as an assemblage of texts to be interpreted by the observer. Though he worked within the tradition of Ricoeur and Dilthey rather than Lévi-Strauss and postmodern critics, Geertz nevertheless tended to reduce social analysis to symbolic "meanings" that could be "read" almost ahistorically as a text. In his *Interpretation of Culture,* as widely read among contemporary scholars of all disciplines as Thomas Kuhn's *Structure of Scientific Revolutions* was read by an earlier generation, Geertz advocated a method of analysis in which the ethnographer thinks of "the culture of a people [as] an ensemble of texts, themselves ensembles, which the anthropologist strains to read over the shoulders of those to whom they properly belong." [42] In this framework, politics, economics, Balinese cockfights, and religious rituals were no longer social actions growing out of particular social structures and created by particular self-interested parties, but "webs of meaning" to be dissected and interpreted by the hermeneutical skills of the observer.

To a point, both Geertz and postmodern criticism served as helpful correctives to social histories that were concerned exclusively with social structure at the expense of culture. [43] But Geertz and, more problematic, postmodernists in both history and anthropology have taken this to its own extreme in a deconstructed world of contextual play, polyvocality, decentering, blurring genres, and deconstructed logosystems that threatens to incur a loss of all method and loss of object. We are in danger of losing the notion of culture as socially embedded in social, economic, and political processes. We have, in a word, lost history as in any sense material social process. In his *Anthropologies and Histories,* William Roseberry points out theoretical and methodological problems that ensue with text as a metaphor for culture (and the ensuing "death" of the author):

> A text is written; it is not writing. To see culture as an ensemble of texts or an art form is to remove culture from the process of its creation. If culture is a text, it is not everyone's text. Beyond the obvious fact that it means different things to different people or different sorts of people, we must ask who is (or are) doing the writing. Or, to break with the metaphor, who is doing the acting, the creating of the cultural forms we interpret. . . . Culture as text is removed from the historical process that shapes it and that it in turn shapes. [44]

Roseberry's criticism brings us back to social history, to institutional process, and to the necessity of grounding cultural products in the context of their social production.

In looking specifically at the loss of center in American religious history, we are struck by the further relativization and fragmentation of the field brought on by Christian particularism. As scholars representing a field that was for the most part excluded—and derided—by history departments in the heyday of the old "New History" of James Harvey Robinson, Charles Beard, and the "Progressives," many religious historians have separated themselves from the "enlightenment objective" foundations of the American historical profession. Citing their own personal Christian epistemology with its critique of modernism and faith in reason, they join forces (at least implicitly) with postmodern criticism in denigrating the whole idea of scientific history and the consequent search for a unified history of the American past "as it really was." By blurring the lines between their personal faith commitments as Christians and their salaried careers as professional historians, they have separated themselves from their origins in social science even as the profession first slighted them.[45] And by distancing themselves from "naturalistic world views" originating in the Enlightenment, they have also distanced themselves from any obligation to relate their scholarship to some professional "field" concerned with "scientific objectivity." Undergirding postmodern and "providentialist" Christian research agendas is an implicit assumption that one's self-interest is at once one's scholarly, academic, and professional legitimation. Freed from all commitments to science or professionalism, they, like postmodernists, are freed to be left with themselves.[46]

One looks at the composite picture of the field emerging from our questionnaire and survey of the recent literature with a feeling of profound unease, a feeling of frustration. There is hardly any sense of a professional community of scholars sharing a common canon. In place of theory, historians all too often simply draw up a shopping list of missing groups to be researched, described, and catalogued as one more puzzle piece in the religious mosaic of America.

Such is American religious history's lack of connectedness to anything larger, that the field is in danger of antiquarianism at the very moment of its triumph in the academy. The fact that Sydney Ahlstrom's synthesis has not been remotely approached in the 20 years since its appearance is not solely owing to Ahlstrom's prodigious genius. It is owing as well to a crisis in the profession of fragmentation without any larger fusion. The divinity school context is lost and nothing constructive has been placed in its stead to encompass an entire field or discipline. Historians are swimming alone in their own particularities. Cut adrift from their origins and oriented overwhelmingly toward the present, many scholars have given up on professional history; some look instead to their ethnic and gendered identities; others point to the particular needs of particular faith communities for whom they are writing their history and sociology. This is a matter of concern to some respondents, one of whom commented: "I think the sociology of religion would be better served if fewer scholars had so much at stake personally [in their subjects]."

Ironically, despite history's purview in the past and in tradition, sociologists may well be role models here in maintaining some semblance of identity as scientists and some reverence for the "classics" in their field. Sociologists continue to offer courses in theory and method; they continue to read Weber and Durkheim; and they self-consciously build their work on the foundations of what went before. To be sure, there is no consensus or common meaning. But there is a common literature. American religious historians do none of these in any sustained way. Yet, if history is to be a discipline, it needs classic texts. Insofar as sociology's founding scholars were at once historians, they may well be the common fount from which all can drink. Weber, Durkheim, Marx, and, for religious historians, Troeltsch, continue to speak to a world where structure matters and where external reality exists and, however incomplete, is socially constructed.

If historians and sociologists renew serious conversations in pursuit of a common field, the learning and borrowing will not be one-way. Sociologists also have a good deal to learn from historians.[47] Historians' and sociologists' greatest strengths are also their greatest weaknesses. We need to begin by recognizing our limitations and the mutual needs that bring us together. One useful voice in this regard is Anthony Giddens, who, in an appendix to his *The Constitution of Society*, addresses the question of the difference between professional history and sociology. The old distinctions between history as preoccupied with the "particular" rooted in time and place, and sociology with the nomothetic "general" that is indifferent to time and space simply will not do. No "particular" is ontologically sui generis, and no "general" is ultimately universal; it is all a matter of shades and gradations. Neither can exist in any meaningful way without the other. Nor, Giddens continues, is the distinction between history as the social science of "dead" people and sociology as the social science of "living" subjects examined in the first person very useful in terms of substantive theoretical and disciplinary difference:

> Social science is done in and through texts and other "secondary" materials as history is. The efforts a social scientist might expend in direct communication with the [living] agents who are the subjects of his or her research investigations are likely to be tiny compared with those which must be spent working through textual materials.

What is the difference then? In the final analysis, Giddens concludes, "nothing." *Nothing* separates history from the social sciences on a conceptual level: "If there are divisions between social science and history, they are substantive divisions of labour; there is no logical or methodological schism." To differences in labor we would add, perhaps, differences in temperament, sensibility, and engagement with the present. We are not advocating the elimination of the labels "sociologist" and "historian." Yet, as Giddens suggests, these differences do not rend the heart of our common enterprise, which is the evolution (Giddens would say "structuration") of American society.[48]

Giddens arrives at this plea for unanimity in part by defining sociology more modestly to include only the study of modern societies in their historical contexts, and leaving premodern to anthropology or archeology. He also rejects grand theory: "The search for a theory of social change . . . is a doomed one. It is flawed by the same kind of logical shortcomings that attach more generally to the supposition that the social sciences can uncover universal laws of human conduct." Historians and sociologists, functionalists and structuralists, cultural and social, quantitative and narrative all represent slightly different labors within a common vineyard. The New Social History and "Narrative" history need each other:

The advocates of narrative history are quite justified in objecting to the indiscriminate importation of the concepts of structural sociology into the work of historians. But they are not right to suppose that such concepts can be ignored altogether. What makes a narrative a persuasive "story" is not just the coherence of the plot but, as [G. R.] Elton says, understanding the "setting, circumstances, and springs" of action. However, the settings and circumstances within which action occurs do not come out of thin air; they themselves have to be explained within the very same logical framework as that in which whatever action described and "understood" has also to be explained.

In like manner, the divisions between "qualitative" and "quantitative" methodologies in both history and sociology are, on close examination, artificial:

> Quantitative techniques are usually likely to be demanded when a large number of "cases" of a phenomenon are to be investigated, in respect of a restricted variety of designated characteristics ["variables"]. But both the collection and interpretation of quantitative material depends upon procedures methodologically identical to the gathering of data of a more intensive, "qualitative" sort. . . . All so-called "quantitative" data, when scrutinized, turn out to be composites of "qualitative"—i.e. contextually located and indexical—interpretations produced by situated researchers, coders, government officials and others. The hermeneutic problems posed by ethnographic research also exist in the case of quantitative studies . . . [and] they lead us to appraise the nature of quantitative data rather differently [i.e. less objectively] from some of the advocates of structural sociology.[49]

Historians should be more interested in sociology now that functionalism, with its general disregard for history and human agency, has declined. The possibilities for mutual borrowing and dialogue are great. So, too, sociologists are more disposed than ever to entertain cultural analysis on its own terms rather than as the creation of social structures.[50] Both disciplines are poised on the edge of new constructions. But they need to do it together.

Giddens recognizes that history and narrative also needs to teach sociology something about their prose and reaching a wide audience of interested Americans. In part, the lesson is methodological. There is in much sociology a confusion of audiences that Giddens terms a "double hermeneutic." This occurs, he notes, at: "the intersection of two frames of meaning as a logically necessary part of social science, the meaningful social world as constituted by lay actors and the metalanguages invented by social scientists; there is a constant 'slippage' from one to the other involved in the practice of the social sciences."[51] There is nothing wrong with "lay language"—the language historians typically employ in recreating the lifeworlds of the subjects they study (usually referred to reconstructing the past "on its own terms"). There is also the metalanguage or theoretical language that is known to the observer as a sort of abstract shorthand, but not to the subject. The problem comes when the two become confused, and sociologists begin writing for their subjects as though they were co-observers, tuned into the special language. Talcott Parsons is perhaps a perfect case example of the bafflement that ensues from this confusion.

Historians have much to teach sociologists about the craft of writing. To a far greater extent than sociology, history has always recognized a dual responsibility to reach their peers in the profession as well as a larger reading audience. The very best historians—Richard Hofstadter, Edmund Morgan, Sydney Ahlstrom, Bernard Bailyn, C. Vann Woodward, Gordon Wood, and James McPherson, to name only a few—were and are also great writers, garnering their fair share of Pulitzer Prizes, National Book Awards, and wide circulations. Sociologists owe it to the public to do the same. To be sure, sociologists like Robert Bellah, Peter Berger, and Robert Wuthnow have reached wide, nonsociological audiences in clear and lucid prose. But more needs to be done.

Sociologists also need to be more self-conscious about "contextualizing" their scholarship in historical settings. Here too they need historians overlooking the *longue durée* to avoid anachronism and hyperbole in the assignment of discontinuous "transformations," or of unprecedented "restructurings," "revolutions," and "culture wars." Relatedly, they need historians' careful work with biography and autobiography to resist the ecological fallacy of confusing correlation with causation, which comes especially easy to studies entailing many individual cases and computer-scored data. It is only when one views an individual over the entire course of a life cycle that the complexities of self and society become fully appreciated in ways that defeat any single sociological, psychological, or cultural reduction.

Even as historians and sociologists trade with their strengths they need to coalesce around common theoretical and empirical concerns. From our survey of the literature and questionnaire, it would appear that the two bodies of theoretical literature with the greatest promise are organizational theory and secularization theory. Both historians and sociologists believe that studies of religion as an organization and movement have enjoyed the greatest advances in the past two decades. Logically, this would appear to be a foundation for further growth. For historians, there is an added bonus in exploring the past within the terms of organizations and the "New Institutionalism"; it will bring them into the twentieth century with the same sophistication they have brilliantly evidenced for premodern periods. How have religion and religious institutions helped to shape the "organizational revolution" that characterizes modern Western societies? And how has that revolution shaped religious organizations and religious meaning in the twentieth century? By building on the insights of organizational sociology, historians are in an ideal position to fill out the story of religion in modern America.[52]

Secularization theory is the other point at which the disciplines of history and sociology converge most directly in studies of American religion.

And here, where definition and context are everything, it appears that sociology has much to gain from history. In his recent and controversial article on the secularization paradigm, Stephen Warner challenges the assumption of secularization as it relates to modern America and grounds his argument largely on "what sociologists have learned from historians."[53] Clearly, the issue of secularization has not been resolved, but it has been advanced by the recognition that it is a problem and not a paradigm. Equally clear is the fact that historians will play a major role in testing the theory throughout American history through their longitudinal case studies. Historians do not need to pursue ever-new topics so much as they need to relate their work to broader, theoretical concerns.

The examples of mutual borrowing and collaboration could be expanded no less infinitely than the menu of needs and opportunities for research we earlier decried. The point in all of this, it seems to us, is that we are at a critical juncture in studies of religion in American society that may not reappear. The workers are there, the institutional networks are in place, and the funding, for the moment anyway, is secure. The time is ripe for a recovery of cross-disciplinary conversation, and consolidation. Who knows, it may even lead to new directions in studies of American religion.

NOTES

1. We acknowledge Yale's Program on Non-Profit Organizations, the Program on Religion sponsored by the Lilly Endowment, and the Pew Evangelical Scholar's program sponsored by the Pew Trusts for financial assistance in this project. We also acknowledge the assistance of Professors Jay Demerath, Rhys Williams, James Davidson, Roger Finke, and Jan Shipps in helping us to construct the 1993 questionnaire. For assistance in mailing and processing the 1993 questionnaire, we thank Jenifer Karyshin, Deborah Stout, and James Stout. Finally, we thank Connie McBirney for assistance with data entry and statistical analysis.

2. The following scholars responded to the 1974 questionnaire: Sydney A. Ahlstrom, Ross W. Beales, Robert K. Berkhofer, Nelson Burr, Richard L. Bushman, William Clebsch, Cedric Cowing, Robert Cummings, Mario DePillis, Robert Doherty, Allen Eister, Ronald Formisano, Lawrence Fuchs, Clarence C. Goen, John C. Greene, Robert T. Handy, Winthrop S. Hudson, William R. Hutchison, Richard J. Jensen, Benton Johnson, Henry Leonard, Jo Ann Manfra, George Marsden, Martin E. Marty, Sister Marie Augusta Neal, Ronald Osborn, Richard Reintz, Ernest R. Sandeen, Daniel Scott Smith, Timothy L. Smith, Harry S. Stout, Robert P. Swierenga, Robert M. Taylor, Jr., John Van Til, James P. Walsh, Robert V. Wells, and Michael Zuckerman.

3. See, for example, Robert F. Berkhofer, Jr., "Clio and the Culture Concept: Some Impressions of a Changing Relationship in American Historiography," in Louis Schneider and Charles M. Bonjean, eds., The Idea of Culture in the Social Sciences (Cambridge, Mass., 1973), 77–100; and Barton J. Bernstein, ed., Towards a New Past: Dissenting Essays in American History (New York, 1968).

4. For historians' sense of a "discipline in ferment" in the 1970s, see Felix Gilbert and Stephen R. Graubard, eds., *Historical Studies Today* (New York, 1972).

5. Henry Warner Bowden traces the formation and early history of the "new" American Society of Church History in *In the Age of Science: Historiographical Patterns in the United States 1876–1918* (Chapel Hill: 1971), 239–46.

6. Of the many essays tracing Miller's post–World War II influence on American history writing, see especially the collection of essays printed in the *Harvard Review* 2 (1964); Robert Middlekauff, "Perry Miller," in Marcus Cunliffe and Robin W. Winks, eds., *Pastmasters: Some Essays on American Historians* (New York, 1969), 167–90; George M. Marsden, "Perry Miller's Rehabilitation of the Puritans: A Critique," *Church History*, 39 (1970): 91–105; and David A. Hollinger, "Perry Miller and Philosophical History," *History and Theory* 7 (1968): 189–202.

7. May's essay is reprinted in Henry F. May, *Ideas, Faiths and Feelings: Essays on American Intellectual and Religious History 1952–1982* (New York, 1983).

8. By 1974, a veritable industry of Puritan-based religious histories, spawned by Miller and his students Edmund S. Morgan and Alan Heimert, appeared in print. The literature is traced in Michael G. McGiffert, "American Puritan Studies in the 1960s," *William and Mary Quarterly* 25 (1968): 36–67, and David D. Hall's essay prepared for this conference. Religion's "recovery" as intellectual history was a *betrayal* of religion in that it confined attention to the Puritans and their legacy. Religion in a modern age was banished to the sidelines and left for "church historians" plying their trade in the obscurity of the divinity schools. In 1974, no scholars— religious or otherwise—challenged secularization theory or its consequences for religious history; instead, secularization functioned as a paradigm—as a taken-for-granted reality that was never tested, and universally believed. Among historians, the secularization paradigm received classic (and for the most part uncontested) articulation in Vernon Parrington's *Main Currents in American Thought* (3 vols.; New York, 127–30), vol. 2, *The Romantic Revolution*. Among sociologists dealing with secularization in the twentieth century, see especially Peter L. Berger, Bridgitte Berger, and Hansfried Kellner, *The Homeless Mind: Modernization and Consciousness* (New York, 1974); and Thomas Luckmann, *The Invisible Religion: The Problems of Religion in Modern Society* (New York, 1967).

9. For optimistic surveys and assessments of the field, see Jerald C. Brauer, "Changing Perspectives on Religion in America," in Jerald C. Brauer, ed., *Reinterpretation in American Church History* (Chicago, 1968), 1–28; Paul A. Carter, "Recent Historiography of the Protestant Churches in America," *Church History* 37 (1968): 95–107; Sydney A. Ahlstrom, "The Problem of the History of Religion in America," *Church History* 39 (1970): 224–35; Eldon G. Ernst, "American Religious History: A Report on the Renaissance Since 1970," *Foundations* 16 (1973): 68–72; Edwin Gaustad, *Religion in America: History and Historiography* (Washington, 1973); John Tracy Ellis, "The Ecclesiastical Historian in the Service of Clio," *Church History* 38 (1969); and David J. O'Brien, "American Catholic Historiography: A Post-Conciliar Evaluation," *Church History* 37 (1968).

10. On the enduring significance of Ahlstrom's writing and teaching, see Henry Warner Bowden, "The Historiography of American Religion," in Charles Lippy and Peter Williams, eds., *Encyclopedia of the American Religious Experience.* 3 vol. (New York, 1989), 11.

In range and coverage there has not been another remotely comparable work to that of Ahlstrom's *A Religious History of the American People*. His "Puritan synthesis" extended Miller's *New England Mind*. Where Miller stopped in the early nineteenth century, Ahlstrom continued the story to its last chapter in the 1960s. Sidney Mead stands alongside Ahlstrom as representing the culmination of the Miller tradition. He, too, wrote religous history as intellectual history and employed a Whiteheadian concept of "religion" to move postcolonial religious history out of the domain of "church history" and the study of denominations and institutions, into the domain of cultural history. See especially Sidney E. Mead, *The Lively Experiment: The Shaping of Christianity in America* (New York, 1973); and *The Nation with the Soul of a Church* (Macon,Ga., 1985). Most of Mead's essays appeared originally as articles in *Church History* and the *Journal of Church and State*. For an assessment of Mead's contribution, see Jerald C. Brauer, "Changing Perspectives on Religion." Mead consolidated America's religious impulses into a form of civil religion he termed the "Religion of the Republic." See especially "The Nation with the Soul of a Church," *Church History* 36 (1967): 262–83; H. Richard Niebuhr, *Radical Monotheism and Western Culture* (New York, 1943); Will Herberg, *Protestant–Catholic–Jew* (Garden City, N.Y., 1960); and Robert Bellah, "Civil Religion in America," *Daedalus* 96 (1967): 1–21.

On the uneasy tension between the Religion of the Republic and the ongoing fact of "sectarianism" and growing pluralism, see Mead's "The Fact of Pluralism and the Persistence of Sectarianism," in Elwyn A. Smith, ed., *The Religion of the Republic* (Philadelphia, 1971), 239–47. The preference in the 1960s and 1970s for pluralism as an ideological good influenced interpretations of religion. Ahlstrom, Marty, and others cast their vote decisively for pluralism as the great American failure. Recognizing pluralism as the appropriate American ideology, students of American religion launched an assault on the themes of civil religion. Besides Ahlstrom, *A Religious History of the American People* (New Haven, 1972); and Martin E. Marty, *Righteous Empire: The Protestant Experience in America* (New York, 1970), see H. Shelton Smith, *In His Image But . . . Racism in Southern Religion. 1780–1910* (Durham, 1972); and Robert T. Handy, *A Christian America: Protestant Hopes and Historical Realities* (New York, 1971). For an incisive review essay of Marty and Handy, see William Clebsch, "Thesis and Theme: Two Histories of American Protestantism," *Journal of Religion* 53 (1973): 99–103. Among sociologists, see especially Peter L. Berger, *The Sacred Canopy* (New York, 1969); and J. Childress and D. Hamed, *Secularization and the Protestant Prospect* (Philadelphia, 1970).

On civil religion see Robert N. Bellah, "American Civil Religion in the 1970s," in Russell E. Richey and Donald G. Jones, eds., *American Civil Religion* (New York, 1974), 255–272. See also Henry F. May, "The Religion of the Republic," reprinted in *Ideas, Faiths and Feelings,* 163–86; Robert T. Handy, "The Protestant Quest for a Christian America, 1830–1930," *Church History* 27 (1953): 8–19; John F. Wilson, "A Historians's Approach to Civil Religion," in Richey and Jones, eds., *American Civil Religion* 115–38; Martin E. Marty, "Two Kinds of Two Kinds of Civil Religion," ibid., 139–60; David Little, "The Origins of Perplexity: Civil Religion and Moral Belief in the Thought of Thomas Jefferson," ibid., 161–83; Franklin H. Littell, "The Churches and the Body Politic," in William G. McLoughlin and Robert N. Bellah, eds., *Religion in America* (Boston, 1968), 24–44; William G. McLoughlin, "Is there a Third Force in Christendom?"

ibid., 45–72; Bryan Wilson, "Religion and the Churches in Contemporary America," ibid., 73–110; Edwin S. Gaustad, "America's Institutions of Faith," ibid., 111–36; Joseph Blau, "Alternatives Within Contemporary American Judaism," ibid., 299–311; Sister Marie Augustana Neal, "Catholicism in America," ibid., 312–38; Cushing Strout, *The New Heavens and New Earth Political Religion in America* (New York, 1974); and Nathan O. Hatch, "The Origins of Civil Millennialism in America: New England Clergymen, War with France, and the Revolution," *William and Mary Quarterly* 31 (1974): 407–30. For many, ethnicity came to define the vital center of religion in America; indeed, for some it served as a surrogate for religion. Coinciding with this trend among religious historians and sociologists, a new group of social and political scholars backed into American religious history through their discovery of the "ethnocultural" variable in social and political behavior. See Timothy L. Smith, "Religious Denominations as Ethnic Communities: A Regional Case Study," *Church History* 35 (1966): 207–26; Martin E. Marty, "Ethnicity: The Skeleton of Religion in America," *Church History* 41 (1972); Harry S. Stout, "Ethnicity: The Vital Center of Religion in America," *Ethnicity* (Winter, 1975) 204–224; John L. Shover, "Ethnicity and Religion in Philadelphia Politics, 1924–1940," *American Quarterly* 25 (1973): 449–515; Wayne L. Bochelman and Owen S. Ireland, "The Internal Revolution in Pennsylvania: An Ethnic–Religious Interpretation," *Pennsylvania History* 41 (1974): 125–60; Owen S. Ireland, "The Ethnic–Religious Dimension of Pennsylvania Politics, 1778–1789," *William and Mary Quarterly* 30 (1973): 423–48; John L. Hammond, "Revival Religion and Anti-slavery Politics," *American Sociological Review* 39 (1974): 175–87.

11. Institutional commitments of senior, divinity-based, scholars inhibited them from following through with research on previously neglected groups, though they agreed on the need for such. Thus, in 1974 we encountered little specificity on which groups ought to be studied and how. Robert Handy voiced this vagueness when answering our question "What are the major immediate areas of needed research in the history of American Religion?" He wanted to give "attention to the emergence of new religious groups of many kinds" in addition to "fresh evaluations of the interrelationships of ethnic groups and religious history." Rather than groups or themes, the respondents singled out neglected periods or regions. Ernest R. Sandeen, for example, asserted that "the twentieth century is the area of most crying need, especially the years from 1918 to 1963." Only a handful of scholars mentioned particular groups outside the mainstream. Jo Ann Manfra stressed "sophisticated studies of [Roman Catholic] religious leadership." No one mentioned fundamentalism, evangelicalism, Pentecostalism, Mormonism, women, or spiritualism. Many mentioned the need to study the "Black Church," without specifying which black church, when, or where.

12. The pioneering works in the New Social History included Philip J. Greven, *Four Generations: Population, Land, and Family in Colonial Andover, Massachusetts* (Ithaca, 1970); Kenneth A. Lockridge, *A New England Town, the First Hundred Years: Dedham, Massachusetts. 1636–1736* (New York, 1970); John Demos, *A Little Commonwealth: Family Life in Plymouth Colony* (New York, 1970); Michael Zuckerman, *Peaceable Kingdoms: New England Towns in the Eighteenth Century* (New York, 1970). Each of these studies borrowed widely from the theories and methods of the social sciences and applied those tools to bodies of historical data dealing with "ordinary people." Almost overnight graduate programs rushed to establish courses on "Theory and Method"

in history writing. Suddenly, it seemed like the whole field of historical studies was shifting underneath. The colonial period enjoyed an unparalleled popularity and influence as Joyce Appleby summarized recently in "A Different Kind of Independence: The Postwar Restructuring of the Historical Study of Early America," *William and Mary Quarterly* 50 (1993): 245–67, see especially page 250.

13. Leading the way in the initiation of historians to sociology and quantitative methods were the Newberry Library summer seminars beginning in 1972. For a summary of increased research in "social history," see David S. Landes and Charles Tilly, *History as Social Science* (Englewood Cliffs, 1971). The particular sociology favored by the New Social historians was the functionalism associated with Talcott Parsons and his "Harvard" school. Among the more important sociological works for historical research in the 1970s were Talcott Parsons, *The Social System* (New York, 1951); Neil J. Smelser, *Social Change in the Industrial Revolution* (Chicago, 1959); Sigmund Diamond, "From Organization to Society," *American Journal of Sociology* 63 (1958): 457–75; R. Bendix and S. Lipset, eds., *Class, Status, Power: Social Stratification in Comparative Perspective* (New York, 1966); Neil J. Smelser, *Essays in Sociological Explanation* (Englewood Cliffs, 1968); much of the methodology in social scientific and demographic research was summarized in Charles M. Dollar and Richard J. Jensen, *Historian's Guide to Statistics* (New York, 1971); and T. H. Hollingworth, *Historical Demography* (Ithaca, 1969). In retrospect, the triumph of functionalism marked the pinnacle of American-based sociology and of its pragmatic faith in legal–rational modern organizations and Enlightenment values to construct a humane, "modern" society. Building on Max Weber's modernization paradigm, metatheories abounded describing modernization within the mechanical and evolutionary context of systems analysis. Above all else, the modern systems were stable and rational, where religion functioned as a component of culture destined to be displaced by more rational symbolic forms. For sociologists no less than historians, "secularization" appeared as an inescapable partner to modernization. Two studies that employed modernization theory to understand American history were Harry S. Stout, "Culture, Structure, and the 'New' History: A Critique and an Agenda," *Computers and the Humanities* 9 (1975): 213–30; and Richard D. Brown, *Modernization* (New York, 1979). For a good review of sociological theory and the paradigmatic (unthinking) linkage of modernization and secularization, see Cyril E. Black, "Dynamics of Modernization," in Robert Nisbet, ed., *Social Change* (New York, 1972), 237–70.

14. We use the term "discontinuous change" in the sense described by Robert Nisbet as a qualitative and categorical change that does "not emerge genetically, in cumulative, growth-like, and sequential fashion from a long line of smaller changes within the system." *Social Change*, 21.

15. Burr's viewpoint might be termed a "Christian particularism," a form of providential historiography that separates out historical explanation from "naturalistic" categories and looks instead to divine providence. In his perceptive article " 'And the Lion Shall Lie Down with the Lamb': The Social Sciences and Religious History," *Fides et Historia* 20 (1988): 20–21, Mark A. Noll summarizes this view as one in which: "events of religious history are regarded exclusively as transcendent and because transcendent, immune to the techniques of the social sciences. In general, the more thorough the divide in a religion between nature and grace, God and the world, revelation and reason, the less room will

be left for social scientific explanation. In America, providential history has flourished most obviously among Protestant fundamentalists, evangelicals, and Pentecostals, Ultramontane Roman Catholics, Mormons, and other adherents of intensely supernaturalistic faiths." For variations on this theme that allow limited room for social scientific explanation within a larger theological framework, see George Marsden and Frank Roberts, eds., *A Christian View of History?* (Grand Rapids, 1975); C. T. McIntire and Ronald A. Wells, eds., *History and Historical Understanding* (Grand Rapids, 1984); or Harry S. Stout, "Theological Commitment and American Religious History," *Theological Education,* 25 (1989), 44–59. For a fuller discussion and critique of some of the implications of this perspective, see below.

16. Jon Butler, "Born-Again America? A Critique of the New 'Evangelical Thesis' in Recent American Historiography," unpublished paper, Organization of American Historians, Spring 1991.

17. In their survey of the rise of religion departments, Harold E. Remus, F. Stanley Lasby, and Linda M. Tober conclude: "The academic study of religion in the last quarter of the twentieth century reflects both the pluralism of American society and of the 'global village' and the steady expansion and specialization of knowledge in academia. The study of religion is thus moving away from definitions and conceptions of religion and attendant methods of study inherited from Christianity, particularly from the Protestant seminary curriculum." See "Religion as an Academic Discipline," in Charles H. Lippy and Peter W. Williams eds., *Encylopedia of the American Religious Experience* (3 vols., New York, 1988), 1664. See also John F. Wilson's introduction to *The Study of Religion in Colleges and Universities,* 3–22; and James M. Gustafson, "The Study of Religion in Colleges and Universities: A Practical Commentary," in ibid., 330–46.

18. For convenient summaries and indexes of recent Roman Catholic scholarship, see the working papers of the Cushwa Center. For "evangelical" historiography see Edith L. Blumhofer and Joel A. Carpenter, eds., *Twentieth Century Evangelicalism: A Guide to the Sources* (New York, 1990); Charles H. Lippy and Peter W. Williams, eds., *Encyclopedia of the American Religious Experience;* Richard T. Hughes, ed., *The American Quest for the Primitive Church* (Urbana, 1988); or Stanley M. Burgess and Gary B. McGee, eds., *Dictionary of Pentecostal and Charismatic Movements* (Grand Rapids, 1988). The expansive literature on religion in the South is indexed and summarized in Charles Lippy, ed., *A Bibliography of Religion in the South* (Macon, 1985); Samuel S. Hill, ed., *Encylcopedia of Religion in the South* (Macon, 1984); and Charles Reagan Wilson, ed., *Religion in the South* (Jackson, 1985). The two defining works on religion in the early Republic are Jon Butler, *Awash in a Sea of Faith: Christianizing the American People* (Cambridge, Harvard University Press, 1990); and Nathan O. Hatch, *The Democratization of American Christianity* (New Haven, 1989).

19. "Report of the Editors," *Church History,* September, 1993: 461.

20. See especially Robert Wuthnow, *The Restructuring of American Religion* (Princeton, 1988); Phillip E. Hammond, "In Search of a Protestant Twentieth Century: American Religion and Power Since 1900," *Review of Religious Research* 24 (1983): 269–89; Robert de V. Brunkow, ed., *Religion and Society in North America: An Annotated Bibliography* (Santa Barbara, 1983); Andrew M. Greeley and William McManus, *Catholic Contributions: Sociology and Policy* (Chicago, 1987); or Robert Wuthnow, ed., *The Religious Dimension: New Directions in Quantitative Research* (New York, 1979).

21. For a recent summary see Steve Bruce, ed., *Religion and Modernization: Sociologists and Historians Debate the Secularization Thesis* (Oxford, 1992).

22. See Peter Dobkin Hall, *Inventing the Nonprofit Sector and Other Essays on Philanthropy, Voluntarism, and Nonprofit Organizations* (Baltimore, 1992). For a fuller discussion of these themes, see below. Letter to the authors, September, 1993.

23. The 1993 questionaire was mailed to 1,974 academics in the fields of history, religion, sociology, and divinity, together with another 1,000 librarians, churchmen and churchwomen, lay subscribers to history and sociology journals and secondary teachers. In distributing our questionnaire, we relied on the mailing lists and membership lists of the ASCH, the Institute for the Study of American Evangelicalism, the Cushwa Center, the American Academy of Religion, and the Society for the Scientific Study of Religion. For purposes of this essay, we were primarily interested in the professional academics, of whom over 500 responded, divided between historians, sociologists, and historians based in religion departments and divinity schools. We do not claim that the 1993 data are broadly representative of the whole field of American religious scholarship, and make no claims for the representativeness of coverage. Indeed, we suspect that major pockets of scholarship eluded our nets or failed to return the questionnaire. For example, not included in our survey (to this point) are American historians who work on religious themes but do not identify themselves in any organizational way as "American religious historians." We hope to pick up many of these generic "American historians" in a follow-up survey. Predictably, our respondents had much to say about the questionaire as well as about religious scholarship. As a rule, historians typically dismissed questionnaires as a "silly" exercise but went on to fill out the questionnaire anyway. Sociologists believed passionately in survey research but found this "instrument" badly flawed. Nevertheless, they too filled it out. The side comments and sometimes separate letters (all of which have been filed for this study) we found of use. All of the statistics cited in this study derive from our survey respondents as of August 1, 1993. A copy of the survey data base will be left on deposit at the Yale Divinity School Library.

24. It is interesting that while Jews are disproportionally numerous in academia generally (see Hollinger essay), their numbers in religion remain as low as their national presence.

25. For a summary of this scholarship by American historians (as distinct from American religious historians), see Jon Butler, "Born-Again History?" One divinity-based respondent pointed out in a separate letter that the instrument we employed itself betrayed a bias to the "religious studies approach" to religion at the expense of church history.

26. We did not include gender because it is only now reaching its ascendancy and permeating the disciplines of religious history and sociology of religion.

27. In a recent survey of religious history funding conducted by Scott Cormode, he discovered that in Guggenheim competitions between 1975 and 1991, only 16 of 141 grants in American history also dealt with religion. ACLS fellowships on religion in the same period averaged only one fellowship per year. Between 1980 and 1991, there were only 13 NEH Research Fellowships for religious research that exceeded $10,000.

28. Substantial funding encourages the acquisition and compilation of substantial archives and data to fuel new generations of scholarship, as has happened

in the past decade with large projects undertaken by Robert Bellah, James Hunter, Robert Wuthnow, James Davidson, Dean Hoge, John Mulder, and the Louisville Institute, and Benton Johnson. These—and other—research projects are listed and updated in the research reports and summaries of the Lilly Endowment, The Pew Charitable Trusts, the Cushwa Center, the Institute for the Study of American Evangelicalism, and the Louisville Institute for the Study of American Protestantism.

29. Beginning with Timothy L. Smith and William Hutchison, the practice has now expanded to include major projects headed by Grant Wacker, Nathan Hatch, George Marsden, and Jay Dolan. Also, conferences sponsored by Pew, Lilly, the Cushwa Center, and ISAE have been funded around a great variety of themes. And finally, scholarly editions have been funded, most notably, *The Works of Jonathan Edwards*. Beyond scholarship, large graduate and junior faculty fellowship programs have been established out of Louisville Seminary, Notre Dame, Princeton University, Harvard Divinity School, and Yale University. Many of the proceedings of the conferences have been published in the "Religion in America" series published by Oxford University Press.

30. The "historylessness" in religious history appeared also in reply to the question: "because of the enormous changes in the religious realm over the past twenty-five years or so, the classic works in my field from the 19th and early 20th century are increasingly irrelevant for both research and graduate training." Historians led the way in agreeing with this proposition. Forty percent of historians find the classics in their field "increasingly irrelevant" compared with 13% of sociologists.

31. But even there, the work is almost solely confined to Protestant institutional and intellectual history. The antimodern bias was not lost on one of our respondents, who recounted: "Once a student came up to me in my survey course on the first half of American history. He questioned why I spent so much time on religion, adding that his friend who had taken my course on the second half said I did not do so in that class. I hadn't really thought about it, but the student was right. That reflects not just my shortcomings but, I suspect, the state of scholarship. I continue to think, as I told the student at the time, religion played a more central role earlier in American history, but American historians have gone too far with the secularization model and do need to develop a better interpretation of the role of religion in American society after the Civil War."

32. Not surprisingly, women's history and religious studies have found common cause with one another. See, for example, Barbara Welter, "The Feminization of American Religion," in Marty Hartman and Lois Banner, eds., *Clio's Consciousness Raised* (New York, 1973); Elizabeth B. Clark, "Women and Religion in America, 1780–1870," in John F. Wilson, ed., *Church and State in America: A Bibliographic Guide*, vol. 1 (New York, 1986), 365–413; and Harry S. Stout and Catherine A. Brekus, "Declension, Gender, and the 'New Religious History,'" in Philip R. Vandermeer and Robert P. Swierenga, eds., *Belief and Behavior: Essays in the New Religious History* (New Brunswick, 1991), 15–37.

33. The five volumes of the Fundamentalism Project Series published by the University of Chicago Press are: Martin E. Marty and R. Scott Appleby, eds., *Fundamentalisms Observed*, vol. 1 (1991); *Fundamentalisms Society: Reclaiming the Sciences, the Family, and Educatiotion*, vol. 2 (1993); *Fundamentalisms the State: Remaking Politics, Militance, and Economics*, vol. 3, (1993) *Accounting*

for Fundamentalisms: The Dynamic Character of Movements, vol. 4 (1994); Fundamentalisms Comprehended, vol. 5 (1995).

34. See especially Roger Friedland and Robert R. Alford, "Bringing Society Back In: Symbols, Practices, and Institutional Contradictions," in Walter U. Powell and Paul J. DiMaggio, eds., The New Institutionalism in Organizational Analysis (Chicago, 1991), 232–66.

35. Jon Butler, Awash in a Sea of Faith; David D. Hall, Worlds of Wonder Days of Judgment: Popular Religious Beliefs in Early New England (New York, 1989); Mark A. Noll, George M. Rawlyk, and David W. Bebbington, eds., Evangelicalism: Popular Protestantism of North America and the British Isles. 1700–1990 (New York, 1994); Jan Shipps, Mormonism: The Story of a New Religious Tradition (Urbana, 1985); Catherine Albanese, America Religions and Religion, 2nd ed. (Belmont, 1992); Nathan O. Hatch, The Democratization of American Christianity; Patricia U. Bonomi, Under the Code of Heaven: Religion, Society and Politics in Colonial America (New York, 1986); David Nord, "The Evangelical Origins of Mass Media in America, 1815–1835," Journalism Monographs, no. 88 (1984); and "Systematic Benevolence: Religious Publishing and the Marketplace in Early Nineteenth-Century America," in Leonard I. Sweet, ed., Communications and Change in American Religious History (Grand Rapids, 1994); David Harrell, Oral Roberts (New York, 1992); Jay Dolan, The American Catholic Experience: A History from Colonial Times to the Present (Garden City, 1985); Robert A. Orsi, The Madonna of 115 Street: Faith and Community in Italian Harlem (New Haven, 1985); Donald G. Mathews, Religion in the Old South (Chicago, 1977); Ann C. Loveland, Southern Evangelicals and the Social Order, 1800–1860 (Baton Rouge, 1980); E. Brooks Holifield, The Gentlemen Theologians (Durham, 1978); Rhys Isaac, The Transformation of Virginia 1740–1790 (Chapel Hill, 1982); David Brion Davis, The Problem of Slavery in the Age of Revolution (New York, 1978); Eugene Genovese, Roll, Jordan Roll: The World the Slaves Made (New York, 1976); Albert Rabateau, Slave Religion: The "Invisible Institution" in the Antebellum South (New York, 1978); George M. Marsden and Bradley J. Longfield, The Secularization of the Academy (New York, 1992); R. Laurence Moore, Religious Outsiders and the Making of Americans (New York, 1986); Ann Braude, Radical Spirits: Spiritualism and Women's Rights in Nineteenth-Century America (Boston, 1989); Steven Stein, The Shakers (New Haven, 1993); Joel A. Carpenter, Revive Us Again: The Recovery of American Fundamentalism, 1930–1950 (New York, forthcoming); and Grant Wacker, "The Holy Spirit and the Spirit of the Age in American Protestantism, 1880–1910," Journal of American History 72 (1985): 45–62.

36. Philip Vandermeer and Robert Swierenga, eds., Belief and Behavior. See also Robert P. Swierenga, "Ethnoreligious Political Behavior in the MidNineteenth Century: Voting, Values, Cultures," in Mark A. Noll, ed., Religion and American Politics From the Colonial Period to the 1980s (New York, 1990), 146–71; and Ronald P. Formisano, "The New Political History and the Election of 1840," Journal of Interdisciplinary History 23 (1993): 661–82.

37. See, for example, Roger Finke and Rodney Stark, The Churching of America; N. J. Demerath III and Rhys H. Williams, A Bridging of Faiths (Princeton, 1994); David G. Hackett, The Rude Hand of Innovation: Religion and Social Order in Albany, New York 1652–1836 (New York, 1991); Nancy Ammerman, Baptist Battles: Social Change and Religious Conflict in the Southern Baptist Convention

(New Brunswick, 1990); K. L. Billingsley, *From Mainline to Sideline* (Washington, D.C., 1990); William D'Antonio et. al., *American Catholic Laity in a Changing Church* (Kansas City, 1989); Allan Figueroa Deck, S. J., *The Second Wave: Hispanic Ministry and the Evangelization of Cultures* (New York, 1989); Charles Y. Glock and Robert N. Bellah, eds., *The New Religious Consciousness* (Berkeley, 1976); Dean Hoge and David Roozen, eds., *Understanding Church Growth and Decline, 1950–1978* (New York, 1979); James Hunter, *Culture Wars* (New York, 1991); Laurence R. Iannaccone, "Religious Practice: A Human Capital Approach," *Journal for the Scientific Study of Religion* 29 (1990), 297–314; Dean Kelley, "Why Conservative Churches are Still Growing," in Patrick H. McNamara, ed., *Religion: North American Style* (Belmont, 1984); Wade Clark Roof and William McKinney, *American Mainline Religion: Its Changing Shape and Future* (New Brunswick, 1987); Stephen R. Warner, *New Wine in Old Wineskins: Evangelicals and Liberals in a Small-Town Church* (Berkeley, 1988); or Robert Wuthnow, *The Restructuring of American Religion.*

38. On the collapse of any center in history, see Francis Fukuyama's provocative essay "The End of History?" *The National Interest* 16 (1989): 3–21. Pauline Marie Rosenau traces the implications of postmodern criticism for history in *Post-modernism and the Social Sciences: Insights, Inroads, and Institutions* (Princeton, 1992). See especially chap. 4, "Humbling History, Transforming Time, and Garbling Geography," 62–76.

39. See Lynn Hunt, "Introduction: History, Culture and Text," in Hunt, ed., *The New Cultural History* (Berkeley, 1989), 1–22.

40. Among postmodern works that have influenced historians most directly are Michel Foucault's "What is an Author?" in Josue Harari, ed., *Textual Strategies: Perspectives in Post-structuralist Criticism* (New York, 1979); and "What is Enlightenment?" in Paul Rabinow and William M. Sullivan eds., *Interpretive Social Science, A Second Look* (Berkeley, 1987); Jacques Derrida, *Positions* (Chicago, 1981); J. Baudrillard, "Modernity," *Canadian Journal of Political and Social Theory* 11 (1987): 63–72; Charles Maier, "The Politics of Time: Changing Paradigms of Collective Time and Private Time in the Modern Era," in C. Maier, ed., *Changing Boundaries of the Political* (Cambridge, 1987); or David Harvey, *The Condition of Postmodernity: An Enquiry into the Origins of Cultural Change* (Cambridge, Mass., 1989). Harold Bloom, *The American Religion: The Emergence of the Post Christian Nation* (New York, 1992), 80, 264. For a trenchant review of Bloom's literary analysis of American religion, see James D. Bratt, "Gnosticism American Style," *Evangelical Studies Bulletin* 9 (1992): 1–3. For other examples of historical works that treat religion as a "literary region," see David Laurence, "Jonathan Edwards as a Figure in Literary History," in Nathan O. Hatch and Harry S. Stout, eds., *Jonathan Edwards and the American Experience* (New York, 1988), 226–45; and R. C. DeProspo, "Humanizing the Monster: Integral Self Versus Bodied Soul in the Personal Writings of Franklin and Edwards," in Barbara O. Oberg and Harry S. Stout, eds., *Benjamin Franklin, Jonathan Edwards, and the Representation of American Culture* (New York, 1993), 204–18.

41. Gordon S. Wood, "Author's Postscript," in The College of William and Mary, *In Search of Early America: The William and Mary Quarterly, 1943–1993* (Richmond, 1993), 77. On this same theme, see Robert Darnton, "The Symbolic Element in History," *Journal of Modern History* 58 (1986): 218–34.

42. Clifford Geertz, *The Interpretation of Cultures* (New York, 1972), 452. See also Geertz's "History and Anthropology," *New Literary History* 21 (1990), 321–35.

43. This was precisely the argument made in response to the 1970s social history in Harry S. Stout, "Culture, Structure, and the New History."

44. William Roseberry, *Anthropologies and Histories: Essays in Culture, History, and Political Economy* (New Brunswick, 1989), 24, 28. See also R. Steven Sangren, "Rhetoric and the Authority of Ethnography: 'Postmodernism' and the Social Reproduction of Texts," *Current Anthropology* 29 (1988): 405–36.

45. For a good discussion of how some self-consciously "evangelical" historians have skirted the objectivity question (without abandoning the ideal), see Leonard I. Sweet, "Wise as Serpents, Innocent as Doves: The New Evangelical Historiography," *Journal of the American Academy of Religion* 56 (1989): 397–416.

46. This is not to say in any way that Christian particularists are proto-postmodernists. Indeed, it may be more accurate to classify them as premodern, that is, as scholars who reject both modernism's faith in reason and postmodernism's nihilism. While sharing postmodernism's skepticism regarding "science as value," Christian particularists have found in Geertz's notion of "culture as text" a quite different meaning. Eschewing all epistemologies of skepticism or nihilism, they interpret "text" quite literally to mean printed religious texts produced by an author. Where postmodernism tends to annhiliate the author—and along with it the possibility of shared knowledge, authentic representation, and theory-grounded interpretation—Christian religious historians celebrate the author and proceed to represent his or her ideas and legitimate their work as "cultural history." Hard social, economic, and psychological studies of writers and their audiences are not part of the agenda. Nor, for the most part, are the life worlds of ordinary people central subjects. In fact, from the questionnaire it appears that for many of our respondents, "cultural history" is the old intellectual history stripped of its apologetic patina, but nevertheless produced in the certainty that ideas can speak for themselves and that intellectual/cultural history carries transcendent "meaning" in a way that structures and functions cannot.

47. See especially Charles Tilly, *As Sociology Meets History* (New York, 1981), 1–52.

48. Anthony Giddens, *The Constitution of Society: Outline of the Theory of Structuration* (Berkeley, 1984), 357, 358.

49. Ibid., 360, 333–34. For a similar formulation from the historians' side, see Charles Tilly, *As Sociology Meets History*, 53–83.

50. For examples of recent turns to the culture concept in sociology, see especially Robert Wuthnow, et. al., *Cultural Analysis: The Work of Peter L. Berger, Mary Douglas, Michel Foucault, and Jurgen Habermas* (Boston, 1984); Roger Friedland and Robert R. Alford, "Bringing Symbols Back In," Richard Munch and Neil J. Smelser, eds., *Theory of Culture* (Berkeley, 1992); N. J. Demerath III, "Culture and Structure in the Decline of Liberal Protestantism and Recent Organizational Analysis," unpublished paper, Project on Religious Institutions at the Program on Non-Profit Organizations, Yale University, 1993; and Rhys H. Williams, "Rhetoric, Strategy, and Institutionalization: Social Movements and Cultural Resources," unpublished paper, Society for the Scientific Study of Religion, 1992.

51. Anthony Giddens, *The Constitution of Society*, 374.

52. Already in 1970, the historian Louis Galambos described "The Emerging Organizational Synthesis in Modern American History," *Business History Review* 44 (1970): 279–90, but the applications to religion were left out, in part because religious historians were not studying religion in the twentieth century. Much recent work in sociology, however, has picked up on the organizational synthesis as a context for understanding modern religion. See, for example, Mayer N. Zald and John D. McCarthy, "Religious Groups as Crucibles of Social Movements," in Mayer Zald and John D. McCarthy, eds., *Social Movements in an Organizational Society* (New Brunswick, 1990), 67–95; Patricia Mei Yin Chang, "An Institutional Analysis of the Evolution of the Denominational System in American Protestantism, 1790–1980," unpublished Ph.D. dissertation, Stanford University, 1993; John Bartholomew, "A Sociological View of Authority in Religious Organizations," *Review of Religious Research* 23 (1981): 118–32; M. R. Louis, "Organizations as Culture-Bearing Milieux," in L. Pondy et al., eds., *Organizational Symbolism* (New Haven, 1983), 39–54; J. W. Meyer and B. Rown, "Institutionalized Organizations: Formal Structure as Myth and Ceremony," *American Journal of Sociology* 83 (1977): 340–63. Among historians, see Russell E. Richey, "Institutional Forms of Religion," in Lippy and Williams eds., *Encyclopedia,* 31–50; John Wilson, "The Sociological Study of Religion," in ibid., 17–30; and D. Scott Cormode, "Secularization, Sacralization and Organizational Fields," unpublished paper, Program on Non-Profit Organizations, 1993.

53. R. Stephen Warner, "Work in Progress Toward a New Paradigm for the Sociological Study of Religion in the United States," *American Journal of Sociology* 98 (1993), 1044–93, quote at 1051. For other suggestive essays arguing both sides of the secularization thesis, see George M. Marsden and Bradley J. Longfield, *The Secularization of the Academy;* Steve Bruce, ed., *Religion and Modernization;* Mark Chaves, "Intraorganizational Power and Internal Secularization in Protestant Denominations," *American Journal of Sociology* 99 (1993): 1–48; Jeffrey K. Hadden and Anson Shupe, eds., *Secularization and Fundamentalism Reconsidered* (New York, 1988); and N. J. Demerath III and Rhys H. Williams, "Secularization in a Community Context: Tensions of Religion and Politics in a New England City," *Journal for the Scientific Study of Religion* 31 (1992): 189–206.

PART II

PROTESTANTISM
AND REGION

2

NARRATING PURITANISM

▦ ▦ ▦

David D. Hall

THREE YEARS OUT OF Harvard College, Jonathan Mitchel was named in 1650 to the office of pastor in the covenanted church of Cambridge, Massachusetts. Thereafter, his ministry to the men and women of the parish unfolded in ways that carried him beyond the training he received at Harvard and the rules of church discipline enshrined in the Cambridge Platform of 1648. Not that he disdained the Platform; it meant much to him, as did the "experimental" preaching of his predecessor in the Cambridge pulpit, Thomas Shepard. Mitchel may have known of Shepard's manuscript diary, with its revelations of that minister's recurrent questioning of his state of grace. The lessons to be learned from this diary were supplemented by the heart-searching meditations Mitchel himself engaged in and by what he observed among his people. While still a student, he heard Shepard preach a "terrible and excellent sermon" on the theme of persons who "seem to be found and saved by Christ, and yet afterwards . . . perish," a sermon that left him "terrified . . . lest [he] should only seem to belong unto Christ." Advising a brother on how to overcome the uncertainty of a "weak" faith, he emphasized the actions of the heart and will: a warm, affective, inward seeking after Christ and the strenuous pursuit of repentance. "Follow hard after God"—such was his advice to all young men—and women. Taking that path himself, he routinely confessed that he was "but vileness and abomination," though in other moments he felt encompassed within the bounds of Christ's mercy.[1]

To his parishioners he preached sermons that reiterated these themes. Some within his congregation surely followed him along the path to fervent spirituality, for he wrote of the church members that "they were a gracious, savoury-spirited people . . . liking an humbling, mourning, heart-breaking ministry . . . ; living in religion, praying men and women." Yet just as surely others were like his brother in doubting the possibility of becoming one of God's favored. There were those who, experiencing illness or hard times, resisted the message that these events were beneficial "afflictions." Now and then a parishioner blamed illness on acts of malice, or witchcraft.[2] But where spirituality as preached contrasted most often with spirituality as lived was in the rhythms of affiliation and participation. Mitchel's predecessor had warned the young people of the parish, some of whom were students at Harvard in their teens, that it would be "a wonder of wonders if ever God show . . . mercy" to unconverted persons over the age of 20.[3] The evangelical catchphrase of "Now or never" summed up the message about time that Shepard and, after him, Mitchel, pressed upon the congregation. The lay men and women of the parish responded to a different imperative. Not as youths, but as young adults about to have children, did they affiliate with the church, and a motive for their doing so was to incorporate the next generation within the community of the godly.[4]

The Cambridge meetinghouse was thus a place where lay and clerical expectations converged, and sometimes clashed. It was a place, moreover, where contradictions became visible in practice. One contradiction arose out of the dual role of the church. Within the framework of Congregationalist discipline, its membership was limited to a selective group of persons who, as "visible saints," satisfied certain criteria for membership. Yet it also had to serve as means of grace to the entire population of the town. Officially a "gathered" body, each congregation was de facto something more akin to an inclusive parish. A second and more basic contradiction concerned the visibility of saving grace. The root premise of the spirituality Shepard and Mitchel described in their sermons was that persons elected to salvation would realize in experience the "new birth," or conversion, that united them with Christ. Yet the course of experience was often baffling to decipher. For reasons both practical and theological, pastors and lay people had to acknowledge that no one really knew who was saved and who was not. Yet this realism did not free them from the effort to achieve or assert such a difference.

The debate that arose in the 1650s and 1660s about the sacrament of baptism and church membership brought these contradictions home to Mitchel. Throughout that debate, he consciously sought an accommodating "middle way" between the "extremes" of "immoderate rigidness" and "wronging either truth, or conscience." This middle way was stitched together out of tradition and social experience, first principles and the family-centered politics of the local situation.[5] As we tell the history of that process, we must always bear in mind that the contradictions to which Mitchel was responding did not go away.

I

What is the understanding of "Puritanism" that emerges from this story? Not a Puritanism of sharply defined boundaries and powerful methods of control, but a way of being religious that involved ongoing negotiation of a passageway between "extremes." Not a Puritanism that was monolithic, but a multilayered system out of which the clergy and the laity could each select motifs or symbols. To be sure, there was much consensus. Mitchel and his parishioners understood themselves as heirs of the Reformation and children of the very covenant that God established with Abraham. Migration to the new world had not severed them from a richly figured mythic and historical past. That past included martyrs and persons of strong conscience who defied Catholicism and the corrupt Church of England. It included certain texts, most especially the vernacular Bible. The memories handed down, the books in circulation, the stories told in sermons, the many modes of oral tradition—all of these connected the people of Cambridge in New England to the Puritan movement that arose in late sixteenth- and early seventeenth-century England and, beyond this, to the Reformed branch of the Protestant Reformation.

Yet in New as in old England this fabric of culture was transmitted not as a whole but in parts, and always through the medium of the life experience of the family. In this manner, culture became differentiated, particular, and local. The learnedness that Jonathan Mitchel shared with his fellow clergy—a learnedness embodied in catechisms, exegetical commentaries on Scripture, and treatises of divinity—helped to constrain the dispersion of culture into fragments. Hierarchy—the felt authority of ministers, magistrates, and collective opinion—was similarly constraining. But the center did not always prevail against the disordering rhythms of everyday life, as in the dispersion of settlement and the decentralizing of economic and political authority. Ordinary people were content to know in part, and even to accept indifference. Perforce, they learned to deal with the "perplexities" stemming from the catechism. Could they be certain of salvation? When did "duties" slip over into being "works"? Was misfortune always and everywhere an act of God's providence? Were prayer and fasting the sole means of relieving illness and pain? Above all, the laity were insistent on pursuing family strategies of incorporation no matter how such strategies complicated a mythic identity as "visible saints."

Continuities and discontinuities, a bounded whole but also fragments, negotiation over boundaries and the recurrent fashioning of a "middle way": such were the characteristics of religion as a culture among the people of Cambridge and their pastor.

This description of Puritanism may seem foreign or tangential to the interpretive traditions that prevail in our teaching and textbooks. But our customary wisdom can be, and in the case of Puritanism all too often is, a matter of half-truths sheltered within paradigms that have shown an astonishing, though undeserved, persistence over time. Toward the end of this essay, I will identify a few of the major paradigms that, all evidence to the contrary notwithstanding, continue to frame our understanding of Puritanism. Here at the outset my purpose is to embark in a "new direction." For me it is a pleasant irony that this venture is sanctioned by and depends on scholarship that spans three generations: from the work of Perry Miller in the 1930s through the revisionists of the 1960s and 1970s to the present day. It is a further irony that the old-fashioned methods of intellectual and institutional history, methods that require a scrupulous exactitude in the reading of texts and the ordering of events, continue to bear rich fruit.[6] Let me also acknowledge my indebtedness to other kinds of work—to cultural anthropology, women's history, the history of religion, and that distended field we sometimes term the "new cultural history." My purpose is not to seek out something new merely for the sake of difference, but to employ an angle of vision that may bring into clearer focus the complexities of the Puritan movement.

The place to begin is with the rules or principles that gave structure and definition to that movement. Afterwards, we shall set these principles in motion.

Theology: Puritanism within the Context of the Reformed Consensus

Puritanism nestled comfortably within the Reformed consensus on theology and, in keeping with this allegiance, represented itself as sustaining the "Orthodox Faith." (For that matter, most of the doctrinal statements issued by the hierarchy of the Church of England before the emergence of an "Arminian" faction in the early seventeenth century were also congruent with the Reformed tradition.)[7] The "Orthodox Faith" involved two forms of "Truth," the one "Doctrinal," the other *practical and experimental.* On the doctrinal side, Reformed creeds affirmed that the Holy Scriptures were the "Rule of Faith and Life," that an all-perfect, sovereign God had issued "eternal decrees" electing some to salvation and others to reprobation, and that the work of redemption unfolded via the stages of effectual call, justification, adoption, sanctification, and faith.[8]

By the close of the sixteenth century, the everyday sermonizing of "godly" ministers concerned itself increasingly with "practical divinity," or what R. T. Kendall has termed "experimental predestinarianism."[9] Elaborating on the mystery of God's secret election of some of humankind to a state of grace, the writers of practical divinity argued that the elect would realize *in experience* their redemption. So God himself had arranged, by linking the work of redemption to the instituted means of grace (Word, church, and ministry) and these, in turn, to the strivings of sinners to achieve renewal or conversion. That is, God had accommodated himself to human nature by deciding of his own will to allow the "means" a certain agency. The means were an agency of persuasion; the ministry of men worked not by force, but by engaging the faculties of the "rational soul" within all humans. What we may term "background theory"—these for the most part being the legacies of scholasticism—pointed in the same direction. Accordingly, the relationship between the divine will and the human actors implementing it was cast in terms of the four Aristotelian categories of causality (formal, efficient, material, final) and a psychology of "will" and "intellect." Woven into the literature of practical divinity were still other scholastic and theological ideas, and the mix included appropriations of certain Scriptural motifs, covenant and law among them.[10]

On this basis the preachers built up their description of the work of grace. In that work the self was fully engaged: acted upon, yet also acting in accordance with Philippians 2:12: "Work out your salvation in fear and trembling."[11] The crucial condition was repentance, which became effective only when and if the participant acknowledged his or her utter unworthiness. Repentance flowed seamlessly into an ethical activism. The inner transformation that repentance helped bring about coincided with obedience of the moral law and the performance of the "duties" it prescribed. In the more formal language of theology, the fulfilling of duties could be phrased as "sanctification," or the holiness that real Christians manifested. Practical divinity was saturated with the language of duty, whether understood as sanctification or as a disciplining first step toward the work of grace; as one historian of Puritanism has remarked, the movement had a "passion for the sanctification of life."[12]

Reclaiming the Apostolic Church: Puritan "Legalism"

"Primitivists" in their understanding of divine history, the Puritans argued that the word of God contained normative instructions on the nature of the Christian church.[13] From the *Admonition to Parliament* of 1572 to the *Platform of Church Discipline* fashioned by a synod of clergy in New England in the late 1640s, the several creeds and manifestoes of the movement located these instructions in the gospels and apostolic letters of the New Testament, with the Old also pertinent in certain respects. According to these creeds, the primitive (in the sense of first or original) church had as its "king" or head no one other than Christ. These same creeds differentiated the "spiritual" powers of the church from the "temporal" powers of the civil state. Regarding the Christian magistrate as crucial to the well-being of the church, and in this respect firmly siding with the "magisterial" Reformation, Puritans insisted that all such civil officers, even up to the rank of monarch, were subject to the spiritual authority of the other realm. The two realms were coequal and in a certain sense independent of each other. Yet they were commonly likened to "twins," an analogy that underscored the unanimity of church and state when each observed God's will.[14]

The true church was a special place. Its marks were the teaching of sound doctrine and the right administration of the sacraments. Some reformers added a third mark, discipline, by which they meant an ecclesiastical structure based strictly on the word of God. A church that lacked this third mark was presumably false, not true. If such were the case, all persons of "conscience" would have to depart from it, just as the early Reformers had departed from the Church of Rome.

The Church as an Ethical Community Engaged in "Edification"

Discipline had another meaning. As invoked within the Puritan movement, it meant that members of the church should be differentiated from the ungodly by their practice of the moral law. Imagining the church as the "body of Christ" and its members as "living stones," Puritans regarded the immoral and the profane as unfit to participate in the community of the godly. They saw that community as caught up in a process of "edification," an ongoing process of spiritual and ethical improvement as the church approximated ever more closely the kingdom of God. The visible church would always fall short of the perfection of the kingdom. But it was the obligation of the godly to use the instrument of discipline, certain practices designed to exclude the ungodly from membership and the sacraments, in order to make the church more like the coming kingdom.[15]

A church made up of Christians in ethical fellowship was a church where everyone (that is, everyone who was male) deserved to participate in decisions like the selection of clergy and acts of exclusion or inclusion with regard to membership. The corollary of discipline was thus a church structure that sanctioned an important role for collective participation or consent, although not to the degree of subordinating the office of the ministry to lay members.

Eschatology and the Rule of the Saints

All of history displayed the workings of God's providence. Within this basic scheme, the pattern that was of more immediate concern was the progress of the community of saints toward the return of Christ and the restoration of His kingdom. In this broad sense, an eschatological imagination pervaded the Puritan movement, an imagination that we may term transformative. Looking forward to a time, as yet far off, when the ordinary structures of society and politics would give way to rule by the saints, the movement sought to enact certain values in anticipation of the coming kingdom. Members of the visible church were to forego anger and conflict, practicing, instead, the rules of love and mutuality. Every household was to become a "little commonwealth." And the nation state was to take on the form of a "Theocracy," with everyone adhering to the will of God.[16]

So much for first principles. As I have already implied, it was one thing to affirm such principles and another to defend them against a variety of opponents. It was still another to put them into practice either in England or New England, for then it became apparent that these ideas caused disturbances of several kinds. From our vantage, we can see that these disturbances had yet another source, the many-sidedness of the principles themselves.

Regarding the church, two problems became powerfully disruptive. The Church of England remained unresponsive to the word of God and the mandate of discipline. Such a church seemed to some an unholy place that came close to forfeiting its legitimacy. This reasoning led a handful of Puritans—most famously, Robert Browne and John Robinson—to invoke the authority of conscience and to proceed down the path of separatism. Once they quit the Church of England, separatists were quick to denounce the lame consciences of those who remained within the Puritan movement.

Separatism forced a reshuffling of the deck. Leaders who had hitherto been "forward" in their thinking suddenly reverted to the argument the defenders of episcopacy had used against them, that in contrast to popery the Church of England was a true church.[17] Others who withdrew in some measure from the Church continued to acknowledge the authority of the Christian magistrate; even among the Puritans who more fully deserved the name separatist, few were totally proscriptive of communion with the Church of England. Given the many possibilities for carving out a space between schism and conformity, separatism must be understood as an unstable category. In certain settings, moreover, it was less a realistic alternative than a specter summoned into being by the vast majority of Puritan moderates and a smaller number of radicals as each group maneuvered for position within the boundaries, both certain and uncertain, of the Church of England.[18]

The nature and extent of these maneuvers varied from one locality to the next. Richard Baxter's father refused to attend the maypole celebrations in his village. He and many others used the emerging practice of Sabbatarianism to differentiate themselves from those they deemed ungodly. The "conventicles" or private gatherings where the godly assembled to enjoy spiritual exercises attracted a certain fraction (although by no means a majority) of those who were dissatisfied with the Church of England.[19] Others took up the practice of household devotions as prescribed by writers like John Dod and Robert Cleaver. "Gadding about," or crossing parish lines to hear the sermons of another minister, was an option that appealed to some. Ministers were endlessly resourceful in picking and choosing among the ceremonies mandated by the Book of Common Prayer and in exploiting the weaknesses of the episcopal system. The zealous Puritan of historians' making was thus a Puritan who adapted fairly easily to the constraints of the English situation; as Stephen Foster has perceptively remarked, the procrustean bed of conformity was "curiously negotiable."[20]

That phrase can also be applied to the speculative systems of church government that "presbyterians" under Elizabeth I proposed in place of the structure and practices of episcopacy; other proposals emerged among separatists and radical Puritans in the early years of the seventeenth century. The role of the civil magistrate, the extent of "democratical" participation by lay (male) church members, the authority of supervisory bodies (if any), and the relationship between gathered communities and the wider society—on these and other issues the word of God failed to speak with perfect clarity. As the conformist John Whitgift pointed out in the 1570s in his critique of Thomas Cartwright, and as a host of critics of the "New England Way" remarked of that experiment, there was much waffling about these arrangements, so much so that Presbyterians often ended up sounding like Congregationalists, and vice versa.[21]

The relationship between church and state posed other problems. Only rarely, as in the "Dedham orders" that Stephen Foster has recently singled out as epitomizing the Puritan program of social ethics, did clergy gain the support of magistrates in proposing a program of discipline for an entire community.[22] Even in their hour of triumph in the 1640s, Puritan magistrates and clergy remained at odds. In the course of preparing a new Directory of Worship for the Church, the Westminster Assembly confronted the question of how to implement the long-desired scrutiny of candidates for the Lord's Supper. Parliament rejected flat out the proposal that clergy play the key role in this scrutiny, and the legislators also wrote into law an exemption from this scrutiny for themselves.[23] When a subsequent and more aggressively Puritan Parliament passed a law imposing a capital sentence for adultery, the actual provisions of the law were such that no one was ever convicted under it. A similar law in Massachusetts resulted in a tiny number of executions.[24] The testiness between magistrates and clergy in New England over matters like church discipline adds to our sense of confusion: when do these actors play their appointed roles?

And what about the transformative possibilities of rule by the saints in the context of expectations of the coming kingdom? Here the turmoil of the 1640s and 1650s in England, when eschatology erupted into apocalyptic and millenarian visions and when schemes proliferated for accomplishing the Christian commonwealth, is a perfect illustration of how ideas can bear unexpected fruit. The colonists faced their own set of paradoxes, as in trying to base the civil franchise on church membership and a code of "laws and liberties" on a primitivist reading of the Old and New Testaments.[25] On each side of the Atlantic, some persons began to argue against a magisterial relation between church and state and in favor of toleration or "Christian liberty." The shock effects of this argument were rivaled by the disturbing realization that saints in power could be as tyrannical as the "popish" rulers they displaced. In the covenanted communities of New England, the saints also proved to be a contentious lot. So much for peace and harmony![26]

Spirituality and the Gathered Church

But the most telling case history of confusion and uncertainty concerns church membership. Out of power, Puritans could extol selectivity and criticize the official church for being lax. In power, they faced the daunting question of how to combine the church as ethical community, which meant being selective, with a state-related church that had to provide instruction and moral discipline for everyone. Could a church be at once inclusive and exclusive? Could the "self-assertion of the godly" be combined with "a campaign to fashion a pervasive Christian society for the many"?[27]

Famously, the founders of congregations in early New England acted to limit membership to "visible saints," and even more famously, some of the founders of these congregations required that prospective members offer a "relation" of spiritual experience. Chapter 3 of the Cambridge Platform, having defined "saints" as "Such, as have not only attained the knowledge of the principles of Religion . . . but also do together with the profession of their faith & Repentance, walk in blameless obedience to the word," went on to specify that "a personall & publick *confession,* & declaring of Gods manner of working upon the soul, is both lawfull, expedient, & usefull."[28] By the mid-1640s "Independents" in England were organizing new congregations or reorganizing existing parishes along similarly restrictive lines. No sooner had each group done so than they found themselves accused by fellow Puritans of confounding the visible church with the invisible, forfeiting the role of the church as means of grace to all,[29] and subordinating the efficacy of the sacraments to the personal faith of communicants.

Thus challenged,[30] and remembering, perhaps, that the same issues arose in the "Admonition" controversy of the 1570s when John Whitgift accused Thomas Cartwright of breaching the distinction between visibility and invisibility in his conception of the church, the immigrants hastily moved to different ground. The apparent daring of the Cambridge Platform could not mask the equivocating language that effectively altered the meaning of "saint": "The weakest measure of faith is to be accepted in those that desire to be admitted into the church . . . . Such *charity* & tenderness is to be used, as the weakest christian if sincere, may not be excluded, nor discouraged."[31] Moving the "judgment of charity" to the center of the process of admission, the clergy in New England conceded that the gathered church contained many who were "hypocrites." John Cotton, hitherto an architect of the gathered church, began to argue that "it were better to admit diverse Hypocrites then to keep out one sincere Child of God from coming into the Church."[32]

The colonists went on to acknowledge a distinction between two kinds of holiness, "external" or "federal" and "internal" or "gracious." Federal holiness could be claimed by everyone in church covenant, even those who entered the covenant as baptized infants. Thus qualified, such persons were entitled to bring their own children to the ordinance of baptism.[33] So it happened that the gathered church incorporated an ever widening constituency of visible saints, many of whom did not satisfy the criteria specified in chapters 3 and 9 of the Cambridge Platform. Indeed the meaning of "visible saint" became remarkably indeterminate. The phrase could variously signify that such persons were (1) regenerate Christians who approximated (as closely as human knowledge allowed) saints in actuality, (2) "morally sincere" and perceived as fulfilling most moral duties, (3) church members by virtue of their ancestors' entering into the church covenant, (4) or hypocrites feigning holiness.[34] Terms like charity and profession proved just as elastic, and for the same reason: they defused the divergent pressures that converged on the gathered church, allowing that institution simultaneously to present itself as an ingathering of the godly, a community "knit together in the bonds of love," and the means of grace, including the wholesome exercise of discipline, to a much wider number of the partially holy.

The governance of gathered congregations provoked another set of questions that the colonists eluded—or endured—in a similar manner. Seeking to implement the transformative possibilities embedded within primitivism, possibilities enhanced by the experience of exodus from England, the colonists ran afoul of critics abroad and at home who denounced the "Congregational Way" as too "democratical" in how it distributed power between the ministry and the laity. Once again the Cambridge Platform bears the marks of compromise. Without repudiating the principles of decentralized governance and the priority of the church covenant, the clergy were able to insert the concept of the "negative voice" and a distinction between "power of office" and the "privilege" of the same. Lay ordinations, only briefly and occasionally employed, became an embarrassment; and to the accusation that voluntary maintenance was depriving the clergy of adequate support, the response was a rapid shift to a town-wide and state-endorsed system of taxation.[35]

These accommodations occurred within the basic framework of Congregationalism, which remained relatively intact. Inheriting this framework and believing, themselves, in the concept of the gathered church, second- and third-generation ministers continued to wrestle with the question of how to reconcile a church that included the many who entered as baptized infants with a church that contained the few who passed into "full" membership. Mitchel's middle way gained wide acceptance as a practical answer to this question. The most important dissenter, Solomon Stoddard, affirmed the importance of conversion but he and his heirs also continued to affirm the significance of the external covenant. In the main, therefore, "Stoddardeanism" coincided with the tradition that descended from Mitchel to Increase and Cotton Mather and their allies.

To insert popular religion into the story, as I will do shortly, is to add another layer of complications. But let us first turn back to orthodoxy.

Orthodoxy

The "experimental predestinarians" wanted sinners to repent and become faithful servants of the law. This model of the spiritual life was paradoxical in one key respect. The ministers who taught it, and the men and women who sought to live by its prescriptions, assumed that the true Christian was differentiated from the hypocrite or reprobate. The line between the two was absolute, and a veritable mountain of sermons and devotional manuals instructed the curious and the needy on how to find out where they stood. Yet in practice this difference became blurred. Evangelical ministers complained that people who merely pretended to be Christians were often taken for the real thing. The paradox of knowing and not knowing had a further dimension. Lay men and women expected to achieve assurance of salvation but instead were "often put to sad doubts of their own Estate."[36]

Theologically, the category of "weak faith" was a departure from the thinking of John Calvin. Other changes emerged as the ministers worked out a response to the "weak believers" they needed to counsel. Within the practical divinity that William Perkins fashioned early in the seventeenth century, the basis of assurance shifted from the Christocentric focus in Calvin's pastoral theology to the process of sanctification and the "practical syllogism."[37]

The inward work of grace was understood to manifest itself in outward signs, including the performance of moral duties and the "profession" of faith. The relationship between these signs and what they signified remained uncertain since no one but God could know for sure "the heart of the Professor." But as one minister reasoned, in demanding evidence of grace we are limited to signs, and therefore to regarding these signs, however outward, as signifying what they seem to be about.[38]

The alternative was an "immediate witness of the Holy Spirit" that, once experienced, swept away all doubts. This alternative to the mainstream erupted in Anne Hutchinson's "Antinomianism" of the 1630s, erupted anew in the agitation that led to the founding of the Society of Friends, or Quakers, in the 1650s, and, a century later, reappeared among the "New Lights" of the revivals known collectively as the Great Awakening. Inevitably, it seems, Puritanism gave rise to an uneasiness, usually expressed as a critique of works or duties, and of clericalism that ripened into seventeenth-century versions of ecstatic religion.[39]

Evangelical orthodoxy held its ground. Responding to the New Lights, Jonathan Edwards drew on Thomas Shepard's defense of sanctification, written in the late 1630s in response to the Antinomians, in advocating godly behavior as the most certain evidence of "true religion." [40] Sanctification thus came to play several roles. Technically it referred to the stage of "evangelical obedience" that concluded the sequence of effectual call and justification. In addition to providing assurance of salvation (in effect, signifying that the entire sequence had occurred), sanctification helped legitimize the preaching of duties at whatever stage. Its place was also large in the process of selecting persons for church membership because it provided a reliable bridge between what was unseen, or invisible, and the visibility of grace that candidates had to display. Moreover, it was a potent weapon against perfectionists of any color, and especially against those who passed over into radical spiritism, rendering unorthodox their claim to assurance grounded on a direct appeal to the Holy Spirit.

It would be interesting to trace how other words in the lexicon of "practical divinity" performed a variety of functions. "Sincerity" would surely be such a term, and "covenant" another.[41] In a controversy that involved both of these words, Jonathan Edwards lamented that the position taken by his thoroughly orthodox cousin Solomon Williams was "a mixture of many schemes, one clashing with, and destroying another." [42] Yet Williams had done no more than reiterate ambiguities that were part of the Puritan tradition, ambiguities that served the clergy well for a century and a half.

Popular Religion

When our framework is enlarged to include the laity, and especially women, these ambiguities become of even more importance. To represent the Puritanism of the laity is to confront an almost impossible task, conceptual and practical. The records reveal a certain number of persons who behave in keeping with the image and idea of "zeal": engaging in self-scrutiny, observing the Sabbath, fluent in the language of spiritual experience, and on guard against allowing hypocrites to enter gathered congregations. These were the religious virtuosi whom almost everyone admired and whose exemplary behavior was recorded in celebratory print. The records also suggest that, for many others, the rhythm of participation in the "means" was uneven and irregular. The practice of Bible reading could not have occurred with much frequency among the 30 or 40% of New England households that had no Bible of their own.[43] Reverence for the clergy coexisted with grudging and tardy contributions to their maintenance. What was later nicknamed half-way church membership satisfied many.

Altogether, the evidence suggests that lay people acted deliberately to establish a certain distance between themselves and the full-blown system of practical divinity. It is plausible to suppose that they did so in order to cope with the tensions that this system generated. The clearest evidence of these tensions and of the pattern of lay response is the data on the timing of affiliation and the rate of participation in the Lord's Supper. Also revealing, though less conclusive, is the eclecticism of healing practices.

Lay men and women approached baptism and the Lord's Supper quite differently. Parents valued baptism for their children, reasoning that children within the external covenant were better off—less threatened by the devil, healthier, and more likely to obtain saving grace. Family preservation, the fundamental goal of the property inheritance system, was equally the goal of those who brought their newborn children to the church almost immediately. These people thought of the church as a place of nurture, a source of protection for the family.[44] Yet the church was also a place where protection was intermingled with judgment and danger. Lay men and women regarded the Lord's Supper as encircled with this double message. As they learned from their ministers and from reading manuals of devotion, the sacrament was only for persons who, beforehand, engaged in stringent self-examination and repentance for sin, persons who could represent themselves as among the redeemed. Anyone who was spiritually unclean ran the risk of "eating and drinking damnation to himself" (I Corinthians 11:28–29). Lacking such assurance, people stayed away. "They have drunk in an opinion, that none but Converted Persons should come to that Ordinance, and so they neglect it," a minister observed in 1707. His observation, widely seconded among his colleagues, is borne out by church records.[45] What the clergy wanted, what they prescribed, was reworked by lay people in keeping with the modes of family culture.

Healing practices reveal a similar selectivity. Lay people craved relief from suffering, be it physical illness or social and psychological distress, as when the emotions of anger and revenge erupted. The practical divinity contained an all-encompassing diagnosis and a set of remedies for these problems. The source was unrepented sin and the chief remedy, repentance or confession and a renewed feeling of dependence on God's will. Collective rituals like the fast day were addressed to the "heats" that infected the body social. On their own as well as in public settings, people turned to prayer to alleviate distress. If they were spiritually adept, they represented suffering as a sign of their dependence on the providence of God, a providence that was ultimately beneficent.

Yet when a woman of Newbury lay ill in the 1670s, the framework of interpretation she preferred was to blame her plight on the malice of an elderly neighbor, Elizabeth Morse, and to nail a horseshoe over her door to keep Goody Morse from entering. A woman of Boston, persuaded that an Irish washerman, already in prison for causing the diabolical "possession" of John Goodwin's children, had also caused her son's illness, came to the jail to ask that the "witch" remove the spell—and afterwards, attributed her son's recovery to this act of magic. Meanwhile, some of John Goodwin's neighbors suggested that he seek the services of a "cunning person." Instead he sought the counsel of ministers.[46] There is no way of telling how many of the colonists chose differently or, indeed, how many were intentionally challenging the ritual processes of fasting, prayer and confession. Only a small handful turned away from orthodoxy to prefer the religio-healing system of the Rogerenes or that of the Quakers, who contrasted the "King of Terrours" present at the deathbeds of the orthodox with their own, more reassuring, approach. Another point of stress was the concept of affliction. To regard illness or misfortune as spiritually beneficial entailed acknowledging responsibility for the sins that brought the situation on. But as Richard Godbeer has suggested, some of the colonists preferred to blame outside forces, like the Devil or the malice of their neighbors.[47] Analytically or in the abstract, though with certain shards of evidence on which to rely, we may suppose that a good many of the colonists entertained and sometimes acted on multiple possibilities for dealing with life crises.[48]

The religious for the laity unfolded, in the main, within the ideal type delineated by the clergy. Yet its relationship to that type was like the blurred reflection in a faded mirror: close but not identical, and revealing of adaptations that imparted a distinctive tone to popular religion.

2

Let me make more explicitly historiographical the implications of my narrative.

Beyond Denominationalism

Nineteenth-century Protestant historians in search of origins and founders, and motivated by a newfound confessionalism, imposed a denominational framework on the history of Puritanism. Historians in the second half of the twentieth century, most of whom have not been writing about their own faith tradition, have discarded this framework. These historians have realized that, on closer inspection, the so-called "Presbyterians" who initiated the Admonition Controversy of the 1570s were not advocating a tidy system of ascending judicial bodies. On the contrary, Elizabethan reformers imagined the proper form of parish church as a community gathered voluntarily out of the world, a description that sounds more like premature Congregationalism. Yet Congregationalism has proved to be a category as slippery as Presbyterianism, and as I have already indicated, Perry Miller's famous distinction between "separating" and "non-separating" Congregationalism rapidly breaks down.[49] The fluidity of ideas in the decades before 1640 arose from the several and conflicting pressures brought to bear on reformers: how to avoid the taint of exclusionary "anabaptism" while introducing a more rigorous discipline; how to manifest proper loyalty to the monarch while pleading the authority of the word of God; how to reconcile a turn toward localism and popular participation with the more hierarchical and centralized ecclesiology of the continental Reformed tradition. Any single manifesto or experiment from these decades cannot be taken as a part that stands for the whole; the variations are too many, and the context becomes all important as particular ministers or congregations negotiated their way among the alternatives. (The most interesting case history of such a congregation may be Murray Tolmie's of the experimental "semi-separatist" church that was gathered in London in 1616 under the leadership of Henry Jacob.)[50]

The confusion did not abate after 1640. Scots Presbyterians were dismayed by the equivocating of their English counterparts. "Independency" swung in a wide arc that at one end included ministers who accepted parish livings and de facto responsibility for everyone within the boundaries of the parish even while attempting some version of a gathered church. The negotiations at the time of the Restoration between Charles II and the Presbyterians revealed anew how moderate most of them were, and how readily they would have remained in the Church had the Restoration Parliament allowed them to forbear a few of the ceremonies. The Act of Conformity of 1662 clarified this issue, but the 1,900 ministers who passed over into Dissent remained of several minds about the nature of the church.

The New England situation was equally fluid; the conciliatory gestures of the Cambridge Platform were echoed in the ever more moderate statements of John Cotton, and by the turn of the century the labels Presbyterian and Congregational were both in use.[51] Here too, local variations proliferated.[52] The fundamental ambiguity that inhered in the concept of discipline—Should it be employed to exclude the impure or serve as a means of grace to incorporate as many persons as possible?—played itself out in a long, agonizing conflict between a handful of laity who resented the dilution of their privileges and the many, both laity and clergy, who wanted a more inclusive church. Jonathan Mitchel's middle way was an attempt to bridge this difference by giving each side some of what it wanted: wider access to baptism and renewal of covenant for adult "children of the church," together with a limiting of access to the Lord's Supper to those who were willing to represent themselves as regenerate.

The point is a simple one: the many layers of negotiation that took place around the nature of the church and ministry render the denominational framework almost useless.

Beyond Calvinism

I have spoken of Puritans as heirs of a theological consensus nurtured within the Reformed tradition. If we name this consensus "orthodoxy," we must immediately beware of imposing a straitjacket on a living, *fully historical* phenomenon. Within the world of international Calvinism, and over the course of two centuries, orthodoxy was spoken in different accents, each articulated in response to shifting challenges.[53] New terms emerged,[54] and the ordering of doctrines in the *Institutes* was rearranged in texts such as Ames's *Medulla* and John Norton's *Orthodox Evangelist.* Moreover, a host of practical sermons arose to surround, and in some sense to supplant, the repertory of creeds and confessions. Only rarely, and more often in the eighteenth than in the seventeenth century, did the everyday routine of sermonizing become polemical.

These realities have displaced the old chestnut of, "Were the Puritans Calvinists?" To Vernon Louis Parrington the answer to this question was unequivocally yes; to Perry Miller, a yes so qualified that many of his readers thought it was a no. The good news is that, in widening their point of view to include other voices within the Reformed tradition, historians since the 1960s have increasingly understood that the Puritans in England and America fall within a "hybrid and broadly-based theological tradition."[55]

The same realities have displaced another feature of the interpretive tradition, the lamentations about Calvinism deteriorating into "hypocrisy." The scholars who in another essay I termed "seminary historians" have shown us through their exacting attention to theological ideas that the abundant references to conditions, activity, "preparation," and duties within the practical divinity left unscathed the doctrines of free grace and predestination.[56] In so doing, they have discarded the interpretive paradigm of "declension" that pervades the whole of Perry Miller's *The New England Mind*, a paradigm premised on the assumption that the colonists were reluctant Calvinists who, as rapidly (and evasively) as they could, introduced works-righteousness in the form of "preparation for salvation." The deeper premise on which Miller's paradigm depends is that the historian can identify an authentic Calvinism that the colonists, perhaps ironically, betrayed.[57] In my opinion this premise is ahistorical, for a fully historical perspective on the Reformed tradition is at odds with a conception of Calvinism as a once and perfect orthodoxy. A living tradition undergoes change. Context mattered, and those who did theology engaged in negotiations of their own kind. The exchange of opinion between John Cotton and his colleagues in the Antinomian controversy is a near-perfect example of this process, as is the texture of John Norton's

The Orthodox Evangelist, for Norton brought the two sides together in a formula that epitomizes how theology is both systematic (in the sense of proceeding from first principles) and improvised, or, as Charles Cohen has remarked, "tactical."[58]

Another near-perfect demonstration of the making of a theological middle way is Brooks Holifield's analysis of the doctrine of baptism among English and American Puritans. Holifield found that the clergy engaged in a form of doublespeak about the ordinance: accepting, on predestinarian grounds, that it was a "seal" of qualities already present in the recipient, they also huffed and puffed to infuse the rite with efficacy. They did so partly in response to Baptists, partly to deal with expectations among the laity (a point more mine than Holifield's) and partly to fill out the significance of the church and other external means. In his words, these clergy turned themselves into "ambidextrous theologians," affirming with the right hand what they denied with the left.[59]

Is it possible to expand upon this reading of theology? Earlier in this essay, I suggested that sanctification may have played a variety of roles depending on the context of debate or the intended audience. Other candidates emerge from the pages of Charles Cohen's *God's Caress* and Norman Fiering's *Moral Philosophy at Seventeenth-Century Harvard:* the "polysemy" of "covenant" and "heart"; the intermingling of "intellectualist" and "voluntarist" theories of psychology; the confusion about ethics and its place in the curriculum.[60] Yet another possibility is the doctrine of providence, which was entangled in a web of motifs: mutability and decay, apocalypticism, and the like.[61]

What do we make of such untidiness, and how does it affect our understanding of Puritanism? The flexibilities of meaning that inhere in terms such as covenant and saint are not symptoms of evasion (as if some proto-Arminian was trying to emerge from his Calvinist skin) or of Protestant scholasticism run wild. Rather does this flexibility indicate that theological categories were making room for religion as lived experience. The "ambidextrous" reasoning of the ministers on matters like infant baptism and the covenant is a superb case in point. When in 1662 they validated the "external" covenant to which children were admitted, the clergy were endorsing the idea, so persuasive that it had the force of custom, that families were entitled to a strategy of preserving and incorporating the next generation. Covenant was the great symbol of this strategy, not the new covenant of the gospel but the ever-enduring family-based covenant of Genesis 17:7 between God and Abraham.[62]

Beyond Conversion: The Rhythms of Practice

The term "conversion," which many historians have made one of the keys to religious self-identity within the Puritan movement, is problematic for other reasons. Patrick Collinson has quietly remarked that William Haller was misled by the spiritual biographies on which he based

The Rise of Puritanism (1938); according to Collinson's reckoning, only a tiny number of these biographies describe anything that resembles a classic conversion. When the "relations" preserved by Thomas Shepard from his Cambridge congregation were published, it became clear that these lay narratives were organized around a distended and diffuse process. Meanwhile, Michael McGiffert and Baird Tipson were each groping for alternatives to convey their analysis of Thomas Shepard's spirituality; Tipson chose "routinized piety" and McGiffert, "renewed conversions," both of them terms that carry us away from the classic model. Drawing on these several sources, Charles Hambrick-Stowe extended the work of revision by recasting "preparation" as a livelong process of disciplined meditation.[63]

The broader question remains of how to interpret Puritan spirituality as a matter of lived experience. Literary historians have approached this question through the aesthetics of figural language.[64] Historians of doctrine, having mapped the complexities of the morphology of conversion, have gone on to wonder whether Puritan spirituality could result in a near-pathological exaggeration of the moment of new birth.[65] From my perspective the basic question may be addressed by turning to a description of religious practices. That description would build on the repertory of possibilities—fast and thanksgiving days, the sacraments, meditation, prayer, psalm-singing, the way of death, modes of healing—which Hambrick-Stowe has analyzed in *The Practice of Piety* and which I expand on in *Worlds of Wonder, Days of Judgment*. Such a description would also acknowledge the plural rhythms of affiliation and participation: to simplify, the strict routine of the religious virtuoso but also the intermittancies in the spirituality of many of the colonists. Only by acknowledging these intermittances can we move to recognizing that the rhythms of religious practice often coincided with stages of the life cycle, in particular the renewing of affiliation that accompanied family formation. Thereby we enlarge the meaning of religious experience in ways that release us from the ahistorical constraints of the category of conversion.

Beyond Religion and Society

Everyone of my generation remembers hearing, and feeling, that the New Social History of ca. 1970 had dismembered Perry Miller's "New England Mind." Lest we forget, the onslaught was led by Darrett Rutman, who in *Winthrop's Boston* derided the coherence of that mind and depicted the gathered churches of Boston as institutions of ever diminishing significance.[66] In those days it was demography that seemed the key to everything. In the spirit of an Elizabethan tragedy, we may observe, How the mighty have fallen! Since the demographers acknowledge the inadequacy of their work (although the evidentiary limitations of, say, Greven's thesis about fathers holding on to their lands, or Demos's thesis about the "breaking of the will" appear not to have diminished the repetition of these arguments elsewhere),[67] historians of religion may begin to rethink the whole matter, and especially the relationship between religion and society.

Here the legacy of the New Social History is twofold. Unable to understand that religion flowed within wider boundaries than as these were imagined by Perry Miller in *The New England Mind,* social historians adopted his scheme of declension, which for them signified that religion became ineffectual or collapsed as society grew more diverse.[68] Alternatively, social historians drew attention to the strength of family culture and the dispersion of authority into local units.[69]

May I offer a series of suggestions that build on the second of these insights?

1. Whether we are dealing with England or New England, the process of differentiation fundamental to the prolonged emergence of modernity was already well advanced. Church and state were not one and the same, but competing interests. Of the truth of this statement we need no further proof than the economic situation of the Church of England in the early seventeenth century.[70] Moreover, church and state were situated within wider spheres of competition and differentiation, like the rivalries and differences between regions.[71] In much of the historical literature, the image and idea of an all-pervasive Puritanism can entice us into assuming that religion and society were one and the same. It was this way of reasoning that social historians found so easy to attack by calling attention to the innumerable episodes in which social behavior was visibly at odds with religious norms or occurred outside any obvious system of regulation. Society and religion thus ended up as unrelated or, at best, in tension, as in the famous episode of John Cotton's vision of a "just price" that the merchant community seems to have ignored.[72]

2. One way out of this impasse is to build on the commonsense argument—advanced by Miller, Morgan, me, and many others—that New England was not a theocracy in the sense of being effectively administered or policed by the clergy.[73] Some historians may want to foreground the differences between the clergy and the magistrates; others, the common ground they surely shared. But as I indicated in my sketch of the Adultery Act of 1650 and of similar laws in New England, the enacting and enforcing of statute law hinged on compromise and accommodation, and the clergy often came away disappointed. Historians of church and state have led the way in pointing out how, in the historically specific social field of the town or, for that matter, within the ranks of the elite, the story is one of compromise rather than of a titanic struggle between freedom and control. As William McLoughlin demonstrated in his exemplary study of "dissent" in early New England, and as Jonathan Chu and Carla Pestana have more recently shown in greater detail at the level of the town and county, the active suppression of the Baptists—who, after all, were Congregationalists and Calvinists uncomfortable with infant

baptism—quickly gave way to forms of acceptance; and although the Quakers posed more of a challenge, local circumstances (for example, kin relationships) usually served to moderate the fines that were levied up front. Pestana has aptly remarked that "toleration was not an either/ or proposition, but developed partially and unevenly." This way of telling the story does not have to diminish the importance of religion or equate it with cohesion and society with diversity and conflict. The very existence of conflict is witness to the contrary; religion mattered to each of the factions that lined up for and against the half-way covenant or for and against acknowledging the monarch after 1660. The endless, never-to-be-resolved debate about the causes of the English Civil War seems to point in the same direction, as does the recent, and admittedly controversial, work of the English historian J. L. D. Clark[74]

As in our times, so in the seventeenth century this situation was bothersome to rigorists who wanted to mobilize the godly against sin. As Richard Gildrie has recently reminded us, English and American Puritanism were engaged in a "reformation of manners" based on a critique of "profane" culture. This campaign for social discipline was embodied in rules about family government and expectations about literacy (the ability to read), both of which were much on the minds of the townspeople of Watertown, Massachusetts, in the 1670s when they acted to ensure that every person in their community owned a printed copy of certain statutes and was able to read. That reading literacy was so pervasive in Watertown is one measure of the success of this campaign; the workings of the legal system in regard to women and families is another. Rigorists were never fully satisfied and from time to time tried to inject fresh urgency into their project. To give an example: the outbreak of King Philip's War in 1675 gained these rigorists a hearing, and the several General Courts quickly passed a burst of reforming legislation as well as orders to enforce laws already on the books. Almost as quickly, however, proclamations that such and such a law would be enforced went the same way as those laws. Certain clergy then turned to the weapon of a special synod (1679–80), which fared little better.[75] These modalities of practice suggest that most social groups in the seventeenth century wanted to restrain the power of moral rules to disrupt or refashion certain relationships. Especially did these groups want to prevent the clergy from deciding univocally who was in violation of those moral rules.

The moral rules that the colonists practiced were, then, somewhat more eclectic than as outlined in any sermon or code of laws; and the enforcement of these rules was not authoritarian but a matter of negotiation between different parties.

3. The clergy and the people participated in a common culture. Yet we may also speak of popular religion, meaning by that term the distinctive ways in which lay men and women fashioned religion for themselves. The concept of popular religion was unavailable to the social historians of the 1960s. Had it been so, we might have been spared the polarizing

of intellectual and social history that eventually led the social historians into a maze of contradictions: witness John Demos's *Entertaining Satan,* where a historian who believes that lay people ignored Puritanism employs it as the explanatory factor for child-rearing practices crucial to his interpretation of witch-hunting.[76] Popular religion has its limitations as an analytical category. If we mean by popular religion the "low" or lay forms Puritanism, we must always bear in mind, as Patrick Collinson once pointed out, that the Puritan program was "unpopular" among many of the English and some of the colonists. Moreover, the category must not prevent us from posing a question on which historians of Tudor-Stuart England disagree strenuously: was there a vacuum in the aftermath of Reformation, a vacuum filled, for ordinary people, not official religion but by other forms of "popular" belief? But let me set aside these interpretive thickets in order to reaffirm the argument I have made in *Worlds of Wonder,* where, borrowing Natalie Z. Davis and Roger Chartieer, I use the term popular in two respects, to indicate that lay people were agents in the making of their culture and to open up a middle where appropriation takes place.[77] Thus defined, the concept spares us the stark extremities (which do not ring true for New England) of domination by a centralizing elite or chasm between elite and people. The people of Jonathan Mitchel's parish who stayed away from the Lord's Supper but wanted baptism for their children fit neatly within this model, and, as I have tried to demonstrate in *Worlds of Wonder,* it has wider implications for understanding witch-hunting, the uses of literacy, and the mentality of the supernatural.

4. The social history of religion in New England must also take account of a distinctive group, the learned. Those who qualified for membership within this group were uniquely privileged. Their authority over interpretation of the Bible and matters of doctrine, though never uncontested, was high. To them fell the task of differentiating true religion from its simulacra like "enthusiasm," a task they performed vigorously in response to the sectarians of mid-century and, a hundred years later, in response to the New Lights. Let us keep these men (no women were involved) in view without romanticizing their power.

5. The structure of the family, and within the family, the agency of wives and mothers, was decisive in establishing the rhythms of affiliation and participation. This point has been documented so thoroughly by Gerald Moran, Maris Vinovskis, Mary Ramsbottom, and Anne S. Brown that I merely reiterate four of their conclusions. By the third quarter of the seventeenth century, wives were preceding husbands into membership by a significant margin; and more wives than husbands were members, also by a significant margin. Within families that stayed put in a town, membership became intergenerational in a manner that steadily increased the numbers of persons affiliated with the church. The moment of affiliation for most persons was linked to family formation: marriage or the birth of a child.[78]

The nexus between family formation and the practice of religion flowed from attitudes that were rarely articulated; my sketch of them in this essay is partly speculative. But I can turn to an intriguing witness from the mid-eighteenth century, no one other than Jonathan Edwards. In his Northampton congregation, it was "visibly a prevailing custom for persons to neglect [the renewal of covenant, or adult profession] till they come to be married, and then to do it for their credit's sake, and that their children may be baptized." The minister of a neighboring parish noted the same conjunction: "nothing induces a Man or Woman to join to the Church, like marrying; and there is scarcely a Child born whose Parents (one at least) did not join to the Church, just before the Birth of the Child." [79] These ministers call attention to a family strategy directed at incorporating the next generation into a framework of relationships, a framework at once symbolic and social. That it was women who initiated church membership suggests that they were less caught up than men in the tensions over clerical assertions of authority. Moreover, the goods that women were especially able to transmit to their children were symbolic or spiritual goods.[80] For the family as a whole, baptism became an instrument and sign of family preservation and family honor.

6. Religion functioned both to bring about what the historian John Bossy has termed a "precarious peace" [81] and as a locus where conflicts that arose elsewhere were reenacted. The ideal was a peaceable kingdom, a brotherhood "knit together in the bonds of love." Yet there was never a time or place where the ideal was perfectly realized; neither the New England town nor the gathered church should be represented as entirely consensual at any moment in their histories.[82] What religion offered was a repertory of practices aimed at overcoming "heats" within the social body: fast days, church discipline, renewal of covenant, witch-hunting, public executions, and the sacrament of the Lord's Supper. Even here, we must attend to the politics that engulfed such practices: a ritual that mimed cohesion, like the fast day, could also generate or reproduce contention (think of witch-hunting), and the animating myth of a "godly people" could be variously appropriated.

A social history that brings into view the role of families and the local setting of conflict and variation is thus a social history that fits well with the multivocality of the several practices of religion. Sabbath observance, the spiritual "relation," prayer, confession, Bible reading, fasting, the sacraments of baptism and the Lord's Supper, witch-hunting—each of these set in motion complex, and even contradictory, frames of meaning. Linking social history and the history of religion in this fashion, we sidestep the impasse that arose from allowing social history to emphasize multiplicity. Declension as a story of religion giving way to the social disappears. And we understand power not as centralized or total, but as brokered and partial.

Puritanism as a "Middle Way"

It is common for historians of Puritanism to speak of the movement as a "middle way," a term much in use in the seventeenth century itself. This device conveys what so many historians sense about the movement, its "inherently paradoxical" nature or what I prefer to identify as ongoing contradictions. The many different scholarly renditions of these paradoxes or contradictions include, most famously, Perry Miller's dichotomy of "piety" and "intellect" and the "federal theology" as a compromise between the two. Another version is Edmund Morgan's in *The Puritan Dilemma,* where the middle ground between perfectionist and pragmatic impulses is summed up in the phrase, "in but not of the world." My study of the Puritan ministry, *The Faithful Shepherd,* was built around the tension between "sacerdotal" and "evangelical" understandings of the ministerial office, and how the "Congregational Way" attempted to accommodate both of these positions. Stephen Foster has complemented Morgan's version in describing a "sectarian" impulse that coexisted uneasily with "magisterial" Puritanism; his Puritans agitate for reform from beneath, in conventicles, and from above, in Parliament.[83] Harry S. Stout has sketched a tension between "purity" and "power." Other historians have turned to near-oxymorons, like Peter Lake's "moderate extremism" or Philip Gura's "radically conservative" colonists.[84]

The ongoing debate among historians of Puritanism in England as to whether the thing-in-itself exists may be understood as a debate over where to situate this middle way. In effect, the nay-sayers want this middle way to encompass much more of the official church than *puritan* has usually implied. Patrick Collinson regards Puritans as, in the main, "conservatives" content to work within the framework of the Church as long as that framework remained doctrinally Calvinist (as it was until the rise of the Laudian party); situating them in this fashion, the historian is entitled to depict Puritans as no more distinctive than the equally elusive "Anglicans." Collinson wants to capture the "now you see it now you don't" quality of a Puritanism that, much of the time, blended into a larger whole. He also acknowledges its "contradictory" nature, and, like the other versions of a middle way I have cited, his underscores the dynamic and contextual qualities of a movement.[85]

This interpretive framework effectively displaces other paradigms. As I have already indicated, it renders almost meaningless the stories of denominational origins, declension, and the struggle to achieve religious liberty. Among historians of Tudor–Stuart England, it places in doubt the very concept of Puritanism with a capitalized "P." Among Americanists, the crucial effect is to set aside what for decades, if not centuries, has been the central paradigm for understanding Puritanism: that the movement assumed a distinctive character in the new world and, in so doing, provided the origins of our national literature, our national identity, our

Americanness.[86] Seedbed of democracy and civic culture, source of our work ethic and millennial sense of mission[87]—this is the exceptionalist, Americanizing Puritanism embodied in most of our teaching, in much of the current scholarship on literature (even as we begin to acknowledge the framework of "colonialism"), and in the classic studies that extend from Miller back into the nineteenth century. Second only to this paradigm is the fable of declension, a tale of a Puritanism that unraveled itself over the course of time. Yet these narratives do not suit the Puritanism of which I have spoken in this essay.[88]

Let me summarize the new directions that emerge out of recent work. As a movement concerned above all else with the practice—the doing—of religion, at the center of Puritanism stood the perennial question of what should constitute the authentically religious. Puritans drew on the resources of the Reformed tradition in answering this question. Hence the transnational dimensions of the movement, dimensions that coexisted with the dispersal of religious practice and authority into families, congregations, and small-scale communities. Moreover, the movement I have sketched was at once coherent and multilayered. Within certain boundaries the play of meanings was remarkably fluid even with regard to such crucial issues as the nature of church membership and the nature of the sacraments. This fluidity had much to do with the structures and differences in everyday life, be these the difference between clergy and laity, men and women, young and old, center and periphery. In acknowledging that religious practices were socially mediated, we move from an essentialist understanding of Puritanism to one that regards it as manifested in practices that themselves were variously appropriated.

This summary description can be recast to provide a narrative history of Puritanism over time. One thread in this narrative would trace how the movement shifted from voluntary affiliation to forms of incorporation based on kinship. To speak more exactly, both modes were present from the start. But over time, and especially in New England, gathered churches evolved into parish-like intergenerational networks, with a corresponding "sacramental renaissance." The transition provoked opposition from persons who preferred to limit the meaning of visible saints; some of these people became Baptists, and a persistent dissatisfaction became a factor in the New Light uprising of the 1740s.[89] Another thread would trace how, from the outset in Tudor England, the movement wrestled with contradictory modes of authority: corporatist, sacerdotal, and magisterial versus the "liberty" of the "Lord's free people." This contradiction intensified during the period of the English Civil War and Commonwealth and during the initial colonization of New England. Ideological conflict was also affected by the decentralized locus of authority in old and New England, which played into the hands of ad hoc liberty. A third strand would trace change and continuity in symbolic identity ("myth") and theological motifs, taking care, in doing so, to acknowledge the possibilities for renewal that change could represent.

In something like this fashion we can bring together social history and the play of ideas, always making central to the story the negotiations that occurred over what constituted the religious. Once again, Jonathan Mitchel is an instructive figure. He drew clear boundaries around spiritual experience: the saints *would* know that they were saved. Similarly, he drew clear boundaries around the Lord's Table: to it he would admit only sincere Christians. For him, religion was a matter of strong rules. Out of those rules, and out of the social history of his manifest authority as an ordained, learned minister, we could write one kind of history of Puritanism—in all probability, a history of Puritanism as authoritarian, controlling, logical, systematic, spiritually intense, and becoming Americanized. Yet such a history would overlook the ways in which the meanings of church, ministry and doctrine were, for Mitchel, uncertain and contested sites. The strong rules he affirmed were, in practice, not so strong after all. As he knew from first-hand experience, hypocrites entered the church. Himself a parent, he deeply mourned the death of a newborn child who never received the sacrament of baptism, and it was in the matrix of this life history, magnified a hundred times among the members of his parish, that he reached out to ensure wider access to baptism and to address the uncertainties of assurance of salvation. As we follow his quest for a middle way, we learn a larger truth about the problems of defining Puritanism: religion as practiced, religion as it unfolds within boundaries or rules, is always and everywhere caught up in negotiations.

NOTES

I thank the members of the American Church History colloquium at Harvard Divinity School, and especially John O'Keefe, for their discerning responses to an earlier version of this essay. I have also benefited from the advice of Richard W. Fox and E. Brooks Holifield.

1. *God's Plot: The Paradoxes of Puritan Piety, Being the Autobiography & Journal of Thomas Shepard*, ed. Michael McGiffert (Amherst: University of Massachusetts Press, 1972); *Mr. Mitchel's Letter to his Brother* (Boston, 1732). Excerpts from Mitchel's diary are included in Cotton Mather, *Ecclesiastes: The Life of the Reverend & Excellent, Jonathan Mitchel* (Boston, 1697); reprinted in Cotton Mather, *Magnalia Christi Americana* (1702. Reprint. 2 vols., Hartford, 1853–54), 2: 80–113; the quotations are from 84–86, 89.

2. Mather, *Magnalia*, 2:92; *Witch-Hunting in Early New England: A Documentary History, 1638–1692*, ed. David D. Hall (Boston: Northeastern University Press, 1991), 134–46.

3. *The Diary of Michael Wigglesworth*, ed. Edmund S. Morgan (New York: Harper Torchbooks, 1965), 119. Wigglesworth as a student and tutor at Harvard recorded a number of Shepard and Mitchel's sermons.

4. This statement is a generalization based on evidence of patterns of church membership in other New England congregations. See note 45 in this chapter.

5. Mather, *Magnalia*, 2:99–100.

6. As in Stephen Brachlow, *The Communion of Saints: Radical Puritan and Separatist Ecclesiology 1570–1625* (Oxford: Oxford University Press, 1988); Peter Lake, *Anglicans and Puritans? Presbyterianism and English Conformist Thought from Whitgift to Hooker* (London: Unwin Hyman, 1988).

7. Dewey D. Wallace, Jr., *Puritans and Predestination: Grace in English Protestant Theology, 1525–1695* (Chapel Hill: University of North Carolina Press, 1982); N. R. N. Tyack, "Puritanism, Arminianism and Counter-Revolution," in *The Origins of the English Civil War*, ed. Conrad Russell (New York: Macmillan, 1973), 119–43; Lake, *Anglicans and Puritans?*; Peter Lake, "Calvinism and the English Church 1570–1635," *Past & Present* 114 (1987): 32–76. See also Basil Hall, "The Calvin Legend," in *John Calvin*, ed. G. E. Duffield (Courtenay Studies in Reformation Theology I: Appleford, England: Sutton Courtenay Press, 1966), 1–18; Basil Hall, "Calvin against the Calvinists," *Proceedings* of the Huguenot Society of London 20 (1962): 284–301; Lynn Baird Tipson, Jr., "The Development of a Puritan Understanding of Conversion" (Ph.D. thesis, Yale University, 1972); Peter Lake, *Moderate Puritans and the Elizabethan Church* (Cambridge, England: Cambridge University Press, 1982), 151–55; Ian Breward, ed., *The Work of William Perkins* (Courtenay Library of Reformation Classics III: Appleford, England: Sutton Courtenay Press, 1970), 78–119.

8. *A Declaration of the Faith and Order Owned and Practised in the Congregational Churches in England* (1658), reprinted in Williston Walker, ed., *The Creeds and Platforms of Congregationalism* (New York: Charles Scribner's Sons, 1893), 355, 356, 368ff. This, the so-called "Savoy Declaration," largely reiterated the Westminster Confession.

9. R. T. Kendall, *Calvin and English Calvinism to 1649* (Oxford: Oxford University Press, 1979).

10. The pioneering recovery of background theory occurred in Perry Miller, *The New England Mind: The Seventeenth Century* (Cambridge: Harvard University Press, 1939), and is significantly extended in Norman Fiering, *Moral Philosophy at Seventeenth-Century Harvard* (Chapel Hill: University of North Carolina Press, 1981). The Aristotelian categories are on view in David D. Hall, ed., *The Antinomian Controversy: A Documentary History, 1636–1638* (Middletown, Ct.: Wesleyan University Press, 1968), 34–36, 38–39, 79–80. See also William K. B. Stoever, *'A Faire and Easie Way to Heaven': Covenant Theology and Antinomianism in Early Massachusetts* (Middletown, Conn.: Wesleyan University Press, 1978). Recent studies that recover the "rationalism" within nineteenth century evangelicalism should make it easier to acknowledge the Puritan version, and to do so without implying that it contradicted the theology. See, for example, E. Brooks Holifield, *The Gentlemen Theologians: American Theology in Southern Culture 1795–1860* (Durham: Duke University Press, 1978).

11. Hall, ed., *Antinomian Controversy*, 70, 72, 73, 124–5, 185.

12. Basil Hall, "The Calvin Legend," 3; Stoever, *Faire and Easie Way*, chap. 5.

13. Theodore Dwight Bozeman, *To Live Ancient Lives: The Primitivist Dimension in Puritanism* (Chapel Hill: University of North Carolina Press, 1988).

14. David D. Hall, *The Faithful Shepherd: A History of the New England Ministry in the Seventeenth Century* (Chapel Hill: University of North Carolina Press, 1972), chap. 6. See also David Little, *Religion, Order and Law* (Chicago:

University of Chicago Press, 1969), chaps. 3–4; Patrick Collinson, *English Puritanism* (The Historical Association, General Series 106: London, 1983), 31.

15. John S. Coolidge, *The Pauline Renaissance in England: Puritanism and the Bible* (Oxford: Oxford University Press, 1970), chap. 2; Lake, *Anglicans and Puritans?*.

16. William M. Lamont, *Godly Rule: Politics and Religion, 1063–1660* (London: Macmillan, 1969); Stephen Foster, *Their Solitary Way: The Puritan Social Ethic in the First Century of Settlement in New England* (New Haven: Yale University Press, 1971), chap. 2.

17. These second thoughts are described in Brachlow, *Communion of Saints*; Lake, *Anglicans and Puritans?*

18. Here I follow Brachlow, Patrick Collinson, Stephen Foster, and others in setting aside Champlain Burrage and Perry Miller's categories of "separating" and "non-separating" Puritan. See Perry Miller, *Orthodoxy in Massachusetts 1530–1650* (1933. Reprint. New York: Harper Torchbooks, 1970).

19. Patrick Collinson, "The English Conventicle," in W. J. Sheils and D. Wood, eds., *Voluntary Religion. Studies in Church History* 23 (1986): 223–59.

20. Stephen Foster, *The Long Argument: English Puritanism and the Shaping of New England Culture, 1570–1700* (Chapel Hill: University of North Carolina Press, 1991), chap. 2 and p. 42.

21. Edmund S. Morgan, *Visible Saints: The History of an Idea* (New York: New York University Press, 1963), chapter 2; Patrick Collinson, *The Elizabethan Puritan Movement* (London, 1967); Lake, *Anglican and Puritan?*; Brachlow, *Communion of Saints*.

22. Foster, *Long Argument*, chap. 1.

23. J. T. Cliffe, *Puritans in Conflict: The Puritan Gentry During and After the Civil Wars* (London: Routledge, 1988), 117–23.

24. Keith Thomas, "The Puritans and Adultery: the Act of 1650 Reconsidered," in *Puritans and Revolutionaries: Essays in Seventeenth-Century History presented to Christopher Hill,* ed. Donald Pennington and Keith Thomas (Oxford: Oxford University Press, 1978), 257–82; John M. Murrin, "Magistrates, Sinners, and a Precarious Liberty: Trial by Jury in Seventeenth-Century New England," in David D. Hall et al., eds., *Saints and Revolutionaries: Essays on Early American History* (New York: Norton, 1984), 152–206.

25. Bozeman, *To Live Ancient Lives,* chap. 5; Richard W. Cogley, "John Eliot and the Millennium," *Religion and American Culture: A Journal of Interpretation* 1 (1991): 227–50; Cogley, "Seventeenth-Century English Millenarianism," *Religion* 17 (1987): 379–89.

26. A. S. P. Woodhouse, ed., *Puritanism and Liberty* (Chicago: University of Chicago Press, 1951).

27. Foster, *Long Argument*, 9.

28. Walker, ed., *Creeds and Platforms,* 205–6, 223.

29. The preface to the Cambridge Platform acknowledges the criticism that "wee provide no course for the gayning, & calling in, of ignorant, & erronious, & scandalous persons, whom wee refuse to receive into our churches, & so exclude from the wholsome remedy of church-discipline." Walker, *Creeds and Platforms,* 196.

30. The transatlantic controversy is described in Hall, *Faithful Shepherd,* chap. 5. "Antinomians" challenged the emerging middle way from the left, as it

were, arguing that true saints could infallibly differentiate between themselves and hypocrites. See Hall, *Antinomian Controversy,* 227.

31. Walker, *Creeds and Platforms,* 222.

32. Baird Tipson, "Invisible Saints: The 'Judgment of Charity' in the Early New England Churches," *Church History* 44 (1975): 1–12; John Cotton, *The Way of the Churches of Christ in New England* (London, 1645), 58.

33. Walker, ed., *Creeds and Platforms,* chap. 11.

34. See, for example, Lake, *Anglican and Puritan,* 36–37 (quoting Theodore Beza).

35. All of these changes are detailed in Hall, *The Faithful Shepherd,* chaps. 5–6, 9.

36. Hall, ed., *Antinomian Controversy,* 73. I have borrowed this and some of the succeeding paragraph from my introduction to *The Works of Jonathan Edwards, vol. 12, Ecclesiastical Writings* (New Haven: Yale University Press, 1994).

37. The practical syllogism: "He that repenteth and believeth the Gospel shall be saved; But I repent and believe the Gospel; Therefore I shall be saved." Hall, *Antinomian Controversy,* 148; the phrase "weak believers" is from the same, 73. Reformed and Puritan modifications in Calvin's doctrine of assurance and, specifically, the shift to "duties," are summarized in Kendall, *Calvin and English Calvinism,* and Charles Lloyd Cohen, *God's Caress: The Psychology of Puritan Religious Experience* (New York: Oxford University Press, 1986), 11.

38. Richard Baxter, *Certain Disputations of Right to Sacraments and the true nature of Visible Christianity* (2nd. ed., London, 1658), 52, 70–71. See also Stoever, *Faire and Easie Way to Heaven,* chap. 4.

39. The theological basis for these movements was the doctrine of the Holy Spirit, of which the classic study remains Geoffrey Nuttall, *The Holy Spirit in Puritan Faith and Experience* (Oxford: Blackwell, 1946). See also David D. Hall, *Worlds of Wonder, Days of Judgment: Popular Religious Belief in Early New England* (New York: Knopf, 1989), 140–43; and *Antinomian Controversy,* 202.

40. Jonathan Edwards, *A Treatise concerning Religious Affections* (1746), where the most common source of quotations were Thomas Shepard, *The Parable of the Ten Virgins* (1660) and *The Sound Believer* (1645).

41. See Cohen, *God's Caress,* chap. 2.

42. Edwards, *Ecclesiastical Writings,* 384.

43. An estimate based on probate inventories (Hall, *Worlds of Wonder,* 247–49), and on Thomas Shepard, Jr.,'s statement that "in multitudes of families there is (it may be) . . . no Bible." *Eye-Salve* (Cambridge, 1673), 50.

44. See Gerald F. Moran, " 'Sisters' in Christ: Women and the Church in Seventeenth-Century New England," in *Women in American Religion,* ed. Janet Wilson James (Philadelphia: University of Pennsylvania Press, 1980), 47–65; Gerald F. Moran, "Religious Renewal, Puritan Tribalism and the Family in Seventeenth-Century Milford, Connecticut," *William and Mary Quarterly,* 3d ser., 36 (1979): 236–54; Mary McManus Ramsbottom, "Religion, Society and the Family in Charlestown, Massachusetts, 1630–1740" (Ph.D. dissertation, Yale University, 1987); Anne S. Brown, " 'Bound Up in a Bundle of Life': The Social Meaning of Religious Practice in Northeastern Massachusetts, 1700–1765" (Ph.D. dissertation, Boston University, 1995). Here and immediately below, I borrow several sentences from *Worlds of Wonder.*

45. Solomon Stoddard suggested in 1708 that four persons stayed away for every one who attended. Stoddard, *The Inexcusableness of Neglecting the Wor-*

ship of God Under Pretence of being in an Unconverted Condition (Boston, 1708), 21 (quotation, p. 18); Hall, *Worlds of Wonder,* 156–61.

46. Hall, ed., *Witch-Hunting in New England,* cases of Elizabeth Morse and John Goodwin; Richard Godbeer, *The Devil's Dominion: Magic and Religion in Early New England* (New York: Cambridge University Press, 1992), chap. 3.

47. Hall, *Worlds of Wonder,* chap. 5; Godbeer, *Devil's Dominion.*

48. As is strongly suggested for their contemporaries in England by Michael MacDonald, *Mystical Bedlam: Madness, Anxiety, and Healing in Seventeenth-Century England* (Cambridge: Cambridge University Press, 1981).

49. See, for example, Patrick Collinson, "Toward a Broader Understanding of the Early Dissenting Tradition," in *The Dissenting Tradition: Essays for Leland H. Carlson,* ed. C. Robert Cole and Michael E. Moody (Athens, Ohio: Ohio University Press, 1979), 3–38.

50. Murray Tolmie, *The Triumph of the Saints: The Separate Churches of London 1616–1649* (Cambridge, England: Cambridge University Press, 1977), chap. 1. Internally diverse, the congregation eventually became the "mother church" of Independent, Separatist, and Baptist congregations.

51. Hall, *Faithful Shepherd,* chap. 12.

52. Paul R. Lucas, *Valley of Discord: Church and Society along the Connecticut River, 1636–1725* (Hanover, N.H.: University Press of New England, 1976), builds his story around these variations without, however, taking into account the theological/mythic boundaries within which they occurred. See also Robert G. Pope, *The Half-Way Covenant: Church Membership in Puritan New England* (New Haven: Yale University Press, 1969), for an even broader survey of variations. And see below, note 69, for reflections on the meaning of the "local."

53. As Patrick Collinson emphasizes in "England and International Calvinism," in Menna Prestwich, ed., *International Calvinism 1541–1715* (Oxford: Clarendon Press, 1985), 213–17.

54. The classic study is Perry Miller, " 'Preparation for Salvation' in Seventeenth-Century New England" (1941), reprinted in *Nature's Nation* (Cambridge, Mass.: Harvard University Press, 1967). Other studies include Kendall, *Calvin and English Calvinism,* and Michael McGiffert, "Grace and Works: The Rise and Division of Covenant Theology in Elizabethan Puritanism," *Harvard Theological Review* 75 (1982): 463–502.

55. C. M. Dent, *Protestant Reformers in Elizabethan Oxford* (Oxford: Oxford University Press, 1983), 1–2, 91–102, quoted in Collinson, "England and International Calvinism," 216. See also the references in note 7, above.

56. David D. Hall, "On Common Ground: The Coherence of American Puritan Studies," *William and Mary Quarterly,* 3rd ser., 44 (1987): 193–229; Stoever, *Faire and Easie Way,* chap. 1; Cohen, *God's Caress,* chap. 1–2. Since so many historians have appropriated Miller's thesis that the language of "conditionality" violated predestination, it is necessary to extend the process of correction to such oft-cited books as Norman Pettit's *The Heart Prepared: Grace and Conversion in Puritan Spiritual Life* (New Haven: Yale University Press, 1966), and to more recent arguments along the same line about presumed difference among the first-generation ministers. For two such corrections, see Cohen, *God's Caress,* 52 n. 16; Norman Pettit, review of Janice Knight, *Orthodoxies in Massachusetts: Rereading American Puritanism* (Cambridge: Harvard University Press, 1994), in *New England Quarterly* 68 (1995): 147–50.

57. This argument is also advanced in Kendall, *Calvin and English Calvinism.*

58. John Norton, *The Orthodox Evangelist* (London, 1654), 289, cited in Cohen, *God's Caress,* 97 n. 85; Cohen, *God's Caress,* 85, in the context of overturning the Miller–Pettit thesis that the first-generation clergy differed on "preparation." His observation has methodological implications that inform the whole of *God's Caress:* in recovering the "polysemic" qualities of Scriptural/theological terms and motifs, Cohen challenges supposed differences in theology from one minister to the next—that is, differences in phrasing that he can rightly understand as "tactical" and not substantial. For another point of view on Norton's hybridity, see Knight, *Orthodoxies in Massachusetts,* 123–28.

59. E. Brooks Holifield, *The Covenant Sealed: The Development of Puritan Sacramental Theology in Old and New England, 1570–1720* (New Haven: Yale University Press, 1974), 45–48 and chaps. 4–5.

60. Cohen, *God's Caress,* 39, and chap. 2. See also his summary of the "congerie of opposites" in practical divinity (6), his observation (55) that "Covenant as testament gave Puritans more flexibility in expositing the meaning of God's compact," and his overall assessment (*idem.*) that "In their sermons, Puritans wove a tapestry whose various threads of meaning from common speech, law, Scripture, and Reformed theology overlay one another in complex and sometimes discordant patterns." Fiering, *Moral Philosophy,* chaps. 1–3.

61. Hall, *Worlds of Wonder,* chap. 2.

62. Anne S. Brown and David D. Hall, " 'That Her Children Might Get Good': Family Strategies and Church Membership in Early New England, " in *Lived Religion in America,* ed. David D. Hall (forthcoming, Princeton: Princeton University Press, 1997).

63. Patrick Collinson, " 'A Magazine of Religious Patterns': An Erasmian Topic Transposed in English Protestantism," in *Godly People* (London: Hembledon Press, 1983), 517; McGiffert, Introduction, *God's Plot*; Baird Tipson, "The Routinized Piety of Thomas Shepard's Diary," *Early American Literature* 13 (1978): 64–80; Charles Hambrick-Stowe, *The Practice of Piety: Puritan Devotional Disciplines in Seventeenth-Century New England* (Chapel Hill: University of North Carolina Press, 1982). See also Patricia Caldwell, *The Puritan Conversion Narrative: The Beginnings of American Expression* (New York: Cambridge University Press, 1983); David Leverenz, *The Language of Puritan Feeling: An Exploration in Literature, Psychology, and Social History* (Brunswick, N.J.: Rutgers University Press, 1980).

64. See, e.g., Barbara Kiefer Lewalski, *Protestant Poetics and the Seventeenth-Century Religious Lyric* (Princeton: Princeton University Press, 1979) and the studies cited in Hall, "On Common Ground," 213–16.

65. Richard F. Lovelace, *The American Pietism of Cotton Mather: The Origins of American Evangelicalism* (Grand Rapids, Mich.: Christian University Press, 1979), chap. 3.

66. Darrett B. Rutman, *Winthrop's Boston: A Portrait of a Puritan Town, 1630–1649* (Chapel Hill: University of North Carolina Press, 1965). Previously, Bernard Bailyn's *New England Merchants in the Seventeenth Century* (1956) had cast Puritanism as "traditional" and ineffective, in contrast to mercantile values that he deemed progressive.

67. Daniel Blake Smith, "The Study of the Family in Early America: Trends, Problems, and Prospects," *William and Mary Quarterly* 39 (1982): 3–28; Gerald F. Moran and Maris A. Vinovskis, "The Puritan Family and Religion: A Critical

Reappraisal," *William and Mary Quarterly* 39 (1982): 29–63 (for corrections of Greven, see 44 n. 43). A much-needed skepticism about the "breaking-of-the-will" thesis is voiced in David Leverenz, *The Language of Puritan Feeling: An Exploration in Literature, Psychology and Social History* (New Brunswick: Rutgers University Press, 1980), 160–61.

68. As Harry S. Stout and Catherine A. Breckus usefully observe in "Declension, Gender, and the 'New Religious History,' " in *Belief and Behavior: Essays in the New Religious History,* ed. Philip R. Vandermere and Robert P. Swierenga (Brunswick: Rutgers University Press, 1991), 15–36.

69. Darrett B. Rutman, "The Mirror of Puritan Authority," in *Law and Authority in Colonial America,* ed. George A. Billias (Barre, Mass., 1965). A few observations are in order on the meaning of the local in the historically specific setting of early New England. Bearing in mind that, ideologically and practically, the Puritan version of Protestantism rejected the authority of the center, we should not allow "local" to stand for difference from or opposition to the "great tradition" (to borrow Redfield's familiar phrase). The presence of a resident learned clergy in almost every New England town means that local culture contained both high and low. Nor should the importance of local units of governance be interpreted as signifying the displacement or breakdown of authority exerted from outside; rather, the two forms of authority coexisted and were often complementary.

70. Christopher Hill, *Economic Problems of the Church,* 3rd. revised ed. (Oxford: Oxford University Press, 1968); Lake, *Anglican and Puritan?,* notes the strain felt by conformist clergy defending the royal supremacy even though the civil state had sanctioned pillaging church property.

71. The several possibilities (or realities) include core/periphery and the dyads of uplands/lowlands or open field/closed field adapted from English agrarian and local history for New England by David Grayson Allen in *In English Ways: The Movement of Societies and the Transfer of English Local Law and Custom to Massachusetts Bay in the Seventeenth Century* (Chapel Hill: University of North Carolina Press, 1981).

72. The relationship between religion and economics is significantly recast in Mark A. Peterson, *The Price of Redemption: The Spiritual Economy of Puritan New England* (Stanford: Stanford University Press, 1997).

73. For a wide-ranging critique of the notion of control, see Margaret Spufford, "Puritanism and Social Control," in *Order and Disorder in Early Modern England,* eds. Anthony Fletcher and John Stevenson (Cambridge: Cambridge University Press, 1985), 41–57. For a study that demonstrates both a remarkable stability of ethical behavior and the complexity of practice, see Roger Thompson, *Sex in Middlesex: Popular Mores in a Massachusetts County, 1649–1699* (Amherst: University of Massachusetts Press, 1986).

74. William McLoughlin, *New England Dissent, 1630–1833: The Baptists and the Separation of Church and State.* 2 vols. (Cambridge, Mass.: Harvard University Press, 1971); Jonathan Chu, *Neighbors, Friends, or Madmen: The Puritan Adjustment to Quakerism in Seventeenth-Century Massachusetts Bay* (Westport, Conn.: Greenwood, 1985); Carla Gardina Pestana, *Quakers and Baptists in Colonial Massachusetts* (New York: Cambridge University Press, 1991), 120 and passim; J. C. D. Clark, *English Society, 1688–1832: Ideology, Social Structure, and Political Practice during the Ancien Regime* (Cambridge: Cambridge University Press, 1985)

75. Richard P. Gildrie, *The Profane, the Civil, & the Godly: The Reformation of Manners in Orthodox New England, 1679–1749* (University Park, Penn.: Pennsylvania State University Press, 1994); *Watertown Records: First and Second Books* (Watertown, Mass.: Watertown Historical Society, 1894), passim. See also Mary Beth Norton, *Founding Mothers & Fathers: Gendered Power and the Forming of American Society* (New York: Knopf, 1996); R. Po-Chia Hsia, *Social Discipline in the Reformation: Central Europe 1550–1750* (London: Routledge, 1989).

76. John Putnam Demos, *Entertaining Satan: Witchcraft and the Culture of Early New England* (New York: Oxford University Press, 1982), 207, 209.

77. Patrick Collinson, "Cranbrook and the Fletchers: Popular and Unpopular Religion in the Kentish Weald," in *Godly People*, 397–428. It is also important to resist the romanticizing tendencies of agency by keeping in view the constraints of tradition. Here I wish to acknowledge the influence of Peter Stallybrass and Allon White's critique of Bakhtin's populism in *The Politics and Poetics of Transgression* (Ithaca: Cornell University Press, 1986).

78. Moran, " 'Sisters' in Christ"; Moran and Vinovskis, "The Puritan Family"; Ramsbottom, "Religion, Society and the Family in Charlestown"; Brown, " 'Bound Up in a Bundle of Life.' "

79. Edwards, *Ecclesiastical Writings,* 316, 213, 318; [Edward Billings], *A Dialogue on the Christian Sacraments* (Boston, 1762), 7.

80. My interpretation assumes that women in New England acted on and found useful the prevailing representation of mothers and motherhood, and discounts the argument that women were overtly or covertly attempting to subvert this representation. The first of these interpretations is advanced in Amanda Porterfield, *Female Piety in Puritan New England: The Emergence of Religious Humanism* (New York: Oxford University Press, 1992), and the second in Carol Karlsen, *The Devil in the Shape of a Woman: Witchcraft in Colonial New England* (New York: W.W. Norton, 1987).

81. John Bossy, "Blood and baptism: kinship, community and christianity in western Europe from the fourteenth to the seventeenth centuries," in Derek Baker, ed., *Sanctity and Secularity: The Church and the World. Studies in Church History* 10 (1973): 142.

82. Here I mean to undo the damage done by Kenneth Lockridge's *A New England Town* (1970) and, again, to critique a long-persisting image of the early town as uniquely ordered around a covenant. See, per contra, James T. Lemon, "Spatial Order: Households in Local Communities and Regions," in Jack P. Greene and J. R. Pole, eds., *British Colonial America* (Baltimore: Johns Hopkins University Press, 1984), 86–122.

83. The phrase "inherently paradoxical" is from Foster, *The Long Argument,* 106. Edmund S. Morgan, *The Puritan Dilemma: The Story of John Winthrop* (Boston: Little, Brown, 1958). Other versions include David Leverenz's psycho-social analysis of Puritan "ambivalence" in *The Language of Puritan Feeling.*

84. Harry S. Stout, *The New England Soul: Preaching and Religious Culture in Colonial New England* (New York: Oxford University Press, 1986); Peter Lake, *Moderate Puritanism,* cited in Brachlow, *Communion of Saints,* 13; Philip F. Gura, *A Glimpse of Sion's Glory: Puritan Radicalism in New England, 1620–1660* (Middletown, Conn.: Wesleyan University Press, 1984), 157.

85. Patrick Collinson, *The Religion of Protestants: The Church in English Society 1559–1625* (Oxford: Clarendon Press, 1982); Collinson, *English Puritanism*, and the essays collected in *Godly People*.

86. See, for example, Sacvan Bercovitch, *The Puritan Origins of the American Self* (New Haven: Yale University Press, 1975). The possible references run into the thousands. One of the pillars of this interpretation, the forging of national identity out of millennialism that William Haller described for Tudor England in *Foxe's Book of Martyrs and the Elect Nation* (London, 1963), has collapsed under closer scrutiny. This revisionism is summarized in Bozeman, *To Live Ancient Lives*, which dismantles the claims that have been made for a similar fusion on this side of the Atlantic. But see Stout, *New England Soul*, for a restatement of a longterm providentialism.

87. Or, as in some recent work, source of "colonialist" and racist attitudes and, in "ideological" literary criticism, of social control. See, for example, Francis Jennings, *The Invasion of America: Indians, Colonialism, and the Cant of Conquest* (Chapel Hill: University of North Carolina Press, 1975); Mitchell Breitwieser, *Puritanism and the Defence of Mourning* (Madison: University of Wisconsin Press, 1990). These perspectives replay one of the oldest paradigms in the interpretation of Puritanism, that it was a fiercely repressive system from which "emancipation" is imperative.

88. Broader changes are involved in the waning of older paradigms. As of the present moment, Puritanism has relinquished its preeminence in the history of Christianity in America. The movement is no longer crucial to the practice of cultural criticism and the discourse about our national identity, as it was to both in the century between 1830 and 1940. Within the community of historians of religion Puritanism has been eclipsed by the proposition that the story of a Christian America dates from the early nineteenth century and the onset of evangelicalism (backdated, perhaps, to the First Great Awakening).

89. Stephen Foster has cast the development of Puritanism in America as involving a shift from sectarianism to a retrieval of the "plentitude of means" the movement had initially elaborated for accomplishing its ends. This analysis is sympathetic to my own focus on incorporation. Foster, *Long Argument*, chap. 5.

3

"CHRISTIANIZING THE SOUTH" — SKETCHING A SYNTHESIS

❖ ❖ ❖

Donald G. Mathews

THE AMERICAN SOUTH WAS and is—as a critic once observed—"haunted by God."[1] Because of this, wrote another observer, the South became "more homogeneous . . . than any other section": more orthodox, more racist, more traditionalist, and less rationalist than the rest of the country. Southern religion was expressed, he believed, in a "haunting ardor" resulting from African Americans' sharing their spirituality with whites, an insight, derived from experience filtered through his racial romanticism and a commitment to interracial cooperation.[2] Edwin McNeill Poteat had grown up in a culture eloquently articulated in the cadences and with the assurance of an evangelical Protestantism that had waxed in confidence and influence especially since the Civil War. Then, defeat and theodicy had fused Southern identity and Christianity in such a way as to make them, to celebrants of the Lost Cause at least, impossible to separate. The Protestant experience in the South, however, was more complex than Poteat, a white minister, conceded because of the various ways in which religion allowed Southerners to exercise, sustain, and resist power; to purge, create, and recreate identity; and to initiate, justify, and withstand change. If the results of Civil War forced white Southerners to create a civic use for Christian faith, it allowed black people to do the same. If religion sustained the defeated in the nadir of their self-consciousness and gave the powerless hope in resisting the powerful; and if a New South divided Southerners along lines of class and gender, race, place, and memory, and if these differences were cast in the language of redemption and authenticity—there is reason to believe that Southern Protestantism embraced not one experience but many.

Among the many experiences was a conversation shaped by asking "How is one to be Christian?" and "How can the world (South) be made Christian?" If the first question implied issues of authenticity and personal struggle, the second suggested aggressive recruitment and confrontation so that conversation often became a shouting match. The answers to such questions could mean the expansion of Christians (Europeans) into the lands of native American peoples; they could also mean ridding the folk of traditional belief and practice inconsistent with Christian worship, doctrine, and discipline.[3] Beyond this usage was that implicit in the evangelical goal of making "real Christians" of those who knew the forms of worship and creed but not their subjective confirmation. A persistent attention to authenticity based on personal experience has historically characterized religion in the South. Another meaning can be inferred from the way in which white Southerners achieved supremacy in the reign of terror after 1890. But this meaning was challenged by whites who believed Christians should fight racism and by a movement of African Americans who, building on their own vision of what it meant to make society Christian, led a civil rights revolution. In the wake of this change, another meaning of Christianizing the world evolved from a conservative political agenda conceived in reaction to the civil rights revolution, birthed in "Christian" academies resistant to secularism, developed in response to gender revolution, and vindicated as a defense of family values. "Christianizing" thus has an ironic and ideological ambiance as much as a descriptive use.

Making the South Christian: Evangelicals and Slavery

Two of the most distinctive influences on Protestantism in the South were the evangelical movement and the presence of African slaves. These, together with a dialectic between the South as a place and as an idea, made religion in the region unique. At the original invasion, the first goal of "Christians" was to dominate native Americans,[4] who became objects of a process that brought missionaries from the Anglican Society for the Propagation of the Gospel in Foreign Parts (SPG) to the New World. The Society failed; the original inhabitants were eventually removed from the South, reduced to isolated areas, or culturally obliterated.[5] Simultaneously, Britons built a church and plantation system, both of which could be said to impose Christian order. Anglican Christianity, Jon Butler writes, created an "absolutist, paternalistic, and violent slavery" that supported an ethic of absolute obedience[6] despite its inability to "achieve disciplinary rigor and authority in pre-revolutionary America."[7] Despite support from colonial legislatures and the favor of colonial elites, Anglican Christianity was unable to stamp its liturgy, doctrine, ministry, and piety upon what became "the South." This fact left the power to do so to others who brought with them to the area their own religious life nurtured from within a reformed tradition, a pietistic community, or the New Light.

From these sources, incipient Southerners began to discover a religious mood affected by a movement personified in the transatlantic revivalist, George Whitefield, who appealed to all three in actions remembered as a Great Awakening. But Southern colonials were so scattered across a vast region that Whitefield's direct influence was limited to small areas of South Carolina and Georgia. His mood and message, however—or those quite similar, were carried by others. From central Virginia, Presbyterianism—owned by peoples from Scotland and Ulster, but preached among the English, too—was the context within which such innovation worked an expanding fault within the substrate of social authority.[8] More confrontational were New Light Baptists who had been nurtured in the revivals of New England, and whose austerity, fellowship, biblicism, and preaching created what Rhys Isaac calls a "counterculture."[9] As the American Revolution began, innovation was amplified from within the established churches of Delaware, Maryland, and Virginia by a itinerant Anglican laymen breaking out of scattered locales of Wesleyan-inspired fellowship to create a broad movement.[10] This preaching—far more than an event 50 years later[11]—spawned southern religion. Wesleyans were a vanguard in that they dispatched young men throughout the region beyond the range or aspiration of settled ministers and gathered churches to organize networks of local class meetings and celebrate communal rituals in conference.[12]

Emphasizing similarities among conversionist Presbyterians, Baptists, and Methodists, historians have understood the phenomena that united them as Evangelical.[13] Evangelical truth and experience retained variations associated with the faith communities within which they were preached, embraced, and enforced, but there was an essential agreement on what was valued even if there were disagreements on ritual and the precise meaning of shared terms. Essential was the personal experience of being convicted of sin after a period of self-examination followed by a further experience of being declared righteous, that is, justified by faith in the efficacious death of Christ Jesus. This experience would be accompanied (or followed) by a further inner assurance that this new found righteousness was authentic (that saints would persevere), that one had indeed been born of the spirit (born again—John 3:3–8) and was committed to living a life guided by study of the Bible, and discipline by fellow believers. Whereas Massachusetts Puritans once exiled those claiming to know they were saved, New Light Baptists, Wesleyans, and others delighted in such knowledge and insisted that all true Christians would do so. This surprising assurance and its complementary expressiveness offended orthodox Calvinists, traditional Episcopalians, and skeptical rationalists, but attracted many others who found the dramas of "experimental Christianity" compelling. The internal, personal drama of the believer was played out in public dramas (ritual) in classes, churches, camp meetings, protracted meetings, and communion seasons throughout the South. If certain believers were suspicious of emotional histrionics or once-and-for-all claims for conversion, the dominant religious mood of the South rested nonetheless on subjective confirmation of Christian truth and personal assurance following repentance and renovation.

Life within the movement is best suggested by Rhys Isaac in *The Transformation of Virginia 1740–1790*.[14] Assuming society to be "a dynamic product of the activities of its members," Isaac calls attention to the "dramatic interaction and structures of everyday life." Seeing this interaction in "knots of dramatic encounter suspended in nets of continuing relationships," he shows how analysis of both reveals the society in which they exist and the nature of power and authority exercised there. Power, authority, and social life are the stuff of religious history in the South even though those who study it have done less to address them than their many opportunities have provided. Isaac's emphasis on dramatic encounters in everyday life relied on an imaginative use of Baptist church books subsequently adopted by others who read disciplinary proceedings within them in order to explain[15] authority, racial interaction, and gender relations. Despite an irrepressible tendency by some interpreters to ascribe greater "equality" among believers in these churches than in the society at large, the word is misleading; it implies a status equity that did not exist. The experience, rather, was one of *fellowship*, which was itself revolutionary within a hierarchical society and one that could allow sharing across race, class, and gender lines. Mechal Sobel, for example, argues that blacks and whites shared with each other and in such a way as to make a world that was neither exclusively black nor white. Testimony to debate, confession, conflict, expulsion, and reconciliation suggests a broad hegemony, perhaps, but resistance as well. The Christianizing process was never complete. Conflict could divide churches against themselves; slaves would resist, avoid, or challenge. Other dissidents could do the same; a continual abrasiveness between the ideal and the real—male assertiveness and Christian restraint, for example—eventually suffused the culture.[16]

The presence of large numbers of Africans in Southern churches affected religion there as much as did the dominance of an evangelical mood. After Africans discovered a resonance between traditional ways of understanding and the preaching, moods, and worship of the evangelical ethos, they worshipped within the same precincts as Europeans—as well as apart. What this meant is the subject of sometimes intense conversation. Scholars emphasize a persistent African religious consciousness among slaves who adapted Christianity to their own purposes, "Christian" commitment being secondary to a higher commitment to African American community.[17] Other scholars understand conversion as bringing Africans into a common Christianity with the implication of acculturation.[18] Scholars who appreciate the tensions and tortured ambiguities in the religious–social process nonetheless insist that being Christian could become a way of being free from the draconian logic of slavery even if it were also a way of being enslaved. Africans discovered that slave and master, when thought of as "sinners," occupied the same position before God; both stood in need of salvation and, in a major contradiction to the logic of enslavement, both belonged in fellowship and because of that relationship could be called to account before the church. This possibility conceded a moral economy in which mutual obligation was implicitly acknowledged and could be as subversive of the masters' claims to authority as it was supportive of the slaves' understanding of themselves as "chosen."[19]

Scholars who privilege African ways and discount Christian commitment among African Americans create a false dichotomy, failing to take into account the syncretic genius of Christianity. Whites' fusion of traditional folk culture was as syncretic[20] as whites' thinking heaven was the extension of family and as whites' penchant for using Christian views of election and millennium to interpret American history. Christianity was not merely a discrete body of doctrine or moral codes, but a way of perceiving the divine, receiving power, and ordering life in a community engaged in various conversations about the Christian way. That this was part of a process of enculturation is obvious, but if it did not create a consensus between black and white or among blacks,[21] it did provide a conceded institutional integrity to the latter. If African Americans created an "invisible" institution beyond the ken and control of whites, they also created a *visible* institution in independent black churches and black congregations of biracial churches and this visibility made claims upon white elites that invisibility did not. As a result, Africans gained public acknowledgment of a privilege becoming a right: having their collective identity respected in a *public* way. Reluctantly and often after violence against insistent black preachers,[22] masters helped establish spaces in which African Americans could celebrate their solidarity and legitimacy.

How many African Americans became members of churches is unknown: estimates range between one-eighth and one-quarter of the 4 million slaves in the South in 1860. How many different faith communities there were, each celebrating and explaining life in its own way, is also unknown: the locality of faith and life in the early South implied a frail uniformity. If the nineteenth century was a constant process of ordering Christian life for both races, there were nonetheless durable themes proceeding from the transformation of self that came from "seeking" or in what whites called "conversion." The difference between black and white here was not as clear as is believed by scholars who accept a Calvinist rather than a Wesleyan model for purposes of comparison. Both races experienced conversion as providing a welcome coherence and hopefulness, although there were, to be sure, differences. Whereas traditional Christian cosmology prepared the unified self to die in Christ and to be reborn with him, African cosmology prepared the self to discover the real person—in opposition to the outer shell of self—who would be guided through vision and trance into freedom. The difference between the African whose real self is set free in an experience of divine presence and the Briton whose real self deserves death but escapes through the grace of the divine is obvious. Yet Africans' sensibilities, values, and insights could be expressed in terms of Christian language and ritual, a fact that enabled slaves to embrace Christian discourse as their own. They discovered in the Old Testament stories an earnest of their future redemption and in the gospel heard justification and hope.[23]

The presence of Africans in the South dictated a dialectic between place and idea that also made the religious history of the region distinctive. The South was born of the world market and the American Revolution. In justifying themselves to each other and the world, Americans discovered that they were attached to republicanism, equality, and liberty in ways affected by estate, interest, and place. The place became an idea as the sons of revolutionaries created a South in creating a Union through conflict between the two that demanded a republican theodicy. This is not to say that whites professed a uniform *southern* identity by 1860—that feat would have been impossible in a society so fractured by local and kinship loyalties. But—challenged in its *place*—the South was willy-nilly becoming an *idea*, too, after 1830, as religion became more identified with both. "Christianizing" the South was not complete by 1860 in the sense that a majority of its people were identified with Christian worship, belief and practice; but networks of Methodist, Baptist, Presbyterian, Disciples, Reformed, Lutheran, and other churches were nonetheless in place to regularize life and develop institutions. Camp meetings ordered the Christian year by setting aside sacred time and space for renewal. The sound of conversion became regular: nondenominational "singing schools" sustained a larger world of music whose form—four shapes—was becoming more important than theology as people sang out of local traditions from Virginia to Texas.[24] Higher culture, too, was claimed by religious leaders who built academies and colleges to educate the spiritual heirs of those who had pilloried a learned clergy and to confirm the elites' sons and daughters in the "refined and enlightened ways"[25] of religion free of sectarian bias.[26]

Nowhere was the service of religion to elites more obvious than in thinking about slavery. Popular denominations had embraced elite members early in their movement despite an original self-conscious disapproval of elite pretensions, and with an improving economy, found large numbers of slaveholders among their members. The ephemeral antislavery impulse of the revolutionary generation came to be remembered as a misguided subversion of religion. The idealism and submissiveness to God's will that had prompted antislavery sentiment came to be expressed in missions to slaves although missionaries would be as scarce as emancipationists.[27] This way of thinking, and the scriptural defense of slavery that developed after 1840, birthed a slaveholding ethic as part of a rapidly expanding corpus of proslavery discourse. Christian apologists insisted that slavery was not a Christian institution unless masters made it so—converting their slaves after themselves falling before the throne of grace. This fusion of Christianity and hierarchy flowed from the sentimental postulate of a common Christianity and owed as much to evangelical self-deceit as discipleship. The assumption rested on a model of the Christian family based on the creative manipulation of biblical texts. The Book of Philemon could be used to justify the Fugitive Slave Act of 1850 and to repeat the conventional bromide that the New Testament— save in this case, perhaps—was silent about slavery. Common belief that relationships (except polygamy) mentioned in the Bible were divinely approved, in addition to an inability to understand the meaning of St. Paul's slavery to Christ, helped create a pervasive cultural fundamentalism justified by biblical texts and masters' subjectively authenticated piety.[28]

The fusion of evangelical religion and slaveholding has encouraged historians to misunderstand the way in which Southerners experienced moral tension. It is possible speciously to contrast *guilt* (tension resulting from failure to obey internalized rules) and *shame* (tension resulting from failure to live up to community expectations), but the actual day-to-day merging of religious and social expectations could easily confuse the two. Evangelicalism had already diluted the doctrine of original sin as organically imputed through the continuities of history, and empowered individuals instead to participate actively in their own salvation. In the process, sin became "taboo": not a condition inherent in the fallen self, but forbidden acts. The distinction between a white Christianity that sustained belief in original sin and a black Christianity enforced through taboo is not as clear as some would like to think. If diaries implied dismay at being tempted or afflicted by persistent "sin," the condition was expressed in the forbidden acts *that dominated disciplinary cases in local churches.* Sin became manageable—a fact suggesting that slaveholders' guilt has been overstated. Probably affected by the writings of Wilbur J. Cash *(The Mind of the South)* and Lillian Smith *(Killers of the Dream)*, Southern historians in the 1950s began to probe slaveholders' internal life. Themselves burdened by the guilt of racism, scholars mistook their own sense of sin for that of the religion they labored to use in their interpretation. They ignored the fact that the guilt of slaveholding evangelicals was that of not perfecting the roles into which they had been called: master, mistress, father, mother, son, daughter, husband, or wife. Those embracing evangelical truth knew that they had been declared righteous in Christ. They could not have imagined guilt inherent in biblically approved relationships.[29]

Making the South Christian: The Lost Cause

The experience of secession, war and defeat allowed Christians to claim the South for Christ by claiming Christ for the South. The process of making Christianity southern received institutional form in 1845 when conflicts initiated by abolitionists resulted in creation of the Methodist Episcopal Church, South and the Southern Baptist Convention.[30] Widespread contest among Christians on the border between free and slave-holding states was part of the conflict then fast separating the sections so that with increasing assurance, the South became—according to its ministers and prominent laymen—the bastion of orthodox Christianity.[31] But because Christian practice was not so pervasive as Southern ministers desired, the war became a "coveted occasion for the pulpit to assert itself as a power in the land."[32] They represented the war in biblical terms and promised that God would vindicate the Confederacy in language of a jeremiadic tradition identified more with the children of New England Puritans than those of Southern Baptists. The South *should* "be the Lord's peculiar people"; it *should* be "the nation to do [God's] work upon earth"; it *should* be worthy of its motto.[33] But conditions for fusing religion with Confederate nationalism were never as compelling as the need. Years of insisting that Southerners were more *Christian* than Yankees could not bond an ambivalent evangelicalism with a bowdlerized republicanism to create national identity. Baptist localism, Methodist perfectionism, and Calvinist exclusiveness combined with democratic suspicion of elites to thwart a broadly evocative southern ideology.[34]

Religion proved to be more suited to the intimate precincts of people suffering fear, agony, and loss. A mood in which death had played so important a role in fixing attention on divine things now provided a familiar way of coping. Conversion could not save men from being killed, but it could save them from the fear of it as it had eased the pain of their womenfolk in a more familiar if no less agonizing travail. Even evangelical taboos such as that against cursing could help sustain morale by calling sacred attention to aspects of everyday life so that the collective enterprise might be understood as sacred, too.[35] For those at home, religion helped to bear the grief that was beyond the power of families to ritualize when loved ones were laid in graves dug by strangers.

Then came defeat. The meaning of widespread death and loss, which might have been understood if capped by victory, became elusive indeed. "Why?" asked a generation of white Southerners. And an answer structured on the dramas of evangelical insight provided passage to a Christian South as apologists fashioned an explanation from the subjectively confirmed assurance that they had been right in their principles and superior in their religion. Defeat was not, however, a simple act inflicted at Appomattox but also the process of Reconstruction through which white Southerners passed in varying degrees until the last Federal troops were withdrawn (1877). Then, certain whites could "remember" the myths and raise the monuments that would justify themselves. Religion was essential to the telling of these tales and erecting public monuments as southern fighting men were memorialized as a "sacramental host."[36] As Christian symbol and metaphor explained southern history, southern heroes such as "Stonewall" Jackson became martyrs and Robert E. Lee was elevated more highly still as the "Christ-symbol for a defeated Confederacy." Overcoming the demonic temptation to fight for the Union, he had served a higher cause and accepted crucifixion on a latter-day Golgotha. The stain of Gettysburg was removed by attributing it to the hated Longstreet, whose resemblance to Judas Iscariot was confirmed by his becoming a Republican after the war.[37] Theodicy explained the (white) South as a people separated from the rest of the nation by its religion, its especially pure devotion to orthodoxy, and therefore its atonement in blood.[38] Military revivals and an identity sanctified by suffering merged to provide a way to interpret military defeat and resolve the social conflict that came afterward.[39] In thus transforming defeat and slighting the requirement of repentance, white publicists collapsed the boundaries between church and world, piety and honor, Old South and New.

Making the New South Christian: Purity and Danger

The dialectic between the South as place and idea continued in the New South as religion adopted the language of capitalism.[40] Industrialization meant cotton mills which in turn meant new kinds of work, living arrangements, and everyday self-understanding. Southerners became entrepreneurs and managers as well as workers. They brought the values of discipline, work, and orderliness to mill and village, applauding evangelists who adapted the concepts of sin, salvation, and sanctification to metaphors of the market. Sinners were told that with "a mortgage on their souls" they could find themselves in "spiritual *bankruptcy*" unless they submitted to Christ who had "paid the *debt*" of sin. In the optimism of growth, Daniel was lionized as a "model *businessman*" capable of keeping the faith in stressful situations. His example suggested that men acting obediently to God in a harsh competitive environment were doing the Lord's work in giving work (salvation) to "humble and virtuous girls" and boys who had been "reduced by misfortune." Men who brought wealth to themselves and employment to others could make industrialism just as Christian as slavery.[41]

Women could make the world Christian, too. Between 1865 and 1920 they were, Ted Ownby has argued, subduing the Satan in men.[42] Evangelical religion had insisted that women should use their moral influence to make husbands live up to "the demands of well-developed womanly integrity."[43] Ownby contrasts the male world of cock-fighting, public carousing, and unregulated hunting with that of the home where women theoretically ruled in splendid piety. But the women went public. The process is unclear; and the fact that it relied on passing legislation suggests that women had male allies who believed restraint good for an industrializing society. As towns became more accessible to the countryside and both genders and races entered "promiscuous" space, public decorum in the presence of white women became a matter of debate that resulted in transforming acts for which churches had once disciplined members into crimes. Essential to the process were the Prohibition campaigns led by a coalition of women, ministers, and middle class men who by 1910 virtually dried up the South when it served the purposes of ruling elites. The implications of merging piety and politics were suggested by such headlines as: "The Saloon and the Rum-Crazed Negro" and "Under Stimulant Furnished by the Saloon He becomes a Brute [Before] Whom Fair and Helpless Womanhood May Well Tremble."[44] Christian activism was associated not only with subduing Satan but also with subduing blacks.

As prohibitionists "Christianized" the South, changes within churches identifying most completely with denominational enterprise created broad discontent. Thousands resisted the Christianity of mill and store as their great grandparents had resisted that of plantation and vestry: they flocked to recapture the fa-so-la singing tradition[45] and the old landmarks of faith.[46] Among Methodists the search for authenticity led to an insistence on entire sanctification as a second, instantaneous blessing after conversion. Sparked north of the Ohio, but crowning like a forest fire in the South, the movement preached against an "indulgent, accommodating, mammonized" Christianity.[47] Some, seeking further authentication, slipped into a Pentecost of charismatic gifts.[48] By the 1920s there were throughout the South a "bewildering array" of preachers who, like the Methodist preachers of the 1780s, used the drama of their own salvation to bring others to "real religion."[49] Expressions of those determined to make Christianity *real* suggest alienation from more than modern churches. The economy was in dreadful shape, and angry farmers slipped easily into the metaphors of apocalypse during the economic crisis and political revolt of the 1890s. When a Georgia Populist leader observed that "religion in the great cities is trying . . . to abolish the simple ways and brotherly teachings of Christ," he knew his audience. People understood that those who wronged them had not only rejected republican values, but also pure religion. They automatically condemned their situation in the radical polarities of Christ and Devil, righteousness and "the money power and Satan."[50]

As elites industrialized the South and as those who failed to benefit from their action sought religious language to justify self and community, innovators made a religion of segregation. The idea that segregation was religion may seem far-fetched because religion is commonly supposed to fix our attention upon the transcendent. Even reference to an immanent God implies meaning beyond the self and society; but religion is what concerns us ultimately and that concern elicits from believers a commitment to meet obligations considered *holy*. Segregation was *a system of symbols* confirmed by law, custom, and practice, and expressed in public signs which *established powerful, pervasive, and long lasting moods and motivations* and created *conceptions of a general order of existence* that stipulated distinctions between races as the very the will of God. Such distinctions, treated as sacred and reinforced by taboo and distance, created, when challenged, a tension that implied violence. The sacred connotations of everyday life *clothed these conceptions with such an aura of facticity* that the *moods and motivations seemed uniquely realistic* and absolutely compelling. The italicized phrases are, as every student of religious history knows, taken from Clifford Geertz's definition of religion as a cultural system and are meant to suggest why segregation should be viewed as a religious system.[51]

Segregation was woven into patterns of social control that could easily become translated into collective violence. The most dramatic characteristic of southern white religion in the late nineteenth century was the violent public expurgation that fused sacrifice, blood, and power in the lynching of black men.[52] Slavery, warfare, defeat, emancipation, politics, and the repressed sexuality of evangelicalism combined to use violence as a way of reaffirming the orderliness and solidarity of (white) communal life. Southern Christians, who so enthusiastically provided prayers, hymns, and sermons in celebrating the South and its religiosity, had for the most part remained mute as elites schemed and murdered their way back into power.[53] Thereafter, the "celebration of hierarchy" found in letters of antebellum elite men, together with the "powerful translation of the personal into the social, [and] the conflation of image and substance," allowed Christian men after the war to do what was "necessary" in order to secure a now hallowed South.[54] Lynching was imbedded in the assumption that (white) community power should discipline unruly blacks; and its romance was nourished by the myth of the Ku Klux Klan,[55] which, although suppressed, rode in spirit as terrorists claimed the South for white supremacy.[56]

Lynching punished men for violating a broad range of racial regulations. The fearful ambiguity of racial etiquette—in which whites could assign taboo by hysterical whim or political calculation—nurtured the terror that policed white supremacy.[57] Ambiguity was resolved in whites' minds by claiming that lynching defended white women from rape—although the chances of a white southern female's being raped by a black man were about the same as those of being struck by lightning.[58] The nature of the alibi is suggested in a comment by a Methodist Bishop that a "possible danger to women" lay in "every offense against the white man." If there was a psychological dimension to the alibi, nourished by a fusion of male domination, sexual anxiety, and folk lore, political culture and economic change also contributed to the likelihood of lynching. Between 1880 and 1910, terror was most likely to occur in areas of new and sustained economic growth into which blacks had recently migrated[59] as well as in areas where the political culture was favorable. That of Virginia was not; conservatives there—unlike those of other states—had come to power through astute political maneuvering rather than violence. The governor's appeal to prevent lynching for "Christian" reasons was not so effective as decisive action of his own.[60] In Georgia, however, an officially "sanctioned racial hysteria" between 1890 and 1910 could allow only an unenforceable antilynching law (1893). When a former governor led a brief campaign for improved race relations, the response was a moving display of effusive sentiment as befitted a culture in which public display of approved emotions was an art form—heedless of action. Few whites challenged racist assumptions that legitimized acts thought to be consistent with the "natural order," writes one scholar, and nature ruled over grace.[61]

Understanding violence as systemic and beneficial to whites—although a commonplace insight among victims and social scientists—has not noticeably affected students of the American Protestant experience. It should be informative to inquire not only into the sexual and psychological dynamics of racial domination and the economic–political benefits derived from them, but also the relation between religion and violence in a culture both evangelical and brutal. The segregating of African Americans, when sexualized through fantasies of rape, made collective punishment of African Americans a sacrificial rite that purified the community.[62] Indeed, awareness of purity and danger suffused segregation as no other aspect of American society. As Southern whites became more committed to Christian practice, developed a professionalized revivalism, founded universities, and expanded the range of their social claims through passing purification laws such as prohibition, they were further securing their purity and therefore their safety by distancing themselves from blacks. The surge for purity was epidemic, carrying certain of the faithful out of corrupted denominations into Pentecostal revival and confirming others in their commitment to pure (Landmark Baptist) churches. Lynching was an essential aspect of this surge because it imposed clear boundaries between safety and danger, purity and pollution. Lynching black men for defying white supremacy rid society of anomalous men who, though black, acted as if they were white. They were dirt, "matter out of place," and being dirt had to be removed. That lynching should have been associated with rape was not surprising in a culture in which white women fulfilled rich symbolic expectations. As an act of purification, it purged its perpetrators of guilt for having allowed pollution to occur and restored the system to equilibrium. Holiness, writes Mary Douglas, is concerned with order, clarity, rectitude, *"unity, [and] perfection of the individual and of the kind."*[63] These, too, were the goals of lynching.[64]

Christianizing (purifying) the South made the region uncomfortable for non-Christians. The Jewish experience is suggestive. Before the Civil War, southern Jews had already adopted a strategy of being as invisible as possible. But during the war, beleaguered white Southerners, who believed themselves elect of the Christian god, found it easy to scapegoat "blasphemous Jews." After the financial crises of the 1890s when hated bankers could be personified by the "Jew," southern Christian culture sustained a dramatic episode of scapegoating when Leo Frank was lynched for the rape and murder of Mary Phagan.[65] This act was but the most violent expression of a pervasive surveillance that continued throughout the twentieth century. Abstracted from their own history and placed in that of Christians who claimed to know them better than they themselves, Jews were not in a serene position. "Be especially careful of the *goyim*" young Eli Evans was told by the men of the synagogue. "Converting a Jew is a special blessing for them." Of Southern Baptists polled in a survey of the 1960s, 90% approved of converting Jews to Christianity (48% of all Protestants); 80% believed that the Jews could never be forgiven (by Christians for the Crucifixion) until they converted. On unforgiving playgrounds of the evangelical South Jewish children grew up susceptible to school mates' curiosity—or if more aggressive— demand: "Why don't you believe in Jesus?"[66] The question implies domination through defining obligation, difference, and value. The challenge is formidable; it makes religious convention the medium of social acceptability. Jews, like blacks, by being themselves were always "different."

Threat was not necessarily intended; it may have come from the best of motives. Its nature is suggested by inference from a partially confessional analysis of religion in the South. In characterizing southern evangelicalism, one critic begins with its emphasis on biblical authority, its self-confident certainty, and its "high degree of personal intensity." He then notices a "clear sense of personal identity" and assertiveness in relating to others, sometimes doing works of charity, sometimes sharing the faith.[67] The tendency of these characteristics, if conceded benign intent, is to encourage self-knowledge articulated in sometimes surprising detail and including firm convictions about right and wrong. Personal intensity in a society where individuals' beliefs are usually matters of taste rather than conviction suggests an admirable strength of character. When self-confidence is merged with making life easy for other people the result is positive. But conviction, self-knowledge, and concern about other people can also lead to an insistence that others really want to be like us—even if they do not know it yet. And personal intensity can become unsolicited intrusion into the sacred precincts of self. Moreover, confidence in acting on the highest authority can result in treating people as objects to be bent to purposes conceived as benevolent but executed in arrogance. Conceding personal integrity to people only if they are like us is not a characteristic peculiar either to evangelicals or Southerners, but it flourished under evangelical dominance and served to reinforce cultural forms that maintained Southern distinctiveness.

Making the New South Christian: Dissidents

That lynching declined after 1910 did not result from the nature of evangelical culture,[68] but from malcontents and outsiders. Important to the process were networks created above the local level that engaged whites and blacks in conversation. A feature of urban culture, these networks transformed people with common interests into a community based not on locale, but upon common values and by whites' beginning to listen to black people. Whites had not been accustomed to doing this, and most did not pay rapt attention now; but after the Atlanta race riot of 1906 gave that city a notoriety from which its elites recoiled, leading white and black citizens began to talk. From within the academy, especially the universities of Georgia, North Carolina, Tennessee, and Virginia, scholars, too, began to work for biracial cooperation, and a handful of Christian groups impressed with the ideas of northern racial liberals became ready to cooperate with blacks. In 1919 a group of white men with ties to northern philanthropy formed a group committed to interracial cooperation, persuading a few blacks to overcome their understandable suspicion to help create a Commission on Interracial Cooperation (CIC). The trajectory of such actions is suggested by Arthur Raper's report of *The Tragedy of Lynching* published later in cooperation with the CIC which located the causes of violence not in African American behavior but in social conditions and the minds of white people: poverty, isolation, and ignorance.[69]

At the same time, there was movement among women as well. In 1920, a group of black women broached the possibility of working with whites on projects of mutual concern, and a cadre of white Southern Methodist women called for their newly enfranchised sisters to join a movement of interracial cooperation. After a preliminary meeting at Tuskeegee, white and black women met at Memphis in October of 1920 to begin conversations[70] that evolved into a Committee on Women's Work (CWW) that initiated exchanges between members of both races throughout the urban South. Cooperation was paralleled by the independent action of white women led by Jessie Daniel Ames, a suffrage activist from Texas. Ames believed that a movement of white women opposed to lynching had more credibility in the South than an interracial movement because it belied the myth that the act was necessary to protect them. She founded the Association of Southern Women for the Prevention of Lynching (ASWPL), which by February 1937 included 109 women's associations with four million members committed to action in their neighborhoods. They asked for pledges from local and state authorities to prevent mob violence and "reassured" them that a constituency would stand by them for acting responsibly. As the result of continued study, the ASWPL women learned the same lessons that Raper had learned about poverty, powerlessness, and white supremacy. They began to see that violence was inherent in the system from which they themselves benefited.[71]

So long as southern whites acted according to traditional evangelical notions of responsibility, they were incapable of criticizing their own institutions. Evangelical bias inclined whites to ignore what whites continued to do to blacks by making the latter objects of invidious comparison. Even the evangelical impulse to do good in mission work to the city and Appalachians suggested the inadequacy of evangelical solutions: *you* change—convert, renew, work hard, and sober up. Some evangelicals did indeed become frustrated by the inadequacy of their analysis and began to seek solutions, as did the ASWPL and CIC, from social science. From such sources and not from the Bible or the purity of a renovated will they discovered that sin lay not in an act—breaking taboo—but in context: the social system.[72] Ironically, however, liberals continued to insist that the South could be reformed by relying upon the best of the Southern tradition.[73] The tradition they had in mind, however, did not include the tradition of emancipation; that was its problem.

Making the South Christian: A Countertradition of Jubilee

The tradition of emancipation came out of the experience and expectations of enslaved African Americans who in the metaphors of Exodus, Liberty, and Judgment (Apocalypse) expected more of Emancipation in 1865 than could be fully realized. African American autonomy and self-determination were at the core of expectation from the first celebrations of Jubilee. Confederate defeat, which made of the Lost Cause a public religion, transformed former slaves into "more than conquerors"—in anticipation of final judgment. During the generation after emancipation, African Americans began through their own action and in their own institutions to transform what it meant to be Christian in a South where the attitudes of slavery persisted. Whites, whose own situation was desperate, were not as supportive as pre-war protestations of missionary responsibility suggested they should have been although a few donated money, buildings, and land. To be sure, there was a brief moment of discovery as blacks and whites groped for the meaning of a common Christianity, but most whites could not abide a transformed fellowship with blacks. And the latter, leaving biracial churches in varying degrees of haste and relief, accepted aid from Yankee missionaries of both races in money, education, and hope.[74] Former slave preachers, too, gathered churches from among their fellow Christians through years of expended energy and amazing ingenuity[75] and, with other resourceful men and women, created networks to bind local churches with each other and the coffers of northern Christians. Black ministers, too, went beyond the boundaries of religion by calling conventions, lobbying elites, and winning seats in state and federal legislatures.[76]

By 1890, such persistence and creativity had thatched the South with a variety of African American denominations[77] although the fit between ubiquitous churches and Christianization was ambiguous. Black and white ministers from the North who came South doubted not that they were bringing Christianity—self-discipline, sobriety, Bible, and theology. Their first encounters with "superstition" and ignorance were disheartening to those carrying the gospel to people who, they discovered, had already preached, dreamed and sung their own salvation. This could have been "Christian" (or at least authentic) in their own ken, perhaps, but to their new teachers and ministers, too exotic and ecstatic. Christianity became negotiable among black Christians of differing backgrounds, classes, and experiences. Authenticity confirmed by experience among people who valued such a theistic epistemology sometimes conflicted with biblical authority. Scattered congregations served only sporadically by semiliterate preachers and isolated from the regularizing influence of denominational bodies made problematic a simple definition of what was normatively "Christian." Dichotomies seemed pervasive: spirituals or hymns, chants or sermons, orality or literacy.[78]

If the full meaning of Jubilee was imagined in the early days of emancipation, it was not soon realized. As white elites bludgeoned their way to regional dominance, a few ministers encouraged emigration to Africa, among them Henry M. Turner. Born free in South Carolina in 1833 and aided in his early education by whites, Turner served African Methodist churches in New Orleans and Washington before going to Georgia as a regimental chaplain. Becoming a Republican party activist, he was elected to the state legislature but then ejected for insisting on equality. Increasingly disillusioned, he realized the futility of his hope that Civil War and Emancipation would evoke a conversion experience in whites. As he had conceded slavery to have been providential for bringing Africans to Christ, he expected whites to concede that its destruction had been providential for bringing America to equality. His anger with white America for its inability to live up to its highest protestations was intense.[79] Concluding that emigration was the only dignified option for blacks, he encouraged them to establish "a great Christian nation" in Africa, but emigration, too, failed. It became clear that African American Christians' nationalism would have to be channeled into the evangelization of Africa and the churches themselves transformed into an infrastructure for African American nationalism.[80] In them, African Americans experienced the authenticity of their humanity in openness to the sacred, continuing to incorporate Bible, Gospel, and African perceptions in the promise of Apocalypse: expectation and judgment.[81]

The tradition of Jubilee maintained the tension between white supremacy and African American community in the South as the institutions of education and religion helped to keep hope alive during years of wandering in the desert of Jim Crow. Historians are just beginning to understand the stories of preparation for the reenactment of Jubilee in the 1950s. The surge came not from the white southern evangelical tradition but rather from pressure by African Americans and the United States Supreme Court, which, after a series of decisions that indicated closer scrutiny of southern society, announced in *Brown v. Board of Education* (1954) that segregated public schools were unconstitutional. The response revealed just how sacred white Southerners believed segregation to be. They hemmed, hawed, ranted, and raged and passed 450 state laws designed to avoid doing what the court told them to do. Employers punished blacks who tried to put *Brown* into effect; school boards, police, and vigilante groups throughout the region tried to force blacks back into place—to maintain the purity of the South. Six years after *Brown*, 1% of black students attended integrated schools in the region.[82]

Gradually and then explosively in the summer of 1963 things changed. An entire people moved in fractured, spasmodic, and increasingly coordinated ways to challenge southern tradition. The cumulative anger, unanticipated insistence, and growing confidence of African Americans shaped a series of skirmishes into a regionwide struggle for civil rights. One man did not cause it, but one man did come to personify the process and to articulate its meaning in ways that both whites and blacks could understand. While completing his doctoral dissertation for Boston University and settling into his first pastorate in Montgomery, Alabama in 1955, Martin Luther King, Jr., was thrust into a leadership role that he transformed into a compelling public persona that soon made him a national figure. He voiced the anguish, hope and determination of blacks in language that enlisted the highest ideals shared across class and ethnic lines; he spoke from Christian hope and the condemning assumptions of Christian love. He brought a voice that promised "Deliverance" and declared "Redemption," themes of the African American experience in the southern tradition. His emphasis on the necessity for love and a true, authentic acting out of the experience of grace made sense to blacks and those whites who were able to confess the imperatives of a shared religious ethos. When the Southern Christian Leadership Conference chose the motto, "To Redeem the Soul of America!" it was proclaiming—as had once the slave preachers—redemption to *both* races at the same time.[83]

As he moved from Montgomery into national consciousness, King never wavered in the commitment to nonviolence that changed southern culture. African American activists were expected to act on the moral basis of doing no harm as they demanded nothing more than that to which their dignity as human beings entitled them. The strategy was homiletic as befitted a preacher within an evangelical tradition and a people who were convinced of God's righteousness: it was to create a crisis in both private and public life through which revulsion at the evil thus revealed could bring about repentance and redemption. The pulpit was transferred from church to street, the sermon was transformed from word to act; the convulsion was evoked collectively, and the audience was changed by television to include the world. The strategy fit the form of traditional evangelical preaching. Nonviolent resistance required discipline, confidence, character, and courage; and many people were equal to the call. If the language was unrelentingly moral and the acts persistently nonviolent, the response was dramatic in contrast: brutality, cruelty, violence, and murder. The impact was shock, shame, outrage, and gradual if partial understanding. The result was action by federal officials, law makers, and judges until legal change came with respect to eating, rooming, learning, working, and voting.[84]

It is customary to refer to King's evangelical religion when explaining the way in which Southerners responded to him. The adjective "evangelical" is meant to convey the style that evoked assent that he spoke the truth; it bespeaks a bonding with people of both races. It refers to the compelling cadence of a richly textured voice expressed in a timbre that transformed familiar metaphor into understanding; it refers to the biblical language that shaped and expressed the experiences of those who listened; it refers to the moral intensity of the man. He himself did assume that a common language of Christian redemption, justice, and morality would touch white Southerners deeply enough to stir a positive response. Moreover, he was impressed enough with the evangelistic crusades of Billy Graham to model after them (with modification) his own crusade for racial redemption. In 1957, he talked with Graham who at that time was acquiring a positive reputation among African Americans. A vision of interracial crusades gradually took shape in King's mind as he discussed strategy with Graham, but it was relinquished when the latter indicated that he could not talk about the "worldly aspects" of race. The evangelical commitment to conversion of individuals overwhelmed Graham's personal decency; as long as that commitment remained paramount—and in evangelical ideology it must, most whites could only be passive.[85]

Evangelical Christians may of course disagree, but the difference between King and Graham in 1957 represented the magnitude of the task facing blacks. Eventually, white evangelicals and liberals alike would concede King's moral authority and the justice of African Americans' surge for equality. The voice in which King spoke, however, can tell us much about the nature of evangelicalism in the surge for freedom. That voice, Keith Miller reminds us in a recent book, was found by entering fully into the oral tradition into which African American preachers are apprenticed. That tradition—even that which whites would call evangelical—was never a religion of applied printed texts or labored exposition, but a lived encounter. African American faith merged current experiences with remembered lives and acts of God's people in Christian lore. Conveying the collective memory were preachers from whose example King learned as he heard his father preach and whose stories made up his own message. He used familiar biblical persons, situations, events occurring at different times as contemporaneous—acting together as one type: Daniel, Ezekiel, Joshua, Moses become together Exodus and Freedom! All fused to evoke a feeling and create an anticipated event. Recurring themes of eternal "events" could become historical. The conjunction occurred immediately with a few words that evoked meaning which so fused social and personal redemption that only a white evangelical could separate them. Experts in this tradition can place hearers within the Bible story and the story itself so within their own situations that the voice of the preacher is lost in the immediate authority of what he is saying.[86]

The other source of King's voice was also significant. It was not evangelical. As in his search for texts and stories from the African American biblical tradition, King sought authority in ways that would allow him to make sense within the liberal European world in which he was so thoroughly educated. The first way was to connect his ideas to men immediately recognizable among educated white Americans: one of these was Mohandus K. Gandhi who was widely admired by liberal American Christians. King interpreted Gandhi through the Indian's American disciples, his own experiences as an African American, and the preaching of his father and grandfather: all emphasized nonviolence as *Christian* love in action. Without harming oppressors, nonviolent confrontation increased social tension until it erupted in a violence that discredited them. The second way to make sense among white liberals was to speak the inclusive language they spoke *as he himself conceived it.* When chided for making the non-Christian, Gandhi, a cult figure, King replied that "God worked through Gandhi, and the spirit of Jesus Christ saturated his life." It was ironic, he thought, but "inescapably true that the greatest Christian of the modern world was a man who never embraced Christianity."[87] This thoroughly unevangelical statement, reflected appreciation for the self-sacrifice of Christian liberals who had been impressed by Gandhi. King admired liberal and social gospel sermons because of the way in which they focused on the responsibility of Christians to reject convention and act to change the world. He borrowed liberals' language even as he spoke that of the African American tradition: both expressed truths for which no one held a copyright.[88]

Making the South Christian: Farewell to Evangelicalism?

The traumatic changes of civil war, emancipation, political conflict, and industrialization, together with the sacralization of violence and white supremacy transformed religion in the American South even as they sealed its social and political importance. Evangelicals whom Isaac dramatized as being in revolt in eighteenth-century Virginia did not achieve cultural hegemony without themselves being changed. The fluidity of the insight that persons receiving gospel and spirit must realize Christ in their own self-consciousness meant that the imposed discipline of slaveholding and segregation as well as the tradition of Jubilee (Exodus and Apocalypse) would be included in the vision of Christian people. The absurdity is obvious; but so is the logic of historical experience. To tell the as-yet-untold story of that transformation will require repudiation of a treasured fallacy on the part of religious historians of the South: the reification of evangelicalism. The need to generalize about the impact of evangelical action in the late-eighteenth-century South led historians to create an evangelicalism of specious concreteness. This innovation was given compelling force by the writings of self-defined evangelicals in the 1970s who held a triumphal vision of their ideology and by the fact that churches dominating the South after the Civil War had been founded or affected by evangelical action. Yet the most renowned scholar of southern religion, believing the evangelical ethos to be normative, nonetheless conceded four different orientations within it by the end of the twentieth century.[89]

Two of these orientations—fundamentalist and ethical (social activism)—are so antithetical that it is difficult to believe they share anything "evangelical" except perhaps the belief that Christian commitment is serious and has concrete results. Indeed, despite conventional wisdom to the contrary, it is difficult to believe that fundamentalism remains evangelical at all, so committed is it to faith as assent to unambiguous "fundamental truths." Evangelical searching of scripture to find God's word for those in travail, which allowed democratic discussion, has been reduced to accepting restricted meanings defined by elites. Those who thus reduce the faith profess homage to evangelical emphases on authentic personal experience (experimental Christianity), biblical authority, recruitment, a disciplined life, and suspicion of formalism, to be sure. But they are not open to creative influences ("the spirit") such as allowed African Americans to participate in the life of antebellum churches; nor do they allow personally authenticated interpretations of scripture that allowed women to justify autonomous action among, for example, black Baptists[90] or white Holiness preachers.[91] As for white social activists, we have seen how, during the early twentieth century, they broke from evangelical emphases and relied instead upon social science—and African Americans—to help them understand racism.

"Evangelical" is most properly an adjective, instead of a noun, and it is most appropriately associated with movement, innovation, and popular appeal (antistructure) than with institutions, reaction and elites (structure).[92] Evangelical movements of the early nineteenth century lost their capacity for sustaining the subversive insight and popular appeal that united African American worship and antislavery radicalism. The institutional logic of denominational structuring that created religious education, erected college buildings, introduced pianos, and installed stained glass windows damped the fire of evangelical enthusiasm and provided impetus for a New South. The popular response was evangelical in a revolt of Holiness, Pentecostal, and parallel activists who sought authenticity and authority once again in scriptural exegesis, subjective experience, and repudiation of elites. This surge for purity prepared the next generation for the Scopes trial, and during the 1880s and 90s disputants began to debate a range of issues eventually identified with the conflict between modernism and fundamentalism.[93] A liberal trend that interpreted texts for their metaphorical rather than their "literal" meaning was so widespread among the middle class that by the 1910s a popular southern novelist could without hypocrisy accept evolution, reject the restricted reading of authoritative texts, and appeal for a return to traditional religion.[94]

This transformation has not yet been studied, although conflict within the Southern Baptist Convention (SBC) over the past century could be a parable for understanding its meaning. The issue of authenticity affected Baptists just as much as those who participated in the Holiness and Pentecostal movements and came to be associated by the turn of the century with attacks on higher criticism and eventually with teaching Darwinian evolution in public schools.[95] In response came a vituperative fundamentalism that offended SBC leaders even though they were also uncomfortable with "modernist" glosses on the faith. Attempting to maintain peace, writes Bill Leonard, these leaders expressed themselves in "the language of Zion." Thereafter, he points out, "whenever controversy seemed irreconcilable, preachers would restore unity with the language of spiritualization, an appeal to personal piety and heart religion, those ideals around which all Southern Baptists could agree and unite."[96] The language disguised the fact that the convention would pass hard-line resolutions against evolution and higher criticism without acting.[97] The discourse could be spoken without hypocrisy because there were very few modernists in churches associated with the Convention.[98] During the 1920s, nonetheless, a hushed suspicion developed that college and seminary professors were teaching heresy and that denominational bureaucrats did not share the values of most Southern Baptists. By the 1960s, officials seemed far too independent: they applauded the Supreme Court decision in *Brown*, defended opposition to the Vietnam War, and attacked poverty. They published books and held conferences on controversial topics. By the early 1970s, conservatives were planning to rescue the SBC for authentic Christianity under the banner of inerrantism. They argued that Baptists were not authentic who conceded that the history and science of the Bible were bound by culture and time. Developing a constituency to take over the presidency of the SBC in 1979, they could purge seminaries, commissions, and boards by 1988.[99]

The SBC is neither the South nor southern religion writ small, but its transformation was nonetheless a significant event. The fundamentalists' victory had been paralleled in the larger society by, and in some ways was associated with, a growing politicization of a New Christian Right. It is significant that Senator Jesse Helms (Republican, North Carolina), who personified both the New Right and southern resistance to civil rights during the 1950s and 60s, was identified with the fundamentalist party of the SBC.[100] During the early 1970s, "Christian" became an ideological rather than a generic term. Early response to the racial desegregation of public schools had come in the form of "Christian" academies, which became so popular throughout the South in the sixties that the Federal government charged them with being segregationist and challenged their tax exempt status.[101] This threw them together with other, less compromised academies outside the South to create fortresses against the siege of secularism. When in the early sixties the Supreme Court struck down devotional reading of the Bible and prayer in the public schools for violating the establishment clause of the first amendment, academies earned greater legitimacy among certain Christians. As the Internal Revenue Service sustained its surveillance of the academies, a "Christian" public interest seemed to be endangered. Academies were defended not for their whiteness, but their commitment to "Christian" principles: work, chastity, patriotism, neatness, obedience, morality (no ambiguity), orthodoxy (no Darwinism), and traditional gender roles.

The constituency of Christian academies was but one among many that became targets of right wing baby boomers and former Goldwater Republicans, who invested funds lavished upon them by conservative money men in the right wing resurgence of the late 1970s. Supported by conservative political action committees, activists used President James Earl Carter's White House Conferences on Families as a reason for organizing counter-conferences (on *the* normal family), which, by condemning abortion, the equal rights amendment, and homosexuality underscored the importance of traditional gender roles to a right wing Christian coalition. Although national in purpose, organizers hoped that the Bible belt of the South could provide them a secure geographical base. That the Moral Majority and Religious Roundtable could be so thoroughly identified with Southerners, and that Senator Helms could be conceded the role of godfather, suggested the strategy of conservatives who hoped that the region's religiosity would benefit them. The measure of political reliability suggested a persistent concern with race. The coalition opposed a treaty with Panama to facilitate extending its sovereignty over the Canal from assumptions reminiscent of the "white man's burden." Opposition to lifting economic sanctions on the white minority government of Rhodesia was designed to support segregation abroad after it had been lost at home. Local control of education, so important in resisting racial integration was also at issue, as academies were encouraged to resist policing by the Internal Revenue Service. Gendered issues (Equal Rights Amendment, abortion, homosexuality) were appropriate in an ethos where race and sex had always meant danger.[102]

Some observers believe that the merger of religion and politics in the Christian Right did not extend southern agendas to the North.[103] Yet it is clear that gender issues associated with the Christian Right are consonant with traditional southern values; only Tennessee of all southern states ratified the woman suffrage amendment; only Texas among southern states allowed ratification of ERA to stand.[104] Religion in the South has contributed to a pervasive cultural fundamentalism obsessed with authority, order, purity, danger, and certainty much as it did in the early twentieth century when associated with race. Feminist attempts to confuse gender, perceived in the ERA, were anathema to religious fundamentalists because of the need to maintain boundaries, sustain authority, assign differences, and separate opposites: that is, to maintain "holiness." [105] If the South is not the only part of the country to carry this demand for purity into the politics of homosexuality, it is nonetheless a southern senator and southern political preachers who use sexuality as Southerners once did race to achieve authenticity and purity—holiness in the face of danger.

What can "Christianizing" the South suggest for new directions in writing American Protestant history? Much of what the study of religion in the South suggests lies not in what it has already accomplished, but in what such a study has yet to achieve. We have assumed the homogeneity of southern religion without looking sufficiently at the *nature* of differences affected by class, region, and theology. The many denominational variations within traditions—such as those among Pentecostals and Baptists of both races, for example—have not been adequately addressed. Making these groups into reified things—Baptist, Pentecostal—ignores the dynamism of southern religion, yet so does the assumption of division between such traditions. Samuel Hill, as we have seen, has tried to solve the problem of reification by suggesting four different orientations among southern evangelicalism.[106] As we have also observed, Hill's typology includes a truth orientation and a social activism that could both be interpreted as having repudiated evangelical tradition. (In addition, he includes emphases on aggressive evangelism and piety.) Hill's insights help in thinking about the richness of the religion intent on Christianizing the South, but to be of use the typology needs to be reshaped by such matters as education, gender, sexuality, race, and violence. Keeping the categories of personal and social relations in mind along with different evangelical types—and the impact of evangelical assertiveness on non-Christians, students could begin to understand more fully the rich texture of religious life. And—as we have argued above—these many categories may even require us to surrender the specious reification of evangelicalism.

In addition, a study of violence and invidious distinction supported by religion in the South forces us to see a broad range of ways in which social action not ordinarily thought of as religious contains elements of interest to historians of religion. Intercollegiate football and spanking in public schools are as interesting as lynching in this respect. So are the civil rights movements through which various themes wafted in varying degrees of intensity. The leaven of religious liberalism to and from which Martin Luther King, Jr., could speak is suggested among those in the SBC wars who heard what he was saying when fundamentalists did not. The "liberal" presence has not been appreciated by students of religion in the South, probably because it is difficult to tease out of what has been written so far just where this liberalism was, although Hill, a former Baptist, thought he saw it in a Methodism gone soft on secularism.[107] Hill pleaded in vain for Southerners to criticize themselves, restate their theology and seek the racial redemption[108] that King sought. Southern Protestantism may have created a "liberalism" different from that in other parts of the country—as suggested by white responses to African Americans' preaching redemption in the movable camp meetings of the civil rights revolution.

"Christianizing" the South is not so much about pacification as conflict and not so much achievement as intent. Because "Christian" includes so many meanings, explaining the role and nature of religion in fabricating southern culture is not a simple task. The predominance of evangelical mood, style and motivation among southern adherents of Christianity made *Christian* identity of a certain kind authentic—indeed, made suspicion of authenticity a characteristic posture of Southerners when confronting dissidents, strangers and opponents. A mood of pious suspicion and psychic conformity when mixed with a commitment to white supremacy made being "Christian" different for whites and blacks. A mixture of racial solidarity, community aspiration, and freedom in the spirit made Christianity inclusive for African Americans even as a generation of whites made it exclusive. Being Christian has become a political threat as well as spiritual promise—and the promise itself expresses a long standing commitment to imposing conformity upon those who share neither the mood nor the faith. The presence of black and white together in the same evangelical culture, too, has been a source of vitality and innovation as well as draconian purity; and the redemptive collective action of African Americans on the public stage contributed something to the whole religious experience of the region yet to be fully appreciated. As Southerners confront the meaning of American pluralism, their experience can provide those interested in the broad range of American faiths with insight into Protestantism as both hegemony and dissidence and can suggest, too, that within a specious homogeneity there can be meaningful conflict, and that in conflict there may also be a common bond.

NOTES

1. James McBride Dabbs, *Haunted by God* (Richmond: John Knox Press, 1972).

2. Edwin McNeill Poteat, "Religion in the South", in William Couch, ed., *Culture in the South* (Chapel Hill: University of North Carolina Press, 1935), 248–69, esp. 251, 253, 258.

3. As it does for Jon Butler in his *Awash in a Sea of Faith: Christianizing the American People* (Cambridge, Mass.: Harvard University Press, 1990). It is from Butler's title that the theme of this essay is borrowed; but as he would be the first to point out, we use the idea in different ways: Butler's usage is more precise.

4. For bibliographies about the religion in the South, see John B. Boles, "The Discovery of Southern Religious History" in B. Boles and Evelyn Thomas Nolen, eds., *Interpreting Southern History* (Baton Rouge: Louisiana State University Press, 1987), 510–48; Charles H. Lippy, *Bibliography of Religion in the South* (Macon: Mercer University Press, 1985).

5. James Axtell, *The Invasion Within: The Contest of Cultures in Colonial North America* (New York: Oxford University Press, 1985) shows the ways in which the religions of Europeans interacted differently from each other in their approach and response to native Americans in the northern colonies.

6. Butler, *Awash in a Sea of Faith*, 147.

7. Ibid., 127–28. Popular religion in the South remains unstudied. David D. Hall's study of popular religious beliefs in early New England has yet to be matched for the southern colonies. See *Worlds of Wonder, Days of Judgment: Popular Religious Belief in Early New England* (New York: Alfred Knopf, 1989). But see also Butler, *Awash in a Sea of Faith*, 65–97.

8. Rhys Isaac, *The Transformation of Virginia 1740–1790* (Chapel Hill: University of North Carolina Press, 1982), 144–57.

9. Ibid., 161–77. See also Donald G. Mathews, *Religion in the Old South* (Chicago: University of Chicago Press, 1977), 17–38.

10. William H. Williams, *The Garden of Methodism* (Wilmington, Del.: Scholarly Resources, 1984); Russell E. Richey, *Early American Methodism* (Bloomington: Indiana University Press, 1991).

11. Catherine Cleveland, *The Great Revival in the West, 1797–1805* (Chicago: University of Chicago Press, 1916); John B. Boles, *The Great Revival 1787–1805: The Origins of the Southern Evangelical Mind* (Lexington: University Press of Kentucky, 1972).

12. Nathan Hatch, *The Democratization of American Christianity* (New Haven: Yale University Press, 1989) understands Methodism as a movement, but not as a vanguard. See Richey, *Early American Methodism*, especially 1–20, 82–97.

13. See Jan Lewis, *The Pursuit of Happiness: Family and Values in Jefferson's Virginia* (Cambridge: Cambridge University Press, 1983), especially 209–30; Samuel S. Hill, Jr., *Southern Churches in Crisis* (New York: Holt, Rinehart and Winston, 1966), 23, 62, 58–62; Rhys Isaac, "Evangelical Revolt: The Nature of the Baptists' Challenge to the Traditional Order in Virginia, 1765 to 1775," *William and Mary Quarterly*, 3d ser., 31 (July 1974): 345–68; Mathews, *Religion in the Old South*, xiv–xvii, 10–38, 40–41, 237–50; Anne C. Loveland, *Southern Evangelicals and the Social Order 1800–1860* (Baton Rouge: Louisiana State University Press, 1980); and Boles, *Great Revival*, 183–203.

14. Isaac, *Transformation of Virginia*, especially 323–46, 350–57.

15. John B. Boles, ed., *Masters and Slaves in the House of the Lord* (Lexinton: University Press of Kentucky, 1988); Margaret Washington Creel, "*A Peculiar People*": *Slave Religion and Community Culture Among the Gullahs* (New York: New York University Press, 1988); Jean E. Friedman, *The Enclosed Garden: Women and Community in the Evangelical South, 1830–1900* (Chapel Hill: University of North Carolina Press, 1985); Mathews, *Religion in the Old South*; Ted Ownby, *Subduing Satan: Religion, Recreation, and Manhood in the Rural South 1865–1920* (Chapel Hill: University of North Carolina Press, 1990). Mechal Sobel, "*Trabelin' On*": *The Slave Journey to An Afro-Baptist Faith* (Westport, Conn.: Greenwood Press, 1979); Sobel, *The World They Made Together: Black and White Values in Eighteenth-Century Virginia* (Princeton:

Princeton University Press, 1987); also Stephanie McCurry, "Defense of Their World: Gender, Class, and the Yeomanry of the South Carolina Low Country, 1820–1860" (unpublished Ph.D. dissertation, State University of New York, Binghamton, 1988), and John Scott Strickland, "Across Space and Time: Conversion, Community, and Cultural Change among South Carolina Slaves," (unpublished Ph.D. dissertation, University of North Carolina, 1985). For attention to Protestant festivals from within the Presbyterian tradition, see Leigh Eric Schmidt, *Holy Fairs: Scottish Communions and American Revivals in the Early Modern Period* (Princeton: Princeton University Press, 1989).

16. See Bertram Wyatt-Brown, *Southern Honor: Ethics and Behavior in the Old South* (New York: Oxford University Press, 1982), and "God and Honor in the Old South," *Southern Review,* 25 (April 1989): 283–96. Richard Rankin, *Ambivalent Churchmen and Evangelical Churchwomen: The Religion of the Episcopal Elite in North Carolina, 1800–1860* (Columbia: University of South Carolina Press, 1993).

17. See Sterling Stuckey, *Slave Culture: Nationalist Theory and the Foundations of Black America* (New York: Oxford University Press, 1987), 30, 38, and 93–97; Creel, *"A Peculiar People,"* 259–75.

18. Boles, *Masters and Slaves in the House of the Lord,* 1–18.

19. Charles Joyner, *Down by the Riverside: A South Carolina Slave Community* (Urbana: University of Illinois Press, 1984), 158–59; Mathews, *Religion in the Old South,* 185–236.

20. Butler, *Awash in a Sea of Faith,* 236–41.

21. See Michael Mullin, *Africa in America: Slave Acculturation and Resistance in the American South and the British Caribbean 1736–1831* (Urbana: University of Illinois Press, 1992), 174–212, 241–67. See also Creel, *"A Peculiar People"*; Eugene D. Genovese, *"Roll, Jordan, Roll": The World the Slaves Made* (New York: Pantheon Press, 1974); Joyner, *Down by the Riverside*; Lawrence W. Levine, *Black Culture and Black Consciousness: Afro-American Folk Thought from Slavery to Freedom* (New York: Oxford University Press, 1977), 3–80; Albert J. Raboteau, *Slave Religion: The "Invisible Institution" in the Antebellum South* (New York, Oxford University Press, 1978); Sobel, *"Trabelin' On,"* 229–47.

22. James M. Simms, *The First Colored Baptist Church in North America* (Philadelphia: J. B. Lippincott, 1888), 13–35.

23. Sobel, *"Trabelin' On,"* 108–28, 182, 221, 412.

24. By the 1840s, shape-note song books had become popular indeed; the *Southern Harmony, Hesperian Harp,* and *Olive Leaf* yielded in popularity to the *Sacred Harp,* published first in 1844, a year before the first Southern Music Convention. See George Pullen Jackson, *White Spitituals in the Southern Uplands* (Chapel Hill: University of North Carolina Press, 1933), 35–38, 57–64, 70–93, 94, 100–102, 151–57. Gavin Campbell has pointed out to me the importance of shape-note singing.

25. Mathews, *Religion in the Old South,* 81–135.

26. Stowe, *Intimacy and Power in the Old South: Ritual in the Lives of the Planters* (Baltimore: The Johns Hopkins University Press, 1987), 122–59, 192–223.

27. Mathews, *Religion in the Old South,* 136–84.

28. See the analysis of Dale B. Martin, *Slavery as Salvation: The Metaphor of Slavery in Pauline Christianity* (New Haven: Yale University Press, 1990), espe-

cially xiii–xxii, 42–49, 136–49. See also Augustus Baldwin Longstreet, *Letters on the Epistle of Paul to Philemon* (Charleston: B. Jenkins, 1845), especially 37–45; Mathews, *Religion in the Old South*, 136–84; Drew Gilpin Faust, ed., *The Ideology of Slavery: Proslavery Thought in the Antebellum South* (Baton Rouge: Louisiana State University Press, 1981).

29. Gaines M. Foster, "Guilt Over Slavery: A Historiographical Analysis," *Journal of Southern History* 56 (November, 1990): 664–94.

30. The major Presbyterian body had already divided after theological dispute caused by antislavery revivalists.

31. Richard Carwardine, *Evangelicals and Politics in Antebellum America* (London: Yale University Press, 1993), 153–74, 255–58, 271–72; C. C. Goen, *Broken Churches, Broken Nation* (Macon: Mercer University Press, 1984).

32. *Southern Christian Advocate* quoted by Drew Gilpin Faust, *The Creation of Confederate Nationalism: Ideology and Identity in the Civil War South* (Baton Rouge: Louisiana State University Press, 1988), 24–5.

33. In a sermon by Georgia's Episcopal Bishop, Stephen Eliott, in January of 1862, ibid., 17 (see also 28); also see Harry S. Stout, "The Life and Death of the Confederate Jeremiad," manuscript of the James A. Gray Lectures, Duke Divinity School, October 1992 (in my possession, kindly loaned by Stout) Lectures 1, 3. Also James W. Silver, *Protestant Churches and Confederate Propaganda* (Tuscaloosa: Confederate Publishing Company, 1957); Harrison Daniel, *Southern Protestantism in the Confederacy* (Bedford, Va.: The Print Shop, 1989), 29–53.

34. Faust, *The Creation of Confederate Nationalism*, 58–76; Paul Escott, "The Failure of Confederate Nationalism: The Old South's Class System in the Crucible of War," in Harry P. Owens and James J. Cooke, eds., *The Old South in the Crucible of War* (Jackson: University Press of Mississippi, 1983), 15–28.

35. Drew Gilpin Faust, "Christian Soldiers: The Meaning of Revivalism in the Confederate Army," *Journal of Southern History* 53 (February 1987), 64–88.

36. Shattuck, *A Shield and a Hiding Place*, 117.

37. Thomas Connelly and Barbara Bellows, *God and General Longstreet: The Lost Cause and the Southern Mind* (Baton Rouge: Louisiana State University Press, 1982), 24, 28–38. Also Charles Reagan Wilson, *Baptized in Blood: The Religion of the Lost Cause 1865–1920* (Athens: University of Georgia Press, 1980).

38. Wilson, *Baptized in Blood*, 45–46.

39. Faust, "Christian Soldiers: The Meaning of Revivalism in the Confederate Army," 88–90; Gaines M. Foster, *Ghosts of the Confederacy: Defeat, the Lost Cause, and the Emergence of the New South* (New York: Oxford University Press, 1987), 195.

40. George Gilman Smith, *Life and Times of George Foster Pierce, D.D, Ll.D.* (Sparta, GA: Hancock Publishing Company, 1888), 560. Hunter Farish, *The Circuit Rider Dismounts: A Social History of Southern Methodism 1865–1900* (Richmond: Dietz, 1938). Also Rufus B. Spain, *At Ease in Zion: Social History of Southern Baptists 1865–1900* (Nashville: Vanderbilt University Press, 1967).

41. Gary R. Freeze, "God, Cotton Mills, and New South Myths: A New Perspective on Salisbury, North Carolina, 1887–1888," in Elizabeth Jacoway et al., eds., *The Adaptable South: Essays in Honor of George Brown Tindall* (Baton Rouge: Louisiana State University Press, 1991), 44–63.

42. Ted Ownby, *Subduing Satan*.

43. Atticus Haygood, ed., *Bishop Pierce's Sermons and Address* (Nashville: Southern Methodist Publishing House, 1885), 290.

44. *The News and Observer,* February 22, 1903.

45. Jackson, *White Spirituals in the Southern Uplands,* 303–15. Jackson, *White and Negro Spirituals: Their Life Span and Kinship* (New York: J. J. Augustin Publisher, 1943), 133–37.

46. Nancy Tatom Ammerman, *Baptist Battles: Social Change and Religious Conflict in the Southern Baptist Convention* (New Brunswick: Rutgers University Press, 1990), 33–34; Bill J. Leonard, *God's Last & Only Hope: The Fragmentations of the Southern Baptist Convention* (Grand Rapids, Mich.: Eerdmans, 1990), 34–35. Other groups had similar debates. See for example David Edwin Harrell, Jr., "Religious Pluralism: Catholics, Jews, and Sectarians," in Charles Reagan Wilson, ed., *Religion in the South* (Jackson: University Press of Mississippi, 1985), 68–69.

47. See Vinson Synan, *The Pentecostal Holiness-Movement in the United States* (Grand Rapids: Eerdmans, 1971), 46, 126, and 33–93. Also J. Lawrence Brasher, "The North in the South: The Holiness Methodism of John Lakin Brasher, 1868–1971," *Methodist History* 27 (October, 1988): 36–47.

48. Synan, *Pentecostal Holiness Movement,* 126 and 94–139; see also Edward L. Ayers, *The Promise of the New South: Life after Reconstruction* (New York: Oxford University Press, 1992), 399ff.

49. Harrell, "Religious Pluralism: Catholics, Jews, and Sectarians," in Wilson, *Religion in the South,* 68–69, 77. See also Erskine Caldwell, *Deep South: Memory and Observation* (Athens: University of Georgia Press, 1980), 46.

50. Bruce Palmer, *"Man over Money": The Southern Populist Critique of American Capitalism* (Chapel Hill: University of North Carolina Press, 1980), 133–37, 201.

51. Clifford Geertz, "Religion as a Cultural System" in Geertz, *The Interpretation of Cultures: Selected Essays* (New York: Basic Books, 1973), 87–125. See also C. Vann Woodward, *The Strange Career of Jim Crow* (New York: Oxford University Press, 1955); Ayers, *Promise of the New South,* 67–68, 126–27, 136–46, 429–34.

52. Wilma Dykeman and James Stokely, *Seeds of Southern Change: The Life of Will Alexander* (Chicago: University of Chicago Press, 1962), 15–16.

53. Allen W. Trelease, *White Terror: The Ku Klux Klan Conspiracy and Southern Reconstruction* (New York: Harper & Row, 1971); George C. Rable, *But There Was No Peace: The Role of Violence in the Politics of Reconstruction* (Athens: University of Georgia Press, 1984).

54. Bruce, *Violence and Culture,* 3–28, 69, 84; Wyatt-Brown, *Southern Honor,* 354, 369; Stowe, *Intimacy and Power,* 250–54.

55. The name could be traced to Charles Lynch of Virginia during the Revolution when he imposed vigilante justice upon suspected Tories. See Trelease, *White Terror,* xv–xlviii.

56. For a brief overview of lynching, see Jacquelyn Dowd Hall, *Revolt Against Chivalry: Jessie Daniel Ames and the Women's Campaign Against Lynching* (New York: Columbia University Press, 1979), 129–57; see also George C. Rable, *But There Was No Peace.* During the period from 1889 to 1899, an average of 188 people a year were lynched. From 1900 to 1909 the toll was 93, the next decade it was 62, from 1920 to 1924 it was 46 and from 1925 through 1929 it was 17. This is derived from data in National Association for the Ad-

vancement of Colored People, *Thirty Years of Lynching* and *Supplements* (New York: NAACP, 1919–28). Arthur Raper, *The Tragedy of Lynching* (Chapel Hill: University of North Carolina Press, 1933), 25.

57. See Neil R. McMillan, *Dark Journey: Black Mississippians in the Age of Jim Crow* (Urbana: University of Illinois Press, 1989), 14–19, 224–53; Hall, *Revolt Against Chivalry,* 148–9; W[illiam] Fitzhugh Brundage, *Lynching in the New South: Georgia and Virginia 1880–1930* (Urbana: University of Illinois Press, 1993), 41–85; Also Joel R. Williamson, *The Crucible of Race* (New York: Oxford University Press, 1984).

58. James R. McGovern, *Anatomy of a Lynching: The Killing of Claude Neal* (Baton Rouge: Louisiana State University Press, 1982), 8.

59. William Fitzhugh Brundage, "Lynching in the New South: Georgia and Virginia, 1880–1930" (Ph.D. dissertation, Harvard University, 1988), 69–101. Ayers, *The Promise of the New South,* 132–159.

60. Brundage, *Lynching in the New South,* 99, 161–70, 187.

61. Ibid., 199–202, 207.

62. René Girard, *Violence and the Sacred,* Patrick Gregory, trans. (Baltimore: Johns Hopkins University Press, 1977), especially 269–71. John W. Cell, *The Highest Stage of White Supremacy: The Origins of Segregation in South Africa and the American South* (Cambridge: Cambridge University Press, 1982), 82–191; Joel R. Williamson, *A Rage for Order: Black–White Relations in the American South since Emancipation* (New York: Oxford University Press, 1986), 98–181.

63. Mary Douglas, *Purity and Danger: An Analysis of Concepts of Pollution and Taboo* (Middlesex, England: Penguin, 1970), 17–72, especially 68.

64. Students of religion can probe beyond lynching to other forms of violence and the way in which religious people understand their universe. Philip Greven, in his recent study of the religious roots of corporal punishment, insists that words and ideas learned from authoritative sources make a difference in how people nurture and teach their children. See Philip Greven, *Spare the Child: The Religious Roots of Punishment and the Psychological Impact of Physical Abuse* (New York: Random House [Vintage Books], 1990), 217. If people could nourish the grotesque ritual of lynching, certainly other forms of behavior linked with such religiously freighted matters as the rearing of children should be studied. The fact that Southern Christian academies in the 1990s would consider a state's forbidding corporal punishment to be a violation of First Amendment guarantees of religious liberty suggests the importance of such research. See Harold G. Grasmick, Carolyn Stout Morgan, and Mary Baldwin Kennedy, "Support for Corporal Punishment in the [Oklahoma] Schools: A Comparison of the the the Effects of Socioeconomic Status and Religion," *Social Science Quarterly* 73 (March, 1992): 177–87.

65. See Leonard Dinnerstein, "Atlanta in the Progressive Era: A Dreyfus Affair in Georgia" in Leonard Dinnerstein and Mary Dale Palsson, eds., *Jews in the South* (Baton Rouge: Louisiana State University Press, 1973), 190 and 170–97. I am grateful to Leah Hagedorn for conversations with her amplified by reading Dinnerstein and Palsson and Eli N. Evans, *The Provincials: A Personal History of Jews in the South* (New York: Atheneum, 1976).

66. Evans, *The Provincials,* 120–39, 211–26, especially 124, 219. See also Caldwell, *Deep South,* 148–49: A shoe salesman complained that he would never tie a black's "shoe laces for him. But the Jews will do it, because they're Jews. That's all need be said about it."

67. Samuel S. Hill, Jr., "The Shape and Shapes of Popular Southern Piety" in David Edwin Harrell, Jr., ed., *Varieties of Southern Evangelicalism* (Macon: Mercer University Press, 1981), 89–114, especially 96–99.

68. Raper, *The Tragedy of Lynching,* 21–23, 49, 72, 81, 91, 122ff.

69. Ibid., 38, also: 6, 11, 15, 16, 18, 20–39, 53–4, 74–84, 119–24, 129–38, 145–171, 191–202, 211–32, 249–60, 281–301, 312–16, 347–55, 367–68, 378–83; Brundage, *Lynching in the New South,* 208–36.

70. Dykeman and Stokely, *Seeds of Southern Change,* 95, 57–95; Hall, *Revolt Against Chivalry,* 58–106.

71. Ibid., 171–91, 195–97, 220–21.

72. John A. Salmond, "The Fellowship of Southern Churchmen and Interracial Change in the South," *North Carolina Historical Review* 69 (April 1992): 179–99; Andrew S. Chancey, " 'A Demonstration Plot for the Kingdom of God': The Establishment and Early Years of Koinonia," *Georgia Historical Quarterly* 75 (Summer 1991): 321–53. Alice Knotts, "Race Relations in the 1920s: A Challenge to Southern Methodist Women," *Methodist History* 26 (Fall, 1988): 199–212.

73. See Morton Sosna, *In Search of the Silent South: Southern Liberals and the Race Issue* (New York: Columbia University Press, 1977); see also Julian Pleasants, "Frank Graham and the Politics of the New South" in Elizabeth Jacoway et al., eds., *The Adaptable South: Essays in Honor of George Brown Tindall* (Baton Rouge: Louisiana State University Press, 1991), 176–211.

74. William E. Montgomery, *Under Their Own Vine and Fig Tree: The African-American Church in the South 1865–1900* (Baton Rouge: Louisiana State University Press, 1993), 56–59.

75. Joseph Baysmore of eastern North Carolina, for example, could establish eight churches in fifteen years and help create the state Baptist Convention before becoming an independent evangelist. Joseph Baysmore, *A Historical Sketch of the First Colored Baptist Church Weldon, N. C.* (Weldon, N.C.: Harrell's Printing House, 1887), 1–2; Montgomery, *Under Their Own Vine,* 100, 308–10.

76. Montgomery, *Under Their Own Vine,* 140–41, 188.

77. Ibid., 97–141, 311–12. Baptists were a majority (54%); Methodists were next, and after them, a few Presbyterians and Episcopalians. There were uncounted independent churches and an impressive number of academies that prepared black professionals.

78. Ibid., 85, 257–65.

79. Ibid., 204. See also Peter Kolchin, "Commentary," in Kees Gispen, ed., *What Made the South Different?* (Jackson: University Press of Mississippi, 1990), 88–96. Also Glenn T. Eskew, "Black Elitism and the Failure of Paternalism in Postbellum Georgia: The Case of Bishop Lucius Henry Holsey," *Journal of Southern History* 58 (November 1992): 637–66.

80. Montgomery, *Under Their Own Vine,* 60, 84–7, 179–87, 203–52. Edwin S. Redkey, *Black Exodus: Black Nationalist and Back-to-Africa Movements 1890–1910* (New Haven: Yale University Press, 1969); Clarence E. Walker, *A Rock in a Weary Land: The African Methodist Episcopal Church During the Civil War and Reconstruction* (Baton Rouge: Louisiana State University Press, 1982); James Melvin Washington, *Frustrated Fellowship: The Black Baptist Quest for Social Power* (Macon: Mercer University Press, 1986).

81. See Theophus H. Smith, *Conjuring Culture: Biblical Formations of Black America* (New York: Oxford University Press, 1994), 55–80, 159–248; Bruce A.

Rosenberg, *Can These Bones Live: The Art of the American Folk Preacher.* Revised ed. (Urbana: University of Illinois Press, 1988), 70–102, 141–70.

82. David R. Goldfield, *Black, White and Southern: Race Relations and Southern Culture 1940 to the Present* (Baton Rouge: Louisiana State University Press, 1990), 76–86, 114.

83. Ibid., 87–117.

84. Ibid., 118–73.

85. Taylor Branch, *Parting the Waters: America in the King Years 1954–63* (New York: Simon and Schuster Inc, 1988), 227–28.

86. Keith D. Miller, *Voice of Deliverance: The Language of Martin Luther King, Jr., and its Sources* (New York: Free Press, 1992), 20–23.

87. Ibid., 92.

88. Ibid., 86–141.

89. Samuel S. Hill, Jr., "The Shapes of Popular Southern Piety" in Harrell, *Varieties of Southern Evangelicalism*, 99–114: "devotional", fundamentalist, evangelistic, and ethical (service).

90. See for example Evelyn Brooks Higginbotham, *Righteous Discontent: The Women's Movement in the Black Baptist Church, 1880–1920* (Cambridge, Mass.: Harvard University Press, 1993).

91. See for example Fannie M. Hunter, *Women Preachers* (Dallas: Berachah Printing, 1905).

92. Victor W. Turner, *The Ritual Process* (Chicago: Aldine Press, 1969); Sally Falk Moore, "Epilogue: Uncertainties in Situations, Indeterminacies in Culture" in Moore and Barbara G. Myerhoff, Editors, *Symbol and Politics in Communal Ideology* (Ithaca: Cornell University Press, 1975), 210–39.

93. See for example the *Quarterly Review* (of the Methodist Episcopal Church, South) 4 (January 1882): 51–58; 5 (July 1883): 551–55.

94. See Corra (White) Harris, *The Circuit Rider's Wife.* 1910. Reprint (Boston: Houghton Mifflin, 1933); *My Book and Heart* (Boston: Houghton Mifflin, 1924), 32, 58–59, 213, 224–26, 311; Clippings of interview of Harris in Corra (White) Harris Papers, University of Georgia, box 102, folder 19.

95. The Scopes trial in Dayton, Tennessee in 1925 was a drama that had already been played out in less publicized ways in colleges, universities, seminaries, and churches throughout the South. See Willard B. Gatewood, Jr., *Preachers, Pedagogues, & Politicians: The Evolution Controversy in North Carolina 1920–1927* (Chapel Hill: University of North Carolina Press, 1966); Ray Ginger, *Six Days or Forever? Tennessee v. John Thomas Scopes* (New York: Oxford University Press, 1958); Ronald L. Numbers, *The Creationists: The Evolution of Scientific Creationism* (New York: Alfred A. Knopf, 1992).

96. Leonard, *God's Last and Only Hope*, 128.

97. William E. Ellis, *"A Man of Books and a Man of the People": E. Y. Mullins and the Crisis of Moderate Baptist Leadership* (Macon: Mercer University Press, 1985), 208.

98. Ammerman, *Baptist Battles*, 44–63.

99. Ibid., 64–125, 212–52; Leonard, *God's Last and Only Hope*, 80–172.

100. Ernest B. Furgurson, *Hard Right: The Rise of Jesse Helms* (New York: W. W. Norton & Co., 1986), 233–51, especially 248–51.

101. Peter Skerry, "Christian Schools versus the I. R. S.," *Public Interest* 61 (Fall 1980): 14–41.

102. See Steve Bruce, *The Rise and Fall of the New Christian Right: Conservative Protestant Politics in America 1978–1988* (New York: Oxford University Press, 1988), 25–49; Donald G. Mathews and Jane Sherron De Hart, *Sex, Gender, and the Politics of ERA: A State and the Nation* (New York: Oxford University Press, 1990), 152–80; Samuel S. Hill and Dennis E. Owen, *The New Religious Political Right in America* (Nashville: Abingdon Press, 1982).

103. Lyman A. Kellstedt, "Evangelical Religion and Support for Social Issue Policies: An Examination of Regional Variation" in Robert P. Steed, Laurence W. Moreland, and Tod A. Baker, eds., *The Disappearing South? Studies in Regional Change and Continuity* (Tuscaloosa: University of Alabama Press, 1990), 123, 107–24.

104. Tennessee and Kentucky ratified but later rescinded. Mathews and De Hart, *Sex, Gender, and the Politics of ERA*, 3–27, 268–69.

105. Donald G. Mathews, " 'Spiritual Warfare': Cultural Fundamentalism and the Equal Rights Amendment," *Religion and American Culture* 3 (Summer 1993): 129–54; Dennis E. Owen, Kenneth D. Wald, and Samuel S. Hill, "Authoritarian or Authority-Minded? The Cognitive Commitments of Fundamentalists and the Christian Right," *Religion and American Culture* 1 (Winter 1991): 73–100.

106. Samuel S. Hill, Jr., "The Shapes of Popular Southern Piety" in Harrell, *Varieties of Southern Evangelicalism*, 99–114.

107. Samuel S. Hill, Jr., *Southern Churches in Crisis*, 209.

108. Ibid., 193–211.

4

"AS CANADIAN AS POSSIBLE UNDER THE CIRCUMSTANCES"

Reflections on the Study of
Protestantism in North America

▨ ▨ ▨

Phyllis D. Airhart

JANUARY 28, 1980, is a memorable date in both American and Canadian history. Since November 1979, North Americans had been following with trepidation the siege of the U.S. embassy in Tehran. But on that day we were offered a momentary respite from our fears for the safety of the hostages. Six American had found their way to the Canadian embassy where they had been, as one reporter described it, smuggled out of Iran "disguised as Canadians." Canada is a country that has acquired a well-deserved reputation for almost obsessive preoccupation with its "identity," and this incident thus occasioned some reflection. How exactly would one disguise a person as a Canadian?

"Just Yodel 'Rose Marie' and Carry a Big Stick," was *Maclean's* columnist Allan Fotheringham's tongue-in-cheek response.[1] An illustration of a "Spot a Canuck ident-a-Kit" accompanied his article and featured a lumberjack sporting an RCMP fedora, wearing mukluks and snowshoes, walking a pet beaver, and clutching a hockey stick and a jug of maple syrup fortified with spirits. His outfit was decorated with a maple leaf pin (the instructions suggested that American exfiltrators wear two), and an object described as a "religious amulet" (upon closer inspection a price tag from Eaton's department store) dangled from his hockey sweater. The dilemma of determining what is distinctively "Canadian" was comically clear.

Being asked to discuss recent work on Canadian religious history in a way that makes a contribution to the recovery of American (used here for the sake of convenience to refer to the United States) religious history is to find oneself in a similar predicament. It would be easy to "over-dress" Canadian scholarship for the occasion—to exaggerate the differences in method and interpretation in a distorting way. In fact a comparison of our lists of accomplishments of the past and agendas for the future would show some striking parallels.

Yet for all the similarities, those knowledgeable about both sides of the border continue to affirm that differences in style and substance do persist. As one Canadian diplomat put it, "The boundary between Canada and the United States is typically a human creation; it is physically invisible, geographically illogical, militarily indefensible, and emotionally inescapable."[2] We have acquired a talent for compromise that sometimes translates into blending of perspectives and approaches in ways that downplay our own creativity in scholarship as in life. We worry that we are dull. We smile at the rightness of the slogan selected as the Canadian counterpart to the expression "as American as apple pie" by CBC radio host Peter Gzowski—"as Canadian as possible under the circumstances." Recognizing that there are many parallels and linkages between Canadian and American religious history, the focus of what follows will be "as Canadian as possible under the circumstances," first analyzing the state of current scholarship and then identifying specific areas for fruitful conversation and collaboration between Canadian and American scholars.

I

The experiences and the expressions of religion in Canada have not always run the same course as elsewhere, nor has historical analysis of those developments proceeded apace. The Canadian—American border seems at times to have served as a buffer, acting as a moderating influence on new ideas and movements as they arrive. Political analysts, historians, and literary critics—Canadian and American alike—note the absence of revolution or civil war in Canada. American Mark A. Noll has dismissed even our "rebellions" of the 1830s as paltry local skirmishes, "hardly the real thing"; Canadian Northrop Frye has remarked that our literary imaginations are "haunted by a lack of ghosts."[3] This attitude appears to have spilled over as well into the writing of our history. As John Webster Grant surveyed the resources available for teaching Canadian church history in 1955, he noted their lack of a sense of magnitude and relevance. Literature dealing with Canada seemed scanty when compared in quality with histories of European churches. More serious was the impression that there was no significant story to tell. With the possible exception of church union in 1925, all the great moments seemed to have happened somewhere else. Canadian historians, he suggested, had not made up their minds what to look for in a mass of material that continued to elude them.[4]

In the four decades that followed, no one succeeded more admirably than Grant himself in accomplishing the tasks he then proceeded to outline. Urging historians of the Canadian church to get inside the Canadian situation and to write about it from that perspective, he warned of the dangers of succumbing to "the subtle temptation to write into Canadian Church history assumptions derived from the study of other countries."[5] He set out four areas that he considered worthy of exploration: the influence of religious issues on the Canadian political tradition; the closely allied problem of church and state in Canada; the Canadian attitude to denominations; and distinctive Canadian features in church life (for example, worship and theological education). These themes were evident in *A History of the Christian Church in Canada,* a three-volume collaboration that he published with H. H. Walsh and John S. Moir. Grant's contribution to the series, *The Church in the Canadian Era,* is still widely regarded as the best available survey of Canadian religious history after Confederation.[6]

Despite the high hopes and solid scholarship of that generation, a contradictory mixture of admiration and disappointment with the results can be detected in subsequent "state of the field" essays. In the 1960s, just as the effort to take a fresh look at religious developments in Canada was getting off the ground, Canada entered a period of rapid change. Both Protestants and Catholics seemed eager to throw off traditional religious loyalties and practices. One result was a declining interest in the history of religious organizations, which paralleled an ebbing involvement in religious institutions. As N. K. Clifford bluntly noted in 1980, few were interested in the historical study of religion in Canada, and still fewer in its historiography. He observed that the Canadian academic community and its journals had ignored *A History of the Christian Church in Canada* while vying with each other to see who could produce the best review of Sydney Ahlstrom's *A Religious History of the American People,* published that same year.[7] In an earlier article written while serving as assistant dean in the University of Chicago's Divinity School, Clifford had assessed the impact of historians' use of "imported theories" to analyze the relationship between religion and the development of Canadian society. He noted that the effort to write distinctively Canadian religious history was not only a search for *Canadian* identity but a search for the identity of the Canadian *church historian* as well. While some historians saw drawing on analogies from other countries as a danger, others like H. H. Walsh had identified the major threat as coming from sociology and urged church historians to look instead to theology for their inspiration.[8]

A decade later, Clifford, now teaching religious studies at the University of British Columbia, proceeded to contest many of the dominant assumptions of the past quarter century. The older perspective had lost its controlling power, he argued, but there was no agreement on the direction in which the study of religion in Canada would take in the future. Citing H. J. Hanham, who had urged that the study of church history not be left solely to seminary historians who were "naturally more concerned with the internal history of church organizations than with the church as a focus of intellectual, political and economic activity," Clifford first challenged the older focus on "the Church." He sought a broader definition of "religion in Canada" which he hoped would come as its study moved to departments of history and religious studies. He also called for greater openness to the social sciences, especially sociology and cultural anthropology, in the framing of questions. Third, and most important in signaling a fork in the road forged by Grant and others, Clifford anticipated "less concern with national distinctiveness, particularly when this is defined primarily in contrast to the United States, and more interest in the way that Canadians have responded to much larger cultural and religious transformations." [9]

Clifford conceded that the perspective he was challenging was likely to continue to function, despite erosion, for there was no other as yet to replace it. Those familiar with Clifford's published work (and, perhaps even more significantly, those with whom he shared his research plans) will recognize something of his own agenda in his critique. [10] Before his sudden death in 1990, he was one of a number of established scholars whose broad vision of the history of Christianity in Canada and interest in methodological innovation helped to nurture a new generation of scholars. This was done with the encouragement of those representing the "earlier generation" who, in a number of cases, invigorated their own scholarship by exploring new trails. Grant, for example, broke important new ground with a fine study of the encounter of native religion and Christianity in *Moon of Wintertime*. Moir was convinced by 1983 that the field was "coming of age but slowly," and urged scholars to be more daring in their approach to religion in Canada. [11]

The 1980s proved to be an important decade, perhaps even a turning point, in a number of ways. "Good Books At Last," Noll observed as he titled his essay reviewing seven books published towards the end of the decade. His positive assessment of recent developments has been matched by a general sense of accomplishment among Canadian historians of religion despite a recognition of how much remains to be done. [12] Most of the authors of the "good books" noted by Noll are well on their way to completing a subsequent publication, a promising sign. It is interesting to compare the direction of this recent work with the three possibilities to which Clifford drew attention at the beginning of the decade. As he expected, a broader vision of Canadian religion has emerged that recognizes its diversity. And there is no longer cause to complain about the

domination of seminary church historians. Mark McGowan has characterized the decade's developments as a "flight from the cloister," com-
mending in particular "the work of social scientists of religion and the
social historians who are pursuing research independent of theological
constructions, and who are analyzing religious questions in light of hu-
manistic and social scientific methods, with as few a priori arguments
from faith as possible."[13] Those fleeing "the cloister" have generally
landed in religious studies departments; there has been surprising little
headway in history departments with the notable exception of Queen's
University.[14]

Historians of religion in Canada in the last decade have also shown a
marked interest in blending historical and social scientific methodologies
to analyze the connections between religion and culture. Francophone
historians in particular have produced an impressive array of social histories drawing on methods associated with the "*histoire des mentalités*"
of the *Annales* school.[15] A number of recent studies by Anglophone
scholars also feature interdisciplinary and multidisciplinary approaches.
William Westfall's *Two Worlds,* to cite one example, makes sophisticated
use of sociological and anthropological theory. Westfall and C. T.
McIntire are currently at work on a "collective biography" of Trinity
College's graduates in divinity that features computer analysis of data.

While recent studies continue to be grounded in Canadian particularity, they have been less preoccupied with highlighting the distinctive features of Canadian religious culture. Perhaps the assumptions of the new
cultural history have created a different ethos; while the "big events" of
religious history may have happened elsewhere, we have plenty of the
"stuff" of good social and cultural history and well-kept records to document it. Furthermore, some Anglo-Canadian historians have benefited
from time spent at American graduate schools or acquaintance with
American scholars and their work through conferences and publications.[16] Questions have thus become transnational and international as
well as national in scope and are framed in a way that is accessible to an
interested "outsider" willing to learn. Clifford thus rightly identified a
conceptual, methodological, and horizontal broadening of the study of
religion that has marked recent work on Protestantism in Canada.[17] One
can still detect the underlying importance of the themes that Grant earlier
identified, but they are being pushed in new directions with growing sophistication.[18]

2

The recovery of Canadian religious history can quite easily be argued to
contribute in substantial ways to understanding Canada's own cultural
experience. But does it have wider import for those dealing with religion
in the American context as they think in comparative terms? Here the
question for the historian is not simply, Shall we do comparative his-

tory?—analysis of change over time always involves comparison in a variety of ways—but, What shall we compare? This is especially the case for the historian of Christianity since the strands that make up its story crisscross and patch together many cultural tapestries. This has been obvious in Canada, where European and American religious influences readily find a place in what we think of as our cultural mosaic. But the key developments of Christianity in the United States have been transnational as well, and considering them in a global context will likely become more pressing as the realities of multiculturalism challenge the myth of America as cultural melting pot. With its promise of fruitful cross-border exchange, Canadian religious history offers an opportunity to begin such an engagement. Robert Handy and Mark Noll are notable examples of American historians whose studies of Christianity in the United States have been enriched by the perspective which their interest in Canada provides. Canadian scholars too are showing an interest in comparative analysis.[19]

The history of the evangelical movement is a subject that is generating much attention on both sides of the border and serves as a good point of entry to illustrate how excursions into the field of Canadian religious history might illumine issues likely to be on the American agenda for some time. Among the most interesting studies are those that are reassessing the role of evangelicalism in shaping the political culture of Canada in the crucial period before the War of 1812. The role of religion in creating and transmitting foundational myths is itself an interesting question for comparative purposes, but also there is the more specific issue of religion as a factor in shaping local and national political traditions. The Loyalist myth has hovered over interpretations of the Canadian past as a counterpoint to Puritan and Republican myths of American destiny. But were British North Americans as staunchly Loyalist as we assume them to be? Recent studies of popular culture in general, and radical evangelicalism in particular, are beginning to challenge our assumptions about British North America's orderly, evolutionary journey toward Confederation and concomitant rejection of revolutionary republicanism. Jane Errington's picture of the decades after the American Revolution presents a much more fluid political situation, with more uncertainty as to whether English-speaking Canada's cultural orientation was to be British or American than is generally recognized.[20]

Canadian historians have tended to assume a staid, respectable, and churchly religious past as well. Now the questions Errington raises about political ideology have been extended to consideration of the implications for religion, with the impact of revivalism drawing particular interest. Nancy Christie, for example, has persuasively argued that in the years leading up to the War of 1812 the relationship of the individual and society was being renegotiated in popular evangelical terms that undercut the authority and assumptions of traditional culture. Those whose interests were allied with traditional culture were alarmed by the revivalism's alternative community, which was "defined by the distinction between the converted and unconverted and built upon personal bonds rather than the impersonal agencies of the established Church and State."[21] George Rawlyk's analysis of early Methodist and New Light revivalism argues for an even more radically democratic, egalitarian, and pristine evangelicalism than the American variety described by Nathan Hatch in *The Democratization of American Christianity* because it was unencumbered by the secular baggage of civic humanism, republicanism, and the covenant ideal.[22] He notes that American Methodist Francis Asbury found his itinerant preachers unable to cope with what he considered the harmful ethos of Maritime revivalism and refused to send them to the region.[23] *The Canada Fire*, Rawlyk's most detailed discussion of radical evangelicalism in the decades after the American revolution, is methodologically noteworthy for its use of social anthropology in exploring the rituals of revivalism—Methodist camp meetings, Baptist believer's baptism, and the Presbyterian long communion.

The study of radical evangelicalism in this period so crucial to the self-understanding of both countries invites analysis of why the two styles developed in such different ways during and after the American revolutionary era. Equally fascinating is what happens after an event remembered only vaguely if at all by most Americans but one that helped create a distinctive and separate sense of identity in Canada—the War of 1812. This unsuccessful attempt by the United States to expand its northern frontier served as a violent reminder of the reality of the border and forced British North Americans to take steps to preserve it both militarily and culturally. Consequently, a period associated with the religious ferment and "disorder" of the Second Great Awakening in the United States looks quite different from a Canadian perspective. The generation of leaders that emerged after the War of 1812 were forced to consider afresh their relationship to England and the United States. For the fast-growing evangelical churches, the aftermath created a set of problems that was to become quintessentially Canadian—how to negotiate the path between a religious experience that to critics smacked of "Americanism" on the one side, and the sometimes unwelcome imposition of order that seemed the price of remaining "British" on the other. Rawlyk argues that radical evangelicalism lost its edge in this context as the anti-Americanism and pro-British feelings unleashed by the War of 1812 "significantly constricted the broad spectrum of permissible belief and practice."[24] Thus began a process involving a shift in "the actual centre of gravity of Canadian evangelicalism" that affected the course of Canadian Protestantism in the nineteenth and twentieth centuries.[25] In the process, radical evangelicalism was tamed.

The stage was set for debates that were to dominate the political landscape for decades. The internal dynamics of Protestantism and the cultural repercussions of its expansion in the last half of the nineteenth century illustrate a second broad area where Canadian developments might well be of interest to American scholars.[26] In Upper Canada (present-day Ontario), for instance, the understanding of the relationship between personal piety and social order were played out in ways that continue to give shape to the province's culture, notably through the distinctive pattern of support for public schools and universities that emerged. Well stocked with rhetoric and resources from religious circles, alliances congealed around platforms identified with two ardent Protestant preachers, Anglican John Strachan and Methodist Egerton Ryerson. The story of the tensions between and eventual transformation of the world views they represented has been well recounted and analyzed by William Westfall.[27] He argues that the divisions between these "two worlds" (which he presents in terms of order and experience) were largely resolved in the decades after midcentury in the creation of a common Protestant culture which hoped that the Dominion of the Lord would be created in the Dominion of Canada.

A growing sense of national identity and purpose was characteristic of both Canada and the United States in this period. At issue in the Civil War was not only slavery but sectionalism, and a number of observers have noted that with the end of the conflict came a new resolve to become one nation rather than a collectivity of states. Canada, meanwhile, was discussing a new political arrangement which was constitutionally formalized in 1867. Developments in Canada offer the historian of American religion an opportunity to assess the religious dimensions of these issues through a different lens. For instance, religious disestablishment and the resulting pluralism came about in different ways but in both cases resulted in a flowering of voluntarism. Voluntary associations are critically important in understanding postdisestablishment Protestantism, for in them we see personal piety expressed and religion intersecting with public life. These associations provided new opportunities (or at least more visibility) for lay leadership that proved to be particularly significant for women.

In the decades following Confederation in Canada, pulpit and press combined to galvanize public support for the new country that evangelicals hoped would become "His Dominion." Sparking the Protestant imagination, this idea provided symbolic coherence for a broadly based consensus. It conveyed their determination to establish the Kingdom of God and was the language in which they spoke of a mission for the new nation. The vision found concrete expression in a variety of voluntary associations to promote the cause of reform and missionary work at home and overseas. Formed in concert with the institutional expansion and denominational expansion and consolidation, these societies suffused Canadian life with religious ideals and provide an interesting parallel to the "Christianizing" of the American people in the nineteenth century described by Jon Butler in *Awash in a Sea of Faith*. Mark Noll's intriguing view is that Canada presents a more convincing history of a "Christian nation" than the United States if their records on such issues as slavery, treatment of native peoples, violence, imperialism, missionary outreach, humane treatment for the poor and weak, provisions for religious education, and impact on public life are compared.[28]

For many Protestants, cultivating Canadian "character" was linked to legitimating the existence of Canada as a nation and was a unifying idea that fostered a sense of identity. A pervasive sense of national righteousness marked the crusades of late-nineteenth-century Protestantism, and there was little internal resistance to the evangelical moralism that undergirded the vision of "His Dominion." Much of the groundwork for developments about which Canadians are most proud was laid in this period by Christian voluntarism. The links forged by missionaries shaped Canada's perspective on international affairs, which involved an emphasis on peacekeeping and mediation. The Social Gospel movement with its legacy of Christian involvement in public life had its roots in large measure in the evangelical activism of the nineteenth century.[29] Temperance and Sabbath observance are examples of issues that first evoked widespread concern among evangelical Protestants, later to become part of the social gospel agenda as the ties to poor conditions at home and in the workplace were perceived.

Yet the gap between "His Dominion" and an ever-changing "current reality" resisted efforts to close it. Social and economic circumstances at first defied Canada's national ideals as the different regions of the country experienced uneven growth. The advantage in a situation of shrinking resources and keen competition often went to denominations with an efficient organizational structure. Even after Canada's economic fortunes improved with the dawn of the twentieth century there were not enough resources to meet the needs of the influx of immigrants to Canada's larger cities and western communities. Theology, economics, and demographics converged in discussions of how to meet these challenges. The typically Canadian solution, blending traditions to create the United Church of Canada, both evoked enthusiasm and provoked controversy.[30] This legacy of Canadian Protestant evangelicalism, both in the achievements and limitations of its moral vision, raises a host of issues that might offer insight into the American religious experience.

3

The radical tendencies of British North American evangelicalism and the effort to create a common Protestant culture in the new nation of Canada are two broad areas where a side-trip through Canadian religious history might suggest new directions to take when revisiting issues central to the American religious story. But there is another way in which attention to Canadian religious history might enrich the work of American historians—part of a more tentative "studies that ought to be but aren't there yet" category. In his presidential address to the American Society of Church History, Nathan Hatch recently identified analysis of Methodism as a glaring omission among studies of American religion. Methodists seem to have fallen between the cracks, perceived as neither "insiders" or "outsiders." Hatch described American Methodism as a historical gold mine, rich in sources and interpretive possibilities. He argued that they, far more than the much-studied Puritans, offer "insight into the distinct character of religious life in the United States."[31] Methodism transcended barriers of gender, class, race, and language and appealed to upstarts and outsiders looking for respect and opportunity. Despite phenomenal growth, Methodists have held little appeal for the intellectual historian. Their own denominational historians have tamed their story in the telling to make the movement appear more respectable. Particularly interesting is Hatch's contention that Methodists "bear the stigma of their petty bourgeoisie origins and identity." They represent what is taken for granted; with their perfectionism, cultural accommodation, and lack of prophetic voice or profound insight, they are "too quintessentially American."[32]

Alfred North Whitehead once remarked that it takes a very unusual mind to undertake analysis of the obvious. Methodism for American religious historians is unquestionably "the obvious." For all its ubiquity, it has only occasionally drawn scholarly attention. Hatch finds it puzzling that in the past no one has proposed questions for which Methodist sources are seen to hold the answers. Yet the importance of finding the right questions and developing strategies for tackling them would seem to be self-evident. Overlooking the obvious is characteristic of Canadian religious history as well and involves the same denominational family. Given its size (the largest Protestant body at the time of Confederation and for many decades after), historians have paid surprisingly little attention to Canadian Methodists. Methodism has suffered from the same lack of attention that Hatch noted in the American case, and for some of the same reasons. As a group they are improbable heroes for intellectual history[33] and are treated with some disdain by Marxists.[34]

Yet the study of Methodism and its progeny, which in Canada would include the United Church of Canada, raises a host of intriguing questions about the relationship between religion and popular (more specifically middle class) culture. Canada's Methodists can lay claim to as much "petite bourgeoisie-ness" as their American coreligionists. Outside observers are often more attuned to what we take for granted and so it is interesting to see this feature of Methodism highlighted by André Siegfried, visitor from France and astute observer of English and French Canadian relations. In *The Race Question in Canada* in 1906 (English translation 1907), he described Methodists as having power and importance unsurpassed by any other of the non-Catholic religious institutions, in large part because of their organizational cohesion and financial resources. Both those who praised and blamed them described them, said Siegfried, as "the respectable bourgeoisie, the class of people who having made the most of their opportunities in this world are conscious that

they have also made satisfactory provision for their welfare in the next."
Despite what Siegfried called an Anglican "smart set" that regarded itself
as superior to the comparatively unfashionable Methodists, it was the
Methodists who were in his view more solid, more wealthy, with more
prosperous commercial establishments and finer churches. With their
stronghold in Ontario, they were also the center of anti-French, aggressive Protestantism.[35]

This aggressive Protestantism, with its vision of a Christian country
that was such a powerful shaping force on both nations in the nineteenth
century, owed as much to Methodism's linking of holiness and social
reform as to either America's Puritan or Canada's Loyalist past. Not surprisingly, the politician who recalled the words of a psalm, "He shall
have dominion from sea to sea," as he participated in creating the new
Dominion of Canada was Methodist Leonard Tilley from New Brunswick. In both contexts, a step toward understanding the significance of
North American Methodism has been made with studies of nineteenth-
century evangelicalism that recognize its connection to broader cultural
developments. This work is now being extended to the twentieth century
as historians of Christianity begin to explore paths that only sociologists
had earlier dared to tread.[36] In the case of Methodism, *Serving the Present Age: Revivalism, Progressivism and the Methodist Tradition in Canada* is one of a number of studies that analyze the continuing significance
of evangelicalism in the twentieth century,[37] exploring the internal dynamics of the denomination as it weathered the erosion of the nineteenth-
century consensus. The book analyzes one aspect central to Methodist
identity—its conversion-centered piety—in relation to changes taking
place in North American Protestantism around the turn of the twentieth
century. It argues that by the time of church union, Methodism had
adopted a nonrevivalist approach to the religious life, one that incorporated new ways of understanding religious experience, an enhanced place
for Christian service, and an openness to innovative approaches to theology. The result was a model of the religious life that was to become as
characteristic of mainstream Protestantism in the first half of the twentieth century as revivalistic piety had been of nineteenth-century evangelicalism.

These studies need to be matched by ones that follow the evangelical
tradition as it took shape in churches associated with twentieth-century
mainstream/liberal Protestantism. As one looks historiographically at the
study of Canadian religious history, the lack of attention given to
twentieth-century mainstream Protestantism, aside from church union
and resistance to it, is even more surprising than the paucity of studies of
Methodism. A glance through the bibliographical essays in *The Canadian
Protestant Experience* finds studies of the Salvation Army, Quakers, Pentecostals, and Doukhobors. Baptists, at around 3% of the population,
have been best served by their historians, with Mennonites not far behind. This is in marked contrast to studies of mainstream Protestant

groups. Judging solely from historical studies of religion in Canada, one would never guess that the United Church has been since its founding in 1925 the largest Protestant denomination; for scholarly purposes, it has been a virtually invisible religion. When its leaders appear in the story of religion in Canada, they are generally cast as characters who undermined religion by, to borrow the title of a recent study, "secularizing the faith." Its author, David Marshall, counts himself as a member of the "new orthodoxy" in religious history: those engaged in telling the story of "the triumph of the forces of secularization."[38] The United Church is dismissed by Marshall as floundering, "hesitant about grasping any new insight or understanding"; by 1940 it is a "defeated church uncertain about its message, mission, and future."[39] By 1990, when Ron Graham recounted his quest "to find the soul of Canada" in *God's Dominion*,[40] he did not feel he had to tarry long among the larger Protestant denominations. They make a cameo appearance in two middle chapters of a seventeen-chapter book where New Age, native, Pentecostal, and non-western religions occupy center stage. Both chapters on mainstream Protestantism deal with conflict over positions taken on social justice issues. "The Raggedy Band" is Graham's title for the chapter on the United Church and its discussion of the ordination of homosexual persons.

Key leaders of the United Church have been so involved in movements of social reform that its national agenda is sometimes assumed to be coterminous with the Social Gospel critique of existing social arrangements. At the same time, like most mainstream groups, its involvement at the local level has been intertwined with the cultural values of the community, paralleling what Hatch has observed about Methodism's place in American culture. When it comes to assessing the relationship between mainstream Protestantism and Canadian culture, there seems to be no separate story to tell. But without a recovery of that story, is it possible to come to terms with the role religion has played in shaping Canadian belief and behavior? Graham describes the United Church as "the most Canadian of churches, and like Canada, its strengths may be the same as its weaknesses: diversity, tolerance, compromise, humility, practicality, and niceness. Truth gets written by committee, mystery gets lost in the negotiation, decency gets translated into dullness, and the spirit gets hamstrung by the bureaucracy. Some jocularly call it the 'Church of Christ Sociologist.' "[41] And yet mainstream Protestant churches like the United Church have been so much a part of the fabric of this nation's life in the twentieth century that it is doubtful whether the much called for "synthesis" of Canadian religious history can be written without first unraveling those particular strands.

4

The analysis of mainstream Protestantism in its cultural context is one area where there is much scope for valuable comparative and collaborative work. Canadian scholars have much to learn from studies of mainstream American Protestantism as well as from scholars in other disciplines as they create their research framework. In turn, the recovery of the history of mainstream Protestantism in Canada may provide additional clues to such "puzzles" as American Methodism. The following three examples using the United Church will serve to illustrate some common issues.[42]

Protestantism as a "Voluntary Establishment"

What happened to the impulse to create the Dominion of the Lord is inexplicable without analysis of the "voluntary establishment" that took shape after the mid-nineteenth-century disestablishment of state-supported churches. At the heart of that voluntary establishment were the denominations which formed the United Church of Canada (Methodist, Presbyterian, and Congregationalist). Our French observer Siegfried noted that connection, and his clever sketches of these Protestant groups were coupled with perceptive observations about Canadian religion and politics. To all appearances, noted Siegfried, "the independence of the these churches in regard to the state has been absolutely established in the New World." On the other hand, he mused, "it would not be safe to say quite so positively that the state's independence of the churches, even the Protestant ones, is established to the same degree." While the Protestant clergy did not attempt to control the government in an ultramontane Catholic fashion, "they do aim at informing it with their spirit."[43] He found Canadian Protestants incapable of even imagining that one could think outside religious forms. While he was convinced that unbelief was not uncommon, it was not publicly expressed: to do so would be "almost an act of infidelity to the Anglo-Saxon race."[44]

This impulse to create a voluntary establishment was carried into the United Church of Canada. The preamble to the United Church's Basis of Union captured remarkably well the hopes of the founders and the vision that shaped the new church's understanding of its mission when it stated, "It shall be the policy of The United Church to foster the spirit of unity in the hope that this settlement of unity may in due time, so far as Canada is concerned, take shape in a church which may fittingly be described as national." Advocates for church union were proud to be considered the conscience of the nation. As General Superintendent S. D. Chown explained to Methodists in 1924, there were many influences—geographic, economic, and political—tending to divide the Canadian people. It was the duty of Christian patriots "to use the bond of religious unity to promote the national oneness of the Dominion that we may attain to a clarified consciousness and conscience concerning the supreme mission of our country in the life of the world."[45] It is difficult to miss the anticipation of increased moral authority in the political realm—more influence in "christianizing" a social order which at that time seemed threatened less by the challenge of French Canada and more by developments associated in the popular mind with western settlement of an influx of immigrants. The creation of the United Church as an institutional expression of the broader North American impulse toward voluntary establishment of religion invites comparison. It parallels, for instance, the process that Robert Handy describes in *Undermined Establishment*.[46] The aims and ambitions of this new "national church" also fueled the United Church's involvement in a worldwide ecumenical movement through missionary and interfaith councils and buttressed the political impulse to shape a "new international order" in ways that suggest a parallel to developments in the United States.[47]

Religious and Cultural Plurality

The growing plurality of twentieth-century Canada has had important ramifications for the self-understanding of mainstream Protestant groups.[48] The complex connections between language, ethnicity, and multiculturalism present much scope for comparison of their religious implications. In recent decades, mainstream Protestant churches have also seemed to lose their touch in relating to popular culture and its plurality.[49] Nowhere is this more obvious than in the United Church, which for so long enjoyed cultural dominance in English-speaking Canada. The challenge of dealing with the immigrants who arrived in Canada in the early decades of the twentieth century coincided with church union negotiations and helped shape the United Church's sense of national mission. "Christianizing" the immigrants was barely distinguishable from "Canadianizing" a culture that, outside Quebec, was primarily Anglo-Saxon in its mores. When C. W. Gordon, Presbyterian pastor and union supporter, wrote *The Foreigner* under the pen name Ralph Connor, his fictional missionary to the prairies expressed these assumptions well. When asked what he was doing in Saskatchewan, he admitted that he could not preach much. His "main line" was "the kiddies," he explained. "I can teach them English, and then I am going to doctor them, and, if they'll let me, teach them some of the elements of domestic science; in short, do anything to make them good Christians and good Canadians, which is the same thing."[50] For a number of years, the United Church found that its ranks were filled with many who drew a further conclusion: that to be Canadian was to be United Church. A different way of coming to terms with religious and cultural plurality has meant the loss of this older identify and contributed to the church's crisis of confidence.[51]

Related to this is the issue of religion and public life in Canada, which for a significant part of the United Church's history has been linked to its social gospel heritage.[52] Recent developments have posed new challenges to the United Church's tradition of affirming public witness, its understanding of the relationship of church and nation, and its assumptions about shaping the character of public leadership (an important but often overlooked issue in understanding the nature of secularization in Canada). To what extent this shift is perception rather than reality is debatable; recent polling data suggest a resilient Christian belief system in Canada, yet public attention to religion in politics and the media creates a quite different picture, and one that differs in the United States. The educational implications of this situation for both laity and professionals are important, particularly in view of the corresponding decline in support for institutional expressions of religion indicated by the poll.[53]

Mainstream Protestant Identity

The experience of the United Church is an important case study in believing and belonging in a mainstream denomination and raises a number of questions. Why, for instance, did both denominational leaders and ordinary Canadian church-goers find the notion of a united church an obvious, common sense idea to support? How did the United Church achieve for a time a hegemony of sorts as compared with other religious cultures? T. J. Jackson Lears's "translation" of Antonio Gramsci's concept of hegemony into historians' language reminds us that the keys to creating a successful hegemony are both economic and ideological: "the leaders of a historical bloc must develop a world view that appeals to a wide range of other groups within the society, and they must be able to claim with at least some plausibility that their particular interests are those of society at large."[54] He notes the importance of attending to the half-conscious psychic needs of social groups and the centrality of language in "cementing a given group's prestige and cultural leadership." He sees as instrumental the examination of the ways that cultural meaning emerges in various historical "texts" (a term that he understands broadly): sermons, advertisements, folklore, popular ritual.[55]

One of the many difficulties in dealing with the United Church as a religious culture is coming to terms with its approach to personal religiosity. The founding generation of the United Church, including those we generally identify with the Social Gospel movement in Canada, continued to value personal religious experience, although they did not necessarily articulate it in Victorian evangelical terms. Part of the transition in the early twentieth century is not simply a shift from preoccupation with "salvation of the individual" to "salvation of society," but rather a changed understanding of what salvation of the individual entailed. It was tied to a different approach to piety impinging on personal and social salvation.[56] This is a type of religiosity which is both pervasive and elusive. Analyzing it involves tracking regional "folkways" in the United Church; assessing the impact of major theological and social developments during the period (for example, Christian socialism, Oxford Group movement, neo-orthodoxy, pacifism, changes in family structures); and examining the "traditioning" process of lay and clerical education. The organizational implications also invite analysis. How does a church committed to breaking down denominational boundaries create its own theological and symbolic boundaries?[57] What do its organizational structures and programs indicate about the kind of institution it hoped to become? How is its service-oriented ethos and sense of community shaped by church-sponsored organizations (for example, Women's Missionary Society, Women's Association, the men's organization As One That Serves, Canadian Girls in Training, Tuxis Boys, Student Christian Movement, Fellowship for a Christian Social Order)?

These are but a few of the ways that geographical and disciplinary boundaries might be tested and crossed. In the case of the United Church, there is no dearth of material—archival documents, personal papers, denominational periodicals and publications, records of proceedings, etc. With the wealth of material readily accessible in the central denominational archives, the temptation to write Toronto-centered "top-down" history is ever present. But those resisting such an enticement will do well to be lured to repositories of congregational histories available in denominational and provincial archives as well as public libraries. The historical analysis often leaves much to be desired, but they give a sense of how congregations situated themselves in local settings.

5

The values and institutions of nations can be understood only in comparative perspective, Seymour Lipset argues, insisting that looking intensively at Canada and the United States sheds light on both of them. "Knowledge of Canada or the United States is the best way to gain insight into the other North American country."[58] The importance of American religious history for better understanding the Canadian context has long been apparent. An instinctive willingness to learn from historical models and methods from Europe, the United States, and occasionally even further afield has added immeasurably to the richness of the study of religion in Canada. Recently, historians have been more venturesome in crossing disciplinary boundaries as well. There is always a danger of lagging behind the pack, arriving on the scene full of enthusiasm to discuss our "latest research" with those for whom that approach is now very "old hat." Perhaps Canadian historians need to overcome their predilection to follow and occasionally lead the way. But in the meantime, it may be enough for Canadians to urge American historians of religion to do unto others as we have done unto you and, by better understanding what American religious history is *not*, to see it more clearly for what it *is*.

NOTES

1. Allan Fotheringham, "Just Yodel 'Rose Marie' and Carry a Big Stick," *Maclean's*, February 11, 1980, 55–56.

2. Hugh L. Keenleyside, cited in *Between Friends/Entre Amis* (Toronto: McClelland and Stewart, 1976), 4.

3. Mark A. Noll, "Christianity in Canada: Good Books at Last," *Fides et Historia* 23 (Summer 1992): 103; and Northrop Frye, "Haunted by a Lack of Ghosts: Some Patterns in the Imagery of Canadian Poetry," in David Staines, ed., *The Canadian Imagination* (Cambridge, Mass.: Harvard University Press, 1977).

4. John Webster Grant, "Asking Questions of the Canadian Past," *Canadian Journal of Theology* 1/2 (1955): 98–99.

5. Ibid., 101. Grant illustrated by references to scholars whose analysis of religion in Canada had been flawed by their use of American analogies.

6. Ibid., 102–3. *The Church in the Canadian Era* (Toronto: McGraw-Hill Ryerson, 1972; 2nd edition Burlington: Welch Publishing Company, 1988). For an excellent and succinct survey of Canadian Protestantism, see Grant's essay in *The Encyclopedia of the American Religious Experience,* ed. Charles H. Lippy and Peter W. Williams (New York: Charles Scribner's Sons, 1988), 239–52.

7. N. K. Clifford, "History of Religion in Canada," *The Ecumenist* 18/5 (1980): 66.

8. N. K. Clifford, "Religion and the Development of Canadian Society: An Historiographical Analysis," *Church History* 38 (1969): 521. The neo-orthodox theological assumptions that he identified (and which were later to come under fire) are evident in H. H. Walsh, "The Challenge of Canadian Church History to Its Historians," *Canadian Journal of Theology* 5/3 (1959): 162–69.

9. Clifford, "History of Religion in Canada," 67–8.

10. For example, his *The Resistance to Church Union in Canada* was significantly influenced by the work of Sidney Mead. He was intrigued with sociological and anthropological theory and how it might be used in the history of the United Church of Canada on which he had begun work.

11. John Webster Grant, *Moon of Wintertime: Missionaries and the Indians of Canada in Encounter Since 1534* (Toronto: University of Toronto Press, 1984), and John S. Moir, "Coming of Age but Slowly: Aspects of Canadian Religious Historiography Since Confederation," Canadian Catholic Historical Association Study Sessions, 1983.

12. For a discussion of recent approaches to religion in Canada assessing various perspectives, see Brian Clarke, "Religion, Culture, and Society: Some Recent Studies on Christianity in Canada," *Method and Theory in the Study of Religion* 2/2 (1990): 267–95; Guy Laperrière and William Westfall, "Religious Studies," in *Interdisciplinary Approaches to Canadian Society,* ed. Alan F. Atibise (Montreal and Kingston: McGill-Queen's University Press, 1990), 39–76; Mark G. McGowan, "Coming Out of the Cloister: Some Reflections on Developments in the Study of Religion in Canada, 1980–1990," *International Journal of Canadian Studies* 1 and 2 (1990): 175–202; A. B. McKillop, "Culture, Intellect, and Context," *Journal of Canadian Studies* 24 (1989): 19–24.

13. McGowan, "Coming Out of the Cloister," 177.

14. This is ironic insofar as McGowan uses Rawlyk as an example of the continuing presence of practitioners of "providentialist" or "devotional" history, written by those whose interest in history has been "engendered by their own faith experience" and more typical of historians in theological colleges. He describes him as one whose perspectival transformation from reductionism to neo-orthodoxy has been facilitated by "his own embrace of evangelical religion"; see McGowan, 178–79, 194 n. 10.

15. See Laperrière and Westfall for an excellent discussion of recent Francophone studies of religion in Canada. For social scientific studies, see the bibliographies in W. E. Hewitt, *The Sociology of Religion: A Canadian Focus* (Toronto: Butterworth, 1993), and Helen Ralston, "Strands of Research on Religious Movements in Canada," *Studies in Religion* 17 (1988): 257–77. From the pioneering work of S. D. Clark to the present, the sociology of religion in English Canada has had a strong historical focus that is important to note.

16. To take the University of Chicago as one example, N. K. Clifford did postdoctoral studies there, after which he served for a few years as assistant dean. The list of scholars who have done master's and/or doctoral work with Brauer and Marty in recent years includes Phyllis Airhart, Robert Choquette, Brian Clarke, Paul Dekar, Tom Sinclair-Faulkner, Bryan Hillis, Roger Hutchinson, and John Stackhouse. George Rawlyk's "conversion" from reductionism to so-called "providential history" noted above was likely intellectual as well as experiential, owing something to his admiration for the quality of work he observed being done on American evangelical history.

17. One important illustration of this recent scholarship is George A. Rawlyk ed., *The Canadian Protestant Experience, 1760–1990.* 2nd ed. (Burlington: G. R. Welch, 1990; Montreal and Kingston: McGill-Queen's University Press, 1993), in which the results of many of the recently published works and doctoral theses were showcased. The book provides a handy introduction to both the main contours and key interpretations of the Canadian story, with a bibliographical essay following each chapter taking stock of the literature on which it was based. The five contributors and the periods covered are Nancy Christie (1760–1815), Michael Gauvreau (1815–1867), Phyllis D. Airhart (1867–1914), Robert A. Wright (1914–1945), and John G. Stackhouse (1945–1990).

18. The interest in gender and religion is an example of the meeting of women's history (which was reluctant to explore religious experience) and religious history (which tended to ignore the role of women). For example, Marguerite Van Die is engaged in study of evangelical Protestantism and the family in nineteenth-century Canada. Ruth Compton Brouwer, "Transcending the 'Unacknowledged Quarantine': Putting Religion into English-Canadian Women's History," *Journal of Canadian Studies* 27/3 (1992): 47–61 explores the new application of religion in women's history.

19. They figure prominently, for example, in a recently published collaborative study of evangelicalism and popular Protestantism; see Mark A. Noll, David W. Bebbington, and George A. Rawlyk, eds., *Evangelicalism: Comparative Studies of Popular Protestantism in North America, the British Isles, and Beyond, 1700–1990* (New York: Oxford University Press, 1994), which includes essays by Canadian scholars Michael Gauvreau, George Rawlyk, Ian Rennie, and Marguerite Van Die.

20. Jane Errington, *The Lion, the Eagle, and Upper Canada: A Developing Colonial Ideology* (Montreal and Kingston: McGill-Queen's University Press, 1987).

21. " 'In These Times of Democratic Rage and Delusion': Popular Religion and the Challenge to the Established Order, 1760–1815" in Rawlyk, *The Canadian Protestant Experience*, 38.

22. George A. Rawlyk, *"The Canada Fire": Radical Evangelicalism in British North America, 1775–1812* (Montreal and Kingston: McGill-Queen's University Press, 1994), xvi; and George A. Rawlyk, "A Total Revolution in Religious and

Civil Government": The Maritimes, New England, and the Evolving Evangelical Ethos," in Noll et al., eds., *Evangelicalism*.

23. Rawlyk, "A Total Revolution," 148.

24. Ibid., 152

25.. *Canada Fire,* xviii.

26. For excellent studies of this period, see Michael Gauvreau, "The Empire of Evangelicalism: Varieties of Common Sense in Scotland, Canada, and the United States" and Marguerite Van Die, " 'The Double Vision': Evangelical Piety as Derivative and Indigenous in Victorian English Canada" in Noll et al., *Evangelicalism*.

27. William Westfall, *Two Worlds: The Protestant Culture of Nineteenth-Century Ontario* (Montreal and Kingston: McGill-Queen's University Press, 1989).

28. Mark Noll, *A History of Christianity in the United States and Canada* (Grand Rapids, Mich.: Eerdmans, 1992), 546–47.

29. The classic work on the rise of the Social Gospel movement is Richard Allen, *The Social Passion: Religion and Social Reform in Canada, 1914–1928* (Toronto: University of Toronto Press, 1971). For a bibliographical introduction to works dealing with voluntary societies in the period between Confederation and the First World War, see Airhart, *The Canadian Protestant Experience,* 135–38.

30. John Webster Grant, "Blending Traditions: The United Church of Canada" in *The Churches and the Canadian Experience* (Toronto: Ryerson Press, 1963), 133–44.

31. Nathan O. Hatch, "The Puzzle of American Methodism," *Church History* 63/2 (1994): 178.

32. Ibid., 185–6.

33. For example, Methodists sit uneasily among those influenced by Common Sense moral philosophy examined by Michael Gauvreau in *The Evangelical Century: College and Creed in English Canada from the Great Revival to the Great Depression* (Montreal: McGill-Queen's University Press, 1991) or the philosophical idealists in A. B. McKillop, *A Disciplined Intelligence: Critical Inquiry and Canadian Thought in the Victorian Era* (Kingston and Montreal: McGill-Queen's University Press, 1991). Methodists fare better as material for intellectual history when taken on their own terms as Marguerite Van Die demonstrates in her fine study of the leading nineteenth-century Methodist theologian; see *An Evangelical Mind: Nathanael Burwash and the Methodist Tradition in Canada, 1839–1918* (Kingston and Montreal: McGill-Queen's University Press, 1989).

34. For example, Methodists and Presbyterian middle-class reformers are not cast in a favorable light in Mariana Valverde, *The Age of Light, Soap, and Water: Moral Reform in English Canada, 1885–1925* (Toronto: McClelland and Stewart, 1991), although the work of the Salvation Army shows off well by comparison.

35. André Siegfried, *The Race Question in Canada* (Paris: Librairie Armand Colin, 1906; English translation 1907; 2nd ed. Toronto: McClelland and Stewart, 1966, 53.

36. See for example John G. Stackhouse, *Canadian Evangelicalism in the Twentieth Century: An Introduction to Its Character* (Toronto: University of Toronto Press, 1993). There will be a number of studies of twentieth-century evan-

gelicalism coming out of George Rawlyk's research project on the Canadian Evangelical Experience.

37. See Phyllis D. Airhart, *Serving the Present Age: Revivalism, Progressivism, and the Methodist Tradition in Canada* (Montreal and Kingston: McGill-Queen's University Press, 1992). In addition to the studies by Gauvreau, Stackhouse, and Van Die noted above, see Brian Fraser, *The Social Uplifters: Presbyterian Progressives and the Social Gospel in Canada, 1875–1915* (Waterloo: Wilfrid Laurier University Press, 1988), which links Presbyterian reform and liberal evangelicalism; Robert Burkinshaw, *Pilgrims in Lotus Land: Conserative Protestantism in British Columbia, 1917–1981* (Montreal and Kingston: McGill–Queen's Unversity, Press, 1995; Robert Wright, *A World Mission: Canadian Protestantism and the Quest for a New International Order, 1918–1939* (Montreal: McGill-Queen's University Press, 1991). A number of these studies raise questions about the way secularization theory had been used to analyze the role of religion in twentieth-century Canada.

38. David B. Marshall, *Secularizing the Faith: Canadian Protestant Clergy and the Crisis of Belief, 1850–1940* (Toronto: University of Toronto Press, 1992), 17. See also Ramsay Cook, *The Regenerators: Social Criticism in Late Victorian Canada* (Toronto: University of Toronto Press, 1985) for a similar view of secularization.

39. Ibid., 229.

40. Ron Graham, *God's Dominion: A Skeptic's Quest* (Toronto: McClelland and Stewart, 1990).

41. Ibid., 222.

42. The section that follows presents some of issues that I am exploring as part of a research project on the United Church of Canada sponsored by the Lilly Endowment. The notes that follow will illustrate some comparative routes that might be explored as well as some works that I have found useful in formulating issues.

43. Siegfried, 55.

44. Ibid., 56.

45. Chown, "A Statement of the Methodist Position Regarding Church Union," Church Union Collection, section 2, box 5/113, 8.

46. See Robert T. Handy, *Undermined Establishment: Church–State Relations in America, 1880–1920* (Princeton: Princeton University Press, 1991). Handy has argued that the patterns of voluntary Christendom were expressed even more fully in Canadian than American life; see "Dominant Patterns of Christian Life in Canada and the United States: Similarities and Differences," in *Religion/Culture: Comparative Canadian Studies, Études Canadiennes Comparées,* eds. William Westfall, Louis Rousseau, Fernand Harvey, and John Simpson. Association for Canadian Studies 7 (1985): 350ff.

47. On the geopolitical involvement of the church, see Wright, *A World Mission* and William M. King, "The Reform Establishment and the Ambiguities of Success" in *Between the Times,* ed. William R. Hutchison (New York: Cambridge University Press, 1989), 122–40. For a fine comparative study of the connection between denominational cooperation and the hope of creating a Christian social order, see Robert T. Handy, "Reflections on the Federal Council of Churches, the United Church of Canada, and the Social Gospel in the 1930s," conference paper presented at Christianizing the Social Order: A Founding Vision of the United

Church of Canada, Toronto, 1992 and forthcoming in *Toronto Journal of Theology* (1996).

48. For discussions of the idea of "His Dominion" and challenges to it, see Noll, *A History of Christianity in the United States and Canada*, 245–285, 423–553; and N. K. Clifford, " 'His Dominion': A Vision in Crisis," *Studies in Religion* 2/4 (1973). For an interesting discussion of the resulting conflict between Catholic and Protestant approaches to religion and nationalism, see Robert Choquette, "Christ and Culture during 'Canada's Century' " in *New Dimensions in American Religious History: A Festschrift for Martin E. Marty*, eds. Jay P. Dolan and James P. Wind (Grand Rapids: Wm. B. Eerdmans, 1993), 83–102; he notes that "Christ's Canadian spokespersons had sold out to two different cultures," 83.

49. For example, Leonard Sweet, "The Modernization of Protestant Religion in America," in *Altered Landscapes: Christianity in America, 1935–1985*, ed. David W. Lotz (Grand Rapids: Eerdmans, 1989), 28, argues that after 1935 mainstream/modernist Protestant became alienated from popular culture: they "made a cult of the cultivated and distanced themselves as never before from their social environment and the religiosity of middle-class Americans."

50. Ralph Connor, *The Foreigner* (Toronto: Westminster, 1909), 253.

51. Hutchison, ed., *Between the Times* and the volumes in the series *The Presbyterian Presence* published by Westminster/John Knox Press are helpful studies of a parallel development in the United States.

52. See Richard Allen, "Religion and Political Transformation in English Canada: The 1880s to the 1930s" in *From Heaven Down to Earth: A Century of Chancellor's Lectures at Queen's Theological College*, ed. Marguerite Van Die (Kingston: Queen's Theological College, 1992), 125–144.

53. See "God Is Alive," *Maclean's*, April 12 1993, 32–50, a report on the results of an Angus Reid Group poll.

54. T. J. Jackson Lears, "The Concept of Cultural Hegemony: Problems and Possibilities," *American Historical Review* 90 (1985): 569.

55. Lears, 588.

56. This is central to the thesis developed in Airhart, *Serving the Present Age*.

57. Michèle Lamont and Marcel Fournier, eds., *Cultivating Differences: Symbolic Boundaries and the Making of Inequality* (Chicago: University of Chicago Press, 1992), especially essays by Diana Crane and Alan Wolfe; Robert Wuthnow, *Communities of Discourse: Ideology and Social Structure in the Reformation, the Enlightenment, and European Socialism* (Cambridge, Mass.: Harvard University Press, 1989), and "Introduction: New Directions in the Empirical Study of Cultural Codes" in *Vocabularies of Public Life: Empirical Essays in Symbolic Structure*, ed. Robert Wuthnow (London and New York: Routledge, 1992).

58. Seymour Martin Lipset, *Continental Divide: The Values and Institutions of the United States and Canada* (New York: Routledge, 1990), xiii. For comparative studies of the two countries dealing specifically with religion, see Handy "Dominant Patterns of Christian Life in Canada and the United States: Similarities and Differences"; Mark Noll, *A History of Christianity in the United States and Canada*; Robert T. Handy, *A History of the Churches in the United States and Canada* (New York, Oxford University Press, 1976); Joseph D. Ban and Paul R. Dekar, *In the Great Tradition: In Honor of Winthrop S. Hudson—Essays on Pluralism, Voluntarism, and Revivalism* (Valley Forge: Judson Press, 1982), especially essays in Part I "Comparative Themes" by Martin E. Marty, Robert T.

Handy, and Paul R. Dekar; Paul R. Dekar, "Church History of Canada: Where From Here?" *Theodolite: A Journal of Christian Thought and Practice* 5/4 (1980): 11–16; John Webster Grant, " 'At Least You Knew Where You Stood With Them': Reflections on Religious Pluralism in Canada and the United States," *Studies in Religion* 2/4 (1973): 340–51; Robert T. Handy, "The 'Lively Experiment' in Canada" in *The Lively Experiment Continued*, ed. Jerald C. Brauer (Macon, Ga.: Mercer University Press, 1987), 203–18.

PART III

THE STAGES
OF AMERICAN
PROTESTANTISM

5

GOD'S DESIGNS

The Literature of the Colonial
Revivals of Religion, 1735–1760

▩   ▩   ▩

Allen C. Guelzo

IN DECEMBER OF 1990, after the completion of a section on Jonathan Edwards at the annual meeting of the American Historical Association in New York City, a dozen or so of mostly younger scholars of Jonathan Edwards swept around the corner from the convention hotel and settled themselves down to a staggering repast at a posh north Italian restaurant. In the midst of some very un-Edwardsean consumption, I offered a question to everyone around the table: What is the most important book which you've ever read on the Great Awakening? With only one exception, the Young Edwardseans gave the palm to an obscure nineteenth-century Congregationalist, Joseph Tracy; the one dissenter held out for a book from the 1960s, but it was the book that most Young Edwardseans are ritually required to despise, Alan Heimert's *Religion and the American Mind: From the Great Awakening to the American Revolution.* These unexpected choices could illustrate, alternately, how disillusioned historians are with virtually all current writing on the Great Awakening, or an entirely lopsided adoption by younger historians of one half of a long-term argument about the Great Awakening, or even what David Hall tactfully called the difficulty early modern historians have in recapturing the meaning of religion to the peoples of early America.[1] The strangest aspect of these responses, however, was the appearance of consensus they suggested, for hardly ever in American history has a single event raised more questions about what an *event* might actually be, or proven so alluring and so elusive of interpretation.

Both of those qualities can be illustrated by considering the enormous interpretive extremes which bracket the Great Awakening. Alan Heimert and Perry Miller, who may be said to have touched off the modern debate over the definition and significance of the Awakening, were confident that the various subevents of the Awakening all fit together as a clear and forceful story of renewal in the face of spiritual declension in America and the creation of a uniquely American set of meanings for American culture. "The Great Awakening was the religious revival that swept through the American colonies between 1739 and 1742," announced Heimert and Miller in the opening of their introduction to the first major anthology in this century of voices from the Awakening—as though there was no question that a single plot governed all the actors of the Awakening. Nor were they in much doubt about its meaning: "The Awakening, in brief, marked America's final break with the Middle Ages and her entry into a new intellectual age in the church and in society." But only fifteen years after the publication of the Heimert–Miller anthology, another major interpreter of early American religion rose to question whether there actually was such a single plot to the Awakening and, if there was, whether it was a story about the imposition of Europeanized establishment religion on the chaos of early American religious experience. The Great Awakening, wrote Jon Butler in 1982, may well be an "interpretive fiction," created by historians to describe a series of isolated, regional subevents whose accomplishments were actually quite modest and whose chief historical use ought to be little more than the polishing of "nearly perfect mirrors of a regionalized, provincial society."[2]

Nor do the alternatives lie only in the extremes. Between Heimert and Butler stretches a considerable amount of interpretive territory, much of which was first explored by the Awakeners themselves, and their critics. Both the friends and the enemies of the Great Awakening were conscious from the beginning that they had been part of an event charged with bitterly contested meanings on numerous levels: on the levels of Christian soteriology (in what ways people are made right with God), ecclesiology (how Christians are to be organized into congregations and who should have the power to rule them), and religious politics (how a Christian society should function and who it should include). But we do not have anything on offer as a historical *interpretation* of the Awakening until 1842, and the publication of Joseph Tracy's *The Great Awakening*. It was Tracy who selected the term *great awakening* from the plethora of descriptions of the revivals used in the eighteenth century and fixed it into place as the modern term of choice, and it was Tracy who for the first time collected and published a broad sampling of documents from the Awakening that he worked into a coherent and accomplished narrative. But the religious questions of the previous century still managed to emerge from Tracy's history as the principal matters of interest. An 1814 graduate of Dartmouth College, Tracy had been trained for the Congregational ministry under the austere eye of Asa Burton of Thetford, Vermont, one of the last major Edwardsean voices in New England; and under that influence, Tracy's book may be read as a major polemic in defense of Edwardseanism as true Christianity, and the Awakening as God's design. "The revival was," Tracy concluded, "in all its valuable features, a manifest example of the power of those doctrines" that Edwards preached. In its train there flowed spiritual enlightenment, the "restoration of the true doctrine concerning church membership."[3]

The reluctance that Tracy's historical narrative exhibited in escaping (or rather, failing to escape) the orbit of the Awakening's religious questions persisted through much of the nineteenth century. Like Tracy, most of those who turned their hand to any historical consideration of the Awakening were usually evangelical Protestant clergy, prompted by the need to reach for historical armor in dealing with later forms of revivalism or later versions of the questions that had so inflamed Jonathan Edwards, Charles Chauncy, Jonathan Dickinson, and the Tennents. As Joseph Conforti has shown, the renewed outbreak of Awakening-like revivals in New England and the trans-Appalachia in the 1820s touched off a major effort to reify the Awakening into a "great, general and formative event" that would justify and rationalize the newer outbursts of revival enthusiasm.[4] The articles on various aspects of the Awakening that splashed up on the pages of theological quarterlies like Edwards Amasa Park's *Bibliotheca Sacra* or Charles Hodge's *Biblical Repertory and Princeton Review,* and the successive editions of the works of Jonathan Edwards and his disciples (principally Hopkins, Bellamy, and Emmons) that were published between 1808 and 1851, were (like the original participants) less consumed with establishing what happened in the Awakening than with establishing whether or not the Awakening was theologically explicable.[5]

Not until the beginning of this century, as an American historical profession was beginning to emerge out of the fledgling nests of late-nineteenth-century university graduate programs and as revivalism was pushed to the margins of public religious concern, did narratives about the Awakening, or that included the Awakening, began to reconfigure themselves around a new set of more strictly historical questions. The first of these questions was a cultural one: To what extent was the Great Awakening a distinctively American event, or an event formative of a uniquely American culture? Long before Alan Heimert, Herbert Levi Osgood asked that question in *The American Colonies in the Eighteenth Century,* and long before Perry Miller, Osgood answered it in the affirmative. The Awakening was "the first great and spontaneous movement in the history of the American people, deeper and more pervading than the wars," Osgood wrote, and he promised that "Curious inquirers, whose purpose it may be to interpret the mind of the American people, will rank this high among the early phenomena which furnish a clue to the elusive thing of which they are in pursuit."[6] A second question was more nearly related to the old religious questions, except that it was now recast as inquiry into the history of ideas: To what extent did the Great Awakening change religious discourse in America? Vernon Louis Parrington addressed that question in *Main Currents in American Thought* in 1926, and concluded that the Awakening was an ironic attempt by hateful Calvinist fanatics to retain their dominance of the public sphere, an attempt that blew up in their own hands and ended up permanently discrediting Puritan (which in Parrington's case meant *fundamentalist*) theology and "thus hastening the decay of Calvinism."[7] The third question was posed by Charles Hartshorne Maxson and Wesley M. Gewehr, who suggested the transposition of the Great Awakening into a metaphor for eighteenth-century political conflict. Gewehr was struck by the parallels between the demands of the New Light Baptists in the 1750s and 60s for religious liberty and the demands of the Virginia patriots in the 1770s for political liberty, and he concluded that "the evangelical doctrine, when brought to bear upon the great mass of the population, produced a democratic feeling, developed a degree of self-respect, and inculcated ideas of self-government . . . and thus accustomed people to self-government." Maxson, likewise, was convinced that "the Great Awakening prepared the way for the Revolutionary War" by creating a "community of feeling," primed for political resistance.[8] Of course, the religious questions did not disappear; in fact, the finest single-volume local study of the Awakening, Edwin S. Gaustad's *The Great Awakening in New England* (1957), was written almost entirely around the same religious controversies that haunted the original actors in the Awakening. But the tone and sense of distance in this writing was much more aloof and historicized, even from historians like Gaustad who had genuine religious interests and commitments as part of the motivations for their work.

Thus, the publication of Alan Heimert's *Religion and the American Mind* (1966) did not so much set out new questions as reinforce a secularization of the Awakening that had been under way for some time. Nevertheless, Heimert's reinforcement was so dramatic and so vividly stated that the sheer critical din that arose around the book forced early American historians to take long new looks at the Great Awakening. In varying degrees, Heimert addressed all three of the modern questions about the Awakening. Like his mentor, Perry Miller, Heimert treated the discourse of Edwards and the Awakeners as an elaborate intellectual code that embodied "a vital competition for the intellectual allegiance of the American people." At the same time, Heimert also discerned an unambiguous political message in the Awakening that placed Charles Chauncy as the forerunner of American liberalism and individualism—although, unlike Vernon Parrington, Heimert meant nothing complimentary about it. For Heimert, liberalism represented a "profoundly elitist and conservative ideology, while evangelical religion embodies a radical and even democratic challenge to the standing order" that stood in judgment against "the increasingly acquisitive and indulgent spirit of the America of the 1730s." That, in turn, led Heimert to see in the Awakening the shape of a new and distinctively American culture, pervaded by longings for evangelical union and the millennium. The Awakening thus became "almost by definition, a quest for the great community," a community that eventually took concrete political shape in a new public citizen who sought "the perfection of a people in righteousness." At each point, Jonathan Edwards was the major player among the Awakeners, and Edwards's magisterial treatise on the will positioned him as an American Rousseau, calling Americans to discover their unity as a people against British tyranny and leading them to the Jeffersonian apotheosis of 1800.[9]

Of course, some early American historians, like Edmund S. Morgan, were less than captivated by Heimert's arguments. Heimert's book "partakes more of fantasy than of history," Morgan snorted, as he catalogued one contradiction after another across Heimert's pages.[10] But *Religion and the American Mind,* and the theses that could be spun off from it, remained too tantalizing and too productive of exploration and exegesis not to attract a host of younger early Americanists to its side. Harry S. Stout, who declared in 1977 that his "point of departure . . . is Alan Heimert's study of *Religion and the American Mind,*" found evangelical itinerant preachers fashioning a new "egalitarian rhetoric" full of messages about free will, self-determination, and liberty that were available a generation later to galvanize resistance to Great Britain.[11] Similarly, Heimert's determination to intertwine religious and political rhetoric paved the way for Gary Nash to identify the urban evangelicals with popular movements that fragmented and democratized hierarchical colonial politics. Just as Heimert had defined the Awakening as a crisis of cultural formation, Nash defined the Awakening as "a profound cultural crisis involving the convergence of political, social, and economic forces," and Nash saw it quickly turn into a "class-specific movement" that promoted "levelling" in the form of lay preaching and a general "expansion of political consciousness and a new feeling of self-importance." Like Heimert, Nash saw the Old Lights as the friends of an emerging liberal capitalist ethic while the Awakeners "heaped scorn" on "the acquisitiveness of the urban elite," and like Heimert again, Nash saw the Awakening as a major formative element in the creation of an "antiauthoritarianism" that shattered the "habit of obedience" among Americans and paved the way to resistance in 1775.[12]

But the great weakness of Heimert's argument and the arguments piled more-or-less haphazardly around his was the ease with which large patches of exceptions could be found in the eighteenth-century record. As Nathan O. Hatch discovered, large numbers of Old Lights cheerfully

joined with the New Lights in supporting the Revolution, almost as
though the distinctions Heimert had drawn did not exist, and Hatch even
found New England Old Lights as firmly fixated on millennialism as the
New Lights. Nor was it at all apparent that the Old Lights were the
apostles of liberal individualism; in fact, the commonest complaint of
the Old Lights and Old Calvinists, during the Awakening and long after
it, was precisely that the Awakeners disrupted and subverted organic notions of community, as symbolized by the Half-Way Covenant and the
conventional New England baptismal rites.[13] Bruce Tucker has pointed
out that the Great Awakening may actually have increased American reliance on British culture, through the transatlantic cooperation of American Awakeners with English Evangelicals, rather than created anything
tending toward an American culture. "By the Revolutionary era, ministers rarely, if ever, invoked the Great Awakening as a crusade upon
which the new political movement could be built," observed Tucker;
"More central was the theme of a religious partnership which had been
betrayed by former friends."[14] And in a later work, *The Democratization
of American Christianity* (1989), Hatch suggested that the real story of
democratization in religion and American culture was the breakup of
established religious institutions under the influence of Jeffersonian political radicalism. Hatch, in essence, turned Heimert upside down by proposing democratization as a process that the Revolution forced on evangelical awakeners in the *second* "great awakening" in the early republic,
and not one that the evangelicals of the first Awakening forced on the
Revolution.

Recognition of these weaknesses in the Heimert thesis led to the administration of a tremendous shock in the form of Jon Butler's 1982
article in the *Journal of American History,* "Enthusiasm Described and
Decried: The Great Awakening as Interpretive Fiction." Butler aggressively assaulted the Heimert thesis on nearly every ground on which it
stood and dragged down a number of Heimert's admirers at the same
time. Butler questioned exactly what was meant by Joseph Tracy's term,
great awakening, and pointed out that the revivals of the 1740s and
1750s were often isolated and incongruent events, and certainly not
nation-shaping cultural upheavals; he questioned the supposed democratic or communitarian valences between revivalism and revolution and
pointed out that the Awakening started and finished securely in the hands
of clerical elites; and he attacked the notion that any common rhetorical
or ideological ground existed between the revivalists and the revolutionaries. The Awakening was no longer "great"; it was, to the contrary, an
unconnected string of regional revivals of various forms of pietist Calvinism, which had little impact on the long-duration growth of either American denominations or American nationalism.

Rarely in the space of one essay has so much damage been done to so
many historical reputations. If Tracy and the nineteenth-century chroniclers offered the spiritual interpretation of the Awakening, and the

twentieth-century historians (climaxing in Heimert) developed a secular-ized political/cultural interpretation of the Awakening, Butler created the anti-interpretation, both in the 1982 essay and more recently in his larger study, *Awash In A Sea of Faith: Christianizing the American People* (1990). Far more serious even than Charles Chauncy, who conceded the importance of the Awakening even while he argued that it was a fraud, Butler argued for the irrelevance of the Awakening, and the fraudulence of its interpretation.

I

With the earth thus leveled by Butler's iconoclasm, it has become possible over the last decade to back off from the macrocultural or political-cum-intellectual paradigms created by Osgood, Parrington, Gewehr, Maxson, and Heimert, and begin reviewing and reconstructing the socio-logical, religious, ethnohistorical and even non-American shape of the Awakening. Without the need to justify one's interest in the Awakening by hitching it to the Revolution, the time has been particularly ripe for bringing the religious meanings of the Awakening back to the fore, espe-cially as cultural anthropologists have impressed historians with the need to fold religion back into their reconstructions of cultures. Even though Gary Nash was largely concerned with political and economic problems in *The Urban Crucible,* he was fully aware that "the Great Awakening in New England was not caused by economic dislocation, spreading pov-erty, or currency problems," and that any adequate understanding of the Awakening had to be rooted, not in anticipations of the Revolution or republican culture, but "deeper into the subsoil of Calvinist Puritan cul-ture." [15]

The most basic of those religious questions concerns the actual mean-ing of revivals or awakenings; few historians have been, as Nash ob-served, overly willing to define these terms, being happier simply to de-scribe the event and debate its details. But one can no more ignore a definition of the Awakening as a religious event than historians of eighteenth-century imperial tensions can avoid a definition of mercantil-ism or capitalism. What that has required, however, is more interpretive empathy than modern historians usually have in store, for religious events that center on revival and conversion necessarily function, espe-cially in early modern cultures like the American colonial eighteenth-century, on levels of meaning that (as anthropologist James Clifford has warned) are not entirely congenial to historians trained up to a "bias toward wholeness, continuity and growth" rather than "contradictions, mutations, and emergencies." As a result, the general predeliction is to read religion as what Martin Marty called a *nothing but* phenomenon— *nothing but* the protest of the poor or the oppressive, *nothing but* the refuge of the timid, *nothing but* this or that—and to read awakenings as events of either resistance or accommodation (to modernism or pluralism, in the fashion of Peter Berger), or as moments along a line of development from dominance to decline or back again (as in Anthony F. C. Wallace's "revitalization" thesis).[16] But a religious awakening can simultaneously be intellectual, mystical, experimental, affectional, and coercive; it can influence and be influenced by many relations, signs, and situations, and it is more likely to speak with a vocabulary of resonance, affinity, and motive than with social causatives.[17] And what is equally important, it is precisely the affectional, the personal, and the mystical that are the components of a revival most compelling to its participants. Even the logically and temporally comprehensible New England doctrinal controversies over baptism, the terms of communion, and the nature of conversion that loom so large as the background to the Great Awakening were charged with devotional, spiritual, and familial meanings which we ignore only at the price of misunderstanding the entire enterprise.[18] Thus, any new history of the Awakening has to begin by readdressing religion in early America as a creative and interactive variable, capable of originating, mediating, and integrating an extraordinary spectrum of experiences.[19]

But such a history cannot stop there: in fact, historians have been calling, somewhat disingenuously, for such interpretive empathy for a generation without ever coming to terms with the terrific ontological and narrative consequences of such empathy. We must go on from mere empathy to ask, in the case of the Great Awakening, whether the current genres of historical narrative are actually capable of conveying anything like the sense of the spiritual or devotional, or whether writing on such subjects would not simply become denatured by the conventional processes of description. The Awakeners were not conscious of being historical; as far as they understood matters, they were participants in an aesthetic and transcendent event that has no respect for the modern metaphysics of history. For the Awakeners, the stories of conversion and supernatural light were not attempts, as ours are, to capture an event in our own hands, but to bring spiritual healing. If this history is to go forward, a new kind of historical language is needed to speak about the Great Awakening—not the sterile and alienated language of modernism, nor the ironic language of the discreetly empathetic, nor yet the self-absorbed and power-hungry language of the postmodern, but a language of awe and terror, and if possible, of reconciliation.

This is not to suggest, however, that the consideration of revivals as historical events—as cultural assimilation or resistance or the like—has yielded no worthwhile fruit. Henry F. May's survey of *The Enlightenment in America* (1976) is helpful for the care with which he integrates the Awakening and the concerns of pietist Evangelicals into the vast mental geography of the Enlightenment, and he treats the Awakening less as a prototype for the American cultural future and more as an angry and self-conscious protest against "the whole social and emotional tendency" of what May called the "Moderate Enlightenment" of eighteenth-century natural religion. Not surprisingly, May had little use for Heimert: "No society could have based its existence" on Jonathan Edwards's treatises on the will or the religious affections, and for May "the marvel is that he affected American culture as deeply as he did." Equally germane to the international context of the Awakening is the even vaster spiritual geography mapped out by W. R. Ward, whose *The Protestant Evangelical Awakening* also situates the Awakeners in a broader eighteenth-century context, only this time the context of Continental pietism and the Counter-Enlightenment. Ward is particularly adept at stressing how the European spiritual revivals rested upon the creation of vast networks of letter writing, travel, the growth of a common popular press, and large amounts of translation and republication, which made printed texts a major vehicle for the spread of religious ideas across national and linguistic boundaries. Ward is also highly effective at making millennialism more than simply a vehicle for the covert expression of American politics.[20] In the end, both of these table-setting studies come to roughly the same conclusion: like May, Ward's general perspective on Protestant Awakenings in the eighteenth century is to see them as movements of resistance to assimilation, which means in the American case that the Great Awakening could be seen less as a movement to establish a new identity and more as an effort to recover or protect old ones.[21]

But the process of assimilation/resistance can cut in various directions, and sometimes simultaneously: Jonathan Edwards lauded small-town, up-river resistance to the "great Noise" of Arminianism that invaded the Connecticut River Valley in the 1730s, but he also wrote and published for large-scale transatlantic audiences. Where Ward has found resistance in the international context, Susan O'Brien, Michael Crawford, Robert Rutter, Harold Simonson, and John Raimo have found an equal measure of enclosure within an Anglo-American system of religious discourse.[22] The question of assimilation/resistance is further complicated in early America as soon as we recognize that the Great Awakening was more than simply an Anglo-American, or Anglophone, event with the dividing lines in communities drawn on the basis of whether people were *for* it or *against* it. As demonstrated by Joyce Goodfriend, Richard W. Pointer, Randall Balmer, Marilyn Westerkamp, A. G. Roeber, Ned Landsman, and Leigh Eric Schmidt in their studies of German, Scottish, Dutch, and Scots-Irish communities in New York and New Jersey, the picture of a single Great Awakening becomes blurred by the mixture of ethnic and religious identities in British North America, to the point where questions of *for* and *against* become almost useless. Balmer, Pointer, and Goodfriend are more-or-less agreed that the Great Awakening (contrary to Ward) was an assimilationist event that helped the Dutch community of New York City find accommodations with the surrounding English colonial culture. However, among the Scots described by Schmidt and Landsman and the German Lutherans described by Roeber in New York and New Jersey, the Awakening becomes much more of what Ward described as a tool for resisting assimilation (in the form of Scottish "communion fairs" that eventually become transmuted into "camp meetings") or even for gobbling up and Scot-ifying colonial Presbyterianism.[23] Concerning Pennsylvania, Dietmar Rothermund, John Frantz, and Stephanie Grauman Wolf all open windows into the German-speaking Protestant communities in and around Philadelphia, although in Wolf's case the principal result is to show how negligible the impact of the Awakening was on German Lutheran and German Reformed churchgoers, while Frantz argues that it had a significant antiassimilationist effect by making the Germans more ethnically and linguistically apart.[24] But even here, generalizations based upon "German" or "Scottish" ethnicity can be treacherous: not only did "German" conceal a variety of distinct and competing regional origins, but non-English colonists showed themselves quite adept at picking and choosing cultural elements from their English neighbors for incorporation without following a particularly coherent plan. Some "Germans," then, might promote English-style Awakenings, but for very different reasons than the English would have employed; and some would have opposed them while being quite loyal to "pietist" constructions of their religion.

If the Middle Colonies have been the major resource for understanding the Awakening as a cultural contest, New England has been home to the sociology of the Awakening, and probably because the general perception of New England as ethnically homogeneous in the eighteenth-century has preempted any expectation of seeing the Great Awakening there as a struggle over assimilation. Some of this attention has been little more than the by-product of the usual New England antiquarian or institutional historical interests.[25] Yale College, which became a center of controversy in the Awakening on more than one occasion, has turned in a rather large share of material on the Awakening through Richard Warch's *School of the Prophets: Yale College, 1701–1740* (1973); Louis L. Tucker's biography of Yale President Thomas Clap, *Puritan Protagonist: President Thomas Clap of Yale College* (1962); and a well-crafted but sadly neglected anthology by Stephen Nissenbaum, *The Great Awakening at Yale College* (1972). But a more important stimulus to the social history of the Awakening in New England was generated by the publication in 1970 of three landmark histories of New England towns by Kenneth Lockridge, Michael Zuckerman, and Philip Greven. With those historians as models, a flurry of essays and monographs by James Walsh, Gerald Moran, John Jeffries, J. M. Bumsted, William Willingham, and Christopher Jedrey seized on the Great Awakening as a means for further understanding or illustrating the demographic and structural dilemmas of eighteenth-century New England.[26] Jedrey's biography of John Cleaveland, for instance, owed a great deal in conceptual terms to Greven's work on inheritance patterns in seventeenth-century Andover, and the central chapter of the book was in fact devoted to showing how Cleaveland, a radical New Light, was situated in a parish that was

wholly devoted to perpetuating traditional patterns of power, landholding, and inheritance, and to resisting the reorganization of village life
along liberal entrepreneurial lines. The story of the Great Awakening in
Cleaveland's parish was thus the story of how older parents and their
dependent (and unwilling) sons stayed loyal to Old Light practices while
the independent and middle-aged were drawn to the New Light.[27] Like
so much else in the literature of the Great Awakening, these studies have
been far from uniform in their conclusions. Stephen Grossbart, for example, analyzed the conversion and membership patterns of five Connecticut parishes between 1711 and 1832, and his results disputed both Gerald Moran's desire to link New Light conversion with maturation and
the life cycle, and Bumsted's penchant for hooking the Awakening to
economic crisis, since the ages of conversion Grossbart computed varied
widely from cohort to cohort irrespective of the age of marriage or settlement, and even went up (rather than down) after 1750.[28] On the other
hand, Rosalind Remer, for example, drew a series of striking connections
between the Land Bank party in Boston in 1739–40 and the New Lights,
and the Silver Bankers and the Old Light churches, and demonstrated
important correlations between church membership, occupation, bank
subscription, and office-holding, so that "clearly, diverging religious beliefs about salvation and piety were closely linked with concerns about
the social order."[29]

By contrast with New England, the sociology of the Awakening in the
Middle Colonies has been almost entirely absorbed by the assimilation
problem. The urtext in the field was, for over fifty years, Charles Hartshorne Maxson's *The Great Awakening in the Middle Colonies*, with Martin Lodge's 1964 dissertation, "The Great Awakening in the Middle Colonies" (University of California, Berkeley), as almost the only useful
complement. This peculiar cloud of inattention began to lift with Jon
Butler's study of the ecclesiastical politics of the Delaware Valley, and the
insistence of Patricia Bonomi and Gary Nash on shifting the focus of
early American religious history out of New England.[30] But for the most
part, the sociology of revivalism in the Middle Colonies has been easily
dwarfed by the attention captured by the theological problems posed by
the Great Awakening to the Presbyterians in Pennsylvania and New Jersey, as well as by one of the finest denominational histories ever written,
Leonard J. Trinterud's *The Forming of an American Tradition: A Re-
examination of Colonial Presbyterianism* (1949). Trinterud's book is not
a study of the Great Awakening per se, but he necessarily devotes an
outsize amount of attention to the Awakening among the mid-Atlantic
Presbyterians in an effort to stand twentieth-century Presbyterian conservatives on their heads by tracing the lineage of Presbyterian liberalism to
the eighteenth-century Awakeners. Beyond Trinterud, Presbyterian biographies like Keith Hardman's dissertation, "Jonathan Dickinson and the
Course of American Presbyterianism, 1717–1740" (University of Pennsylvania, 1971), and Milton J. Coalter's *Gilbert Tennent, Son of Thun-*

der: A Case Study of Continental Pietism's Impact on the First Great Awakening in the Middle Colonies (1986) take over as the principal narratives of the Presbyterian Awakening in the Middle Colonies. For the non-Protestant or non-Calvinist groups who actually constituted the numerical majority in the Middle Colonies, the available literature is ludicrously thin (except, again, as a study of assimilation), which suggests rather strongly that the impact of the Awakening needs in the future to be assessed not only in terms of those who received it but those who resisted it or who were indifferent to it. Pennsylvania German Lutherans, for instance, were resistant to "pietism" even when it came in the form of German Lutheran missionaries like Henry Melchoir Muhlenberg who had no assimilationist agendas, and in fact American Lutheranism managed to develop a theological and institutional identity quite apart from the evangelicalism of the Awakening.[31] Ironically, no single person in the Middle Colonies has come in for greater attention in connection with the Awakening than one whose principal interest in it was to make money from it, and that was Benjamin Franklin.[32]

The bibliographical terrain for the social history of the Awakening in the southern colonies was almost as flat until very recently. Much of this neglect, as Jack P. Greene has complained, was surely due to the overall propensity of early American historians to treat Massachusetts rather than the Chesapeake as the normative early American society. Greene has argued relentlessly that early modern societies like colonial British North America underwent a developmental evolution involving *simplification, elaboration,* and then finally *replication* (the copying and appropriation of imperial British cultural norms), which fits the Chesapeake and not Massachusetts. Greene and his model have undergone severe criticism at times, especially for Greene's inability to fit the Chesapeake's overwhelming reliance on slave labor into anything that seems to "replicate" Georgian English society. But the involvement of prominent English figures like Whitefield in the American revivals (and over a prolonged period of time, until Whitefield's death in Massachusetts in 1770) and the thick network of intellectual exchange between American and British Awakeners, implies that the Awakening could act as an important demonstration of "replication," provided that more evidence of its operation could be demonstrated in the South. It is not so much Greene who takes up that note as it is Jon Butler, who interprets the Awakening (such as it was) not as an assertion of American cultural identity but as the continuation of a steady process of imposing formal institutional religious authority on populations who had heretofore escaped it. "Europeans in America did not flee their past; they embraced it," Butler wrote in 1990, "They moved toward the exercise of authority, not away from it, and they understood that individual religious observance prospered best in the New World environment through the discipline of coercive institutional authority." In so saying, Butler has produced what amounts to yet another argument about assimilation, with the Awakenings as examples of "religious, social, and economic maturation" in the colonies that often aimed at homogenizing various "ethnic dimensions in religious observance, both Scottish and German," into a single imperial evangelical form.[33]

Greene, unfortunately, preferred to by-pass the Awakening as he had by-passed slavery, and studies of Virginia community like Darrett and Anita Rutman's *A Place in Time: Middlesex County, Virginia, 1650–1750* (1984) usually come to conclusion in midcentury, before any form of the Great Awakening arrived in Virginia. Consequently, our understanding of the Awakening in the South, and especially Virginia, relies very largely on Richard Beeman's and Rhys Isaac's work on the Virginia New Light Baptists, which clearly hooked evangelical Awakeners, in Heimert-like style, to the Revolution and a new American political ideology and away from assimilation.[34] The attractiveness of Isaac's story turns on the variety of sources he used to illustrate it—not the elite texts used by Heimert, but passers-by on roads and highways, the patriarchal organization of buildings, the hierarchical message of Anglican church architecture. Although Isaac's overall message is about the transformation of Virginia culture from a provincial hierarchy to a fragmented, contentious republican society, the New Light Baptists and the Awakening in Virginia play the catalytic role in this transformation, in that the New Light Baptists created a counterculture of austerity, ecstatic and extempore preaching, and social fellowship to which Virginia elites were eventually forced by the Revolution to concede, and then surrender, power. Given the fact that the Awakening in Virginia continues into the 1760s, Isaac represents a formidable bid to reestablish the political and revolutionary significance of the Awakening as its central plot; unfortunately, it is precisely the fact that Isaac's Awakening occurs so conveniently in the 1760s that raises legitimate questions about whether his New Light Baptists have any meaningful connection with the New England and Pennsylvania events of 1739–1742. Without that connection, Isaac's New Light Baptists become merely an isolated and local phenomenon, whose relationship to the Revolution is a freak of the Virginia environment, not Heimert's Awakening political ideology.

Of course, even if Isaac is right about Virginia, that does little to dislodge the justice of Jon Butler's complaints about Heimertizing the rest of the Awakening. And indeed, if one looks at evangelicals in the 1760s in places like Philadelphia, the papers and records of the "second-generation" evangelicals like William Bradford reveal a behavior of assimilation to imperial culture and "replication" almost inverse to that of Isaac's Baptists. Isaac is also on unsteady ground when dealing with Virginia's slave population in the Awakening, especially since Isaac claims that African Americans were moved only marginally by his New Light Baptists and created an evangelical ethos with none of Isaac's critical interest in republican self-control. Recent articles by Leigh Eric Schmidt, Stephen J. Stein, Alan Gallay, and Frank Lambert have pointed out that white Awakeners in the South were indeed culpably timid in confronting the racial status quo, but Lambert and Albert Raboteau have taken particular pain to show that African Americans appropriated the Awakening for their own purposes and equipped it with their own meanings quite apart from the intentions of Whitefield or the other white Awakeners.[35] Indeed, it is seriously worth wondering how much the affectional style of the Awakeners found a major pool of support in the response of African Americans, for whom traditional religion had always contained strong affectional elements. Historians have paid unaccountably little attention to the repeated observations of the Awakeners about the large numbers of African American hearers and converts whom they encountered, and it may well turn out to be no accident that New England towns with the most serious outbreaks of radical separatism were those like Groton and New London, which had unusually large concentrations of free and enslaved African Americans in the eighteenth century.[36]

Another problem with giving Isaac too long an interpretive leash is the short shrift he gives the Presbyterians in Virginia. George W. Pilcher has given us at least one study of a major New Side Presbyterian in Virginia in *Samuel Davies: Apostle of Dissent in Colonial Virginia* (1971), and the late Lefferts Loetscher provided another biography of a Scots-Irish Virginia Presbyterian who was greatly affected by New Side revivalism in the Shenandoah in his *Facing the Enlightenment and Pietism: Archibald Alexander and the Founding of Princeton Theological Seminary* (1983). But beyond that, the Virginia Presbyterians are still in need of the kind of description that Isaac provided for the Baptists.[37] If Heimert is right, then such a study should demonstrate a substantial set of interconnections between the various ethnic and regional revivals that dotted the British American seaboard. For the Virginia Presbyterians, far more so than Isaac's Baptists, were much better placed, in terms of the ethnic geography of the mid-Atlantic, to sustain such interconnections. After all, Samuel Davies was originally a Pennsylvanian, moved to northern Virginia with the tide of Scots-Irish immigration there in 1749, attempted to lure both Edwards and Joseph Bellamy to Virginia, and ended up moving to New Jersey to take up what became the central post of New Light leadership in the 1760s at Princeton. If the Great Awakening was a single event that possesses a coherence beyond the New England and Pennsylvania events of 1739–1742, the evidence of it will lie, not with Isaac's Baptists, but with people like Davies and his migratory evangelical Scots.

2

The mention of biographies highlights the odd way in which the Awakening, however else it may want for sociological, ethnocultural, or demographic analysis, has never lacked for biographers, and sometimes hagiographers.[38] The most potent subject for biography in the Awakening has always been George Whitefield, and the Great Itinerant's most useful

biographer has always been himself, since Whitefield unhesitatingly par-
layed his own *Journals* and ostensibly private correspondence into public
propaganda and publicity for his revivals.[39] Hardly a year passed after
his death, however, before a crowd of biographers began jostling together to recreate his image. Luke Tyerman's 1200–page *The Life of the
Rev. George Whitefield* (1876–1877) was the standard biography of
Whitfield for almost a century. But Tyerman was tipped off that pedestal
by the Canadian Baptist Arnold Dallimore in his two-volume *George
Whitefield: The Life and Times of the Great Evangelist of the Eighteenth-
Century Revival* (1970, 1980), for although Dallimore's biography was
plainly written that ye may believe, it represents a major effort to move
Whitefield out of the shadow of Wesley, to redeem him from the picture
of public buffoon that the enemies of the Awakening retailed, and to
establish in painstaking detail Whitefield's transatlantic goings and com-
ings over three decades.

Whitefield has subsequently become the centerpiece of two of the most
innovative interpretations of the Awakening, by Harry Stout and Frank
Lambert, where the questions shift from assimilation to modernization.
Stout's biography of Whitefield is closely connected to both his earlier
studies of New Light preaching rhetoric and his long-term sympathies
with Heimert. Accordingly, Stout's Whitefield is primarily a preacher; in
fact, more than a preacher, Whitefield is an actor, a "divine dramatist,"
who skillfully links evangelical religion with the new public culture of
"theatricality" in the eighteenth century. But true to Heimert, Stout's
Whitefield is also a harbinger of the Revolution, bravely standing up for
the interests of Americans in the 1760s and warning his English brethren
not to press the colonies unrighteously. For Lambert, who stands in the
shadow of Timothy Breen (his dissertation advisor) rather than Heimert,
Whitefield is primarily an entrepreneur who manipulates the eighteenth-
century "consumer revolution" and commodifies evangelical religion
through his published journals and sermons.[40] Lambert's Whitefield, unlike Stout's, has virtually no message about politics or revolution, but he
does have tremendous significance as a cultural shaper of a new
Habermas-like "religious public sphere" in which abstract public debate
is substituted for class-based authoritarian pronouncements. Lambert's
Whitefield seized control of "the expanding network of colonial newspapers" through a deliberate "print and preach" strategy; "crafted a new
religion out-of-doors, beyond parish boundaries"; and "employed the
language of reason," rather than ecclesiastical authority, which appealed
to the newly rationalized audience in an age of expanding commerce.[41]
From both Lambert and Stout, there emerges a picture of the Awakening
as a swiftly moving, sophisticated, coordinated, and dynamic communi-
cative event that in some measure belies the localized and New England–
dominated image of Butler's critique, as well as leaving earlier images
of the Awakening as a desperate (or valiant) reaction against modernity
seriously wanting.

Oddly, it is not individual clergymen as much as the clergy considered as a whole who have come under some of the most sophisticated scrutiny in the literature of the Great Awakening. The social state of the ministers has fascinated a number of historians, since the role of the clergy as public intellectuals in the eighteenth century has eerie valences for modern academics. James W. Schmotter, George Harper, J. W. T. Youngs, David Harlan, and Donald Scott all address in varying ways the decay of religious and social authority in the clergy both before and after the Awakening, while the first three chapters of E. Brooks Holifield's *A History of Pastoral Care in America: From Salvation to Self-Realization* (1983) lay out the changes in pastoral theory and practice that the Awakening induced.[42] Once again, however, the conclusions that emerge from such specialized professional studies have been strangely contradictory. Schmotter, for instance, insisted that "New Englanders aroused by the spirit of revivalism" deserted their respectable parsons to "turn to Baptist or Separatist meetings," while the "ties of professionalism" that had bound the clergy together as a professional caste disintegrated during their "internecine squabbling" over the Awakening. Holifield and Youngs saw the relationships of clergy and people change, too, but less in terms of a decrease of political authority and more in terms of an adjustment of clerical style to accommodate the increasing demands of the people that the clergy make "concern for the people the *essence* of clerical leadership."[43]

If the preachers of the Awakening can call forth such a conflicting body of analysis, then it has to be said that their rivals and critics have summoned forth almost as much. That the Old Lights have survived with any shred of attraction left is largely due to Conrad Wright's deeply sympathetic account of their response to the Awakening and to Edmund S. Morgan's beautiful biography of Ezra Stiles.[44] On the other side of the spectrum, New Light radicalism, whether in the form of the Separate Congregationalists, Free Will Baptists, or Universalists, became the focus of the late Clarence C. Goen, in his benchmark study of the Separates, *Revivalism and Separatism in New England, 1740–1800: Strict Congregationalists and Separate Baptists in the Great Awakening* (1962); David Lovejoy, in his broad survey of *Religious Enthusiasm in the New World: Heresy to Revolution* (1985); and Stephen Marini, in his colorful and provocative monograph on *Radical Sects of Revolutionary New England* (1982). The uproar over James Davenport and the Separates in New London has garnered the most significant scholarly attention, especially in articles by Richard Warch, Peter Onuf, and Harry Stout, but Leigh Eric Schmidt has also focused attention on the Boston Separate Andrew Crosswell, whose publications in defense of New Light radicalism gave more theological heft to the Separates than the social "shock tactics" used by Davenport and Timothy Allen. Those "shock tactics," as Onuf and Stout have shown, were not without their own rhyme and reason, since Davenport's theatrical defiance of the Standing Order in New London was carefully calculated to encourage an "assertive role" for audiences and congregations. As Stout and Onuf conclude, "By successfully calling into question the integrity of the religious establishment and enjoining these people to act for themselves, Davenport demonstrated how tenuous were the bonds of social order and how fragile traditional controls could be in a rapidly changing society. . . . This awakening—which released so much anger and discord—offered a glimpse into things as they were and were becoming in a world at war with itself."[45]

This brings us at last to Jonathan Edwards. No survey of the literature of the Awakening can honestly avoid Edwards, just as none can safely try to do him bibliographical justice. He is, as Martin Marty remarked in the midst of an even more ambitious bibliographical survey, "the single one-purpose industry among American historians."[46] As with Whitefield, the most important sources on Edwards are by Edwards himself, and the twelve current volumes of the Yale University Press *Works of Jonathan Edwards,* each with an introduction that could stand alone as a work of scholarship, offer the best introduction to the man whom George Bancroft advised students to give their days and nights to if they wished to understand America. Approaching the secondary literature on Edwards is more daunting, since Edwards's theological students fashioned a formidable school of Calvinistic theology around his writings known as the New Divinity, and the flourishing of the New Divinity between 1760 and 1840 left a lengthy trail of commentary and controversy on Edwards through the major theological quarterlies of the new republic. With the passing of the New England Theology, Edwards's general popularity declined, and by the 1920s, studies of Edwards by Progressives like Parrington and Henry Bamford Parkes had fixed him as a reactionary but tragically talented figure that Americans had safely left behind them. Even Ola Elizabeth Winslow's lengthy and largely sympathetic biography of Edwards in 1940 could not escape a measure of regret that Edwards had chained himself to a backwards and anti-intellectual religious mentality.[47] Largely in response to this, Perry Miller's 1949 biography of Edwards, riding high on the neo-orthodox critique of liberalism popularized by Reinhold Niebuhr, restructured Edwards as a Niebuhr-like critic of modern acquisitiveness whose admiration for Lockean sensationalism clearly fixed him as a thoroughly American thinker and whose Calvinism was a weapon a "tamed cynic" could feel comfortable with.[48]

It is to Miller, whose dramatic style and fierce championship of Edwards are written large across every page of *Jonathan Edwards,* more than anyone else that we owe the modern revival of interest in Edwards, and it may be worth wondering if the entire historiography of the Great Awakening since 1949 is simply an indirect beneficiary. But, as if to confirm Marty's comment about the industriousness of Edwards scholars, Miller has been rendered increasingly out-of-date by the tide of Edwards studies published in the 1980s and the early 1990s. Clearly, the most important of these publications are the ones that have attempted to call a halt to the wave of biographical modernizations: Norman Fiering's *Jonathan Edwards's Moral Thought and Its British Context* (1981), which corrects many of the more egregious interpretive errors in Miller's reading of Edwards (principally, Fiering weans Edwards off Locke and puts him back within the context of Continental theocentric rationalism) without sacrificing any of the intellectual excitement Miller imparted to him, and William S. Morris's *The Young Jonathan Edwards: A Reconstruction* (1991), a book that developed a legendary—almost cult—following among Edwardseans but that had to wait almost thirty years to make the transition from a University of Chicago dissertation to publication. Morris, like Fiering, sets Edwards against the background of Edwards's own reading in Continental rationalism and Protestant scholasticism as a student at Yale, and opened up a view of the Edwards who went up to Yale and met, not Locke, but de Maastricht.

Fiering helped to ignite a flurry of reexaminations of Edwards's philosophical writings and pushed intellectual historians into a radical reconsideration of Edwards's long-term place in American philosophy.[49] One of the best samplings of the various forms that the intellectual history of Edwards has taken is the volume of essays collected from the papers given by Henry May, Norman Fiering, Wilson Kimnach, and others at a major conference on Edwards at Wheaton College in 1984, and published by Nathan Hatch and Harry Stout as *Jonathan Edwards and the American Experience* (1988). Ironically, as Edwards's philosophical reputation ascended, his preeminence as a theologian seemed to dim. I remember thinking, as a graduate student attending the 1984 Wheaton conference, how peculiar it was that a meeting dedicated to Jonathan Edwards, and held in the Billy Graham Center at Wheaton College, could get through three days of papers on Edwards and never once mention "Sinners in the Hands of An Angry God." Perhaps this is because the theologians have turned out, ironically, to be the ones most concerned with making Edwards "modern," and most of them are unaccountably chary of talking about Edwards's role in the Great Awakening. Two recent and lengthy theological surveys of Edwards's thought by Sang Hyun Lee and Robert W. Jenson, both theological seminary professors, quixotically pleaded for Edwards's "modernity" and invoked as their pole-star the name, not of Fiering, but Perry Miller (in Lee's case, in the first sentence of his book).[50]

This has meant, oddly, that the most successful work on Edwards and the Great Awakening has been that which grounds Edwards in the mentality and context of western Massachusetts in the mid–eighteenth century. Gregory H. Nobles, Patricia J. Tracy, and Kenneth P. Minkema (in his unpublished dissertation on the Edwards family) have presented surveys of the social and familial world of the upper Connecticut River Valley, and Tracy in particular draws close connections between the pressures exerted on Northampton's youth and the theological and spiritual message Edwards was presenting to them.[51] The picture of Edwards that emerges from Tracy's book is not particularly happy: as a student of Stephen Nissenbaum, Tracy had picked up on a suggestion Nissenbaum embedded at the close of the book he and Paul Boyer coauthored on the Salem witch trials, a suggestion that asked for some consideration of the Great Awakening and the 1692 witch frenzy as being two sides of the same response to social and economic pressure in New England.[52] In that light, Edwards becomes a desperate figure, struggling to preserve clerical authority in an atmosphere of economic stress and instability, and turning to the most vulnerable part of the Northampton community, the young and landless (just as the young and landless turned out to be the chief accusers at Salem), to build a power base. The Great Awakening thus becomes Edwards's bid to succeed Solomon Stoddard, turning the children against the parents, and then ultimately the children against himself in 1750 when he failed to deliver on the promises of redemption and security that the Awakening had offered to them. The question that lingers in the mind after these works, however, is still the question of awe and terror: would Jonathan Edwards have recognized himself on these pages? Or do these studies, useful as they are, only underscore that Edwards may be the first place where the new language of the Awakening must be written?

3

There are several ways to measure the impact of an event or a movement. Alan Heimert made his measurements almost entirely on the basis of elite texts, an approach with weaknesses that have only become more glaring the more we have understood the dynamic relationship that exists between texts and readers. Part of the ease with which Butler made his critique of Heimert rested on his understanding of how closely confined the influence of those texts could be in the eighteenth century's public sphere, and it was Butler's knowledge of both the geographical and perceptual constraints of elite religious texts that undergirded the punishing assertions he made in 1982 about the Awakening's regional limitations and the few real challenges to elite religious leadership offered by the revivals. What we have learned about the economic and social constraints on the eighteenth-century Protestant clergy, and their dependence for marginal livelihoods on the good will of their congregations, makes it even more problematic that they could have assumed the directing role Heimert imputed to them. Even if the clergy were in some way important to the Revolution, it probably had little to do with whether they were New Lights or not.

And yet, most of the work that has been published on the Awakening since 1982 has demonstrated that there were limitations in Butler's critique, too. Butler's Gramscian portrayal of eighteenth-century Americans being herded by a clerical hegemony toward "Christianization" ignored the work of European popular culturalists, which stressed the shared spiritual and intellectual interactions of clergy and laity.[53] Similarly, new research on the radicalism of New Light laypeople in the Revolutionary era has given a subtle and unexpected restorative to Heimert's demand to see the Awakening and the Revolution as a single chain of ideological events. Add to this the recovery of the transatlantic evangelical networks performed by Ward, O'Brien, Crawford, and others, and the extraordinarily sophisticated manipulation of rhetoric and print for lay audiences and readers that Stout and Lambert have shown in Whitefield, and the various regional pieces of the Awakening begin to take on far more coherent and interwoven shape than we had supposed (although caution will interrupt to suggest that *transatlantic* is not the same as *intercolonial,* that New Light radicals shared their radicalism with numbers of Old Lights, deists, Anglicans, Catholics, and Jews, and that bits of connection do not guarantee coherence).

That caution is what leads me to deflect discussion of the importance of the Awakening away from the preoccupation with the creation of a *political* mentality that prepared Americans for the Revolution, and to urge pursuit of the very substantial role that the Awakening played in shaping the American *evangelical* mentality. The Awakening crystallized a particular religious ideology, shaped around the experience of direct conversion, disinterested benevolence, and a peculiar connection between individualistic assent to religious experience and the possibility for a new, heightened shape of communal order. When one surveys the religious establishments of Virginia and New England, and the sectarian chaos of the middle colonies in the eighteenth century, there is comparatively little in the religious history of those communities that foreshadows what we have come to recognize as modern evangelicalism; even among the most direct offspring of the Radical Reformation, one finds pietism and quietism but not evangelicalism. That in large measure was the offspring of the Awakening, and the Awakening remains the formative event of the American evangelical mentality—it gave methods, psychology, and (in the form of Edwards, Brainerd, and Whitefield) role-models and heroes.[54] It may be true that Edwards's influence in the 1740s extended little beyond the Connecticut River Valley, but that influence had grown gigantic by the end of the century, and personalities as volatile as Charles Grandison Finney and John Brown all have connections to the ideas Edwards and the New Divinity developed to define the Awakening. Alongside the question of a persistent evangelical ideology formed by the Awakening, there must also be the question of how that ideology institutionalized itself. One real but remarkably unappreciated accomplishment of the Awakening in New England was the dominance it gave to Yale College in western New England. Riding the same tide of institutionalization into the nineteenth century were the explicitly New Light colleges like Dartmouth, Brown, and Princeton (all more-or-less offspring of Yale) and their nineteenth-century spin-offs, Oberlin, Knox, the Oneida Institute, Mount Holyoke, Wheaton—all of whom transmitted and transformed the New Light and the New Divinity in radical ways.

Still, the influence of elite texts, if not the clergy elites themselves, on
the political ideology of the Revolution cannot be waved entirely aside.
Even if we concede the criticism that an American Revolution led by
Thomas Jefferson and Tom Paine seems to wear little of the impress of
Jonathan Edwards or George Whitefield, that concession may be in danger of ignoring the long-duration meaning of the texts of the Awakening
for American political culture. *Freedom of the Will* and *The Religious
Affections* might have had little formative power over the Enlightened
minds of the Continental Congress, but they staged a dramatic comeback
in the early nineteenth century when the deism of the Founding Fathers
had mostly gone to seed. As John Murrin observed, "If we are determined to attribute a major political and military upheaval to revival fervor, we would do far better to choose the Civil War, not the Revolution." Perhaps not in 1775, but far more certainly in 1861, the children
of the Awakening "imposed their social vision upon their fellow citizens
until their reformist ardor drove an angry South to secession." And it is
in that long-term influence, rather than the short-term connections to the
Revolution, that we may have to find the long-sought political meanings
of the Awakening. "Without the Great Awakening and its successors,
there would have been a revolution in 1775," Murrin concedes, "but in
all probability, no Civil War in 1861."[55] There are several other such
connections that have gone curiously undrawn between the Awakening
and the nineteenth century, not the least of which concerns the relationship of religion and capitalism. After all, the Awakening took place simultaneously with the development of international commercial capitalism over the century between 1730 and 1830; and yet, apart from Mark
Valeri's essay on Edwards, no serious effort has been made to situate the
correspondence of the Awakening and the capitalist transformation of
the Anglo-American economy.[56] This does not mean that we should be
looking simply for a bigger and better version of the Osgood–Miller–
Heimert paradigm. Recent historians of early American radicalism have
found a striking connection between the Awakeners and revolutionary
radicalism among agrarian Regulators, artisans, and urban mechanics
and slaves. In surveying the work of Alan Taylor on the Maine land
rioters of the 1780s and 90s, and Michael Merrill and Sean Wilentz on
the New Divinity laborer William Manning, Alfred Young has concluded
that the political resistance of early republican radicals was "as their language alone suggests . . . often rooted in religion, especially in the evangelical dissenting faiths. Evangelical religion surfaces in protest throughout these essays."[57] Thus, Heimert may have been right after all, but not
for the reasons he thought.

The possible connections of the evangelical ideology of the Awakening, Revolutionary radicalism, and the evangelicalized political culture of
nineteenth-century politics have only been tentatively explored as yet. But

within the orbit of that interest, the most important story about radicalism and the Awakening is that of gender more than class. We have known for a long time about the predominance of women as members of colonial churches, but we have not known how to translate that demographic fact into a statement of gender, and so, oddly, we know very little about the formative influence of gender in the Awakening. What makes this odder still in the context of the Awakening is that we do know that the spiritual experience of women plays a significant role in the accounts of Edwards, the Tennents, and Whitefield. We are also becoming more dimly aware that the evangelical communications networks were highly gendered: women wrote to women even as men wrote to men, although curiously (in generational terms) daughters seem to have imbibed their evangelicalism from their fathers to transmit to their children. Beyond that, however, whatever else we know of women in the Awakening underscores a paradoxical combination of submission and assertiveness, and assertiveness clearly did not win the day. Susan Juster has pointed out how New Light Baptists, in the crux of the Awakening, were willing to let down the walls of patriarchy —only to build them up again after the passage of a generation and the fervor of revival. Similarly, we do not know much about womens' participation in the revivals themselves.[58] Mary Beth Norton and Charles Hambrick-Stowe have succeeded in recovering the experiences of Sarah Osborn, a disciple of Samuel Hopkins's in Newport, Rhode Island, and Osborn's career as an organizer and promoter of revival interest in the 1750s and 1760s may offer a pattern for understanding still further the opportunities and limits imposed on gender by the Awakeners. But even as sparse as these explorations may be at present, they already decisively question Ann Douglas's "feminization" thesis, for contrary to Douglas's assertion that women "feminized" and debased the masculine Calvinism of post-Awakening New England into a thin gruel of sentimentalism, Edwardsean women from Sarah Pierpont Edwards to Mary Lyon of Mt. Holyoke not only embraced the most ultra forms of New Light Calvinism but were remarkably successful in promoting them.[59] That, in turn, may help to open up a larger question of ambiguity in American evangelicalism, which concerns its persistent capacity to involve itself in both radical individualism and self-absorbed communalism, in both radical antielitism and complacent bourgeois conservatism.

Much as there is new ground to turn over, there is also some old ground that is far from exhausted. Donald Weber's *Rhetoric and History in Revolutionary New England* (1988), as well as the Stout and Lambert biographies of Whitefield, have demonstrated that the rhetorical meanings of the Awakening are far from well understood. Tied to further consideration of rhetoric and speech must be a consideration of public ritual (along the lines hinted at by Rhys Isaac). Evangelical religion has always been a religion of signs, but the perception of those signs has usually been occluded by the prominence of evangelical speech, as though evangelical Protestantism in the eighteenth century (and the Great Awakening with it) was an exercise in gnosticism rather than pietism. That the Awakening invented participatory rituals other than Davenport's breeches-burning has only been faintly touched on, and then usually in the context of ethnic exceptionalism. What is yet to be done is the identification and elaboration of the larger patterns of evangelical performance that were established in the Awakening (the concert of prayer, the emergence of a folk hymnody in the singing schools and shaped-note hymnody of Daniel Read and Jeremiah Ingalls) and preserved in nineteenth-century evangelicalism. And not only in evangelicalism: Charles Grandison Finney is frequently described as a revivalist who appropriated the style of lawyers to win his "retainer for the Lord Jesus Christ," but Richard D. Brown is right to question whether the shoe may really be on the other foot, and whether the rhetorical culture of early American lawyers (like Tapping Reeve, in the heart of New Divinity country in Connecticut's Litchfield County) may have instead imitated New Light preaching.[60] Above all, we are desperately impoverished in our understanding of the spirituality of the Awakening, despite the fact that a sizeable proportion of the Awakening's texts were devotional rather than polemic, and despite the fact that Edwards and Prince consciously hoped to prove the unrevolutionary nature of the Awakening by deploying reprintings of seventeenth-century devotional texts. However, persuading historians, not to mention the editors of scholarly periodicals, to take spirituality with any seriousness may be a far more difficult task than the actual work of research and analysis.[61]

The Great Awakening was not as revolutionary or culturally unique an event as some of its admirers have claimed, but neither was it as unsophisticated, provincial, and resultless as its decriers have asserted. Its immediate effects tended to be localized, but the strength of transatlantic connections and intercolonial communications guaranteed that those effects would be described, read, internalized, and exemplified across a broad mental and physical geography in British North America. It was in many respects a backwards-looking and by no means American event, in that it borrowed freely from Scottish and Continental precedents— from communion fairs to childrens' conversions —and gave a renewed lease to what David Hall called "the mentality of wonders," and yet it also galvanized separation, conflict, and new forms of communal action, and dissipated the elite solidarities upon which deference, force, and persuasion rested. If the interpretive wind still blows from any direction, it is still from Heimert's and not Butler's, although it blows in ways that Heimert paid little attention to. The Great Awakening occupies a peculiar borderland between intellectual history and religious history, between the history of influential elites and large social movements. Much of the difficulty we have experienced in discussing the Awakening lies precisely in how it straddles these boundaries in its odd ungainly way, and much of the standoff we have witnessed about the Awakening's long-duration significance in American history has arisen from seeing it only on one side of those boundaries. There is much that we do not know about the Awakening, much more in fact than we realize (estimates of the actual numbers of converts, for instance, still rest on Benjamin Trumbull's and Joseph Tracy's educated guesses in the early nineteenth century), while at the same time, the moment is long past for a large-scale synthetic history of the Awakening.[62] More than a narrative of surprising conversions, I fully expect that it will be a narrative of surprising convergences.

NOTES

I wish to thank Rose Beiler, Donna Rilling, Cathy McDonnell, Jane Merritt, James Pearson, Liam Riordan, Marianne Wokeck, Michael Zuckerman, and the friends and Fellows of the Philadelphia Center for Early American Studies for their helpful commentary on a preliminary draft of this chapter.

1. Hall, "Religion and Society: Problems and Considerations," in *Colonial British America: Essays in the New History of the Early Modern Era* (Baltimore, 1984), 317.

2. Heimert and Miller, "Introduction," *The Great Awakening* (Indianapolis, 1967), xiii–xv; Butler, "Enthusiasm Described and Decried: The Great Awakening as Interpretive Fiction," in *Journal of American History* 69 (September 1982): 324.

3. Tracy, *The Great Awakening: A History of the Revival of Religion in the time of Edwards & Whitefield* (Boston, 1842), 402, 406, 414.

4. Conforti, "The Invention of the Great Awakening, 1795–1842," in *Early American Literature* 26 (September 1991): 99–118, and "Edwardseans, Unitarians, and the Memory of the Great Awakening, 1800–1840," in *American Unitarianism, 1805–1865*, ed. Conrad E. Wright (Boston, 1989), 31–50.

5. See Noah Porter, "President Edwards on Revivals," in *Quarterly Christian Spectator* 1 (1827): 295–308; Daniel T. Fiske, "New England Theology," in *Bibliotheca Sacra* 22 (July–October, 1865): 467–512, 568–87; Edwards Amasa Park, "New England Theology," in *Bibliotheca Sacra* 9 (January 1852): 170–219; Edwards Amasa Park, "Introductory Essay," in *The Atonement: Discourses and Treatises by Edwards, Smalley, Maxcy, Emmons, Griffin, Burge, and Weeks* (Boston, 1859), pp. ix–xlvii; Charles Hodge, *The Constitutional History of the Presbyterian Church in the United States of America* (Philadelphia, 1851), part 2, 11–101; Archibald Alexander, *The Log College: Biographical Sketches of William Tennent and his students, together with an account of the revivals under their ministries* (1851; London, 1968), 7–13; Benjamin Trumbull, *A Complete History of Connecticut, Civil and Ecclesiastical* (1818; New London, 1848), volume 2, 103–219; for a modern survey of this literature, see, Mark Noll, "Jonathan Edwards and Nineteenth-Century Theology," in *Jonathan Edwards and the American Experience*, Nathan O. Hatch and Harry S. Stout, eds. (New York, 1988), 260–87.

6. Osgood, *The American Colonies in the Eighteenth Century* (New York, 1924), volume 3, 409; it also has to be noted that one other secular response to the Awakening was to ignore it entirely—Lawrence Henry Gipson's great multi-

volume history of the Anglo-American empire in the eighteenth century hardly notices the Awakening from either British or American perspectives, and only *The British Isles and the American Colonies: The Southern Plantations, 1748–1754* (New York, 1960) and *The British Isles and the American Colonies: The Northern Plantations, 1748–1754* (New York, 1965) actually managed to give the Awakening a total of five pages of notice; similarly, Carl Bridenbaugh's urban histories, *Cities in the Wilderness: The First Century of Urban Life in America, 1625–1742* (New York, 1938), gave only two of its 481 pages to the Awakening, while his sequel, *Cities in Revolt: Urban Life in America, 1743–1776* (New York, 1955), only managed to mention the Awakening on four of its 425 pages, and Bridenbaugh's history of Philadelphia, *Rebels and Gentlemen: Philadelphia in the Age of Franklin* (New York, 1942), devoted all of two paragraphs to it; even Stephanie Graumann Wolf's recent *As Various As Their Land: The Everyday Lives of Eighteenth-Century Americans* (New York, 1993) only has space on four of its 279 pages for the Great Awakening.

7. Parrington, *Main Currents in American Thought: An Interpretation of American Literature from the Beginnings to 1920* (New York, 1926), volume 1, 160–61.

8. Gewehr, *The Great Awakening in Virginia* (Durham, N.C., 1930), 187; Maxson, *The Great Awakening in the Middle Colonies* (Chicago, 1920), 150.

9. Heimert, *Religion and the American Mind from the Great Awakening to the Revolution* (Cambridge, Mass., 1966), 9–10, 12, 100, 300, 532.

10. Morgan's review of Heimert appeared in the *William and Mary Quarterly* 24 (July 1967): 454–59.

11. Stout, "Religion, Communications, and the Ideological Origins of the American Revolution," in *William and Mary Quarterly* 34 (October 1977): 521, 533; Stout, *The New England Soul: Preaching and Religious Culture in Colonial New England* (New York, 1986), 193, 218–19, 286.

12. Nash, *The Urban Crucible: Social Change, Political Consciousness, and the Origins of the American Revolution* (Cambridge, Mass., 1979), 204, 208, 218, 223, 384. Even when historians were not modeling themselves directly on Heimert's thesis, it was still clear that his book had exerted a tremendous pull on their interpretations of the Awakening. Richard Bushman's *From Puritan to Yankee: Character and Social Order in Connecticut, 1690–1765* (New York, 1967), was critical of Heimert's overemphasis of "the political significance of the New Divinity" at the expense of "religious issues," but Bushman still lauded the "valuable insights" of Heimert's book (302) and developed an argument structurally similar to Heimert's which saw the Awakening as the catalyst for transforming Connecticut from a provincial and hierarchical society to an individualistic "Yankee" democracy.

13. Mark A. Noll, "Ebenezer Devotion: Religion and Society in Revolutionary Connecticut," in *Church History* 45 (September 1976): 293–307, and "Moses Mather (Old Calvinist) and the Evolution of Edwardseanism," in *Church History* 49 (September 1980): 273–85.

14. Hatch, *The Sacred Cause of Liberty: Republican Thought and the Millennium in Revolutionary New England* (New Haven, 1977), 25–26; William K. Breitenbach has also shown that Edwards's disciples, the New Divinity, were deeply ambivalent about commitments to individualism and community, in "Unregenerate Doings: Selflessness and Selfishness in New Divinity Theology," in *American Quarterly* 34 (Winter 1985): 479–502; Tucker, "The Reinvention of

New England, 1691–1770," in *New England Quarterly* 59 (September 1986): 315–40.

15. Nash, *The Urban Crucible*, 204, 219.

16. Wallace, "Revitalization Movements," in *American Anthropologist* 58 (April 1956): 265, and "Paradigmatic Processes in Culture Change," in *Rockdale: The Growth of an American Village in the Early Industrial Revolution* (New York, 1978), 477–485; see also William G. McLoughlin, *Revivals, Awakenings, and Reform: An Essay on Religion and Social Change in America, 1607–1977* (Chicago, 1978), 12–23.

17. James Clifford, *The Predicament of Culture: Twentieth-Century Ethnography, Literature, and Art* (Cambridge, Mass.: 1988), 337–38; Martin Marty, "Explaining the Rise of Fundamentalism," in *The Chronicle of Higher Education* (October 28, 1992), A56; Lewis R. Rambo, *Understanding Religious Conversion* (New Haven, 1993), 32–35, 41–42, 87; Clifford Geertz, *The Interpretation of Cultures* (New York, 1973), 25–310; see also Andrew Smout's "Born Again at Cambuslang: New Evidence on Popular Religion and Literacy in 18th Century Scotland," in *Past and Present* 97 (November 1982): 114–27, and Steven Bruce's "Social Change and Collective Behaviour: The Revival in 18th-Century Ross-shire," in *British Journal of Sociology* 34 (December 1983): 554–72, which are both critical of material reductionism, and which use literacy, reading patterns, and "affinity" of world views to describe religious decisionmaking as an independent variable in social formation.

18. See James P. Walsh, "The Pure Church in Eighteenth-Century Connecticut" (unpublished Ph.D. dissertation, Columbia University, 1970) and "Solomon Stoddard's Open Communion: A Re-examination," in *New England Quarterly* 43 (March 1970): 97–114; Gerald F. Moran, "The Puritan Saint: Religious Experience, Church Membership, and Piety in Connecticut, 1636–1776" (unpublished Ph.D. dissertation, Rutgers University, 1973); Robert G. Pope, *The Half-Way Covenant: Church Membership in Puritan New England* (Princeton, 1969), 251–75; Paul Lucas, *Valley of Discord: Church and Society along the Connecticut River, 1636–1725* (Hanover, N.H., 1976), 169–202; Ralph Coffman, *Solomon Stoddard* (Boston, 1978), 48–102; and James W. Jones, *The Shattered Synthesis: New England Puritanism Before the Great Awakening* (New Haven, 1978), 104–28.

19. Lovelace, *Dynamics of Spiritual Life: An Evangelical Theology of Renewal* (Downers Grove, Il., 1979), 21–22, 61–200, esp. 75; Michael Crawford offers a summary of the distinctions and materials used by the eighteenth-century revivalists in observing the Awakening in "The Morphology of Religious Revivals" in *Seasons of Grace: Colonial New England's Revival Tradition in its British Context* (New York, 1991), 180–95.

20. For the politicization of millennialism and its connections with the Awakening, see Ruth Bloch, "The Social and Political Base of Millennial Literature in Late 18th-Century America," in *American Quarterly* 40 (September 1988): 378–96; and *The Visionary Republic: Millennial Themes in American Thought, 1756–1800* (Cambridge, 1985), 10–21, and James West Davidson, *The Logic of Millennial Thought: Eighteenth Century New England* (New Haven, 1977), 213–54; and Sacvan Bercovitch, "The Typology of America's Mission," in *American Quarterly* 30 (Summer 1978): 135–55. For an approach to eighteenth-century millennialism that pushes the millennialism of the Awakeners into an international context instead, see Gerald R. McDermott, *One Holy and Happy Society:*

The Public Theology of Jonathan Edwards (University Park, Pa., 1992), 50–92.
21. May, *The Enlightenment in America* (New York, 1976), 49–50; Ward, *The Protestant Evangelical Awakening* (Cambridge, 1992), 2–10, 16–49, 353–55; see also, W. R. Ward, "Power and Piety: The Origins of Religious Revival in the Early Eighteenth Century," in *The Bulletin of the John Ryland University Library of Manchester* 63 (Autumn 1980): 231–52, "The Protestant Frame of Mind," in *History Today* 40 (September 1990): 18–24, and "The Relations of the Enlightenment and Religious Revival in Central Europe and in the English-Speaking World," in *Reform and Reformation: England and the Continent, 1500–1700,* ed. Derek Baker (Oxford, 1979), 281–305.

22. Susan O'Brien, "A Transatlantic Community of Saints: The Great Awakening and the First Evangelical Network, 1735–1755," in *American Historical Review* 91 (October 1986): 811–32; Rutter, "The New Birth: Evangelicalism in the Transatlantic Community During the Great Awakening, 1739–1745" (unpublished Ph.D. dissertation, Rutgers University, 1982); Raimo, "Spiritual Harvest: The Anglo-American Revival in Boston, Massachusetts, and Bristol, England, 1739–1742" (unpublished Ph.D. dissertation, University of Wisconsin, 1974); Simonson, "Jonathan Edwards and His Scottish Connections," in Journal of American Studies 21 (December 1987): 353–76; Crawford, *Seasons of Grace,* 19–28, 37–42, 53–65, 82–104, 141–79, 192–239.

23. Goodfriend, "The Social Dimensions of Congregational Life in Colonial New York City," in *William and Mary Quarterly* 46 (April 1989): 252–278, and *Before the Melting Pot: Society and Culture in Colonial New York City, 1664–1730* (Princeton, 1992), 81–94, 108–10, 121–32; Pointer, *Protestant Pluralism and the New York Experience: A Study of Eighteenth-Century Religious Diversity* (Bloomington, In., 1987), 29–52; Balmer, *A Perfect Babel of Confusion: Dutch Religion and English Culture in the Middle Colonies* (New York, 1989), 99–140; Westerkamp, *The Triumph of the Laity: Scots-Irish Piety and the Great Awakening, 1625–1760* (New York, 1989); Roeber, *Palatines, Liberty and Property: German Lutherans in Colonial British America* (Baltimore, 1993), 328; Schmidt, *Holy Fairs: Scottish Communions and American Revivals in the Early Modern Period* (Princeton, 1989); Landsman, *Scotland and Its First Colony, 1683–1765* (Princeton, 1985), 183–91, 227–55; see also Elizabeth Nybakken, "New Light on the Old Side: Irish Influences on Colonial Presbyterianism," in *Journal of American History* 68 (March 1982): 813–32.

24. Rothermund, *The Layman's Progress: Religious and Political Experience in Colonial Pennsylvania, 1740–1770* (Philadelphia, 1961), and "Political Factions and the Great Awakening," in *Pennsylvania History* 27 (October 1959): 317–31; Frantz, "The Awakening of Religion among the German Settlers of the Middle Colonies," *William and Mary Quarterly* 33 (April 1976): 266–88; Wolf, *Urban Village: Population, Community, and Family Structure in Germantown, Pennsylvania, 1683–1800* (Princeton, 1976), 203–42, 333–34.

25. See, for instance, Thomas Henry Billings, "The Great Awakening," in *Essex Institute Historical Collections* 65 (January 1929): 89–104, or Mary H. Mitchell, *The Great Awakening and Other Revivals in the Religious Life of Connecticut* (New Haven, 1934).

26. Bumsted, "Religion, Finance and Democracy in Massachusetts: The Town of Norton as a Case Study," *Journal of American History* 57 (March 1971): 817–31; Walsh, "The Great Awakening in the First Congregational Church of Woodbury, Connecticut," *William and Mary Quarterly* 28 (October 1971): 543–

62; Moran, "Conditions of Religious Conversion in the First Society of Norwich, Connecticut, 1718–1744," *Journal of Social History* 5 (Spring 1972): 331–43; Willingham, "Religious Conversion in the Second Society of Windham, Connecticut, 1723–1743: A Case Study," *Societas* 6 (1976): 109–19; Jeffries, "The Separation in the Canterbury Congregational Church: Religion, Family and Politics in a Connecticut Town," *New England Quarterly* 53 (December 1979): 522–49.

27. Jedrey, *The World of John Cleaveland: Family and Community in Eighteenth-Century New England* (New York, 1979), 52, 58–94; Robert Gross also links division and agitation over the Awakening in Concord, Massachusetts, to larger contentions over inheritance patterns and landholding, in *The Minutemen and Their World* (New York, 1976), 18–29.

28. Grossbart, "Seeking the Divine Favor: Conversion and Church Admission in Eastern Connecticut," *William and Mary Quarterly* 46 (October 1989): 696–740; for similar questions, see also Edward M. Cook, Jr., *The Fathers of the Towns: Leadership and Community Structure in Eighteenth Century New England* (Baltimore, 1976), 128–29.

29. Remer, "Old Lights and New Money: A Note on Religion, Economics and the Social Order," *William and Mary Quarterly* 47 (October 1990): 566–73.

30. Butler, *Power, Authority, and the Origins of American Denominational Order: The English Churches in the Delaware Valley, 1680–1730* (Philadelphia, 1978), 75–78, where Butler presents an early version of his attack on the Heimert thesis; Bonomi, *Under the Cope of Heaven: Religion, Society, and Politics in Colonial America* (New York, 1986), 72–92, 168–81; Nash, *The Urban Crucible*, 219–21, 227–32; see also Lodge's "The Crisis of the Churches in the Middle Colonies, 1720–1750," in *Pennsylvania Magazine of History and Biography* 95 (April 1971): 195–220.

31. See Frederick Tolles, "Quietism and Enthusiasm: The Philadelphia Quakers and the Great Awakening," in *Pennsylvania Magazine of History and Biography* 69 (January 1945): 26–49, where the Awakeners are interpreted as an immature version of the same enthusiasm that gave rise to Quakerism and that consequently embarrassed Quakers eager to disassociate themselves from their century-old roots in religious radicalism; see also E. G. Alderfer's history of the Ephrata community, *The Ephrata Commune: An Early American Counterculture* (Pittsburgh, 1985), where Whitefield is mentioned only once (101) and the Great Awakening not at all. The essays on *Continental Pietism and Early American Christianity* edited by F. Ernest Stoeffler (Grand Rapids, Mich., 1976) make almost no connection at all between the Awakening and the various forms and communities of German Reformed, Lutheran, Brethren, and Mennonite pietism in the American colonies, while Marianne Wokeck effectively demonstrates how German-speaking Lutheranism insulated itself from the concerns of the Awakeners in two as-yet unpublished papers, "The Desert Is Vast and the Sheep Are Dispersed: Henry Melchoir Muhlenberg's Views of the Immigrant Church" and "German Settlements in the North American Colonies: A Patchwork of Cultural Assimilation and Persistence."

32. John R. Williams, "The Strange Case of Dr. Franklin and Mr. Whitefield," in *Pennsylvania Magazine of History and Biography* 102 (October 1978): 399–421; David T. Morgan, "A Most Unlikely Friendship—Benjamin Franklin and George Whitefield," in *The Historian* 47 (February 1985): 208–18; Lambert, "Subscribing for Profits and Piety: The Friendship of Benjamin Franklin and George Whitefield," in *William and Mary Quarterly* 50 (July 1993): 529–

48; see also chap. Four, "The Spirit and the Press," in Melvin Buxbaum, *Benjamin Franklin and the Zealous Presbyterians* (University Park, Pa., 1975), 116–52.

33. Butler, *Awash in a Sea of Faith: Christianizing the American People* (Cambridge, Mass., 1990), 128, 179.

34. Beeman, "Social Change and Cultural Conflict in Virginia: Lunenburg County, 1746 to 1774," in *William and Mary Quarterly* 35 (July 1978): 455–76, and *The Evolution of the Southern Backcountry: A Case Study of Lunenburg County, Virginia, 1746–1832* (Philadelphia, 1984); and Isaac, *The Transformation of Virginia, 1740–1790* (Chapel Hill, N.C., 1982), 165–73, 278–95, 315, 322, and "Religion and Authority: Problems of the Anglican Establishment in Virginia in the Era of the Great Awakening and the Parsons' Cause," in *William and Mary Quarterly* 30 (January 1973): 3–36, and "Evangelical Revolt: The Nature of the Baptists' Challenge to the Traditional Order in Virginia, 1765–1775," in *William and Mary Quarterly* 31 (July 1974): 345–68; see also Jack Stephen Kroll-Smith, "In Search of Status Power: The Baptist Revival in Colonial Virginia, 1760–1776" (unpublished Ph.D. dissertation, University of Pennsylvania, 1982), 157–78, 185–218. Outside of Virginia, see Daniel T. Morgan, "The Great Awakening in North Carolina, 1740–1775: The Baptist Phase," in *North Carolina Historical Review* 45 (1968): 264–83.

35. Isaac, *Transformation*, 307; Schmidt, "The 'Grand Prophet' Hugh Bryan: Early Evangelicalism's Challenge to the Establishment and Slavery in the Colonial South," in *South Carolina Historical Magazine* 87 (October 1986): 238–50; Gallay, "The Origins of Slaveholders' Paternalism: George Whitefield, the Bryan Family, and the Great Awakening in the South," in *Journal of Southern History* 53 (August 1987): 369–94; Stein, "George Whitefield on Slavery: Some New Evidence," in *Church History* 42 (June 1973): 243–56; Lambert, "I Saw the Book Talk: Slave Readings of the First Great Awakening," in *Journal of Negro History* 77 (Fall 1992): 185–98; Albert Raboteau, *Slave Religion: The Invisible Institution in the Antebellum South* (New York, 1978), 95–128.

36. Noel Ignatiev, "The Revolution as an African-American Exuberance," in *Eighteenth-Century Studies* 27 (Summer 1994): 605–13.

37. See Ernest T. Thompson, *Presbyterians in the South, Volume 1: 1607–1861* (Richmond, Va. 1963), 41–66; Robert F. Scott, "Colonial Presbyterianism in the Valley of Virginia," in *Journal of the Presbyterian Historical Society* 35 (June 1957): 71–92, and 35 (September 1957), 171–92.

38. There are four major sources of short but highly useful biographical material in W. B. Sprague, *Annals of the American Pulpit; or Commemorative Notices of Distinguished American Clergymen of Various Denominations* (New York, 1859), volume 1; Clifford K. Shipton, *Sibley's Harvard Graduates: Biographical Sketches of Those Who Attended Harvard College* (Boston, 1937–1960), volumes 5–11, covering the classes of 1701 through 1745; F. B. Dexter, *Biographical Sketches of the Graduates of Yale College, October 1701–May 1745* (New York, 1885); and James McLachlan, *Princetonians, 1748–1768: A Biographical Dictionary* (Princeton, 1976). For individual Great Awakening–related biographies, see Joseph Conforti, *Samuel Hopkins and the New Divinity Movement: Calvinism, the Congregational Ministry, and Reform in New England Between the Great Awakenings* (Grand Rapids, Mich., 1981), 23–40; Stanley Grenz, *Isaac Backus—Puritan and Baptist* (Macon, Ga., 1983), 55–91; Edward M. Griffin, *Charles Chauncy of Boston, 1705–1787* (Minneapolis, 1980), 46–108; and Charles Lippy, *Seasonable Revolutionary: The Mind of Charles*

Chauncy (Chicago, 1981), 20–77. The single major prorevival voice among the Church of England clergy in Virginia was Devereaux Jarratt, whose memoirs were edited and published by Douglass Adair as "The Autobiography of the Rev. Devereaux Jarratt," in *William and Mary Quarterly* 9 (July 1952): 346–93; New Light Baptists also turn up frequently on the pages of Charles Woodmason's famous Journal, which was edited and published by Richard J. Hooker as *The Carolina Backcountry on the Eve of the Revolution: The Journal and Other Writings of Charles Woodmason, Anglican Itinerant* (Chapel Hill, N.C., 1953), and somewhat less frequently in Henry Melchoir Muhlenberg's *The Journals of Henry Melchoir Muhlenberg*, eds. T. G. Tappert and J. W. Doberstein (Philadelphia, 1942–1958), 3 volumes.

39. Whitfield's autobiographical *A Short Account of God's Dealings with the Reverend Mr. George Whitefield, A.B.* (Philadelphia, 1740) and *A Further Account of God's Dealings with the Reverend Mr. George Whitefield* (London, 1747), along with his eight *Journals*, were first published together by Whitefield himself in 1756, and then republished by William Wale in 1905 and again by Iain Murray as *George Whitefield's Journals* (Edinburgh, 1960); Whitefield's letters were published in the first three volumes of his six-volume *Works* (London, 1771), the first volume of which was reprinted with an introduction and the addition of thirty-four additional letters by S. M. Houghton as *Letters of George Whitefield* (Edinburgh, 1976).

40. Stout, *The Divine Dramatist: George Whitefield and the Rise of Modern Evangelicalism* (Grand Rapids, Mich., 1991), xvi, xxii, 262–67, 287; in the end, Stout cannot resist connecting Whitefield with the Revolution by pointing to Whitefield's condemnation of the Stamp Act and the American episcopate proposal before his death in 1770: "He died a Pauline evangelist *and* an American patriot" (287).

41. Lambert, "The Great Awakening as Artifact: George Whitefield and the Construction of Intercolonial Revival, 1739–1745," in *Church History* 60 (June 1991): 223–46; Lambert, "Pedlar in Divinity: George Whitefield and the Great Awakening, 1737–1745," in *Journal of American History* 77 (1990): 812–37; and Lambert's full-scale biography, *"Pedlar in Divinity": George Whitefield and the Transatlantic Revivals* (Princeton, 1993). On the construction of the "public sphere," see William J. Gilmore, *Reading Becomes a Necessity of Life: Material and Cultural Life in Rural New England, 1780–1835* (Knoxville, 1989), and Michael Warner, *The Letters of the Republic: Publication and the Public Sphere in Eighteenth-Century America* (Cambridge, Mass., 1990), xiii.

42. Schmotter, "Ministerial Careers in Eighteenth-Century New England: The Social Context, 1700–1760," in *Journal of Social History* 9 (Winter 1975): 249–67; Harper, "Clericalism and Revival: The Great Awakening in Boston as a Pastoral Phenomenon," in *New England Quarterly* 57 (December 1984): 554–66; Harlan, *The Clergy and the Great Awakening in New England* (Ann Arbor, Mich., 1980), esp. 49–69.

43. Schmotter, "Clerical Professionalism in the Great Awakening," in *American Quarterly* 31 (Summer 1979): 148–68; Youngs, *God's Messengers: Religious Leadership in Colonial New England, 1700–1750* (Baltimore, 1976), 139–40.

44. Wright, *The Beginnings of Unitarianism in America* (Boston, 1955), 28–58; Morgan, *The Gentle Puritan: A Life of Ezra Stiles, 1727–1795* (New Haven, 1962), 20–77.

45. Richard Warch, "The Shepherd's Tent: Education and Enthusiasm in the Great Awakening," in *American Quarterly* 30 (Summer 1978): 177–98; Onuf, "New Lights in New London: A Group Portrait of the Separatists," in *William and Mary Quarterly* 37 (October 1980): 627–43; Stout and Onuf, "James Davenport and the Great Awakening in New London," in *Journal of American History* 71 (December 1983): 556–78; Schmidt, "A Second and More Glorious Reformation: The New Light Extremism of Andrew Crosswell," in *William and Mary Quarterly* 43 (April 1986): 214–44.

46. Marty, "American Religious History in the Eighties: A Decade of Achievement," in *Church History* 62 (September 1993): 367.

47. Parkes, *Jonathan Edwards: The Fiery Puritan* (New York, 1929), 249–55; Winslow, *Jonathan Edwards, 1703–1758* (New York, 1940), 325–30.

48. Miller, *Jonathan Edwards* (New York, 1949), 119–26, 270–72, 324–26.

49. Donald Weber, "The Figure of Jonathan Edwards," in *American Quarterly* 35 (Summer 1983): 556–64; James Hoopes, "Jonathan Edwards's Religious Psychology," in *Journal of American History* 69 (March 1983): 849–65; Allen C. Guelzo, *Edwards on the Will: A Century of American Theological Debate* (Middletown, Conn., 1989); Bruce Kuklick, *Churchmen and Philosophers: From Jonathan Edwards to John Dewey* (New Haven, Conn., 1985), 15–32.

50. Lee, *The Philosophical Theology of Jonathan Edwards* (Princeton, 1988), 3, and Jenson, *America's Theologian: A Recommendation of Jonathan Edwards* (New York, 1988), viii, 194–96; a far better example of a theologically oriented study of Edwards, rooted in Edwards's unpublished sermons and far more attentive to questions of historical context, is McDermott's *One Holy and Happy Society*, 43–92.

51. Nobles, *Divisions Throughout the Whole: Politics and Society in Hampshire County, Massachusetts, 1740–1775* (New York, 1983), 12–106; Tracy, *Jonathan Edwards, Pastor: Religion and Society in Eighteenth-Century Northampton* (New York, 1979), esp. 188–94; Minkema, "The Edwardses: A Ministerial Family in 18th-Century New England," (unpublished Ph.D. dissertation, University of Connecticut, 1988), volume 1, 206–70.

52. Boyer and Nissenbaum, *Salem Possessed: The Social Origins of Witchcraft* (Cambridge, Mass., 1974), 215–16.

53. See A. G. Roeber, "The Problem of the Butler Transatlantic *Problematique* and American Religious History," unpublished paper read at the German Historical Institute Conference on Cultural Transfer, October 29–31, 1992.

54. Joseph Conforti, "Jonathan Edwards's Most Popular Work: 'The Life of David Brainerd' and Nineteenth-Century Evangelical Culture," in *Church History* 54 (June 1985): 188–201.

55. Murrin, "No Awakening, No Revolution? More Counterfactual Speculations," in *Reviews in American History* 11 (June 1983): 169.

56. Valeri, "The Economic Thought of Jonathan Edwards," in *Church History* 60 (March 1991): 37–54; see also McDermott, *One Holy and Happy Society*, 138–42.

57. Rhys Isaac, "Preachers and Patriots: Popular Culture and the Revolution in Virginia," in *The American Revolution: Explorations in the History of American Radicalism* (DeKalb, Il., 1976), 125–56; Alfred F. Young, "How Radical was the American Revolution?" in *Beyond the American Revolution: Explorations in the History of American Radicalism* (DeKalb, Il., 1993), 322; see also Richard D.

Birdsall, "The Reverend Thomas Allen, Jeffersonian Calvinist," in *New England Quarterly* 30 (June 1957): 147–65; and Lovejoy, *Religious Enthusiasm in the New World*, 202–06.

58. Juster, "Sexual Politics: Gender and Authority in the Evangelical Church" (paper delivered at the American Historical Association, December 28, 1991); see also Jay Fliegelman, *Prodigals and Pilgrims: The American Revolution Against Patriarchal Authority, 1750–1800* (New York, 1982), 155–94.

59. Norton, "My Resting Reaping Times: Sarah Osborn's Defense of Her 'Unfeminine' Activities," in *Signs: Journal of Women in Culture and Society* 2 (1976): 515–29; Hambrick-Stowe, "The Spiritual Pilgrimage of Sarah Osborn (1714–1796)" in *Church History* 61 (December 1992): 408–21; see also Joseph Conforti, "Mary Lyon, the Founding of Mount Holyoke College, and the Cultural Revival of Jonathan Edwards," in *Religion and American Culture* 3 (Winter 1993): 69–89; and Barbara E. Lacey, "Women and the Great Awakening in Connecticut," unpublished paper, Princeton Theological Seminary, 1982.

60. Brown, *Knowledge is Power: The Diffusion of Information in Early America, 1700–1865* (New York, 1989), 101.

61. Charles E. Hambrick-Stowe, "The Spirit of the Old Writers: The Great Awakening and the Persistence of Puritan Piety" in *Puritanism: Transatlantic Perspectives*, ed. Francis J. Bremer (Boston, 1993); and Allen C. Guelzo, "The Spiritual Structures of Jonathan Edwards," in *The Bulletin of the Congregational Library* 62. 44 (Fall 1993): 4–15.

62. On numbers of converts, see Trumbull, *History of Connecticut*, volume 2, 218; Tracy, *The Great Awakening*, 389. Two general surveys of the Awakening were published in the 1970s, the first of which was Cedric Cowing, *The Great Awakening and the American Revolution: Colonial Thought in the 18th Century* (Chicago, 1971), followed by J. M. Bumsted and John E. Van de Wetering, *What Must I Do to Be Saved? The Great Awakening in Colonial America* (Hindale, Il., 1976). Both, however, are very short (the Bumsted-Wetering volume is only 165 pages, while Cowing is only 225 pages and actually devotes less than half its length to the Awakening) and heavily dependent on Tracy and Heimert.

6

RELIGION AND THE
AMERICAN REVOLUTION

▦ ▦ ▦

Gordon S. Wood

THE RELATION OF RELIGION to the American Revolution has always been a problem. We sense that there should be a relationship, but we are not at all clear what it is or even ought to be. Although the eighteenth century was still a deeply religious age, at first glance the Revolution does not seem to have much to do with religion. To be sure, there was a good deal of talk about the people's inalienable right to worship God according to the dictates of their conscience or about the separation of church and state.[1] But these liberal and enlightened beliefs, culminating in the First Amendment to the Constitution, seem to emphasize less the significance of religion than its subordination to politics and other more important matters. As the new 1777 state constitution of New York put it, the Revolution was very much designed to end the "spiritual oppression and intolerance wherewith the bigotry and ambition of weak and wicked priests" had "scourged mankind."[2]

If truth be told, most of the Founding Fathers, enlightened men in an enlightened age, were not all that enthusiastic about religion, certainly not about religious enthusiasm.[3] At best, the gentry leaders of the Revolution only passively believed in organized Christianity and, at worst, they scorned and ridiculed it. Although few were outright deists, most, like the South Carolinian physician David Ramsey, described the Christian Church as "the best temple of reason." No doubt George Washington was a frequent churchgoer, but he scarcely ever referred to God as anything but "the Great Disposer of events" and in twenty volumes of his papers never mentioned Jesus Christ. Even puritanical John Adams thought that the argument for Christ's divinity was an "awful blasphemy" in this new enlightened age. Like the principal sources of their Whig liberalism—whether John Locke or the Commonwealth publicist "Cato"—the Revolutionary leaders viewed religious enthusiasm as a kind of madness, the conceit "of a warmed or overweening brain." Thomas Jefferson's hatred of the clergy knew no bounds, and he repeatedly denounced the "priestcraft" for converting Christianity into "an engine for enslaving mankind . . . into a mere contrivance to filch wealth and power to themselves." For Jefferson and his liberal colleagues, sectarian Christianity was the enemy of most of what they valued—the free and dispassionate inquiry of reason into the workings of nature. As enlightened gentlemen addressing each other in learned societies, they abhorred "that gloomy superstition disseminated by ignorant illiberal preachers" and looked forward to the day when "the phantom of darkness will be dispelled by the rays of science, and the bright charms of rising civilization."[4]

Because the enlightened Founding Fathers set such a secular tone and sponsored all those ringing declarations about freedom of conscience and separation of church and state, most historians either have tended to reduce religion to its role in politics or have decided that religion does not have much to do with the Revolution at all. Nearly all of the early historians of the Revolution—from David Ramsey to George Bancroft—saw little place for religion. And many present-day historians have agreed. Edmund S. Morgan has argued that the Revolutionary generation not only displaced religion with politics and clerical leadership with lawyers, but transformed and secularized the intellectual character of the culture.[5] Certainly, the proportion of publications devoted to religious matters greatly declined during the Revolution while those devoted to politics increased enormously. Although Bernard Bailyn admits that religion necessarily pervaded all aspects of American life in the eighteenth century, he believes that it had no unique influence on the Revolutionary movement, whose effective determinants, he says, were political. As if to confirm this point, Jon Butler in his recent widely acclaimed survey of early American religious history concedes that "at its heart, the Revolution was a profoundly secular event."[6]

Even the eighteenth-century clergy seemed to conspire in making religion the servant of politics and the Revolution a secular event. Many of the religious leaders, including the Calvinists, endorsed the Revolution and its enlightened liberal impulses wholeheartedly. For most Protestant groups, the great threat to religion came from the Church of England,

and enlightened rationalists like Jefferson and James Madison had little trouble in mobilizing Protestant Dissenters against the established Anglican church. The Enlightenment's faith in liberty of conscience that justified this disestablishment of the Anglican church scarcely seemed dangerous to American religion. Even in Massachusetts and Connecticut, where religious establishments existed but were Puritan, not Anglican, Congregational and Presbyterian clergy invoked enlightened religious liberty against the dark twin forces of British civic and ecclesiastical tyranny without fear of subverting their own peculiar alliances between church and state. Since it was an axiom of enlightened political science that virtue among the people was necessary for the sustenance of republican government, the clergy excitedly claimed that religion was the principal promoter of virtue and thus inadvertently contributed to the widespread notion that religion was simply the handmaiden of republicanism in creating the moral regeneration the country needed.

Much of the historical work of the past generation has therefore made religion seem to be of less importance to the Revolution than Enlightenment beliefs and political ideology. Yet this subservience of religion to other matters runs against much of what we know of the prevailing beliefs of ordinary people in this premodern age. Despite the growth of Enlightenment among elites in the eighteenth-century America, Protestantism in one form or another still remained the principal means by which most common people ordered and explained the world and made it meaningful. Not everyone could get emotional fulfillment from contemplating a declaration of rights or from participating in representative government. For most ordinary people, religion met personal and social needs not comprehended by rational philosophy or Whig ideology. Could such a prevalent, popular, and powerful mode of understanding and emotional fulfillment as religion have been so easily smothered by Whig political ideas and the reason of the Enlightenment? After all, the period preceding the Revolution experienced such a vast outpouring of religious passion that later commentators could only call it a Great Awakening, and the period following the Revolution outdid even that initial explosion of evangelical religious feeling to become the Second Great Awakening. Could religion during the Revolutionary decades have simply dropped out of sight? Was popular religion like a raging river that suddenly went underground only to reemerge downstream with more force and vigor than ever?

So totally did religion seem to disappear during the Revolution that historians have naturally concluded that the American people's religiosity itself must have receded. They have argued that the Revolution destroyed churches, interrupted ministerial training, and politicized people's political thinking. The older established churches, now either dismantled or under attack, were ill equipped to handle a rapidly growing and moving population. The proportion of college graduates entering the ministry fell off, and the number of church members declined drastically, with, it is estimated, scarcely one in twenty Americans being members of a church.[7] At the same time, the influence of enlightened liberalism eroded the premises of Calvinism, indeed, of all orthodox Christian beliefs. The Enlightenment told people they were not sinful but naturally good, possessed of an innate moral sense, and that evil lay in the corrupted institutions of both church and state. For some enlightened gentlemen, Christianity became simply the butt of dinner party jokes. However, this rational deism could not be confined to the drawing rooms of the sophisticated gentry, but spilled out into the streets. The antireligious writings of Ethan Allen, Thomas Paine, Comte de Volney, and Elihu Palmer reached out to new popular audiences and gave many ordinary people the sense that reason and nature were as important (and mysterious) as revelation and the supernatural. For a moment, at least, the Enlightenment seemed to have suppressed the religious passions of the American people.[8]

All this accumulated evidence of religious apathy and growing rationalism has convinced many historians that the Revolutionary decades were "the most irreligious period in American history." For much of the nineteenth and twentieth centuries, historians repeated over and over that the Revolution saw "the lowest low-water mark of the lowest ebb-tide of spiritual life in the history of the American church." For at least a few decades Americans appeared simply to have lost much of their earlier spiritual vitality and gone into what Martin Marty once called "a big sleep."[9]

We are now only beginning to realize how misleading these common historical interpretations of popular infidelity and religious indifference in Revolutionary America are. The mass of Americans did not suddenly lose their religiousness in 1760 only to recover it several decades later. Certainly, the low proportion of church membership is no indication of popular religious apathy, not in America where church membership had long been a matter of an individual's conversion experience and not, as in the Old World, a matter of birth.[10] As Bernard Bailyn has pointed out, in traditional societies where involvement with a dominant religion was automatic, the significant religious decision for a person was to break with the religious association into which he or she had been born. Consequently, religious indifference could exist along side extensive, though merely formal, church membership. "In the colonies the opposite became true: to do nothing was likely to mean having no religious affiliation at all, and the significant decision involved joining, not withdrawing from, a religious association. As a result, broad waves of religious enthusiasm could go hand in hand with low church membership."[11] There were of course fierce expressions of popular hostility to the genteel clergy with their D. D.'s and other aristocratic pretensions during the Revolutionary years. Yet this egalitarian anticlericalism scarcely represented any widespread rejection of Christianity by ordinary people.

The notion that Americans suffered a religious recession during the Revolution is an optical illusion, a consequence of historians' looking for religion in the wrong places. One kind of American religion may have declined during the Revolution, but it was more than replaced by another kind. Religion was not displaced by the Revolution; instead, like other central elements of American life, it was radically transformed.

Some historians during the past generation or so, beginning perhaps with Perry Miller in his 1961 essay "From the Covenant to the Revival," have sensed that religion had more to do with the Revolution than simply separating church from state and promoting virtue on behalf of republican governments.[12] No doubt the boldest and controversial of these attempts to link religion and the Revolution was that of Alan Heimert in 1966. Not only did Heimert try to find the origins of the Revolution in the Great Awakening of George Whitefield, Jonathan Edwards, and Gilbert Tennent, but he sought to link the midcentury effusions of evangelical Christianity to the development of Jeffersonian democracy and American nationalism. By reading through and beyond the lines of eighteenth-century sermons Heimert created a Manichaean world divided between the elitist, legal-minded "liberals" and the populist, emotion-laden evangelicals. Heimert's liberals were prissy, conservative, prudent men, disdainful of the vulgarity of ordinary people and frightened of the enthusiasm of the Awakening and, indeed, of all change, and reluctant to participate in the Revolution. His New Light revivalists, on the other hand, were backed up by common, ordinary people, simple plowmen with their hearts on their sleeves who knew more than sophisticated professors with their heads in the clouds. These populist evangelicals were the real force behind the Revolution; they provided Americans with a radical, even democratic, social and political ideology—one that resembled more the communalism of Rousseau than it did the individualism of Locke.[13]

Heimert's book was much too personal, much too much of a cri de coeur against bourgeois conservatism and stuffiness, to be entirely convincing. At times, his book appears so imaginatively separated from the reality of the eighteenth century as to be scarcely history; his argument certainly cannot be verified in any conventional manner. His dichotomy between the rational and evangelical traditions is too simple, too rarified, too detached from the concrete and complicated world of real people; it cannot, for example, account for the fact that most of the intellectual and political leaders of the Revolution were rational liberals and yet were anything but reluctant rebels. Thomas Jefferson and John Adams were hardly evangelical in their outlook, and yet they were passionate revolutionaries who in 1776, at least, were as devoted to the good sense and equality of the common man as any New Light.

Although Heimert's book was subjected to devastating criticism by historians, his positing of a connection between religion and the Revolution was too important and too intriguing to be ignored. Since his book appeared several historians, including William McLoughlin, Harry Stout, Rhys Isaac, and Patricia Bonomi, have continued to explore and refine that connection. In fact, Nathan O. Hatch claims that over the past several decades "no single issue in all of American history has attracted more talent than that of linking the Great Awakening and the Revolution."[14] McLoughlin, who wrote one the few favorable reviews of Heimert's book, saw the Awakening as a kind of emotional and spiritual preparation for the Revolution, especially in a common enthusiasm for liberty; and he assumed a dichotomy in American society between rationalists and pietists that was as stark as that of Heimert—a division between those who took the world as it is and accommodated themselves to it and those who saw the world as it ought to be and yearned to change it.[15]

Stout, for his part, redefined Heimert's argument and perhaps made more of it than Heimert ever intended. Heimert, Stout said, was not trying to establish any direct intellectual links between religious thought and political rebellion but instead was trying to demonstrate that the evangelicals' contribution to the Revolution lay in the creation of a new popular rhetoric, a new form of oral public persuasion that recast the norms of the traditional culture and indirectly undermined the authority of the established social order.[16] In his prize-winning book, Isaac brilliantly developed this point in his anthropologically rendered interpretation of the challenge mounted by the Baptist evangelicals in Virginia against the hierarchical Anglican establishment.

In her recent book, *Under the Cope of Heaven,* Patricia Bonomi has gone beyond McLoughlin, Stout, and Isaac to make an even more explicit connection between religion and the Revolution. She has suggested that in a world where religious orthodoxy and establishment were taken for granted the challenge of American dissenting Protestantism to the Anglican monarchy had to be as much political as religious. It was natural, she argued, for the colonists to think of religious and civil liberty as connected; witness, for example, John Adams's coupling of the canon and feudal law as the common enemy of freedom. So that in Anglicanism itself and in its periodic suggestions for an American bishop lay an inherent monarchical obstacle to the freedom and flourishing of the dissenting churches of America. In such circumstances, Protestant dissent was instinctively republican and thus primed for rebellion against the British monarchical establishment.[17]

J.C.D. Clark in his new book, *The Language of Liberty, 1660–1832,* has brought together all these suggested connections between religion and the coming of the Revolution and has exploited them as never before.[18] In fact, in his book Clark lays out nothing less than a full-scale religious interpretation of the Revolution. He argues that in the eighteenth-century religion was still the major means by which most people identified themselves and ordered their lives. Americans, says Clark, were brought together and made revolutionary not by a common adherence to something called a "radical whig commonwealth" tradition (which Clark believes is an invention of twentieth-century historians) but by their religion. Such unity that Englishmen on both sides of the Atlantic had came from their Protestantism; but for the colonists, or most of them, that unity was strengthened by their common dissent against the Anglican monarchical establishment. It was a pluralistic unity, however, one that divided them as much as it held them together; for the various peoples of the New World were separated not as much by their ethnicity (which Clark contends is a modern conception) as by their religious sectarianism. Indeed, much of the factional politics and the petty rebellions of the eighteenth century were grounded in religious differences.

Historians of eighteenth-century America, says Clark, have been too ready to apply modern categories to that very different age. Political discourse in the English-speaking world of the eighteenth century, he writes, was inevitably preoccupied with religious issues. This was especially so in the colonies, since the colonists' religious experience was very different from that of England. Matters of church polity and church order that had been settled in England itself in the decades following 1689 remained problematic and unfinished in the colonies and hence open to continual challenge and controversy. Where dissent in the home island of England gradually lost adherents and largely failed to devise strong institutional structures, the opposite was true in the colonies. During the first half of the eighteenth century, the dissenting churches, says Clark referring to the recent work of Jon Butler, extended their institutional and disciplinary hold over their adherents. Indeed, in New England the dissenting churches were nearly as established, coercive, territorial, and ceremonial as was the Church of England in the mother country. Only the Anglican church in the colonies failed to build an organizational and disciplinary framework commensurate with its ambitions and its position at home—a failure that, as Clark remarks, was one of the many ironies of American religious developments.

Yet these dissenting American denominations, however strong, could never feel secure in a transatlantic English world dominated by a monarchy that drew its strength from its connection to the orthodoxy of the Church of England. In the end, Clark argues, the ancient Protestant dissenting fears of an ecclesiastical establishment were decisive in bringing on the Revolution. By the middle of the century, many Americans had come to associate tyranny with an Anglican ascendancy; even popery had come to mean the exercise of power by any established episcopal church. Nursing their atavistic hatreds, the various religious sects carried on a guerrilla struggle against what was perceived to be a militant imperial Anglicanism, a struggle that in the 1770s finally became what Clark calls a "civil war of religion." Since in Clark's view politics in the premodern world was merely a manifestation of underlying religious passion, religion had to be the fundamental source of this civil war. Dry and rational constitutional arguments over rights and liberties by themselves could never have led to armed rebellion. Only impassioned religious enthusiasm and excitement could have produced the frenzied rhetoric and virulent hostility that characterized the Revolution and turned it into what Clark describes as "the last great war of religion in the western world."[19] It is hard to imagine a more extravagant interpretation of religion's role in bringing on the Revolution than this.

Clark's argument is far more complicated and sophisticated than the simple fear of a bishop being sent to America invoked earlier by some historians to help explain the Revolution.[20] Yet despite its many qualifications and subtleties, his argument seems much too extreme, much too thinly supported by research, and much too dismissive of contrary evidence (for example, the fact that a majority of the signers of the Declaration of Independence were Anglican) to be acceptable to most historians, though it should help force a healthy reexamination of the religious ancien régime in eighteenth-century America.

As his convoluted prose suggests, Clark at least is aware of the complexity involved in a religious explanation of the Revolution; many other religious interpreters of the Revolution seem not to be. The connections many historians seek between religion and the Revolution appear too simple and straightforward. Jon Butler can contend that "the link between the revivals and the American Revolution is virtually nonexistent" because too many historians have suggested that the link is direct and causal.[21] Even John Murrin's intriguing and whimsical counterfactual speculation of what would have happened in the 1760s and 70s if there had been no Awakening suffers from too much emphasis on intentionality and from too close an identification of motives with consequences.[22]

Trying to establish an identification, for example, between the evangelicals and the Revolutionaries or between the Old Lights and the loyalists seems mistaken. Whether the New Lights actually became enthusiastic patriots or not appears irrelevant. Instead, it is what their revivalism inadvertently did to the structure of the society and the character of the culture that ultimately matters. Butler, for example, argues that the Awakening was more local and more fragmented, less antiauthoritarian and less democratic than we have thought and thus is not easily related to the Revolution. But this seems to misunderstand the nature of the historical process. No one ought to be arguing that the Awakening "caused" the Revolution; it no more "caused" the Revolution than did the growth of popular politics and competitive elections in the colonies during the decades after 1730. The growth of popular politics in the 1740s, 50s, and 60s did not by any means create a democratic polity on the eve of the Revolution; indeed, in many respects politics in the 1760s was just as elitist and premodern as it had been in 1720. But beneath the surface much had changed in colonial political life. The same seems true of American religious life as a consequence of the midcentury Awakening or awakenings. It seems evident that in one way or another the Great

Awakening helped to prepare American society and culture for the Revolution, but of course not in any direct, deliberate, or intentional manner. The midcentury New Light revivalists and evangelicals were not consciously trying to change the political order or to foment rebellion or to create a radical ideology; they were simply trying to save souls. Nonetheless, there is little doubt that they contributed to new social and cultural circumstances out of which the Revolution arose.

Perhaps one helpful way of breaking out of the difficulty of having to choose between religion and politics as an explanation for the Revolution is to see both religious and political developments as consequences of more deeply rooted determinants, as manifest responses to massive demographic and economic changes taking place in the society. This does not mean, however, that religion any more than politics can be reduced to a mere matter of social circumstances; it was always possible for some individuals to have religious or political beliefs totally out of accord with their social condition. Yet religion was that aspect of the culture that gave the highest level of meaning, order, and value to people's experience; indeed, for many of them religious belief made possible their social experience. Religious assertions of meaning and value did not occur randomly in the population; they were usually related to people's differing psychological and social experiences. Consequently, we have to make some effort to explain why at specific times some Americans of a particular sort believed one thing and other Americans of another sort believed something else; otherwise, we will never understand the relation of religion to the Revolution.

The religious developments in the Chesapeake that Isaac has written so sensitively about, for example, clearly had their bases in what was happening socially. A surging population and changing marketing relationships were unsettling traditional hierarchies throughout the region. In the two and a half decades after 1750, one quarter of the parishes of the established Anglican Church in Virginia were dissolved, and by the time of the Revolution two quarters more had petitioned to be dissolved. Hundreds and thousands of Virginians found themselves separated from customary paternal and patronage connections and in need of new meanings to make sense of their new experience. Growing numbers of them left the established Church of England and began forming new evangelical communities that rejected outright the high style, the luxurious living, and the preoccupations with rank and precedence of the dominant Anglican gentry. In the decades after the 1740s, succeeding waves of enthusiastic New Light Presbyterians, Separate Baptists, and finally Methodists swept up new converts mostly from among the common people of the Chesapeake. Between 1769 and 1774, the number of Baptist churches in Virginia alone increased from seven to fifty-four.[23]

What was taking place in Virginia at midcentury was just one manifestation of the general religious upheaval taking place throughout all the colonies that we have come to know as the Great Awakening. Up and down the continent the religious stirrings of the midcentury were often diverse, complicated, and local in their origins; but in general they grew out of people's attempts to adjust to the changes taking place in their social relationships.

Probably the most important of these changes in social relationships resulted from the rapid expansion of trade and money-making in the middle decades of the eighteenth century. It is not surprising, for example, that New Light religious awakenings in Connecticut centered precisely in those eastern counties most disrupted by commerce and paper money emissions.[24] Or that many New Light leaders in central Massachusetts were deeply involved in the Land Bank.[25] But the connection between the Awakening and the expansion of capitalism was not simple and direct; it was subtle and not easily grasped. Some historians have seen the Awakening as a simple reaction to the growth of commerce, a product of the resentment of the lower classes against those who dominated the colonial economy.[26] Even Heimert, for all of his disclaimers that the divisions of the Awakening were economic, nevertheless believed that its spirit was "profoundly hostile to the emerging capitalistic ethic of eighteenth-century America."[27] But such judgments are misleading, to say the least; for, as John Brooke has suggested, it was not those impoverished or victimized by commerce who were most deeply involved in the Awakening; rather, it was those most impatient and ambitious and most recently implicated in "capitalistic" activities of one sort or another and as yet unacculturated to them who needed the moral reassurance and moral restraints for their behavior offered by the New Light message.[28] People out of joint with their culture—on the move and challenging the existing social hierarchy—required new criteria other than the traditional visible means of determining status and place in the community. "New births" that transcended all man-made measures of worth not only justified new activities but undermined the existing structures of the social and ecclesiastical order.

By challenging clerical unity, shattering the communal churches, and cutting people loose from ancient religious bonds, the Great Awakening represented in one way or another a massive defiance of traditional authority. The logic of Protestantism was drawn out further than ever before. Revivalist clergymen urged the people to trust only in "self-examination" and their own private judgments, even though "your Neighbours growl against you, and reproach you." Some New Lights went so far as to assert the "absolute Necessity for every Person to act singly . . . as if there was not another human Creature upon Earth." The burden of people's new religious attachments now rested clearly on themselves and their individual decisions.[29] Such conditional loyalties could contribute little to the deferential faith and obedience on which the colonists' monarchical social order ultimately rested. And thus, the Awakening's religious challenge to established authority inevitably but indirectly prepared many Americans for the subsequent political challenge that would become the American Revolution.

There were many other religious expressions of deep-lying social developments in these years. The New Divinity movement—the extreme Calvinist movement that eventually came to dominate half the Congregational ministerial posts in New England—was, for example, a response in part to the rapidly growing population of New England.[30] By midcentury, after three generations of dividing and subdividing family land holdings, many successful New England farmers found themselves without sufficient land to satisfy their sons.[31] Many of them provided capital and watched thousands upon thousands of their children set out for new and distant places, some as far away as Florida and the lower Mississippi but most to other areas of New England—to the Berkshires, to Maine, and up the Connecticut River to what became Vermont. Others, however, sought to send more of their sons to college. Since the two existing New England colleges, Harvard and Yale, were incapable of absorbing the increasing numbers, there were increased demands for new colleges to be established in the west—demands that eventually resulted in the founding of Amherst and Williams in the post-Revolutionary years.

In the meantime, many ordinary farmers did manage to place their sons in Harvard or Yale, and a high proportion of these sons became ministers who eventually constituted a substantial part of the evangelical and particularly the New Divinity movement. Indeed, a vast majority of the New Divinity clergy were from modest or obscure social backgrounds, as evidenced by their ranking as entering students at Harvard and Yale—a ranking that was essentially based on the social status of the students' families. By midcentury many of highest ranked students at Harvard and Yale were rejecting the ministry for alternative opportunities in other professions. Consequently, students from modest or obscure backgrounds came to make up an increasing proportion of the Congregational clergy of New England; in fact, these students from lowly or middling origins in time came to constitute a very significant majority (seven out of ten) of those Congregational ministers who became New Lights during the Awakening. And of these New Light clergymen the most modest in origins and the most likely to take posts in the most obscure areas of western New England were those who were identified with the New Divinity movement. Not only were these ministers from humble social backgrounds eager to promote the ideal of equality that became so important in the Revolution (as college students, for example, they were instrumental in abolishing class ranking at Harvard and Yale on the eve of the Revolution), but they became deeply involved in reform movements of the early Republic.[32]

Elsewhere it was the same: far-reaching and profound social developments were manifesting themselves in important midcentury religious movements. The transformation of the Society of Friends that took place in these years was at bottom a response to fundamental social changes. The Society had begun in the seventeenth society as an enthusiastic sect that appealed largely to lowly and middling social groups. By the mid-eighteenth century, however, the Society had increasingly compromised with the world, had grown and prospered, and in Pennsylvania at least had become an aristocracy dominating social, political, and economic life. In reaction, some Friends sought to recover some of the Society's original ascetic and sectarian qualities that had been lost since the seventeenth century. They sought to withdraw the Society from the world in order to purify it and then return it to the world as a reforming sect—promoting philanthropic projects and humanitarian reform, including abolishing slavery, providing schooling for poor children, and sending missions to the Indians. At the same time, the Society transformed its membership by disowning those Quakers who were unwilling to live up to the Society's reforming ideals and by recruiting new converts like Moses Brown of Providence, Rhode Island, from the growing middling ranks of colonial society. Many of these new Quaker converts renounced the aristocratic world of leisure, luxury, and gentility and devoted themselves to the reform and improvement of ordinary people. Brown, for example, eventually became a celebrated middle-class reformer—a vegetarian advocate, a temperance booster, an opponent of slavery, a promoter of practical education for common people, and a developer of manufacturing and industry.[33]

As newly rising middling groups were resolving the problems of their lives through religion, so too were the topmost ranks of the society. With the growth of gentility in the mid-eighteenth century and the increasing search for distinction more and more people with aristocratic aspirations moved into the sanctuary of the Church of England. Although the Anglican church often appealed to the poorest and most powerless of the colonists, as the king's church it was also especially attractive to the top of the social scale—to royal officials and other elites and those who dreamed of becoming elites. Amidst the disarray and confusion of the Great Awakening the Church of England appeared as a refuge in a storm and consequently gained numerous new adherents. By the eve of the Revolution there, were 400 Anglican congregations in the North American colonies, and in New England at least the church seemed poised to make further inroads into the Puritan establishment.[34] Everywhere in New England, as elsewhere, religion revealed the tensions of a changing society.

In this context we can understand the conflicting responses of the orthodox Calvinist clergy of New England to varying social and theological circumstances. Some ministers had to fend off the Anglican threat to their congregations from without; at same time, however, others had to worry about the possibility of subversion from within their Congregational ranks by New Light evangelicals. The direction of the threat depended ultimately on the kind of congregation the clergyman had. If the minister's congregation was made up of successful but ordinary people of modest origins just probing the fringes of respectability or gentility, then his concern had to be with the attractions of the New Lights. But if his congregation was made up of very wealthy and genteel people—merchants or professionals—who were moving on the edges not of respectability but of the highest circles of the local aristocracy, then his concern had to be with the temptations of Anglicanism.

Liberal Congregationalism, which eventually led to Unitarianism, developed in part as a response to this threat posed by Anglicanism.[35] By midcentury there were more and more established well-to-do and genteel New Englanders who were uncomfortable with too much Calvinist enthusiasm for public confession, depravity, and human helplessness in the face of God's sovereignty. Puritan ministers with such congregations had to find some sort of fine middle line—a supernatural rationalism that would avoid the embarrassing enthusiasm of fervent Calvinism and yet would be orthodox enough to avoid slipping into the Arminianism of Anglicanism.

Jonathan Mayhew, who took over the wealthy ministry of West Church in Boston because the previous occupant had upped and converted to Anglicanism, was faced with just such a congregation. The members of West Church were well-to-do arrivistes, merchants and others who paid their minister better than any other Puritan minister in Massachusetts but expected in return a reasonable and respectable religion that did not make them bare their souls and wallow in sin. Mayhew's task was to meet the conflicting desires of his wealthy congregation. Through his liberal brand of Congregationalism and his fiery denunciations of Anglicanism—so passionate as to bewilder even his supporters—he sought to keep the ambitious members of his church from following their previous minister into the Church of England; he did so by offering them as much respectability, formality, and Arminian methods of self-salvation as was possible within Congregationalism. He allowed his parishioners their prosperity but at the same time condemned the luxury and avariciousness of the Anglican world that tempted them.[36]

These are some of the attempts that historians have made to demonstrate the different ways that religion reflected the social transformations of these years surrounding the Revolution. Yet ultimately these attempts do not do justice to the vitality of meaning religion had for many, if not most, people and to the radicalism of the changes the Revolution brought about in America's religious landscape. In just a few years the centuries-old traditions of religious orthodoxy and establishment, already weakened by New World circumstances and the Great Awakening, were finally destroyed, and modern Christian denominationalism was born. The Revolution released more religious energy and fragmented Christendom to a greater degree than had been seen since the upheavals of seventeenth-century England or perhaps since the Reformation.

Historians are just beginning to appreciate the extent of religious change that took place in the Revolution. We have always known about the Second Great Awakening, of course, but only recently are we beginning to get studies that concentrate on the Revolutionary years themselves and that attempt to understand how Americans got from the First to the Second Great Awakening.[37] The most important of these studies are several essays by Stephen A. Marini that grow out of his earlier book on the *Radical Sects of Revolutionary New England.*[38]

In both his essays and his book Marini is reluctant to assume any social determinants of religious activity, and thus he is not able to explain fully why religion developed the way it did in the Revolutionary era. Indeed, in his book he found that the members of the evangelical sects he studied in western New England were not socially or economically or politically deviant but instead were representative of the hill country communities they lived in. Hence, he concluded that "the decisive factor in the gathering of the sects was not social or economic or political; it was the intrinsic religious message of the founders broadcast in compelling evangelistic strategies to the settlers of the hill country." Yet because Marini's measure of social position is extremely crude—mere wealth holding—it cannot capture all those social and cultural nuances that separate one person from another; and because these settlers did not responded randomly to the evangelical message, we are still left with the problem of explaining why some persons did and others did not respond to it.[39] Still, his work is now the starting point for any further study of religion and the Revolution.

Basing his studies on the statistical findings of church historian Frederick Weis and of sociologists Roger Finke and Rodney Stark, Marini has uncovered such radical changes in religious growth and religious affiliation between 1760 and 1790 that he can only conclude that Americans of this period were experiencing what he calls a Revolutionary Revival.[40] No one before has ever so clearly and so positively identified the Revolutionary years themselves as a period of religious vitality and enthusiasm. Marini's work suggests that there were in fact no distinct First and Second Great Awakenings but instead one long period of evangelical revival from the mid-eighteenth century to the early decades of the nineteenth century. Everything about religion that we used to think happened later, in the early nineteenth century or in the Age of Jackson, actually had its beginnings in the Revolution or earlier, and much future research is likely to document and fill out this point. Thus, the Revolutionary years witnessed no decline in the American people's religiosity. Indeed, the total number of church congregations doubled between 1770 and 1790 and even outpaced the extraordinary growth of population in these years; and the people's religious feeling became stronger than ever, though now devoted to very different kinds of religious groups.[41]

The older state churches that had dominated colonial society for a century and a half—the Anglican, Congregational, and Presbyterian—were suddenly supplanted by new and in some cases unheard-of religious denominations and sects. As late as 1760, the two great European-like establishments—the Church of England in the South and the Puritan churches in New England—had accounted for more than 40% of all congregations in America. By 1790, however, that proportion of religious establishment had dropped below 25% and was threatened with further erosion.[42] At times Marini's description of the dramatic collapse of the age-old state traditions of orthodoxy and establishment in the face of new evangelical sectarian movements resembles Clark's account of the Revolution as "a civil war of religion." Only a war, it seems, could explain such a sudden turnabout in religious sentiment. Although Marini does not assess the sources of this collapse, he implies that it represented a radical shift in the American people's social relationships and cultural consciousness.

All the old eighteenth-century monarchical and aristocratic hierarchies, enfeebled and brittle to begin with, fell apart under the impact of long-developing demographic and economic forces. In thousands of different ways, connections that had held people together for centuries were strained and severed, and people were set loose in unprecedented numbers. The Revolution shattered traditional structures of authority, and common people increasingly discovered that they no longer had to accept the old distinctions that had separated them from the upper ranks of the gentry. Ordinary farmers, tradesmen, and artisans began to think they were as good as any gentleman and that they actually counted for something in the movement of events.[43] Not only were the people being equated with God, but half-literate ploughmen were being told (by the likes of Thomas Jefferson no less) that they had as much common or moral sense as learned professors.[44]

Historians, especially historians of religion, have spent a lot of ink trying to determine the ways in which the so-called Scottish Common Sense tradition influenced American Protestantism.[45] The entire endeavor seems much too mechanistic; it assumes that ideas such as those concerned with the theory of moral sense were reified entities that people self-consciously adopted or not. That may have been true of scholars in their studies, but it was not the way most people, including someone like Jefferson, got their ideas about common sense morality. Such notions were much too widespread in the eighteenth-century English-speaking world to have to come from a few books written by a few Scotsmen such as Francis Hutcheson and Adam Smith or for that matter by a few Englishmen such as Lord Shaftesbury and Bishop Butler. In fact, a few great minds do not all by themselves invent such ideas; the great thinkers of an age merely conceptualize and work into theoretical consistency thoughts and impulses that are prevalent in the culture. These eighteenth-century Common Sense ideas—that there was a natural social instinct or sympathy in people that linked them to others, and that there was a natural sense of right and wrong, a kind of moral gyroscope, in every person regardless of social position or education—met the needs of a democratizing society in which obscure ordinary people were for the first time in history contesting the superiority of their hitherto presumed betters.[46] They required a moral sense that did not depend on literacy or learning and a social instinct that would hold them together in the absence of the monarchical ties of blood and patronage that the Revolution had destroyed.

The Revolutionary decades were therefore filled with discussions of the ways Americans might relate to one another—it was a central issue of the Revolution.[47] Fraternity became as important to Revolutionary Americans as liberty and equality. Americans who had never read Thomas Reid or Francis Hutcheson nevertheless devoted an extraordinary amount of intellectual energy to describing the moral instincts of unlettered people and the natural affections and sympathy that people had for one another. The Enlightenment's stress on modern civility and common sense morality came together with the traditional message of Christian charity to make the decades following the Revolution a great era of benevolence and communitarianism. Figures as diverse as Jefferson, Samuel Hopkins, and Thomas Campbell told people that all they had to do in the world was to believe in one God and to love other people as themselves.[48]

While educated gentry formed new cosmopolitan connections, countless numbers of common people found comfort in the creation of new egalitarian and affective communities. From the Revolution on, all sorts of voluntary associations—from mutual aid societies to freemasonry—sprang up to meet the needs of newly detached individuals; but most important for ordinary folk was the remarkable growth of hitherto insignificant religious communities and the spectacular emergence of new sectarian groups.[49]

While nearly all of the major colonial churches either declined or failed to gain relative to other groups in the years between 1760 and 1790 (which helps explain many historians' notion of "a religious recession" in these years), the Methodists and Baptists multiplied by manyfold the number of their congregations during this period. The Baptists grew from 94 congregations in 1760 to 858 in 1790 to become the single largest religious denomination in America. The Methodists had no adherents at all in 1760, but by 1790 they had created over 700 congregations to rival in national numbers the older Congregational and Presbyterian churches. Organized nationally into circuits and locally into classes and served by uneducated itinerant preachers, the Methodist ecclesiastical structure and the revival it inspired became, writes Marini, "unquestionably the most important single religious development of the Revolutionary Revival."[50] But this growth in the numbers of these evangelical congregations with ties to the institutional churches of the former mother country, remarkable as it was, was less startling than the sudden emergence of new sects and utopian religious groups that no one had ever heard of before—Shakers, Universal Friends, Universalists, and a variety of other schismatics. As early as 1790, says Marini, revivalist groups of Baptists, New Light Presbyterians, and Methodists, together with numbers of splinter groups and utopian sects, had moved from the margins to the center of American society and thereby laid the foundations for nineteenth-century evangelical America. Almost overnight the entire religious culture was transformed.

Nowhere else in Christendom was religion so fragmented. Yet nowhere else was it so vital. American Protestantism was broken into a multiplicity of groups called denominations, none of which claimed a monopoly of orthodoxy yet out of whose competition emerged Christian truth. There was no religious situation like it in the western world.

The disintegration of traditional structures of authority opened new religious opportunities for the illiterate, the lowly, and the dependent. Both the Baptists and the Methodists encouraged public exhortation by women, and even the more conservative Protestant churches began emphasizing a new and special role for women in the process of redemption.[51] Religion was in fact the one public arena in which women could play a substantial part. By the time of the Revolution nearly 70% of church members of the New England churches were women, and in the decades following the Revolution this feminization of American Christianity only increased.[52] Some of the most radical sects, like Mother Ann Lee's Shakers and Jemima Wilkinson's Universal Friends, even allowed for female leadership; the Shakers, in fact, became the first American religious group to recognize formally the equality of the sexes at all levels of authority.[53]

The democratic revolution of these years made it possible for the most common and humble of people to assert themselves and their emotions and values in ways they could not have earlier. Genteel learning, formal catechism, even literacy no longer mattered as much as they had in the past, and the new religious groups were able to recruit converts from among hitherto untouched elements of the population. Under the influence of the new popular revivalistic sects, thousands of African American slaves became Christianized, and blacks, even black slaves, were able to become preachers and exhorters. In the 1780s and 90s a black preacher, Andrew Bryan, organized several Baptist churches in Georgia, including the first Baptist church that whites or blacks in Savannah had ever seen; and in the early nineteenth century a free black named Henry Evans founded the first Methodist church for whites and blacks in Fayetteville, North Carolina. Both the Baptists and the Methodists condemned slavery and welcomed blacks to full membership in their communion. In fact, in parts of the South the first Methodist adherents were black slaves; in Wilmington, North Carolina, for example, the first Methodist congregation formed in 1784 was all black. By 1800 nearly one out of three American Methodists was an African American. Mainly because whites eventually objected to integrated churches, African Americans like Methodist Richard Allen began organizing dozens of independent black congregations throughout much of America. During the first third of the nineteenth century, for example, blacks built in the city of Philadelphia alone fourteen churches of their own, twelve of them Methodist or Baptist. Although we know very little of the actual religious practices in the black churches, white observers emphasized praying, preaching, and especially singing as the central elements of black worship. The black churches stressed the expression of feelings and mixed African traditions with Christian forms, hymns, and symbols.[54]

But it was not just African Americans who brought more emotion to religion. Everywhere in America, among ordinary white folk as well as black, the open expression of religious feelings, along with singing, praying, and preaching, became more common than in the colonial period. The Revolution seems to have released torrents of popular religiosity and passion into American life—the extent of which we have just begun to measure. Visions, dreams, prophesies, and new emotion-soaked religious seekings acquired a new popular significance, and common people were freer than ever before to express publicly their hitherto repressed vulgar and superstitious notions. Divining rods, fortune-telling, astrology, treasure seeking, and folk medicine thrived publicly as they had not for a half century or more. Long-existing subterranean folk beliefs and fetishes emerged into the open and blended with traditional Christian practices to create a new popular religious syncretism—a subject attracting much current historical interest; witness, for example, John Brooke's remarkable investigations into the folk and magical origins of Mormonism.[55]

Yet this new religiosity, like other popular aspects of the culture, did not repudiate the reason and the ideals of the Enlightenment; instead, it absorbed and vulgarized them. The democratic revolution forged a new popular amalgam out of traditional folk beliefs and the literary culture of the gentry. Ordinary people became semi-enlightened and thought that they had suddenly become wise. Through newspapers, almanacs, tracts, chapbooks, periodicals, lectures, and other media, common people increasingly acquired smatterings of knowledge about things that hitherto had been the preserve of educated elites. And at the same time they were told that their newly acquired knowledge was as good as that possessed by those who were "college learnt."[56] Under such egalitarian circumstances, truth itself became democratized, and the borders the eighteenth century had painstakingly worked out between religion and magic, science and superstition, naturalism and supernaturalism, were blurred. Animal magnetism seemed as legitimate as gravity. Dowsing for hidden metals appeared as rational as the workings of electricity. Popular speculations about the lost tribes of Israel seemed as plausible as scholarly studies of the origins of the Indian mounds of the Northwest. And crude folk remedies were even thought to be as scientific as the bleeding cures of enlightened medicine.

The result was an odd mixture of credulity and skepticism among people. Where everything was believable, everything could be doubted. All claims to expert knowledge were suspect, and people tended to mistrust anything outside of their own immediate observation. Yet because people prided themselves on their shrewdness and believed that they now were capable of understanding so much, they could be easily impressed by what they did not comprehend. A few strange words spoken by a preacher, or hieroglyphics displayed on a document, or anything written in highfalutin language could carry great credibility. In such an atmosphere, hoaxes of various kinds and charlatanism and quackery in all fields flourished.[57]

Religion was powerfully affected by these popularizing developments. In the confusion of the Revolution's demographic and commercial changes, many ordinary people became seekers looking for signs and prophets and for new explanations for the bewildering experiences of their lives. They came together without gentry leadership anywhere they could—in fields, barns, taverns, or homes—to lay hands on one another, to bath each other's feet, to offer each other kisses of charity, to form new bonds of fellowship, to let loose their feelings both physically and vocally, and to Christianize a variety of folk rites. Mathews, Isaac, Marini, and others have captured some of this, but there is much more to be done.[58]

From the "love feasts" of the Methodists to the dancing ceremonies of the Shakers, isolated individuals found in the variety of evangelical "bodily exercises" ungenteel and sometimes bizarre but emotionally satisfying ways of relating to God and to each other. When there were no trained clergy to minister to the yearnings of these often lost men and women, they recruited leaders from among themselves. New half-educated enterprising preachers emerged to mingle exhibitions of book-learning with plain talk and appeals to every kind of emotionalism. Their revivalistic techniques were effective because such dynamic folk-like processes were better able to meet the needs of rootless egalitarian-minded men and women than were the static churchly institutions based on eighteenth-century standards of deference and elite monopolies of orthodoxy. These common people wanted a religion they could personally feel and freely express, and the evangelical denominations offered them that, usually with much enthusiastic folk music and hymn singing. Not only was the period 1775–1815 the golden age of hymn writing and singing in America, but it was also the period in which most religious folk music, gospels, and black spirituals first appeared. The radical Baptist Elias Smith by himself produced at least fifteen different editions of colloquial religious music between 1804 and 1817.[59]

Obviously, this religious enthusiasm tapped long-existing veins of folk culture, and many evangelical leaders had to struggle to keep the suddenly released popular passions under control. Some enthusiasts drew on folk yearnings that went back centuries, and in the new free environment of republican America saw the opportunity to establish long-desired utopian worlds in which all social distinctions would be abolished, diet would be restricted, and goods and sometimes women would be shared. Although we have many studies of these utopian groups in the nineteenth century, we have not always acknowledged how much a product of the Revolution and late eighteenth-century circumstances most of them were.

Thanks especially to the work of Marini and others, we are now better able to recognize the Revolutionary origins of this religious upheaval that became known as the Second Great Awakening. This long Awakening, like the democratic impulse of the Revolution, was very much a movement from below, fed by the passions of very ordinary people. To describe it, as some historians have done, as a conservative, antidemocratic movement is to miss its popular force and significance.[60] To be sure, some Congregational clergy in New England saw in evangelical Christianity a means by which Federalists might better control the social disorder resulting from the Revolution. But these Federalist clergy like Timothy Dwight scarcely comprehended, let alone were able to keep up with the surging emotional needs of people. Jon Butler's notion that the revivals and proliferation of churches encouraged a strengthening of authority or what he calls "republican hierarchicalism" seems to have the proportions of the story backwards.[61] Of course, there were extensive efforts to reverse the extreme fragmentation, and in time these efforts at establishing some evangelical order would develop into the middle-class discipline, self-improvement, and respectability that Daniel Walker Howe and Richard L. Bushman talk about.[62] But because the chauvinistic accounts of most early denominational historians tended to telescope this growth of refinement and organizational coherence in their particular churches, we have not always fully appreciated just how disorderly the denominations' origins were.[63] Evangelical authoritarianism and respectability were slow to develop out of the social confusion of the immediate post-Revolutionary decades. As Nathan O. Hatch points out, for example, it was at least a generation before the Methodists were able to tame and domesticate the evangelical camp meeting.[64]

In the South recent studies suggest that revivalism was more complicated than we have thought and that the evangelical religions were not as initially successful in recruiting communicants as we have often been led to believe. By 1790, according to Christine Leigh Heyrman, only about 14% of southern whites and less than 4% of blacks belonged to Baptist, Methodist, or Presbyterian churches, and much of this growth had come from the Scots-Irish migrations before the war and the collapse of Anglicanism following independence. The "evangelicals," she says, "had yet to show much strength among the South's large unchurched population, white or black." And the situation did not change much over the next quarter century. By 1815 "the combined membership of Baptists, Methodists, and Presbyterians inched up to just 17 percent of the white population and 8 percent of the black." Part of the explanation of slow growth came from the social disorder created by the war and migrations. But more important in limiting growth were the radical egalitarian and antipatriarchal impulses of the eighteenth-century evangelical religions. In 1784 the newly constituted Methodist Episcopal Church climaxed more than a decade of fierce antislavery preaching in America by enacting a rigorous set of rules designed to rid its membership of slaveholders. But such egalitarian and antislave sentiments could not be sustained: they did too much violence to the traditions and beliefs of ordinary southern whites. It was only a matter of months, in fact, that stiff opposition from the southern laity forced the Methodist leaders to back down and to repeal most of the new restrictions on slaveholding.

But even when the evangelical denominations made accommodations to slavery their growth among common southerners remained for decades slow and gradual. Ordinary southern farmers, according to Heyrman, steadily resisted the appeal of evangelical preachers, frightened by "the ways in which Baptists and Methodists struck at those hierarchies that lent stablility to their daily lives: the deference of youth to age; the submission of children to parents and women to men; the loyalties of individuals to family and kin above any other group; and the rule of reserve over emotion within each person. Because the Baptists and Methodists threatened the most fundamental ways in which ordinary people structured their neighborhoods, their households, and their very selves, these churches drew lay suspicion for nearly a century." In these curcumstances many evangelical leaders eventually concluded that "the ultimate success of evangelicalism in the South lay in appealing to those who confined the devil to hell, esteemed maturity over youth, put family before religious fellowship, upheld the superiority of white over black and of men over women, and prized their honor abouve all else." But even with these concessions to southern realities the earlier egalitarian and antipatriarchal impulses were never entirely lost, and southern evangelicalism became a complex mixture of disparate elements.[65]

Heyrman's impressive book certainly complicates and enriches our understanding of the origins of southern evangelicalism. Yet it does not deny, indeed, it supports, the view that social disorder may have been the most important circumstance lying behind the appeal of evangelical religion. It seems obvious that the system of slavery could not long tolerate social disorder; it necessarily shaped all dependency relationships in most southern households. As Rachel Klein has pointed out, even southern backcountry yeomen tended to incorporate slavery into their notion of family order.[66] The maintenance of slavery required a hierarchical southern social world that became increasingly differentiated from the dynamic and disorganized societies in the rest of America.

Because of slavery evangelical religion thus may have developed more slowly in the South. But elsewhere the situation was different. In the most disordered and fluid areas of the North and West the newly released religious yearnings of ordinary people often tended to overwhelm traditional religious instituions. Between 1803 and 1809, for example, more than half the Presbyterian clergy and church members of Kentucky were swept away by the torrents of popular revivalism.[67]

As a result of Donald G. Mathews's *Religion in the Old South* and especially of Nathan O. Hatch's *The Democratization of Christianity*, we can understand more clearly the dynamic and democratic character of this evangelical revolution. Both Mathews in his work, especially in his pathbreaking article on "The Second Great Awakening as an Organizing Process," and Hatch in his very important book assume a traditional aristocratic world that has fallen apart as a consequence of the Revolution and that has to be put back together by common ordinary people on new democratic terms.[68] Just as the people were taking over their governments, so, it was said, they should take over their churches. Christianity had to be republicanized. The people were their own theologians and had no need to rely on others to tell them what to believe. We must, declared the renegade Baptist Elias Smith in 1809, be "wholly free to examine for ourselves what is truth, without being bound to a catechism, creed, confession of faith, discipline or any rule excepting the scriptures."[69] From northern New England to southern Kentucky, Christian fundamentalists called for an end to priests, presbyters, associations, doctrines, confessions—anything and everything that stood between the people and Christ. The people were told that they were quite capable of running their own churches, and even clerical leaders of the conservative denominations like Presbyterian Samuel Miller were forced to concede greater and greater lay control.[70]

Everywhere, said the renegade Presbyterian Barton Stone—who was a product, as Hatch has correctly pointed out, not of the frontier but of the American Revolution—the people were "awakened from the sleep of ages" and saw "for the first time that they were responsible beings" who might even be capable of bringing about their own salvation.[71] Although Calvinists still tried to stress predestination, limited atonement, and the sovereignty of God, conversion more and more seemed to be within the grasp of all who desired it—a mere matter of letting go and trusting in Christ. By emphasizing free will and earned grace, the Methodists especially gathered in great numbers of souls and set the entire evangelical movement in a decidedly Arminian direction. The Universalists who promised salvation for everyone were widely condemned, but they were only starkly drawing out the logic implied by others.[72] Sin was no longer conceived as something inherent in the depravity of human beings but as a kind of failure of a person's will and thus fully capable of being eliminated by individual exertion. Even some of the Calvinist Presbyterians and Separate-Baptists felt compelled to soften their opposition to Arminianism in the face of the relentless challenges by free will believers; many of them came to believe, as Richard Rabinowitz has so brilliantly demonstrated, that the external moral behavior of people—their "character"— was more central to religious life than the introspective conversion of their souls.[73]

With ordinary people being told, as one preacher told them in 1806, that each individual was "considered as possessing in himself or herself an original right to believe and speak as their own conscience, between themselves and God, may determine," religion in America became much more personal and voluntary than it had ever been; and people were freer to join and change their religious affiliation whenever they wished.[74] They thus moved from one religious group to another in a continual search for signs, prophets, or millennial promises that would make sense of their disrupted lives. With no church sure of holding its communicants, competition among the sects became fierce. Each claimed to be right, called each other names, argued endlessly over points of doctrine, mobbed and stoned each other, and destroyed each other's meeting houses.

The result was a further fragmenting of Christianity. "All Christendom has been decomposed, broken in pieces" in this "fiery furnace of democracy," said a bewildered Harrison Gray Otis.[75] Not only were the traditional Old World churches fragmented, but the fragments themselves shattered in what seemed at times to be an endless process of fission. There were not just Presbyterians, but Old and New School Presbyterians, Cumberland Presbyterians, Springfield Presbyterians, Reformed Presbyterians, and Associated Presbyterians; not just Baptists, but General Baptists, Regular Baptists, Free Will Baptists, Separate Baptists, Dutch River Baptists, Permanent Baptists, and Two-Seed-in-the Spirit Baptists. Some individuals cut their ties completely with the Old World churches and gathered around a dynamic leader like Barton Stone or Thomas Campbell. Other seekers ended up forming churches out of single congregations, and still others simply listened in the fields to wandering preachers like the eccentric Methodist Lorenzo Dow, who in the single year of 1805 traveled some 10,000 miles.[76]

Some radical evangelicals even thought they could end what the young Joseph Smith, the founder of Mormonism, called "this war of words and tumult of opinions" among the sects by appealing to the Bible, and especially the New Testament, as the lowest common denominator of Christian belief.[77] The Scriptures were to be to democratic religion what the Constitution was to democratic politics—the fundamental document that would bind all the competitive American Christian sects together in one national communion. The biblical literalism of these years became, in fact, popular religion's ultimate concession to the Enlightenment—the recognition that religious truth now needed documentary proof. In that democratic age where all traditional authority was suspect, some concluded that individuals possessed only their own reason and the Scriptures—the "two witnesses," said Joseph Smith's grandfather, "that stand by the God of the whole earth."[78] Sects like the Shakers and later the Mormons came to believe that they needed some sort of literary evidence or written testimony to convince a skeptical world that their beliefs were not, as the Shakers were anxious to show, "cunningly devised fables" but rather manifestations of "the spirit of Eternal Truth."[79]

But, of course, reliance on the literalism of the Bible or on other literary evidence hardly stopped the confusion and fragmentation. Church publications and collections of testimonies proliferated, but there was no final authority, no supreme court of Christianity, to settle the interminable disputes among the sects over the Bible or any other testimony. And so the splintering went on.

In some areas, churches as such scarcely existed, and the traditional identification between religion and society, never very strong in America to begin with, now finally dissolved. The church no longer made any effort to embody the community, and it became for many little more than the building in which religious services were conducted. By concentrating on the saving of individual souls, the competing denominations essentially abandoned their traditional institutional and churchly responsibilities to organize the world here-and-now along godly lines. Church membership was based now not on people's position in the social hierarchy but on their evangelical fellowship. Consequently, the new evangelical denominations were less capable than the traditional eighteenth-century churches had been in identifying with the whole community and in encompassing a variety of social ranks within their membership.[80]

Despite religion's separation from society, however, some Americans thought that it was the only cohesive force holding the nation together— "the central attraction," said Lyman Beecher in 1815, "which must supply the deficiency of political affinity and interest."[81] Yet these new religious sects and movements not only Christianized American popular culture and brought many people together and prepared them for nineteenth-century middle-class respectability, but they also helped to legitimate the freedom and individualism of people and to make morally possible their commercial participation in an impersonal marketplace.[82] As Tocqueville pointed out, "The Americans combine the notions of Christianity and of liberty so intimately in their minds that it is impossible to make them conceive of the one without the other."[83] Conversion experiences did not leave people incapacitated and unworldly; indeed, their "new births" seemed to fit them better for the tasks of this world. Religion increased their energy as it restrained their liberty, got them on with their work as it disciplined their acquisitive urges; it gave them confidence that even self-interested individuals subscribed to absolute standards of right and wrong and thus could be trusted in market exchanges and contractual relationships. As William Breitenbach has so brilliantly argued, even the New Divinity movement within New England Calvinism, despite its strong repudiation of selfishness, ultimately grounded Samuel Hopkins's famous concept of universal disinterested benevolence on the enlightened self-interest of people, and thus set credible moral limits to their individualism and acquisitive behavior.[84]

From the disruptions and bewilderments of their lives many people could readily conclude that the world was on the verge of some great transformation—nothing less than the Second Coming of Christ and the Day of Judgment predicted in the Bible. As we have been told by a number of recent historians, millennialism of various kinds, both scholarly and popular, grew out of the turbulent Revolutionary decades at the end of the eighteenth and the beginning of the nineteenth centuries and became the means by which many justified and explained the great social changes of the period. In fact, the recent historical literature on Revolutionary millennialism is approaching in complexity and sophistication the finespun discussions eighteenth-century clergymen themselves had on the subject.[85]

Militant patriot clergy pictured the struggle against Britain optimistically as a means of bringing about the millennium and infused the political arguments of the Revolutionaries with a transcendent religious significance that tended to overwhelm the traditional pessimistic apocalyptic thinking about the coming end of the world. During the 1780s and 90s, however, all sorts of millennial theories, both pessimistic and optimistic, were vigorously debated. By the early nineteenth century, the optimistic interpretations had revived, and many of the Adventist beliefs took on a progressive character appropriate to a new improving American society.

Older pessimistic Christian beliefs in the millennium usually had assumed that Christ's coming would precede the establishment of a new kingdom of God. The literal advent of Christ would be forewarned by signs and troubles, culminating in a horrible conflagration in which everything would be destroyed. Christ would then rule over the faithful in a New Jerusalem for a thousand years until the final Day of Judgment. Those who held such premillennial beliefs generally saw the world as so corrupt and so evil that only the sudden and catastrophic intervention of Christ could create it anew. Although in post-Revolutionary America some fundamentalist sects clung to these older apocalyptic interpretations of the millennium, most of the leading American churches began to picture the Second Coming of Christ following rather than preceding the thousand years of glory and bliss.[86] And such an approaching age of perfection seemed to be beginning in America itself.

This new postmillennialism represented both a rationalizing of revelation and a Christianizing of the Enlightenment belief in secular progress. It was optimistic and even worldly; it promised not the sudden divine destruction of a corrupt world but a step-by-step human-directed progression toward perfection in this world. Since the United States was itself leading humanity toward the earth's final thousand years of bliss, millennial hopes came to focus on contemporary events occurring in America as signs of the approaching age of perfection—a perfection that would be brought about, some said, "not by miracles but by means," indeed, "BY HUMAN EXERTIONS."[87] Every move westward across the continent and every advance in material progress—even inventions and canal-building—were now interpreted in millennial terms. Such millennial beliefs identified the history of redemption with the history of the new Republic. They reconciled Christianity with American democracy, and they explained and justified the anxious lives and the awakened aspirations of countless numbers of ordinary Americans for whom the world had hitherto never offered any promise of improvement.

These, then, were the basic elements of the evangelical Protestantism that resulted from the American Revolution—a new unprecedented kind of popular Christianity for a new democratic society: a proliferation and splintering of sects, a complete separation between church and society, a weakening of clerical authority and a strengthening of lay control, a growing tendency toward Arminianism in the process of conversion, a blurring of theological distinctions and doctrines, and an increased emphasis on an activist and progressive postmillennialism. By the end of the second decade of the nineteenth century, the evangelical Protestantism of ordinary people had come to dominate American culture to an extent the Founding Fathers had never anticipated. Although America's religion was almost everywhere voluntary, lacking the coercive power of the state, the United States nevertheless had become the most thoroughly Christian nation in the world.

And the Revolution had been crucially responsible in creating this new religious situation, both by democratizing the society and releasing the latent evangelical energy of many common ordinary people. Although we may now sense the broad outlines of what happened religiously during the Revolutionary era, we do not yet have most of the data or the details. Modern biographies of many of the principal religious figures are missing; even careful studies of the rise of Methodism are lacking.[88] We have lots of studies of the separation of church and state, freedom of conscience, and the First Amendment, but as Stephen Marini correctly points out, we still do not have "a general overview of American religious development during the period, let alone a careful analysis of it."[89] If recent studies and works in progress are any indication, this neglect of religion and the American Revolution is about to end.

NOTES

1. The best recent survey of church-state relations in early America is Thomas J. Curry, *The First Freedoms: Church and State in America to the Passage of the First Amendment* (New York, 1986).

2. Evarts B. Greene, *Religion and the State: The Making and Testing of an American Tradition* (Ithaca, 1959), 80.

3. Among historians' repeated and sometimes desperate attempts to show that the founding fathers were really religious, the most recent is Ellis Sandoz, *A Government of Laws: Political Theory, Religion, and the American Founding* (Baton Rouge, La., 1990). "If Thomas Jefferson was a believer," writes Sandoz, "who disbelieved? The answer that is persuasively suggested is *nobody*. The founders were united in what John Adams long after called the general principles of Christianity, . . . which for him meant especially the Ten Commandments and the Sermon on the Mount" (149). It is true that Jefferson was no atheist, but he had no interest whatsoever in organized Christianity and scarcely possessed a Christian sensibility in any traditional meaning of that term. If enlightened gentlemen like Jefferson and Franklin praised Jesus, it was, as Jon Butler says, not because

of any belief in Christ's divinity but because they found value, as Jefferson put it, in Christ's "universal philanthrophy, not only to kindred and friends, but also to all mankind." See Butler, "Coercion, Miracle, Reason: Rethinking the American Religious Experience in the Revolutionary Age," in Ronald Hoffman and Peter J. Albert, eds., *Religion in a Revolutionary Age* (Charlottesville, Va., 1994), 22.

4. Henry May, *The Enlightenment in America* (New York, 1976), 72–73; Jon Butler, *Awash in a Sea of Faith: Christianizing the American People* (Cambridge, Mass., 1990), 195–96, 214–15; George H. Knoles,"The Religious Ideas of Thomas Jefferson," *Mississippi Valley Historical Review*, 30 (1943–44), 194; Nicholas Collins, "An Essay on those Inquiries in Natural Philosophy Which at Present are Most Beneficial to the United States of North America," American Philosphical Society, *Transactions*, 2 (1793), vii

5. Morgan, "The American Revolution Considered as an Intellectual Movement," in Arthur M. Schlesinger, Jr., and Morton White, eds., *Paths of American Thought* (Boston, 1963), 11–33.

6. Bernard Bailyn, *Faces of Revolution: Personalities and Themes in the Struggle for American Independence* (New York, 1990), 104; Jon Butler, *Awash in a Sea of Faith*, 195.

7. Russel B. Nye, *The Cultural Life of the New Nation, 1776–1830* (New York, 1960), 230; Franklin Hamlin Littell, *From State Church to Pluralism: A Protestant Interpretation of Religion In American History* (New York, 1962), 32.

8. On deism see Kerry S. Walters, *The American Deists: Voices of Reason and Dissent in the Early Republic* (Lawrence, Kansas, 1992).

9. John W. Chandler, "The Communitarian Quest for Perfection," in Stuart C. Henry, ed., *A Miscellany of American Christianity* (Durham, N.C., 1963), 58; William Warren Sweet, *The Story of Religions in America* (New York, 1930), 322; Douglas H. Sweet, "Church Vitality and the American Revolution: Historiographical Consensus and Thoughts towards a New Perspective," *Church History*, 45 (1976), 342, 344.

10. Jon Butler stresses the low proportion of church members or communicants among the eighteenth-century colonists while Patricia U. Bonomi and Peter R. Eisenstadt emphasize the high proportion of church attendance. Butler, "Coercion, Miracle, Reason," in Hoffman and Albert, eds., *Religion in a Revolutionary Age*, 19; Bonomi and Eisenstadt, "Church Adherence in the Eighteenth-Century British American Colonies," *William and Mary Quarterly*, 3d ser., 39 (1982), 245–86.

11. Bernard Bailyn et al., *The Great Republic*, 4th ed. (Lexington, Mass., 1992), 1: 174.

12. Miller, "From the Covenant to the Revival," in *Nature's Nation* (Cambridge, Mass., 1967).

13. Alan Heimert, *Religion and the American Mind from the Great Awakening to the Revolution* (Cambridge, Mass., 1966).

14. Hatch, *The Democratization of American Christianity* (New Haven, 1989), 221.

15. William G. McLoughlin, "The American Revolution as a Religious Revival: 'The Millennium in One Country,' " *New England Quarterly*, 40 (1967), 99–110; McLoughlin, " 'Enthusiasm for Liberty': The Great Awakening as the Key to the Revolution," in Jack P. Greene and William G. McLoughlin, *Preachers and Politicians: Two Essays on the Origins of the American Revolution* (Worcester, Mass., 1977), 47–73.

16. Stout, "Religion, Communications, and the Ideological Origins of the American Revolution," *William and Mary Quarterly*, 3d ser., 34 (1977), 519–41.

17. Patricia U. Bonomi, *Under the Cope of Heaven: Religion, Society, and Politics in Colonial America* (New York, 1986). In a recent article Bonomi reached this conclusion: "We may stop well short of proposing religious differences as the primary 'cause' of the American Revolution. It may nonetheless be asserted that the state of mind in which American colonials moved toward separation is nowhere better seen than in the realm of religion." Bonomi, "Religious Dissent and the Case for American Exceptionalism," in Hoffman and Albert, eds., *Religion in a Revolutionary Age*, 51.

18. J.C.D. Clark, *The Language of Liberty, 1660–1832: Political Discourse and Social Dynamics in the Anglo-American World* (Cambridge, Eng., 1993).

19. Ibid., 305.

20. Arthur L. Cross, *The Anglican Episcopate and the American Colonies* (New York, 1902); and Carl Bridenbaugh, *Mitre and Sceptre* (New York, 1962).

21. Jon Butler, "Enthusiasm Described and Decried: The Great Awakening as Interpretive Fiction," *Journal of American History*, 69 (1982), 324.

22. John M. Murrin, "No Awakening, No Revolution? More Counterfactual Speculations," *Reviews in American History*, 11 (1983), 161–171.

23. Joan Rezner Gunderson, "The Myth of the Independent Virginia Vestry," *Historical Magazine of the Protestant Episcopal Church*, 44 (1975), 133–141; Gunderson, *The Anglican Ministry in Virginia, 1723–1766: A Study of a Social Class* (New York, 1989); Rhys Isaac, *The Transformation of Virginia 1740–1790*, (Chapel Hill, 1982), 173; Christine Leigh Heyrman, *Southern Cross: The Beginnings of the Bible Belt* (New York, 1997), 13.

24. Richard L. Bushman, *From Puritan to Yankee: Character and the Social Order in Connecticut, 1690–1763* (New York, 1967), 107–95.

25. John L. Brooke, *The Heart of the Commonwealth: Society and Political Culture in Worcester County, Massachusetts, 1713–1861* (Cambridge, Eng., 1989), 69, 70, 83–84.

26. John C. Miller, "Religion, Finance, and Democracy in Massachusetts," *New England Quarterly*, 6 (1933), 29–58.

27. Heimert, *Religion and the American Mind*, 55.

28. Brooke, *In the Heart of the Commonwealth*, 90.

29. Bonomi, *Under the Cope of Heaven*, 158–160; Brooke, *Heart of the Commonwealth*, 68, 74–76, 83, 187–88.

30. Joseph A. Conforti, *Samuel Hopkins and the New Divinity Movement: Calvinism, the Congregational Ministry, and Reform in New England Between the Great Awakenings* (Grand Rapids, Mich., 1981), 1–22. On the intellectual connection between the New Divinity movement and the Revolution, see Mark Valeri, "The New Divinity and the American Revolution," *William and Mary Quarterly*, 46 (1989), 741–69.

31. Philip J. Greven, *Four Generations: Population, Land, and Family in Colonial Andover* (Ithaca, 1970), 246–51.

32. Conforti, *Hopkins and New Divinity Movement*, 9–58, 175–95.

33. Sydney V. James, *A People Among Peoples* (Cambridge, Mass., 1963); Jack D. Marietta, *The Reformation of American Quakerism, 1748–1783* (Philadelphia, 1984); Mack Thompson, *Moses Brown: Reluctant Reformer* (Chapel Hill, 1962).

34. Frederick V. Mills, "Anglican Expansion in Colonial America, 1761–1775," *Historical Magazine of the Protestant Episcopal Church* (1970), 315–24.

35. Conrad Wright, *The Beginnings of Unitarianism in America* (Boston, 1955).

36. Charles W. Akers, *Called Unto Liberty: A Life of Jonathan Mayhew, 1720–1766* (Cambridge, Mass., 1964).

37. See especially Douglas H. Sweet, "Church Vitality and the American Revolution: Historiographic Consensus and Thoughts Towards a New Perspective," *Church History,* 45 (1976), 343–57

38. Stephen A. Marini, *Radical Sects of Revolutionary New England* (Cambridge, Mass., 1982); Marini, "Religion, Politics, and Revolution," in Hoffman and Albert, eds., *Religion in a Revolutionary Age,* 184–217; Marini, "The Religious World of Daniel Shays," in Robert A. Gross, ed., *In Debt to Shays: The Bicentennial of an Agrarian Rebellion* (Charlottesville, Va. 1993), 239–277; and Marini, "The Revolutionary Revival in America," (unpublished paper). On religion in the Revolution, see also Brooke, *In the Heart of the Commonwealth,* 176–88.

39. Marini, *Radical Sects,* 95–101.

40. Marini cites the following works: Frederick Lewis Weis, *The Colonial Churches and Colonial Clergy of New England* (Lancaster, Mass., 1936); Weis, *The Colonial Churches and Colonial Clergy of the Middle and Southern Colonies, 1607–1776* (Lancaster, Mass., 1938); Weis, *The Colonial Clergy of Maryland, Delaware, and Georgia* (Lancaster, Mass., 1950); Weis, *The Colonial Clergy of Virginia, North Carolina, and South Carolina* (Boston, 1955); Weis, *The Colonial Clergy of New York, New Jersey, and Pennsylvania* (Lancaster, Mass. 1957); Roger Finke and Rodney Stark, "American Religion, 1776–1860: A Statistical View," *Sociological Analysis,* 49 (Spring, 1988), 39–51; Finke and Stark, "How the Upstart Sects Won America: 1776–1850," *Journal for the Scientific Study of Religion,* 38 (1989), 27–44; and Finke and Stark, *The Churching of America, 1776–1990* (New Brunswick, N.J., 1992). Marini works with the numbers of congregations, which are much more easily determined, rather than attempting to extrapolate from the number of congregations the actual number of church members. For other attempts to calculate church membership in the eighteenth century and the Revolutionary era see Bonomi and Eisenstadt, "Church Adherence in the Eighteenth-Century British American Colonies"; and Heyrman, *Southern Cross,* 261–66.

41. Marini, "Religion, Politics, and Ratification," in Hoffman and Albert, eds., *Religion in a Revolutionary Age,* 188–199, and Marini, "Revolutionary Revival," 15.

42. Marini, "Religion, Politics, and Ratification," in Hoffman and Albert, eds., *Religion in a Revolutionary Age,* 193–96, and Marini, "Revolutionary Revival," 18–19

43. See Nathan O. Hatch, *The Democratization of American Christianity* (New Haven, 1989), for the Revolution's popular effects on religion.

44. Koch, *Religion of the American Enlightenment,* 181; Jefferson to Peter Carr, 10 Aug. 1787, in A. A. Lipscomb and A. E. Bergh, eds., *The Writings of Thomas Jefferson* (Washington, D.C., 1903–04), 6, 257–58.

45. Sydney E. Ahlstrom, "The Scottish Philosophy and American Theology," *Church History,* 24 (1955), 257–72; Henry F. May, *The Enlightenment In*

202 THE STAGES OF AMERICAN PROTESTANTISM

America (New York, 1976), 307–62; Mark. A Noll, "Common Sense Traditions and American Evangelical Thought," *American Quarterly,* 37 (1985), 216–38.

46. Thomas Reid, the Scottish moral sense theorist, declared that it was wise to trust "the vulgar" or the "unlearned" who "are guided by the dictates of nature" and who "express what they are conscious of concerning the operations of their own mind" when they "believe that the object which they distinctly perceive certainly exists." Noll, "Common Sense Traditions," *American Quarterly,* 37 (1985), 218.

47. On attaching people to one another see Gordon S. Wood, *The Radicalism of the American Revolution* (New York, 1992), 215–25.

48. On the similarity of the messages of Jefferson, Hopkins, and Campbell see H. Shelton Smith, Robert T. Handy, and Lefferts A. Loetscher, *American Christianity: An Historical Interpretation with Representative Documents* (New York, 1960), 1: 516, 543–44, 579–86.

49. On philanthropic societies see Conrad Edick Wright, *The Transformation of Charity in Postrevolutionary New England* (Boston, 1992); on Freemasonry see Steven C. Bullock, *Revolutionary Brotherhood: Freemasonry and the Transformation of the American Social Order, 1730–1840* (Chapel Hill, 1996).

50. Marini, "Revolutionary Revival," 45–46; Hatch, *Democratization of Christianity,* 81–93.

51. Ruth Bloch, *Visionary Republic: Millennial Themes in American Thought, 1756–1800* (Cambridge, Eng., 1985), 225; Hatch, *Democratization of Christianity,* 78–80.

52. Ann Douglas, *The Feminization of American Culture* (New York, 1977); Elaine Forman Crane, "Religion and Rebellion: Women of Faith in the American War for Independence," in Hoffman and Albert, eds., *Religion in a Revolutionary Age,* 80.

53. Marini, "Revolutionary Revival," 28; Stephen J. Stein, *The Shaker Experience in America: A History of the United Society of Believers* (New Haven, 1992), 43, 48–49.

54. Hatch, *Democratization of Christianity,* 102–113; Albert J. Raboteau, *Slave Religion: The "Invisible Institution" in the Antebellum South* (New York, 1978); Mechal Sobel, *Trabelin' On: The Slave Journey to an Afro-Baptist Faith* (Princeton, 1988); Sylvia R. Frey, " 'The Year of Jubilee Is Come': Black Christianity in the Plantation South in Post-Revolutionary America," in Hoffman and Albert, eds., *Religion in a Revolutionary Age,* 87–124, esp. 97, 99, 103, 112. Charles Joyner, *Down By the Riverside: A South Carolina Slave Community* (Urbana, Ill., 1984); Margaret Washington Creel, *"A Peculiar People": Slave Religion and Community Culture Among the Gullahs* (New York, 1988); and Paul E. Johnson, ed., *African-American Christianity: Essays in History* (Berkeley, 1994).

55. John L. Brooke, *The Refiner's Fire: The Making of Mormon Cosmology, 1644–1844* (Cambridge, Eng., 1994). Even enlightened Freemasonry became more of a religious institution in the decades following the Revolution. See C. Bullock, *Revolutionary Brotherhood,* 163–83.

56. Hatch, *Democratization of Christianity,* 45.

57. Wood, *Radicalism of the Revolution,* 361–62.

58. Donald G. Mathews, *Religion in the Old South* (Chicago, 1977).

59. Marini, *Radical Sects,* 158; Hatch, *Democratization of Christianity,* 129, 146–161.

60. Dixon Ryan Fox, "The Protestant Counter-Reformation in America," *New York History*, 16 (1935), 19–35; Clifford S. Griffin, "Religious Benevolence as Social Control, 1815–1860," *Mississippi Valley Historical Review*, 44 (1957), 423–44; Charles I. Foster, *An Errand of Mercy: The Evangelical United Front, 1790–1837* (Chapel Hill, 1960).

61. Butler's own evidence shows that the Baptists were dividing and subdividing even as they attempted to organize themselves. Butler, *Awash in a Sea of Faith*, 276. Yet Butler is surely right to stress the way religious denominations built powerful institutions to harness the religious authority abandoned by the state at the Revolution—an important theme that needs more study. Ibid., 285; Hatch, *Democratization of Christianity*, 95.

62. Daniel Walker Howe, "The Evangelical Movement and Political Culture in the North during the Second Party System," *Journal of American History*, 77 (1991), 1216–39; Richard L. Bushman, *The Refinement of America: Persons, Houses, Cities* (New York, 1992).

63. Hatch, *Democratization of Christianity*, 97, 272n. For some of the evangelical sects' initial efforts at establishing order, see Marini, *Radical Sects*, 116–35; Hatch, *Democratization of Christianity*, 201–206.

64. Hatch, *Democratization of Christianity*, 52.

65. Heyrman, *Southern Cross*, 23–27, 255–56. On the conservatism of southern white laymen in the face of the radical evangelical appeal see also Rachel N. Klein, *Unification of a Slave State: The Rise of the Planter Class in the South Carolina Backcountry, 1760–1808* (Chapel Hill, 1990); and Stephenie McCurry, *Masters of Small Worlds: Yeoman Households, Gender Relations, and the Political Culture of the Antebellum South Carolina Low Country* (New York, 1995).

66. Klein, *Unification of a Slave State*, 271.

67. Ralph E. Morrow, "The Great Revival, the West, and the Crisis of the Church," in John Francis McDermott, ed., *the Frontier Re-Examined* (Urbana, Ill., 1967), 78.

68. Donald G. Mathews, "The Second Great Awakening as an Organizing Process, 1780–1830: An Hypothesis," *American Quarterly*, 21 (1969), 23–43; Hatch, *Democratization of Christianity*.

69. Smith, *The Loving Kindness of God Displayed in the Triumph of Republicanism in America . . .* (n.p., 1809), 27. For Mathew's article, see *American Quarterly*, 21 (1969), 23–43.

70. Belden C. Lane, "Presbyterian Republicanism: Miller and the Eldership as an Answer to Lay-Clerical Tensions," *Journal of Presbyterian History*, 56 (1978), 311–14.

71. John Rogers, *The Biography of Elder Barton Warren Stone . . .* (Cincinnati, 1847), 45; Hatch, *Democratization of Christianity*, 70.

72. For the appeal of Universalism among workingmen in Philadelphia see Ronald Schultz, "God and Workingmen: Popular Religion and the Formation of Philadelphia's Working Class, 1790–1830," in Hoffman and Albert, *Religion in a Revolutinary Age*, 138.

73. Marini, *Radical Sects*, 88; Marini, "Revolutionary Revival," 53–54; Richard Rabinowitz, *The Spiritual Self in Everyday Life: The Transformation of Personal Religious Experience in Nineteenth-Century New England* (Boston, 1989), 3–151.

74. Abel M. Sargent, *The Destruction of the Beast in the Downfall of Sectarianism . . .* (n.p., 1806), 15.

75. Otis, quoted in Josiah Quincy, *The History of Harvard University* (Cambridge, 1840), 2: 663.

76. On Dow see Charles C. Sellers, *Lorenzo Dow: The Bearer of the Word* (New York, 1928); and Hatch, *Democratization of Christianity,* 36–40. On these religious developments see in general Whitney R. Cross, *The Burned-Over District: The Social and Intellectual History of Enthusiastic Religion in Western New York, 1800–1850* (New York, 1965); John R. Boles, *The Great Revival, 1787–1805* (Lexington, Ky., 1972); Donald G. Mathews, *Religion in the Old South* (Chicago, 1977); and Anne C. Loveland, *Southern Evangelicals and the Social Order, 1800–1860* (Baton Rouge, 1980).

77. Joseph Smith, *The Pearl of Great Price* (Salt Lake City, 1974), 47.

78. Asael Smith (1799), in William Mulder and A. Russell Mortensen, eds., *Among the Mormons: Historic Accounts by Contemporary Observers* (New York, 1958), 24.

79. Stein, *Shaker Experience,* 80–86.

80. Donald M. Scott, *From Office to Profession: The New England Ministry, 1750–1850* (Philadelphia, 1978), 34, 47–48.

81. Lyman Beecher, *On the Importance of Assisting Young Men of Piety and Talents in Obtaining an Education for the Gospel Ministry* (New York, 1815), 16.

82. Some historians have questioned Hatch's interpretation in his *Democratization of Christianity* on the grounds that he equates democratization with the rise of capitalism. See, for example, Paul E. Johnson, "Democracy, Patriarchy, and American Revivals, 1780–1830," *Journal of Social History,* 24 (1990–91), 843–49. While the development of a market society was certainly a dominant force in the early Republic, and was accelerated if not made possible by the social fragmentation coming out of the Revolution, there was no necessary connection between being evangelically religious and being a supporter of capitalism; indeed, some of the most religious people were critics of the emerging market world. See Jama Lazerow, *Religion and the Working Class in Antebellum America* (Washington, D.C., 1995), which argues that religion decisively affected the nature of antebellum labor protest.

83. Alexis de Tocqueville, *Democracy in America,* ed. Phillips Bradley (New York, 1956; 1st ed. 1835), 1: 306.

84. William Breitenbach, "Unregenerate Doings: Selflessness and Selfishness in New Divinity Theology," *American Quarterly,* 34 (1982), 479–502. See also James D. Berman, "The Social Utility of Wicked Self-Love: Calvinism, Capitalism and Public Policy in Revolutionary New England," *Journal of American History,* (1995), 965–98.

85. On millennialism see J. F. Maclear, "The Republic and the Millennium," Elwyn A. Smith, ed., *The Religion of the Republic* (Philadelphia, 1971), 183–216; David E. Smith, "Millenarian Scholarship in America," *American Quarterly,* 17 (1965) 535–49; Ernest Lee Tuveson, *Redeemer Nation: The Idea of America's Millennial Role* (Chicago, 1968); James West Davidson, *The Logic of Millennial Thought: Eighteenth-Century New England* (New Haven, 1977); Sacvan Bercovitch, *The American Jeremiad* (Madison, Wis., 1978); J.F.C. Harrison, *The Second Coming: Popular Millenarianism, 1780–1850* (New Brunswick, N.J., 1979); Melvin B. Endy, Jr., "Just War, Holy War, and Millennialism in Revolutionary America," *William and Mary Quarterly,* 3d ser., 42 (1985), 3–25; and Ruth

Bloch, *Visionary Republic: Millennial Themes in American Thought, 1756–1800* (Cambridge, Eng., 1985).

86. Bloch, *Visionary Republic*, 217; Davidson, *Logic of Millenial Thought*, 275–76.

87. Timothy Dwight (1813) and Elephalet Nott (1806) cited in Davidson, *Millenial Thought* 275, 276.

88. Hatch, *Democratization of Christianity*, 220–26.

89. Marini, "Revolutionary Revival," 10. For another attempt to connect religion and the Revolution, see Mark A. Noll, "The American Revolution and Protestant Evangelicalism," *Journal of Interdisciplinary History*, 23 (1993), 615–38. The closest we have to an overview is Edwin S. Gaustad's brief book *Neither King nor Prelate: Religion and the New Nation, 1776–1826* (Grand Rapids, Mich., 1993).

7

PROTESTANTISM, VOLUNTARISM, AND PERSONAL IDENTITY IN ANTEBELLUM AMERICA

◈ ◈ ◈

Daniel Walker Howe

"NOW THAT THE REPUBLIC—the *res publica*—has been settled, it is time to look after the *res privata*—the private state." So declared Henry David Thoreau in 1854.[1] Many of his neighbors, on this much at least, agreed with the great iconoclast and undertook their own brave experiments with shaping a new personal life for themselves. In this respect, the individualism of Walden Pond may serve as a symbol for a mass movement: of innumerable quests for new identities, for new births, to reexamine past lives, to reshape human nature. Although many evangelists undertook to organize and collectivize this movement, it remained at heart voluntary and individual, a matter of personal choices.

The Declaration of Independence proclaimed that all men had an unalienable right to the pursuit of happiness. In practice, Americans defined this pursuit not only in economic and political terms but also in moral and spiritual ones. The decades following the American Revolution and establishment of the Constitution witnessed an extraordinarily rich and varied experimentation by the people of the new nation with new lifestyles, faiths, and manners. Much of this seeking took religious form. In the instructive hyperbole of Nathan Hatch, it was "an age when most ordinary Americans expected almost nothing from government institutions and almost everything from religious ones." [2] Not only were many versions of Christianity transplanted to America from overseas, but indigenous religious movements also sprang up. As Jon Butler has written, "To be religious in America [in this period] was not only to make choices, but to choose among astonishing varieties of religion created in America and duplicated nowhere else." [3] The scholarship of recent years has enriched our understanding and appreciation for this great outburst of energy in all its diversity.

Most of American religion during antebellum times was Protestant, though heavy immigration of Roman Catholics during the 1840s made theirs the largest single denomination by the end of the decade, provoking a strong nativist reaction. This essay will treat American Protestantism between about 1815 and the 1850s. It will be historiographical, in the sense that it will discuss recent scholarly writings, but it will also be historical, in the sense that it will use these works in an attempt to fashion a coherent interpretation of the subject. Though the historians who have written on it have approached the subject in very different ways, and have sometimes disagreed with each other, I have tried to discern the outlines of a pattern within which their works can be be comprehended. More importantly, I think that this pattern helps us understand the lives of the antebellum Americans whom we study. The essay must be selective, for there has been a veritable explosion of writing about antebellum Protestantism; I shall pay most attention to works published since 1987. The need for selectivity is all the greater because I wish to show that American Protestantism can only be understood if it is placed within a wider cultural context, which requires relating religion to politics, moral philosophy, and polite culture. But if my subject is broadened in some respects it is narrowed in others: I say little about ethnicity, race, gender, Canada, the South, foreign missions, or the market revolution, important as all of them are, because those themes have been assigned to other contributors.

Voluntarism and Self-Discipline

That white Americans of the antebellum period were freer and more individualistic than people had ever been before is a historical commonplace, and a number of powerful explanations have been offered to account for it. What these people chose to do with their freedom has been studied much less, but it is the subject of this essay. The people of that extraordinary time and place undertook not only to reform (that is, reshape) society, but also to reform or reshape themselves, their own identities and characters. The political history of the time, with its struggles over issues like temperance, sabbatarianism, nativism, and the restriction of slavery, can only be understood in terms of this larger reform context, much of which was quite nonpolitical, but some of which eventually spilled over, so to speak, into the political arena.

The word that is usually used to refer to the aspect of antebellum American society that concerns us is "liberal." To explain why American society was liberal a number of hypotheses, by no means mutually exclusive, have been advanced. Among them are the absence of feudalism (Louis Hartz), the material abundance of the continent in relation to its population (David Potter), the experience of repeatedly reconstructing political institutions on the frontier of white settlement (Frederick Jackson Turner), the consequences of the American Revolution (Gordon Wood), and the relatively free military security enjoyed by a country with no powerful foreign enemies nearby (C. Vann Woodward).[4] A major contributory cause to which I wish to call attention, however, was the ecclesiology of sectarian Protestantism, which had given a large portion of the population practical experience with contractual forms of responsible authority that could be—and were—readily transferred from the religious to the civil realm. The Protestant Reformed tradition taught men and women to read and interpret Scripture for themselves, to experience divine grace for themselves, and to covenant together to form churches. This kind of sectarian experience had been going on ever since the seventeenth century (in European conventicles, even earlier) and continued to flourish more than ever in antebellum America. Although liberalism was destined to become a secular ideology, its origins and prevalence in America owe much to religion, especially the faith and practice of Calvinists and Anabaptists.[5] In antebellum times, practical experience with creating churches and other voluntary societies, religious and secular, was even more widespread among Americans than the founding of political institutions on the frontier.

In recent years, historians have reminded us of the limitations of antebellum freedom: that a majority of the population, including African Americans, women, and others, were denied its full benefits. In antebellum America, political life was actually less democratic than other aspects of culture, including religion, which were more inclusive in the scope of their participation. If we widen our universe of discourse to include nonpolitical activities, one finds that working-class people, women, minority groups, and yes, even slaves, were able to participate to a significant degree in certain kinds of voluntary activities related to religion, manners, and self-discipline. Although I shall not here pursue the history of the oppressed groups as fully as they deserve, one of the interesting aspects of this kind of cultural history is the widespread nature of participation in it.[6]

Antebellum Americans were a nation of volunteers.[7] Freer than people had ever been to decide things for themselves, they used their freedom to reshape their physical surroundings, their society, and themselves. The first we call technological progress, the second, social reform. The third, their experimentaton with new identities and social roles, is perhaps no less important. Americans redefined themselves as members of new organizations and denominations, as Masons or Anti-Masons, as militiamen

or Associationists or Shakers. They joined labor unions, women's auxilia-
ries, and volunteer fire brigades. They undertook to live Christian lives,
temperate lives, disciplined lives, and polite lives. Members of restorationist religious movements, like colonial Puritans, undertook to live ancient lives.[8] New gender roles were debated, and experiments in complex
marriage, celibacy, and polygamy conducted. Political participation for
women was demanded at Seneca Falls in 1848. Secondary education for
women was expanded and the first colleges open to women founded.[9]
People sought to improve themselves (as they put it) through education,
and they pursued this not only in schools and universities but also in
lectures, lyceums, seminaries, and conversation groups. Economic and
political life provided their own opportunities for self-definition. There
was a wider range of occupational choices. The market revolution also
enabled people to redefine themselves through their choices from an ever-
widening selection of consumer goods. Even the political parties of the
period can be seen as one manifestation of the widespread quest for identity: the ethnoreligious school of political history has shown that affiliation with a political party (of which there were many in this period)
might be as much an assertion of personal identity as a judgment on the
questions of the day.[10]

The pursuit of identity almost always had two sides: freedom and discipline. Most of the new religious faiths and secular lifestyles required
voluntary commitment but also imposed novel restraints. These might
involve anything from the temperate use of alchohol (or total abstinence
from it), to unpaid labor in a utopian community, to the proper use of a
fork. Historically, the members of Reformed and sectarian churches had
assumed collective responsibility for each other's behavior, a "watch and
ward" over church discipline. The new American religions had their own
versions of church discipline. Sometimes Americans went beyond self-
reformation and the discipline of those in their own group to a concern
with the reformation and discipline of others: to redeem the insane
through asylums or convicts through penitentiaries, for example. Feeling
accepted by God, these believers also felt commissioned by him. From
this outreach derives the evangelical reformers' reputation as promoters
of social control. It is useful, however, to recognize that concern with
social control was one aspect of a concern with discipline and character
formation that typically began with the self and was then extended to
others.

An illuminating recent case study of antebellum church discipline is
Curtis D. Johnson's examination of rural Cortland County in western
New York. He distinguishes those denominations that became concerned
with reforming the larger American society from those that concentrated
on their own members and explains how this distinction arose. Johnson
emphasizes the serious interest taken in theology, especially the question
of free will, by large numbers of ordinary people, as well as the important role played by women as agents of religious activism.[11]

A New Birth

Most antebellum American Protestantism was, in one way or another, evangelical. As recently as 1983 it was possible for Leonard Sweet to write that it was "indisputable" that American evangelicalism was "understudied." A decade later, this is no longer indisputable; indeed, it has even been suggested that American evangelicalism may now be *over*studied.[12] Be that as it may, scholarly writing on American evangelicalism has become quite substantial in both quantity and quality. Within the history of American evangelicalism the antebellum period is pivotal, for it was then that modern revivalism became institutionalized. The antebellum period was also the time when evangelical religion exerted its greatest culture-shaping power since the settlement of Puritan New England.[13]

The distinguishing feature of evangelicalism among the varieties of Christianity is its insistence upon a "new birth," that is, a conscious commitment to Christ, undertaken voluntarily at an identifiable moment, generally conceived (depending on the theology of the particular evangelical group) as a response to divine grace. How the offer of grace and the human response to it should be described was a central issue for rival schools of American evangelical theology during the antebellum period. Theologians—both learned and unlearned—reconsidered the Reformation soteriological formulations, and, for the most part, strengthened assertions of the freedom of the human will rather than assertions of the irresistibility of divine grace. Protestant theological discussion of the freedom of the will constituted one of the most sophisticated dialogues in antebellum America.[14]

"Conversion," that is, commitment to Christ, initiated what was expected to be a long process on the part of the convert to lead a better life, to remake himself or herself. Assisted by devotional programs such as John Wesley's famous "method," from which his followers got their name, this process too had elaborate and various theological descriptions. The goal, which might be termed "sanctification" or "holiness" or "perfection," was needless to say elusive, but its pursuit involved believers in self-examination, repentance, and efforts at improvement. The discipline and supportiveness of their fellow church members were intended to encourage these efforts. Despite its importance, there has been only a little scholarly work on this subject, most of it on the colonial rather than the antebellum period. Conversion itself and the preparation for it have been better studied than the subsequent struggle for personal improvement.[15]

The individualism of evangelical religion is modified during a religious revival, which has come to mean an evangelical undertaking to secure mass, rather than individual, conversion experiences. Conversions during a revival are typically public rather than private, and induced by preaching rather than meditation or other private devotions. The promotion of organized revivals became a central feature of antebellum American society. The modern study of antebellum revivalism takes as its point of departure Whitney Cross's regional study of upstate New York and has continued in a number of noteworthy subsequent works in the past generation.[16]

The study of antebellum revivalism has reached a high point of sophistication in two recent case studies. Randolph A. Roth examines the Connecticut River Valley in Vermont. He finds revivals were a way of promoting Christianity within a liberal society; they put religion on a voluntary rather than traditional or coercive basis. Roth portrays his subjects as people trying "to reconcile their commitment to competition, toleration, and popular sovereignty with their desire to defend an orderly and pious life." Like others before him, Roth interprets the antebellum revivals as having been conditioned by economic circumstances, though his work represents an advance beyond the class-conflict model. Roth believes revivals flourished best in manufacturing towns because there they represented a conjuction of the values and interests of the owners and the workers. He combines his sensitive interpretive constructs with carefully recreated statistical data.[17]

David G. Hackett examines Albany, New York, relating revivalism there to ethnic, economic, and ideological changes across several generations. While theoretically sophisticated, he never lets theory get in the way of empirical fact. He points out the similarity in values between the evangelicals and the Workingmen's political party, both affirming self-discipline and temperance. Hackett's interpretation of the Second Great Awakening is broadly similar to Richard Bushman's interpretation of the First (which bypassed Albany): evangelicalism is identified with a personality type arising out of the breakdown of early-modern European (in this case, Dutch) organic community and the rise of individualism and the power of choice.[18]

Religious bodies are by nature transnational, and to study Protestantism in the United States is in some respects to define the subject artificially. Most of the American branches of Protestantism were imported by migrants from Europe. Conversely, Mormonism, a religion usually thought to be archtypally American, won hundreds of thousands of converts in Britain and Scandinavia. The more we know about the history of evangelical activity, the more we realize its transatlantic nature. Itinerant revivalists have moved back and forth across the water from George Whitefield's day to Billy Graham's, and the nineteenth century was a time of particularly close international cooperation among evangelicals. Occasions like the great conventions of the Evangelical Alliance held in London in 1846 and in New York in 1873 exemplify the international quality of evangelicalism.[19]

One of the salient characteristics of the best work on revivalism and evangelicalism in recent years has been the introduction of a long-overdue transnational dimension. A pioneer in this regard was Richard Carwardine, whose study of transatlantic revivalism showed the influence exerted in Britain, especially Wales, by Charles G. Finney and his "modern revival" techniques.[20] In this respect antebellum history will undoubtedly continue in the path so ably marked out for the colonial period by the transatlantic works of Marilyn Westerkamp, Leigh Eric Schmidt, Michael J. Crawford, and W. R. Ward.[21] Here, as so often happens, the historians of the middle period move in the same directions as the historians of early America, with the latter often in the lead. The past overemphasis on uniquely American environmental factors in discussing evangelical religion is well on its way to being corrected.[22]

In the long run, revivals proved less effective as means of perpetuating and consolidating religious gains than institutional structures: seminaries, schools, colleges, missions, benevolent associations, and, of course, churches themselves.[23] For some reason, historians have been inclined to overestimate the effects of revivals and underestimate those of institution-building. The institutionalization of charisma (as Max Weber termed it) is a process that has found few fans among historians. Institutions and their administrators have seemed dull at best, oppressive and reactionary at worst.[24] Actually, however, two of the most exciting and prominent of the antebellum revivalists—Lyman Beecher and Charles G. Finney—turned in their later years toward the administration and development of educational institutions, and their instincts were sound.[25] Among Methodists, it was the founders of chapels and churches rather than the itinerant exhorters who made the more lasting contribution. On the whole, the Second Great Awakening was more successful than the First in institutionalizing its objectives. Indeed, it was the genius of nineteenth-century reformers, religious and secular, on both sides of the Atlantic, to embody their moral reforms in institutions so as to perpetuate them.[26]

The gigantic problem of slavery presented antebellum reformers with the most difficult task of giving institutional expression to their moral imperatives. For the generation after the Civil Rights movement of the 1960s, historians were inevitably primarily interested in studying the abolitionists. During the last few years, however, historical work has broadened somewhat, to look also at how mainstream Northern churches responded to the demands of antislavery, whether through restriction, colonization, or outright abolition.[27] An excellent microhistorical study of the trial of a woman abolitionist who challenged the authority of her minister illuminates the tensions between ultraist perfectionism and moderate comprehensiveness.[28]

Several recent trends in the study of revivalism are well exemplified in Terry Bilhartz's carefully researched study of the churches in Baltimore between 1790 and 1830. Bilhartz attributes the emergence of revival techniques in large part to the needs of the clergy to find a way to gain converts among adult white males, a group that was notoriously hard to win over yet critical to the economic security of the churches. He devotes attention to the collective discipline of church communities, particularly among Methodists and Quakers. He attributes the growth of the Methodists to their ardent evangelism, yet also argues that, in the final analysis, revivals mattered less than such institutional developments as the organization of new congregations. Bilhartz concludes his fascinating study with the observation that the Second Great Awakening must be judged a failure when measured by the ambitions of its proponents.[29] But this may be less a judgment on the antebellum evangelicals' accomplishments than on the extravagance of their postmillennial expectations.

Evangelicalism and Politics

Historians are generally agreed that evangelical Protestantism in the United States, as elsewhere in the Atlantic world, was concerned (among other things) with the imposition of order or a sense of order. It is not surprising, then, that the connection of evangelical religion to antebellum politics should have attracted attention. But "order" is a word that can mean many things; the orderliness that antebellum evangelicals sought was associated with improvement, not complacency, with conscious planning, not acceptance of tradition. In other words, it was the social analogue of the rational order they sought to introduce into their private lives.

Just as there were various schools of theological thought about the process of individual improvement, there were different strands of political perfectionism too. At the perfectionist extreme were groups whose political radicalism derived from radical theological views, such as Hicksite Quakers. Most famous of these perfectionists were the Garrisonian abolitionists, who rejected party-political involvement yet demanded drastic social change (the immediate abolition of slavery and equal rights for women).[30] Mainstream evangelicals tended to support the Whig party, whose policies involved a greater measure of national planning and public responsibility across a wide range of economic and cultural issues than those of their Democratic adversaries. The political historian Harry Watson sums up the reasons for such a choice: "The Democrats saw themselves as the party of liberty, while Whigs claimed to be the party of improvement. Whether the subject was a bank, a road, or a school for the deaf, Whigs usually lined up in favor of a systematic program for social uplift, while Democrats worried that such projects might limit personal freedom or serve paternalistic purposes." In such a situation, religious and cultural attitudes dovetailed with economic ones in determining party loyalty. If one considers party identification as an aspect of personality or temperament, this congruence is not surprising.[31]

Evangelical reform antedated the Whig party and indeed helped create it. Three movements that were particularly significant in this regard were sabbatarianism, the missions to the American Indians, and the opposition to Freemasonry. The political significance of sabbatarianism has been judiciously examined in Richard R. John's innovative work.[32] The Presbyterian mission to the Cherokees turned out to have enormous political consequences when President Andrew Jackson sided with the State of Georgia in dispossessing the tribe, and missionaries defended the rights of the Indians to their land, which had been guaranteed by treaty. Imprisoned by the state for defying its authority, two missionaries took the case to federal court and won vindication of the Cherokees' rights from Chief Justice John Marshall, only to see the president find a way to circumvent the decision and drive the Cherokees westward along the Trail of Tears.[33]

The Anti-Masonic movement was triggered in 1826 by the unsolved kidnapping/murder of an ex-Mason who had threatened to reveal the order's secrets and the successful subsequent coverup by officials who were Masons. Most strongly based in evangelical areas of Yankee settlement, the Anti-Masonic movement declared there was no legitimate place in American society for a secret, elitist organization that apparently aspired to set itself above the law. The two antagonistic voluntary societies, Masonry and Anti-Masonry, constitute a paradigm of antebellum American life; each reflected, among other things, its members' quest for identity. The conflict between Mason and Anti-Mason will never be satisfactorily studied until there is more examination than there has been of the Masonic Order in the period.[34] The most thorough account so far, Paul Goodman's book on the Anti-Masons, amasses much fascinating material, especially on Anti-Masonry's links with abolitionism and its protofeminist critique of the male exclusiveness of Masonry. However, Goodman's overall interpretation of Anti-Masonry as anti-industrial, antimodern, and an example of "paranoid delusions now better forgotten" is not born out by his own evidence, much of which indicates the rationality of the Anti-Masons and the legitimate basis of their accusations.[35] The historical profession has not yet escaped from the antievangelical and antireformer bias that colored so much of the writing on antislavery until recently.

Richard J. Carwardine's new book, *Evangelicals and Politics in Antebellum America*, is by far the largest study of its subject.[36] The author commences his account in 1840 and finds a twofold significance in the election of that year: (1) the campaigners embraced the popular style of the revival camp meeting, and (2) a substantial portion of the evangelical community mobilized behind the candidacy of William Henry Harrison. (How the Whig party managed to exploit the symbol of "hard cider" without losing their temperance constituency is explained with wry humor.)[37] In 1840 and afterwards, Carwardine explains, the Whigs presented themselves to the electorate not so much as the party of the prosperous as the party of the "hard-working, self-improving, sober, and thrifty of all classes."[38] Mainstream evangelicals were among those who defined themselves this way.

The climax of Carwardine's narrative is the story of the key role played by the evangelicals in the transition from the second to the third party systems. When the evangelicals became dissatisfied with the response of the Whig party leadership to their concerns over temperance, the political power of Catholic immigrants, and the extension of slavery, they abandoned the party. One possible alternative, the American Party (better known by its derisive nickname, "Know-Nothings"), did not succeed in rallying disaffected evangelicals effectively enough to became the Whigs' permanent successors, for reasons Carwardine carefully sets out. Ultimately, the Republican party successfully embodied the values of Northern political postmillennialism: "conscience, obedience to the higher law, Calvinistic duty, self-discipline, and social responsibility."[39] In the Republican party, as in public school systems, the nineteenth-century moral reformers built one of their most successful institutional monuments.

More than thirty years ago, Lee Benson observed that the Whig party pursued as its goal a "positive liberal state" that facilitated the individual's pursuit of self-improvement; the Democratic party, finding this goal presumptuous and paternalistic, endorsed a "negative liberal state" that left individuals alone to improve themselves or not. Lawrence Frederick Kohl's recent book seeks to build upon this insight, arguing that the discourse of Whig-Democratic party politics should be read as "a dialogue over the proper nature of the individual's relations with his fellow men in an individualistic social order." Democrats were preoccupied with the individual's need to shake off external controls, Whigs with the need to maintain self-control. Kohl does not do all that might be done with his theme, partly because he says little about religion, partly because he couches his argument in a terminology ("inner-directed" Whigs versus "tradition-directed" Democrats) whose origins and full significance he does not explore. But in emphasizing "the ability of political discourse to touch and intensify basic psychological conflicts within individuals" he has performed a service.[40]

As we have seen, evangelicalism was larger and more durable than the Whig party. The dominant strand of American evangelicalism backed first the Whigs and then, having lost faith in them, helped create a viable constituency for the Republicans. But Richard Carwardine is careful to identify and characterize those evangelical groups who supported other parties, including abolitionists and Democrats, or who withdrew from the corruptions of politics altogether. Those evangelicals who did not identify their community with society as a whole, "for whom the state's only proper role was to protect men and women from religious tyranny," backed the Democrats, as did those who felt threatened by the evangelical social program, including most nonevangelical, liturgical Christians and those indifferent or hostile to religion. In religion, as in other respects, the Democratic party represented an alliance of outgroups, the social periphery resisting the encroachments of the core.[41]

The Outsiders

This section will deal with Protestants outside the evangelical Whig establishment. For an understanding of religious outgroups as such, the most important recent work is Laurence Moore's *Religious Outsiders and the Making of Americans*. The powerful insight on which this book rests is that the status of "outsider" in American religion has to a considerable extent been self-imposed: people voluntarily chose to define themselves as dissenters and were quite capable of spurning ecumenical or irenic overtures. In an unstructured society, religious differentiation provided people with a sense of identity. "One way of becoming American was to invent oneself out of a sense of opposition." The Mormons, for example, were different from other Americans "because they said they were different. . . . Mormon difference, that is, was a deliberate invention elaborated over time."[42] Moore has transcended the conventional American nationalist piety that we are all pretty much alike and anyone who calls attention to differences must be imagining things, must be, as the great consensus historian Richard Hofstadter put it, "paranoid." After Moore's insight has been absorbed, one can see that the anti-Mormon, anti-Catholic, Anti-Mason, and anti-slave-power publicists (among others) were no more and no less paranoid than their respective adversaries.[43]

Nathan O. Hatch's wide-ranging and original account of *The Democratization of American Christianity* during the antebellum period is written with an enthusiastic warmth that contrasts with Moore's ironic detachment, yet it teaches a similar lesson. Hatch treats five groups, which overlap with Moore's: Methodists, Baptists, "Christians," Mormons, and African American churches. Hatch does not claim that these denominations were particularly democratic in their internal structure; indeed, he concedes they were sometimes authoritarian (more so than the mainstream Whig evangelicals, one could add). Although he makes occasional reference to the party of Jefferson and Jackson, and to working-class affiliation, he is not directly concerned with either politics or social structure, and he provides no statistics on the social origin of the people he treats. The "democratization" of his title refers essentially to popular culture, to a vernacular medium of communicating the Christian message through preaching, congregational singing, and mass-circulation periodicals. Like Moore's people, Hatch's are gutsy volunteers. They defy convention and "storm heaven by the back door."[44] Their Christianity is authentic Christianity, but their democratic version of that ancient faith is very much a freely chosen matter of personal style.

Hatch proposes to redefine the term "Second Great Awakening," so that it will refer primarily to the vernacular movements he has described. The evangelical Whigs were merely reactive, he insists, "only a secondary theme in the awakening's story."[45] One trouble with such a redefinition, however, is that it ignores or marginalizes much of the social reform impulse associated with the Awakening. Rather than recognize the innovative quality of antebellum evangelical Whig reformers, Hatch reverts to calling them a declining elite struggling to maintain social control—a description that one thought recent scholarship had substantially modified. In an effort to recover the historical role of "his" people, Hatch seems, ironically, to shortchange the historical role of the antebellum Awakening as a whole. Would it not be more accurate to see the Second Great Awakening, in all its rich Christian diversity, of which Nathan Hatch has done so much to remind us, as empowering middle-class reformers as well as populists—in the words of the Book of Common Prayer, "all sorts and conditions of men"?

The strength of Jon Butler's highly original synthesis of colonial and antebellum American religious history lies in its cultural breadth. Picking up on the example of Sir Keith Thomas and historians of the French *Annales* school, Butler writes about Christianity in relation to other forms of popular supernaturalism such as magic, witchcraft, spiritualism, and dowsing. Like the cultural historians of early-modern Europe, Butler shows how the different versions of Christianity were in competition with these other belief systems, which they sometimes tried to stamp out but which often coexisted with Christianity in forms of religious syncretism. This explains the paradox of the title of Butler's book, *Awash in a Sea of Faith,* which implies that there is more than enough generalized religion around; but the subtitle, *Christianizing the American People,* implies that Christianity itself is in short supply and has to be fostered by its promoters.[46]

Butler is reluctant to interpret American religion in voluntaristic terms. He quite rightly calls attention to the authoritarianism and intolerance of many religious movements. In his account of the disestablishment of religion by the various individual states, he emphasizes the practical and the contingent rather than issues of high principle, leaving one to draw the conclusion that the most powerful guarantor of religious freedom in the new nation was simply its enormous religious diversity. At the end of the day, however, even Butler has to concede that the multiplication of religious sects, movements, reforms, and institutions in the antebellum period mightily empowered multitudes of people—including not only "white, Anglo-Saxon, Protestant, and middle- and upper-class males," but also "women, American blacks, and newly arrived immigrants."[47]

Of liturgical Protestants, the most important were the Episcopalians. A peculiar feature of the historiography of nineteenth-century American Protestantism until very recently has been the paucity of writing about the Episcopal Church. Once the Revolution and its attendant disestablishment are over, Episcopalianism drops out of general accounts of American history. However, the Episcopal church provided an alternative Christian identity to the dominant American evangelical and Reformed tradition. Throughout the nineteenth century, it offered a haven for refugees from other denominations, particularly people who came to find the Reformed tradition too theologically confining, morally intrusive, or culturally stark. Partly because of this, the evangelical wing of the American Episcopal church became weaker than its counterparts within the

Anglican churches of other countries. Perceived as a bastion of resistance to evangelical moral and social reform, the Episcopal church became during the course of the antebellum period a bastion of the Democratic party in the North.[48] The impact of the Oxford Movement in the United States (which was quite substantial) is perhaps the greatest untold story of American Anglicanism.

Indigenous American denominations, by contrast, have been the subject of considerable attention from historians. Richard T. Hughes and C. Leonard Allen treat a group of "restorationist" religious movements, which they interpret as sharing a desire to escape from the historical and conditioned back to some unconditioned, original absolute. They interpret the evolution of Alexander Campbell's "Christian" movement from ecumenical to sectarian, like the rejection of pluralism by the Mormons, as examples of the fundamental intolerance of primitivism.[49] Although millenarianism might be thought even more vulnerable to criticism than primitivism, the Adventist movement started by William Miller has recently been receiving sympathetic treatment. The sudden emergence of Adventist historiography is the product of a change in the attitude of the church itself toward its history. The thrust of the new writing, in which Adventists themselves have taken a leading part, is toward showing (quite persuasively) that Miller's arguments were rationally plausible for their time, and that his followers were not demented or marginalized, but normal people from a wide range of social and religious backgrounds. There was substantial overlap between Millerites and abolitionists (including Angelina Grimké Weld, for example), and although mainstream evangelicals were quick to condemn the Millerites, they actually had much in common.[50] Eventually the Adventists, illustrating Laurence Moore's model, separated themselves out into a sect with its own distinctive lifestyle, including observance of Saturday as the sabbath and conscientious objection to military service.

Some of the best-remembered perfectionist experiments of antebellum America were utopian communities. Three of these communities, have received superb extended treatments lately. Stephen Stein's book on the Shakers is a model of sober common sense, as the author sifts through the layers of romanticization that have built up around the famous furniture-makers. Stein is particularly hard-headed in his estimate of the importance of institutionalization over charisma. Carl J. Guarneri's book on the American followers of Charles Fourier, and Christopher Clark's book on the Northampton Association, although not strictly religious histories, are wonderfully evocative descriptions of how many thousands of Americans in the 1840s embarked on a new life in planned communities as disciples of a kind of secular millennialism.[51] One way of understanding Henry David Thoreau's *Walden* is to read it as the account of an experiment in a one-man utopian community.

One religious group illustrates all of the themes in this section: the Mormons. The Mormons were the examplars par excellence of Laurence

Moore's voluntary outsiders and Nathan Hatch's populist rebels. They provided Jon Butler with wonderful illustrations of syncretism in their borrowings from fortune-telling, treasure-seeking, and miracle-working (from Freemasonry too, Butler might have added).[52] The Mormons were also restorationists of a lost-and-found gospel, millenarians, and utopian communitarians. They experimented with alternative lifestyles, practicing both socialism and polygamy before abandoning them under outside pressure, and continuing to live by the healthful abstinence enjoined in the Word of Wisdom. The Mormons have shown a genius for institutionalizing their undertakings, for example, in their Mutual Improvement Associations. Although their religion is indigenous to America, the Mormons' successful overseas missions make good subjects for transatlantic history.[53]

The historiography of Mormonism has undergone a remarkable maturation. For a long time, even the best historians of Mormonism did not locate their subject in the context of American religion; when Mormonism was contextualized it was treated as an aspect of the regional history of the American West. Then, with the work of historians like Klaus Hansen and Jan Shipps, the context in which Mormonism was viewed dramatically broadened.[54] At the present time, the historiography of Mormonism is flourishing more than ever. The Latter-day Saints Church itself includes many excellent historians who work on the history of their religion; their work is by no means necessarily apologetic in tone or purpose.[55] The variety of different kinds of recent work shows how historians are taking advantage of the richly rewarding material Mormonism offers. There are excellent new treatments of Mormon millennialism (Grant Underwood), Mormon music (Michael Hicks), the Mormon use of the Bible (Philip Barlow), and the institutionalization of charisma (Irene Bates and E. Gary Smith).[56] The political dimension of early Mormonism, touched on suggestively by Hatch, has been pursued further by Kenneth Winn, who shows how both Mormons and anti-Mormons made use of classical republicanism. Winn gets carried away by his thesis to the point of attributing classical sources to aspects of Mormonism that obviously have other origins. But his book contains much valuable information on the relations of the Mormon church to the Whig and Democratic parties as well as Joseph Smith's presidential campaign of 1844.[57]

In the last analysis, what set the outsiders apart from the mainstream Whig evangelicals was their attitude toward American society. The Whig evangelicals were seeking to create the functional equivalent of an established church, within which evangelicals would take the lead in reforming society as a whole along their own moral lines. The outsiders pulled back from the larger society, concentrating not on transforming it but on maintaining their own distinctiveness from it. The categories were not immutable, however, and groups like the Methodists were quite capable of evolving from "outsider" to "mainstream" status, as they came to place greater reliance on institutions than on charisma, and on a civilizing mission rather than on populist rhetoric.[58] How some forms of evangelical religion made their peace with respectability will be the subject of the next section.

Protestantism, Polite Culture, and Moral Philosophy

The rise of polite culture is one of the great themes of the history of the middle class. It represents a giant undertaking of voluntary self-reconstruction. Like religious reform movements, polite culture undertook to make the world a better place while also reshaping individuals into better people. Polite culture served somewhat the same individual and social purposes that church discipline had served among early-modern Protestant sectarians; it became a form of secular discipline common to middle-class persons everywhere. It taught people to control their passions and appetites, and to show consideration for the feelings of others. As obedience to the discipline of the church defined its membership, so good manners defined a person as a member of polite society—the name the Victorian middle class called itself.

The best recent treatment of polite culture in nineteenth-century America is John F. Kasson's *Rudeness and Civility*. Kasson treats politeness as an aspect of the new middle-class world of striving. He tells how Benjamin Franklin challenged the older view that human nature was hopelessly passionate and depraved and taught instead that people could become rational, prudent actors. Franklin's program of self-improvement taught that polite behavior was also prudent behavior, since it would be rewarded in this life. Kasson shows how, in the new middle-class urban world, such prudential politeness replaced the hierarchy of traditional society as the approved basis of human relations. Etiquette books propagated what was in effect an ideology of politeness. The new ideology, unlike traditional hierarchy, was inclusive rather than exclusive, open to all who would adopt it.[59] But the progress of politeness found tough going in the United States, where the temptations to unbridled self-aggrandizement were great. European visitors during the antebellum period typically complained about the state of American manners.

In Britain, middle-class polite culture originated in the early eighteenth century, propagated by publications like the *Spectator* and the *Tatler*. Like the political philosophy of John Locke, it was associated with the Whig regime that came to power after the Revolution of 1688 and with latitudinarian Anglicanism. The ideology of politeness applied to literary taste as well as interpersonal relations. It emphasized the control of the irrational passions and deplored religious appeals to such passions as "enthusiasm."[60] To many eighteenth-century British and American evangelicals, however, the conjunction of politeness and religious latitudinarianism was unappealing. These evangelicals tended to embrace a more austere life-style and reject polite society, treating it as a negative reference group. In America, the Great Awakening revealed differences in the

style of communication: extemporaneous evangelical preaching sometimes repudiated polite standards of literary taste (based on the proper
supremacy of reason over passion) in favor of more frankly emotional
appeals. This tradition of popular rhetoric was continued in antebellum
times by some of the aggressive sectarian preachers and pamphleteers of
the Second Great Awakening.[61]

A remarkable feature of the Second Great Awakening, however, was
how many evangelicals came to embrace polite culture as a welcome ally
in the struggle to civilize America. Instead of regarding politeness and
evangelicalism as rival codes, they forged a remarkable synthesis of the
two. There was actually a strong basis for such an alliance: polite culture
can be considered as a kind of secular perfectionism, sharing many of the
goals of religious perfectionism. Both polite and evangelical culture were
concerned with disciplining wayward human nature, and in the tumultuous society of antebellum America, each might well welcome the aid of
the other. Many evangelical leaders, after all, felt a strong commitment
to reason and did not wish their message to be dependent upon appeals
to the irrational passions. The desire to synthesize evangelical Christianity with polite culture became a typical characteristic of mainstream
Whig evangelicals in both North and South, as indeed of many evangelicals in other countries. In the end, both evangelical and nonevangelical
versions of polite culture came into existence, with the evangelical version the more restrictive of the two.[62]

To some extent this alliance was a natural consequence of the evangelicals moving away from an exclusively oral culture and into the world of
print. The prevailing literary standards were polite, and when evangelicals enlisted printed media in their service it would have seemed unnatural never to conform to them. Polite culture taught respect for classical
education, and so had Christianity ever since the founding of the medieval universities. Literacy and education accordingly became important
vehicles for cooperation between evangelicalism and politeness. Other examples of the alliance of the evangelical movement and politeness would
include efforts to control violence, sexuality, and alcohol, and to promote
respect for women.[63] In general, the emphasis on cultivating "character,"
which came to be typical of the Victorian middle class in both Britain
and America, represented the confluence of evangelical Christian discipline and polite culture.

At the core of this ideological synthesis was what was then called
moral philosophy. Originating in eighteenth-century Scotland, this transatlantic academic discipline reached the height of its influence in
nineteenth-century Britain and the United States. As then defined, it was
a science of human nature and human values, including not only ethical
theory but also aesthetics, rhetoric, and all of what we now consider the
social sciences, including political economy.[64] In its origins, the Scottish
school of moral philosophy provided a formal academic rationale for
polite culture. It was the creation of thinkers associated with the Moder-

ate wing of the Church of Scotland: Arminian in theology, Whig and Lockean in politics.[65] It organized the human faculties into a hierarchical model, in which reason and morality should rule over passion. Unfortunately, as the moral philosophers acknowledged, passion was a stronger motivating force in human nature, so that overcoming it posed major difficulties of psychological conditioning and social engineering.[66]

In late-eighteenth and early-nineteenth century America, the Scottish school of moral philosophy was taken over by evangelical scholars of energy and vision and made their own. The leading figures in this process were John Witherspoon and Samuel Stanhope Smith of Princeton, who synthesized evangelical Christianity with the science, the republicanism, and the polite standards of the Enlightenment. In a model work of intellectual and institutional history, Mark Noll has described the ambitions and strengths of their vision, along with the ironies and shortcomings of its implementation.[67] The Princeton version of moral philosophy, along with other versions developed at Yale and Harvard, exerted enormous cultural power. The influence of Scottish-American moral philosophy was not confined to Princeton Presbyterians, Yale Congregationalists, or Harvard Unitarians, but extended beyond the socially elite denominations, for example, to the "Christian"/Disciples movement. It provided much of the intellectual rationale for the interventionist political program of the Whig party.[68]

Although educational institutions could play an important part, America polite culture was always propagated primarily in the home, and its progress went hand in hand with the cult of domesticity and an increasing anxiety about the proper child-rearing techniques. Parents tried to shape their children's lives and characters, to make them both Christian and polite.[69] Horace Bushnell, America's greatest nineteenth-century theologian, was much indebted to the ideology of politeness in the creation of his own system of Christian Nurture, conceived as an alternative to revivalism. Ironically, out of the concern of middle-class American society with individual identity, Bushnell created an organicist and deterministic social theory.[70]

In the antebellum era, what defined the outgroups in American society was often their refusal to conform to middle-class standards of character as these were defined by moral philosophy and polite culture. For example, the Millerites were accused of being undisciplined and mentally unbalanced because their belief in the imminent Second Coming rendered the virtues of hard work and thrift irrelevant.[71] Irish Catholics were considered both drunken and violent. And the accusation that Southern slavery was licentious proved one of the most effective weapons in the abolitionist arsenal. Sometimes outgroups voluntarily embraced such distinctions. High-church Episcopalians, while endorsing politeness, distinguished themselves from evangelicals by countenancing activities like dancing and card-playing.[72] The followers of Charles Fourier believed that the human passions should be indulged rather than restrained and

designed their utopian communities with this in mind. Mormon polygamy and Oneida "complex marriages" deliberately defied conventional
morality.[73]

One of the important recent books on this subject continues the contest between polite culture and its "outsider" critics. The eminent Mormon historian Richard Bushman, writing on "the refinement of America," describes not only the rise of polite standards of behavior but also
the improved standards of material culture that went with it, in architecture, food, and home furnishings. Bushman addresses the relationship
between religion and polite culture and describes how some Christians
denounced refinement, some embraced it, and others were ambivalent. He takes note of Horace Bushnell's essay on "Taste and Fashion,"
which argues that the two are different: "taste" is aesthetic and creative,
an application of powers evident in God's own creative acts; "fashion"
is unworthy, self-seeking deference to human opinion. The distinction
is one Jonathan Edwards would have made, but Bushman does not endorse it. Although he grants that "the spread of parlor culture was one
of the great democratic movements of the nineteenth century," for Bushman, taste is ultimately snobbery. Looking behind the middle-class functions of Victorian politeness, Bushman recurs to its more remote origins
in the courtly behavior of earlier centuries. "Considering its tainted origins in the discredited royal courts, gentility exercised unlikely influence in republican America," he observes ruefully.[74] After describing the
nineteenth-century synthesis of Christianity and refinement, and its wide-
ranging manifestations in (for example) literature, theology, and the
Gothic revival in church architecture, Bushman declares that all such attempts to reconcile the gospel with politeness and aesthetic taste are fundamentally misconceived. "The advocates of tasteful religion lost sight of
gentility's fundamental commitment to court hierarchies and the cultural
elevation of a superior class, hardly the aim of Christianity."[75]

There is an old LDS Sunday-school song about a boy who admits he
may not "look quite genteel" but boasts nonetheless, "I might be envied
by a king, for I am a Mormon boy."[76] In his sense of opposition between
polite culture and true religion, Richard Bushman perpetuates this traditional Mormon outlook.

Unitarianism, Literature, and Self-Culture

Unitarianism was a small denomination in antebellum times, and even
today, after uniting with the Universalist church, it remains tiny. Nevertheless, the Unitarians occupied a crucial position in the religious and
cultural history of antebellum America. Unitarian clergymen like William
Ellery Channing, Theodore Parker, and Samuel Gilman were among the
country's leading intellectuals. The Unitarians were important propaga-
tors of polite culture, both as a standard of behavior and as a standard
of literary criticism. They maintained close contacts with the British Uni-

tarians, although in several respects the Yankees were less radical.[77] While their Christology followed the heterodox formulation of the ancient theologian Arius, the New England Unitarians of the generation after 1815 still considered themselves Christians. What made the Unitarians distinctive among American Protestants was their carrying a widespread rejection of Calvinist theology to unusually explicit extremes. Other Protestants accordingly took them seriously as rivals and worked hard to refute them in debate. Yet despite the important part played by the antebellum Unitarians in the religious history of their time, their historiography has diverged away from that of the rest of American Protestantism.[78] Most of the writing on antebellum Unitarianism treats the movement in its relationship to literature rather than religion. I recognize this historiographical situation by treating Unitarianism separately here, while at the same time arguing for the reintegration of Unitarianism into the mainstream of antebellum Protestant history.

The antebellum Unitarians carried on a tradition of moral philosophy that retained the Arminianism of the Scottish founders. Within the framework of this philosophy, the cultivation of the range of human "faculties" was important. While the evangelical Calvinist moral philosophers like Witherspoon would have agreed with the need to train the faculties, they tended to put more emphasis upon controlling them, that is, on self-discipline. The Unitarian thinkers emphasized the positive development of the faculties, in James Freeman Clarke's term, self-culture. Unitarian self-culture and evangelical self-discipline had much in common, and both could motivate Whig philanthropy and social reform.[79] But Unitarians played a disproportionately important part in promoting reforms designed to educate or develop human potential. The two most influential of nineteenth-century American educators were both Unitarians: Horace Mann, the organizer of public school systems, and Charles William Eliot, who transformed Harvard, the center of Unitarian intellectual life, into a model modern university. So also were some of the most energetic crusaders on behalf of the disadvantaged: Samuel Joseph May, the abolitionist; Charles Sumner, who fought against racism in both North and South; and Dorothea Dix, founder of mental hospitals. The list could go on and on.[80]

Among the faculties that Unitarians sought to cultivate were not only the reason but also the "affections," that is, benevolent emotions. In this respect they were the heirs of theologically liberal pietists in the seventeenth and eighteenth centuries.[81] The Unitarians shared with evangelical revivalists the goal of awakening the religious affections.[82] Yet the Unitarians disapproved of much of what went on in revivals as superficial, manipulative, and anti-intellectual. The principal alternative vehicle they developed for the nurture of religious and moral sentiments was literature. From the Christian Unitarians came the didactic and sentimental writing we call the genteel tradition in American letters. From their iconoclastic offspring in the village of Concord came the outburst of literary creativity we call transcendentalism: no longer Christian, but every bit as concerned with spiritual and moral objectives.[83]

Modern literary scholars have shown little interest in the writers of the genteel tradition like Longfellow, Lowell, and the elder Holmes, but they have shown enormous interest in Emerson and Thoreau, and some in the other transcendentalists as well. Accordingly, much of the writing on antebellum Unitarianism has been undertaken by literary scholars looking at the background of transcendentalism and other romantic literature. Some of the literary scholars who have written on Unitarianism in the past generation have been captive to the anti-Unitarian bias of the late great Perry Miller, an atheist who found liberal Christianity distasteful even though he respected what he considered the toughness of Calvinism. Transforming the master's irony into a principle of perverse interpretation, they have been led into confusions and distortions.[84] On the other hand, some of the best literary scholarship on the transcendentalist movement in recent years has been that which located it properly within the context of New England Unitarianism.[85]

What is called the "New Historicism" in literary studies has reached a high point in Lawrence Buell's *New England Literary Culture from Revolution through Renaissance,* a book that integrates literary and religious history to their mutual benefit. One of the strengths of Buell's wide-ranging work is the breadth of his definition of literature, which includes history and oratory as well as poetry and fiction. He is able to show how all these genres were influenced by religion, both Unitarian and trinitarian.[86] Another superb work of recent years is Charles Capper's biography of the transcendentalist Margaret Fuller, the first volume of which has appeared. Capper shows how indebted Fuller was to Unitarian concepts of self-culture. He also begins the process of examining the relationship between Unitarian self-culture and the American discovery of European art forms like symphonic music, sculpture, and dance—art forms long distrusted by the Puritan–evangelical religious tradition dominant in America.[87] Still another approach to the literary influence of Unitarianism is provided by David S. Reynolds. His excellent book, *Faith in Fiction,* examines popular sentimental writings as vehicles of liberal religion.[88]

But the Christian Unitarianism of antebellum America was also significant as a religious movement, not simply as background for literary movements. The leading practitioner of Unitarian church history in the past generation has been Conrad Wright.[89] Recent years have witnessed significant additions, including David Robinson's denominational history (the first volume in Henry Warner Bowden's series), the collection of scholarly essays edited by Conrad Edick Wright (son of Conrad Wright), and, most valuable of all, Jonathan Carey's completion of Sydney Ahlstrom's long-awaited anthology of Christian Unitarian writings, entitled *An American Reformation.*[90] Such studies enable us to appreciate the significance of the antebellum Christian Unitarians as precursors of the much more widespread liberal Protestantism of the post–Civil War era.

In 1988 I was able to write a new introduction to a revised edition of *The Unitarian Conscience*.[91] What we have learned since the first edition appeared in 1970 has confirmed the importance of Scottish moral philosophy in both Britain and America and underscored the representativeness of the small, distinctive community of American Unitarian Christians. Their commitments to rationality, education, and politeness were widely shared among the middle-class Protestant clergy.[92] Their synthesis of Protestantism with Enlightenment moral philosophy anticipated many features of the culture of Victorian times. In short, the antebellum Unitarians reward study because they were an articulate and organized group heading in the same direction as the rest of their culture, a little faster and more explicitly.

One of the improvements in historical understanding that has taken place since the first publication of *The Unitarian Conscience* is that we are now much more aware of the importance of Unitarian moral philosophy and its ideal of self-culture in transforming the self-image of women. Among those influenced by the antebellum Unitarian model of the faculties and their cultivation were Louisa May Alcott, Elizabeth Palmer Peabody, Lydia Maria Francis Child, Josephine Shaw Lowell, Julia Ward Howe, and Margaret Fuller.[93] Women's rights, like American literature, derived much of their initial impulse from the small Unitarian denomination.

Conclusion

Out of the efforts of antebellum Americans at self-definition there emerged a multiplicity of value conflicts: evangelical versus nonevangelical, Unitarian versus trinitarian, Whig versus Democrat, Mason versus Anti-Mason, northern Yankee versus southern cavalier, polite versus popular culture, to mention but a few. American religious diversity and freedom of religious choice were central to this massive effort at self-definition that helped usher in individualism and the pluralism of the modern world. What religious faith has meant in the lives of individuals in America—what might be called the historical psychology of religion—is a subject that we have only just begun to study.[94]

In the antebellum period, one of the most important features of the history of personal identity was the voluntary embrace of some form of self-discipline (from many forms available). In the absence of strong social or political institutions, such self-discipline provided both personal identity and a sense of social order. To possess "character" in the meaning that nineteenth-century Americans attached to it was to have one's passions under control. This made one worthy of the respect of others and, among white males, worthy of civic responsibility. The moral philosophers of the Scottish school worked out the theoretical guidelines for the practice of self-discipline. Under the intellectual leadership of evangelical scholars at Yale and Princeton, many American evangelicals came to embrace this moral philosophy and the prudential, considerate polite culture that went with it as allies in a campaign to civilize the country. There were other evangelical Christians, however, for whom true religion remained too stark, too highly personal, or too closely identified with their own ethnic subculture for such a synthesis to be acceptable. In the antebellum era, those who supported the synthesis of evangelicalism and polite culture tended to support the redemptive initiatives of the Whig party; those who remained outside this synthesis tended to be Democrats. At the moment it seems that a majority of American historians, whether their own outlook is religious or secular, find it easier to sympathize with the "outsiders" than with those who undertook to redeem the nation as a whole. No doubt this preference is related to the struggles of minorities and dissenters for cultural autonomy that are going in in our own time.[95] The tensions we experience today, on campuses and elsewhere, between universalism and multicultural particularism are not new. The need to define an identity has always been part of the pursuit of the American Dream.[96]

NOTES

1. "Life Without Principle" [delivered as a lecture in 1854], in Henry David Thoreau, *Reform Papers,* ed. Wendell Glick (Princeton: Princeton University Press, 1973).

2. Nathan O. Hatch, *The Democratization of American Christianity* (New Haven: Yale University Press, 1989), 14.

3. Jon Butler, *Awash in a Sea of Faith: Christianizing the American People* (Cambridge, Mass.: Harvard University Press, 1990), 256.

4. Still valuable on these and related themes are the essays collected in C. Vann Woodward, ed., *The Comparative Approach to American History* (New York: Basic Books, 1968).

5. See Daniel Walker Howe, "The Impact of Puritanism on American Culture," in *The Encyclopedia of American Religious Experience,* ed. Peter W. Williams and Charles Lippy (New York: Charles Scribner's Sons, 1988), 2: 1057–74.

6. See the autobiographical accounts discussed in Robert M. Calhoon, *Evangelicals and Conservatives in the Early South, 1740–1861* (Columbia: University of South Carolina Press, 1988), chap. 5. Also see Donald Yacovone, "The Transformation of the Black Temperance Movement," *Journal of the Early Republic* 8 (Fall 1988): 281–98: C. Eric Lincoln and Lawrence H. Mamiya, *The Black Church in the African American Experience* (Durham, N.C.: Duke University Press, 1990), 50–55, 92, 116, 240–44; Nancy A. Hardesty, *Your Daughters Shall Prophesy: Revivalism and Feminism in the Age of Finney* (Brooklyn: Carlson, 1991); Nancy A. Hewitt, *Women's Activism and Social Change: Rochester, New York, 1822–1872* (Ithaca, N.Y.: Cornell University Press, 1984).

7. The classic discussion of antebellum voluntary associations, political and religious, is Alexis de Tocqueville, *Democracy in America,* ed. Phillips Bradley (New York: Alfred A. Knopf, 1945; first pub. in French in 1835), 1: 191–98,

301–18; 2: 20–32, 106–20. See also Milton B. Powell, ed., *The Voluntary Church: American Religious Life, 1740–1860, Seen Through the Eyes of European Visitors* (New York: Macmillan, 1967).

8. Richard T. Hughes and C. Leonard Allen, *Illusions of Innocence: Protestant Primitivism in America, 1630–1875* (Chicago: University of Chicago Press, 1988); cf. Theodore Dwight Bozeman, *To Live Ancient Lives: The Primitivist Dimension in Puritanism* (Chapel Hill: University of North Carolina Press, 1988).

9. See, e.g., Kathryn Kish Sklar, "The Founding of Mount Holyoke College," in *Women of America: A History*, ed. Carol Berkin and Mary Beth Norton (Boston: Houghton Mifflin, 1979), 177–201; and Joseph Conforti, "Mary Lyon, the Founding of Mount Holyoke College, and the Cultural Revival of Jonathan Edwards," *Religion and American Culture* 3 (Winter 1993): 69–90.

10. On the ethnoreligious interpretation of the Second Party System, see Daniel Feller, "Politics and Society: Toward a Jacksonian Synthesis," *Journal of the Early Republic* 10 (Summer 1990): 135–62; and Robert P. Swierenga, "Ethnoreligious Political Behavior in the Mid-Nineteenth Century," in *Religion and American Politics*, ed. Mark Noll (New York: Oxford University Press, 1990), 146–171.

11. Curtis D. Johnson, *Islands of Holiness: Rural Religion in Upstate New York, 1790–1860* (Ithaca: Cornell University Press, 1989).

12. Leonard Sweet, *The Evangelical Tradition in America* (Macon, Ga.: Mercer University Press, 1984), 1; Jon Butler, "Born-Again History?" paper presented to the American Historical Association, annual meeting, Washington, D.C. (December, 1992).

13. See George M. Marsden, *Religion and American Culture* (San Diego: Harcourt, Brace, Janovich, 1990), esp. 47–94; Daniel Walker Howe, ed., *Victorian America* (Philadelphia: University of Pennsylvania Press, 1976), esp. 4–28.

14. See, e.g., William R. Sutton, "Benevolent Calvinism and the Moral Government of God: The Influence of Nathaniel W. Taylor on Revivalism in the Second Great Awakening," *Religion and American Culture* 2 (Winter 1992): 23–47; George M. Marsden, *The Evangelical Mind and the New School Presbyterian Experience: A Case Study of Thought and Theology in Nineteenth-Century America* (New Haven: Yale University Press, 1970); Glenn Hewitt, *Regeneration and Morality: A Study of Charles Finney, Charles Hodge, John W. Nevin, and Horace Bushnell* (Brooklyn: Carlson, 1991).

15. On the colonial period, see Charles Hambrick-Stowe, *The Practice of Piety: Puritan Devotional Disciplines in Seventeenth-Century New England* (Chapel Hill: University of North Carolina Press, 1982); and Charles Lloyd Cohen, *God's Caress: The Psychology of Puritan Religious Experience* (New York: Oxford University Press, 1986).

16. Whitney R. Cross, *The Burned-Over District: The Social and Intellectual History of Enthusiastic Religion in Western New York, 1800–1850* (Ithaca: Cornell University Press, 1950); Timothy Smith, *Revivalism and Social Reform in Mid-Nineteenth Century America* (New York, 1957); William G. McLoughlin, *Modern Revivalism: Charles Grandison Finney to Billy Graham* (New York: Ronald Press, 1959); William G. McLoughlin, *Revivals, Awakenings, and Reform* (Chicago: University of Chicago Press, 1978); Paul E. Johnson, *A Shopkeeper's Millennium: Society and Revivals in Rochester, New York, 1815–1837* (New York: Hill and Wang, 1978).

17. Randolph A. Roth, *The Democratic Dilemma: Religion, Reform, and the Social Order in the Connecticut River Valley of Vermont, 1791–1850* (Cambridge: Cambridge University Press, 1987); quotation from p. 6.

18. David G. Hackett, *The Rude Hand of Innovation: Religion and Social Order in Albany, New York, 1652–1836* (New York: Oxford University Press, 1991). Cf. Richard Bushman, *From Puritan to Yankee: Character and Social Order in Connecticut, 1690–1765* (Cambridge, Mass.: Harvard University Press, 1967).

19. Enduringly useful is Frank Thistlethwaite, *The Anglo-American Connection in the Early Nineteenth Century* (Philadelphia: University of Pennsylvania Press, 1959); see also David Brion Davis, *The Problem of Slavery in the Age of Revolution* (Ithaca: Cornell University Press, 1975).

20. Richard Carwardine, *Transatlantic Revivalism: Popular Evangelicalism in Britain and America, 1790–1865* (Westport, Conn.: Greenwood Press, 1968).

21. Marilyn Westercamp, *The Triumph of the Laity: Scots-Irish Piety and the Great Awakening* (New York: Oxford University Press, 1988); Leigh Eric Schmidt, *Holy Fairs: Scottish Communions and American Revivals in the Early Modern Period* (Princeton: Princeton University Press, 1989); Michael J. Crawford, *Seasons of Grace: Colonial New England's Revival Tradition in Its British Context* (New York: Oxford University Press, 1991); W. R. Ward, *The Protestant Evangelical Awakening* (Cambridge: Cambridge University Press, 1992).

22. See Mark Noll, ed., *Evangelicalism* (New York: Oxford University Press, 1993); and Daniel Walker Howe, *American History in an Atlantic Context* (Oxford: Clarendon Press of Oxford University Press, 1993).

23. For the early period, this point is well made in Patricia Bonomi, *Under the Cope of Heaven: Religion, Society, and Politics in Colonial America* (New York: Oxford University Press, 1986).

24. For typically negative judgements on antebellum institution-building, see David J. Rothman, *The Discovery of the Asylum* (Boston: Little, Brown, 1971); and Michael Katz, *The Irony of Early School Reform* (Cambridge, Mass.: Harvard University Press, 1968).

25. See James W. Fraser, *Pedagogue for God's Kingdom: Lyman Beecher and the Second Great Awakening* (New York: University Press of America, 1985); and Keith J. Hardman, *Charles Grandison Finney, 1792–1875: Revivalist and Reformer* (Syracuse: Syracuse University Press, 1987).

26. Still valuable is Lois Banner, "Presbyterianism and Voluntarism in the Early Republic," *Journal of Presbyterian History* 50 (Fall 1972): 187–205.

27. See John R. McKivigan, *The War Against Proslavery Religion* (Ithaca: Cornell University Press, 1984); Victor B. Howard, *Conscience and Slavery: The Evangelistic Calvinist Domestic Missions, 1837–1861* (Kent, Ohio: Kent State University Press, 1990); Hugh Davis, *Joshua Leavitt: Evangelical Abolitionist* (Baton Rouge: Louisiana State University Press, 1990); and David Brion Davis, "Reconsidering the Colonization Movement," *Intellectual History Newsletter* 14 (1992): 3–16.

28. Glenn C. Altschuler and Jan M. Saltzgaber, *Revivalism, Social Conscience, and Community in the Burned-Over District: The Trial of Rhoda Bemet* (Ithaca: Cornell University Press, 1983).

29. Terry D. Bilhartz, *Urban Religion and the Second Great Awakening: Church and Society in Early National Baltimore* (Rutherford, N.J.: Farileigh Dickinson University Press, 1986).

30. See H. Larry Ingle, *Quakers in Conflict: The Hicksite Reformation* (Knoxville: University of Tennessee Press, 1986); Lawrence J. Friedman, *Gregarious Saints: Self and Community in American Abolitionism, 1830–1870* (Cambridge: Cambridge University Press, 1982).

31. Harry Watson, *Liberty and Power: The Politics of Jacksonian America* (New York: Hill and Wang, 1990), quotation from p. 186; Daniel Walker Howe, *The Political Culture of the American Whigs* (Chicago: University of Chicago Press, 1979), esp. 3–5, 35–37, 149, 235, 301, and 380 n. 5.

32. Richard R. John, "Taking Sabbatarianism Seriously: The Postal System, the Sabbath, and the Transformation of American Political Culture," *Journal of the Early Republic* 10 (Winter 1990): 517–67.

33. William G. McLoughlin, *Cherokees and Missionaries, 1789–1839* (New Haven: Yale University Press, 1984) records the courage of the missionaries and their wives, though the author subordinates it to his basic disapproval of their goals (Christian evangelism and the acculturation of the Indians). Idem, *Champions of the Cherokees: Evan and John B. Jones* (Princeton: Princeton University Press, 1990), is a more sympathetic account of two Baptist missionaries.

34. A good beginning has been made in Steven C. Bullock, "A Pure and Sublime System: The Appeal of Post-Revolutionary Freemasonry," *Journal of the Early Republic* 9 (Fall, 1989): 359–73. See also Dorothy Lipson, *Freemasonry in Federalist Connecticut, 1789–1835* (Princeton: Princeton University Press, 1977).

35. Paul Goodman, *Towards a Christian Republic: Antimasonry and the Great Transition in New England, 1826–1836* (New York: Oxford University Press, 1988); quotation from p. 245.

36. New Haven: Yale University Press, 1993.

37. Carwardine, *Evangelicals and Politics*, 61–62. Watson explains the domestic associations of hard cider in *Liberty and Power*, 224.

38. Carwardine, *Evangelicals and Politics*, 109.

39. Ibid., 321.

40. Lee Benson, *The Concept of Jacksonian Democracy: New York As a Test Case* (Princeton: Princeton University Press, 1961); Lawrence Frederick Kohl, *The Politics of Individualism: Parties and the American Character in the Jacksonian Era* (New York: Oxford University Press, 1989); quotations from pp. 229 and 17. The terms "inner-directed" and "other-directed" were invented in David Riesman et al., *The Lonely Crowd: A Study of the Changing American Character* (New Haven: Yale University Press, 1950, rev. ed. 1961).

41. Quotation from Carwardine, *Evangelicals and Politics*, 111. For a fuller presentation of this argument and the relevant secondary scholarship, see Daniel Walker Howe, "The Evangelical Movement and Political Culture in the North During the Second Party System," *Journal of American History* 77 (March 1991): 1216–39.

42. Laurence Moore, *Religious Outsiders and the Making of Americans* (New York: Oxford University Press, 1986), quotations from pp. 45 and 31.

43. Richard Hofstadter, *The Paranoid Style in American History* (New York: Knopf, 1965).

44. Hatch, *The Democratization of American Christianity*, quotation from pp. 13 and 219.

45. Ibid., 226.

46. Butler, *Awash in a Sea of Faith: Christianizing the American People* (cited in n. 3).

47. Ibid., 288.

48. See Robert Bruce Mullin, *Episcopal Vision/American Reality: High Church Theology and Social Thought in Evangelical America* (New Haven: Yale University Press, 1986). On Episcopal evangelicalism, fine new works are Richard Rankin, *Ambivalent Churchmen and Evangelical Churchwomen: The Religion of the Episcopal Elite in North Carolina, 1800–1860* (Columbia: University of South Carolina Press, 1993); Allen C. Guelzo, *For the Union of Evangelical Christendom: The Irony of Reformed Episcopalians* (University Park, Penn.: Penn State University Press, 1994); and Diana Hochstedt Butler, *Standing Against the Whirlwind: Evangelical Episcopalians in Nineteenth-Century America* (New York: Oxford University Press, 1995).

49. Richard T. Hughes and C. Leonard Allen, *Illusions of Innocence: Protestant Primitivism in America, 1630–1875* (Chicago: University of Chicago Press, 1988).

50. Gary Land ed. *Adventism in America: A History* (Grand Rapids, Mich.: Eerdmans, 1986), chaps. 1 and 2; Ronald L. Numbers and Jonathan M. Butler, eds., *The Disappointed: Millerism and Millennialism in the Nineteenth Century* (Bloomington: Indiana University Press, 1987); Ruth Alden Doan, *The Miller Heresy, Millennialism, and American Culture* (Philadelphia: Temple University Press, 1987).

51. Stephen J. Stein, *The Shaker Experience in America: A History of the United Society of Believers* (New Haven: Yale University Press, 1992); Carl J. Guarneri, *The Utopian Alternative: Fourierism in Nineteenth-Century America* (Ithaca: Cornell University Press, 1991); Christopher Clark, *The Communitarian Moment* (Ithaca: Cornell University Press, 1995).

52. Butler draws with profit upon D. Michael Quinn, *Early Mormonism and the Magic World View* (Salt Lake City: Signature Books, 1987).

53. Richard Jensen and Malcolm Thorp, eds., *Mormons in Early Victorian Britain* (Salt Lake City: University of Utah Press, 1989).

54. Fine examples of the former historiographical tradition include Fawn Brodie, *No Man Knows My History: The Life of Joseph Smith* (New York: Knopf, 1945); Dale L. Morgan's unfinished history, printed in part in *Dale Morgan on Early Mormonism: Correspondence and a New History*, ed. John Phillip Walker (Salt Lake City: Signature Books, 1986); and Leonard Arrington, *Great Basin Kingdom: An Economic History of the Latter-day Saints, 1830–1900* (Cambridge, Mass.: Harvard University Press, 1958); for the newer tradition, see Klaus J. Hanson, *Mormonism and the American Experience* (Chicago: University of Chicago Press, 1981); and Jan Shipps, *Mormonism: The Story of a New Religious Tradition* (Urbana: University of Illinois Press, 1985).

55. For example, Marvin S. Hill, *Quest for Refuge: The Mormon Flight from American Pluralism* (Salt Lake City: Signature Books, 1989). More conventional by LDS standards are Richard Bushman, *Joseph Smith and the Beginnings of Mormonism* (Urbana: University of Illinois Press, 1984); and Leonard J. Arrington, *Brigham Young: American Moses* (New York: Knopf, 1985).

56. Grant Underwood, "The Millenarian World of Early Mormonism," Ph.D. dissertation, UCLA, 1988; Michael Hicks, *Mormonism and Music: A History* (Urbana: University of Illinois Press, 1989); Philip L. Barlow, *The Mormons and the Bible* (New York: Oxford University Press, 1991); Irene Bates and E. Gary Smith, *Lost Legacy: The Mormon Office of Presiding Patriarch* (Urbana: University of Illinois Press, 1996).

57. Kenneth H. Winn, *Exiles in a Land of Liberty: Mormonism in America, 1830–1846* (Chapel Hill: University of North Carolina Press, 1989).

58. See A. Gregory Schneider, "Social Religion, the Christian Home, and Republican Spirituality in Antebellum Methodism," *Journal of the Early Republic* 10 (Summer 1990): 165–89.

59. John F. Kasson, *Rudeness and Civility: Manners in Nineteenth-Century Urban America* (New York: Hill and Wang, 1990). Although it does not mention politeness as such, see also Louise L. Stevenson, *The Victorian Homefront: American Thought and Culture, 1860–1880* (New York: Twayne, 1991).

60. On the progress of politeness in England, see Paul Langford, *A Polite and Commercial People: England, 1727–1783* (Oxford: Oxford University Press, 1992), chap. 3.

61. On the eighteenth century, see Harry S. Stout, "Religion, Communication, and the Ideological Origins of the American Revolution," *William and Mary Quarterly* 34 (October 1977): 519–41; on the nineteenth, see Nathan Hatch, *Democratization of American Christianity*, 3–11, 146–61.

62. On the Southern synthesis of evangelical Christianity with politeness, see Brooks Holifield, *The Gentlemen Theologians: American Theology in Southern Culture, 1795–1860* (Durham, N.C.: Duke University Press, 1978), esp. 36–49.

63. Among many works, see Dickson D. Bruce, *Violence and Culture in the Antebellum South* (Austin: University of Texas Press, 1979).

64. The starting-point for modern scholarship is Gladys Bryson, *Man and Society: The Scottish Inquiry of the Eighteenth Century* (Princeton: Princeton University Press, 1945). On the transatlantic dimension of Scottish moral philosophy, see Daniel Walker Howe, *The Unitarian Conscience: Harvard Moral Philosophy, 1805–1861*, rev. ed. (Middletown, Conn.: Wesleyan University Press, 1988); and idem, "Why the Scottish Enlightenment was Useful to the Framers of the American Constitution," *Comparative Studies in Society and History* 31 (July 1989): 572–87.

65. On the Lockean nature of Scottish philosophy, see Ronald Hamowy, "Jefferson and the Scottish Enlightenment," *William and Mary Quarterly* 36 (July 1979): 503–23.

66. See Daniel Walker Howe, "Franklin, Edwards, and the Problem of Human Nature," in *Benjamin Franklin, Jonathan Edwards, and the Representation of American Culture*, ed. Barbara B. Oberg and Harry S. Stout (New York: Oxford University Press, 1993), 75–97; Kasson, *Rudeness and Civility*, 147–81.

67. Noll's work is one of the most impressive achievements of American religious historiography, but it falls chronologically mainly outside the purview of this essay. Mark A. Noll, *Princeton and the Republic, 1768–1822* (Princeton: Princeton University Press, 1989). See also idem, "The Irony of the Enlightenment for Presbyterians in the Early Republic," *Journal of the Early Republic* 5 (Summer 1985): 149–76; and Calhoon, *Evangelicals and Conservatives in the Early South*, 80–84.

68. See Donald H. Meyer, *The Instructed Conscience: The Shaping of the American National Ethic* (Philadelphia: University of Pennsylvania Press, 1972); Hughes and Allen, *Illusions of Innocence*, 153–58; Howe, *Political Culture of the American Whigs*, 27–31.

69. See Mary P. Ryan, *Cradle of the Middle Class: The Family in Oneida County, New York, 1790–1865* (Cambridge: Cambridge University Press, 1981). Of course, parents who could afford it enlisted the services of professional educa-

tors in the cause of Christian politeness; see James S. McLachlan, *American Boarding Schools* (New York: Charles Scribner's Sons, 1970).

70. See Daniel Walker Howe, "The Social Science of Horace Bushnell," *Journal of American History* 70 (September 1983), 305–22.

71. Ruth Doan, *The Miller Heresy*, 143–67.

72. Mullin, *Episcopal Vision/American Reality*, 79.

73. See Lawrence Foster, *Women, Family, and Utopia: Communal Experiments of the Shakers, the Oneida Community, and the Mormons* (Syracuse: Syracuse University Press, 1991).

74. Richard Bushman, *The Refinement of America: Persons, Houses, Cities* (New York: Knopf, 1992), 273, 326–31, 411, 446.

75. Ibid., 352.

76.

Kind friends, as here I stand to sing,
  So very queer I feel,
That now I've made my bow, I fear
  I don't look quite genteel;
But, never mind, for I'm a boy,
  That's always full of joy—
A rough and ready sort of chap—
  An honest "Mormon" boy.
Chorus:
A "Mormon" boy, a "Mormon" boy, I am a "Mormon" boy;
  I might be envied by a king,
For I am a "Mormon" boy.

—Evan Stephens, "The 'Mormon' Boy" (1881), *Deseret Sunday School Songs* (Salt Lake City: Deseret Sunday School Union, 1909), #269.

77. Especially in the antislavery network. See Douglas Stange, *Patterns of Antislavery among American Unitarians, 1831–1860* (London: Associated University Presses, 1977); and idem, *British Unitarians Against American Slavery, 1833–1865* (London: Associated University Presses, 1984).

78. For example, Mark Noll, in his comprehensive *History of Christianity in the United States and Canada* (Grand Rapids, Mich.: Eerdmans, 1992), refers to Unitarianism only incidentally and cites no works on it.

79. James Freeman Clarke, *Self-Culture: Physical, Intellectual, Moral, and Spiritual* (Boston, 1880); Conrad Edick Wright, The Transformation of Charity in Postrevolutionary New England (Boston: Northeastern University Press, 1992).

80. I chose examples that illustrate the historiography. Jonathan Messerli, *Horace Mann* (New York: Knopf, 1971); Hugh Hawkins, *Between Harvard and America: The Educational Leadership of Charles W. Eliot* (New York: Oxford University Press, 1972); Donald Yacovone, *Samuel Joseph May and Dilemmas of the Liberal Persuasion* (Philadephia: Temple University Press, 1991); David Herbert Donald, *Charles Sumner and the Rights of Man* (New York: Knopf, 1970); David Gollaher, "Dorothea Lynd Dix and the Frontiers of Madness in America," Ph.D. dissertation, Harvard University, 1990.

81. See Daniel Walker Howe, "The Cambridge Platonists of Old England and the Cambridge Platonists of New England," *Church History* 57 (December

1988): 470–85; Teresa Toulouse, *The Art of Prophesying: New England Sermons and the Shaping of Belief* (Athens, Ga.: University of Georgia Press, 1987); and John Corrigan, *The Hidden Balance: Religion and the Social Theories of Charles Chauncy and Jonathan Mayhew* (Cambridge: Cambridge University Press, 1987).

82. Smith, *Revivalism and Social Reform*, 95–102; Howe, *The Unitarian Conscience*, 151–73; Anne C. Rose, *Transcendentalism as a Social Movement, 1830–1850* (New Haven: Yale University Press, 1981), 28–37.

83. See Lawrence Buell, *Literary Transcendentalism* (Ithaca: Cornell University Press, 1973), 1–139; William R. Hutchison, *The Transcendentalist Ministers: Church Reform in the New England Renaissance* (New Haven: Yale University Press, 1959).

84. Ann Douglas, *The Feminization of American Culture* (New York: Knopf, 1977); Andrew Delbanco, *William Ellery Channing: An Essay on the Liberal Spirit in America* (Cambridge, Mass.: Harvard University Press, 1981).

85. For example, David M. Robinson, "The Legacy of Channing: Culture as a Religious Category in New England Thought," *Harvard Theological Review* 74 (April 1981): 221–39; idem., "Margaret Fuller and the Transcendental Ethos," *PMLA* 97 (January 1982): 83–98; Richard A. Grusin, *Transcendentalist Hermeneutics: Institutional Authority and the Higher Criticism of the Bible* (Durham, N.C.: Duke University Press, 1991).

86. Lawrence Buell, *New England Literary Culture from Revolution through Renaissance* (Cambridge: Cambridge University Press, 1986).

87. Charles Capper, *Margaret Fuller: An American Romantic Life. The Private Years* (New York: Oxford University Press, 1992).

88. David S. Reynolds, *Faith in Fiction: The Emergence of Religious Literature in America* (Cambridge, Mass.: Harvard University Press, 1981).

89. Conrad Wright, *The Beginnings of Unitarianism in America* (Boston: Beacon Press, 1955); idem, *The Liberal Christians: Essays on American Unitarian History* (Boston: Beacon Press, 1970); idem, ed., *A Stream of Light: A Sesquicentennial History of American Unitarianism* (Boston: Unitarian Universalist Association, 1975).

90. David Robinson, *The Unitarians and the Universalists* (Westport, Conn.: Greenwood Press, 1985); Sydney E. Ahlstrom and Jonathan S. Carey, eds., *An American Reformation: A Documentary History of Unitarian Christianity* (Middletown, Conn.: Wesleyan University Press, 1985); Conrad Edick Wright, ed., *American Unitarianism, 1805–1865* (Boston: Massachusetts Historical Society and Northeastern University Press, 1989). See also Olive Hoogenboom, *The First Unitarian Church of Brooklyn* (New York: First Unitarian Church, Brooklyn, 1987).

91. Cited above, note 64.

92. The parallels are especially noteworthy in Mark Noll, *Princeton and the Republic*, and Brooks Holifield, *The Gentlemen Theologians*.

93. See, for example, Bruce A. Ronda, ed., *Letters of Elizabeth Palmer Peabody: American Renaissance Woman* (Middletown, Conn.: Wesleyan University Press, 1984); Joan Waugh, *Unsentimental Reformer: The Life of Josephine Shaw Lowell* (Cambridge, Mass.: Harvard University Press, forthcoming).

94. For fascinating starts, see Richard Rabinowitz, *The Spiritual Self in Everyday Life: The Transformation of Personal Religious Experience in Nineteenth-Century New England* (Boston: Northeastern University Press, 1989); and James

Hoopes, *Consciousness in New England: From Puritanism and Ideas to Psychoanalysis and Semiotic* (Baltimore: Johns Hopkins University Press, 1989).

95. The connection is made explicit in Lawrence Levine, *Highbrow/Lowbrow: The Emergence of Cultural Hierarchy in America* (Cambridge, Mass.: Harvard University Press, 1989).

96. The continuity between antebellum religious developments and the present is illuminated in Frances FitzGerald, *Cities on a Hill: A Journey Through Contemporary American Cultures* (New York: Simon & Schuster, 1986), esp. 383–414.

PART IV

PROTESTANTISM
AND THE
MAINSTREAM

8

ETHNICITY AND AMERICAN PROTESTANTS

Collective Identity in the Mainstream

■ ■ ■

John Higham

THE "ETHNIC REVIVAL" of the 1960s began in the early years of the decade. It was nourished by the contrasting but fertilizing background of the Civil Rights movement, which already had a strong popular base and unambiguous political goals. The revival had neither. It started gently enough among scholars, engaged in an academic discussion of pluralism. At the heart of this discourse was a strikingly new emphasis on the power of race, religion, and ethnicity in structuring American society.

Describing deep fissures along religious as well as racial and ethnic lines, several notable sociological treatises argued that the fissures were here to stay. The books' titles alone will indicate the interest they must have aroused among historians of religion: *Protestant–Catholic–Jew: An Essay in Religious Sociology* (1955); *The Religious Factor: A Sociological Study of Religion's Impact on Politics, Economics, and Family Life* (1961); *The Protestant Establishment: Aristocracy & Caste in America* (1964); *Assimilation in American Life: The Role of Race, Religion, and National Origins* (1964). A similar message of persistent ethnic differences was conveyed by Nathan Glazer's and Daniel Patrick Moynihan's influential *Beyond the Melting Pot: The Negroes, Puerto Ricans, Jews, Italians, and Irish of New York City* (1963).[1]

In the second half of the decade, quickened by an explosive upsurge of black power and pride, the sense of ethnic differentiation within white America grew more insistent, more freighted with grievance. Foundations, educational administrators, and ethnic intellectuals added their voices and resources.[2] The rhetoric of the revival, with its increasingly hard-edged assertion of particular group identities, obviously clashed with liberal Protestant hopes for an ecumenical Christianity. Nevertheless, historians of American Protestantism were not altogether unready to join in such socially sanctified work. At a time of falling confidence in the status quo and rising respect for the durable strength of distinctive ethnic groups, a new incentive to rediscover the social foundations of religious differences was clearly tempting.

Two historiographical initiatives prepared the way for considering Protestants as ethnic in nineteenth- and twentieth-century America. Significantly, both of them were launched in the melioristic climate of the early sixties, when ideas about pluralism and assimilation were not sharply polarized.[3]

Political historians took the first of these initiatives in the course of challenging a predominantly economic interpretation of American history. Beginning in the late 1950s, Lee Benson undertook a rigorous analysis of election statistics all across New York state. His object was to identify the constituencies that supported each of the principal political parties during the antebellum decades. Were they class-based coalitions? Contrary to the standard progressive view, Benson's *The Concept of Jacksonian Democracy: New York as a Test Case* (1961) demonstrated a prevailing partisan alignment of religious and ethnic groups rather than a division of classes. Years later, a poll of professional historians rated Benson's powerful monograph one of the five most influential books on American political history since World War II. By then an "ethnocultural school" of younger historians, whom Benson and Samuel P. Hays had inspired, was busily extending and refining their cardinal distinction between native-born evangelical Protestants and other ethnic or religious groups—Catholics prominent among them—who were far less willing to use government as a means of civic improvement.[4]

The "new political history," as it was often labeled, was largely secular; it had a stronger allegiance to quantitative methods than to any religious tradition. Concurrently, however, a "New Social History," microscopically targeted on local communities, offered specialists in religious history a vehicle for exploring the ethnic roots and the everyday experiential contexts of different kinds of believers. Here a second ethnocultural trail was blazed by Timothy Smith.

A professor of history and education at the University of Minnesota, Smith was keenly interested in the ways in which evangelical Protestantism fostered "a generalized Protestant faith," common schools, and a common American culture.[5] Eager to widen the perceived reach of that inclusive American faith, Smith in 1962 organized an ambitious collaborative research project that examined in minute detail the religious and social acculturation of eastern European immigrants in the raw mining towns of northern Minnesota in the early twentieth century. A preliminary report on the project, which Smith published in 1966, stressed "an astonishingly rapid adjustment in all groups to prevailing American folkways" under the leadership of their own businessmen and clergy. More than ever, apparently, public schools in the Minnesota iron range towns were bringing disparate groups together. Soon, however, Smith was taken aback by the divisive splintering in religion and politics that tore many of those immigrant communities apart, leaving the fragments (as he reported but did not attempt to explain) encased in their own insularity.[6]

The project dragged on, turning gradually into a splendid archive—the Immigration History Research Center at the University of Minnesota. Eventually, Smith developed a characteristically optimistic interpretation of the religious lessons that could be drawn from the experience of America's immigrants. In eastern Europe as in America, he argued in the *American Historical Review* in 1977, ethnic identities have formed around religious traditions. The religious core of those ethnic communities has given them an expansive, hopeful orientation toward the future, rather than a static, backward outlook; that is what religion does. Smith acknowledged in passing that some ethnic groups may lack a progressive spirit; but static backward-lookers never entered his story.[7]

Furthermore, Smith contended, the psychologically wrenching experience of migration deepens people's need for religion, which in turn has enabled them to join in new, enlarged communities adapted to change. Thus, Smith managed to accept the durability of ethnicity while finding in it a capacity for change and a promise of universal redemption. But he was no longer writing about specific ethnic groups in a concrete historical setting.

Throughout the late 1960s and 1970s, surrounding the systematic initiatives that Smith launched in social history and that the ethnocultural school awakened in political history, was a far wider outpouring of specialized ethnic studies from every part of the country. A careful bibliography of all doctoral dissertations on immigration and assimilation written in the United States between 1899 and 1972 revealed that half of that entire output was completed in the last ten years of the period, 1962 to 1972.[8] The overwhelming majority dealt with a single ethnic group to which the author felt related. Only a few, such as Philip Gleason's *The Conservative Reformers: German-American Catholics and the Social Order* (1968) and Kerby A. Miller's *Emigrants and Exiles: Ireland and the Irish Exodus to North America* (1985) have been works of distinction. Fewer still have the broad, comparative span of Stephan Thernstrom's *The Other Bostonians: Poverty and Progress in the American Metropolis, 1880–1970* (Cambridge, Mass., 1973), although we are seeing a slowly growing number of comparative histories of two or three groups in a common locale.[9]

What is more specifically germane to my own subject is the relatively small proportion of this huge literature that highlights religious aspects of the immigrant experience. Jay Dolan reported that of all the books reviewed over a twenty year span (1965–85) in four major historical journals that cover immigration history and history of religion, only 58 featured both immigration and religion. Dolan considered that number quite meager, since one journal alone reviewed about 400 books on American history each year.[10]

These figures may give an unduly negative impression, however. Historians of immigration have long known that among the foundations of an immigrant settlement the church was second only to the family. In the nineteenth century, acquiring a place of worship usually engaged the immigrants' earliest collective efforts. The church or synagogue then sustained and nurtured the fledgling community. Yet the institution that established the community could also become a cockpit of internecine strife. Surveys of the major immigrant groups typically cover in some fashion (if they do not always emphasize) both the centrifugal and the centripetal energies of religion.[11] A multitude of more specialized studies examine the immigrant religions in depth. It is not altogether surprising that the first substantial and impressive scholarly monograph on a topic in American immigration history was George Stephenson's now-classic *Religious Aspects of Swedish Immigration* (1932).[12]

Not all ethnics, of course, identify themselves with immigration. Many have been here too long for that; they have forgotten remote external origins and have acquired new identities in this country. Dolan would have found a far larger corpus of writing if he had counted works treating religion and ethnicity rather than religion and immigration. African Americans, American Indians, and the various white ethnic minorities that are indigenous to the United States, such as Mormons, Southerners, and Down-Easterners would have come within his purview. Nearly all of these have received abundant scholarly appraisal in recent years.

I mention these far-flung extensions of my assigned topic not because I propose to cover them but rather to make clear how much this essay must leave out. Lacking the competence to assess the enormous range of ethnic identities that have drawn upon one or more threads in the great tapestry of Protestantism—or have taken shape in resistance to it—I shall limit myself to one central subject: the making and unmaking of a specifically ethnic consciousness within the so-called "mainstream" of American Protestantism. This is the truly neglected dimension in the abundant ethnic and immigration history that scholars have produced during the last three decades. With rare exceptions that will appear in due course, historians have not written about an overall Protestant identity. I shall try to explain why, and also to sum up what—on the basis of present knowledge—can be said about this curiously unpopular subject.

Some may feel that I exaggerate the avoidance of ethnic issues by Protestant historians. Perhaps I do. But consider the early initiatives that have never been effectively followed up. The ethnocultural school of political historians had much to offer to historians of religion, yet the latter made almost no response. Among the large number of graduate students whom Timothy Smith trained, I know of only one who has actively pursued Smith's interest in the interaction between religion and ethnicity.[13] The others have reverted either to one or to the other, and Smith himself has returned to the internal history of religion. Jon Butler might also be listed as a dropout from the field of immigrant religion. His first book was a sophisticated study of French Huguenots and their assimilation in early America. Yet only in a brief footnote does his recent article, "The Future of American Religious History," makes room for scholarship linking religion and ethnicity.[14]

Why, among important American historians in the 1970s and 1980s, an initial fascination with the ethnicization of religion seemed to shrivel and fragment may be only too easy to understand. As differentness gathered ever more respect and affirmation in the milieu in which historians worked, ethnicity became the possession, the solace, and the shield of the "other." It belonged to minorities, and thus by definition excluded any majoritarian identity, however mistaken such an exclusion might be. Mainstream Protestantism, trapped in entanglements with dominant institutions and burdened by its own fast eroding power and status, had scant access to the language of ethnic grievance.

Still, there remain two offbeat historians who have tried to discern what an ethnic Protestantism might mean. Before comparing their theses and relating my own suggestions to their work, we will need a little more definition of ethnicity than I have supplied so far.

Ethnicity is one of those elusive and elastic concepts that lend themselves to many cross-purposes. It generally refers to "a segment of a larger society whose members are thought, by themselves and/or others, to have a common origin and to share important segments of a common culture."[15] Ethnic groups coalesce through a perception of difference from other collectivities that also claim a special, supposedly distinctive heritage. Since the group's differentness is perceived as a legacy from the past, in order to endure the group must transmit an identity from one generation to the next and reenact that identity in compelling symbols. Whatever commonly shared possessions the group can lay claim to—such as language, religion, race, and territory—are used to maintain the boundary between itself and others or to alter the boundary to its own advantage.

As Smith, Martin Marty and others have pointed out, ethnicity is often the "skeleton," or supporting framework, around which religious traditions cohere, or (depending on how you look at it) religion is the energizing force behind ethnicity. Yet the relations between the great world religions and ethnicity are fundamentally ambiguous. Christianity in its largest dimensions struggles explicitly against ethnocentric closure. For centuries it has lent itself to imperial or to universal purposes. To assess the bearing of ethnicity on American Protestantism, both the ethnic and the supraethnic aspects of Christianity will have to be considered.

Two recent works provide, in contrasting ways, a useful starting point. R. Laurence Moore's widely and justly appreciated book *Religious Outsiders and the Making of Americans* (1986) lays out our first sustained interpretation of what ethnicity has contributed to the vitality of the major American religions. Harry S. Stout's brief, obscurely published article "Ethnicity: The Vital Center of Religion in America" (1975) presents a more systematic but almost totally contrary view of how "ethnic allegiance [has] assumed both the function and authority of religion" in America.[16] Moore and Stout agree on the importance of ethnicity in the development of Protestantism, Catholicism, and Judaism. They disagree on almost everything else.

Moore writes against the ideal that used to govern Protestant historiography: anticipation of a unified church. More vigorously than anyone hitherto, he applies to American religions our contemporary appreciation of pluralistic diversity. Wherever Protestants or Catholics or Jews—dividing over their own religious beliefs and practices—spawn new sects, Moore discerns an "everlasting centrifugal force" that answers multitudinous needs for "a wise variety of social identities" in a bewilderingly formless society. Some of this fissiparous energy has flowed from ethnic minorities, whom Moore discusses with insight and empathy. Some of it has sprung from indigenously American creations, such as Christian Science and Jehovah's Witnesses. All of it has enabled "outsiders" to resist absorption while simultaneously claiming a place of their own in America.[17]

Religious Outsiders exemplifies the best contributions that cultural pluralism is making to contemporary scholarship; it also betrays the cardinal shortcoming of a pluralist perspective. I have argued elsewhere that pluralism is a philosophy of minority rights that has no place for majorities.[18] It may presuppose, but it can not effectively analyze, a center or a "mainstream." Accordingly, Moore delivers a powerful challenge to any dominant tradition without either affirming or denying the presence in American history of a normative, mainline Protestantism. It is simply left in the shadows, unexamined and undefined. The most that Moore gives us is an unanswered question. "Is the notion of Protestant hegemony a myth?" he asks. "Must we . . . renounce attempts to say what has been dominant or typical in America's religious past?" [19]

This is the very question that Harry Stout, writing eleven years earlier, had explored through the lens of ethnicity. Moore would say little about the dynamics of ethnicity. His attention would focus not on a process but on a status: the outsider status that both ethnic and nonethnic minorities have often deliberately sought. Their behavior, Moore thought, seems to owe less to their own distinctive characteristics than to the mysterious centrifugal energy that he found everywhere in American culture. For Stout, however, ethnic allegiances are the generative force and primary subject. They have dictated the changing shape and structure of religion throughout American history.

According to Stout, a transcendent faith, addressing all sectors of society, has rarely in America risen above its ethnic base. To counter the alienation that threatens people in a society as fluid and heterogeneous as ours, religion characteristically becomes "ethnoreligion," committed to maintaining and reinforcing a specific ethnic solidarity. What has changed over time is not group centeredness but rather a steady enlargement of the relevant group. In the first phase of this process, exemplified by Puritan New England, the ethnoreligion centered in one locally based church. It looked inward, endeavoring above all to preserve the integrity of its own community. From the late eighteenth century onward, a second phase followed, when the multiplication of outsiders threatened the established group. Through the instrument of the revival, white Protestants "expanded their ethnic consciousness." They built a pan-Protestant religious community, a benevolent empire that could retain hegemony by doing good. A similar evolution among other newcomers gradually produced four major ethnic communities: Protestant, Catholic, Jew, and black. At present, in a third phase, "faith" is merging with "success," and the ethnic identities of the four communities are slowly blending into a bland, all-embracing civil religion, "The American Way of Life." In this culminating phase the communal involvement and sense of identity present in the earlier phases dissolve. All are swallowed up in "mass society."

This bleak vision, so heavily charged with the spiritual despair of the Vietnam War era, preserves the traditional idea of a unifying mainstream while specifying its ethnocentric origin and stripping it of any universalizing purpose. In the end, the mainstream can no longer provide even a sustaining fellowship. America, Stout concludes, has never been a Christian nation and shows no sign of becoming one.

Most readers today will doubtless find Moore's cheerful pluralism—with its refusal to make grand claims for or against Christianity—more persuasive. Stout brushes aside too much of the variousness and contradiction in American life, too many of the tensions between collective self-interest and wider values. Nevertheless, his deployment of secondary sources and sociological theories does begin to historicize a center or mainstream. The construction of an American Protestant identity has been a powerful aspiration, and no history of American Protestantism that neglects it will be adequate. The pursuit of a generalized Protestant identity can be studied anew by examining Stout's framework in the context of Moore's pluralistic insights.

As Stout suggests, white Americans probably began to discover a Protestant communal identity—an interdenominational affiliation with one another—under the impact of the disestablishment of their churches and the resulting turn to an outreaching revivalism. Many of them had certainly regarded themselves in some sense as Protestants, that is, non-Catholic Christians. In nearly all of the Anglo-American colonies, however, that had been an attribute rather than an identity. The colonists had been Protestant in the same way that most of them knew themselves as civilized, or married, or among the "middling sort" of people. An ethnic identity requires more than some shared attributes. Let us remember that it entails a recognizable social boundary, maintained in order to defend a particular heritage from others who are thought to lack it.

Before the Revolution Protestants in the English colonies felt no need to league together, except in Maryland. Elsewhere, Catholics were not sufficiently visible to create a significant ethnic boundary. A close comparison between Puritan sermon literature in New England and in old England would probably show a striking difference in attention to "Romish priests" and papal plots, simply because removal from England left the Catholic threat far behind.[20]

By the eighteenth century expanding French settlements to the north and west were bringing Catholic power closer to the Anglo-American colonies. Even then, however, when Britain's Quebec Act of 1774 gave a wide sanction to the Roman Catholic religion on the very frontiers of Massachusetts and New York, the colonial reaction was less viscerally outraged than one might have expected. Nothing remotely comparable to the savage Gordon Riots, which ravaged Catholic premises in London for six days in 1780, ever occurred in British North America.[21]

During and after the Revolution, a swirl of competing beliefs kept religious attachments loose and unsettled. For several years, adherents of the former Church of England called it simply the Protestant Church, doubtless to protect it from angry, self-righteous patriots.[22] In reality, however, there was no Protestant church, not even the possibility of one—until the separation of church and state, together with the growing rationalism and secularism of the revolutionary era, inspired in some evangelical Christians a protoethnic reaction. They joined together as the destined guardians of virtue and order in the new republic.[23]

Ironically, the huge but incomplete success of the revival in the early nineteenth century denied conservative evangelicals the commanding role they sought. Revivalism democratized evangelical culture, opening it to vast numbers of people who had no sense of belonging to a "Standing Order" or of constituting a bounded community of Americans *par excellence*. Theirs was a movement aimed at converting everyone, not at a fixed or exclusive identity. They cared and quarreled about doctrine, not about descent.[24]

Had the evangelical movement carried everything before it, an ethnic Protestantism might have crystallized in the Jacksonian era, perhaps in connection with the Mexican War. The subsequent history of the United States could then have been very different. That did not happen, however, and the inability of anyone to speak unequivocally of American Protestants as a body was unintentionally confirmed by the first considerable historian of religion in America. Robert Baird's book *Religion in America* (1844) divided the religious scene into two parts: Evangelicals, whom Baird approvingly called "Orthodox Protestants" and all others, whom he labeled "Unevangelical." The Evangelicals "faithfully exhibit the fundamental and saving truths of the Gospel." The Unevangelical folk are the negative side of American religion because they neglect or reject the "great doctrines." This latter group includes Roman Catholics, Unitarians, Jews, Socialists, and Mormons.[25] Baird's categories reflect the consolidation not of a Protestant identity but of a strong evangelical identity that was increasingly displayed in lifestyles as well as in "saving truths." Yet that evangelical identity cut sharply across any larger Protestant presence. Between these highly moralistic, middle-class Evangelicals and more latitudinarian Protestants who frequently occupied a higher rank in society, social distance was wide and mutual antipathy sometimes acute.[26] An even greater gulf yawned between Evangelicals and a large part of the urban poor.[27] Evangelicals divided the public they sought to unite.

Not only were American Protestants in the early nineteenth century too disunited and unfamiliar with one another to constitute a people. Any consciousness of Protestantism as a collective heritage was entirely overshadowed by a larger attachment that was also more intimately personal. Evangelicals talked all the time about being or becoming Christians. To judge from the language they used, a Christian identity was far more intensely self-referential than was being a Protestant. When aspirants prepared themselves for conversion, they "determined to be Christians." When they joined a congregation, they rejoiced in "Christian fellowship." When they wanted political action, they called on "Christian patriots" to put "God and religion" above party and to remember that the United States was founded as a "Christian nation." All the while, these "professors" of Christianity gave their newspapers such names as *Christian Advocate, Christian Index, Christian Monitor, Christian Record, The Religious Herald*, and *Biblical Recorder.*[28] Until the nativist movement arose, no one seemed to think it worth while to put the word "Protestant" in the title of a religious paper. In the early republic, Protestantism was eclipsed on one side by a wider and deeper Christian identity and on the other by more specific denominational, doctrinal, and class allegiances.

Beginning in the 1830s, titles such as the *American Protestant Vindicator* appeared occasionally on the streets of New York City and Philadelphia. These papers marked the emergence of an anti-Catholic movement activated by the onset of mass immigration from Europe. For the first time organizations appealing explicitly to native white Protestants of every doctrinal persuasion presented themselves as the saviors, not only of Protestantism, but of the American republic.[29] Here was ethnicity, full-blown and rampant, and fired by an association of Protestant group consciousness with American nationalism.

In the extensive literature on nativism in the mid-nineteenth century historians have tried repeatedly to explain the astounding eruption in 1854–55 of a self-proclaimed American party. It elected eight governors, more than a hundred congressmen, and the mayors of Philadelphia, Chicago, and Boston, along with thousands of other officials, while mobs burned churches and devastated foreign quarters in numerous cities. For a while, the Americans seemed on the verge of replacing the Whigs as one of the two major political parties. Something momentous and baffling was happening.

Some historians have attributed these events primarily to the collapse of the "Second Party System," arising from the breakup of the Whig party and from popular disgust with politicians. Others have sought psychosocial explanations for irrational fantasies of papal conspiracies aimed at subverting republican institutions. In the same vein they have written about a displacement of anxieties, aroused by the escalating sectional conflict, which were projected on to a European despotism. Recently, scholars who emphasize the anti-immigrant rather than the anti-Catholic side of the upheaval have called attention to the enormous scale of immigration in the 1850s—resulting in foreign-born majorities in half a dozen leading cities—and the real strain this dramatic transition placed on civic order, political organization, and social services.[30]

All these factors were important. Yet they seem insufficient to account for the utter novelty in American history of a mass movement that was so socially divisive. One senses a need to look further to comprehend the nativist explosion of the 1850s not only in the context of immediate events but also in the perspective of long-term changes in American national consciousness.

It is a historiographical commonplace that American national feeling originated during the Revolution through agreement among American elites on a set of liberal principles as the foundation of a new republic. Scattered, decentralized, and ethnically heterogeneous, the infant nation had little adhesive force beyond a fervent belief in its political theory and a pride in the weak government the theory prescribed. Ethnic nationalism, in the sense of a popular consciousness of being a distinct, cohesive people, was virtually nonexistent. For some decades, therefore, the American Union seemed to contemporaries a frail experiment.[31] Yet public education, writers, newspapers, theaters, and perhaps above all the simple accumulation of shared memories gradually formed a recognizable American culture and even an uncertain sense of familiarity among those who shared it. Critics frequently predicted that a national character, though not yet achieved, was in the making.[32]

This aspiration for a more cohesive national feeling received significant impetus from a major shift in cultural sensibilities: the onset of romanticism. Unimpressed by abstract principles, romantic thinkers valued the organic solidarity and dynamic growth of living communities. History and tradition became essential sources of both ethnic and national identities. Except where a Puritan heritage lingered in New England, most white Americans in the early nineteenth century seem to have had little sense of comprising either an ethnic or a national community. Then romanticism, together with democracy, brought both to the fore.[33] Those mingled aspirations—partly for a more rooted sense of belonging to a distinctive place, partly for a closer feeling of identification with fellow citizens—produced an intense national fervor. It infused the nativist movement on one hand and the Civil War on the other.

Organic nationalism has often been an exclusionary force, intended to preserve racial hierarchies and reinforce ethnic boundaries. Alternatively, however, it can promote inclusiveness. It can weaken boundaries and foster a larger sense of interdependence among groups of very different origins, as in Herman Melville's Edenic vision of a gathering of "all tribes and peoples . . . into one federated whole . . . on this Western Hemisphere." What is more, both exclusionary and inclusive impulses can take hold, simultaneously and symbiotically, in the same population; for the integrative urge that drives people to uphold the solidarity and preeminence of their own group can also spur a widening fraternity among those who look to the future, not just the past. In the middle years of the nineteenth century, ethnic Protestantism and an increasingly inclusive American nationalism challenged and invigorated one another.[34]

Since romantic nationalism relied above all on a living past, we may turn to a leading mid-century American historian for the outlines of a national identity that combined an Anglo-Protestant core with an ever more cosmopolitan ethnic mixture. George Bancroft's *History of the United States of America* was the first eloquent and powerful history of this country. Until the end of the nineteenth century, it was also the greatest. By 1848 Bancroft had published five volumes and had established the scheme he pursued undeviatingly to completion in 1882. A romantic nationalist who drew heavily on German idealism during student years at Göttingen, Bancroft traced the unfolding in Anglo-America of a divinely ordained spirit of freedom, derived not only from immemorial customs of the Teutonic race and from English precedents but also from Christianity in general and Protestantism more particularly. In effect, Bancroft made a Protestant ethnic heritage an essential component of the genius of America.

Yet this celebration of Protestant and Anglo-Saxon origins said little that could feed the prejudices of the nativist movement, which Bancroft rebuked and disdained. More original than his interpretation of the sources of freedom was his constant, insistent focus on a gradual unification of the American colonies and the new nation. To mid-century Americans who felt deeply troubled over the obstacles that slavery and Catholic immigration posed to the march of freedom, Bancroft's *History* preached a thousand reassuring lessons in the ability of earlier generations to overcome external tyrannies and internal conflicts. His contrapuntal narrative was carefully structured to reflect creditably on each of the colonies. Above all, it dramatized a dialectical responsiveness of dissimilar colonies and different religions to one another. "The spirit of the colonies [Virginia and Maryland as well as New England] demanded freedom from the beginning," Bancroft declared. Therefore, the great achievement of the American people was the gradual nationalization of freedom through compromise, practicality, and popular sovereignty.[35]

In telling that story, Bancroft imbedded the formative ideology of the early republic in a long and growing tradition that pointed forward beyond the limitations of its origins. The unfinished work of the American people, he declared, was "building up the home of humanity . . . . By giving a welcome to every sect, America was safe against narrow bigotry . . . . as truth never contradicts itself, the collision of sects could but eliminate error; and the American mind, in the largest sense eclectic, struggled for universality, while it asserted freedom." [36] Accordingly, Bancroft's history acclaimed both Anglo-Protestant origins and an ever-expanding national identity. In effect, *The History of the United States* legitimated the preeminence of a Protestant heritage by blurring the boundaries between Protestants and others in a more inclusive, freedom-loving nation.

A similarly nonexclusive indistinctness invested the Protestant origins of various voluntary societies, including libraries, fraternal orders, and historical societies. All such projects, which multiplied steadily from the 1840s onward, resembled the nativist movement in wanting a more homogeneous civic life; but they sought it by a strategy of inclusion. Perhaps the most instructive of these enterprises, in terms of ethnicity, were cemeteries.

Burial grounds that maintain a link between generations are a powerful symbol as well as a literal sign of rootedness. Wherever ethnic groups insist on exclusive possession of a terrain—as in wars of "ethnic cleansing"—the bodies underground are likely to count in the struggle. They are therefore at risk of defilement or deportation.[37] In societies with easier intergroup relations, burial in a common location can readily signify permanent belonging and fellowship.

In early America, however, graveyards were feeble markers of either continuity or community. Land did not belong to tenaciously possessive ethnic groups. It belonged to individual families. So long as most of the English colonies and the states that succeeded them had scant history and even less tradition, burial places were casually maintained and fell readily into neglect. In towns they were adjuncts of particular houses of worship; in the countryside they gathered a family or an assortment of neighbors. For the most part, they registered loss, separation, and forgetfulness far more than any promise of continuity. Even George Washington's tomb, unattended, crumbled into ruins by the 1830s.[38]

Beginning in the 1830s, when the first monuments commemorating American heroes were erected—and then much more widely in the 1840s and 1850s—urban cemeteries underwent major face-lifting. New ones were designed as idyllic rural retreats, where townspeople could commune with nature while pondering markers of their common past. By featuring local worthies of an earlier era and by honoring the sons whom the community lost in the nation's wars, rural cemeteries offered Americans a powerful site of common memory. As collective memorials, these well kept, park-like shrines served (in the words of one scholar) to subdue "a strongly particularized memory" of individual loss and its associated grief "by eliciting contemplation of the integration of the dead into what was seen as a beneficent natural order."[39] Although inspired by European examples, this new form of civic display enjoyed a popularity in this country that astounded European visitors. In 1866 the *New York Times* described Brooklyn's Green-Wood Cemetery as an attraction on a par with Central Park and Fifth Avenue.[40]

The "rural" cemeteries were also distinctive in blending an unostentatiously Protestant sponsorship with a broadly patriotic and civic appearance. Working through nonsectarian corporations established solely to manage each cemetery, the Protestant civic leaders who created them took care to offer lots to people of modest as well as substantial means, to receive the dead of any religion, and at least in the early years to set aside sections for immigrants who (in the words of one advertisement) may "wish to lie side by side . . . far away from the homes and graveyards of their Fatherland."[41]

In sum, the new cemeteries resembled Bancroft's *History* in structure and purpose. Both offered glimpses of a nondenominational Protestant identity emerging from sectarian competition and functioning as the core of a larger national unity. In contrast to the nativist movement, both the rural cemetery and the romantic historian pursued a goal of integration through a strategy of inclusion. The cemetery was a symbolic ground where Nature's Nation could enfold its diverse population in a sacred unity. The *History* was a sacred text assuring the continuation of the process.

Still, inclusiveness under Protestant leadership was hardly more than an aspiration in the mid-nineteenth century. For the cities of the North, the overwhelming reality from the 1840s onward was a fracturing of consciousness and an extension of government under the pressure of a huge, predominantly Catholic immigration. The inclusive ideal of the rural cemetery quickly confronted a resolute resistance from other religious traditions. Adapting to American conditions, Catholics and orthodox Jews laid out their own separate graveyards, hallowed by their own rituals of consecration. Especially among Catholics, burial on their own ground was a compelling need. In 1850, for example, the City Inspector of New York reported that almost a third of the New Yorkers who died during the preceding year were interred in the new Catholic cemetery in Williamburgh. This was many times the number of interments in the already famous Greenwood Cemetery. It also substantially exceeded burials in Potter's Field or in any other graveyards nearby.[42]

In short, the disposition of the dead reflected both sides of a growing ethnic and national consciousness among the living. The desire of some elite Protestants to belong to a broadly national community, and to stand collectively preeminent within it, prefigured a more inclusive American-ism on one hand and a more ethnocentric feeling on the other. One result was to endow American cities with their first vivid symbols of civic unity and natural harmony. At the same time, however, effervescent Christian identities rooted in interdenominational competition were in some mea-sure condensing into a generalized Protestantism defined by native de-scent. Cities were now seen as composed of groups, not individuals. And prominent among the groups was a "plague of strangers."[43]

The ethnic landscape, then, was already shifting when an immigration crisis in the mid-1850s, coming on top of a sectional crisis, produced an earthquake. To many Americans the threats from a Slave Power in the South and an invasion of Catholic immigrants in the East looked much alike. In both cases the agents of a reactionary despotism—slaveholders and mentally enslaved foreign voters—seemed to be dividing the country and turning back the advance of freedom and righteousness. Against the corrupt politics associated with popery and slavery, the American (or Know-Nothing) party offered itself as an instrument of moral purifica-tion.

On the positive side, the Know-Nothings succeeded briefly as a patri-otic reform movement rooted in mainstream values. Some of the cities and states they controlled benefited from legislation on women's rights, public health and order, and imprisonment for debt. Yet their success was short-lived. Antislavery, proving stronger than nativism, soon found in the Republican party a vehicle of its own, uncontaminated by religious intolerance.[44] That negative side of nativism antagonized many Protes-tants and other Americans as an unpardonable violation of the core val-ues of American freedom.

So the nativist eruption of the 1850s subsided with its goals unat-tained and its fears unrealized. Nevertheless, it dramatized a new era in the structuring of American ethnicity. A native-born white Protestant community had come into being. Although still relatively weakly linked to one another and compelled to recognize themselves as one people within a larger nation, these older white Americans had learned to use a key lesson of romanticism: descent from the founding fathers of the country conferred indisputable cultural authority.

According to a close student of the period, the nativist outburst—for all the rancor that it spawned—gave Americans of Protestant or native descent some of the communal feeling and ethnic warmth that the Irish and Germans had always enjoyed. In Buffalo and probably in other mul-tiethnic cities, it fostered among Americans a new capacity to subordi-nate their own internal divisions to larger civic purposes.[45]

As nativism receded, this enhanced sense of interdependence—together with an ethic of cultural responsibility—widened the stream of civic voluntarism that had risen in the 1840s. The Civil War called forth prodigies of voluntary organization, especially through the United States Sanitary Commission, and after the war the Protestant community busied itself endlessly in founding more hospitals, libraries, historical societies, and fraternal orders, organizing pioneer celebrations, building grandly imposing churches, and sponsoring large interdenominational projects such as Chautauqua, the YMCA, and the Woman's Christian Temperance Union. At an elite level, intercollegiate athletics and the first socially prominent athletic clubs in major cities belonged to the same loose, far-flung network of social cohesion.[46]

The moral issues and ethnocultural conflicts that had engaged evangelical Protestants and nativists before the Civil War persisted long after it. Time and again problems of immigration, strong drink, political corruption, and the regulation of schools mobilized Protestant voters. Yet little changed in social relations or political power, and no crisis comparable to that of the 1850s broke until the 1920s. It is true that social separation in private life between the major ethnoreligious groupings prevailed, and true also that by the end of the nineteenth century blatant discrimination in employment was becoming widespread. Catholic girls were sought, for example, for clerical work, while advertisements for bookkeepers and other higher level white collar positions often specified "Protestant preferred."[47]

In such ways the invisible boundary between "mainstream" Protestants and other Americans sharpened as racial nationalism intensified throughout the western world. Nevertheless, the boundary was seldom openly defended. On some sides (though not on all) it was fairly porous. In comparative perspective, one may ask why and how the United States in the late nineteenth century avoided a punishing *Kulturkampf*. Surely, part of the answer must be that outside of the South the Protestant community retained its cultural authority without insisting on political predominance, without extending its social boundaries aggressively into the public sphere, and without repressing its internal diversity. Protestants lived within a larger national community that did not as a matter of principle inquire too closely into religious beliefs or into the ethnic origins of the white population.

Accordingly, the Protestant community in the late nineteenth and early twentieth century depended far more on the vitality and influence of its leadership in politics, culture, business, and philanthropy than it did on the strength of uncertain and shifting boundaries. This was the golden age of ethnic Protestantism. Its universities, richly endowed and open to students of all antecedents, rivaled the best in Europe. Its art museums attained equal distinction; so did its architects. Its urban planners filled the cities with parks. Its greatest foundations developed international programs of public health and literacy. Its political leadership reached an apogee in Woodrow Wilson, and the growth of Protestant church membership in the major cities culminated about the same time. Winthrop

Hudson has rightly called the period from 1890 to 1914 "the halcyon years" of American Protestantism.[48]

Nevertheless, in those same years the intellectual and social elites on which Protestantism relied so heavily were drifting away from the rank and file of the ethnic community. The Protestant Ascendancy, as Joseph Alsop has styled the northeastern upper class, was sealing itself off from the rest of society, including the Protestant middle class. At the same time, in rebellion against their own ethnic origins, a generation of "young intellectuals" of heterogeneous antecedents redefined America as a pluralistic nation without a legitimately dominant culture.[49] By the 1920s, intellectuals ceased to be guardians of the inherited culture. They became its adversaries or critics.

Consider the dismay that provincial Protestants after World War I, especially in the South and Midwest, must have felt at the changes sweeping through a nation they had been taught to regard in some special way, though not exclusively, as their own. The autonomy of their home towns was yielding to national advertising, marketing, and mass culture. The cities were awash in alcohol and alien peoples, the movies full of sex and sin. Many periodicals publicized a widespread concern that America was losing its Protestant character.[50]

Perhaps most threatening of all was the inescapable recognition that the leaders who had customarily spoken for the Protestant masses, and provided them with a model of aspiration and conduct, were giving way to faceless bureaucrats in the business world, cosmopolitan secularists in the universities, and corrupt politicians in both political parties. These changes lend a poignant significance to a confession in 1926 by the Imperial Wizard and Emperor of the Ku Klux Klan. "We are a movement of the plain people," wrote Hiram Wesley Evans, "very weak in the matter of culture, intellectual support and trained leadership." This "makes it very hard for us to state our case and advocate our crusade. If the Klan should ever fail, it would be from this cause."[51]

So the *Kulturkampf* came in the 1920s, and with it a shattering defeat for a futile and often vicious effort to close ranks, purge evildoers, and somehow restore a purified, Protestant society in which government by the people would once more prevail, as Klansmen imagined it had in the past. The nativists of the 1850s had been much less exclusionistic. Only in California had they tried to legalize economic discrimination against foreigners or to prohibit the entry of any immigrant group.[52] The failure of the mid-nineteenth-century nativist movement had been tactical but far from humiliating. The Klan's was complete. In contrast to the Know-Nothing party, which was superseded by a stronger reform movement, the Klan was simply driven from the field by its own crimes and the superior strength of its enemies. In dozens of cities far more outrages were committed against the Klan than it succeeded in perpetrating.[53]

To simplify a complex scene of cultural conflict in the 1920s, it may be sufficient to say that the Klan was a desperate, last-ditch effort to reimpose by intimidation a Protestant moral code to which other Americans—including business elites, intellectuals, universities, and mass media—would no longer submit.[54] A sense of impending dispossession and of the urgency of closing ranks against invading forces hangs over all of the moral rearmament and struggles for power that the Klan undertook. But the country had spun out of the control of any single ethnic group.

The collapse of the Ku Klux Klan and the subsequent breakup of ethnic Protestantism during the 1940s and 1950s taught a lesson that has since been faithfully observed: Protestantism in America cannot depend on defending its boundaries. It must have enlightened leaders who rise above ethnic enclosures. This is not the kind of lesson that contemporary ethnic studies feature. It does not fit very well with the ethnic historian's characteristic theme of endurance and survival in a painful or hostile environment. Perhaps that is why the history of a general Protestant identity has been neglected, and also why that story has a troubling but hopeful message for all Americans.

NOTES

1. For a sympathetic overview of the progress of ethnic scholarship in the 1960s and 1970s, see Rudolph J. Vecoli, "Return to the Melting Pot: Ethnicity in the United States in the Eighties," *Journal of American Ethnic History* 5 (1985): 7–20.

2. For a succinct account of the white-ethnic revival as an organizational project see Arthur Mann, *The One and the Many: Reflections on the American Identity* (Chicago, 1979), 1–45.

3. Philip Gleason, "American Identity and Americanization," in *Harvard Encyclopedia of American Ethnic Groups,* ed. Stephan Thernstrom (Cambridge Mass., 1980), 45–55. This entire essay is essential background to the present chapter.

4. Allan G. Bogue, "The New Political History in the 1970s," in *The Past Before Us: Contemporary Historical Writing in the United States,* ed. Michael Kammen (Ithaca, 1980), 231–251.

5. Timothy L. Smith, "Protestant Schooling and American Nationality, 1800–1850," *Journal of American History* 53 (March 1967): 679–695. The quoted phrase is on 694.

6. Cf. Timothy L. Smith, "New Approaches to the History of Immigration in Twentieth-Century America," *American Historical Review* 71 (July 1966): 1265–1279, with his "Religious Denominations as Ethnic Communities: A Regional Case Study," *Church History* 35 (June 1966): 1–20. The unacknowledged contrast between the generalities of the first paper and the close-up view of local ethnic communities in the second could hardly be more startling. Smith's original emphasis on convergence between immigrant aspirations and preexisting American values was renewed in his "Immigrant Social Aspirations and American Education, 1880–1930," *American Quarterly* 21 (Fall 1969): 523–43.

7. "Religion and Ethnicity in America," *American Historical Review* 83 (December 1978): 1155–1185.

8. Jay P. Dolan, "Immigration and American Christianity: A History of Their Histories," in *A Century of Church History: The Legacy of Philip Schaff*, ed. Henry W. Bowden (Carbondale, Ill., 1988), 136.

9. The first of these, perhaps, was Josef J. Barton's *Peasants and Strangers: Italians, Rumanians, and Slovaks in an American City* (Cambridge, Mass., 1975). One of the most powerful is Ramón Gutiérrez's *When Jesus Came the Corn Mothers Went Away: Marriage, Sexuality, and Power in New Mexico, 1500–1846* (Stanford, 1991), in which two religions and their interaction are a major theme.

10. "Immigration and American Christianity," 138. The journals Dolan studied were: *Journal of American History, American Historical Review, Church History,* and *Catholic Historical Review.*

11. See, for examples of titles that do not reveal their substantial religious content, Oscar Handlin, *The Uprooted* (Boston, 1951); Henry S. Lucas, *Netherlanders in America: Dutch Immigration to the United States and Canada, 1789–1950* (Ann Arbor, 1955); Arthur Hertzberg, *The Jews in America: Four Centuries of an Uneasy Encounter* (New York, 1989); Odd S. Lovoll, *The Promise of America: A History of the Norwegian-American People* (Minneapolis, 1984); Victor R. Greene, *American Immmigrant Leaders, 1800–1910: Marginality and Identity* (Baltimore, 1987); and the valuable scholarly articles in *Ethnicity on the Great Plains,* ed. Frederick C. Luebke (Lincoln, Neb., 1980). I am especially indebted, however, to a splendid reprint collection of scholarly articles, *The Immigrant Religious Experience,* vol. 19 of *American Immigration & Ethnicity,* ed. George E. Pozzetta (New York, 1991).

12. Minneapolis, 1932.

13. Richard W. Pointer, *Protestant Pluralism and the New York Experience: A Study of Eighteenth-Century Religious Diversity* (Bloomington, 1988).

14. Jon Butler, "The Future of American Religious History," *William & Mary Quarterly* 42 (April 1985): 167–83. Martin E. Marty's presidential address, "Ethnicity: The Skeleton of Religion in America," *Church History* 41 (March 1972): 5–21, was an especially vivid summons to students of religion to repair their neglect of the ethnic history of native-born white Protestants. The road Marty pointed down, however, remains almost untraveled.

15. J. Milton Yinger, "Ethnicity," *Annual Review of Sociology* 11 (1985): 159. A similar definition, which adds that "ethnic groups are larger than kin or locality groups and transcend face-to-face interaction," is in Wendell Bell, "Comparative Research on Ethnicity: A Conference Report," Social Science Research Council *Items* 28(4) (December 1974): 61–64. Additional theoretical papers are in *Ethnicity, Ethnic Identity, and Language Maintenance,* vol. 16 of *American Immigration & Ethnicity,* ed. George E. Pozzetta (New York, 1991).

16. *Ethnicity* 2 (1975): 204–224 (quote from 207). I would never have discovered this article had not George E. Pozzetta included it in his admirable anthology, *The Immigrant Religious Experience.*

17. Thus, depicting the "outsider"—the other—as a beneficiary of religious pluralism, Moore disputes the preoccupation with victimization that had become characteristic of pluralist historiography. See the elaboration of his argument in "Insiders and Outsiders in American Historical Narrative and American History," *American Historical Review* 87 (1982): 390–423.

18. John Higham, *Send These to Me: Immigrants in Urban America.* Revised ed. (Baltimore, 1983), 198–232.

19. Moore, *Religious Outsiders,* 21.

20. References to Rome or to Catholicism appear nowhere, for example, in the indexes to Perry Miller's two-volume *The New England Mind* (Cambridge, Mass., 1939, 1953), and Harry S. Stout tells me that his own "fairly extensive reading of Puritan sermons . . . found relatively little Catholic-bashing (though it was certainly present in small degrees)."

21. C. Shibata, "'Most Fatally Mischeivous [sic] to the British Colonies': Changing Colonial Reactions to the Quebec Act," American history seminar paper, The Johns Hopkins University, October 6, 1993. On English anti-Catholicism, see John Brewer, *The Common People and Politics, 1750–1790s* (Cambridge, 1986), 38–39, 138–39.

22. *Dictionary of American English on Historical Principles*, ed. William Craigie, 4 vols. (Chicago, 1936–44), 3: 1845.

23. Charles I. Foster, *An Errand of Mercy* (Chapel Hill, 1960).

24. Walter B. Posey, *Religious Strife on the Southern Frontier* (Baton Rouge, 1965). See also Nathan O. Hatch, *The Democratization of American Christianity* (New Haven, 1991).

25. Robert Baird, *Religion in America, or, an Account of the Progress, Relation to the State, and Present Condition of the Evangelical Churches in the United States with Notices of the Unevangelical Denominations* (New York, 1844), extracted in *The American Evangelicals, 1800–1900: An Anthology*, ed. William G. McLoughlin (New York, 1968), 30–40.

26. Kathryn K. Sklar, *Catharine Beecher: A Study in American Domesticity* (New Haven, 1973), 123. The origins of this psychosocial cleavage are examined in Philip Greven, *The Protestant Temperament: Patterns of Child-Rearing, Religious Experience, and the Self in Early America* (New York, 1977).

27. Elliott J. Gorn, "'Goodbye Boys, I Die a True American': Homicide, Nativism, and Working-Class Culture in Antebellum New York City," *Journal of American History* 74 (September 1987): 398–410.

28. Anne C. Loveland, *Southern Evangelicals and the Social Order, 1800–1860* (Baton Rouge, 1980), 1, 93, 109, 111, 123; Donald G. Mathews, *Religion in the Old South* (Chicago, 1977). By midcentury, however, Evangelical writers were applying to their own interdenominational activity a different global term—"the Church"—which hints at an emerging pan-Protestant identity. C. C. D., "Fidelity in the Church," *The Independent* 10 (January 7, 1858), 6; and "The Revival," *New York Weekly Tribune*, March 13, 1858, p. 4.

29. See the excellent bibliography in Ray Billington, *The Protestant Crusade, 1800–1860: A Study of the Origins of American Nativism* (New York, 1938). In Boston one of these early champions of "the sun of Protestantism" against "the dark cloud of Popery" was edited by a Unitarian. J. Elaine Frantz, "Through the *Eagle's* Eye: Anti-Catholicism and Self-Reflection in *The Daily American Eagle*, 1844–1845," American history seminar, The Johns Hopkins University, March 31, 1993. On the beginnings of anti-Catholicism in New York City, see Sean Wilentz, *Chants Democratic: New York City & the Rise of the American Working Class, 1788–1850* (New York, 1984), 85–86.

30. All these have been effectively synthesized in David H. Bennett, *The Party of Fear: From Nativist Movements to the New Right in American History* (Chapel Hill, 1988), 27–155.

31. John M. Murrin, "A Roof without Walls: The Dilemma of American National Identity," in *Beyond Confederation: Origins of the Constitution and American National Identity*, ed. Richard Beeman et al. (Chapel Hill, 1987).

32. Paul C. Nagel, *One Nation Indivisible: The Union in American Thought 1776–1861* (New York, 1964), 170–72. See also Joseph M. Torsella, "American National Identity, 1750–1790: Samples from the Popular Press," *Pennsylvania Magazine of History and Biography* 112 (April, 1988): 168–87; "American Society as a Field for Fiction," in *Prose Writings of William Cullen Bryant*, ed. Parke Godwin. 2 vols. (New York, 1901), 2:351–60; Nathaniel Hawthorne, *Our Old Home: A Series of English Sketches* (Columbus, Ohio, 1970), 325.

33. On the deepening of memory and tradition in the mid-nineteenth-century, see Michael Kammen, *Mystic Chords of Memory: The Transformation of Tradition in American Culture* (New York, 1991), 78–90.

34. My argument here will not find favor among those who conceive of loyalty as a zero–sum game, and are convinced that large, impersonal collectivities tend to victimize smaller communities.

35. George Bancroft, *History of the United States,* 14th ed. (Boston, 1848), 1: vii, 2: 451–54. See also the valuable abridgement of the entire work by Russel B. Nye (Chicago, 1966).

36. Nye, 223; Bancroft, 2: 464. For a more explicit statement of Bancroft's universalist and antinativist bent, see his powerful address to the New York Historical Society, "The Necessity, the Reality, and the Promise of the Progress of the Human Race" (1854) in his *Literary and Historical Miscellanies* (New York, 1855), 504–17. For comparisons between Bancroft and other contemporary historians see J. V. Matthews, "'Whig History': The New England Whigs and a Usable Past," *New England Quarterly* 51 (June 1978): 193–208.

37. *New York Times,* October 28, 1992, A9; February 3, 1993, A6; and January 18, 1996, A6.

38. David Charles Sloane, *The Last Great Necessity: Cemeteries in American History* (Baltimore, 1991), 3–27, 80. See also *Cemeteries and Gravemakers: Voices of American Culture,* ed. Richard E. Meyer (Ann Arbor, 1989), and for comparison John Matturri, "Windows in the Garden: Italian-American Memorialization and the American Cemetery," in *Ethnicity and the American Cemetery,* ed. Richard E. Meyer (Bowling Green, Ohio, 1993), 14–35.

39. Matturri, "Windows in the Garden," 15; Sloane, *Last Great Necessity,* 80–81. Sloane records the creation in New York state of just two rural cemeteries in the 1830s, followed by eight in the 1840s and fifteen in the 1850s, 93.

40. Kenneth T. Jackson and Camilo Jose Vergara, *Silent Cities: The Evolution of the American Cemetery* (New York, 1989), 19.

41. Jackson and Vergara, *Silent Cities,* 52. Many rural cemeteries in the North accepted African Americans. Some did not. See Sloane, *The Last Great Necessity,* 83, and Ann and Dickran Tashjian, "The Afro-American Section of Newport, Rhode Island's Common Burying Ground," in Meyer, *Cemeteries and Gravemarkers,* 163–96.

42. New York City, Common Council *Manual of the Corporation, 1850,* 328, 331. On Jewish burial grounds, see Jackson, *Silent Cities,* 56.

43. Alan I. Marcus, *Plague of Strangers: Social Groups and the Origins of City Services in Cincinnati, 1819–1870* (Columbus, Ohio, 1991).

44. Tyler Anbinder, *Nativism and Slavery: The Northern Know Nothings and the Politics of the 1850s* (New York, 1992).

45. David A. Gerber, *The Making of an American Pluralism: Buffalo, New York 1825–1860* (Urbana, 1989), 377–91.

46. Jeffrey Charles summarizes the explosive growth of fraternal orders in *Service Clubs in American Society: Rotary, Kiwanis, and Lions* (Urbana, Ill., 1993), 11–18. On the emergence of a grand style in church architecture, see Michael Frisch, *Town into City: Springfield, Massachusetts, and the Meaning of Community, 1840–1880* (Cambridge, Mass., 1972), 145. On postwar athletic organizations, see Benjamin G. Rader, *American Sports: From the Age of Folk Games to the Age of Spectators* (Englewood Cliffs, N.J., 1983), 50–57, 70–80, 108–11, 149–52.

47. Walter Licht, *Getting Work: Philadelphia, 1840–1950* (Cambridge, Mass., 1992), 78–79, 95, 133–38. On the social separation of Anglo-Protestants from other religious and ethnic groups, see Olivier Zunz, *The Changing Face of Inequality: Urbanization, Industrial Development, and Immigrants in Detroit, 1880–1920* (Chicago, 1982), 55–59, 68.

48. Winthrop Hudson, *American Protestantism* (Chicago, 1961), 124–27. For statistics, see Kevin J. Christiano, *Religious Diversity and Social Change: American Cities, 1890–1906* (New York, 1987).

49. *I've Seen The Best of It: The Memoirs of Joseph W. Alsop* (New York, 1992); David A. Hollinger, "Ethnic Diversity, Cosmopolitanism and the Emergence of the American Liberal Intelligentsia," *American Quarterly* 27 (1975): 133–51; Lawrence J. Oliver, "Theodore Roosevelt, Brander Matthews, and the Campaign for Literary Americanism," *American Quarterly* 41 (1989): 93–111.

50. David Reimers, "Protestantism's Response to Social Change, 1890–1930," in Frederic C. Jaher, ed., *The Age of Industrialism in America* (New York, 1968), 369–78; Gregory H. Singleton, *Religion in the City of Angels: American Protestant Culture and Urbanization, Los Angeles, 1850–1930* (Ann Arbor, 1979).

51. Quoted partly in Bennett, *Party of Fear*, 221, and partly in Stanley Coben, *Rebellion Against Victorianism: The Impetus for Cultural Change in 1920s America* (New York, 1991), 157. An older study reports that the heads of local "klaverns" in Pennsylvania were with few exceptions ordinary tradesmen or small businessmen, many of them with only elementary education. Emerson H. Loucks, *The Ku Klux Klan in Pennsylvania: A Study in Nativism* (Harrisburg, 1936), 60. See also: Kenneth T. Jackson, *The Ku Klux Klan in the City, 1915–1930* (New York, 1967); William D. Jenkins, *Steel Valley Klan: The Ku Klux Klan in Ohio's Mahoning Valley* (Kent, Ohio, 1990); Leonard J. Moore, *Citizen Klansmen: The Ku Klux Klan in Indiana, 1921–1928* (Chapel Hill, 1991).

52. The maximum demand of the Know-Nothing party was for restrictions not on immigration but on naturalization and alien voting. Cf. Anbinder, *Nativism and Slavery*, and Robert F. Heizer and Alan J. Almquist, *The Other Californians: Prejudice and Discrimination under Spain, Mexico, and the United States to 1920* (Berkeley, 1971).

53. Coben, *Rebellion*, 151–55.

54. For an informed review of recent scholarly literature, see Stanley Coben, "Ordinary White Protestants: The KKK of the 1920s," *Journal of Social History* 28 (1994): 155–65.

9

PROTESTANTS AND
ECONOMIC BEHAVIOR

▨ ▨ ▨

Robert Wuthnow
Tracy L. Scott

"IT IS INSTRUCTIVE TO TRACE . . . the influence of religious ideas on economic development. It is not less important to grasp the effect of the economic arrangements accepted by an age on the opinion which it holds of the province of religion." So wrote R. H. Tawney in his 1930 foreword to Max Weber's *Protestant Ethic and the Spirit of Capitalism.*[1] The half century since those words were written has witnessed a profusion of efforts to examine these reciprocal effects. The literature generated may not, as one recent review suggests, be as extensive as that concerned with, say, religion and politics, or revivals and religious movements.[2] Yet, in another sense, it is considerably richer because virtually all these other topics also include discussions of how religion and economic conditions have intertwined. Indeed, it becomes necessary to focus on studies that specifically address questions about the impact of religion on economic behavior (rather than simply the reverse) in order to delimit the topic at all.

Weber's own work has remained a prominent point of departure. How religious orientations may have contributed to the shaping of American capitalism has thus received much attention. Historians and sociologists have examined the impact of Puritanism and of subsequent variants of Protestantism on the American work ethic, asking how this ethic may have furthered economic development. Plausibility has been provided by Weber's argument that economic development depends heavily on individual motivation and that religious conviction can be a significant source of this motivation. To study the religious roots of economic behavior has thus been, as it was for Weber, a way of challenging economistic perspectives that associate economic development strictly with such factors as supply and demand, markets, technology, and labor management.

In the course of investigating the economic effects of religious ideas, recent inquiries have nevertheless moved in a number of new directions as well. Some have challenged Weber's special emphasis on the Puritan work ethic, showing that Puritanism was a complex of doctrines and practices that carried ambiguous economic consequences. Others have questioned whether ideological expressions of the work ethic in public life were adhered to as rigorously in the daily lives of Protestants themselves. Still others have emphasized the role of religious communities at the local level as a potentially more powerful influence than religious ideas alone. Tawney's appeal for investigations of the impact of economic conditions on religion has also been heard. Implicitly at least, most studies of the effects of religion on economic behavior have also made assumptions about how these effects may have been shaped by a particular stage of economic development.

This chapter provides an overview of the major lines of investigation into the relationships between Protestantism and economic behavior that have been evident in studies conducted during the past quarter century.[3] It argues that religious beliefs and practices have been demonstrated to have a significant impact on economic behavior, and thus remain relevant in efforts to understand the trajectory of American economic development. It also argues that the nature of this impact has become increasingly unclear, both in studies of more recent periods and in more recent studies of earlier periods. Thus, it seems doubtful that scholarship can turn as easily to studies of religion for straightforward evidence that economistic models are inadequate. Rather, future research will need to pay closer attention to the complexities of religious institutions and to the changing character of economic conditions.

Colonial America

Studies of colonial America, while raising questions about the relevance of Protestantism to a wide range of economic activities,[4] have been particularly interested in the fact that this period witnessed exceptional economic growth. Foreign and domestic trade, agriculture, settlement, population, profits, and artisanal industries all expanded. By 1765, the social order of the colonies had been markedly transformed. What had once functioned as close-knit communities, governed by biblical principles institutionalized in a strict code of civil and ecclesiastical law,[5] now seemed to revolve more around individual initiative and economic freedom. Religious ideas had undoubtedly contributed to these changes, for, as Weber suggests, the ascetic doctrines of the colonists encouraged them to work hard and to lead lives of sobriety and frugality. Yet the same ideas did not prevent wealth from being accumulated or discourage those who prospered from investing their wealth in larger enterprises. The question, then, is whether these very ideas, in a sense, became their own gravediggers. Did they inadvertently produce new economic conditions that they could no longer control? This possibility is, of course, consistent with Weber's own assertions. In his view, capitalism quickly became an all-encompassing system that no longer needed religious legitimation. If the question is consistent with Weber, the manner in which it has been addressed is, however, less concerned with ideas than with communities and social institutions. Research has emphasized the extent to which religious ideas in the American colonies were integrated with community structures that legitimated and enforced these ideas. As economic conditions changed, it was thus not so much a question of ideas ceasing to be relevant, but of strain developing in communities. Studies of religion and economic behavior in colonial America have thus been particularly concerned with the question of whether community broke down and, if so, to what extent and with what consequences.

Richard Bushman's study of colonial Connecticut has remained one of the most influential examinations of the relationships between Protestantism and economic behavior.[6] His argument, in brief, is that a radical transition took place between 1690 and 1765 from a homogeneous, close-knit, tightly controlled community of settlers to a more heterogeneous, loosely structured, individualistic society of traders, trappers, and farmers. Religion figures prominently at every phase of this transition: Puritanism initially undergirds civil authority and seeks to restrain worldliness; its doctrines are vulnerable to change, however, because they inadequately distinguish between laudable industry and the aggressive pursuit of wealth; resultant economic growth thus puts pressure on established religious institutions; their leaders respond by creating a more individualistic theology; and when this theology takes root during the Great Awakening, further economic change is legitimated. The upshot of these developments, in Bushman's analysis, is that community did indeed break down, economic expansion inevitably led to a more pluralistic and individualistic ethos, and Puritanism adapted to the transition, contributing further to the demise of community. On balance, religion functions in this account much as the Puritans themselves might have seen it: as a moral and spiritual force seeking to restrain the unruly and sinful passions of human nature but, in the short term at least, being unable to do so for the society at large.

In focusing as much as it does on the Great Awakening, Bushman's account tends to portray Puritanism as a static doctrine that essentially needed to be replaced in order for Protestantism to adapt to new economic circumstances—a view that has been challenged in research concerned with the ambiguous and internally diverse qualities of the Puritan settlements.[7] For example, Stephen Foster's study of colonial New England, focusing more on the seventeenth century, places greater emphasis on the dynamic character of Puritanism itself.[8] It imported traditional ideas from England but developed new ones unique to the experience of the New World as well. It emphasized not only communal authority but also individual conscience, championing both "order" and "love," and in doing so provided for a stronger and more inclusive ethic than one less fraught with ambiguities. The fact that Puritanism could not fully withstand later economic developments was, therefore, not so much a sign of weakness but evidence that it contained seeds of growth within itself. Foster's account nevertheless focuses ultimately on the same ambiguities that Bushman does. Puritanism encouraged diligence and thrift but sought to discourage the love of money. Scarcely anybody could devote their energies fully to the economic activities that were encouraged without also showing an interest in them. Thus, according to Foster, a strong element of guilt resulted that may have contributed to the eventual rise of conversionist beliefs during the Great Awakening.

That the authority of Puritan community gradually eroded is not in question. This erosion is, however, challenged in Christine Heyrman's more recent study of colonial Massachusetts.[9] She argues that commercial growth and prosperity did not precipitate drastic social and cultural changes but continued traditional Puritan values and behavior. Basing her conclusions on evidence from Gloucester and Marblehead between 1690 and 1750, she traces a dramatic shift from agriculture to trade and fishing and shows how the new mercantile economy included sharper differences between rich and poor, a more differentiated occupational structure, increased opportunity for social mobility, and a more fluid social order. These changes, however, did not bring about individualism, an entrepreneurial ethic, a decline in community authority, or an increased emphasis on conscience. Traditional ideas remained strong, restricting economic change but also surviving in the face of this change.

If Heyrman's study is concerned with showing the survival capacity of Puritan ideas, it nevertheless raises serious questions about how important a role these ideas may have played in colonial Massachusetts. They were, it appears, malleable to a great extent by local elites. In the conflict between locals and outsiders, control over prestigious positions in congregations and in town councils was sometimes fought out on the basis of religious creeds. New economic realities made conflict more likely but also gave resources to some established elites as well as to newcomers. Puritanism survived in Gloucester and Marblehead because the balance of power was in its favor. By inference, it probably did not fare as well in Boston or in Connecticut because the balance of power was not in its favor.

Puritanism was not the only important Protestant influence on economic life in colonial communities. Quakerism has long been connected with a successful economic ethic and strong community life in Pennsylvania. Frederick Tolles's classic study of the Quaker merchants of Philadelphia shows how their economic ethic of industry, prudence, honesty, and order contributed to the successful founding of the city.[10] However, soon after establishing this "holy experiment" the Quaker merchants experienced increasing tension between successful economic endeavors and religious participation and community. Participation in economic and political life—the "holy experiment"—inevitably led to a loss of simplicity and spirituality, essential elements of Quaker life. By the time of the Revolution, many Quaker leaders withdrew from the world in order to regain a holy community.

In his study of the Welsh and Cheshire Quakers of colonial Pennsylvania, Barry Levy finds a similar tension between an economic ethic encouraging discipline, hard work, and economic profits, and the "worldliness" that this ethic inevitably produced.[11] However, Levy traces this ethic to a more fundamental Quaker ideal of "domesticity," originating in the Quaker communities of northwest England.

The lesson from these studies, then, is that religious beliefs in colonial New England were concerned with how people should work and how they should regard their money; they were at the start a force in community life because of the authority of the clergy as well, and in some cases they continued to figure in disputes among local elites. None of these studies, however, demonstrates convincingly that religious beliefs placed effective curbs on material appetites or even that these appetites may have been channeled into productive enterprise by religious beliefs. Because Puritanism was such a prominent feature of public life, people did of course draw connections between it and economic behavior. It provided a language in which transactions could be interpreted, and in this sense it promoted community, whether in tightly bounded settings or in the culturally more diverse circumstances of the eighteenth century. Indeed, as J. E. Crowley shows, public discourse about work and work-related activities was embedded in a rich tapestry of language about morality, benevolence, civic obligation, and community responsibility.[12] Well into the eighteenth century, religious language was relevant to the ways in which people talked about economic behavior, but its emphasis on community was seldom powerful enough to inhibit the dynamics of economic development itself. As language, it was malleable, and therefore it survived by adapting to new circumstances. Historians disagree about how much was new and how much was retained, but they agree that adaptation was the case.

None of this should be very surprising—except for the fact that Weber believed people needed motivation for what they did and that religion provided such motivation. Yet more recent understandings of motivation regard it less as a stimulus guiding behavior in one direction or another than as a language for making sense of one's behavior.[13] Puritanism played its part eloquently. People made moral sense of events by imbuing them with sacred meaning, of coincidences and misfortunes by attributing them to demons and poltergeists, of themselves and their families through carefully chosen biblical names, and of their work by describing it as a calling. To work hard was evidence of doing God's will. But to want success so badly that cutting corners became necessary or that work itself ceased to be meaningful was considered excessive. The "calling" gave merchants a way to tell themselves why they were pursuing a particular line of work. But the same language allowed them to say why they were content not being more wealthy than they were or why they felt it was appropriate to open a new shop or to understand why their pastor had chosen to preach on a particular topic. The memoirs of London artisan Nehemiah Wallington capture what many of his Puritan counterparts in the New World probably felt as well. For him, the calling was not so much a decisive message causing him to enter a particular line of work as a constant reminder to discipline himself, observe godly priorities, work hard, trust in God, and refrain from envying his neighbors.[14] People worked long hours, some considerably longer than others, no doubt, but Puritanism also provided a way of understanding time that gave work meanings other than the sheer expenditure of energy. Time was part of a cosmic drama, it could consist of reverie, and it could be penetrated by the voices of angels. The mental world of Boston merchant Samuel Sewall (1652–1730), for example, was layered with multiple meanings of time that linked the everyday world directly to the divine. "Historical time, like the phases of a war and events in Massachusetts politics," writes David Hall, "was really prophetic time, and Sewall struggled to decipher the relationship between the two. Time for him was also a complex structure of coincidences. And time was finally 'God's time' . . . in that he alone determined what would happen."[15] Kenneth Silverman's biography of Cotton Mather also demonstrates clearly how Puritanism supplied a language for interpreting the smallest of everyday occurrences. For Mather, avoiding greed was not so much a matter of wanting a low salary (he wanted a higher one) or of doing without books (he had thousands), but of praying daily and attempting to balance evil with acts of charity.[16] Different ministers, congregations, and families also interpreted Puritan doctrines quite differently, some emphasizing moral discipline much more rigorously than others.[17] Had there been no Great Awakening, it is conceivable that commercial expansion would have taken place much as it did anyway, and that the War of Independence would also have been fought. But the Great Awakening would not thereby have been insignificant. Nor could its significance be understood strictly in religious terms. It supplied a language that enriched the daily lives of those who experienced it, gave them a way of understanding their spiritual longings as well as the new freedom they enjoyed in business, and made it possible for them to communicate with their neighbors.

An emphasis on language and meaning leaves open the question of larger influences on religion and economic behavior and is, for this reason, somewhat less intellectually satisfying than the approach of earlier studies. However, language does not exist in a social vacuum. Its meanings are conditioned by social circumstances. The important question, therefore, shifts from one about ideas influencing behavior and behavior influencing ideas, to one about contexts and meanings. Social contexts shape the ways in which ideas and behavior take on meaning. If it is assumed that people create meaning—that is, interpretations that make sense of their lives—by stitching their thoughts, speech, and actions together, then it would seem likely that these meanings might differ from situation to situation. Circumstances and events provide some of what requires interpretation as well as interests and goals that may shape the nature of those interpretations, and even the symbolic resources used to make them.

How such a perspective applies to the colonial period is illustrated by Gary Nash's study of Boston, New York, and Philadelphia in the years leading up to and including the Great Awakening.[18] Nash is especially concerned to show the rising importance of class conflict. His work is, accordingly, skewed at points by arguments about the disparities between lower and upper classes. With appropriate modifications, this emphasis nevertheless helps to illuminate how different economic circumstances may condition the interpretation and application of religious ideas. Further evidence comes from the fact that the three cities at issue provided different circumstances as well. In each of the three Nash perceives a strong influence in the seventeenth century from the relative stability of economic and political relationships. A hierarchical social order dominated by merchants encourages religious ideas to be interpreted in ways that restrain overzealous behavior on the part of elites and that account for (but do not attempt close supervision of) the behavior of the lower classes. The calling, for example, advocated acceptance of one's lot in life, and diligence in one's particular vocation, as all callings were of equal worth to God. Nash argues that this belief contributed to "the [only] modest ambitions" of laborers in the late seventeenth century. People still valued community—and their place in it—more than individual advancement and acquisition of wealth. During the next half century, the three towns underwent different paths of economic development, thereby conditioning the way in which the new ideas associated with the Great Awakening were interpreted.

John Brooke's study of pre-Revolutionary Massachusetts, focusing especially on the religious and political rhetoric of the period, shows in greater depth how the corporate life of towns was undergirded by arguments about sacred purpose.[19] Towns were economically regulated for the common good. Townspeople were expected to fulfill their "duty" to the town but also to reap rewards as part of a "covenant community" chosen by God. By analyzing sermons, Brooke traces the rhetoric of how material contributions to the community are linked to spiritual rewards. In practice, mutual benefit was legally mandated by a household monetary assessment that supported the town minister. All aspects of town life—spiritual, political, and economic—merged, and thus the town government regulated these realms to assure both contributions by and rewards to all inhabitants. The Great Awakening brought a change in public culture, Brooke argues, not simply by initiating new religious ideas but by shifting public discourse from its religious underpinnings to a republican vision of voluntary contractualism.

Research of this kind remains importantly concerned, therefore, with the mutual impact of religion and economic behavior, and recognizes that colonial America must be understood as a time of large-scale change in both religious thought and economic conditions. It challenges the view, however, that ideas led straightforwardly to particular kinds of behavior, or that economic conditions necessarily resulted in specific kinds of new ideas. The fact that economic *downturn,* if Nash is correct, was more conducive to the new ideas of the Great Awakening than economic prosperity, for example, presents a fundamental challenge to arguments that associate the latter simply with wider markets and expanding trade. Substantively, the result is a more variegated picture of the relationships between religious ideas and economic conditions in colonial America. This also means that more nuanced interpretations of the regional differences (for example, in the Great Awakening as experienced in Boston and in New York) must be taken into account. Theoretically, it suggests that the relationship between religion and economic behavior was contingent on different circumstances.[20]

The Era of Industrialization

Much of the research concerned with religion and economic behavior during the nineteenth century focuses on questions similar to those posed in studies of the colonial period. Questions about the religious motivations for working, the rise of individualism, and the breakdown of community continue to be prominent concerns. Many studies are concerned with the religious and moral responses to economic conditions accompanying industrialization.[21] Increasingly, questions about the relationships between religion and the legitimation of social class positions also become important. Studies focusing on the antebellum period emphasize the mixing of religion and economic interests among the rising middle classes, while studies of the postbellum period raise questions about these relationships among the urban and industrial working classes.[22]

Paul Johnson's study of Rochester, New York, during the 1820s and 1830s has been a particularly influential contribution to the literature on the relationships between religion and industrialization. He argues that the introduction of large-scale manufacturing in the 1820s involved an attendant attempt to subject workers to factory discipline and diligence in work. Johnson agrees with other historians of the early nineteenth century who assert that businessmen's preoccupation with Christian discipline and reform was, in part, a way to adapt to a new and growing market economy, and a new way to exercise power and control over others. Self-control was "the moral imperative around which the northern middle class became a class" (p. 6). However, he also argues that the motivation of the managerial classes included a sincere conviction that they were "civilizing" and "saving" their workers.[23]

Johnson's argument has been criticized by scholars who believe its emphasis on social control has been overstated. In their judgment, Johnson's Rochester industrialists are described as being more manipulative than they probably were.[24] Other studies of antebellum America, while frequently taking issue with Johnson, nevertheless give additional support to the idea that changing economic conditions encouraged religious practices emphasizing individual salvation and moral discipline, and that these practices in turn seem to have flourished among those in the vanguard of changing conditions.[25] John Hammond shows that revivals in the 1830s in New York state, Ohio, and Kentucky were more numerous in counties with small farms and large proportions of recent immigrants from New England.[26] His main concern is with the long-term political consequences of the revivals, but he also argues that revivalism represented a new set of religious beliefs concerned with the ability of individuals to change themselves and their world. Following Hammond, Richard Rogers demonstrates revivalism to have been positively associated with the rise of manufacturing and with commercial centers.[27] In subsequent work, Rogers has also argued that the content of religious movements during this period was shaped by circumstances other than market forces themselves.[28]

Anthony Wallace's study of Rockdale, a mill town near Philadelphia, traces the interplay of religious and economic factors during a period of rapid mechanization (1835–1850) by examining the influences of socialist utopianism and evangelical millennialism.[29] The former held that small rural communities were the natural human economic institution and that property and machinery should be owned by the community as a whole. The latter asserted that human nature is sinful and that only faith in God can make humans good and consequently produce a good society. Thus, in order to cure social ills, conversion was a necessary first step. Most of the prominent manufacturing families were evangelical Protestants and, by virtue of their influence and numbers, succeeded in silencing the socialist views.

Though it is based on data from later in the century, George Thomas's research provides further evidence of a relationship between changing economic conditions and religious beliefs. He demonstrates an "isomorphism" between religious individualism and that implied in the spread of capitalist agriculture, namely, the need for ascetic discipline to compete in long-distance markets.[30] Reviewing these and other studies of the period, Nathan Hatch concludes, "The Methodist regime of voluntarism and of disciplined collective action did not automatically translate into political or economic action, but it did become for thousands of Americans a profound shaper of behavior, a way of life, culturally attuned to the politics of self-professed interest groups and the economics of unabashed enterprise."[31]

For the latter half of the nineteenth century, attention shifts decidedly toward the relationships between religion and the behavior of the rising working class. Daniel T. Rodgers's study of the work ethic in industrial America provides a valuable point of departure.[32] Though religion figures only marginally in his account, Rodgers is centrally concerned with the transition from an eighteenth-century work ethic, born among Puritanism, farmers, and artisans, to the new realities of work in the expanding factory system of the late nineteenth century.[33] He senses that new economic conditions made older moral ideals antiquated. Factory work could scarcely be considered a function of moral virtue; for most people it was a matter of economic necessity. Work was chosen, not because of a divine calling, but because it was available, and people exerted themselves in their labors, not to glorify God, but to avoid being fired. Whereas earlier transitions (as we have seen) have generally been approached by asking how new ideas more compatible with new circumstances came into being, Rodgers develops a more complex argument. As the traditional work ethic became less relevant to working conditions themselves, it was not so much reshaped as elevated, becoming an official ideology filled with more bombast than ever.

If the work ethic, as it were, sailed off under its own steam, the question remains as to what members of the industrial working class may themselves have thought and believed. Although no study of the magnitude of E. P. Thompson's *Making of the English Working Class*[34] has been produced for the American case, Herbert Gutman's research has been particularly sensitive to questions of working-class attitudes and culture, including the role of religion.[35] Gutman argues that workers need to feel that their actions are justified by a value system that transcends their own individual self-interests, thereby making them feel morally and psychologically right about their actions. Religious beliefs provide such legitimation, although (with Weber) Gutman suggests that different beliefs can serve equally well, nevertheless channeling behavior in different directions. Premillennialism, for example, sometimes proved attractive to the working class because rapid industrialization generated extraordinary psychological strains, causing the distressed to reject the secular order and seek solace in a religion of "doom, despair, and destruction" (p. 89). Gutman, however, is more interested in the religious ideas that may have influenced the labor movement to take political action against the established industrial order. He argues that all types of labor reforms and movements drew from a common Christian tradition, and that this tradition offered a framework to challenge the dominant industrial ideology.

In focusing on labor organizers, Gutman's work is as much about the ideas of a particular segment of the work force as Rodgers's is. Other studies pay more attention to the beliefs and practices of workers themselves, but provide neither a comprehensive picture nor one that yields a clear interpretation of the role of religion. Research among shoemakers in Lynn, Massachusetts, for example, suggests that the churches contributed to the rise of an industrial work ethic in the 1820s that encouraged frugality, diligence, and temperance.[36] This ethic appears to have been shared widely among shoemakers as well as among merchants and factory owners, and it differed significantly from earlier notions of work that situated it in understandings of community and family responsibility. If the churches fostered it, they nevertheless did so half-heartedly, espousing more traditional values as well. After the Civil War, the shoe industry expanded and underwent mechanization. One segment of the work force remained loyal to management, while another engaged in strikes and other acts of resistance. Among the former, loyalty may have been reinforced by common moral and religious values. Among the latter, however, the same values were often evident as well, but workers reinterpreted the work ethic as a form of discipline necessary to their own interests. Religion thus provided a language for making sense of work, but was malleable. Loyalty or resistance depended more on working conditions themselves and on political constraints than on religious views.

In a quite different setting (postbellum Missouri), David Thelen also finds no clear connection between religion and the promotion of, or resistance to, economic change.[37] In fact, his thesis is that Missourians in this period are best characterized by ambivalence: on the one hand, recognizing the economic value of the railroads and expanded markets for grain and other commodities; on the other hand, wanting to preserve ethnic customs, local power arrangements, and a slower and simpler way of life. Churches were a vital gathering place at the local level and sometimes helped in mobilizing resistance movements. They also espoused an individualistic work ethic that was not unconducive to economic expansion. A similar ambivalence is found among the Missourians in Michael Cassity's study of nineteenth-century Sedalia and Pettis County.[38]

Following more closely in the footsteps of Gutman, Ken Fones-Wolf addresses the neglect of historical research into the uses of Christianity by antebellum labor movements.[39] Focusing on the working class of Philadelphia, he critiques simplistic assessments of religion as a tool of employers for social control, or as a divisive element among the working classes, blocking unified efforts for reform. In chapters dealing variously with the Knights of Labor, liberal reformers battling the conservative YMCA and YWCA, and the Labor Forward Movement, Fones-Wolf demonstrates that religion, especially Protestantism, was used by labor organizations in their dealings with capitalists.

To suggest that religion promoted only ambivalence or that it was too amorphous to have any discernible economic consequences is, however, too simple. Tocqueville's term "self-interest rightly understood" provides a better characterization than "ambivalence." The prevailing religious ethos seldom stood headlong in the way of industrialization but sought to temper self-interested activities with a sense of moral obligation to God, family, community, and self. It saw, for example, that the ruthless robber barons in control of the railroads needed to be restrained for the long-run economic good of farmers and shopkeepers alike. It was a widely shared ethos, but not monolithic. Methodist section gangs, for example, had different views of how to restrain the railroads than Mennonite farmers did. But for both, religion was an important enough factor that their economic lives cannot be understood without it. Churches provided the kind of meeting space that guild halls did in Europe. While workers in Lyon sang the Marseillaise and remembered the French revolution, those in Lynn sang hymns[40] and remembered revivals. Religion was a resource that provided them with a shared tradition, with meaningful rallying cries, and with an encouraging faith.

The Twentieth Century

Research on the twentieth century differs from the foregoing because a decidedly larger share has been produced by sociologists and anthropologists working with contemporary data than with archival materials. Ethnographic studies in local communities and systematic opinion surveys add richness to the empirical base from which conclusions can be drawn. The major questions, however, are strikingly similar to those raised in studies of the nineteenth century. Weberian themes remain much in evidence, as do questions about the breakdown of community. Despite major technological innovations and general expansion in economic well-being, the high levels of church attendance and religious conviction evident in the United States have also led many studies to focus on the relationships between religious commitment and economic behavior, rather than assuming the society had simply become too secular for such relationships to matter.

Studies of these relationships during the first half of the century are understandably less abundant than for the second half of the century (when the social sciences have flourished on a larger scale). For the earlier period, more attention has been paid to the effects of changing economic conditions on religious behavior than on the reciprocal effects of religious commitment. Much of this research has been stimulated by theoretical assumptions about secularization. Economic growth was expected to undermine religious commitment. Empirical results, however, have largely disconfirmed this expectation. Protestant churches and church membership grew steadily from the start of the century until about 1960, despite advancing industrialization, and did so in cities as well as in small towns and rural areas.[41] Among the reasons for this growth are increasing competition among Protestant denominations and between Protestants and Catholics as a result of immigration, which added ethnic diversity, and rising literacy rates, which made people more attentive to confessional differences (both of which were, in turn, dependent on an expanding economy).[42] Other important factors include easier access to neighborhood churches in cities than on farms and an increase in male church attendance, generally thought to be a result of urbanization and the mechanization of farm labor.[43] If religious participation increased, concerns were nevertheless widespread that some qualitative erosion was also taking place as a result of economic developments. After World War I, fewer churches offered services in immigrants' native languages, and other distinctive ethnic customs began to be abandoned; radio and motion pictures were said to have dampened attendance at Sunday evening services; and the automobile may have increased religious voluntarism by placing a wider variety of churches within easy commuting distance. Some research has also suggested that liberal theology and "modernist" outlooks in mainline Protestant churches were linked with the expanding urban and suburban middle classes, while fundamentalist reactions to these developments were associated with poorer segments of the urban population and with rural and small-town populations in the Midwest, West, and South, whose local communities were being threatened by large-scale manufacturing, long-distance commerce, and industrialization, much as their forebears in upstate New York had been a century earlier.[44] Other studies focus on broader shifts in American culture and offer various evaluations of Protestantism's response to the emerging values of rationality and regulation associated with the urban-industrial order, from the social and economic critiques of Protestantism[45] to the liberal Protestant contribution to a therapeutic ideology of self-realization and spiritualization of the corporate system.[46]

Some attention has also been devoted to particular points of intersection between Protestantism and economic behavior during the pre–World War II period. The Social Gospel movement, for example, remains a subject of continuing interest.[47] Apart from the substantive interest it inspires, it is also important because it shifts attention away from questions about the religious legitimation of the work-and-wealth ethic[48] to questions about economic justice, assistance for the poor, and the churches' responsibilities to the industrial working class. Recent research has emphasized the ways in which the Social Gospel movement sought to address new economic conditions but with limited success because of its adherence to traditional middle-class values,[49] and has pointed to other connections between religious thought and industrialization during the same period.[50] The role of religion in the labor movement has also drawn increasing attention. Allen Tullos's *Habits of Industry*, for example, traces continuities in the Protestant work ethic embodied in Presbyterian, Methodist, and Baptist churches in the Carolina Piedmont region during the transition from a rural economy after the Civil War to the textile industry that characterized the region in the 1920s.[51] Another study has examined the relationships between the religious composition of the United States (taking states as the unit of analysis) and voting for leftist candidates in the 1920s, concluding that religion was not an "opiate" (as Marx suggested) because variations can be accounted for more easily by ethnicity (the presence or absence of Scandinavians) than by religious factors.[52] Other research has paid greater attention to movements, ranging from Pentecostal and Holiness churches, to socialist labor communes, to conservative Americanist movements, to black churches, all of which appealed to the interests and needs of the dispossessed, and some of which appear to have been instrumental in the upward social mobility of these groups, for example, by encouraging temperance, hard work, moral discipline, self help, and family loyalty.[53]

Since World War II, a significant share of the research on religion and economic behavior has been based on opinion surveys. These studies have made it possible to determine how widely held various beliefs and values are and to relate them systematically with other beliefs and values. The landmark study of religion and economic behavior was Gerhard Lenski's 1958 Detroit Area Survey in which the contemporary relevance of the Weber thesis was examined.[54] Lenski found that commitment to work as an intrinsic value was widespread, that it was somewhat more common among Protestants than among Catholics (which he took as support for the Weber thesis), and that it was reinforced by religious "devotionalism" (claiming to have a personal relationship with God). Subsequent studies have, however, challenged Lenski's conclusions and pointed to diminishing religious effects. Charles Glock and Rodney Stark, for example, criticized Lenski for lumping Protestants together and sought to establish the importance of denominationalism as a factor associated with widespread differences in religious beliefs and practices.[55] Andrew Greeley, examining Protestant-Catholic differences with greater attention to regional and ethnic influences, pronounced the Weber thesis dead and called for a moratorium on discussing it.[56] Larry Blackwood compared data from the 1970s with Lenski's earlier data and showed an overall decline in commitment to the work ethic rooted largely in occupational, rather than religious, factors. His research showed that work was still held as an intrinsic value more often by churchgoers than by nonattenders, but there were no differences between Protestants and Catholics and no effects attributable to differences in religious belief.[57]

Tracy Scott's analysis of national data suggests that intrinsic commitment to work may be only weakly associated with religious involvement and with religious affiliation.[58]

The main thrust of this research, then, is to suggest that religious commitment may be declining as a significant influence on economic behavior. Studies of special populations sometimes challenge this conclusion. For example, Benton Johnson's research on Jehovah's Witnesses remains provocative in suggesting that ascetic moral and spiritual values in this group may contribute positively to their economic well-being.[59] Nancy Tatom Ammerman's study of a fundamentalist congregation in Connecticut shows how religious convictions help working-class people to cope psychologically with unfulfilling jobs and with the rising demands of dual-career households.[60] Matthew Lawson's research in a charismatic congregation emphasizes that religious conceptions of authority may provide models for behavior in the work place that promote cooperation and diminish interpersonal tension.[61] Thomas Fuechtmann has examined the role of churches in Youngstown's effort to block plant closings in the steel industry.[62] Some research on the new religious movements of the 1970s also suggested a significant impact on economic values, in this case, legitimating the pursuit of alternative careers and nonmaterialistic lifestyles.[63] Qualitative research on religious views of economic justice also suggests some significant connections. Stephen Hart, for instance, shows that deeply religious people are often quite thoughtful about economic justice and that their arguments reflect understandings of God, human nature, equality, and the causes of suffering.[64] Broad surveys of the literature, however, generally indicate diminishing influence. James Riccio, for example, concludes a comprehensive review by suggesting that few studies demonstrate clear relationships between measures of religious commitment, such as affiliation, preference, or attendance, and measures of economic factors, such as socioeconomic status, social mobility, achievement motivation, or commitment to the work ethic. He also cautions that the research strategies employed in many of these studies have been inadequate.[65]

It is perhaps not surprising, therefore, that some of the most influential qualitative studies of American society have paid little attention to the economic role of religion. Paul Leinberger's and Bruce Tucker's replication of William Whyte's *Organization Man* research, for example, suggests (largely by omission) that the current generation of young professionals and business managers are seldom guided by religious convictions and are seldom involved in local churches the way their parents were.[66] Robert Bellah and his associates emphasize the importance of religious values for the long-range health of American society, but their empirical work indicates that these values may be too private and too closely rooted in idiosyncratic personal needs to have much influence on individual decisions about work, community, or politics, let alone on public discourse about collective values.[67] Christopher Lasch decries the erosion of the Protestant work ethic but suggests that such virtues simply "no longer excite enthusiasm" and envisions them being replaced by expressivist values from secular sources.[68]

At this writing there is, however, some research in progress that may shed new light on the relationships between religion and economic behavior in the last decade of the twentieth century. One study examines current changes in the American middle class, especially the rising fortunes of the top quintile compared to the growing economic pressures experienced by the remainder, to see if these changes may be aggravating tensions between religious liberals and religious conservatives, and to see if religious conservatism may also be gaining ground, or becoming more closely linked with racial discrimination, traditional family values, and a stricter work ethic, as a result of economic pressures.[69] Other research, drawing inspiration from literature suggesting that a new class of college-educated professionals and knowledge workers is coming into power, bringing with it a secular, antireligious ethic,[70] is examining the extent to which these arguments are correct and what their implications may be for strategic segments of the work force. One study, for example, demonstrates that religious conflict may be particularly pronounced in the so-called semi-professions (nursing, teaching, and clerical work) because of differential exposure to new class values and because of gender issues in traditionally female occupations.[71] Another study shows that members of evangelical Protestant denominations remain underrepresented in professional and managerial occupations, perhaps because of parental background as well as religious values, but that these denominations are also being absorbed into the new class at a steady rate; thus, questions arise about the ways in which individuals in largely secular occupations, such as the social sciences, journalism, and therapy, may be able to reconcile their religious beliefs with the values of these occupations.[72]

Future Directions

It is impossible in a brief review to take account of the full variety of research that has been conducted on the relationships between Protestantism and economic behavior. Certain dominant patterns are, however, evident. One is the enormous uniformity that prevails in the questions this relationship evokes: Does religious belief legitimate certain kinds of economic behavior, especially hard work and the pursuit of wealth? Does religious belief lead to unanticipated economic consequences? Do economic developments undermine religious commitments and encourage the breakdown of religious communities? Is religious commitment capable of restraining economic behavior? These questions remain as significant today as they did at the end of the nineteenth century. Studies of the relationship between religion and economic behavior are thus (potentially at least) a window into the more abiding quandaries of the modern epoch itself. They provide ways to consider larger questions about ideology, economic determinism, community, and moral restraint. Another conclusion is that studies provide no single answer to these questions. Contrary to some reviews that have identified shifts from Weberian to Marxist, or from Marxist to Tocquevillian perspectives, for example, this review finds no evidence of such orthodoxies or of movement away from them. Instead, the evidence indicates that religious belief always has ambiguous consequences, that it legitimates the pursuit of wealth but also restrains it, that communities break down but are also preserved, and that belief gradually adapts to new circumstances but never adapts completely. If the literature yields no definitive view of the effects of religion on economic behavior, it has, however, accumulated much in the way of substantive knowledge and, on the whole, points to a number of promising directions for research in the future.

1. The study of religion and economic behavior has been an exceptionally productive area of research during the past quarter century (though not as rich as some observers would like) and it needs to be encouraged in the years to come. The studies reviewed here are in essential agreement about the fact that changing economic conditions in American history have had a decided impact on the character of religion. They show less consensus on the question of how religion may have influenced economic development. They do not support simplistic arguments, for example, about religious asceticism being a driving force in economic growth. Nor do they suggest that religion was a champion of traditionalism or that it stood in the way of economic change. What they do demonstrate beyond doubt is that religion and economic behavior have coexisted in uneasy tension with each other. Seldom has American religion instructed believers *not* to work hard, *not* to invest their talents wisely, or *not* to engage in gainful activities. But—with a few glaring examples that have been widely popularized—seldom has it argued that God loved the rich and not the poor, or that the chief end of life was simply to work, to reap profits, or to bask in material pleasures. Religion has, many studies demonstrate, been sufficiently pliable to remain relevant in new economic circumstances. When it could no longer rely on civil authorities to enforce its moral injunctions, it turned toward more internalized conceptions of self control. And when these no longer made as much sense, it found new relevance in messages about happiness and inner peace. In its various instantiations, religion has, however, remained of special interest for understanding the economic realm because it asserted the importance of commitments that transcended this realm. It told people that they should work to feed their families, but in so doing also made clear that family was a value, perhaps more worthy than, or at least not to be subsumed by, work. It reminded people of moral obligations to their neighbors, their community, and their nation that could not (classical economists to the contrary) be fulfilled simply by producing pins in larger volume and with greater efficiency. It perhaps assuaged middle-class guilt by providing occasions for charitable giving, but in the

process it also kept visions of kindness alive. Thus, when historians interested in the development of American society have paused to ask what else besides farms and railroads and steel mills made the nation what it is, they have inquired into the beliefs and values of the people themselves, and in so doing have discovered that these were embedded in a rich language of religious symbolism. None of this, of course, is to deny the value of historical studies examining the spread of railways or the financial development of American business. As those studies produce new understandings of economic conditions, however, there will be a continuing need to know how people made sense of these conditions, how they viewed themselves, and how they inscribed their circumstances with moral importance and with transcendent meaning.

2. The study of religion and economic behavior, perhaps more so than most topics in American history, demonstrates the value of interdisciplinary collaboration among historians, sociologists, and scholars in religious studies.[73] Reading studies produced by historians concerned with Protestantism and economic developments in the eighteenth and nineteenth centuries, for example, sociologists cannot help being impressed with how prominently the figures of Weber and Durkheim loom in these studies. This of course is not surprising, for Weber and Durkheim were principally concerned with the social and cultural consequences of changing economic conditions. Both were also inspired by the theoretical weaknesses they saw in classical economics. Their aim, as Parsons was to demonstrate clearly,[74] was to show that human behavior could not be understood strictly in terms of rational, self-interested, utilitarian calculations. They found the moral obligations manifested in religion particularly valuable in this endeavor. Historical studies asking about the ways in which moral obligations may shape economic development, or be shaped by it, are thus consistent in seeking inspiration from Weber and Durkheim. Marx's legacy, filtered through Tawney, H. Richard Niebuhr, and E. P. Thompson, is also evident in this literature. Why class conflict has not been more acute in American history has often been attributed to the muting effects of common religious assumptions and to the crosscutting cleavages separating Protestants and Catholics or black Baptists and white Methodists. But studies of American labor history also turn more often to religious themes than comparable studies of European labor movements do. Historical studies of religion and economic behavior have thus been concerned with some of the broadest questions posed in classical sociological theory. Other studies, focusing on more tractable issues, have also found inspiration in the sociological literature. Work on religion, gender, and domestic labor, for example, has drawn on theories of role behavior for conceptual guidance.[75] Among sociologists, there have been significant efforts to move directly into the historians' terrain. Although historical sociology has progressed on many fronts in recent years,[76] it has been especially concerned with the relationships between religion and economic factors,[77] again perhaps because of the theoretical

questions raised by Weber, Durkheim, Marx, and others. These forays have forced a new historical awareness on sociologists of religion,[78] causing them to move beyond the simple generalizations found in theories of cultural change, and have probably introduced new methods and conceptual innovations into the historical literature.[79] It is nevertheless evident that work at the intersection of history and sociology remains sorely in need of critical reflection. Much of the work to date is rooted in simplistic assumptions about the ways in which religious ideas may legitimate economic interests, and about the psychological motivations that may link individual beliefs with individual behavior. Recent attempts to view Weber, Durkheim, and Marx in a different light have been little utilized. Johnson's work represents a significant advance in its effort to pay closer attention to actual social relationships, rather than individual psychology, and yet this work has often been misinterpreted.[80] Efforts to pay closer attention to the power relationships among clergy and laity, or among other significant producers of new ideas, remain insufficiently developed. Indeed, little has yet been done to incorporate insights from the literatures on social movements, organizational ecology, production of culture, or cultural articulation.[81] Research on religion and economic behavior is thus ripe for continued efforts but also in need of new frameworks.

3. The new quantitative history, popularized by Robert Fogel and Stanley Engerman,[82] Lee Benson,[83] and others in the 1960s and 1970s, has produced some notable studies of religion and is likely to be a fruitful avenue of inquiry in the future.[84] Its relevance to the study of religion and economic behavior is indicated by the fact that questions about these relationships often focus on broad social patterns, such as the effects of industrialization or the spread of market agriculture, and that evidence on economic factors is often readily available from censuses of manufacturing, business records, and so on. Quantitative analysis of such data can lead to generalizations about the correlates of religious variables and can provide tests of alternative hypotheses (for example, whether religious change is more closely associated with growth in manufacturing, the capitalization of agriculture, or population growth). At the local level, community and congregational studies can sometimes utilize quantitative data as well, showing, for example, how religious membership patterns may vary by occupation, or how household inventories vary among the members of different churches. In the future, more can probably be done with quantitative historical data on organizations than has been done in the past. For example, little has been done on the economic conditions under which new congregations were founded in the nineteenth century, on the relationships between religiously sponsored service institutions (such as colleges and hospitals) and the economic development of cities, or on the ways in which business failures during the Great Depression may have contributed to tensions within denominations.[85] For many other purposes, however, the value of quantitative history is clearly limited. If, as suggested here, religion often provides a language

for making sense of economic behavior, rather than a force channeling it in one direction or another, then studies of sermons, diaries, letters, and biographical materials are likely to be more illuminating than correlational studies of occupations and church membership statistics. Apart from this, the main questions that studies of religious and economic change have addressed are concerned with subtle changes in the meanings of religious teachings; for example, with changing conceptions of moral discipline or of free will in choosing one's religious views under more complex economic circumstances. For these questions, quantitative history has helped in establishing the fact that circumstances were changing, but has done less to illuminate the content of changing moral understandings.

4. The study of religion and economic behavior provides an interesting commentary on the so-called secularization thesis. If a generalization can be risked, historians of American religion have tended to eschew the idea of secularization, regarding it as a sociological fallacy easily refuted with evidence of religious revivals and the lingering vitality of sacred tradition. Sociologists of religion have found it more difficult to abandon the term, but increasingly use it as a straw person against which to pose other interpretations of American religion. The literature on religion and economic behavior bears directly on this issue, whether it invokes the term or not. It indicates both that the idea retains considerable merit and that it needs further refinement. The notion of secularization that seems largely to be consistent with this literature is not that religion has diminished numerically but that it has been transformed qualitatively in ways that render it more palatable to new economic circumstances and yet perhaps reduce its influence in public life.[86] The clearest support for this contention comes from the literature on colonial America. If Puritanism played an enormous role in the corporate life of New England society, undergirding its legal system, its penal code, and influencing the manner in which merchants conducted business, the Great Awakening made faith more a matter of conscience, more easily adapted to the complexities of commercial life, more voluntary, more amenable to a pluralistic setting, and less capable of exercising direct restraint on social institutions. Some of the work on the nineteenth century suggests that this type of secularization deepened during and after the Second Great Awakening. Revivalism further privatized religion, making salvation itself a matter of emotion and removing faith from the relationships between employers and workers. With credit to the debate over how much or how little of the traditional patterns were retained, one can read much of this literature and feel basically at home with the arguments of Talcott Parsons,[87] Peter Berger,[88] Thomas Luckmann,[89] and other proponents of the secularization thesis. Indeed, it might be ventured that none of this literature undermines the idea that economic change is an exogenous force that operates largely without respect to religious restraint and that it significantly alters the character of faith in the process. Where further refinement

is needed is largely with respect to understanding more clearly what changed and what did not. There is a persistent danger in taking the Puritan colonies as the inevitable starting point against which to measure all other developments. They were, as is sometimes suggested, a deviant case compared to religion in England and elsewhere in Europe at the time. More importantly, questions must be asked about the extent of religious conformity within the Puritan colonies themselves. The celebrated case of Robert Keayne, the Boston merchant who was tried and found guilty for earning excessive profits, provides an example worth considering.[90] Keayne's own testament reveals that he was scarcely convinced of the propriety of the accusation. A deeply moral and religious man, he nevertheless emphasized the counsel of his own conscience much in the way that people were supposed to have done only a century later. It may have been important for religious and civil authorities to control a prominent merchant like Keayne, yet as Bernard Bailyn and others who have studied the episode suggest, the political economy of Boston did not require the majority of the population to undergo such restraint.[91] Sailors, trappers, explorers, and small farmers may have been much more loosely tied to the church and to the center of economic power. Thus, what Johnson depicts as a loosening of the moral order in the 1830s as a result of the separation of work from households may not have been characteristic of the broader population at all. Country traders may have relied on such order, but the domestic households of independent farmers or the livelihood of long-distance traders probably did not. If more needs to be known about the starting point from which secularization embarked, better understanding is also needed of the new ideas that developed. The Great Awakening allegedly placed greater emphasis on internalized moral discipline than before, but so did many of the religious movements of the nineteenth century. Were their conceptions of moral discipline the same or different? Weberian arguments would suggest that they may well have been different and that the differences may have been associated with the increasing rationalization of industrial society. In the earlier period, conscience may have been instructed by divine voices or by coincidences deemed to be the work of divine agents. By the end of the nineteenth century, such counsel may have been less common, while systematic attention to the development of one's spiritual muscles may have become more important. Plain living and neighborliness may have been the hallmark of Christian living in one period; punctuality and careful planning, in another. Some attention has of course been devoted to examining these changes. But further work is needed if the connections between faith and economic behavior are to be made with greater precision.

5. A promising future direction for studies of religion and economic behavior is to pay closer attention to language, discourse, and the symbolic construction of meaning. Questions about economic development have inevitably led to an emphasis on religious change. In the effort to

show that religion was proactive as well as reactive, studies have also sought evidence of behavior being shaped by religious ideas. Common to many of these studies is the contemporary view of ideas that regards them as attitudinal predispositions, significant primarily because they in fact influence behavior. Thus, belief in hard work becomes more interesting if people actually work harder, just as a racial stereotype does if it leads to racist behavior. Few of the studies, historical or contemporary, show compellingly that religious attitudes had very much of an effect on economic behavior. The reasons why need to be considered. Theories of structuration,[92] or of structure and agency,[93] may be helpful in this regard. When religion could influence individual behavior through the coercive powers of government, significant effects could sometimes be experienced (a merchant could be tried for unbiblical business practices or his wife could be prevented from owning property at all). When religion came to be a matter of moral suasion, it could then be expected to have an influence only on behavior subject to individual discretion. A merchant, for example, who can choose how many hours to work may be influenced by a religious work ethic, whereas a factory worker who has to work a specified schedule each day may not be. Yet, even the merchant may be subject to norms of the marketplace to the point that deciding when to open or close is seldom a matter of individual initiative. In that event, religion may have greater influence on his thinking about his work than on his work itself. In short, *meaning* becomes the relevant issue. But meaning has played a relatively small role in the literature on religion and economic behavior. The early Weber who was concerned with acquisitive behavior is more evident than the later Weber who emphasized the meaning of social action. Nor is there much impact from the anthropological history espoused by Clifford Geertz,[94] Robert Darnton,[95] Natalie Zemon Davis,[96] and others,[97] or of the discursive emphasis evident in Foucault[98] or Bakhtin.[99] Whatever models may be chosen, the important point is to reckon with the fact that religious language has provided an enduring framework for making sense of economic behavior. Ordinary men and women in the seventeenth century were lauded for being Christian in all their "words and ways,"[100] not simply in their ways. The parable of the good steward or the biblical description of the virtuous woman provided them with a way to speak about what they were doing. Two centuries later, union organizers encouraged their members to sing "Onward Christian Soldiers" for the same reasons. The language itself was significant, enhancing the meaning of routine economic behavior, but also turning that behavior into something that could be understood collectively. Clearly, a fruitful direction for research on religion and economic behavior, therefore, is to examine more carefully how this behavior has actually been presented in religious discourse.

 6. Future research must not overlook the fact that so much of the literature produced in recent decades has concentrated on special moments of change, such as the first and second Great Awakenings, when

economic conditions seemed to be changing rapidly and when revivals and new denominations highlighted religious change as well. Earlier accounts of these periods that emphasized the role of psychological anxiety as a factor in new religious ideas have largely given way to efforts to understand them in different ways. In focusing on economic conditions, these studies sometimes give the impression that the new realities of economic life were largely determined by economic forces themselves and that religious ideas simply adjusted to these realities. For example, markets required greater individual initiative, so religious ideas were invented that stressed such initiative. Such arguments not only run the danger of suggesting that necessity is the mother of invention but also shortcircuit the processes by which these adjustments were actually made. An alternative view is suggested by the examples just given of religious effects on economic behavior being "structured" by the realities institutionalized in any given set of economic arrangements. If these arrangements are thought of as a set of rules, then individuals would be expected to play the game according to these rules, but have opportunities to improvise according to their own religious convictions (and some of the rules themselves might derive from religious sources). But some historical moments might be characterized, again not so much by an immediate replacement of one set of rules by another, but by the rules themselves being uncertain and up for grabs. Under such circumstances, the players might be especially eager to talk about the rules and to seek new ideas about what the rules should be.[101] They might also have greater freedom than at other times in making up their own rules or in selecting idiosyncratic combinations of rules. Mary Ryan's account of family patterns in the 1830s and 1840s, for example, suggests that parents in these decades found older patriarchal models unworkable and had not yet invented new models, so they turned increasingly to new sources for advice.[102] In this situation, she suggests, revivalists and leaders of moral reform movements were able to have a relatively large impact on the ways in which people thought. What this example also suggests is that transitional periods are characterized by competition among various movements seeking to redefine the moral order.[103] New denominations competed with established ones, and more extreme cults also emerged. Bruce Laurie's study of Philadelphia, for example, shows how various evangelical, traditional, radical, and secular movements competed for the loyalty of workers in the 1840s as well.[104] New ideas are eventually institutionalized through a process of selection. Some become more attractive than others, depending on their ability to deploy resources and how well they make sense of new conditions. Future research might do well to examine this process in order to understand better why some ideas succeed better than others.

7. An extension of the previous point is to suggest that the relationships between Protestantism and economic behavior may need to be examined with a more critical eye toward systematic comparisons, especially bringing in comparisons among different political conditions. The

danger in discussing religion–economy connections is that other institutional factors may be neglected. As some of the literature suggests, family and child-rearing patterns compose one set of relevant factors. Political factors are likely to be another, if only because government has been used so often to stimulate and control economic behavior.[105] In the United States, separation of church and state has perhaps made it more plausible for studies to focus on the effects of religious ideas on market relations without reference to government. The Puritan case, however, suggests that subsequent changes in religion–economy connections should not be understood simply as a function of economic growth but as a feature of religious disestablishment. The increasing relevance of moral discipline in religious arguments about work-related activity, for example, needs to be seen in comparison with the role that government played in reinforcing such discipline in colonial America. For broader comparisons between the United States, Europe, and other nations, the role of political conditions must also be taken into account.[106] Efforts to control the industrial labor force in the nineteenth century, for example, are typically understood to have focused more on religion in the United States than in Germany or France because church–state alliances in those countries alienated workers from religion. It may also be the case, as some studies suggest, that these differences are attributable to insufficient "administrative capacity" in the United States,[107] or to a more complex interaction among officials, social reformers, and religious leaders that channeled ameliorative social legislation away from broad-based redistributive programs and into "matriarchal" welfare programs concerned with the needs of women and children.[108] As government has become more active in regulating economic behavior in the twentieth century, churches have also shifted some of their attention away from purely voluntaristic activities toward lobbying and legislation. One of the needs is thus for historical and sociological studies to focus more on the ways in which religious organizations have worked with government agencies to achieve economic reforms, such as workmen's compensation laws, child labor legislation, the right to strike, or family-leave policies.

8. Another need is for greater care in considering the role of gender, race, ethnicity, and religious diversity. Virtually all research on religion and economic behavior has focused on men, partly because data have been more readily available and because men were more likely to have been involved in the labor force. The recent inclusion of women in the labor force in large numbers raises new questions about the effects of this inclusion on religious participation and about possible differences in the ways in which men and women may draw on religious resources for assistance with workplace problems, such as childcare, stress, and sexual harassment. Gendered conceptions of work and of family responsibilities, often placing greater demands on women, also raise questions about the roots of such conceptions in religious traditions. Gender is not an issue only for contemporary studies, however. Puritan women bore significant

responsibilities in the household economy, producing food and clothing, as well as mentoring children and fulfilling many of the family's spiritual obligations to the church and to neighbors.[109] How the household economy was influenced by religious commitment is thus a topic sorely in need of further investigation. Nineteenth-century studies have documented how gender played a large role in the relation between religion and economic life. By dividing the spheres of work and home along gender lines, middle class Protestants could hold together Christian virtues and entrepreneurial self-interest. The pious domestic woman would exercise moral influence over her husband and son, while the man would strive for business success and abundant provision for his Christian home.[110] Yet, studies have concentrated on the experiences of women in this division of labor,[111] and the accompanying "feminization" of religion,[112] while implicitly assuming Protestantism's contribution to this larger cultural phenomenon. Future research needs to examine the explicit role of religion in the development of this ideal of separate spheres and in the actual practice of a gendered division of labor. Teresa Murphy's study of the relationships between gender and reform in the 1840s represents another promising line of inquiry, suggesting, for example, that evangelicalism served importantly in the efforts of working-class women to organize in New England mill towns, as Jama Lazerow also finds.[113] Other issues now receiving attention with promising results include the role of women as financial guardians of the church in African American communities,[114] historic and contemporary conceptions of vocation and calling among women,[115] the cultural and religious roots of gendered conceptions of money,[116] and the role of churches in mobilizing women against unfair labor practices.[117]

Race, ethnicity, and religious diversity pose comparative challenges to the literature that has been based primarily on white Protestant males. Some important work on the juncture of religious and economic behavior has of course been done on slavery[118] and on African American communities in the late nineteenth and twentieth centuries.[119] The relevance of interaction between Protestants and Native Americans is also becoming more important in historical studies. Joel Martin's study of missionary activities among Native Americans in Alabama in the early nineteenth century, for example, suggests that such locations provide new insights into the ways in which the work ethic and a religiously inspired drive for economic expansion came into conflict with humanitarian and communal ideals from the same religious roots.[120] Religious diversity creates sensitivity to the economic teachings and practices of particular groups, such as Mormons, Shakers, and Methodists, but also suggests a greater need, in the context of considering Protestantism, to do so with recognition of competition between Protestants and Catholics, and by taking advantage of opportunities for comparisons among Protestants, Catholics, and Jews. Comparative studies may be especially valuable in the future as ways of sharpening generalizations about the effects of specific religious teachings on economic behavior.[121]

9. Sociological studies of the relationships between religion and economic behavior can be usefully directed toward understanding how the present transition from industrial to postindustrial society may be altering these relationships. Such studies, based primarily on contemporary data, can also benefit by drawing comparisons with historical studies of previous stages of economic development. The rise of postindustrial society has of course been much discussed in the social sciences.[122] It emphasizes the diminishing role of heavy-goods manufacturing in economically advanced societies and their increasing emphasis on the marketing of human services, consumer goods, and information. The religious implications of this transition have been largely ignored, except for the literature on the so-called new class of knowledge workers as a carrier of secular assumptions and lifestyles.[123] As a result, contemporary discussions continue to emphasize religious teachings on economic issues that may have been relevant during the era of industrialization but of declining interest in postindustrial society. The Protestant work ethic, for example, may at one time have been associated with long working hours and with rigid conformity to the demands of the job. But in postindustrial society long hours and rigid conformity may have little to do with material success (or at least may be perceived that way).[124] The workplace may be governed more by professional norms and by complex decision-making processes than by straightforward rules requiring moral discipline. If religion is to have any effect on work, it may therefore exercise its influence on feelings, for example, providing reassurance that one has made the right decision in the face of moral uncertainty. Money and consumer goods may be subject to similar shifts in the potential relevance of religion.[125] Postindustrial society provides higher standards of affluence for most people than in previous times. Frugality is less likely to be freighted with moral significance as slogans such as "buy American" or "raise the level of consumer confidence." At the same time, postindustrial productive capacity, together with mass media, make the modern consumer more aware of goods and services that are beyond the family budget than at any time in the past. Thus, religious teachings may be needed to tell people who have it all, so to speak, why they do not have more (and should not worry about having more). Changing understandings of gender roles, the demise of the extended family, the anonymity of suburban life, and huge gaps between rich and poor are also characteristic features of postmodern society. If evidence from historical studies of previous transitions is an indication, American religion will adjust to these features, rather than ceasing to be relevant at all. What the nature of these adjustments may be is, however, a question remaining to be examined.

10. Finally, future research needs to include studies of the more subtle ways in which religion and economic behavior may connect. Most of the

studies reviewed here focus on institutionalized religion, raising questions about churches, church participation, and the teachings of churches. Such studies must of course be given prominence if the emphasis is on Protestant*ism*. However, *Protestants* (or individuals in general) may well mix the sacred and economic behavior in more complex ways. In other contexts, for example, the study of wills and burial practices has provided an intriguing glimpse at the ways in which sacred values may influence the disposal of material wealth. In American society, especially since the late nineteenth century, an interesting issue may be the ways in which sacred values have been absorbed by other institutions. One interpretation of secularization has suggested, in fact, that religion has not so much declined in influence as in visibility.[126] Thus, healing rituals that at one time may have been performed by the church are now performed in secular hospitals, yet the Judeo-Christian *value* of caring and compassion may be retained in these practices. Another argument is that the moral discipline advocated by religious reformers in the eighteenth and nineteenth centuries has become less essential in twentieth-century society because economic relationships are more fully institutionalized and provide alternative ways of governing behavior.[127] Examples might include codes of ethical conduct in the professions, government regulations restraining corrupt transactions in the stock market, health and safety standards that require electricians to install proper wiring whether they are religiously devout or not, and an elaborate system of schooling, standardized tests, and job recruitment procedures that channel people into suitable careers whether they have received a divine calling or not. From one perspective, the transfer of such functions from churches to secular institutions can be taken as evidence of secularization. Yet religious values, or some other sense of sacredness, may be preserved in the process. Clergy, for example, may devote special energy to the passage of clean water legislation because they believe this to be a religious value that can nevertheless be achieved more effectively by government than by the churches. Students may regard standardized tests with as much awe and foreboding as they once did being grilled by church elders on the Westminster Confession. Or, in the face of institutionalized work schedules, health codes, and tax laws, special moments of transcendence that break through these routines may become occasions for prayer and rejoicing. Besides institutions, ideologies can also become repositories of the sacred. For example, much attention has been given to the ways in which Puritanism contributed to the rise of modern science, which, in turn, has provided its own mythologies about economic progress.[128] Similar attention could probably be devoted to economic theory itself, regarding it as a set of assumptions about human nature that has gained sacred status in contemporary life.[129] Especially when economic theory provides scholars with metaphors about markets, rational choice, and preference maximization that are then used to explain away the essence of religion, the circle would seem to have become complete.

In conclusion, Tawney's suggestion that it is "instructive" to trace the connections between religion and economic behavior remains as true today as it was in 1930. The reason is not that the effort produces straightforward conclusions, but that it generates conundrums about the wider contours of social life. Weber and Durkheim had no personal affinities with religious convictions yet found them worth examining in order to understand better the character of economic development itself.[130] There is continuing reason for historians and sociologists to do the same, especially in a society with as rich and as continuing a religious tradition as the United States. Religious convictions may be found to have relatively modest consequences for the economic behavior of individuals or of the nation as a whole. The questions they raise about the nature of economic life, however, remain valuably unsettling.

NOTES

1. R. H. Tawney, "Foreword," in Max Weber, *The Protestant Ethic and the Spirit of Capitalism*, trans. by Talcott Parsons (New York: Charles Scribner's Sons, 1958), 11.

2. Michael Zuckerman, "Holy Wars, Civil Wars: Religion and Economics in Nineteenth-Century America," *Prospects* 16 (1991): 205–40, is an exceptionally valuable review but gives a false impression by stating that "scholars of the current generation have mounted no concerted effort to conceptualize the relation of spiritual or ethical life to economic activity [and] have disdained even to engage in any sustained dialogue on the subject" (205).

3. Our aim is not to offer a comprehensive review of the literature, but a discussion of selected works and commentary about directions that research might usefully take in the future. In addition to the published literature, we benefited from correspondence and discussions with a number of the scholars whose work is represented herein.

4. The following suggest the range of topics that have been examined: Robert C. Ritchie, "God and Mammon in New Netherland," *Reviews in American History* 2 (1974): 353–57; R. J. Lahey, "The Role of Religion in Lord Baltimore's Colonial Enterprise," *Maryland Historical Magazine* 72 (1977): 492–511; Michael R. Bradley, "The Role of the Black Church in the Colonial Slave Society," *Louisiana Studies* 14 (1975): 413–21; T. H. Breen, "Looking Out for Number One: Conflicting Values in Early Seventeenth-Century Virginia," *South Atlantic Quarterly* 78 (1979): 342–60; T. H. Breen, *Puritans and Adventurers: Change and Persistence in Early America* (New York: Oxford University Press, 1980); and Jon Butler, *The Huguenots in America: A Refugee People in New World Society* (Cambridge, Mass.: Harvard University Press, 1983).

5. George Lee Haskins, *Law and Authority in Early Massachusetts: A Study in Tradition and Design* (New York: Macmillan, 1960); and especially on economic grievances, see Richard Gaskins, "Changes in Criminal Law in Eighteenth-Century Connecticut," *American Journal of Legal History* 25 (1981): 309–42.

6. Richard L. Bushman, *From Puritan to Yankee: Character and the Social Order in Connecticut, 1690–1765* (Cambridge, Mass.: Harvard University Press, 1967).

7. See, for example, Philip F. Gura, *A Glimpse of Sion's Glory: Puritan Radicalism in New England, 1620–1660* (Middletown, Conn.: Wesleyan University Press, 1984); and David D. Hall, "Understanding the Puritans," in Herbert J. Bass, ed., *The State of American History* (Chicago: Quadrangle, 1970), 330–49.

8. Stephen Foster, *Their Solitary Way: The Puritan Social Ethic in the First Century of Settlement in New England* (New Haven: Yale University Press, 1971).

9. Christine Leigh Heyrman, *Commerce and Culture: The Maritime Communities of Colonial Massachusetts, 1690–1750* (New York: Norton, 1984).

10. Frederick B. Tolles, *Meeting House and Counting House: The Quaker Merchants of Colonial Philadephia, 1682–1763* (Chapel Hill: University of North Carolina Press, 1948).

11. Barry Levy, *Quakers and the American Family: British Settlement in the Delaware Valley* (New York: Oxford University Press, 1988).

12. J. E. Crowley, *This Sheba, Self: The Conceptualization of Economic Life in Eighteenth Century America* (Baltimore: Johns Hopkins University Press, 1974).

13. On motivation as language, see the convergence evident in C. Wright Mills, "Situated Actions and Vocabularies of Motive," *American Sociological Review* 5 (1940): 904–13; Marvin B. Scott and Stanford M. Lyman, "Accounts," *American Sociological Review* 33 (1968): 46; Kenneth Burke, *A Grammar of Motives* (Berkeley: University of California Press, 1969); Ellen Rooney, *Seductive Reasoning: Pluralism as the Problematic of Contemporary Literary Theory* (Ithaca: Cornell University Press, 1989); Bertrand Very, "Milan Kundera on the Hazards of Subjectivity," *Review of Contemporary Fiction* 9 (1989): 79–87; Anthony Giddens, *Modernity and Self-Identity* (Stanford: Stanford University Press, 1991), 35; and Robert Wuthnow, *Acts of Compassion* (Princeton: Princeton University Press, 1991), esp. chap. 3.

14. Paul S. Seaver, *Wallington's World: A Puritan Artisan in Seventeenth-Century London* (Stanford: Stanford University Press, 1985), 124.

15. David D. Hall, *Worlds of Wonder, Days of Judgment: Popular Religious Belief in Early New England* (Cambridge, Mass.: Harvard University Press, 1990), 219.

16. Kenneth Silverman, *The Life and Times of Cotton Mather* (New York: Columbia University Press, 1985), esp. chap. 8.

17. Philip Greven, *The Protestant Temperament: Patterns of Child-Rearing, Religious Experience, and the Self in Early America* (Chicago: University of Chicago Press, 1977).

18. Gary B. Nash, *The Urban Crucible: Social Change, Political Consciousness, and the Origins of the American Revolution* (Cambridge, Mass.: Harvard University Press, 1979).

19. John L. Brooke, *The Heart of the Commonwealth: Society and Political Culture in Worcester County, Massachusetts, 1713–1861* (New York: Cambridge University Press, 1989).

20. Contingency in interpretations of Weberian arguments is also emphasized in Wuthnow, *Experimentation in American Religion* (Berkeley: University of California Press, 1978), chap. 4; and Wuthnow, *Rediscovering the Sacred* (Grand Rapids, Mich.: Eerdmans, 1992), chap. 5.

21. A classic study in this regard is Henry F. May, *Protestant Churches and*

Industrial America (New York: Harper & Brothers, 1949). Related is the extensive literature on benevolence societies and their connection to religious institutions and ideas; one definitive study is Clifford Griffin, *Their Brother's Keepers: Moral Stewardship in the United States, 1800–1865* (New Brunswick, N.J.: Rutgers University Press, 1960). See also the detailed study of Protestantism's efforts at urban moral reform: Paul Boyer, *Urban Masses and Moral Order in America, 1820–1920* (Cambridge, Mass.: Harvard University Press, 1978).

22. Two notable exceptions to this pattern are David Montgomery, "The Shuttle and the Cross: Weavers and Artisans in the Kensington Riots of 1844," *Journal of Social History* 5 (1972): 411–46; and Jama Lazerow, "Religion and the New England Mill Girl: A New Perspective on an Old Theme," *New England Quarterly* 60 (1987): 429–53.

23. Paul Johnson, *A Shopkeeper's Millennium: Society and Revivals in Rochester, New York, 1815–1837* (New York: Hill and Wang, 1978).

24. Lois W. Banner, "Religious Benevolence as Social Control: A Critique of an Interpretation," *Journal of American History* 60 (1973): 23–41, while preceding Johnson, provides an alternative view of the period.

25. Some additional studies are discussed in Michael Zuckerman, "A Different Thermidor: The Revolution Beyond the American Revolution," in James A. Henretta, Michael Kammen, and Stanley N. Katz (eds.), *The Transformation of Early American History: Society, Authority, and Ideology* (New York: Oxford University Press, 1991), chap. 5.

26. John L. Hammond, *The Politics of Benevolence: Revival Religion and American Voting Behavior* (Norwood, N.J.: Ablex, 1979).

27. Richard L. Rogers, "American Evangelicalism and the Market Economy: Revivalism in New York State, 1825–1835," unpublished paper, Department of Sociology, Princeton University, 1986; also presented at the annual meeting of the American Sociological Association, Chicago, 1987.

28. Richard L. Rogers, "Millennialism and American Culture: The Adventist Movement, 1831–1851," unpublished paper presented at the annual meetings of the Society for the Scientific Study of Religion, 1986; and "The Role of Elites in Setting Agendas for Public Debate: A Historical Case," in Wuthnow (ed.), *Vocabularies of Public Life* (London: Routledge, 1992), chap. 12.

29. Anthony Wallace, *Rockdale: The Growth of an American Village in the Early Industrial Revolution* (New York: Knopf, 1978).

30. George M. Thomas, *Revivalism and Cultural Change: Christianity, Nation Building, and the Market in the Nineteenth-Century United States* (Chicago: University of Chicago Press, 1989).

31. Nathan O. Hatch, "The Second Great Awakening and the Market Revolution," unpublished paper, University of Notre Dame, 1992.

32. Daniel T. Rodgers, *The Work Ethic in Industrial America, 1850–1920* (Chicago: University of Chicago Press, 1978).

33. For a useful study of public commentary (including religious sources) on manual labor in the antebellum period see Jonathan A. Glickstein, *Concepts of Free Labor in Antebellum America* (New Haven: Yale University Press, 1991).

34. E.P. Thompson, *The Making of the English Working Class* (New York: Vintage, 1966).

35. Herbert G. Gutman, "Protestantism and the American Labor Movement: The Christian Spirit in the Gilded Age," *American Historical Review* 72 (1966),

74–101; reprinted in (and cited from) Herbert G. Gutman, *Work, Culture, and Society in Industrializing America: Essays in American Working-Class and Social History* (New York: Knopf, 1976), 79–118.

36. Paul Faler, "Cultural Aspects of the Industrial Revolution: Lynn, Massachusetts Shoemakers and Industrial Morality, 1826–1860," *Labor History* 15 (1974): 367–94; and Alan Dawley and Paul Faler, "Working-Class Culture and Politics in the Industrial Revolution: Sources of Loyalism and Rebellion," *Journal of Social History* 9 (1976): 466–80.

37. David Thelen, *Paths of Resistance: Tradition and Dignity in Industrializing Missouri* (New York: Oxford University Press, 1986).

38. Michael Cassity, *Defending a Way of Life: An American Community in the Nineteenth Century* (Albany: State University of New York Press, 1989).

39. Ken Fones-Wolf, *The Trade Union Gospel: Christianity and Labor in Industrial Philadelphia, 1865–1915* (Philadelphia: Temple University Press, 1989).

40. An intriguing study emphasizing the links between religion and labor protest songs is Clark D. Halker, *For Democracy, Workers, and God: Labor Protest Song-Poems and Labor Protest, 1865–1895* (Urbana: University of Illinois Press, 1991).

41. W. Seward Salisbury, *Religion in American Culture* (Homewood, Ill.: Dorsey Press, 1964); Roger Finke and Rodney Stark, *The Churching of America* (New Brunswick, N.J.: Rutgers University Press, 1992).

42. Kevin J. Christiano, *Religious Diversity and Social Change: American Cities, 1890–1906* (Cambridge: Cambridge University Press, 1987).

43. For an alternative interpretation see Gail Bederman, "'The Women Have Had Charge of the Church Work Long Enough': The Men and Religion Forward Movement of 1911–1912 and the Masculinization of Middle-Class Protestantism," *American Quarterly* 41 (1989): 432–65.

44. Some of these studies are discussed but not given great credence in George M. Marsden, *Fundamentalism and American Culture: The Shaping of Twentieth-Century Evangelicalism, 1870–1925* (New York: Oxford University Press, 1980), esp. chap. 22.

45. See Robert Wiebe, *The Search for Order, 1877–1920* (New York: Hill and Wang, 1967).

46. T. J. Jackson Lears, *No Place of Grace: Antimodernism and the Transformation of American Culture* (New York: Pantheon Books, 1981).

47. Readable, but largely descriptive, for example, is Susan Curtis, *A Consuming Faith: The Social Gospel and Modern American Culture* (Baltimore: Johns Hopkins University Press, 1991).

48. Emphasized, for example, in the widely read book by Peter Baida, *Poor Richard's Legacy: American Business Values from Benjamin Franklin to Donald Trump* (New York: Morrow, 1990).

49. A brief, fair-minded assessment of the Social Gospel movement is included in William R. Hutchison, *The Modernist Impulse in American Protestantism* (Durham, N.C.: Duke University Press, 1992), esp. 264–74.

50. Philip Benjamin, *The Philadelphia Quakers in the Industrial Age, 1865–1920* (Philadelphia: Temple University Press, 1976).

51. Allen Tullos, *Habits of Industry: White Culture and the Transformation of the Carolina Piedmont* (Chapel Hill: University of North Carolina Press, 1989).

52. Rodney Stark and Kevin J. Christiano, "Support for the American Left, 1920–1924: The Opiate Thesis Reconsidered," *Journal for the Scientific Study of Religion* 31 (1992): 62–75.

53. The literature on these movements is vast; one recent study that includes an ample bibliography is Brian J. L. Berry, *America's Utopian Experiments: Communal Havens from Long-Wave Crises* (Hanover, N.H.: University Press of New England, 1992).

54. Gerhard Lenski, *The Religious Factor* (Garden City, N.Y.: Doubleday, 1961).

55. Charles Y. Glock and Rodney Stark, *Religion and Society in Tension* (Chicago: McGraw-Hill, 1965).

56. Andrew M. Greeley, *The American Catholic: A Social Portrait* (New York: Basic Books, 1977), esp. chap. 3.

57. Larry Blackwood, "Social Change and Commitment to the Work Ethic," in Wuthnow, ed., *The Religious Dimension* (New York: Academic Press, 1979), 241–56.

58. Tracy L. Scott, "Religion and Attitudes toward Work," unpublished paper, Department of Sociology, Princeton University, 1992.

59. Benton Johnson, "Do Holiness Sects Socialize in Dominant Values?" *Social Forces* 39 (1961): 309–16.

60. Nancy Tatom Ammerman, *Bible Believers: Fundamentalists in the Modern World* (New Brunswick, N.J.: Rutgers University Press, 1987).

61. Matthew P. Lawson, "Religious Principles and the Dynamics of Power in a Catholic Charismatic Prayer Group," unpublished paper presented at the annual meetings of the Society for the Scientific Study of Religion, Washington, D.C., 1992.

62. Thomas G. Fuechtmann, *Steeples and Stacks: Religion and Steel, Crisis in Youngstown* (Cambridge: Cambridge University Press, 1989).

63. Wuthnow, *The Consciousness Reformation* (Berkeley: University of California Press, 1976).

64. Stephen Hart, *What Does the Lord Require: How American Christians Think about Economic Justice* (New York: Oxford University Press, 1992).

65. James A. Riccio, "Religious Affiliation and Socioeconomic Achievement," in Wuthnow, *The Religious Dimension*, chap. 9.

66. Paul Leinberger and Bruce Tucker, *The New Individualists: The Generation after the Organization Man* (New York: HarperCollins, 1991), see esp. 307.

67. Robert N. Bellah, Richard Madsen, William M. Sullivan, Ann Swidler, and Steven M. Tipton, *Habits of the Heart: Individualism and Commitment in American Life* (Berkeley: University of California Press, 1985), esp. chaps. 3 and 9.

68. Christopher Lasch, *The Culture of Narcissism: American Life in an Age of Diminishing Expectations* (New York: Norton, 1978), esp. chap. 3.

69. Timothy T. Clydesdale, "Money, Faith, and Divided America: A Study of How Religious and Economic Differences Influence Attitudes toward Race Relations, Poverty, Work, and Family," unpublished Ph.D. dissertation, Department of Sociology, Princeton University, 1993.

70. On the "new class," see the essays in B. Bruce-Briggs, ed., *The New Class?* (New Brunswick, N.J.: Transaction Books, 1979); Barbara Ehrenreich and John Ehrenreich, "The Professional Managerial Class," *Radical America* 11

(1977): 7–31; Steven Brint, "'New Class' and Cumulative Trend Explanations of the Liberal Political Attitudes of Professionals," *American Journal of Sociology* 90 (1984): 30–69; and Daniel Yankelovich, *New Rules* (New York: Bantam, 1981).

71. Sara M. Wuthnow, "Convergences among Nurses and the New Class," unpublished doctoral dissertation, Rutgers University, 1983.

72. John Schmalzbauer, "The Rise of the Evangelical Knowledge Sector, 1945–1992," unpublished paper presented at the Religion and Culture Workshop, Center for the Study of American Religion, Princeton University, 1992.

73. On this intersection more generally, see Charles Tilly, *As Sociology Meets History* (New York: Academic Press, 1981).

74. Talcott Parsons, *The Structure of Social Action* (New York: Free Press, 1937).

75. For example, see Laurel Thatcher Ulrich, *Good Wives* (New York: Knopf, 1982).

76. Philip Abrams, *Historical Sociology* (Ithaca: Cornell University Press, 1982).

77. This interest, it is worth noting, has not been recognized widely among historical sociologists.

78. One indication of this awareness is the historical work of sociologists of religion such as George M. Thomas, Roger Finke, Rodney Stark, Kevin Christiano, and Mark Chaves; another, a growing number of sessions at professional meetings focusing on such studies.

79. For a brief overview, see David G. Hackett, "Sociology of Religion and American Religious History: Retrospect and Prospect," *Journal for the Scientific Study of Religion* 27 (1988): 461–74.

80. Johnson, *Shopkeeper's Millennium*; Zuckerman, "Holy Wars, Civil Wars."

81. These lines of investigation are illustrated further in Wuthnow, *Communities of Discourse: Ideology and Social Structure in the Reformation, the Enlightenment, and European Socialism* (Cambridge, Mass.: Harvard University Press, 1989).

82. Robert William Fogel and Stanley L. Engerman, *Time on the Cross: The Economics of American Negro Slavery* (Boston: Little, Brown, 1974).

83. Lee Benson, *The Concept of Jacksonian Democracy: New York As a Test Case* (Princeton: Princeton University Press, 1961).

84. Many of these studies are mentioned in Philip R. Vangermeer and Robert P. Swierenga, eds., *Belief and Behavior: Essays in the New Religious History* (New Brunswick, N.J.: Rutgers University Press, 1991).

85. Some work on these issues is presented in Robert C. Liebman, John Sutton, and Robert Wuthnow, "Exploring the Social Sources of Denominationalism: Schisms in American Protestant Denominations, 1890–1980," *American Sociological Review* 53 (June 1988): 343–52; and in Edward P. Freeland, "Public and Private Hospitals and Colleges, 1890–1980," unpublished Ph.D. dissertation, Princeton University, 1992.

86. This view is consistent with Bryan Wilson, *Religion in Sociological Perspective* (New York: Oxford University Press, 1982).

87. Talcott Parsons, "Christianity and Modern Industrial Society," in Edward Tiryakian, ed., *Sociological Theory, Values, and Sociocultural Change* (New York: Free Press, 1963), 385–421.

88. Peter L. Berger, *The Sacred Canopy: Elements of a Sociological Theory of Religion* (Garden City, N.Y.: Anchor, 1969).

89. Thomas Luckmann, *The Invisible Religion: The Transformation of Symbols in Industrial Society* (New York: Macmillan, 1967).

90. Bailyn, Bernard, ed, *The Apologia of Robert Keayne: The Last Will and Testament of Me, Robert Keayne, All of It Written with My Own Hands and Began by Me, Mo: 6: I: 1653, Commonly Called August, The Self Portrait of a Puritan Merchant* (Gloucester, Mass.: Peter Smith, 1970).

91. Bernard Bailyn, *The New England Merchants in the Seventeenth Century* (Cambridge, Mass.: Harvard University Press, 1955).

92. Anthony Giddens, *The Constitution of Society: Outline of the Theory of Structuration* (Berkeley: University of California Press, 1984), esp. chaps. 1 and 6.

93. Donald Davidson, *Essays on Actions and Events* (Oxford: Clarendon Press, 1980); Randall Collins, "On the Micro-Foundations of Macro-Sociology," *American Journal of Sociology* 86 (1981): 955–78; Abrams, *Historical Sociology.*

94. Clifford Geertz, *The Interpretation of Cultures* (New York: Basic Books, 1973).

95. Robert Darnton, *The Great Cat Massacre and Other Episodes in French Cultural History* (New York: Basic Books, 1984).

96. Natalie Zemon Davis, *Society and Culture in Early Modern France* (Stanford: Stanford University Press, 1975).

97. See also the broader discussion in Hayden White, *The Content of the Form: Narrative Discourse and Historical Representation* (Baltimore: Johns Hopkins University Press, 1987); and for a critique of the Geertzian approach, David G. Hackett, "Culture and Social Order in American History," in David G. Bromley, ed., *Religion and the Social Order: New Developments in Theory and Research* (Greenwich, Conn.: JAI Press, 1991), 73–90.

98. Michel Foucault, *The Archeology of Knowledge* (New York: Random House, 1972).

99. M. M. Bakhtin, *The Dialogic Imagination* (Austin: University of Texas Press, 1981); Gary Saul Morson and Caryl Emerson, eds., *Rethinking Bakhtin: Extensions and Challenges* (Evanston: Northwestern University Press, 1987); Michael Holquist, *Dialogism: Bakhtin and His World* (London: Routledge, 1990).

100. Ulrich, *Good Wives*, 1.

101. Ann Swidler, "Culture in Action: Symbols and Strategies," *American Sociological Review* 51 (1986): 273–86, offers generalizations of this kind about the role of symbols in "unsettled" times; Hackett, "Culture and Social Order in American History," gives some examples focusing on episodes of religious change.

102. Mary P. Ryan, *Cradle of the Middle Class: The Family in Oneida County, New York, 1790–1865* (Cambridge: Cambridge University Press, 1981).

103. Wuthnow, *Meaning and Moral Order* (Berkeley: University of California Press, 1987), esp. chaps. 5 and 7.

104. Bruce Laurie, *Working People of Philadelphia, 1800–1850* (Philadelphia: Temple University Press, 1980), and *Artisans into Workers: Labor in Nineteenth-Century America* (New York: Noonday Press, 1989).

105. The literature on changing relationships between government and American religion is surveyed in John F. Wilson, ed., *Church and State in America: A Bibliographic Guide*, 2 vols. (New York: Greenwood Press, 1986).

106. Suggestive discussions that make such comparisons include David Martin, *Toward a General Theory of Secularization* (New York: Harper & Row, 1976); Mary Fulbrook, *Piety and Politics* (Cambridge: Cambridge University Press, 1983); and the essays in Wuthnow, ed., *Between States and Markets* (Princeton: Princeton University Press, 1991).

107. Theda Skocpol and Kenneth Finegold, "State Capacity and Economic Intervention in the Early New Deal," *Political Science Quarterly* 97 (1982): 255–78.

108. Theda Skocpol, *From Soldiers to Mothers* (Cambridge, Mass.: Harvard University Press, 1992).

109. Ulrich, *Good Wives.*

110. See Barbara Welter, "The Cult of True Womanhood, 1820–1860," *American Quarterly* 18 (1966): 151–74; Nancy F. Cott, *The Bonds of Womanhood: "Woman's Sphere" in New England, 1780–1835* (New Haven: Yale University Press, 1977); Ryan, *Cradle of the Middle Class.*

111. Barbara L. Epstein, *The Politics of Domesticity: Women, Evangelism, and Temperance in Nineteenth Century America* (Middletown, Conn.: Wesleyan University Press, 1981); Nancy Hewitt, *Women's Activism and Social Change: Rochester, New York, 1822–1872* (Ithaca: Cornell University Press, 1984).

112. Barbara Welter, "The Feminization of American Religion, 1800–1860," in Hartman and Banner, eds., *Clio's Consciousness Raised: New Perspectives on the History of Women* (New York: Octagon Books, 1976); Ann Douglas, *The Feminization of American Culture* (New York: Knopf, 1977).

113. Teresa Anne Murphy, *Ten Hours' Labor: Religion, Reform, and Gender in Early New England* (Ithaca: Cornell University Press, 1992). Jama Lazerow, "Religion and the New England Mill Girl: A New Perspective on an Old Theme," *New England Quarterly* 60 (1987): 429–53.

114. For example, Jualynne Dodson, "African-American Women, Power, and the Church," unpublished paper presented at the Religion and Culture Workshop, Princeton University, 1992; and Evelyn Brooks Higginbotham, "The Female Talented Tenth," unpublished paper presented at the Religion and Culture Workshop, Princeton University, 1991.

115. Rosemary Skinner Keller, *Calling and Career: Vocational Journey in the American Experience* (Louisville: Westminster/John Knox Press, 1993).

116. Viviana Zelizer, "The Social Meaning of Money: 'Special Monies,' " *American Journal of Sociology* 95 (1989): 342–77.

117. Nancy A. Hewitt, "Varieties of Voluntarism: Class, Ethnicity, and Women's Activism in Tampa," in Louise A. Tilly and Patricia Gurin, eds., *Women, Politics and Change* (New York: Russell Sage Foundation, 1990), chap. 3; and Ruth Milkman, "Gender and Trade Unionism in Historical Perspective," in Ibid., chap. 4.

118. Eugene D. Genovese, *Roll Jordan Roll: The World the Slaves Made* (New York: Vintage, 1976); Albert J. Raboteau, *Slave Religion: The "Invisible Institution" in the Antebellum South* (New York: Oxford University Press, 1978).

119. Hans Baer, *The Black Spiritualist Movement* (Knoxville: University of Tennessee Press, 1984); C. Eric Lincoln, *The Black Church Since Frazier* (New York: Schocken, 1974); C. Eric Lincoln and Lawrence H. Mamiya, *The Black Church in the African American Experience* (Durham, N.C.: Duke University Press, 1990); and Arthur Paris, *Black Pentecostalism* (Amherst: University of Massachusetts Press, 1982).

120. Joel Martin, *Sacred Revolt* (Boston: Beacon, 1992).

121. For example, see Ewa Morawska, "Small Town, Slow Pace: Transformations of the Religious Life in the Jewish Community of Johnstown, Pennsylvania (1920–1940)," *Comparative Social Research* 13 (1991): 127–78, which also emphasizes the role of gender.

122. Still of special value is Daniel Bell, *The Coming of Post-Industrial Society* (New York: Basic Books, 1973).

123. On the "new class," see B. Bruce-Briggs, ed., *The New Class?* (New Brunswick, N.J.: Transaction Books, 1979); Peter L. Berger, "American Religion: Conservative Upsurge, Liberal Prospects," in Robert S. Michaelsen and Wade Clark Roof, eds., *Liberal Protestantism* (New York: Pilgrim Press, 1986); Peter L. Berger, *A Far Glory: The Quest for Faith in an Age of Credulity* (New York: Free Press, 1992), esp. chap. 2; and James Davison Hunter, *American Evangelicalism* (New Brunswick, N.J.: Rutgers University Press, 1983).

124. Lasch, *The Culture of Narcissism*, chap. 3; evidence from the Religion and Economic Values Project points to a widespread perception that hard work and material success are no longer related.

125. Worth special attention, though of less relevance to United States than to British history, is Colin Campbell, *The Romantic Ethic and the Spirit of Modern Consumerism* (Oxford: Basil Blackwell, 1987). See also, T. J. Jackson Lears, "Beyond Veblen: Rethinking Consumer Culture in America, 1840–1920," in Simon Bronner, ed., *Consuming Visions: Accumulation and Display in America, 1880–1920* (New York: Norton, 1989).

126. Parsons, "Christianity in Industrial Society."

127. John Boli, "The Economic Absorption of the Sacred," unpublished paper presented at the conference on "Rethinking Materialism," Center for the Study of American Religion, Princeton University, 1993.

128. Most of the best essays in this literature have been collected in I. Bernard Cohen, *Puritanism and the Rise of Modern Science: The Merton Thesis* (New Brunswick, N.J.: Rutgers University Press, 1990).

129. Donald N. McCloskey, *If You're So Smart: The Narrative of Economic Expertise* (Chicago: University of Chicago Press, 1990); Alan Wolfe, *Whose Keeper? Social Science and Moral Obligation* (Berkeley: University of California Press, 1989), esp. chap. 1; and Neil J. Smelser, "Economic Rationality as a Religious System," unpublished paper presented at the conference on "Rethinking Materialism," Center for the Study of American Religion, Princeton University, 1993.

130. For a discussion of the theoretical legacy of Weber and Durkheim, see Wuthnow, "Religion and Economic Life," in Neil J. Smelser and Richard Swedberg, eds., *Handbook of Economic Sociology* (Beverly Hills, Calif.: Sage, 1994).

IO

PROTESTANT SUCCESS IN THE NEW AMERICAN CITY, 1870–1920

The Anxious Secrets of Rev. Walter Laidlaw, Ph.D.

▦ ▦ ▦

Jon Butler

Jesus wept over Jerusalem, wept because an exact knowledge of its conditions was in His mind; He weeps to-day over the conditions of our human institutions, because in His omniscience He is aware of their every detail, and the Church which is the organ to express His love to the world, must become equipped with His omniscience, so far as it can be, in order that His love may be a larger blessing.

> The Federation of Churches and Christian Workers in New York City,
> *First Sociological Canvass: The Fifteenth Assembly District*
> (New York, 1896), 5

. . . an electric machine seeks out the secrets recorded on the cards, tabulates them, and permits an inventory of a district's population, not only by denominations, but by blocks.

> The Federation of Churches and Christian Workers in New York City,
> *Fourth Annual Report* (1899–1900), 13.

TWO THEMES—and one relationship—dominate historians' work on Protestantism and the city between 1870 and 1920: urbanization, Protestant decline, and the implicit causal connection between them. Subtleties abound, of course, and the stark characterization suggested here could be modified in many ways. But if one were answering students' classroom questions about how historians usually describe the relationship between Protestantism and the American city between 1870 and 1920, the answer surely would turn in the direction of our opening observation. Moreover, this habit of thinking is old, not new. Between the Civil War and World War I, most Protestants perceived the city only as a "problem" and certainly not as an opportunity. The language of the pathologist dominated Protestant rhetoric about the city. Like historians now, Protestants then employed images of decline, decay, and denouement—rather than nurture, growth, or maturity—to describe their fate in the city.[1]

Yet, other themes also emerged in contemporary accounts, and they offer instructive guides to reassessing Protestantism in the late nineteenth-century American city. Many are surprisingly positive, if not Pollyannish. Others reflect a sophistication often unappreciated by men and women of the time as well as by later historians. If properly exploited, they suggest possibilities in the later nineteenth-century American society that our historical literature currently obscures. Taken together with an understanding of Protestantism's quite different fate in the European city, we might ponder just what we have been emphasizing when we discuss the city and Protestantism between 1870 and 1920.

Three books, two of them more than forty years old, dominate the historiography of Protestantism and the new American cities: Aaron Abell's *Urban Impact upon American Protestantism,* published in 1943 during World War II; Henry May's *Protestant Churches and Industrial America,* published in 1949 as part of the first great wave of post–World War II scholarship that reshaped modern American university and intellectual life; and Paul Boyer's *Urban Masses and Moral Order in America, 1820–1920,* published in 1978, the most comprehensive study of the city as moral problem in nineteenth-and early twentieth-century America.

The brevity of this list reveals the remarkable paucity of work on Protestantism in the age of the new American city. Even were the literature mammoth, these books would remain important for obvious reasons. They command their topics in unmatched ways. They treat, in broad fashion, the rise of the new American city, Protestantism in a wide variety of forms, and the prescriptions for urban disorder that obsessed late nineteenth-century American Protestant leaders. They also are superbly researched and well written, reflecting the sureness of superior history. Still, given the depth of literature on the Puritans, for example, it is remarkable how few general studies treat Protestantism and the city after 1870. We know far more about 5,000 early American Puritans than we know about 500,000 urban Presbyterians. This gap is well revealed in the astonishing lack of suitable books available for classroom use on late nineteenth-century urban Protestantism. Abell and May have long been out of print, and although Boyer's *Urban Masses and Moral Order* now is available in a paperback edition, one book does not a choice make.

What happened between Protestantism and the city? In the historiography, the relationship is clear: the city acted and Protestants reacted. To what did Protestants react? Three issues stand out: the city itself, the rise of industrialism, and the threat to the Protestant domination of American culture. Abell's opening assessment targets the city as the both the Protestant focus and the culprit. "The rapid growth of industrial cities after 1865 burdened religion to the breaking point," Abell argues, and he stresses the Protestants' clear view of the burden: "the city was the hothouse of every cancerous growth—of new evils like industrial war and class hatred and of the older evils of pauperism and crime, of intemperance and vice."[2]

For May, industrialism accelerated intellectual challenges first broached during the eighteenth-century Enlightenment (about which May would write his last major book) and deepened the dramatic social and economic changes created by urbanization. Unprecedented poverty, blight, hunger, disease, and crime became the result.[3] For Boyer, urbanization threatened the Protestants' apparent command of American culture, and they reacted by creating a vast array of movements and institutions, ranging from the Sunday School to the settlement house and urban planning bureaus, to cope with challenges arising from the urban transformation and foreign immigration.[4]

In general, these and other historians view the American Protestant–urban encounter as tragic rather than abject failures; or, invoking non-Christian Greek metaphors, Protestants were condemned to play the role of Sisyphus rather than Hercules. If Abell ends on a negative note— "Protestantism had not solved the urban religious problem"—he allows that the Social Gospel and its allied movements "reproduced the compassionate life of Jesus Christ and contributed immeasurably to the growth of humanitarian democracy," although these achievements fell far short of Social Gospel aims. Boyer, writing about a century of Protestant–urban encounters, describes the Protestant achievement as one of modest goals modestly met. Although May offers the most critical account, even he finds something of value in the encounter, although it is political rather than religious: the Social Gospel laid a valuable foundation for Progressive victories, but these successes never satisfactorily addressed industrialism's social problems.[5]

A second group of books concentrates on the Social Gospel and assesses the Protestant–urban encounter on its terms. In these books, the city comes into play because Social Gospel issues impinged on it. The city is not an independent topic of study in them; indeed, it is a "problem" because it was *the* "problem" that brought forth the Social Gospel.[6] Here, too, the earliest work, C. Howard Hopkins's *The Rise of the Social Gospel in American Protestantism, 1865–1915*, published in 1940, was particularly impressive. Preceding Abell and May, Hopkins established the principal mode of Social Gospel analysis: the heart of Social Gospel analysis is a largely intellectual enterprise with a course in practical ethics thrown in for good measure. The Social Gospel historian thus assesses the origins of the movement, especially its relationship to European theology and secular thought from the higher criticism and the rise of sociology to social Darwinism, then turns to two kinds of secular questions: the challenge and impact of the Social Gospel. Yet, as this analysis proceeds, the historians move far from the issue that many Social Gospelers saw at the center of their work: would Christianity survive the industrial, immigrant city?[7]

Thus, aside from Hopkins, few historians of the Social Gospel concentrate on either theology or religion. They seldom claim Social Gospel leaders as "theologians" of any substance, perhaps rightly, and the Social Gospel emphasis on "applied Christianity" scarcely improves things; perhaps it is to theology what a "trade school" is to the professions—a shallow imitation of the real thing. The term "theology" winds its way through Hopkins's *Rise of the Social Gospel.* But it occupies little attention in other books on the Social Gospel and does not even appear in the index to Ralph Luker's recent *Social Gospel in Black and White,* where, as in most studies since Hopkins's, the emphasis is on activism and its successes and failures, not intellectual life. At best, theology is brought in as a kind of final rite for Protestantism, the Gilded Age representing the decades when the old marriage of theology and American intellectual life ends in divorce after an increasingly difficult separation. This is, one thinks, a principal point of Bruce Kuklick's *Churchmen and Philosophers.* Kuklick emphasizes the "tangential" role of theology in the Social Gospel and describes Social Gospelers as dependent on the new "social scientists" for their distinctiveness and their legitimacy, not on classical theologies. It is no accident that Kuklick concludes with the sad portrait of the aged and almost blind Edwards Amasa Park uselessly attempting to resuscitate Jonathan Edwards's individualistic Calvinism in an urbanizing and industrializing nation where social process had long since displaced personal effort or even God in determining the fate of both individuals and society.[8]

Thus, most books on the Social Gospel focus on an instrumental question and leave theology aside. "Did the Social Gospel transform America as it had promised?" The answer is simple for most historians: not at all or only in limited ways. May gives a particularly acerbic judgment. He finds most Social Gospelers insipid, however much they gave "encouragement to developing American progressivism." At best, he credits the few "radical" Christians, meaning Christian socialists, who "made a distinct contribution to the ethical, idealistic wing of developing American radicalism." His conclusion about interaction among Protestantism, the city, and the coming of industrialism, hardly could have made his 1949 readers optimistic as they contemplated the further transformation of urban

America after World War II: "Whether Christian social doctrine has an important role in the present confused and desperate period of American social thought remains an open question. It seems likely however that whatever group prevails will make use, in some form or another, of the goals and motives which religion has always provided."[9]

More recent books give the Social Gospel somewhat better but still decidedly mixed reviews. For example, Susan Curtis's recent book, *A Consuming Faith*, treats the Social Gospel as a movement that ultimately—and quickly—degenerated into a self-serving provider of goods and services for an expanding middle class that by the 1920s had long since lost sight of its original social outreach to whole populations.[10] Ralph Luker's *Social Gospel in Black and White* is an exception. Luker argued that a tradition of positive Social Gospel action on American racial issues, often ignored by previous historians, including Abell and May, directly shaped Martin Luther King's ministry and the 1960s Civil Rights movement.[11]

Finally, a special group of studies on Protestantism and the city focus on relations with laboring men and women. In the main, they constitute a special variety of labor history. The most expansive and mature works are those by Herbert Gutman, originally in a 1966 *American Historical Review* article, and David Montgomery, who has engaged relations between religion and labor in a number of studies. More specialized work has appeared from Ken Fones-Wolf, John Bodnar, Matthew Lee, and John Buckowczyk. Most of them focus on the so-called "labor" or "working-men's churches" and on Christian socialism, and most of them ultimately describe the failure of these efforts, both among workers and within the American denominations, to make modern Christianity effect the ethics of Christ's sermon on the mount, the efforts themselves often constituting a "lost moment" in American labor and religious history.[12]

Was the American Protestant encounter with the city largely a failure? Certainly not in numerical terms, whatever qualitative judgments are made about the Protestant effect on social ethics and morality after 1870. Amidst images of intellectual decay, political compromise, declining influence, and sheer puzzlement, the work of the New York City reformer Walter Laidlaw, suggests re-examining our most common approaches to late nineteenth-century American Protestantism and taking up the burden, if not of success, then of a remarkable survival, and of the contemporary and historiographical burdens that accompany it.

I

The city is the Gibraltar of civilization. . . .
[It] is the great center of influence, both good and bad. It contains that which is fairest and foulest in our civilization. It is the mighty heart of the body politic, which sends its streams of life pulsating to the very finger-tips

of the whole land and when the blood becomes poisoned, it poisons every fiber of the whole body. Hence the supreme importance of city evangelization.

Josiah Strong, "Introduction," in Samuel Lane Loomis,
Modern Cities and Their Religious Problems (1886)

American Protestant leaders invented the Social Gospel because they prophesied and feared that the rise of the city meant the end of traditional Christian command of society. This demise would come in two forms: a loss of Christian authority in society and a dramatic decline of substantial Christian affiliation in the population. The loss of authority would stem from intellectual and political "secularization." The decline of Protestant "weight" in society would, in turn, result from two causes: the shift from rural to urban society that would destroy traditional face to face Christian worship and foreign immigration that would shatter the already declining Protestant domination of the population. Historians often treat these predictions as symptoms of rural provincialism and anti-Catholic and anti-Semitic bigotry. In turn, they seldom address the threats themselves, and this failure produces substantial misunderstandings. It misperceives the central dynamics of religious change and persistence in urban America, and it obscures the patterns that set the United States on a remarkably different religious course than its Western European counterparts. Protestant leaders probably were wrong about the "traditional" Protestant hegemony in rural society. But their concerns about the coming urban threat were based on more than irrational (or even theologically informed) worries about an approaching institutional apocalypse.

European developments clearly demonstrated why American Protestant leaders were concerned about their fate in the new American city. England especially offered a looming vision of urban industrialism's secular leviathan. The famous 1851 religious census and the late Victorian religious surveys of London by Charles Booth and Richard Mudie-Smith graphically demonstrated that Protestantism was losing its hold on the English population. The 1851 religious census, which measured church attendance and which was conducted with a fanfare intended to boost Sabbath turnout, turned up an attendance rate of only about 50%. Roughly half the population failed to attend church at all, a quarter attended either nonconformist Protestant congregations or expanding Catholic churches, while the state church counted less than a quarter of England's adults as worshipers. Charles Booth's studies of the 1890s and Richard Mudie-Smith's 1904 survey of religious life in London offered even more grotesque pictures of city religion—or irreligion. By 1904 only about one in four Londoners attended church at all, leaving 75% of the adult population without substantial institutional ties to Christianity, and nonconformists and Catholics again accounted for more than half of those who did attend, so that the Church of England could claim only a minority of a minority. In short, the Queen's Church was, indeed, patronized by few people besides the Queen.

The 1851 religious census and the Booth and Mudie-Smith studies did not falsely represent England's urban spiritual blight. Robert Currie and others have described England's long descending church adherence patterns in *Churches and Churchgoers: Patterns of Church Growth in the British Isles since 1700,* and Alan Gilbert, K. S. Inglis, Hugh McLeod, and James Obelkevitch have confirmed the pattern in detailed studies ranging from the late eighteenth century into the early twentieth century. While their views are not identical and while they point up methodological problems in the attendance surveys, all are agreed on one point: Christianity's hold on the English population—irrespective of whether it was actually declining from some difficult to measure previous high point—was in serious trouble throughout Britain as industrialization, urbanization, and modernization advanced.[13]

Nor was the picture brighter on the Continent for either Protestants or Catholics. Hugh McLeod's *Religion and the People of Western Europe 1789–1970* describes substantial decline in Scandinavian Sabbath attendance in both rural and urban settings. If the anticlericalism of the French Revolution was succeeded by a return to Christianity in substantial portions of the population and even by the development of new forms of popular Christian, the patterns were uneven and were, in turn, succeeded by growing secularism after 1870, with substantial segments of the French population not merely indifferent to Christianity but openly and often bitterly anticlerical. In urban Germany, particularly Berlin, Sabbath attendance scarcely reached 5%, though McLeod and others point up a greater urban–rural difference there than in England or France. The pattern was remarkably different than it was 300 years earlier, for in that time, the cities appear to have throbbed with the urgency of religious reform, their efforts often being described as the very heart of the Reformation.[14]

Twentieth-century patterns only confirm the progress of the late nineteenth-century European urban spiritual crisis. Sabino Acquaviva's 1970 book, *The Decline of the Sacred in Industrial Society,* proclaimed cause as well as reality. In his concluding chapter, Acquaviva held out hope for the sacred by uncovering anomalies in European "dechristianization." But even Acquaviva acknowledged the difference between hope and reality. By the 1950s only about a third of nominal French Catholics took part in Easter communion, and weekly mass attendance ranged between 9% and 40% in the cities. English Protestant weekly church attendance hovered at between 10% and 20%, and a survey of London, Leeds, and Birmingham housewives showed that between 56% and 69% of them simply "never" attended church and that they lacked substantial institutional religious contact at any point in their lives. Indeed, Poland excepted, Acquaviva's digest of studies of institutional religious indifference in twentieth-century Europe suggests that the Iron Curtain measured surprisingly little difference between East and West and that the Western campaign against "Godless Communism" might also have been directed toward institutional irreligiosity at home.[15]

Indeed, had Americans of the 1890s looked to statistics assembled in their own past, they might have increased their worry about the present. As early as 1760, Baptists began keeping denominational membership statistics, not merely of "membership" but of births, deaths, baptisms, and of members who had been disciplined, who had moved, and who had been "dismissed by letter," all to determine the flow of adherence in rampantly mobile society. Ezra Stiles filled his notebooks with drawings of New England church buildings and estimated their seating capacity to determine if the churches were large enough for the population. Mary Ryan describes the work of the Reverend John Frost of Oneida County, New York, who counted rural Protestants between 1813 and 1816 and whose surveys revealed worrisome patterns: only half the rural households in Oneida County contained even a single church member or adherent; the other half lacked any at all. Nor was counting church members an interest merely of the clergy. Between 1845 and 1875 the New York state census, taken in the fifth year of each decade, kept religious statistics furnished by local churches and synagogues that calculated the number of members, seats, and attendance.[16]

The urban crises of the Gilded Age produced the first large-scale surveys of individual religious preference taken in American cities. The surveys were avowedly instrumental: they were taken to boost church membership; their sponsors thought that only by knowing what people actually were doing could Protestant church leaders accurately assess the extent of the proselytizing necessary and the means of accomplishing it. The first known urban survey, taken by New Haven's Reverend John C. Collins in 1880, typified the pattern. Modifying a proposition made to the city's ministers, perhaps by the young Graham Taylor, the future University of Chicago sociologist then at Hartford Seminary, "to take a religious census of the city, and find out what proportion of the people did not go to church, who they were, what children did not attend Sunday school, and other facts of the same import," Collins hired two "Christian young men" "to go to every house in the city" to compile facts that would determine institutional religious affiliation in the city. The young men canvassed the entire city, ward by ward. They would "bring their note-books to me," Collins reported, "and I then had the facts copied into a large book, and also upon large sheets of paper." Collins sent abstracted results to all city ministers who supported the survey, and included the names and addresses of unchurched residents to facilitate Protestant proselytization.[17]

Collins himself found the results worrisome because the once Puritan town contained too many unchurched residents and too many Catholics.

But the survey also contains the first statistical evidence that American urban church patterns were already diverging from those in Europe, especially in London. The New Haven survey reported roughly 25,000 church members among 11,500 families and that some 40,000 persons attended church regularly; only about 10,000 persons, none claiming to be either Catholics or Jews, said they did not attend church at all.[18]

Ultimately, New York City stimulated the most extensive urban religion surveys. The precise background of the surveys is not yet known, but they most likely emerged out of concerns voiced in such publications as Samuel Lane Loomis's *Modern Cities and Their Religious Problems* (New York, 1887). Loomis focused on urbanization's threat to Protestant church-going specifically and to Christian adherence generally and largely bypassed the late nineteenth-century theological crises. He noted the problems that separated American cities from their European counterparts (American cities were far more heterogeneous), described London and Parisian programs as models for American urban proselytizing, and then outlined an "efficient" parish system that would, in effect, divide blocks into areas supervised by cooperating local churches that stress neighborhood worship rather than doctrinal purity. Josiah Strong's introduction reinforced the concern about simple church-going: "In six Assembly Districts of New York," meaning Manhattan, "the aggregate population is 360,000, for which there are thirty-one Protestant churches and 3,018 saloons"; Manhattan's First Assembly District contained "44,000 people, seven Protestant churches, and 1,072 saloons—one hundred and fifty-three saloons for every church"; and in the 20th Assembly District, only three Protestant churches could be found amidst a population of 60,000 people. Under such circumstances, how could Protestantism and Christianity survive, much less prosper?[19]

By 1896 the Federation of Churches and Christian Workers of New York City was conducting religious surveys to determine if the city had become America's Protestant charnel house. The survey director was Walter Laidlaw, an immigrant from Canada and a Presbyterian. Born in rural Ontario in 1861, Laidlaw received a B. A. (1881) and M.A. (1886) from the University of Toronto, studied sociology at the University of Berlin (1885–86), and received a Ph.D. (1896) in philosophy from New York University (the dissertation was entitled "A Christian Propaedeutic"). In 1895, while at the Collegiate Dutch Reformed Church and studying for his Ph.D., Laidlaw became executive secretary of the Federation of Churches and Christian Workers of New York City (the origins of the group are obscure, but it probably had connections to the "Convention of Christian Workers" held in Chicago in 1886 to which John Collins reported the results of his 1880 New Haven survey). In the next decade Laidlaw directed at least ten "sociological canvasses" of New York City using assembly districts and wards as the boundaries for his laboratories and published the results in the Federation's annual reports or in its sometime journal, *Federation*.[20]

Laidlaw's Federation surveys were unprecedented in their breadth, depth, and methodological sophistication. Laidlaw secured funding from a broad group of churches and organizations. He used assembly districts to define boundaries and hired workers to survey every household in the district; he claimed that Federation survey workers visited every household at least four times in the course of the survey. No previous American religious survey had been so sophisticated or assessed religious commitment with such technological prowess. Perhaps the only exception was the ill-fated 1880 U.S. census, which was so complicated that the census managers drowned in its data and little of its extensive information on religion, for example, ever was processed or published and much was simply thrown away.[21]

The New York City surveys typically asked between forty and fifty questions, a strong contrast to the 1880 New Haven survey, which asked twelve questions, and the 1889 Hartford census, which asked six. The information ranged from name, address, nationality, and religion to age and gender, home facilities, length of residence in the home, city, and country, ownership of Bible, church and Sunday school attendance, occupational information including wages and condition of home (clean or dirty). Survey workers also categorized household members under 30 years of age by categories, and then determined if they attended public school, Sunday School, or church, whether they were church communicants or members, whether they were baptized, their occupations, whether they possessed "insurance," belonged to a club, the number of days they worked, whether they belonged to a labor union, and how much they earned.

The stunning detail of the Federation surveys reflected Laidlaw's immersion in modern technology, not any aversion to it. Laidlaw's survey workers recorded the responses on printed survey forms that they carried to Federation headquarters where office workers transferred data to "Hollerith cards," the predecessor of the modern "IBM card" and first used for the 1890 U.S. census. By 1899, the Federation possessed two "Hollerith machines" to process the cards (the inventor of the machine, Carl Hollerith, gave them to the Federation himself), which tabulated the punched data (see Plates 1 and 2). These procedures allowed the Federation to bring the results down to the "block level" and gave cooperating Protestant churches a complete list of possible members, together with unparalleled information about their backgrounds. By 1903, the Federation claimed to have surveyed nearly 100,000 New York City families, distributing the results to local cooperating churches who were, quite literally, proselytizing on an explicitly sociological base.[22]

Two views should be taken of Laidlaw's results. Laidlaw himself believed that they confirmed the Protestant urban crisis and used the results to lobby for the "cooperative parish," a scheme similar to the one Loomis proposed a decade earlier in *Modern Cities and Their Religious Problems*.[23] After 1900, however, Laidlaw's pessimism eased, not so much because he believed the Protestants' urban woes had waned or even that the New York religious situation seemed better that that in London (Laidlaw made no references to the Booth and Mudie-Smith London surveys in his Federation reports), but because he could point to substantial results from interdenominational cooperation, if not from the cooperative parish system he touted but which never prospered. From Laidlaw's perspective, the surveys had revealed needs and opportunities that brought forth new congregations, settlement houses, and even parks in the city that the mainline Protestant denominations supported through political lobbying and financial help.

After 1910 Laidlaw spent the remainder of his career backing both ecumenism and statistics. He remained executive director of the Federation of Churches and Christian Workers until 1920, publicly backed United States entry into World War I, and aided the Interchurch World Movement. In 1921, Laidlaw became executive secretary of the Cities Census Committee, with whom he published two books, *Statistical Sources for Demographic Studies of Greater New York, 1920* (New York, 1922) and *Population of the City of New York, 1890–1930* (New York, 1932). His entry in the 1932 *Who's Who in America* proudly noted his appointment, at age 64, as supervisor of tabulation for the 1925 New York state census, and his funeral in May 1936 at Harry Emerson Fosdick's Riverside Church revealed how far he had come, denominationally and intellectually, from his Canadian Presbyterian upbringing. Laidlaw was credited for inventing the "small census tract" (its origins lay in his survey work with the Federation), and his New York *Times* obituary proclaimed him a "census authority" as well as a church figure, noting that at age 75 he still was serving as a city population consultant and had "dropped dead . . . as he was returning from lunch to the offices of the Mayor's Committee on City Planning."[24]

Laidlaw's Federation surveys in New York City open up important new views of the Protestant encounter with the new American city. Most importantly, they suggest a remarkable urban Protestant resilience amidst the late nineteenth-century American spiritual crisis. Comparing Laidlaw's New York City surveys with London surveys by Booth and Mudie-Smith suggests that the American urban religious experience was veering sharply from European patterns, and that, particularly by comparison with their European counterparts, the most remarkable strength in the United States urban landscape of religious institutions was found in the often criticized "mainstream" denominations.[25]

The Federation's 1896–1903 surveys report substantially higher denominational adherence than in London and markedly higher than in Berlin. The ten Federation surveys did, of course, describe different results in different districts. Still, the general picture proved remarkably consistent. Nominal Protestants accounted for about 40% of the households surveyed, nominal Catholics for another 40%, and nominal Jews for the remaining 20%, with less than 5% reporting no nominal affiliation. Moreover, Protestant affiliation or adherence did not lag nearly as far behind comparable rates for Catholics as might be thought: half the nominal "Protestants" claimed "church homes" (there are interesting variations among the different denominations; Baptists, for example, reported the highest rate of "church homes" outside the "district"), and about half seemed to be attending services with some regularity.[26]

The surveys of Manhattan's 14th Assembly District and Brooklyn's 17th Ward, taken in 1900 and printed in Tables 1 and 2, offer intriguing samples of the general patterns. Household heads who could be categorized as "unclassified Protestants," "unspecified," and "agnostics" amounted to less than 5% of the total in each ward; over 90% of households reported containing "baptized persons," although the vagueness of the categorization leaves considerable room for doubt about its meaning; about half the Protestants and 80% of the Catholics reported attending church regularly (only about 10% of Jews reported regular attendance at a synagogue or temple, a figure Laidlaw was hard-pressed to explain, in part because he seems to have been unaware of the quite different historical relationship between family and synagogue among Christians and Jews); and more than 95% of the households described themselves as endogamous (only 741 Brooklyn households reported parents of different denominations compared with 11,215 who reported parents of the same denomination).[27]

Laidlaw's findings were confirmed both by other brief contemporary surveys and by Laidlaw's later efforts to bring a historical perspective to his figures. A less systematic survey of Manhattan church attendance in November 1902 (see Table 3) showed about 38% of Christian church members attended church regularly, the high being registered by Methodists and Catholics (about 50% each), the low by Lutherans (about 5%)—a rate that more than doubled the rate Mudie-Smith found in London two years later and was almost ten times higher than known rates of church attendance by nominal Protestants in Berlin in the same decade.[28]

At the end of his life, Laidlaw drew attention to the apparent rise rather than decline in New York City religious institutional affiliation between 1845 and the 1920s. His *Population of the City of New York, 1890–1930*, published in 1932, used statistics drawn from the 1855 New York state census, Federation surveys done in 1901, and the United States religious censuses of 1906, 1916, and 1926 (see Table 4) to conclude that religious institutional affiliation in New York City rose from about 21% in 1855 to about 40% in 1916 (Laidlaw also calculated adherence for 1926, but the calculation is compromised by the Census Bureau decision to count all "ethnic Jews" as synagogue members, a practice that also compromises the 1936 figures). In fact, numbers from the 1845, 1855, 1865, and 1875 New York state censuses generally confirm Laidlaw's assessment (see Table 5). The percentage of church and synagogue members rose slightly between 1855 and 1875 despite an apparent dramatic decline in both membership and attendance in New York City

TABLE 1 Summary Religious Statistics, 14th Assembly District, New York City, 1900

Denominations	Total Families	Home Owners	Lesees	With Communicants	No Communicants	With Church Attendants	No Church Attendants	With Church Home	No Church Home	Church Home in District	No Church Home in District	With Baptized Persons	Without Baptized Persons	Sunday School	No Sunday School	Parents Same Denom.	Parents Different Denom.
Baptist	65	2	63	31	34	49	16	35	30	27	38	59	6	37	28	57	8
Congregational	6	0	6	3	3	3	3	1	5	1	5	5	1	3	3	3	3
Episcopalian	1083	27	1056	577	506	967	116	934	149	863	220	1033	50	568	515	966	11
Evangelical Association	33	1	32	9	21	19	11	4	29	0	33	27	6	23	10	33	0
Friends	3	0	3	1	2	1	2	1	2	0	3	2	1	1	2	3	0
Lutheran	1280	48	1232	569	711	946	334	646	634	453	827	1206	74	779	501	1196	84
Methodist	124	1	123	60	64	98	26	92	32	81	43	115	9	66	58	108	16
Free Methodist	3	1	2	3	0	3	0	2	1	2	1	3	0	2	1	3	0
Moravian	9	0	9	3	6	7	2	7	2	5	4	9	0	5	4	9	0
Presbyterian	239	9	230	140	99	207	32	183	56	130	109	225	14	152	87	214	25
Reformed Dutch	117	2	115	61	56	103	14	89	28	61	56	111	6	75	42	105	12
Reformed German	5	1	4	3	2	4	1	3	2	0	5	5	0	2	3	5	0

Category	1	2	3	4	5	6	7	8	9	10	11	12	13	14	15	16	Total
Ethical Culture	0	2	1	1	1	1	2	0	2	0	1	1	2	0	2	2	2
Unitarian	0	2	1	1	0	2	2	0	2	0	1	1	1	1	2	0	2
Unclassified Protestant	59	651	256	454	120	590	678	32	615	95	413	297	569	141	687	23	710
Unspecified	0	364	107	257	269	95	364	0	363	1	344	20	353	11	356	8	364
Agnostic	0	11	2	9	7	4	11	0	11	0	11	0	11	0	10	1	11
Protestant	324	3732	1621	2435	564	3492	2401	1655	1963	2093	1330	2726	2443	1613	3932	124	4056
TOTAL																	
Roman Catholic	206	4383	2466	2123	245	4344	2413	2176	1783	2806	781	3808	1858	2731	4520	69	4589
Greek Catholic	1	2	0	3	0	3	2	1	1	2	0	3	0	3	3	0	3
Jews	8	1740	1196	552	1595	153	1690	58	1628	120	1280	468	1686	62	1716	32	1748
Buddhist	0	1	0	1	1	0	1	0	1	0	1	0	1	0	1	0	1
SUBTOTAL	215	6126	3662	2679	1841	4500	4106	2235	3413	2928	2062	4279	3545	2796	6240	101	6341
GRAND TOTAL	539	9858	5283	5114	2405	7992	6507	3890	5376	5021	3392	7005	5988	4409	10172	225	10397

Source: *The Federation of Churches and Christian Workers in New York City, Fourth Annual Report, 1899–1900* (New York, 1900), 48.

TABLE 2 Summary Religious Statistics, 17th Ward, Brooklyn, 1900

Denominations	Total Families	Home Owners	Lesees	With Communicants	No Communicants	With Church Attendants	No Church Attendants	With Church Home	No Church Home	Church Home in District	No Church Home in District	With Baptized Persons	Without Baptized Persons	Sunday School	No Sunday School	Parents Same Denom.	Parents Different Denom.
Baptist	474	63	411	243	231	365	109	382	92	360	114	429	45	299	175	421	53
Congregational	21	6	15	11	10	13	8	10	11	6	15	20	1	13	8	18	3
Disciples	82	7	75	49	33	68	14	79	3	75	7	81	1	49	33	68	14
Adventist	1	0	1	1	0	1	0	1	0	0	1	1	0	0	1	1	0
Episcopalian	643	81	562	324	319	460	183	451	192	360	283	627	16	365	278	564	79
Reformed Episcopalian	83	18	65	45	38	66	17	72	11	71	12	81	2	54	29	71	12
Evangelical Association	55	13	42	36	19	50	5	53	2	52	3	53	2	31	24	46	9
Christian Alliance	35	2	33	22	13	32	3	35	0	29	6	34	1	23	12	30	5
Friends	5	1	4	2	3	3	2	4	1	0	5	3	2	1	4	5	0
Lutheran	1925	211	1711	930	995	1265	660	1228	697	1004	921	1896	39	994	931	1821	104
Methodist	953	132	821	517	436	768	185	801	152	753	200	922	31	600	353	880	73
Primitive Methodist	97	8	89	39	58	79	18	94	3	91	6	90	7	53	44	81	16
Moravian	2	1	1	0	2	1	1	2	0	1	1	2	0	1	1	1	1
Presbyterian	572	92	480	330	242	443	129	445	127	386	186	556	16	329	243	518	54
Reformed Dutch	365	69	296	242	123	329	36	262	103	237	128	355	10	202	163	280	85
Reformed German	14	4	10	7	7	6	5	12	2	5	9	12	2	6	8	14	0

Salvation Army	0	14	8	6	2	12	9	5	2	12	5	9	7	7	10	4	14
Ethical Culture	0	1	0	1	1	0	1	0	1	0	1	0	1	0	1	0	1
Spiritualist	1	0	1	0	1	0	1	0	1	0	1	0	1	1	2	0	1
Swedenborgian	0	2	0	2	0	2	2	0	0	2	1	1	1	1	1	0	2
Unitarian	0	1	1	0	0	1	1	0	1	0	0	1	0	0	1	0	1
Universalist	5	53	27	31	10	47	15	43	10	48	12	46	34	24	46	12	58
Unclassified Protestant	20	216	87	149	60	176	227	9	202	34	193	43	201	35	222	14	236
Unspecified	4	189	78	114	128	64	190	2	186	6	176	16	178	14	167	25	192
Agnostic	0	7	2	5	5	2	7	0	7	0	7	0	7	0	6	1	7
Protestant TOTAL	539	5292	2504	3327	381	5450	2344	3487	1807	4024	1767	4064	2953	2878	5069	762	5831
Roman Catholic	197	5538	3048	2687	74	5661	1830	3905	477	5258	573	5162	1086	4649	5178	556	5735
Greek Catholic	2	23	14	11	2	23	6	19	3	22	3	22	4	21	25	0	25
Jews	3	362	247	118	294	71	296	69	279	86	268	97	288	77	330	35	365
SUBTOTAL	202	5923	3309	2816	370	5755	2132	3993	759	5366	844	5281	1378	4747	5533	592	6125
GRAND TOTAL	741	11215	5813	6143	751	11205	4476	7480	2566	9390	2611	9345	4331	7625	10602	1354	11956

Source: *The Federation of Churches and Christian Workers in New York City, Fourth Annual Report, 1899–1900* (New York, 1900), 49.

TABLE 3 Christian Church Attendance, Manhattan, November 1902

Denomination	Churches	Membership	Total Attending	Percentage Attending	Men Attending	Women Attending
Dutch Reformed	15	9,218	10,241	111	4,298 (42%)	6,038 (58%)
Presbyterian	48	25,742	18,920	74	7,958 (42%)	10,962 (58%)
Episcopal	50	56,050	33,137	59	11,124 (34%)	22,013 (66%)
Methodist	45	14,749	20,191	137	9,085 (45%)	11,016 (55%)
Congregational	6	2,379	2,153	90	1,087 (50%)	1,066 (50%)
Disciples of Christ	2	667	848	127	350 (41%)	498 (59%)
Lutheran	27	18,808	7,542	39	(41%)	4,471 (59%)
Baptist	40	27,863	27,226	98	11,440 (42%)	15,777 (58%)
Christian Science	5	1,950	1,784	97	645 (36%)	1,120 (64%)
Other Protestant	43	16,956	12,946	76	5,455 (43%)	7,491 (57%)
Catholic	81	522,130	317,454	61	86,335 (27%)	231,119 (73%)
TOTAL	362	696,512	452,433	65	132,326 (31%)	311,571 (69%)

Source: New York *Times*, Nov. 24, 1902

in 1865. Moreover, the New York City pattern was remarkably similar to the state pattern even though the city reported one congregation for every 2,816 residents while counties outside the city reported one congregation for every 588 persons.[29]

Finally, the Federation surveys confirm the broad patterns of urban denominational affiliation exemplified in United States Census Bureau statistics assembled first in the 1890 United States census and then in special religious censuses taken in 1906, 1916, 1926, and 1936. All the United States religious censuses had important flaws. First, the reported results made it appear as though virtually every American belonged to one kind of religious organization or another because Henry Carroll, who assembled them, left the unchurched out of statistical pie charts that divided the United States population by denominations. Second, the statistics did not derive from surveys of individuals but, like the New York state censuses, came from numbers submitted by religious organizations. Third, the basis for the figures submitted by the religious organizations was not identical nor consistently handled; Catholics counted members differently than Protestants, for example, and in 1926 and 1936 the Census Bureau changed the meaning of the term "Jews" from one indicating synagogue or temple membership to one meaning "ethnicity," with a consequent expansion in the number of "Jews." [30]

Still, figures from five cities—Atlanta, Chicago, Cincinnati, New York, and Philadelphia—between 1890 and 1916 largely confirm the pattern of expansion in adherence to religious institutions suggested by the detailed New York City Federation surveys. In Atlanta, for example, religious institution affiliation hovered at about 42% in 1890 and 44% in 1916; in Chicago, the percentage of church members grew from 35% in 1890 to 43% in 1916; in Cincinnati it rose slightly from 39% in 1890 to 44% in 1916; and in Philadelphia it grew dramatically from 32% in 1890 to 46% in 1916. Moreover, in these cities, Protestantism fared remarkably well, both by comparison with the visions of impending doom drawn years before by leaders like Josiah Strong and Samuel Loomis and by comparison with the substantial difficulties encountered by Protestants throughout early twentieth-century Europe, all of whom would have envied the secrets borne out in Walter Laidlaw's "electric" surveys.[31]

Conundrums mark the past as much as the present, and the relationship between Protestantism and the new American city surely exhibits its share. We could, of course, eliminate one conundrum merely by declaring it nonexistent. Most of our classroom lectures to the contrary, perhaps we should say that the late nineteenth-century "spiritual crisis" transfixed only effete and unimportant intellectuals and that the age of the new American city should be best known for a remarkable advance in institutional religious commitment that separated America from Europe and finally made America's long-touted "exceptionalism" a reality. But such revisionism is not suitable everywhere. Rather, any substantial new direction in the history of American Protestantism after 1870 probably will

TABLE 4 Summary of Members of Religious Bodies of New York City, 1855, 1901, 1906, 1916 and 1926

Religious Bodies	1855 Congregations	1855 Members	1855 Percentage	1901 Congregations	1901 Members	1901 Percentage	1906 Congregations	1906 Members	1906 Percentage	1916 Congregations	1916 Members	1916 Percentage	1926 Congregations	1926 Reported Members	1926 Confirmed Members	1926 Percentage	1926 Under 13 Yrs.	1926 Sunday School Members
I Adult baptism	49	10,222	1.12	124	38,335	1.05	162	49,029	1.14	174	54,354	1.02	208	67,941	67,941	1.04	2,652	28,014
II Infant baptism	345	65,298	7.19	630	221,361	6.06	661	251,249	5.82	674	285,326	5.33	678	341,850	311,749	4.79	39,405	144,168
II Both modes	24	4,964	.55	56	23,162	.64	113	17,755	.14	101	17,556	.33	122	20,312	20,270	.31	1,378	11,002
IV Lutheran	7	2,228	.24	114	43,488	1.19	125	51,285	1.19	152	62,046	1.16	192	110,430	78,029	1.20	32,401	39,080
Protestant total		82,712	9.10	924	326,346	8.94	1,061	369,318	8.29	1,101	419,285	7.84	1,200	540,533	477,989	7.34	75,836	222,264
V East Orthodox	—	—	—	4	5,700	.15	9	18,067	.42	17	39,279	.73	22		25,690	.39	3,669	1,298
VI Catholic	53	110,448	12.17	224	945,602	25.90	278	1,413,775	32.70	337	1,545,562	28.85	430		1,733,954	26.62	447,099	101,939
VII Jewish	11	40	.00	104	18,366	.50	615	30,414	.70	721	93,819	1.75	1,044		1,765,000	27.09	—	13,295
VIII Mormons	—			1	70	.00	3	270	.01	3	515	.01	3		1,109	.02	200	334
IX Miscellaneous	—			1	500	.01	27	3,266	.07	21	2,772	.05	75		7,333	.11	4	343
X Christian Scientist	—			7	1,809	.05	9	3,372	.08	—	—	—	35		5,882	.09	—	4,606
Totals	489	275,912	21.27	2189	1,624,739	35.55	3,063	2,207,800	42.27	3,301	2,520,514	39.23	4,009	1,081,066	4,494,946	61.66	602,644	566,343

Source: Walter Laidlaw, ed., *Population of the City of New York, 1890–1930* (New York: Cities Census Committee, Inc., 1932), 297; Laidlaw's categorizations of Protestants and others, drawn from the detailed statistics printed in *ibid.*, 282–288, are listed below.

I: Adult Baptism Bodies:	**IV: Lutheran Bodies**
White	Augustana Synod
Brethren (Dunkers)	Ch. of Lutheran Brethren
Christadelphians	Danish Evangelical
Christian Israelites	Finnish Evangelical
Church of God (Anderson, Ind.)	Finnish National
Churches of Christ	Independent Lutheran
Disciples of Christ	Joint Synod Ohio
Independent Baptist	Norwegian
Life and Advent Union	Slovak
Northern Baptist Convention	Synodical Conference of Missouri
Plymouth Brethren	Unclassified Lutheran
Primitive Baptist	United Danish
Seventh Day Adventist	United Lutheran Church
Seventh Day Baptist	United Norwegian

Negro
Church of God and Saints of Christ
Church of God in Christ
Churches of Christ, Holiness
Churches of God, Holiness
National Baptist Convention

II: Infant Baptism Bodies

White
Church of New Jerusalem
General Church
General Convention
Congregational
Methodist Congregational
Free Methodist
Methodist Episcopal
Methodist Protestant
Primitive Methodist
Moravian
Presbyterian Bodies:
Presbyterian In U.S.A.
United Presbyterian
Synod of Reformed Presbyterian
Welsh Calvinistic
Protestant Episcopal
Reformed Bodies:
Christian Reformed
Free Magyar
Hungarian Reformed
Reformed in America
Reformed in U.S.
Universalist

Negro
African Methodist Episcopal
African Methodist Episcopal Zion
African Orthodox
African Orthodox of New York
Colored Methodist Episcopal
Union American Methodist Episcopal

III: Both Modes Baptism
American Rescue Workers
Assemblies of God, G. Coun.
Catholic Apostolic
Christian Missionary Alliance
Christian Church General Convention
Church of the Nazarene
Evangelical Church
Evangelical Synod
Friends
Hicksites
Orthodox
Independent Churches
Liberal Catholic
New Apostolic
Old Catholic
American Catholic Church
North American Old Roman Catholic
Pentecostal Assemblies
Pillar of Fire
Reformed Episcopal
Reformed Catholic
Salvation Army
Scandinavian Evangelical
Norwegian-Danish Free Church
Swedish Mission Covenant
Unitarian
Volunteers of America

V: Eastern Orthodox
Church of Armenia
Greek Orthodox
Jacobite Assyrian
Polish National Catholic
Russian Orthodox
Syrian Orthodox

IX: Miscellaneous Bodies
American Ethical Union
Bahais
Chinese Temples
Spiritualist Bodies
National Alliance
National Association
Progressive
Theosophist Bodies
American Theosophical Society
Theosophical Society in America
Theosophical Society of New York
Vedanta Society

X: Scientist Bodies
Christian Science Parent Church
Church of Christ Scientist
Church of Divine Science

TABLE 5   Church and Synagogue Affiliation New York 1845-1875

Year	County Population	Number of Institutions	Seatings	Number Usually Attending	Communicants or Members
New York City					
1845	371,223	176 (1/2,109 persons)[a]	nd[b]	nd	nd
1855	629,904	252 (1/2,500 persons)	234,730	222,550 (35.3%)	135,406 (21.5%)
1865	726,386	258 (1/2,815 persons)	266,980	161,403 (22.2%)	78,674 (9.2%)
1875	1,041,886	370 (1/2,816 persons)	292,343	nd	247,772 (23.8%)
New York State					
1845	2,604,495	3,822 (1/681 persons)	nd	nd	nd
1855	3,466,212	5,077 (1/683 persons)	2,141,159	1,124,211 (32.4%)	702,384 (20.3%)
1865	3,827,818	5,388 (1/710 persons)	2,157,173	1,070,662 (28.0%)	741,831 (19.4%)
1875	4,698,958	6,320 (1/743 persons)	2,537,470	nd	1,177,537 (25.1%)

Sources: *Census of the State of New York, for 1845* (Albany, 1846); Franklin B. Hough, *Census of the State of New York, for 1855* (Albany, 1857); Franklin B. Hough, *Census of the State of New York, for 1865* (Albany, 1867); C. W. Seaton, *Census of the State of New York for 1875* (Albany, 1877).

[a] 1/n = one institution for every *n* persons in population.

[b] nd = no data available.

wisely wallow in conundrums, among them that America Protestantism not only survived urbanization and industrialization but did so as Gilded Age spiritual crises raged and as diametrically opposite results emerged in Europe. Thus, the most pressing new direction needed in the study of Protestantism and the American city is a full and sophisticated understanding of how Protestant churches survived and even expanded in urban America even as they withered in Europe.

If a new "problématique" hides anywhere in American Protestant history, it surely resides within this story of divergences. Certainly, stressing the different paths of modern religious development in Europe and America undermines the two most common conclusions drawn by historians about Protestantism's fate in twentieth-century America. One conclusion employs the "O. Henry ending." Here, like the short story writer, historians employ what amount to "surprise endings" as they shift from narratives of multiple spiritual crises between 1870 and 1970 to the sudden rise of conservative Protestant evangelicalism to political and cultural power after 1975, little of it well explained or even anticipated. A second conclusion employs the romantic myth of spiritual constancy, in which religion is deemed to have been a persistent force in American life from the colonial era to the late twentieth century that historians and journalists often have ignored, a view Garry Wills espouses in *Under God: Religion and American Politics.* The first is unsatisfying, and the second is untruthful. In their place, a new, more perceptive, and more critical American Protestant history will widely accent religion's bumptious "progress" in the United States—tumultuous change as well as persistence, dead-ends as well as brilliant successes, and above all, complex paths to the variegated present in a spiritually diverse society.[32]

Three kinds of historical study bear the greatest promise in clarifying the light of Protestant survival amidst a historiography dark with metaphors of spiritual decay: imaginative studies of institutional adherence after 1870, studies that assess causal explanations for those patterns, and studies that discuss the implications of Protestantism's survival as the nation simultaneously modernized, urbanized, and industrialized.

If the thought of studying church membership patterns glazes one's eyes, perhaps suggesting a parallel to Puritan studies in the 1960s and 1970s will lift the spirits. The "new community studies," which concentrated in part on who adhered and who did not (or, perhaps more appropriately, on who was excluded and who was not), gave us more than a thoroughly new view of Puritan society and religion. It also reenergized early American intellectual history, though this may have been neither intended nor anticipated. Not even the most committed intellectual historian would think of going back to the pre-1960 Puritan historiography, and for at least two reasons. Three decades of community studies have given us more sophisticated insights into the ways Puritanism worked than we possess for any other aspect of American history except, possibly, slavery. We all rightly laugh at Edmund Morgan's wonderful aphorism that we "know more about the Puritans than any sane person should want to know." And we do so because we know we can afford to laugh, long having reveled in the knowledge itself, however much centered on one region and one century. In addition, community history became a major foundation for transforming intellectual history. David Hall's *Worlds of Wonder, Days of Judgment,* just to consider one of the most successful histories to bridge the gap between intellectual history and popular culture, simply would have been impossible without the community studies of Sumner Chilton Powell, Darrett Rutman, Philip Greven, John Demos, G. B. Warden, and Michael Zuckerman, among others, all of which focused on the ways Puritanism and the populace actually interacted.[33]

Assessing urban adherence patterns after 1870 must occur in the context of both European and broad American patterns. The European historiography is broadly developed, and if the language is almost entirely pathological, the ability to examine cadavers (in many if not all countries) has allowed or encouraged European historians to make deeper probes into their subjects than their American counterparts have accomplished, although one could claim that the latter are at least put off by still squirming patients. Hugh McLeod's essay, "Secular Cities?" offers a superb beginning to the problem and to the available European sources, and if his explanations assume too much consistency in the American pattern and attach too much importance to voluntarism as a cause for American success, they nonetheless lay down important outlines of both inquiry and explanation. For statistical models, American historians would do well to begin with several important studies of the 1851 British religious census, especially the 1960 article by K. S. Inglis, "Patterns of Religious Worship in 1851," in the *Journal of Ecclesiastical History,* then turn to Robert Currie et al., *Churches and Churchgoers: Patterns of Church Growth in the British Isles since 1700* (1977). Together with Currie's *Methodism Divided,* Alan Gilbert's *Religion and Society in Industrial England,* James Obelkevitch's *Religion and Rural Society,* and Albion Urdank's *Religion and Society in a Cotswold Vale,* these studies remind us how much American historians can learn from their European counterparts about methods and problems in assessing church adherence and its implications as rural society declined and urban society advanced—and here I artificially limit myself only to English scholarship.[34]

Understanding national American trends and their local variations is equally important. Kevin Christiano's *Religious Diversity and Social Change* is the most impressive recent study of urbanism and pluralism because it combines sophisticated quantification with a strong historical sense. If it stops short of assessing grand causes, it also does not descend into the vague abstractions that limit George Thomas's otherwise interesting *Revivalism and Cultural Change,* nor does it project the bitter invective and partisan "history" that disfigure Roger Finke's and Rodney Stark's *Churching of America.* More traditional historical studies of church membership patterns, such as David Hackett's *Rude Hand of Innovation* and Curtis Johnson's *Islands of Holiness,* and the voluminous early twentieth-century local surveys catalogued in Earl D. C. Brewer and Douglas W. Johnson, *An inventory of the Harlan Paul Douglass collection of religious research reports* (1970), highlight the superb numerical sources awaiting historical dissection. Certainly, it is remarkable how seldom national church adherence patterns have been studied and how our ignorance of the simplest numerical relationships among the churched, the unchurched, and the partially churched or historical issues of region, gender, and class between 1870 and 1920 makes it difficult to write persuasive social, intellectual, and political history about religion's fate, much less its role, in a modernizing America.[35]

National patterns also must be understood in the light of secular urban history. Surely Protestantism survived the urban onslaught because consciously and unconsciously, at least some American Protestants successfully manipulated the urban experience in ways Europeans did not. Just as historians of theology customarily probe their topic in the light of secular thought, so American religious historians must engage the secular setting. Eric Monkkonen's *Making America Urban* provides a superb overview of the urban process as it unfolded from the colonial period to the late twentieth century, with an emphasis on peculiarities in the combination of population density, advancing (but often sporadic) technical advances, and organizational development ranging from organization—indeed, invention—of the modern police to new schemes in city financing. Likewise, Terrence McDonald's *Parameters of Urban Fiscal Policy* remind one how thoroughly both urbanization and industrialization changed American public finance, most obviously in government but possibly also in religion. Both books—together with many of the European studies—also reinforce the call to greater methodological sophistication among American religious historians and the need for far better skills in both quantification and theoretical modeling.[36]

Of course, single-city studies constitute one of American urban history's most distinctive features, and if there is a peculiar parallel between American urban and religious history in practice—most urban historians have "their city" and most religious historians have "their group"—the two should be more frequently combined. A recent example of the benefits of doing so, although it begins at the very end of our period, is James Lewis's *Protestant Experience in Gary, Indiana, 1906–1975,* which focuses on the comparative history of a Methodist and Presbyterian congregation. Other models include Altina Waller's *Reverend Beecher and Mrs. Tilton,* which explores an obviously lurid topic but also offers a superb and rare glimpse at a Gilded Age congregation. Likewise, several ethnic group studies, such as June Alexander's *The Immigrant Church and Community: Pittsburgh's Slovak Catholics and Lutherans, 1880–1915* and Stanley Nadel's *Little Germany,* on mid-nineteenth century New York City, provide extremely useful views of the urban Protestant immigrant group.[37]

Ideally, the new case studies should be comprehensive, even though the mounting piles of evidence from the nineteenth and twentieth centuries discourage such breadth. This is because American Protestantism survived and ultimately prospered in raucously complex settings where many segments of the population belonged to no religious groups, where many others belonged to different religious groups, and where the groups that all of them honored or ignored did not necessarily contain or constrain their spiritual views and choices. Single-group studies, refined by their very precision, seldom convey this turbulence. Perhaps, then, it is time to promote group projects as a way of comprehending religious behavior across whole cities after 1870. One such project already is under way in Indianapolis, and others are perfectly feasible *if* humanists overcome a strong traditional bias against collaborative work. The expansive and variegated complexities of late nineteenth- and early twentieth-century American urban spirituality probably cannot be comprehended by lonely individual effort. Historians generally, including American religious history, have been far more resistant to change than were late nineteenth-century Protestant leaders. Most of us possess fewer numerical skills than did Walter Laidlaw—this being *our* anxious secret—and the methodological advances that seemed so promising fifteen years ago appear to be receding rather than advancing.[38]

What caused the Protestant survival in urban America? Although it is difficult to assess this question until we know more about the survival itself, several issues seem particularly important. One is institutional power. Clearly, it is time for greater systematic study of Protestant American denominational organization and life and for greater sophistication in appreciating its complexities. One recent discussion suggests why. Finke and Stark offer a stark "consumerist" explanation for American urban church adherence: "people in cities, and even in small towns, are more likely to have access to a church that is right for them." In their view, the choice seldom changes and is reinforced by the fact of others going to other churches—the latter being Kevin Christiano's argument that pluralism subtly reinforced lay inclinations toward church adherence in late nineteenth- and early twentieth-century America. Surely, however, the explanation for the survival and subsequent advance of American Protestantism after 1870 lies in the deft match of producer with consumer, to continue the market vocabulary. Granted that we know relatively little about the consumer, I would suggest that we know equally little about the producers. And here, the principal producers were the "mainstream" denominations Finke and Stark so consistently denigrate— Episcopalians, Presbyterians, Methodists, Baptists, and, later, Lutherans. Despite attention to growth among Protestant evangelicals and alleged decline in American mainstream groups, if the mainstream denominations had slumped as badly in America as they did in Europe between 1870 and 1920, all the highly touted evangelical growth could not have salvaged American Protestantism.[39]

To understand why Protestantism survived in a rapidly urbanizing, industrializing society, we need to understand how mainstream Protestants actually operated, how they shaped their denominations, how they exercised authority, how they maneuvered clergy, congregations, and laity into successful confluence. Indeed, thinking only of financial issues, it would be useful to apply Terrence McDonald's approach to the transformation of public finance in postbellum San Francisco to Methodist or Episcopal denominational organization. Similarly with organization. Did the Protestant denominations "incorporate" as America incorporated, as both Alan Trachtenberg and Olivier Zunz have described for the late nineteenth century? Whatever the criticisms leveled at the mainstream denominations by dissidents, sects, and historians, it is important to remember that, like the Big Three car makers, they have survived and dominated nonetheless, far beyond the expectations and hopes of their critics.[40]

At the same time, it also is crucial to understand the appearance of new groups whose absence clearly would have severely crippled Protestant survival after 1870. The most effective models here probably exist in American women's history. A wide number of books, from Ann Boylan's *Sunday School* to Edith Blumhofer's *Aimee Semple McPherson: Everybody's Sister,* demonstrate how women not only participated in Protestant worship but came to shape it in ways that separated them—and American Protestantism—from their European counterparts, who exercised far less influence in their churches, either locally or nationally. Kathryn Dvorak's *African-American Exodus,* a book on the separation of southern black Protestants from their white congregations after 1865, describes institutional creativity and expansion among another people. It reminds one how thoroughly the postbellum urban experience reshaped black Protestantism, and how slow this process might have been, since both the Laidlaw surveys (in portions not analyzed here) and the United States census figures (see those for Atlanta) suggest that black adherence to Protestant churches before 1920 was by no means as widespread as it was later. Michael Harris's *The Rise of Gospel Blues,* a study of Thomas Dorsey and the creation of the "black spiritual," also offers a crucial model. Harris demonstrates, through meticulous scholarship, how the "gospel blues" emerged from Thomas Dorsey's conscious, deliberate labor and was far from a "natural" outgrowth of slave religion. Harris does *not* argue that Dorsey's work increased black urban church adherence; rather, his book spotlights the deliberate creative process that recast an emerging black worship, much as one suspects that parallel processes recast white worship—and denominational organization—in the same period.[41]

We also must better appreciate the relationship between religion and the rise of the state in American public life after the Civil War. The great bulk of United States Supreme Court church–state decisions occurred after the so-called "Jehovah's Witnesses" cases of 1940 (*Cantwell v. Connecticut* and West Virginia *State Board of Education v. Barnette*). But the recent and relatively narrow debate over "church-state" issues pales before the great and broad debate about religion and American society between 1870 and 1920. It was Philip Schaff, not Josiah Strong, who wrote, in "Church and State in the United States," published by the American Historical Association in 1892: "Destroy our churches, close our Sunday-schools, abolish the Lord's Day, and our republic would become an empty shell, and our people would tend to heathenism and barbarism."[42]

Schaff and other Protestant leaders believed that American public and private life would be determined largely by the health of a public religion dominated by institutional Protestantism, hence the challenge of Roman Catholicism and Judaism. Yet images of real physical coercion in religion were not far distant. For more than seventy-five years, American Christian denominations, Catholic as well as Protestant, accepted the allocation of proselytizing rights by the federal government on American Indian reservations and reaped the benefits of government suppression of traditional non-Christian religious practice among American Indians with little dissent, a "voluntarism" only fully disbanded after passage of the American Indian Religious Freedom Act in 1978.[43]

This leads, in turn, to another dark side—bigotry and prejudice, not just as rhetorical or intellectual constructions but as possible causes of the Protestant persistence after 1870. Did the idioms of Josiah Strong, Philip Schaff, Samuel Lane Loomis merely fall on deaf ears? How did they affect the churched laity, the unchurched, and the partially churched? Did Protestant anti-Catholicism and anti-Semitism help sustain Protestant institutional adherence in this period, particularly in the cities? The answers to these questions are important because if they are negative, one could wonder why and how Protestant leaders indulged this bigotry to no profitable end for so long, while if the answers are yes, it is important to know how, why, and to what extent this bigotry "worked" to keep people in the churches or lure them there. John Higham's *Strangers in the Land* and Leo Ribuffo's *The Old Christian Right* both suggest that Protestant anti-Catholicism and anti-Semitism exploited American resentment over eastern and southern European immigration, but the precise ways in which it succeeded at the congregational level and fitted other aspects of congregational life need substantial new study.[44]

Of course, Protestant leaders knew well that Protestant views could be projected into American public life in many ways, the church–state relationship aside, and the shifts occurring in the context of urbanization and modernization indeed reshaped much of American public life. George Marsden and others have described how Protestantism once commanded American higher education, particularly in the late nineteenth century when the great public universities came into being, and then how Protestantism slowly slipped from view in both presidents' offices and classrooms. Studies of moves in other directions would prove extremely helpful, particularly when one remembers that whatever the fate among academics of Robert Bellah's much criticized views about "civil religion," it would be hard to dismiss the importance of religion, and especially Protestantism, in American presidential politics since 1870. How did the trappings of public religion, much of it reflecting exclusively Protestant forms, shift even as, seemingly, government became simultaneously more powerful and more "secular"? What of the role of wars in shaping public perceptions about the need for and desirability of religion, from the Spanish–American War through World Wars I and II and beyond? And, again, if these themes were important, why did they appear to reap rewards in America but not in Europe where, superficially at least, they were present in equal measure?[45]

Finally, we should determine if a causal relationship existed between Protestantism's survival and the spiritual crisis of the "old order." Could it be that the spiritual crisis of the Gilded Age was the best thing that ever happened to American Protestantism, at least if adherence in modern times is concerned? Historians have waxed eloquently on Protestant intellectual difficulties after 1850. Yet the Protestantism that succeeded it receives less systematic, less eloquent study. Histories of the new Protestantism often carry a snide tone when discussing prescient figures like Henry Ward Beecher, a mildly dismissive tone when discussing Social Gospel advocates, and an unbelieving tone when discussing revivalists, especially Dwight Moody, Billy Sunday, or Aimee Semple McPherson.[46]

We need to know much more about how the new Protestantism worked in the congregations, whatever the justice of verdicts about well-known preachers. We know relatively little about how average clergymen managed the transition to urban milieus. The subject is vast, but it would be extremely useful to apply the techniques long applied to the seventeenth-century Puritans or that Donna Merwick pioneered in *Boston Priests, 1848–1910: A Study of Social and Intellectual Change* to the late nineteenth- and early twentieth-century Protestant clergy. How did they minister to their flocks, and how did the flocks respond? Did the Protestant survival stem from the vigor of relationships between clergy and laity or did these relationships constitute yet more obstacles to be survived? How did average clergymen really handle the controversy over science, education, and morals? Did clergymen adopt "success" orientations and "positive thinking" earlier than we have believed? What about heaven and hell, rewards and punishments, and substantial theological inquiry? In short, did the American Protestant clergy really draw the laity in, or did lay men and women remake the churches in their own images, the 1950s "suburban captivity of the churches" being preceded by middle-class urban captivity seventy-five years earlier?[47]

Having thought about causes of the Protestant survival in urban America, understanding its implications becomes our final task. We could begin with a seemingly frivolous topic—architecture—because, in fact, it is a topic of immense symbolic importance. Here, an especially persuasive model comes from the unlikely locale of Anglican Virginia, Del Upton's *Holy Things and Profane*. Upton's book has the habit of making readers unable to pass church buildings without contemplating their cultural and social significance. European cathedrals may be older, but in America, places of worship are far more numerous and redolent of the broad constituencies that created them. How were these buildings constructed? Why were they designed in their own distinctive fashion, and why and how did these designs change over the years? Who wanted these designs, and what did they mean to both laity and clergy? Given frequent congregational disputes over new buildings, few knew better than the laity that buildings represented far more than bricks and mortar.[48]

It also would be crucial to know how the persisting denominations integrated views on economic life with the shifting realities of the American economy. We understand Social Gospel criticisms of the emerging corporate economic order reasonably well. But we know far less about what happened in the face of Social Gospel failures, again, particularly at the local level. Here especially, historical investigations have concentrated largely on the northeast and midwest, often on relationships with organized labor, and relatively little work is available on the south and west. Did the Protestant denominations literally sell out to American capitalism in most regions of the country, or did they sustain tension-ridden relationships with capitalism and its creators? What regional and denominational variations are important? How did the Protestant denominations advance or retard American economic development between the Civil War and the Depression? Here, one can only say that the work of Herbert Gutman, Dan Rodgers, Ken Fones-Wolf, David Thelen, and Clark Halker (who, like Michael Harris, studies music) needs to be expanded.[49]

New scholarship on religion, family, and children should become as commonplace for urbanizing America as it has become for the colonial era and the nineteenth century. By every account, the era of the new American city dramatically changed American family life. The scale required for postbellum family studies clearly makes such work daunting and may indeed also be most efficiently accomplished with group studies. Still, studies on earlier period provide enticing models for late nineteenth- and early twentieth-century work: the most obvious are the many studies that now exist of the so-called "Puritan family" (or, as Gerald Moran and Maris Vinovskis suggest, perhaps we should just say, the English Calvinist family in New England), but also books like Philip Greven's *Protestant Temperament,* Barry Levy's *Quakers and the American Family,* and Jan Lewis's *Pursuit of Happiness.*[50]

Finally, politics. Between 1870 and 1920 and perhaps the Depression, American politics came close to repeating the divisive patterns that characterized antebellum politics, with remarkable election shifts, party instability, and a political invective to match, although not hinged on sectional conflict. Yet many of the voting studies of the 1960s and 1970s linked certain religious groups indelibly to certain voting patterns. If this is true, how can we explain the lurching shifts in local and national elections? Here, it may be necessary to recalculate the earlier equations of religious affiliation and voting behavior, in part as George Thomas did in *Revivalism and Cultural Change,* not only to appreciate subtleties in Protestant political interests and voting patterns but also because, despite Protestant survival, the voting rate still tended to be considerably higher than the church-going rate; that is, a much higher percentage of the adult population voted than belonged to or attended religious institutions between 1870 and 1920. Here, Mark Noll's edited book, *Religion and American Politics, from the Colonial Period to the 1980s,* and Michael Leinesch's *Redeeming America: Piety and Politics in the New Christian Right* offer convenient points of departure. The essays in the Noll volume, running from the colonial period to the later twentieth century, demonstrate the persistent influence of religion on a variety of American politics, even as they also reveal puzzling and erratic patterns that often defy comprehensive explanation. And the Leinesch volume offers a particularly intelligent account of the relationship between piety and political activism, which when buttressed by sociological studies, such as Steve Bruce's *Pray TV: Televangelism in America,* or Bruce's *Rise and Fall of the New Christian Right: Conservative Protestant Politics in America, 1978–1988,* describes complex and often surprising relationships between religion and politics in a thoroughly urbanized, industrialized society that American Protestantism, mainstream and nonconsensus alike, not only survived but helped make.[51]

In short, in politics as elsewhere, the "problématique" of survival and success, however strong its moral ambiguities, constitutes the principal challenge to historians of Protestantism in the new American city between 1870 and 1920. Only by understanding how American Protestants endured and even prospered as industrialization and urbanization displaced rural America with a spiritually fearful urban one, can we understand the power—and to some, the specter—of religion in late twentieth-century America, to say nothing of understanding the past in its own rich, complex terms.

NOTES

1. A. I. Abell, *The Urban Impact upon American Protestantism* (Cambridge, Mass., 1943); Paul Boyer, *Urban Masses and Moral Order in America, 1820–1920* (Cambridge, Mass., 1978); Henry F. May, *Protestant Churches and Industrial America* (New York, 1949).

2. Abell, *Urban Impact on American Protestantism,* 3.

3. May's opening chapter is entitled "The Battle with Radicalism," and it elucidates Protestant confrontation with "radical" reformers from the Enlightenment to antebellum freethinking.

4. Boyer does not, however, deal systematically with nineteenth-century prejudice and bigotry, for which John Higham's *Strangers in the Land: Patterns of American Nativism, 1860–1925* (New York, 1966) remains the most compelling account.

5. Abell, *Urban Impact on American Protestantism,* 254.

6. Among the variety of works on the Social Gospel are Susan Curtis, *A Consuming Faith: The Social Gospel and Modern American Culture* (Baltimore, 1991); Robert T. Handy, *The Social Gospel* (New York, 1966); Matthew C. Lee, "Onward Christian Soldiers: The Social Gospel and the Pullman Strike," *Chicago History* 20 (1991): 4–21; Ralph Luker, "The Social Gospel and the Failure of Racial Reform, 1877–1898," *Church History* 46 (1977): 80–99; Ralph Luker, *The Social Gospel in Black and White: American Racial Reform, 1885–1912* (Chapel Hill, 1991); Robert Moats Miller, "Fourteen Points on the Social Gospel in the South," *Southern Humanities Review* 1 (1967): 126–40; Gary Scott Smith,

"Conservative Presbyterians: The Gospel, Social Reform, and the Church in the Progressive Era," *American Presbyterians* 70 (1992): 93–110; R. Glenn Wright, *The Social Christian Novel* (New York, 1989).

7. C. Howard Hopkins, *The Rise of the Social Gospel in American Protestantism, 1865–1915* (New Haven: Yale University Press, 1940).

8. Bruce Kuklick, *Churchmen and Philosophers: From Jonathan Edwards to John Dewey* (New Haven, 1985), 227.

9. May, *Protestant Churches and Industrial America*, 261.

10. Curtis, *A Consuming Faith*.

11. Luker, *The Social Gospel in Black and White*.

12. John R. Aiken and James R. McDonnell, "Walter Rauschenbusch and Labor Reform: A Social Gospeller's Approach," *Labor History* 11 (1970): 131–50; George H. Nash III, "Charles Stelzle: Apostle to Labor," *Labor History* 11 (1970): 151–74; William B. Faherty, "The Clergyman and Labor Progress: Cornelius O'Leary and the Knights of Labor," *Labor History* 11 (1970): 175–89; George C. Suggs Jr., "Religion and Labor in the Rocky Mountain West: Bishop Nicholas C. Matz and the Western Federation of Miners," *Labor History* 11 (1970): 190–206; Henry F. Atkinson, *The Church and Industrial Warfare: A Report on the Labor Troubles in Colorado* (New York, 1920); John Bodnar, *Workers' World: Kinship, Community, and Protest in an Industrial Society, 1900–1940* (Baltimore, 1982); J. J. Bukowczyk, "The Transforming Power of the Machine: Popular Religion, Ideology and Secularization among Polish Immigrant Workers in the United States 1880–1940," *International Labor and Working Class History* 34 (1988): 22–38; Kenneth Fones-Wolf, "Religion and Trade Union Politics in the United States, 1880–1920," *International Labor and Working-Class History* 34 (1988): 39–55; Herbert Gutman, "Protestantism and the American Labor Movement: the Christian Spirit in the Gilded Age," *American Historical Review* 72 (1966): 74–101; Lee, "Onward Christian Soldiers," 4–21; McLeod, "The Culture of Popular Catholicism in New York City in the Later Nineteenth and Early Twentieth Centuries," in L. H. van Voss and F. van Holthoon, eds., *Working Class and Popular Culture* (Amsterdam, 1988), 71–82; Bruce C. Nelson, "Revival and Upheaval: Religion, Irreligion, and Chicago's Working Class in 1886," *Journal of Social History* 25 (1991): 233–53; F. Perry, "The Working Man's Alienation from the Church," *American Journal of Sociology* 4 (1898–99): 621–29; Charles Stelzle, *The Workingman and Social Problems* (Chicago, 1903); Richard B. Stott, *Workers in the Metropolis: Class, Ethnicity, and Youth in Antebellum New York City* (Ithaca, 1990); Robert A. Wauzzinski, *Between God and Gold: Protestant Evangelicalism and the Industrial Revolution, 1820–1914* (Rutherford, N. J., 1993).

13. A fair sampling of contemporary surveys and scholarship on religious adherence and attendance in Victorian Britain might include the following: *Census of 1851 Report on Religious Worship (England and Wales)* (1851); *The Religious Census of London, reprinted from the British Weekly* (London, 1888); "Our Religious Census of London," *British Weekly*, Nov. 5, 1886, 1–2; "Notes and Queries on the Mission Hall Census," *British Weekly*, Jan. 13, 1888, 1, special supplement; Alan Gilbert, *Religion and Society in Industrial England: Church, Chapel and Social Change 1740–1914* (London, 1976); K. S. Inglis, "Patterns of Religious Worship in 1851," *Journal of Ecclesiastical History* 11 (1960): 74–86; Richard Mudie-Smith, *The Religious Life of London* (London, 1904); James Obelkevich, *Religion and Rural Society: South Lindsay, 1825–1875* (Oxford,

1976); David M. Thompson, "The Churches and Society in Nineteenth Century England: A Rural Perspective," in G. J. Cuming and Derek Baker eds., *Popular Belief and Practice* (Cambridge, 1972), 267–76. Probably because of the presumption that all British subjects were at least nominal "members" of the Church of England unless they formally declared adherence to a nonconformist congregation, religious surveys in Victorian Britain concentrated on attendance; in contrast, American surveys, as well as the religious censuses conducted between 1906 and 1936, usually assessed membership or adherence.

14. Hugh McLeod, *Religion and the People of Western Europe, 1789–1970* (New York, 1981).

15. Sabino S. Acquaviva, *The Decline of the Sacred in Industrial Society* trans. Patricia Lipscomb (Oxford, 1979), esp. chap. 2, "The Crisis of Religion in Industrial Society," 36–84.

16. The early Baptist statistics can be found in A. D. Gillette, *Minutes of the Philadelphia Baptist Association from A.D. 1707 to A. D. 1807* (Philadelphia, 1851); Ezra Stiles's comments about churches and their capacities are scattered through both Franklin Bowditch Dexter, *Extracts from the Itineraries and other miscellanies of Ezra Stiles, D.D., LL.D. 1755–1794 with a Selection from his Correspondence* (New Haven, 1916), and Franklin Bowditch Dexter, *The Literary Diary of Ezra Stiles* (New York, 1901); the Reverend John Frost's survey is discussed in Mary P. Ryan, *Cradle of the Middle Class: The Family in Oneida County, New York, 1790–1865* (New York, 1981), 75–77 and Table C.1., "Church membership by family status, 1813–16," based on Frost's survey, is printed on 257.

17. John C. Collins, "Religious Statistics," *Proceedings of the First Convention of Christian Workers in the United States and Canada*, Chicago, 1886, 8–10.

18. Ibid. Collins's numbers are, in fact, confusingly presented and are not broken down by city ward. Also see *A Religious Census of Hartford, taken by the Connecticut Bible Society, 1889* (Hartford, Connecticut, 1889).

19. Josiah Strong, "Introduction," in Loomis, *Modern Cities and Their Religious Problems*, 5–12.

20. "Walter Laidlaw," *Who Was Who in America* (Chicago, 1942), 1: 698. The Federation's annual reports sometimes are confused with its journal, *Federation*, in part because some annual reports constituted whole issues of the journal but also were printed separately.

21. See Kevin J. Christiano, *Religious Diversity and Social Change: American Cities, 1890–1906* (New York, 1987), 26–29, for a discussion of the ill-fated 1880 census.

22. For example, the survey taken in Brooklyn's 17th Ward, printed in the *Fourth Annual Report, 1899–1900* (39), asked residents about address, floor, location (front or rear), number of rooms, rooms with outside windows, monthly rent, was home a "rear Tenement," bath, water closet, hot and cold water, family name, number in household, length of residence in house, New York City, and in the U.S., "Circulating Library Member," did the family own a Bible, family size, number of boarders and were the boarders relatives and church attenders, and number of domestics and did the domestics attend church. The form changed from survey to survey, though usually only in details. Thomas J. Jones describes his survey work for Laidlaw in *The Sociology of a New York City Block* (New York, 1904). On the Hollerith card and its technology, see *Hollerith Punched Card Code: Category, Hardware Standard: Subcategory, Interchange Codes and*

Media (Washington, D.C., 1971); Geoffrey Austrian, *Herman Hollerith, Forgotten Giant of Information Processing* (New York, 1982); Philadelphia. Committee on Science and the Arts Franklin Institute, *Report on the Hollerith Electric Tabulating System. [By The] Committee on Science and the Arts* (Washington, D. C., 1890); Keith S. Reid-Green, "The History of Census Tabulation," *Scientific American* 260 (1989): 98–103; and Leon E. Truesdell, *The Development of Punch Card Tabulation in the Bureau of the Census, 1890–1940 : With Outlines of Actual Tabulation Programs* (Washington, D.C., 1965). On United States census tabulation methods, see Margo Anderson, *The American Census: A Social History* (New Haven, 1988), 102–07.

23. Walter Laidlaw, "A Cooperative Church Parish System," *American Journal of Sociology* 3 (1898): 795–808.

24. *New York Times*, May 21, 1936, p. 21. "Walter Laidlaw," *Who's Who in America* (Chicago, 1934), 1397. For brief comments on Laidlaw's census work, see Benjamin P. Bowder, Evelyn S. Mann, and Martin Oling, *Census Data with Maps for Small Areas of New York City 1910–1916: A Guide to the Microfilm* (Woodbridge, Conn., 1981).

25. Like literary evidence, these statistical materials are not without limitations and flaws. The Federation undertook its surveys to aid Protestant proselytizing, not for scholarly purposes; its questions often were patronizing (as in its evaluations of worker housing) and the reports sometimes revealed underlying prejudices, both against Catholics (Laidlaw described them as "dirty") and against Jews (whose aloofness from synagogues puzzled Laidlaw). Yet, Laidlaw's own apparent convictions about urbanism and Protestantism should have led him to underestimate church adherence, not overestimate it, and there is no evidence that Laidlaw "cooked" his results by skewing questions or altering results.

26. For the European comparisons, see McLeod, "Secular Cities? Berlin, London, and New York in the Later Nineteenth and Early Twentieth Centuries," in Steve Bruce, ed., *Religion and Modernization: Sociologists and Historians Debate the Secularization Thesis* (Oxford, 1992), 59–89. Since this essay was written McLeod has published his important book-length study, *Piety and Poverty: Working-Class Religion in Berlin, London and New York, 1870–1914* (New York, 1996).

27. "Summary Religious Statistics," *The Federation of Churches and Christian Workers in New York City, Fourth Annual Report, 1899–1900*, 48–49.

28. McLeod, "Secular Cities," 69. McLeod describes the rates as percentages of the population at large, but the *New York Times* article cited by McLeod describes them as proportions of church members.

29. See tables in this article drawn from Walter Laidlaw, ed., *Population of the City of New York, 1890–1930* (New York, 1932), 297. Also see the following New York state censuses: *Census of the State of New York for 1845* (Albany, 1846); Franklin B. Hough, *Census of the State of New York, for 1855* (Albany, 1857); Franklin B. Hough, *Census of the State of New York, for 1865* (Albany, 1867); C. W. Seaton, *Census of the State of New York for 1875* (Albany, 1877).

30. The most complete discussion of the federal religious censuses, including problems in their collection and analysis, is found in Christiano, *Religious Diversity and Social Change*, 24–41. As will be discussed later, several difficulties mar the interpretation in Roger Finke and Rodney Stark, *The Churching of America, 1776–1980: Winners and Losers in our Religious Economy* (New Brunswick,

N.J., 1992). A sample of the work of Henry K. Carroll is found in *The Religious Forces of the United States, Enumerated, Classified, and Described on the Basis of the Government Census of 1890; with an Introduction on the Condition and Character of American Christianity* (New York, 1893).

31. See Tables 5; Bureau of the Census United States, *Religious Bodies: 1906* (Washington, D. C., 1910); Bureau of the Census United States, *Religious Bodies: 1916* (Washington, D. C., 1919); Bureau of the Census United States, *Religious Bodies: 1926* (Washington, 1930); Bureau of the Census United States, *Religious bodies: 1936* (Washington, 1941); Bureau of the Census United States, *[1890 US Census] Report on Statistics of Churches in the United States at the Eleventh Census: 1890. . . . by Henry K. Carroll, special agent.* (Washington, D. C., 1894). Historians interested in additional statistical information on church membership should be aware of three bibliographies that deal explicitly with surveys—Earl D. C. Brewer and Douglas W. Johnson, *An Inventory of the Harlan Paul Douglass Collection of Religious Research Reports* (New York, 1970) (the collection of more than 1000 such reports, most dating from 1925 to 1965, formerly housed at the National Council of Churches in New York City, has been disbanded, but the Brewer and Johnson bibliography served as the basis for a microfiche edition of the collection, one copy of which can be found at the Center for Research Libraries in Chicago); Allen Eaton and Shelby M. Harrison, *A Bibliography of Social Surveys: Reports of Fact-Finding Studies Made as a Basis for Social Action; Arranged by Subjects and Localities* (New York, 1930); Zenas L. Potter, *The Social Survey: a Bibliography* (New York, 1915). In addition, the Methodist Archives at Drew University, has recently accessioned papers of H. Paul Douglass which contain original surveys conducted by the Institute for Social and Religious Research, which Douglass headed. No original surveys taken by the Federation of Churches and Christian Workers in New York City have been located.

32. See, for example, Winthrop S. Hudson and John Corrigan, *Religion in America*, 5th ed. (New York, 1992). Garry Wills's views are expressed in *Under God: Religion and American Politics* (New York, 1990), esp. 3.

33. The historiography on Puritanism and even on Puritan historiography is nearly endless. For a convenient beginning, see David Hall, "Puritanism: Another Try," in this volume.

34. See the sources cited in note 13, as well as Robert Currie et al, *Churches and Churchgoers: Patterns of Church Growth in the British Isles since 1700* (Oxford, 1977); McLeod, *Secular Cities;* Robert Currie, *Methodism Divided: A Study in the Sociology of Ecumenicalism* (London, 1968); Albion Urdank, *Religion and Society in a Cotswold Vale; Nailsworth, Gloucestershire 1780–1865* (Berkeley, 1990).

35. Christiano, *Religious Diversity and Social Change;* Finke and Stark, *The Churching of America;* David G. Hackett, *The Rude Hand of Innovation: Religion and Social Order in Albany, New York 1652–1836* (New York, 1991); Curtis D. Johnson, *Islands of Holiness: Rural Religion in Upstate New York, 1790–1860* (Ithaca, 1989); George M. Thomas, *Revivalism and Cultural Change: Christianity, Nation Building, and the Market in the Nineteenth-Century United States* (Chicago, 1989).

36. Terrence J. McDonald, *The Parameters of Urban Fiscal Policy: Socioeconomic Change and Political Culture in San Francisco, 1860–1906* (Berkeley, 1986); Eric H. Monkkonen, *America Becomes Urban: The Development of U. S. Cities and Towns 1780–1980* (Berkeley, 1988).

37. June G. Alexander, *The Immigrant Church and Community: Pittsburgh's Slovak Catholics and Lutherans, 1880–1915* (Pittsburgh, 1987); James L. Lewis, *The Protestant Experience in Gary, Indiana, 1906–1975: At Home in the City* (Knoxville, Tenn., 1992); Kenneth D. Miller and Ethel Prince Miller, *The People Are the City: 150 Years of Social and Religious Concern in New York City* (New York, 1962); Stanley Nadel, *Little Germany: Ethnicity, Religion, and Class in New York City, 1845–80* (Urbana, Ill., 1990); Altina L. Waller, *Reverend Beecher and Mrs. Tilton: Sex and Class in Victorian America* (Amherst, 1982). Also see Marion I. Bell, *Crusade in the City: Revivalism in Nineteenth-Century Philadelphia* (Lewisburg, Pa., 1977); James Borchert, *Alley life in Washington: Family, Community, Religion, and Folklife in the City, 1850–1970* (Urbana, 1980); James F. Bundy, *Fall from Grace: Religion and the Communal Ideal in Two Suburban Villages, 1870–1927* (New York, 1991); Jay Dolan, *Catholic Revivalism: The American Experience, 1830–1900* (Notre Dame, 1978); James M. Findlay, *Dwight L. Moody: American Evangelist, 1837–1899* (Chicago, 1969); Jack Kugelmass, *The Miracle of Intervale Avenue: The Story of a Jewish Congregation in the South Bronx* (New York, 1986); Gary A. Kunkelman, *The Religion of Ethnicity: Belief and Belonging in a Greek American Community* (New York, 1990); Thomas E. Lenhart, "Methodist Piety in an Industrializing Society: Chicago 1865–1914," Ph.D. dissertation, Northwestern University, 1981; F. Michael Perko, *A Time To Favor Zion : The Ecology Of Religion And School Development On The Urban Frontier, Cincinnati, 1830–1870* (Chicago, 1988); Linda K. Pritchard, "The Soul of the City: A Social History of Religion in Pittsburgh," in Samuel P. Hays, ed., *City at the Point: Essays on the Social History of Pittsburgh* (Pittsburgh, 1989); Stephen J. Shaw, *The Catholic Parish as a Way-Station of Ethnicity and Americanization: Chicago's Germans and Italians, 1903–1939* (New York, 1991); Leslie W. Tentler, *Seasons of Grace: A History of the Catholic Archdiocese of Detroit* (Detroit, 1990); Wauzzinski, *Between God and Gold;* Francis P. Weisenburger, "God and Man in a Secular City: The Church in Virginia City, Nevada," *Nevada Historical Quarterly* 14 (1971): 3–23; Ira G. Zepp, *The New Religious Image Of Urban America : The Shopping Mall As Ceremonial Center* (Westminster, Md., 1986). For a French example, see Louis Perouas, *Le Diocese de La Rochelle de 1648 a 1724: Sociologie et Pastorale* (Paris, 1964).

38. For one collaborative effort, see Theodore Hershberg, ed. *Philadelphia: Work, Space, Family, And Group Experience In The Nineteenth Century: Essays Toward An Interdisciplinary History Of The City* (New York, 1981).

39. Finke and Stark, *The Churching of America,* 205.

40. McDonald, *Parameters of Urban Fiscal Policy;* Alan Trachtenberg, *The Incorporation of American Society* (New York, 1982); Olivier Zunz, *Making America Corporate, 1870–1920* (Chicago, 1990); *American Denominational Organization: A Sociological View,* ed. Ross Scherer (Pasadena, 1980).

41. Katharine L. Dvorak, *An African-American Exodus: The Segregation of the Southern Churches* (New York, 1990); Anne M. Boylan, *Sunday School: The Formation Of An American Institution, 1790–1880* (New Haven, 1988); Daniel Mark Epstein, *Sister Aimee: The Life of Aimee Semple McPherson* (New York, 1993). Michael W. Harris, *The Rise of Gospel Blues: The Music of Andrew Dorsey in the Urban Church* (New York, 1992).

42. Schaff, quoted in John Wilson and Donald Drakeman, *Church and State in American History* (Boston, 1986), 153, which also offers an excellent guide to the general problem. Among the diverse approaches, one might consult Stephen

Botein, "Religious Dimensions of the Early American State," in Richard Beeman et al., ed. *Beyond Confederation: Origins of the Constitution and American National Identity* (Chapel Hill, 1987), 315–30; Thomas J. Curry, *The First Freedoms: Church and State in America to the Passage of the First Amendment* (New York, 1986); N. J. Demerath III and Rhys H. Williams, *A Bridging of Faiths: Religion and Politics in a New England City* (Princeton, 1992); John Eidsmoe, *Christianity And The Constitution: The Faith Of Our Founding Fathers* (Grand Rapids, Mich., 1987); Edwin Scott Gaustad, *Faith Of Our Fathers: Religion And The New Nation* (San Francisco, 1987); Ellis Sandoz, *A Government of Laws: Political Theory, Religion, and the American Founding* (Baton Rouge, 1991).

43. On church–state issues and on broader issues concerning religion and the state, see, among others, Chester J. Antieau et al., *Freedom from Federal Establishment: Formation and Early History of the First Amendment Religion Clauses* (Milwaukee, 1964); Chester J. Antieau et al., *Religion under the State Constitutions* (Brooklyn, 1965); Stephen Colwell, *The Position of Christianity in the United States, in its Relations with our Political Institutions, and specially with Reference to Religious Instruction in the Public Schools* (Philadelphia, 1854); Robert L. Cord, *Separation of Church and State: Historical Fact and Current Fiction* (New York, 1982); Edwin B. Firmage, *Zion in the Courts: A Legal History of the Church of Jesus Christ of Latter-day Saints* (Urbana, 1988); Robert T. Handy, *Undermined Establishment: Church–State Relations in America, 1880–1920* (Princeton, 1991); Mark DeWolfe Howe, *The Garden and the Wilderness: Religion and Government in American Constitutional History* (Chicago, 1965); Dean M. Kelley, *Government Intervention in Religious Affairs* (New York, 1982); Richard E. Morgan, *The Supreme Court and Religion* (New York, 1972); Benjamin Franklin Morris, *Christian Life and Character of the Civil Institutions of the United States, Developed in the Official and Historical Annals of the Republic* (Philadelphia, 1864); Mark A. Noll et al., *The Search for Christian America* (Westchester, Ill, 1983); John Webb Pratt, *Religion, Politics, and Diversity: The Church–State Theme in New York History* (Ithaca, 1967); Frank J. Sorauf, *The Wall of Separation: The Constitutional Politics of Church and State* 1976); Keith Tolman, "The Sacramental Wine Case of 1917–18," *Chronicles of Oklahoma* 42 (1984): 312–24. On American Indians and religion, see Jill E. Martin, "Constitutional Rights and Indian Rites: An Uneasy Balance," *Western Legal History* 3 (1990), 245–70; R. Pierce Beaver, *American Missions in Bicentennial Perspective* (South Pasadena, Ca., 1977); R. Pierce Beaver, *Church, State, and the American Indian* (St. Louis, 1966); Francis P. Prucha, *American Indian Policy in Crisis: Christian Reformers and the Indian, 1865–1900* (Norman, Okla., 1976).

44. The best recent study of more modern prejudice is Leo P. Ribuffo, *The Old Christian Right: The Protestant Far Right from the Great Depression to the Cold War* (Philadelphia, 1983), while Higham's *Strangers in the Land* remains the best general study of the earlier period. Also see Kathleen M. Blee, *Women of the Klan: Racism and Gender in the 1920s* (Berkeley, 1991); Stewart J. D'Alessio and Lisa Stolzenberg, "Anti-Semitism in America: The Dynamics Of Prejudice," *Sociological Inquiry* 61 (1991): 359–66; Leonard Dinnerstein, "The Historiography of American Anti-Semitism," *Immigration History Newsletter* 16 (1984), 2–7; David A. Gerber, *Anti-Semitism in American History* (Urbana, 1987); David A. Gerber, "Cutting Out Shylock: Elite Anti-Semitism and the Quest for Moral Order in the Mid-Nineteenth-Century American Market Place,"

Journal of American History 69 (1982): 615–37; Larry R. Gerlach, *Blazing Crosses in Zion: The Ku Klux Klan in Utah* (Logan, Utah, 1982); Oscar Handlin, "American Views of the Jew at the Opening of the Twentieth Century," in Abraham J. Karp, ed., *Jewish Experience in America: Selected Studies from the Publications of the American Jewish Historical Quarterly* (New York, 1969), 1–22; William F. Holmes, "White Capping: Anti-Semitism in the Populist Era," *American Jewish Historical Quarterly* 63 (1974): 244–61; Glenn Jeansonne, *Gerald L. K. Smith, Minister of Hate* (New Haven, 1988); Robert A. Rockaway, "Anti-Semitism in an American City: Detroit, 1850–1914," *American Jewish Historical Quarterly* 64 (1974): 42–54; Timothy C. Weber, "Finding Someone to Blame: Fundamentalists and Anti-Semitic Conspiracy Theories in the 1930s," *Fides et Historia* 15 (1992): 40–55.

45. George M. Marsden and Bradley J. Longfield, *The Secularization of the Academy* (New York, 1992); George M. Marsden, *The Soul of the American University* (New York, 1994). Aside from observations about American anti-Catholicism in the Spanish–American War and charges of Christian boosterism and huckerism during World War I, more general and powerful relationships between religion and American wars have attracted little attention from historians—the most obvious instance being World War II, which is all but ignored in most American religious history texts.

46. On Beecher, see Waller, *Rev. Beecher and Mrs. Tilton*, and Clifford E. Clark, *Henry Ward Beecher: Spokesman for Middle Class America* (Urbana, 1978); on Moody see Findlay, *Dwight L. Moody*; Gene A. Getz, *MBI: The Story of Moody Bible Institute* (Chicago, 1969); and S. N. Gundry, *Love Them In: The Proclamation Theology of D. L. Moody* (Chicago, 1976); on Billy Sunday see Roger A. Bruns, *Preacher: Billy Sunday and Big-Time American Evangelism* (New York, 1992); Lyle W. Dorsett, *Billy Sunday and the Redemption of Urban America* (Grand Rapids, Mich., 1991); and on Aimee Semple McPherson see Epstein, *Sister Aimee*; Edith L. Blumhofer, *Aimee Semple McPherson: Everybody's Sister* (Grand Rapids, Mich., 1993) Gloria Ricci Lothrop, "West of Eden: Pioneer Media Evangelist Aimee Semple McPherson in Los Angeles," *Journal of the West* 27 (1988): 50–60; and Gregg D. Townsend, "The Material Dream of Aimee Semple McPherson: A Lesson in Pentecostal Spirituality," *Pneuma* 14 (1992): 171–183.

47. David D. Hall, *The Faithful Shepherd: A History of the New England Ministry in the Seventeenth Century* (Chapel Hill, 1972); Harry S. Stout, *The New England Soul: Preaching and Religious Culture in Colonial New England* (New York, 1986); Donald M. Scott, *From Office to Profession: The New England Ministry, 1750–1850* (Philadelphia, 1978); Donna Merwick, *Boston Priests, 1848–1910: A Study of Social and Intellectual Change* (Cambridge, Mass., 1973); Gibson Winter, *Suburban Captivity Of The Churches: An Analysis Of Protestant Responsibility In The Expanding Metropolis* (New York, 1961).

48. Del Upton, *Holy Things and Profane: Anglican Parish Churches in Colonial Virginia* (Cambridge, Mass., 1986); Del Upton and John M. Vlach, eds., *Common Places: Readings in American Vernacular Architecture* (Athens, Ga., 1986).

49. Ken Fones-Wolf, *The Trade Union Gospel: Christianity and Labor in Industrial Philadelphia, 1865–1915* (Philadelphia, 1989); Gutman, "Protestantism and the American Labor Movement"; Daniel T. Rodgers, *The Work Ethic in Industrial America, 1850–1920* (Chicago, 1978); David Thelen, *Paths of Resis-*

tance: Tradition and Dignity in Industrializing Missouri (New York, 1986); Clark D. Halker, *For Democracy, Workers, and God: Labor Song-Poems and Labor Protest, 1865–1895* (Champagne Urbana, Ill., 1991).

50. John Demos, *A Little Commonwealth: Family Life in Plymouth Colony* (New York, 1970); Sanford Fleming, *Children and Puritanism: The Place of Children in the Life and Thought of the New England Churches, 1620–1847* (New Haven, 1933); Philip J. Greven Jr., *The Protestant Temperament: Patterns of Child-Rearing, Religious Experience, and the Self in Early America* (New York, 1977); Barry Levy, *Quakers and the American Family: British Settlement in the Delaware Valley* (New York, 1988); Jan Lewis, *The Pursuit of Happiness: Family and Values in Jefferson's Virginia* (New York, 1983); Gerald F. Moran and Maris A. Vinovskis, "The Puritan Family and Religion: A Critical Reappraisal," *William and Mary Quarterly* 39 (1982): 29–63; Gerald F. Moran and Maris A. Vinovskis, *Religion, Family, and the Life Course: Explorations in the Social History of Early America* (Ann Arbor, 1992); Edmund Morgan, *The Puritan Family: Religion and Domestic Relations in Seventeenth-Century New England* (New York, 1966); Daniel Blake Smith, *Inside the Great House: Family Life in Eighteenth-Century Chesapeake Society* (Ithaca, 1980); Daniel Blake Smith, "The Study of the Family in Early America: Trends, Problems, and Prospects," *William and Mary Quarterly* 3d ser., 39 (1982): 3–28; Maris Vinovskis, "A Ray of Millennial Light: Early Education and Social Reform in the Infant School Movement in Massachusetts, 1826–1840," in Tamara K. Hareven, ed., *Family and Kin in Urban Communities, 1700–1930* (New York, 1977), 62–99; Helena M. Wall, *Fierce Communion: Family and Community in Early America* (Cambridge, Mass., 1990); Rosemarie Zagarri, "Morals, Manners, and the Republican Mother," *American Quarterly* 44 (1992): 192–215.

51. Mark A. Noll, *Religion and American Politics from the Colonial Period to the 1980s* (New York, 1990); Michael Lienesch, *Redeeming America: Piety and Politics in the New Christian Right* (Chapel Hill, 1993); Steve Bruce, *Pray TV: Televangelism in America* (New York, 1990), and Bruce, *The Rise and Fall of the New Christian Right: Conservative Protestant Politics in America, 1978–1988* (Oxford, 1988).

I I

THE SPIRIT AND THE FLESH

Gender, Language, and Sexuality in American Protestantism

▨ ▨ ▨

Susan Juster

RELIGION HAS ALWAYS, it seems, belonged more in the "female world of love and ritual" than in the male world of politics and profit. We have known for some time now that women have constituted the majority of church members in most denominations since the mid-seventeenth century; we have been reminded by literary scholars and historians alike of the erotic dimension of religious discourse, with its tropes of marriage and sexuality; we have belatedly recognized the vital role that organized religion, with its many voluntary societies and church-sponsored associations, played in providing a middle ground for American women between the (male) public sphere and the (female) domestic sphere. We have learned, too, not to be misled by the pervasive theme of declension in American religious history into assuming that a feminized faith is necessarily a marginal one. The relationship between the feminization of American Protestantism and its declining hegemony in American political and cultural life, however much lamented by contemporary observers from Cotton Mather to Billy Sunday, is more a convenient fiction than historical reality. Celebrations of the positive contributions of a feminized faith to national concerns (such as abolition, the suffrage, and civil rights) have accompanied our recovery of a distinctive female presence and voice within American Protestantism itself.

I would like in this essay to unravel several aspects of this scholarly consensus on the "natural" alliance of women and American Protestantism. Because so much good work has been done to uncover the varied religious behaviors of American women over time, from joining churches to teaching Sunday school to missionary work, I will focus here on exploring the "ideological work" of gender in religious discourse from the seventeenth through the nineteenth centuries.[1] How has gender functioned as a system of symbols—a way of organizing perception into categories that correspond to "masculine" and "feminine"—in Protestant discourse? What have been the ideological and political consequences of assigning certain religious practices to the category of "female" and others to the category of "male"? What is the relationship between the gendered symbolism of religious discourse and the lived experiences of men and women? How, to quote Robert Orsi, "do people live in, with and against, the discourses which they inherit"?[2] These kinds of questions have sparked a revival of interest in the study of religion as language and as cultural practice among scholars arrayed across a wide spectrum of theoretical positions, from poststructuralism to cultural studies.

My goal here is not to explore the merits and limits of different theoretical approaches to religious studies, but rather to ground the discussion that follows in the basic proposition that gender is a fluid and dynamic element in the construction of faith rather than an eternal and unchanging category of human existence. "Maleness" and "femaleness" have meant different things to different generations of American Protestants as they searched for ways to describe their faith, even while the language of gender has provided a remarkably constant framework for understanding the progression from sin to redemption that is the grand narrative of the Protestant experience. This essay takes up four themes in American Protestant history that center on the perceived opposition of masculine to feminine: the trope of female piety, male and female languages, changing constructions of sexuality, and the gendered bias of the Protestant "nation." The chronological and topical limits of the essay will be immediately apparent; I rarely venture beyond the antebellum period, and I devote far more space to the experience of whites than to blacks—biases that reflect the current state of historical scholarship as well as my own interests. New England also looms larger than it should, which is unfortunate though not surprising given the prominence of Puritan studies in the general field of American religious history. Though the connections between the four sections may seem tenuous, each raises the vexed but vital question of how American Protestants see their sexual identities and desires as inextricable from their spiritual experiences and aspirations.

Gendering the Soul: The Language of Female Piety in Puritan New England

The earliest settlers of Puritan New England were caught between two discursive traditions of Western Christendom: one that insisted on the androgynous nature of the soul and another that described the relationship of the soul to God in gendered terms. Believing that "in God there is neither male nor female," as the Scripture declared, Anglo-American Puritans also envisioned faith as the sexual union between a feminized believer and a masculine God. "The Soule's the Wombe," the poet Edward Taylor rhapsodized, "Christ is the Spermodote / And Saving Grace the seed cast thereinto."[3] The tension between these two constructions of the soul—one androgynous, one female—was complicated in early New England by the politics of dissent, as Puritans struggled to establish a new orthodoxy free of the taint of sexual disorder that had dogged them in the Old World. The long-standing association of religious dissent with disorderly gender relations proved both an obstacle and an opportunity for New England Puritans as they created a new feminized language of piety.[4]

There has been an upsurge of interest among both literary scholars and historians in the gendered imagery of Anglo-American Puritan discourse, where converts of both sexes commonly portrayed themselves as "brides" of Christ who shared a sexual as well as spiritual union with the divine bridegroom.[5] "Looke what affection is between Husband and Wife," John Cotton demanded in 1655; "hath there been the like affection in your soules toward the Lord Jesus Christ? Have you a strong and hearty desire to meet him in the bed of loves, when ever you come to the Congregation, and desire you to have the seeds of his grace shed abroad in your hearts, and bring forth the fruits of grace to him, and desire that you may be for him, and for none other?" As God shed his "seed" abroad in the hearts of his people, so the experience of conversion "delivers" the fruit of this seed.[6] The conflation of spiritual and maternal powers in the literature on religious conversion is powerfully evoked in Patricia Caldwell's description of the "deliverance" of the English Puritan Elizabeth White from sin to life at the same time she was delivered of her first child.[7]

This rhetorical tradition was not new to colonial New England, but Walter Hughes has argued that the act of transplantation imbued American Puritanism with a greater appreciation for the sensual side of religious experience. Early New England was, in his words, a "kind of cultural hothouse in which many Puritan ideas underwent exotic growth and even bore forbidden fruit." A burning *desire* for God's love replaced the more filial emotions that inspired English Puritans.[8] In eroticizing their spiritual longings, Puritans exploded the association of femininity with marginality that had constituted the very core of early modern religious discourse. Unable (or unwilling) to shake off the association of dissent with sexual disorder, New Englanders brilliantly converted this liability (as they converted so many other obstacles, from stony fields to an unforgiving climate) into a spiritual asset; rather than repudiate the femininizing implications of their faith, Puritans embraced a language of religious affection that was unabashedly erotic. Dissent was now orthodoxy, and the trope of female sanctity became an important cultural myth of colonial New England.

Of course, the continued attachment to a sensual language of religious affection did not preclude Puritan authorities from denouncing deviants within their own midst in the same terms that they themselves had been denounced. Throughout the seventeenth century, the most threatening of all protest movements (antinomianism, Quakerism, witchcraft) were routinely depicted as sexually deviant.[9] Castigating dissenters for their sexual excesses helped Puritan authorities resolve the paradoxes of their own feminized faith, which could induce powerful anxieties, especially in men. We need not delve too deeply into psychological speculation to see the gender panic at work in the Puritans' vigorous repression of religious dissent through the coupling of spiritual and sexual disorder. In perhaps the cruelest example of such psychological displacement, the massacre of the Pequot Indians in 1637 was justified by invoking the spectre of Anne Hutchinson and her "monstrous" sexual deformities: as interchangeable victims of iconoclastic violence, Indians and antinomians were sacrificial lambs to the male anxieties of Puritan authorities who saw in both a demonic female face. Witches, later, would share in the same fate.[10]

However powerful such images of sanctified and demonic femininity were for American Puritans, the social implications of the rhetoric of female piety are far from clear. Margaret Masson and Amanda Porterfield suggest that the typological equation of converts with brides contributed to a general leveling of sexual differences in more prosaic ways. Men who were able figuratively if not literally to cast themselves in a feminine image in their spiritual lives were, Masson argues, less likely to endorse rigid sex roles outside the church; they also, suggests Porterfield, glorified women as mothers in their domestic arrangements just as they deferred to those "nursing Fathers" who had guided them to the New World.[11] On the other hand, Philip Greven has underscored the psychological costs of this feminine imagery for men who were forced to supress their masculine identity when addressing God; the latent homosexuality of the Puritan typology of the regenerate was responsible, in his view, for much of the anger and hostility that Puritan men exhibited in their secular lives.[12]

This search to link the rhetorical position of men and women in the language of Puritan piety with actual sex roles in Puritan society has led to a number of misunderstandings. Metaphors cannot be taken literally; as Joan Scott has cautioned, we must be careful "not to confuse masculine/feminine with male/female. The former are a set of symbolic references, the latter physical persons, and though there is a relationship between them, they are not the same."[13] Our efforts to comprehend how Puritans understood the relation between religious metaphor and social position have been hampered by problems of translation—terms that meant one thing in the spiritual realm often meant something very different in the profane world. To be utterly "dependent" upon God, for instance, was the ultimate mark of sanctification for pious Puritans; to be "dependent" in the economic or political realm was, in constrast, the ultimate sign of marginality for these same Puritans. The trope of female sanctity made a virtue out of qualities (humility, dependency, subordination) that signified powerlessness outside the walls of the meetinghouse. It is difficult to see how the feminized metaphors of Puritan faith provided much room for women to gain in stature or autonomy outside the church.

There has also been a persistent tendency in the literature on Puritan imagery to misunderstand the metaphorical structure underlying these images. Puritans envisioned the spiritual not so much as a place where feminized saints met a male God, but as an expansive realm of unbounded sexuality. The images of God found in the poetry of Edward Taylor, for instance, are sexually multivalent; God is portrayed simultaneously as ravishing bridegroom and lactating mother, as male and female. In one poem sinners "suckle" the breasts of God; in another, they are "ravished" by his seed.[14] The indeterminate nature of these metaphors suggests the porosity of sexual identity itself in Puritan ecclesiology. The "melting" together of human and divine that occurred in the act of spiritual union was possible because the boundaries of self (including those of gender) were not conceived of as unbreachable fortresses but as permeable frontiers.

To say that Puritan saints entered into such a protean relationship with God is not to deny that they were in some sense metaphorically "feminized"; indeed, the changeling nature of grace signaled its peculiarly female quality. Converts could so easily assume female roles because women were considered the less bounded sex. Early modern religious theorists envisioned women as empty vessels, to be filled by either divine or demonic substances; hence the endless vacillation between images of women as sainted and as damned in the iconic and devotional literature of both late medieval Catholicism and Reformed Protestantism. The powerful association of women with both witchcraft and ecstatic prophecy provides one context for understanding the Puritan tendency to envision saints as female. As Phyllis Mack argues in her superb book on visionary women in seventeenth-century England, women were commonly portrayed in popular discourse as "liminal creatures" who inhabited the borderlands of conventional cultural dichotomies: nature vs. culture, sacred vs. profane.[15] Puritan saints were thus "feminized" not because they played the role of bride to the divine groom, but paradoxically because they had to forgo any stable sexual identity whatsoever in order to be fit "vessels" of God's grace.

After the cataclysmic events of 1692, Amanda Porterfield has argued, the trope of female sanctity lost much of its cultural power in Puritan New England. The Salem witch hunt of 1692, in which the rhetorical coupling of sexuality and religious dissent was used to justify the hanging of 18 witches (most women), repelled many Puritan authorities who increasingly turned away from erotic imagery in their sermons and prescriptive writings. The enhanced professionalism of the New England clergy after 1700 was reflected not only in ministerial consocations and a higher premium on seminary learning, but in the adoption of a language of "enlightened patriarchalism" which stressed the paternal authority of ministers over their flocks, and of men over women within the godly household.[16]

Such a masculinization of religious language was consistent not only with the growing self-confidence of the ministerial elite but also with the increasing complexity of New England's social and economic life in the eighteenth century. The displacement of sexual metaphors reflects the diminished sense of organic unity among a people who increasingly felt themselves to be strangers to one another.[17] Although there is fierce disagreement about the pace and timing of New England's transformation from agrarian village to commercial center, there is little question that the spread of market relations in the later colonial period had important consequences for religious discourse that have gone largely unappreciated. While we have become properly cautious about assuming that an agrarian economy offered women more opportunities for autonomous activity than a commercialized one, it remains true that the model of social relations embedded in agricultural practices speaks more to the experiences of women than men in these societies. Organized largely around the rituals of reproduction, agrarian societies share a cosmological as well as material affinity with the female world of birth and nurture. Organic metaphors of social relationships, whether in the household or the church, closely approximate the social reality of preindustrial villages like those of early New England. Commercial societies, on the other hand, are organized around rituals of exchange rather than of sexual reproduction. The story of economic change in the eighteenth century is the story of how the "invisible hand" of the market freed men and women from the imperatives of the family economy to act autonomously in their own self-interest. Autonomous individuals began to engage in unrestricted exchanges with other autonomous individuals, or so the ideology of capitalism goes. It has come as no surprise to feminist scholars that the autonomous individual enshrined at the core of the market revolution was a male figure; nor should it surprise historians of religion that the prevailing metaphors of spiritual union came to center less on female than on male forms of exchange.

The meetinghouse had become as much a marketplace of religious belief as a sanctuary from secular entanglements by the mid-eighteenth century, as Harry Stout's fine new biography of George Whitefield attests.[18]

The complex relationship between commerce and religious culture in colonial New England defies easy categorization; on the one hand, as Christine Heyrman demonstrates, capitalist practices were condemned by Puritan ministers for their corrosive effect on social relations while, on the other hand, Puritan values of cooperation and localism continued to shape the practice of commercial exchange well into the eighteenth century. Heyrman's study points to the resiliency of the Puritan ethos in accommodating unfamiliar and potentially damaging economic practices, and allows us to see how religious concerns were grafted onto the language of economic exchange.[19]

There is much work yet to be done in tracing out the implications of this nexus between religion and the market for women, who came to dominate the membership rolls of organized churches in every Protestant denomination even as a feminized language of religious affection was giving way to a masculinized language of economic exchange. What exactly did it mean for women whose social identity continued to be defined by their domestic relationships (that is, by their position in a web of mutual dependencies) when evangelists like George Whitefield spoke in a "language of consumption" that presumed autonomous economic actors? The genius of Whitefield's ministry, Stout writes, lay in his unparalleled ability to "encourage pious souls to become actors themselves and to transform the world from a profane stage to a sacred stage."[20] Such a call may have been especially difficult for women to answer. But however disabling the market model of religion may have been for individual women seeking redemption, it posed even greater challenges to the tradition of feminine religious discourse that New England Puritans had imported from abroad. True, many critics of the new commercial order were quick to draw parallels between the fickleness and instability of credit and the unrestrained sexuality of women; for them, there was no contradiction between the language of passion and the language of the market.[21] Colonial Americans, however, were protected from both the excesses of financial speculation that sparked such misogynistic polemics and the extremes of sectarian warfare that an uncontrolled marketplace of religious ideas invariably created. Secure from the highs and lows of financial and sectarian strife, Americans were free to develop a market-based language of religion that was remarkable for its rationality and restraint—and for its masculine tone.

We can see this evolution in the maritime communities of Marblehead and Glouceser studied by Heyrman, where it was women who experienced the greatest loss as capitalism was reconciled to Puritanism. The aggressive sexuality of maritime women, evoked so vividly in the civil and criminal court records of the seventeenth and early eighteenth centuries, had no place in a maturing commercial society. Ironically, the only outlet for women's sexuality by the middle of the eighteenth century was radical religion. In the revivals of the 1740s, sexual impulses were channeled into spiritual experience in ways that seventeenth-century Puritans would have found familiar but which later generations found disconcerting. Heyrman's account of the sublimation of sexuality in the radical phase of the Great Awakening (a phase dominated by marginal groups— women, blacks, and unskilled laborers) provides indirect evidence that a feminine religious language now occupied the fringes of Puritan culture.

This conclusion is reinforced by studies that focus on dissident religious groups within New England Puritanism. Orthodox New Englanders had to contend not only with the multiple economic and social changes that combined to erode the feminine nature of Puritan piety but with internal dissension that often pulled in the opposite direction. My own work on New England Baptists and Separates in the eighteenth century, as well as George Rawlyk's work on evangelicals in Maritime Canada, suggests that among those who dissented from dissent, a radical commitment to the "ravishing" experience of grace held sway well into the early nineteenth century. Indeed, the feminine nature of Puritan piety may have been exacerbated by the politics of dissent—by the need to demonstrate one's superior commitment to the "pure" faith among those who lacked the ecclesiastical and social credentials of the orthodox. The revivals of the Great Awakening, as several scholars (myself included) have argued, were particularly important in reinvigorating the passionate underside of New England Puritanism that had been eclipsed since the late seventeenth century. Proudly proclaiming their indifference to the conventional structures of Puritan ecclesiology, from the territorial parish to the prepared sermon to the tribal congregation, the Awakeners resurrected a model of religious community that was defiantly female: sensual, sublime, suspended outside of time and space. As had been the case a century before, the feminine nature of Puritan revivalism was underscored by the long-standing association of religious dissent with sexual deviance. Like their orthodox forbears, New Lights did not shun the more female aspects of their piety (however uncomfortable they proved to be in the long run)—even to the extent of allowing women to exhort publicly and occasionally serve in a governing capacity.[22]

Thus, religious dissenters resurrected the language of erotic female spirituality that had supposedly been discredited by the enlightened humanism of eighteenth-century Congregationalism. There was, however, a crucial difference in the social and political functions of female piety among these later radicals as opposed to first-generation Puritans: more and more, a feminized piety would come to be associated with marginality. The original Puritan émigrées had masterfully articulated a language of the sensual and sublime to the political interests of those who governed the colony. Transformed suddenly by the simple act of migration from the periphery to the center, these early Puritan leaders found themselves in the perhaps unique situation of combining a language of dispossession with broad social and political powers. Eighteenth-century evangelicals were not so fortunate; for them, a feminized religious language was the clearest indication of how far removed they were from the center of American religious culture.

This scenario, in which the feminized, erotic religious discourse of seventeenth-century Puritanism gave way to a masculinized, market-oriented discourse in the eighteenth century, should not be overdrawn. Indeed, Whitefield's mastery of the metaphors and techniques of the market enabled him, in Stout's words, to "let the woman in him speak in a lion-like voice that startled hearers everywhere."[23] The key to Whitefield's phenomenal success as a revivalist lay in his ability to fuse female passions with the language of consumption, a lesson too often ignored by historians who tend to create a false dichotomy between religion and the market, between "feminized" faith and "masculine" reason—a dichotomy that few colonial Americans would recognize in such stark terms. However polarized the worlds of religion and business would seem to Victorian Protestants (and of course they remained deeply integrated in practice if not in principle), colonial Americans moved easily back and forth between the two. Like Whitefield, they may have found it easier to move back and forth between male and female personas as well, since gender was conceived more as a set of discrete roles than a psychosexual identity. In the colonial world, "gender restrictions were structural rather than psychological," Laurel Ulrich has argued, and this relative flexibility afforded religious figures a wide field of play in which to experiment with new modes of self-presentation and religious communication.[24]

Gendering the "Word": From Oral to Print Culture

As Americans were busy transforming their economy from its agrarian base to the bustling commercial hub of the Anglo-American colonial world, they were also engaged in another momentous cultural undertaking: the transition from an oral to a print culture. The two processes were closely related. A commercialized economy demanded certain skills from those who would profit from its financial and technological innovations, including basic literacy and the ability to figure.[25] The world of print culture, as it took shape in the multiplying coffee houses, lyceums, academies, and presses of the eighteenth century, was also a distinctly masculine world. Female literacy (defined as the ability to write one's name) lagged considerably behind male literacy during the entire colonial period, though David Hall has argued that the number of women able to read may have been much more greater than these figures suggest.[26] More than the simple ability to read or write one's name, however, print culture entailed a wider familiarity with like-minded persons scattered across the globe and the ability to engage in transatlantic networks of communication (literary, scientific, religious, as well as commercial). This world was largely restricted to men and those few widows prominent and prosperous enough to be able to maintain their husbands' cosmpolitan affairs after their death. As Richard Brown notes, communication among women primarily took place in face-to-face encounters confined to the informal circle of family and neighborhood.[27]

The gendered divide between oral and print culture went deeper than the practical division of labor which segregated male and female activities in the eighteenth and nineteenth centuries. The fraternal nature of these networks, which collectively constituted what Jürgen Habermas has called the "bourgeois public sphere," was ideological as well as pragmatic. The qualities that set this new public sphere apart from older forms of association all reflected the masculine side of a set of oppositions that were commonly understood in gendered terms: public/private, reason/emotion, nature/art, equality/hierarchy, universal/particular. As Joan Landes has shown so brilliantly in the case of France, the expanded networks of print culture allowed men to break free of the constraining world of private dependencies associated increasingly with women. In the world of print, as in the world of commerce, men addressed each other as autonomous individuals.[28]

Dominated by men and ideologically defined by masculine attributes, the rise of print culture has also been credited with creating more masculine forms of religion. Orality and literacy have often been portrayed as, respectively, feminine and masculine modes of communication in religious culture. Sharon Farmer, for instance, argues that the "embodied" nature of the spoken word (with hearer and speaker in close physical contact) helps explain why women were associated with the power of oral persuasion in ancient and medieval literature.[29] Religious traditions that place a strong emphasis on the "Word" as the source of divine authority have been described as particularly masculine in orientation, whereas those that privilege the more mystical elements of religious faith, like that of personal revelation, are seen as more feminine.[30] Carla Pestana locates the appeal of Quakerism to women in its elevation of the mystical experience of the inner light over the bible-centered ecclesiology of the Congregationalists and the Baptists in seventeenth-century New England.[31]

Within those religious traditions which deferred to the spiritual authority of the Bible and cultivated a learned respect for the power of print, women's cultural affinity for speech could be deeply menacing. The relationship between femininity and the spoken word was an uncomfortable one in the early modern world, for religious authorities no less than civil authorities who routinely prosecuted women scolds and gossips.[32] Although David Hall has argued that print culture is inherently less conservative than oral communication, because the printed word can be read individually at a physical remove from the authority of the author, ministers and magistrates alike considered "heated" speech (especially when uttered by women) far more troubling than heretical printed material.[33] Ministers periodically confronted women whose unbridled tongues posed serious challenges to the religious order. The celebrated case of Anne Hutchinson, whose "fluent Tongue" earned her the undying enmity of the Puritan governor John Winthrop and banishment from Massachusetts in 1637, is but one example of the kinds of subversive speech women dissenters engaged in throughout the centuries. Hutchinson's paradigmatic status in the Puritan construction of disorderly female speech is attested to by a number of literary scholars. For Ann Kibbey, "the resolution of the antinomian controversy did much to make 'women' a symbolic category of threat to Puritan authority."[34] For Amy Schrager Lang, the persistent attempts of Puritan divines and later chroniclers to associate Antinomianism with a corrupt and deformed sexual nature, manifest in the supposed monster-births of Anne Hutchinson and several of her female followers, proved an enduring narrative strategy from the seventeenth through the nineteenth century.[35] The lesson hinted at in Hutchinson's trial —that an "ungoverned tongue" bespoke a diabolical nature—became explicit in later witchcraft trials; indeed, Jane Kamensky goes so far as to suggest that "the witch's crime was, at root, a crime of female speech."[36]

Only when women's religious challenges were safely confined to the written page, where their emotional and psychological force could be better contained, would they be allowed a legitimate "voice" in their religious communities; surely, it is not coincidental that the transformation of the image of woman from evil seductress to spiritual guardian of the home occurred at the same time that print culture emerged triumphant in the nineteenth century. The most concerted attacks on women preachers occurred in this century, as denominational authorities sought to deny their female membership access to any public forum.[37] The iconoclasm of earlier religious traditions, in which the living "Word" was elevated above material signs, seems to have been replaced by an almost reverent worship of the printed word in the nineteenth century. With the congealing of private expressions of faith into literary conventions, the Victorian period seems to have effected a synthesis of the public and private worlds of religion.

Women's penchant for oral communication did not disappear in the nineteenth century, despite the best efforts of religious authorities to suppress all forms of female speech. Rather, female self-expression took increasingly unorthodox forms, ranging from spiritualism to mystical revelation.[38] At bottom, exercises such as trance-speaking and supernatural visitation entailed a radical disjuncture of self and langauge; female mystics did not claim any authorship over their visionary utterances, but instead saw themselves as passive conduits for the Word of God. Ann Braude sees in Victorian spiritualism an important avenue for female empowerment; "Spiritualism helped an entire generation of American women find their voice. It produced both the first large group of female religious leaders and the first sizable group of American women to speak in public. Whether one views the medium's voice as inspired by an external intelligence or by some remote region of her own mind, the trance state liberated it." [39] This ringing endorsement needs to be qualified on two levels. First, spiritualists were not the first important group of religious women to assume a public voice; female preachers in the eighteenth and early nineteenth centuries blazed a path of words across the religious landscape that spiritualists could never equal. Second, and more importantly, it mattered a great deal whether the medium's voice emanated from "some remote region" within or from an "external intelligence." One need only compare the defensive posture of trance speakers who insisted they were merely "unconscious instruments" of a greater intelligence to the supremely self-confident stance of Anne Hutchinson (who never doubted her own immense intelligence) to sense the enormous gulf that separated women's religious expression from the seventeenth to the nineteenth centuries.

Gendering the Body: The Feminization of Victorian Religion

As women crossed the divide from oral culture to print culture, they inevitably entered into the Victorian era's literary preoccupation with sexuality as a simultaneously cohering and corrupting force in the social universe. When historians speak of the "feminization" of American religion in the nineteenth century, they usually mean that a distinctly feminine sensibility came to characterize the language and theology of the Protestant faith, among liberals and evangelicals alike.[40] There is more to this proposition than first meets the eye, however, for it actually conflates two distinct processes into one. The language of the Old Testament, with its terrifying images of a wrathful God who consigns helpless infants to the flames of hell, may have been supplanted by more tender images of a loving and merciful Christ, but such sentimentalized language would hardly have been considered "feminine" by earlier generations of American Protestants. A far more fundamental transformation in cultural perceptions of womanhood had to take place before the romantic language of Victorian religion could be justly perceived as feminine.

As Nancy Cott argued in an important essay several years ago, constructions of women's sexuality underwent a sea-change between the seventeenth and the nineteenth centuries. Once regarded as the more carnal sex, "roving wombs" that devoured men as they wreaked havoc on the social and political order men had created, women were transformed into "passionless" creatures by Victorian ideologues intent on erecting a new sexual regime more conducive to the economic imperatives of mature capitalism. Urging that men and women restrain their sexual appetites as well as their other appetites, medical theorists elaborated a vision of the "spermatic economy" in which the conservation of sexual energies was necessary for sound management of the country's economic resources. Women, as guardians of the home, bore the brunt of this new sexual economy more than the men they were supposed to be guarding. A certain amount of lust was, after all, a good thing in the competitive world of the marketplace, but could fatally undermine the delicate balance between desire and restraint that a chaste homelife sustained.[41]

A sanitized version of feminine religious language thus characterized Victorian religious discourse, one which emphasized the emotional side of spiritual union with God instead of its erotic dimension. Rather than the ravishing bridegroom of the early colonial period, Christ appeared in nineteenth-century devotional literature as, in Barbara Welter's words, "a very cosy Person" into whom the sinner is urged to "nestle."[42] The nature as well as the language of ecstatic worship changed dramatically in the nineteenth century. Whereas female visionaries in the medieval and early modern periods used their proximity to the carnal world to bridge the gap between the natural and supernatural, ecstatic female experience (such as spiritual mediumship) in the Victorian era was premised on the *asexual* nature of women. The flesh was, for the first time, seen as an impediment to spiritual communion and only those who could suppress their carnal selves altogether had direct access to the divine.[43] The desexualizing of feminine religious discourse reached its height in the efforts of several religious groups (most headed by women) to abolish sexuality altogether. The Shakers and the Society of the Publick Universal Friend made celibacy the capstone of their respective religious visions, while the collective fraternity of the Methodist circuit riders exhibited a sexual ascetism that Jon Butler has compared to the Catholic priesthood.[44]

Far more sexually charged descriptions of spiritual union, however, continued to circulate on the fringes of Protestant America. Backcountry mystics who provided the spiritual leadership for much of the agrarian unrest that plagued the country in the early republican period were as prone as seventeenth-century Puritans or eighteenth-century Awakeners to draw explicit analogies between sexual and spiritual desire. Alarmed conservatives were quick to condemn the ecstatic physical exercises of these democratic ranters and their deluded followers; "The *pitching* of *breath, sighs* and *groans* of preacher and hearer," wrote one, "was *awful* and *tremendous*. I know not what to compare it to, unless a number of swine shut up in a yard, with furious mad-dogs rushing upon 'em . . . all wallowing in their distress, groaning, squaling and pausing for life."[45] Like animals, the "soul-sick" men and women depicted in conservative harangues "wallowed" in the kind of carnal excesses that inevitably accompanied the revivalists' call. The sight of an entire congregation reduced to this bestial condition seemed to confirm the worst fears of Victorian pedagogues who saw sexual, economic, and political disorder as hopelessly entangled on the American frontier.

The coupling of religious, sexual, and political disorder in the mind of middle-class America may also explain the extraordinary resistance to the evangelizing of the African-American community in the white South. While Christianity would ultimately became a powerful prop of the slaveholding ethos, worried planters saw only the threat of slave insurrection in the early efforts of white missionaries to bring the Word of God to the heathen slaves. Resistance was greatest whenever evangelicals sought to import the sensually charged revivalistic model of the First Awakening into the slave quarters. The Baptists, in particular, spoke the language of ravishment to white and black audiences alike in the eighteenth century—a language that superimposed the image of unbridled black sexuality onto the image of spiritual communion, a gutsy move indeed. It is difficult to conceive of an image more capable of arousing the worst fears of white slaveowners.

Worse yet, evangelicals articulated such a potent image in "promiscuous" congregations in which men and women, whites and blacks, assembled together in defiance of the unstated rules of southern society. While the language of spiritual ravishment may seem especially menacing when spoken to an audience that included black men and white women, the presence of black women in these congregations also accounted for much of the slaveholders' opposition. African American women did not share in the cultural reevaluation of Victorian womanhood as pious and chaste. Slave women confounded all the basic tenets of "true womanhood" because they crossed the boundary between work and home without apparent contradiction; Jacqueline Jones suggests, in fact, that in stark contrast to the "cult of domesticity" which confined white women to the home, black women who chose to remain at home and "play the lady" were denounced as "unnatural." [46] To the white imagination, black women— even more than black men—were "icons for black sexuality in general." [47] The sexualization of the African race served crucial political and disciplinary functions in the slaveholding South, but it also "perpetuated an enormous division between black people and white people in the 'scale of humanity': carnality as opposed to intellect and/or spirit; savagery as opposed to civilization; deviance as opposed to normality; promiscuity as opposed to purity; passion as opposed to passionlessness." [48] Such oppositions, I would suggest, were also central to the mainstream Protestant task of distinguishing respectable religion from its degraded evangelical variant.

This overdetermined identification of black women with promiscuity may explain the eagerness of some spiritual women like the Shaker Rebecca Jackson to embrace celibacy. Darlene Clark Hine notes that one response to assaults upon black sexuality was the creation of a politics of silence, a "culture of dissemblance." [49] Rebecca Jackson was certainly not unique among Shaker women for her advocacy of celibacy, but she perhaps went to extraordinary lengths to purge her private and public life of all hints of a corrupting carnality. Other African American women responded not by suppressing but by affirming their sexual powers in their spiritual lives; black women in the African Methodist Episcopalian church were, Jean Humez notes, "among the most passionate defenders of an 'old-fashioned' revivalistic emphasis on spiritual and ecstatic experience and expression as the 'heart' of religion." [50] Humez does not elaborate on what she means by "old-fashioned," but I suspect it refers to the embodied model of ecstatic experience that previous generations of American Protestants had found so empowering.

To ask why African American women preferred one form of religious expression over another is to venture into uncharted territory. The syncretic yet defiant stature of slave religion, in which the values and beliefs of white Christianity were both accommodated and challenged, has been explored with great sophistication, yet we still know very little about the gendered nature of slave worship. [51] Did slave women, like the Native American women studied by Carol Devens, resist more fiercely than men the evangelizing efforts of white Christians? [52] Or did women, in their capacity as faith-healers and nurses, help mediate between white and black visions of Christian communion? [53] We know that "hidden" churches existed in the slave community side by side with the formal religious societies formed by Baptists and Methodists in the eighteenth and nineteenth centuries, and slave women—in their role as spiritual healers—may well have formed the principal link between the two. Whether the story heard in the "hush-harbors" of the slave quarters was an eroticized version of the officially sanctioned one, we may never know. But we do know that sexual desire and religious aspirations mingled uneasily in the plantation South, a constant reminder of the volatile basis of slavery itself.

Gendering the Nation: Religion and Politics in Republican America

This fragile balance between sexual restraint and secular authority characterized the new nation itself as it took shape after the Revolution. Historians have been as reluctant to concede the erotic content of political discourse in revolutionary America as the "founding fathers" themselves. By shifting our focus for a moment from religion to politics, we can see how persistent inattention to the fissures of gender in American democratic culture has led to a skewed appreciation for the liberating potential of Protestant revivalism in the nineteenth century.

Following the lead of Gordon Wood and Nathan Hatch, historians have increasingly come to see the evangelical revivals of the early nineteenth century as emblematic of the "democratic pulse" of America itself. The revivals of the Second Great Awakening followed closely upon the heels of the social, economic, and political disruptions of the revolutionary era. Thrust into unfamiliar political relationships, unsure of their social moorings and thirsting for a more expansive economic life, Americans faced the nineteenth century with a mixture of elation and dread. The boisterous tenor of Jacksonian democracy, with its extravagant celebration of the vernacular, seemed to be confirmed by the "democratic"

revivals of the 1820s and 30s in which conventional social and ecclesiastical hierarchies fell by the wayside. Seen from this perspective, the unprecedented participation of women and African Americans in the evangelical revival was a striking indication of their populist roots and
democratic message.[54]

I would like to suggest here an alternative reading of the "democratic"
revivals of the nineteenth century, one rooted in a consideration of the
massive cultural assault on female and black sexuality that cast a dark
shadow over the triumphal path of American democracy and Protestant
revival alike. The "two faces of republicanism" that Stephanie McCurry
has identified—the public face of natural rights and political equality and
the private face of gender and racial inequality—were reconciled in the
"natural" subordination of women to men.[55] Rejecting all conventional
sources of hierarchy, from wealth to aristocratic privilege, republican theorists came to depend more and more on "natural" forms of distinction
to demarcate lines of authority both within the home and in the wider
republic. The sexual division between men and women who occupied
separate but complementary roles in society, because authorized by nature, became the prototypical model for relations of authority in all aspects of republican society. Republican men, in fact, needed republican
women in order to fulfill their civic responsibilities. "There was a direct
relationship between the developing egalitarian democracy among men
and the expectation of continued deferential behavior among women,"
Linda Kerber has written. "Just as planters claimed that democracy in
the antebellum South rested on the economic base of slavery, so egalitarian society was said to rest on the moral base of deference among a class
of people—women—who would devote their efforts to service: raising
sons and disciplining husbands to be virtuous citizens of the Republic."[56]
Here we see the inexorable logic of revolutionary discourse, which yoked
the fates of women and slaves together as the negative referents of republican virtue.

McCurry's astute observations about the alliance of republican politics
and proslavery ideology in antebellum South Carolina point to the critical role of evangelical religion in forging a unified vision of southern
society around the symbolic likeness of blacks and women. However often they resorted to paternalistic metaphors to defend the "peculiar institution," she notes, slaveholding ideologues "found a great deal more psychological satisfaction in likening slaves to women than to children." The
metaphor of marriage, with its suggestion of voluntary consent, served
to mask the authoritarian nature of gender and race relations alike. "By
insisting that women *chose* to submit . . . men were, in effect, denying
the personal power they knew women to have over them, however tem-
porarily, in romantic and sexual love." The spectre of female rebellious-
ness that McCurry argues loomed large over proslavery justifications was
thus, at bottom, the spectre of uncontrolled female sexuality. Proslavery

theorists went to such great lengths to compare the authority of masters over slaves to that of husbands over their wives because both were rooted in sexual domination.[57]

And, Doris Sommer would add, in sexual desire. Sommer's provocative study of the intertwining of passion and patriotism in the "foundational fictions" of Latin America digs further beneath the benign surface of republican rhetoric to expose an even deeper layer of sexual meaning. Drawing on the seminal work of Michel Foucault on the history of sexuality and Benedict Anderson on the history of nationalism, she notes that the late eighteenth century was the formative era for both discourses. Sex became an object of intense scrutiny at the same time that the modern nation-state was arising out of the ashes of the traditional monarchy, and the two processes were intimately linked. Sexual desire was yoked to national patriotism through the fictive metaphor of marriage, which in the national romances penned by Latin American authors brought together men and women of different economic, racial, ethnic, and religious groups. National unity, in other words, was achieved through the erotic union of disparate elements within the nation.[58] As in the United States, the sexual relationship of husband to wife came to stand for all those voluntary bonds (political, commercial, social) that held the republic together.[59] Sommer's insistence on the importance of desire as well as domination in the sexual metaphors of republican rhetoric complicates considerably our understanding of the place of women (and blacks) in democratic politics and religion. The patriarchal authority republican men strove for in their domestic relations was always in danger of being undercut by the passionate feelings such relations engendered.[60] No wonder, then, that Americans in the Jacksonian era struggled so hard to contain the threatening sexuality of women and blacks as they consolidated the political gains of the Revolution.

From this perspective, the extraordinary appeal of evangelical religion to women and slaves—both of whom had been classified as "naturally" dependent members of the polity—is perhaps an indication of the deeply conservative function of religion in the early republic. The revivals of the Second Great Awakening may have been less an affirmation of the democratic political revolution begun in 1776 than a consolation prize for those who did not share in the fruits of independence. Conflating the patriarchal power of men over women with the authority of whites over blacks, mainstream Protestant churches reaffirmed a central message of Victorian culture—that society was to be truly a home where men governed their dependents. To suggest that women and slaves occupied analogous positions in the political and religious culture of antebellum America is not to discount the very real material and legal disabilities that uniquely afflicted the African American community. But their common designation as dependent elements in a culture that prized independence above all placed them in a comparable dilemma. As sexual objects, women and slaves were not to possess but to *be* possessed.[61]

Despite its stirring rendition of the democratic tenor of antebellum religion, Nathan Hatch's recent survey of those populist religious groups that emerged after the American Revolution provides evidence for a contrary reading. For the religious primitivists of the early republican period described by Hatch display little of the sexual latitude of earlier evangelicals. Populists they might be in their rejection of the traditional hierarchies of class and education, but patriarchs they remained to the core. As one of the new brand of populist leaders, the Prophet Matthias, preached in the 1830s, "Everything that has the smell of woman must be destroyed. Woman is the capsheaf of the abomination of desolation—full of all deviltry."[62] Similarly, the democratic populism of Joseph Smith and the Mormons cannot be separated from their less savory attempts to revive biblical patriarchy and rural familism. The intense misogyny displayed by many of these "Old Testament Patriarchs" was, as Paul Johnson has argued, inextricable not incidental to their democratic pretensions. Those populists who found the "smell of woman" noxious betray the deep sexual ambivalence of American democrats for whom passion and power were uncomfortably linked.

It is, I think, highly suggestive that George Rawlyk's recent review of radical evangelicals in British North America in the postrevolutionary era concludes that Canadian evangelicalism was "more radical, more anarchistic, more democratic and more populist than its American counterpart." The radical thrust of Canadian evangelicalism is attested to above all by its tolerance of sexual disorder. The inspired antics of the "New Dispensationalists," who practiced spiritual wifery and other antinomian excesses in the 1780s and 1790s, had no counterpart in the United States, where "enthusiastical" displays of any kind were discouraged. Rawlyk rightly locates the source of this discrepancy in the secular "baggage of civic humanism, republicanism, and the covenant ideal" carried by American evangelicals, although I would argue that it was not the *secular* nature of this ideology that was so constraining but rather its internal contradictions.[63] Sexual desire may have been necessary for the republic to exist, as the pervasive marital representations of republican union suggest, but it also destabilized the domestic and political authority of those who governed.

Postscript

If Americans had succeeded in synthesizing evangelical religion and democratic politics into a sweeping "Christian republicanism"[64] by the early decades of the nineteenth century, incorporating populist and patriarchal elements into an undifferentiated whole, how might we expect Protestantism to respond to the gradual unraveling of this synthesis in the later nineteenth and early twentieth centuries?

The story of Protestant fortunes in the late-Victorian era is commonly told in terms of a declining cultural and political hegemony, manifest in the rise of sizeable Catholic and Jewish communities with the resources and will to challenge the stranglehold of Protestantism over the national institutions and symbols of middle-class America.[65] Faced with the loss of cultural and ecclesiastical dominance, Protestant leaders responded in the same way so many other beleagured professional groups responded to the challenges of the late nineteenth century: with a shrill assertion of masculinity. As Gail Bederman explains, between 1880 and 1920 "many middle-class men experienced the social and cultural changes tied to the development of a corporate, consumer-oriented society as dangerous challenges to their manhood." The Protestant clergy was no different; dreading the "effeminacy" that they believed inevitably attached to an ennervated religious establishment, Protestant leaders issued a collective cry for a more virile form of religion, a kind of "muscular Christianity" to rescue their sagging fortunes from the grip of women.[66] Hardened images of Jesus and God, for instance, began to take shape in more liberal Protestant circles as male reformers envisioned a robust, muscular Christ to complement their own sense of manly mission. There was "nothing mushy, nothing sweetly effeminate about Jesus," Social Gospelers insisted; rather, Jesus was "a man's man."[67] The culmination of this masculinizing impulse may well have been the triumph of fundamentalism in the early decades of the twentieth century, which, as Betty DeBerg argues, "functioned in popular American culture to support the gender roles and ideology of the Victorian era well into post-Victorian times."[68]

If "femininization" was the problematic of early Victorian religion, then "masculinization" had become the critical issue for late Victorian Protestants. In both eras, gender identity was central to the way American Protestants conceived of their faith and its larger social purpose. There is a neat symmetry about the literature on gender and religion in the nineteenth century as American believers seem to have substituted a masculine persona for a feminine one under the pressures of a maturing corporate society: virility took the place of tenderness, a hard-headed pragmatism succeeded the visionary hopes of earlier seekers, and Jesus metamorphosed from gentle Savior to rugged carpenter. The underlying premise of this scenario is that the alliance between women and religion that the early Victorians succeeded so well in forging was inimical to the cultural and political imperatives of industrial America. As the business of America increasingly became business itself, the function of the church shifted accordingly. No longer a sanctuary from the vicissitudes of industrial life, as it had been earlier in the century, the church by 1890 was seen as an integral component of corporate culture.[69]

Rather than focusing exclusively on structural changes in the economy, we can also understand the "crisis of masculinity" that Protestants apparently faced by examining the ideological assumptions of a democratic culture that yoked the fate of "the common man" to the continued submission of women and blacks. For the marriage between populism and patriarchy that was consummated in the Jacksonian era came apart in the late nineteenth century. The emancipation and franchisement of African Americans after the Civil War and the birth of the first organized women's rights movement in the middle decades of the century helped bring the two faces of republicanism—public and private—together for the first time. Hence it was possible for democratic populists of the 1880s and 1890s to envision a republic of racial cooperation, just as the massive women's movement of the Gilded Age envisioned women as "social housekeepers" who had a duty to become active in politics and the professions.[70] The National Farmers Alliance and Industrial Union and its political offshoot, the People's Party, brought millions of American farmers together in a powerful populist insurgency, aggressively enlisting the aid of black sharecroppers and in the process experimenting with "new modes of interracial political coalition." Although these efforts at interracial cooperation were ultimately thwarted by the "brooding presence" of white supremacy that was so deeply engrained in democratic culture, the populist movement of the 1890s nonetheless represents a significant moment in American political culture. For a brief time, populism reached beyond the racial divide that had been erected in the early nineteenth century to address the democratic aspirations of both blacks and whites. Their moment in the sun was all too fleeting, however, as the People's Party disbanded in 1896 and a new era in "Jim Crow" segregation was ushered in at the turn of the century.[71]

Given what we know of the imbrication of sexual and racial anxieties in American democracy, it is not surprising that the 1890s also saw the first calls for a revitalized masculine religious culture. The Men and Religion Forward Movement, for example, made little effort to disguise its commitment to creating a masculinized church that was also racially pure. Booker T. Washington, the only African American who participated in the movement, exploited white anxieties about black encroachment on the masculinized church in his fundraising speeches, warning that "unless northern white Protestants donated large amounts of money to the southern black churches, the needy blacks would migrate to the northern cities where most of his audience lived."[72] The church could not be effectively masculinized unless the corrupting influence of black Americans, who continued to represent uncontrolled sexuality in white popular culture, was safely contained within the independent black churches.

In important respects, then, the "muscular Christianity" of the late-Victorian era represented a last-ditch effort by embattled patriarchs to restore the two faces of American republicanism that the various populist and feminist movements of the 1870s, 80s, and 90s had threatened to unite. That they were ultimately successful is hard to dispute: female suffrage would not be accomplished for another generation, a rigid caste system was imposed upon black Americans that was not seriously challenged until the 1960s, and the Protestant churches were reclaimed by men for the masculine purposes of corporate capitalism, as women's charitable and missionary organizations were disbanded or coopted by male authorities. And the political successes of fundamentalism on the national level in the twentieth century seem to confirm the central message of manly Christianity, that power and patriarchy go hand-in-hand. But the long-term consequences of this resurgent masculinity are difficult to gauge. The feminine aspects of Protestant faith are not so easily dislodged, as witnessed by the charismatic renewal of the 1960s and 70s and the revival of communitarian ethics.[73] Pentacostalism is "the world's most dynamic, most rapidly growing form of Christianity," Mark Noll reports in his recent history of Christianity in Canada and the United States; it may be the most "femininized" as well, in its emphasis on the ecstatic experience of grace, unstructured language (speaking in tongues), and sexual egalitarianism.[74] However successful mainstream Protestantism has been in repudiating the language and forms of female piety at various critical moments in American history, more feminine versions of spiritual communion continue to circulate on the fringes and even at the core of American culture.

NOTES

1. For the best treatment of gender as "ideological work," see Mary Poovey, *Uneven Developments: The Ideological Work of Gender in Mid-Victorian England* (Chicago, 1988).

2. Orsi, " 'He Keeps Me Going': Women's Devotion to Saint Jude Thaddeus and the Dialectic of Gender in American Catholicism, 1929–1965," in Thomas Kselman, ed., *Belief in History: Innovative Approaches to European and American Religion* (Notre Dame, Ind., 1991), 155.

3. Quoted in Walter Hughes, " 'Meat Out of the Eater': Panic and Desire in American Puritan Poetry," in *Engendering Men: The Question of Male Feminist Criticism,* eds. Joseph A. Boone and Michael Cadden (New York, 1990), 103.

4. For a discussion of early modern associations of religious dissent with sexuality and femininity, see Phyllis Mack, *Visionary Women: Ecstatic Prophecy in Seventeenth-Century England* (Berkeley, 1992). As Denise Riley notes, the soul itself was increasingly gendered female in the seventeenth and eighteenth centuries; *"Am I That Name?": Feminism and the Category of 'Women' in History* (Minneapolis, 1988), 18–43.

5. See Amanda Porterfield, *Female Piety in Puritan New England* (New York, 1991); Ivy Schweitzer, *The Work of Self-Representation: Lyric Poetry in Colonial New England* (Chapel Hill, 1991); Margaret Masson, "The Typology of the Female as a Model for the Regenerate: Puritan Preaching, 1690–1730," *Signs* 2 (1976): 304–315; and Donald Maltz, "The Bride of Christ is Filled with His Spirit," in *Women in Ritual and Symbolic Roles,* ed. Judith Hoch-Smith and Anita Spring (New York, 1978), 222–52.

6. Quoted in David Leverenz, *The Language of Puritan Feeling: An Exploration in Literature, Psychology, and Social History* (New Brunswick, 1980), 129.

7. Patricia Caldwell, *The Puritan Conversion Narrative: The Beginnings of American Expression* (New York, 1983).

8. Hughes, "Meat Out of the Eater," 103.

9. For examples of this rhetorical coupling of sexual and religious disorder, see Kathleen Verduin, " 'Our Cursed Natures': Sexuality and the Puritan Conscience," *New England Quarterly* 56 (June 1983): 200–37; Carol Karlsen, *The Devil in the Shape of a Woman: Witchcraft in Colonial New England* (New York, 1987); Carla Pestana, "The City Upon a Hill Under Siege: Puritan Perceptions of the Quaker Threat to Massachusetts Bay 1656–1661," *New England Quarterly* 56 (September 1983): 323–53; and Philip Gura, *A Glimpse of Sion's Glory: Puritan Radicalism in New England, 1640–1660* (Middletown, Conn., 1984).

10. Ann Kibbey, "Mutations of the Supernatural: Witchcraft, Remarkable Providences, and the Power of Puritan Men," *American Quarterly* 34 (1982): 125–48.

11. Masson, "The Typology of the Female as a Model for the Regenerate"; Porterfield, *Female Piety in Puritan New England.*

12. Philip Greven, *The Protestant Temperament: Patterns of Child-Rearing, Religious Experience, and the Self in Early America* (New York, 1977).

13. Joan Scott, "Language and Working-Class History," in her *Gender and the Politics of History* (New York, 1988), 63.

14. See his cycle on sacramental meditations, especially "Meditation 3," first series, and "Meditation 150," second series, in *The Poems of Edward Taylor,* ed. Donald Sanford (New Haven, 1960), 7–8, 354; and "Meditation 12," in *The Poetical Writings of Edward Taylor,* ed. Thomas H. Johnson (New York, 1939), 132.

15. Phyllis Mack, *Visionary Women: Ecstatic Prophecy in Seventeenth-Century England* (Berkeley, 1992), 24–44. On the disorder of women in early modern culture, see Natalie Zemon Davis, "Women on Top," in her *Society and Culture in Early Modern France* (Stanford, 1965), 124–151; and Lyndal Roper, "Will and Honor: Sex, Words, and Power in Augsburg Criminal Trials," *Radical History Review* 43 (Jan. 1989): 45–71. On the instability of the female subject in English Renaissance literature and culture, see Catherine Belsey, *The Subject of Tragedy: Identity and Difference in Renaissance Drama* (New York, 1985), Part 2.

16. John Corrigan, *The Prism of Piety: Catholic Congregational Clergy at the Beginning of the Enlightenment* (New York, 1991). On the professionalization of the clergy, see Corrigan's lucid account of the moderate Congregational temperament in the early eighteenth century does not pay adequate attention to the role of gender anxieties in pushing Puritan ministers in a more restrained direction. For an alternative reading of these "moderates," one that identifies the tension between manliness and effeminancy as the "central pivot" of their worldview, see Greven, *The Protestant Temperament,* 243–250; David Hall, *The Faithful Shepherd: A History of the New England Ministry in the Seventeenth Century* (Chapel Hill, 1972); Patricia Bonomi, *Under the Cope of Heaven: Religion, Society, and Politics in Colonial America* (New York, 1986); Jon Butler, *Awash in a Sea of Faith: Christianizing the American People* (Cambridge, Mass., 1990); Donald Scott, *From Office to Profession: The New England Ministry 1750–1850* (Philadelphia, 1978). The quotes are from Corrigan, 12–13.

17. Helena M. Wall, *Fierce Communion: Family and Community in Early America* (Cambridge, Mass., 1990).

18. Harry S. Stout, *The Divine Dramatist: George Whitefield and the Rise of Modern Evangelicalism* (Grand Rapids, Mich., 1991).

19. Christine Heyrman, *Commerce and Culture: The Maritime Communities of Colonial Massachusetts, 1690–1750* (New York, 1984).

20. Stout, *The Divine Dramatist*, xx.

21. J. G. A. Pocock, *Virtue, Commerce, and History: Essays on Political Thought and History, Chiefly in the Eighteenth Century* (New York, 1985); Deborah Laycock, "Exchange Alley: The Sexual Politics of South Sea Investment," Paper presented at the Western Society of Eighteenth Century Studies conference, San Diego, February 1991.

22. Susan Juster, *Disorderly Women: Sexual Politics and Evangelicalism in Revolutionary New England* (Ithaca, 1994); George Rawlyk, *Ravished by the Spirit: Religious Revivals, Baptists, and Henry Alline* (Kingston, Ontario, 1984); Catherine Brekus, " 'Let Your Women Keep Silence in the Churches': Female Preaching and Evangelical Religion in America, 1740–1845," Ph.D. dissertation, Yale University, May 1993, chapter 1; Henry Abelove, *The Evangelist of Desire: John Wesley and the Methodists* (Stanford, 1990).

23. Stout, *Divine Dramatist*, 43.

24. Laurel Thatcher Ulrich, *Good Wives: Image and Reality in the Lives of Women in Northern New England 1650–1750* (New York, 1982), 38. For a more theoretical account of the shift from relatively porous notions of gender, in which men and women were arrayed along a single continuum of sexual identity, to essentialist notions of gender bipolarity, see Thomas Lacqueur, *Making Sex: Body and Gender from the Greeks to Freud* (Cambridge, Mass., 1989).

25. Richard D. Brown, *Knowledge is Power: The Diffusion of Information in Early America, 1700–1865* (New York, 1989), provides a more qualified analysis of the connection between commerce and print culture; most merchants, until the late eighteenth century, apparently prized face-to-face conversations over printed matter such as newspapers or letters as a source of vital information about trade. Yet the kinds of "conversations" that merchants participated in resemble the transatlantic networks that similarly engaged other genteel men from doctors to ministers. See chap. 5, "Communication and Commerce."

26. For literacy figures derived from signatures, see Kenneth Lockridge, *Literacy in Colonial New England* (New York, 1974); for a discussion of literacy which argues for a broader definition, see David Hall, *Worlds of Wonder, Days of Judgment: Popular Religious Belief in Early New England* (Cambridge, Mass., 1990), chap. 1.

27. Brown, *Knowledge is Power*, 160–163.

28. Jürgen Habermas, *The Structural Transformation of the Public Sphere: An Inquiry into a Category of Bourgeois Society*, trans. Thomas Burger and Frederick Lawrence (Cambridge, Mass., 1989); Joan B. Landes, *Women and the Public Sphere in the Age of the French Revolution* (Ithaca, 1988), esp. chap. 2.

29. Sharon Farmer, "Softening the Hearts of Men: Women, Embodiment, and Persuasion in the Thirteenth Century," in Paula Cooey, Sharon Farmer, and Mary Ellen Ross, eds., *Embodied Love: Sensuality and Relationship as Feminist Values* (San Francisco, 1987), 115–133.

30. Phyllis Mack, "Women as Prophets during the English Civil War," *Feminist Studies* 8 (Spring 1982): 19–45; Deborah Valenze, *Prophetic Sons and Daughters: Female Preaching and Popular Religion in Industrial England* (Princeton, N.J., 1985); Caroline Bynum, "Women Mystics and Eucharistic Devotion in the Thirteenth Century," *Women's Studies* 11 (1984): 179–214; Richard Bauman, *Let your Words be Few: Symbolism of Speaking and Silence Among*

Seventeenth-Century Quakers (New York, 1983). David Hall's contention that speech and writing were interchangeable in early New England calls into question the gendered distinction drawn above; "Holy books were also living speech," he argues, *Worlds of Wonder, Days of Judgment,* 38.

31. Carla Pestana, "Religious Conversion and Gender in Massachusetts, 1660–1700," unpublished paper, Ohio State University. E. Brooks Holifield similarly argues that Quakers were able to justify and encourage preaching by women because they were not constrained by the biblicism of the other religious groups in the American colonies; *Era of Persuasion: American Thought and Culture, 1521–1680* (Boston, 1989).

32. The association between women and evil speech is a long and venerable one in the Anglo-American world; for women as scolds and gossips, see David Underdown, "The Taming of the Scold: The Enforcement of Patriarchal Authority in Early Modern England," in *Order and Disorder in Early Modern England,* eds. Anthony Fletcher and John Stevenson (New York, 1985), 116–136; Lynda E. Boose, "Scolding Wives and Bridling Scolds: Taming the Woman's Unruly Member," *Shakespeare Quarterly* 42 (Summer 1991): 179–213.

33. Hall, *Worlds of Wonder, Days of Judgment*; Robert St. George, " 'Heated' Speech and Literacy in Seventeenth-Century New England," in David D. Hall and David Grayson Allen, eds., *Seventeenth-Century New England* (Boston, 1984), 275–322; Jane Kamensky, "Governing the Tongue: Speech and Society in Early New England," Ph.D. dissertation, Yale University, May 1993.

34. Kibbey, *Interpretation of Material Shapes,* 93.

35. Amy Schrager Lang, *Prophetic Woman: Anne Hutchinson and the Problem of Dissent in the Literature of New England* (Berkeley, 1987).

36. Jane Kamensky, "Words, Witches and Woman Trouble: Witchcraft, Disorderly Speech, and Gender Boundaries in Puritan New England," *Essex Institute Historical Collections* 128 (October 1992): 286–307. See also Karlsen, *Devil in the Shape of a Woman,* for the association of witchcraft with disorderly speech and ungodly behavior.

37. Catherine Brekus narrates the displacement of women from positions as public speakers in the late 1830s and 1840s in her dissertation, "Let Your Women Keep Silence in the Church." For the first three decades of the nineteenth century, she argues, women experienced unprecedented opportunities to preach and exhort in the newer evangelical sects like the Free Will Baptists and the Christians. As these groups moved closer to the ecclesiastical center in the middle decades of the century, however, they retreated from their commitment to sexual egalitarianism in the church. See also Louis Billington, " 'Female Laborers in the Church': Women Preachers in the Northeastern United States, 1790–1840," *Journal of American Studies* 19 (1985): 369–94.

38. Ann Braude, *Radical Spirits: Spiritualism and Women's Rights in Nineteenth-Century America* (Boston, 1989).

39. Ibid., 201.

40. For discussions of the "feminization" of American Protestantism in the late eighteenth and early nineteenth centuries, see Ann Douglas, *The Feminization of American Culture* (New York, 1977); Richard Shiels, "The Feminization of American Congregationalism 1730–1835," *American Quarterly* 33 (1981): 46–62; Barbara Welter, "The Feminization of American Religion 1800–1860," in her *Dimity Convictions: The American Woman in the Nineteenth Century* (Athens, Ga.: 1976), 83–102; David Schuyler, "Inventing a Feminine Past," *New England*

Quarterly, 51 (1978): 291–308; David Reynolds, "The Feminization Controversy: Sexual Stereotypes and the Paradoxes of Piety in Nineteenth-Century America," *New England Quarterly* 53 (1980): 96–106.

41. Nancy F. Cott, "Passionlessness: An Interpretation of Victorian Sexual Ideology, 1790–1850," *Signs* 4 (1978–79): 219–36; Ben Barker-Benfield, "The Spermatic Economy: A Nineteenth-century View of Sexuality," *Feminist Studies* 1 (1973): 45–74; R. R. Neuman, "Masturbation, Madness, and the Modern Concepts of Childhood and Adolescence," *Journal of Social History* 9 (1975): 1–27.

42. Welter, "The Feminization of American Religion."

43. Braude, *Radical Spirits,* chap. 4. For the medieval period, see Caroline Walker Bynum, "Bodily Miracles and the Resurrection of the Body in the High Middle Ages," in *Belief in History: Innovative Approaches to European and American Religion,* ed. Thomas Kselman (South Bend, 1991), 68–106; and her *Holy Feast and Holy Fast: The Religious Significance of Food to Medieval Women* (Berkeley, 1987), which argues that medieval writers treated the body less as a trap or hindrance than as a means of access to the divine.

44. Lawrence Foster, *Religion and Sexuality: The Shakers, the Mormons, and the Oneida Community* (Urbana, 1981); Jon Butler, *Awash in a Sea of Faith: Christianizing the American People* (Cambridge, Mass., 1990), 237. See also Russell Richey's discussion of the intense male bonding that occurred among Methodist itinerants—a bond that was threatened by women and marriage—*Early American Methodism* (Bloomington, Ind., 1991), 5–11.

45. Quoted in Alan Taylor, *Liberty Men and Great Proprietors: The Revolutionary Settlement on the Maine Frontier, 1760–1820* (Chapel Hill, 1990), 136.

46. Jacqueline Jones, *Labor of Love: Labor of Sorrow* (New York, 1985); Dorothy Burnham, "The Life of the Afro-American Woman in Slavery," *International Journal of Women's Studies* 1 (1978): 366–77; Deborah Gray White, *Arn't I a Woman? Female Slaves in the Plantation South* (1985); Victoria E. Bynum, *Unruly Women: The Politics of Social and Sexual Control in the Old South* (Chapel Hill, 1992).

47. Sander L. Gilman, "Black Bodies, White Bodies: Toward an Iconography of Female Sexuality in Late Nineteenth-Century Art, Medicine, and Literature," in Henry Louis Gates, ed., *"Race," Writing and Difference* (Chicago, 1986), 223–40. Evelyn Brooks Higginbotham explores the racial configurations of gender in her important essay, "African-American Women's History and the Metalanguage of Race," *Signs* 17 (1992): 251–74. Winthrop Jordan's now classic study of racial attitudes between the sixteenth and nineteenth centuries argues that black women's bodies epitomized European perceptions of Africans as primitive, animal-like, and savage; *White Over Black: American Attitudes Toward the Negro, 1550–1812* (New York, 1977).

48. Higginbotham, "African-American Women's History," 263.

49. Darlene Clark Hine, "Rape and the Inner Lives of Black Women in the Middle West: Preliminary Thoughts on the Culture of Dissemblance," *Signs* 14 (Summer 1989): 912–20. See also Hazel Carby's discussion of how black women reconstructed the sexual ideologies of the nineteenth century to produce an alternative discourse of womanhood; Carby, *Reconstructing Womanhood* (New York, 1987).

50. On Rebecca Jackson, see Jean M. Humez, ed., *Gifts of Power: The Writings of Rebecca Cox Jackson, Black Visionary, Shaker Eldress* (Amherst, 1981).

See also Humez, " 'My Spirit Eye': Some Functions of Spiritual and Visionary Experience in the Lives of Five Black Women Preachers, 1810–1880," in *Women and the Structure of Society,* eds. Barbara Harris and JoAnn McNamara (Durham, 1984), 130.

51. For examples of the syncretism between African and European religious systems, see Mechal Sobel, *Trabelin' On: The Slave Journey to an Afro-Baptist Faith* (Westport, Conn., 1979); Sobel, *The World They Made Together: Black and White Values in Eighteenth-Century Virginia* (Princeton, 1987); and Albert Raboteau, *Slave Religion: The "Invisible" Institution in the Antebellum South* (New York, 1978). For an alternative view that stresses the defiant nature of slave religion, see Sylvia Frey, *Water From the Rock: Black Resistance in a Revolutionary Age* (Princeton, 1991); and Lawrence Levine, *Black Culture and Black Consciousness: Afro-American Folk Thought From Slavery to Freedom* (New York, 1977). Jon Butler argues that true syncretism only came about after Christianty filled the void left by the "spiritual holocaust" of slavery and came face-to-face, for the first time, with significant numbers of recently imported slaves. *Awash in a Sea of Faith,* 247–52.

52. Carol Devens, *Countering Colonization: Native American Women and Great Lakes Missions, 1630–1900* (Berkeley, 1992).

53. See Sharla Fett, " 'It's a Spirit in Me': Spiritual Power and the Healing Work on African American Women in Slavery," in *A Mighty Baptism: Race, Gender, and the Creation of American Protestantism,* ed. Susan Juster and Lisa Mac-Farlane (Ithaca, 1996), 189–209, for a discussion of female faith-healers. For a discussion of the role of the "slave mammy" as cultural liaison between blacks and whites on the plantation, see Eugene Genovese, *Roll, Jordan, Roll: The World the Slaves Made* (New York, 1974). For other examples of black women's role as cultural and spiritual mediators, see Margaret Washington Creel, *"A Peculiar People": Slave Religion and Community-Culture Among the Gullahs* (New York, 1988), 291.

54. Gordon Wood, "Evangelical America and Early Mormonism," *New York History* 61 (Oct. 1980): 359–86, and *The Radicalism of the American Revolution* (New York, 1992); Nathan Hatch, *The Democratization of American Christianity* (New Haven, 1989).

55. Stephanie McCurry, "The Two Faces of Republicanism: Gender and Proslavery Politics in Antebellum South Carolina," *Journal of American History* (March 1992), 1245–64.

56. Linda Kerber, *Women of the Republic: Intellect & Ideology in Revolutionary America* (New York, 1980), 285.

57. McCurry, "The Two Faces of Republicanism, 1253.

58. Doris Somer, *Foundational Fictions: The National Romances of Latin America* (Berkeley, 1991).

59. Jan Lewis, "The Republican Wife: Virtue and Seduction in the Early Republic," *William and Mary Quarterly* 78 (1987): 689–721; Jay Fliegelman, *Prodigals and Pilgrims: The American Revolution against Patriarchal Authority 1750–1800* (New York, 1982), esp. chap. 5. Lewis, especially, has refocused attention on the role of women as republican *wives* as opposed to *mothers* in political discourse of the late eighteenth century; not until the failures of the republican vision were manifestly apparent by the 1820s and 30s would political theorists come to extoll the maternal responsibilities of women over their conjugal ones.

See her "Motherhood and the Construction of the Male Citizen in the United States, 1750–1850," in *Constructions of the Self,* ed. George Levine (New Brunswick, 1992), 143–64.

60. For an eloquent discussion of how passion can subvert patriarchy, see Kenneth Lockridge, *On the Sources of Patriarchal Rage: The Commonplace Books of William Byrd and Thomas Jefferson and the Gendering of Power in the Eighteenth Century* (New York, 1992).

61. Winthrop Jordan cautions against a too facile comparison of the fate of women and blacks in the revolutionary era in his essay, "On the Bracketing of Blacks and Women in the Same Agenda," in *The American Revolution: Its Character and Limits,* ed. Jack Greene (New York, 1987), 276–81.

62. Quoted in Paul Johnson's review of Hatch's book, "Democracy, Patriarchy, and American Revivals, 1780–1830," *Journal of Social History* 24 (Summer 1991): 846.

63. Rawlyk, *Radical Evangelicalism in British North America from the American Revolution to the War of 1812,* unpublished paper, Queen's University, May 1993, 28, 34–35. Jon Butler has explored these contradictions in *Awash in a Sea of Faith,* in which he describes the "republican hierarchicalism" of Protestant denominations in the postrevolutionary years. As he writes, "Denominations were republican not only in their love of virtue . . . but in their conviction that not quite all were equal in matters of governance." Women and blacks, he notes, were prominently excluded from denominational politics in the early republic (272, 280–82).

64. See Mark Noll, "The American Revolution and Protestant Evangelicalism," *Journal of Interdisciplinary History* 23 (Winter 1993): 615–38, for a clear discussion of how evangelicalism, republicanism, and common sense moral reasoning came together to form a powerful ideology in the postrevolutionary era.

65. Douglas Frank, *Less than Conquerers: How Evangelicals Entered the Twentieth Century* (Grand Rapids, Mich., 1986); Margaret Bendroth, *Fundamentalism and Gender, 1875 to the Present* (New Haven, 1993).

66. Gail Bederman, " 'The Woman Have Had Charge of the Church Work Long Enough': The Men and Religion Forward Movement of 1911–1912 and the Masculinization of Middle-Class Protestantism," *American Quarterly* 41 (Sept. 1989): 435. On the "masculinity crisis" see Joe Dubbert, "Progressivism and the Masculinity Crisis," reprinted in Elizabeth and Joseph Pleck, eds., *The American Man* (Englewood Cliffs, N.J., 1980), 302–20; David Pugh, *Sons of Liberty: The Masculine Mind in Nineteenth-Century America* (Westport, Conn., 1983); Peter G. Filene, *Him/Her/Self: Sex Roles in Modern America* (Baltimore, 1974), 69–93; Elliot J. Gorn, *The Manly Art: Bare Knuckle Prizefighting in America* (Ithaca, 1986), 179–206; Michael S. Kimmel, "The Contemporary 'Crisis' of Masculinity in Historical Perspective," in *The Making of Masculinities,* ed. Harry Brod (Boston, 1987), 121–54. For a critique of the "crisis" scenario, see Clyde Griffen, "Reconstructing Masculinity from the Evangelical Revival to the Waning of Progressivism: A Speculative Synthesis," in Mark C. Carnes and Clyde Griffen, eds., *Meanings for Manhood: Constructions of Masculinity in Victorian America* (Chicago, 1990), 183–204.

67. Susan Curtis, "The Son of Man and God the Father: The Social Gospel and Victorian Masculinity," in *Meanings for Manhood,* 72.

68. Betty DeBerg, *Ungodly Women: Gender and the First Wave of American Fundamentalism* (Minneapolis, 1990), 147.

69. Bederman, "The Men and Religion Forward Movement," 435–36. On the Victorian synthesis of church and home, see Janet Forsythe Fishburn, *The Fatherhood of God and the Victorian Family* (Philadelphia, 1981); and Colleen McDannell, *The Christian Home in Victorian America, 1840–1900* (Bloomington, Ind., 1986).

70. Ruth Bordin, *Women and Temperance: The Quest for Power and Liberty, 1873–1900* (Philadelphia, 1980); and Barbara Leslie Epstein, *The Politics of Domesticity: Women, Evangelism, and Temperance in Nineteenth-Century America* (Middletown, Conn., 1981).

71. Lawrence Goodwyn, *The Populist Moment: A Short History of the Agrarian Revolt in America* (New York, 1978), xxii, 122.

72. Bederman, "Men and Religion Forward," 439, note 34.

73. David Edwin Harrell, Jr., *All Things Are Possible: The Healing and Charismatic Revivals in Modern America* (Bloomington, Ind., 1975); Robert Bellah et al., *Habits of the Heart: Individualism and Commitment in American Life* (1985).

74. Mark A. Noll, *A History of Christianity in the United States and Canada* (Grand Rapids, Mich., 1992), 541.

12

FROM MISSIONS TO MISSION
TO BEYOND MISSIONS

The Historiography of American Protestant Foreign Missions Since World War II

▦ ▦ ▦

Dana L. Robert

IN 1964, PROFESSOR OF HISTORY of Missions at the University of Chicago R. Pierce Beaver wrote *From Missions to Mission,* a reflection book published by the YMCA. In his small book, this eminent American mission historian of the mid–twentieth century reviewed the early part of the century and saw a Christianity that had ridden to success on the coattails of Euro-American imperialism and prestige. Two world wars, however, had demonstrated to growing nationalist movements in the developing world that Christianity was not part of a superior culture, but was an agent of colonialism. Beaver went on to analyze the current climate for world missions—militant nationalism, urbanization, secularization, repudiation of the West, and revivals of non-Christian religions. To move forward in such a context, he said, missions must begin to cooperate among themselves and with younger nonwestern churches on behalf of Christ's mission. Beaver saw embodied in the World Council of Churches the beginning of new approaches to mission that would stress reconciliation over competition, and peace and justice issues alongside proclamation. Missions from the west should become a common worldwide enterprise: pluralism must give way to unity.

Beaver's small volume, its prescience notwithstanding, illustrates the danger of historians drawing on the past in order to predict the future. The ecumenical movement that Beaver touted as the source of new forms of mission had within ten years so modified the definition of mission that confusion over its meaning was widespread in mainline churches. When Beaver retired from the University of Chicago in 1971, his post was eliminated, a practice followed in numerous mainline institutions during the 1970s. "Foreign missions" had become "universal mission," only to evaporate into generalizations. Oddly enough, the North American evangelical missionaries whom Beaver described in 1964 as "sectarian and partisan," and as disrupting the unity of mission "for the first time in three hundred years," (98) surpassed mainline missionaries in number and vigor. Today, with pluralism celebrated and competition among religions fierce, with nondenominational missions dwarfing the efforts of the old mainline, with indigenous Pentecostalism exploding in nooks and crannies around the world, the prospect for mission in the twenty-first century is dynamic and diverse but bears little resemblance to the top-down, unified witness Beaver envisioned in 1964. The vibrancy of multicultural Christianity on every continent has completed the shift from "mission" to "beyond missions."

The road traveled so painfully by American Protestantism since the Second World War, from separate "missions" to unified "mission" to "beyond missions," has been trod as well by historians. Mission history prior to World War II was largely a denominational affair, told from the perspective of efforts by individual denominations to spread their form of Christianity around the globe.[1] R. Pierce Beaver and other mission historians of the post–World War II generation saw their vision of Protestant foreign missions through the lens of ecumenical unity. Similarly, American secular historians were captivated by an interpretation of Protestant missions as a symbol of American identity. Important to both the secular and the church historians was the transition from missions to mission, from a pluralistic enterprise to the symbol of either national or ecclesiastical cooperation. However, the social changes that Beaver described in 1964 accelerated throughout the 1960s and early 1970s, narrowing not only the common religious vision but the secular one as well. By the late 1960s, there was scarcely a work written on American Protestant missions that did not focus on their role in promoting imperialism. Historical concern for mission died like the chairs of missiology in mainline Protestant institutions: interest was either gone or confined to the negative.

The 1980s witnessed an explosion of renewed scholarly interest in the history of American Protestant missions. The acknowledgment of pluralism both in American society and within American Protestantism freed mission history from its captivity to unity. Intellectual historians discovered a full range of American mission theory that had lain forgotten in mission libraries for decades. Feminist historians recognized the dominance of women in the missionary movement and used the ample documentation provided by mission sources to uncover hidden angles on American women. The "sectarian" evangelicals excoriated by Beaver in 1964 had reached a level of institutional maturity and ecclesiastical dominance where critical historical analysis had become both possible and necessary. Church historians realized that missions were a central preoccupation of not only the "mainline," but of ethnic Americans, women, assorted subcultures, and Roman Catholics as well. From the ashes of "mission" reemerged "missions," a lively and diverse enterprise, no longer able to fit comfortably into the outgrown garb of denominational history, Christian unity, or American identity.

Before the historiographic trail from mission singular to missions plural is explored, a caveat is in order. This essay seeks to cover only "foreign" missions, defined as those efforts to spread Protestant Christianity from North America to cultures and contexts outside its borders. The United States as a mission field itself, including outreach to immigrants and to indigenous peoples of North America, deserves another full essay and cannot be considered adequately without including Roman Catholicism. Arguments can be made that foreign missions should include missions to native Americans prior to the conquest of their territory by the United States, or that the convenient but missiologically archaic term "foreign" should be replaced by the nongeographic term "cross-cultural." However, for the sake of convenience and to remain true to the way that American Protestants have generally used the term "foreign," this essay will exclude the historiography of North America itself as a mission field.

Protestant Foreign Missions and the Mission of America

Intellectual history's search for national identity, for a central unifying idea of what it means to be an American, dominated the study of Protestants and foreign missions during the mid–twentieth century. When the field of American intellectual history emerged between the two world wars, historians anchored the meaning of America to its concept of national mission. Unable to base their unity on common ethnic backgrounds, Americans apparently drew their identity from common purpose—shared commitment to democracy, voluntarism, individual rights, and free enterprise.

With the United States entering the fray against both fascism and communism, Ralph Gabriel published *The Course of American Democratic Thought.*[2] To Gabriel and his followers, the public function of the mission idea was so compelling that it diverted attention from its historic roots in American Protestant missions to non-Christians. When Gabriel, Perry Miller, and others created "American intellectual history" in the 1930s and 1940s, they loosened the idea of mission from its theological context, secularized it, and made it the basis for Protestant-dominated national identity. For American intellectual historians, to be an American meant de facto to be a Protestant. To be a Protestant meant to be in mission. Therefore, the syllogism concluded, to be an American was to participate in mission. Foreign missions, in the plural, became a manifestation of the singular mission of America.

By the mid–twentieth century, intellectual historians had subsumed the specifically religious dimensions of the American mission impulse under the issue of nationalism. In 1952, Perry Miller, who had rescued the intellectual life of American Puritans from oblivion, published the important essay "Errand into the Wilderness," in which he traced the origins of American identity to the Puritans' desire to propagate pure religion through emigration from Europe.[3] The abundance of land, however, worked against disciplined purity and created the national mission from the failure of the religious one. Adapting to their environment, the American Puritans did not abandon their "errand to the wilderness" but transformed it into the process of Americanization. Miller's essay symbolized for a generation of thinkers the essential unity of American tradition and identity, and the captivity of religious motivations to secular ones.

Following World War II, a new generation of church historians deepened the focus on mission's relationship to nationalism. With the World Council of Churches being founded in 1948 as the "United Nations of Christendom," the 1950s was not only the heyday of "consensus history," but of the Protestant ecumenical movement, a powerful force that deeply influenced mainline church historians. Although they acknowledged that spiritual motives were primary in Protestant mission, church historians like R. Pierce Beaver at the University of Chicago, William Richey Hogg of Southern Methodist University, and Robert T. Handy at Union Theological Seminary nevertheless examined missions through the prism of unity, either in terms of national identity or as a basis for ecumenical cooperation.[4]

Robert Handy's interest in church–state relations, the ecumenical movement and in other Protestant efforts to initiate the kingdom of God on earth, such as the Social Gospel and home missions, made him a perceptive analyst of Protestant mission's contribution to nationalism. Handy explored how turn-of-the-century Protestants used foreign missions to propagate so-called Christian civilization.[5] Missions became an imperialistic crusade to spread western civilization throughout the world, as well as the motivating force behind the ecumenical movement. Mission-oriented Protestants "felt themselves part of one crusade for the evangelization, the Christianization, and the civilization of the world" (135). In the first twenty years of the twentieth century, Protestants, according to Handy, "easily idealized the culture and democracy of America. There was a considerable transfer of religious feelings to the civilization and the nation" (139). Missionary forces had unwittingly become involved in "religious nationalism."

The idea that Protestant foreign missions were a tool of nationalism and by extension abroad, imperialism, proved to be an irresistible thesis that has generated numerous monographs from the late 1950s until the present. After consensual interpretations of American history were challenged by the social upheavals of the 1960s, and the ecumenical movement splintered on the shoals of secularized theologies and political disunity, mission increasingly became a metaphor not for national virtue but for imperialistic excesses. The mission of America and by association Protestant foreign missions no longer represented America's virtue, but its fatal flaw.

Monographs on American missions and imperialism tended to focus on a particular geographic region or moment in history. One of the earliest works to explore the foreign policy implications of missionary nationalism was an excellent book produced in 1958 on China by Paul H. Varg.[6] He concluded that the struggle initiated by missionaries between Chinese and western culture was so severe that "American nationalism threatened to triumph over the religious" (ix). In 1961, Kenneth MacKenzie wrote on the Philippines, showing how foreign missions were a reason for President William McKinley's decision to keep the Philippines as a colony in 1898.[7] The role of New England in early-nineteenth-century missionary imperialism was explored by John A. Andrew III.[8] Andrew argued that American foreign missions were in fact the result of "cognitive dissonance" by Congregationalists who sought to compensate for their loss of power at home by extending it abroad to places like the Pacific Islands. One of the finest examinations of missionary involvement in American foreign policy was Joseph Grabill's study of the Protestant missionary impact on the Near East. Running aginst the current of seeing missions as supportive of American imperialism, Grabill argued that missionaries promoted internationalism and the protection of minorities in the Ottoman Empire.[9]

Other more recent monographs on American missions' relationship to nationalism and imperialism include Rosa del Carmen Bruno-Jofre's study of Methodist mission education in Peru.[10] Based on primary sources and written by a Peruvian, *Methodist Education in Peru* argues that Methodist educational missionaries imported American ideologies couched in theological formulations and the theories of John Dewey. In 1986, Kenton Clymer produced a finely nuanced study of American missionary attitudes toward American colonialism and Filipino culture.[11]

Following the pattern set by intellectual historians, the historiography of American Protestants and foreign missions evolved from identifying the Protestant missionary impulse as the source of American identity (from missions plural to mission singular), to mission as the source of both ecclesiastical and national unity, and from nationalism to imperialism. Given the historical reality that Americans engaged in political imperialism far less than Europeans, who carved out empires in Asia, Africa, and Latin America, it has been important to define the precise relationship between missionary activity and imperialism.

Two valuable articles have been written on the nature of American missionary imperialism in general. The first of these was by Arthur Schlesinger, Jr., whose essay "The Missionary Enterprise and Theories of Imperialism" equated American missions with cultural imperialism.[12] Missionaries may not have personally wielded economic or political power, he argued, but they represented the purposeful aggression of American culture against the ideas and cultures of other people. In 1982, William R. Hutchison reasoned that the broad support of Americans for foreign missions at the turn of the century was because of the shared belief that "Christianity as it existed in the West had a 'right' not only to conquer the world, but to define reality for the peoples of the world."[13] Apologists for American missions were not so much agents of American colonialism as the ideologues of the movement, providing a "moral equivalent" for American imperialism.

The tendency inherited from intellectual history to evaluate Protestant foreign missions in relation to American nationalism has had both strengths and weaknesses as an interpretive framework. The greatest strength has been its refusal to evaluate the mission movement apart from the larger stream of American history: American missionaries, after all, retained American attitudes no matter where they worked. The benefits, however, must be held in tension with the weaknesses of nationalist mission history. For one thing, nationalist mission history could turn the mission impulse into a hireling at the service of national identity. In the 1950s, parallel support for national and church unity made missionaries into heroes, the shock troops of the eminently compelling "American way"; by the late 1960s, the missionary had become the villain of American foreign policy. In either case, until the 1980s missionary thought and activity was seldom studied in its own right, nor was the role of the missionary as transmitter of cross-cultural information to America taken seriously. In sinologist John K. Fairbank's words, "the invisible man of American history" was the missionary.[14]

Another weakness of nationalist mission history was that its focus on identity led it to concentrate on the so-called mainline churches as the "thought leaders" of American Protestantism. Consensus intellectual history was biased toward texts produced primarily by white male New Englanders, to the exclusion of women, conservative evangelicals, Anabaptists, African Americans, Pentecostals, and other groups deemed marginal or nonexistent. Popular piety was ignored in favor of formal theological and political pronouncements. Intellectual sources superseded other forms of documentation, with the social biography of the missionary force seldom examined except where it fed nationalist identity or

Christian unity, as in the case of the Student Volunteer Movement for Foreign Missions.[15]

One of the most egregious failures of nationalist mission history was, surprisingly enough its parochialism. With the exception of studies of the ecumenical movement or of missionaries in China, scarce were assessments of Protestant missionary activity in relation to the mission work of other nations, or in relation to the indigenous cultures and religions affected by the missionary. Seldom was the question raised about how people of other cultures viewed the mission enterprise; indigenous converts became by implication "running dogs" of American imperialism. In effect, the study of Protestant foreign missions leaned toward becoming a subsidiary of a political agenda, either in the service of national identity or in the debunking of the same.

The Discovery of Mission Theory

Despite the use of selected mission thought as a basis for constructing national identity, until the 1980s American intellectual historians seemed uninterested in the full range of mission thinking regardless of its undeniable importance for American history and culture. The causes for neglect were several: the captivity of missions to the national mission of America, the embarrassment of secular historians at ideas smacking of either conservatism or "proselytization," and neglect of cross-cultural issues in history generally. Interest in mission theory was confined to the missiologists, who were seldom in dialogue with intellectual historians. The noteworthy exception was R. Pierce Beaver, whose commitment both to missiology and to history caused him to write books with "cross-over" value. In the 1950s he produced two of the earliest articles written on American mission theory from an historical perspective.[16]

In 1967, Beaver collected the works of the most important nineteenth-century mission theorist, Rufus Anderson of the American Board.[17] In rediscovering Anderson, Beaver uncovered the source of much mission theory that Americans had long taken for granted, particularly the indigenous church principles of self-support, self-government, and self-propagation. Another valuable source book for mission thought was Beaver's collection of early American missionary sermons.[18] In 1968 he contributed a groundbreaking overview of American missionary motivation.[19] Although outside the scope of this essay, Beaver also wrote pioneer scholarly works on the relationship of missions to American Indians.[20]

In the 1970s, a smattering of works on the history of mission thought appeared to whet the appetite of historians. In 1970 Denton Lotz wrote a dissertation at the University of Hamburg, " 'The Evangelization of the World in This Generation': The Resurgence of a Missionary Idea Among the Conservative Evangelicals." While Lotz's dissertation was never published, it was important because not only did it deal seriously with American mission thought, but it also traced a key idea from its origins in the late-nineteenth-century evangelical mainline to conservative groups in the present. Also, 1970 saw the publication in Holland of J. A. DeJong's work on millennialism and missions, which traced a particular theme in mission thought prior to the beginning of explicitly American foreign missions.[21] Charles Chaney in 1976 published a thorough study of mission thought in the seventeenth and eighteenth centuries.[22] Despite the importance of Chaney's work for American intellectual history, the book did not attain the recognition it deserved because it was published by a mission press. In 1977 appeared the seminal essay by missiologist and historian Charles Forman of Yale, "A History of Foreign Mission Theory."[23] Forman had discovered in the mission library of Yale Divinity School 150 serious works written by American mission theorists between 1890 and 1950, virtually none of which had been read by intellectual historians. Roger Bassham placed American mission thought in its global context in a work on ecumenical, evangelical, and Roman Catholic mission theology since World War II.[24]

The academic study of American mission theory received a major boost when in 1977 missiologist Gerald Anderson revived the periodical *Occasional Bulletin* from the Missionary Research Library that in 1981 became the *International Bulletin of Missionary Research,* now the largest circulation scholarly mission periodical in the world. Anderson had written a doctoral dissertation in 1960 that was the first comprehensive study of twentieth-century Protestant mission theory.[25] With an historian's training and sensibilities, Anderson began a series on the legacies of major nineteenth- and twentieth-century mission theorists, recruiting experts to write biographical sketches of such mission thinkers as E. Stanley Jones, Daniel Fleming, Rufus Anderson, and A. J. Gordon. The series continues today, and every quarter the mission thought of another hitherto neglected mission theorist is brought to light. Probably more than anything else, Anderson's legacy series has created scholarly interest in mission theory among missiologists and evangelical church historians. Apart from the series, the *International Bulletin of Missionary Research* publishes other articles relevant to American mission theory.[26] In 1988, Anderson's own article, "American Protestants in Pursuit of Mission: 1886–1986" appeared in a centennial volume for the American Society of Church History.[27] His article was a helpful overview of both mission thought and activity over a century. One further recent article of Gerald Anderson's extensive corpus requires mention, namely, his overview of the entire field of mission research, including history.[28] Currently, Anderson is editing the *Biographical Dictionary of Christian Missions,* which when published will be the first-ever work of its kind.

Mission theory moved out of the missiological ghetto and into mainstream history with the 1987 publication of William R. Hutchison's eagerly awaited history of American Protestant mission theory.[29] As an intellectual historian rather than a missiologist, Hutchison examined mission theory "as American." While granting integrity to the body of mission thought, Hutchison's book descended from intellectual history's quest for national identity. *Errand to the World* represented the first book-length attempt to grapple with a full range of mission thought. Its sources were nevertheless limited almost entirely to "high texts" from the Reformed tradition, broadly defined. Hutchison's book, while a brilliant piece of work, was the beginning rather than the end of mainstream historical research into Protestant mission theory.

Hutchison's focus on the "American-ness" of Protestant mission thought has been shared by historians of nonwestern Christianity. In 1970 Norman Etherington wrote "An American Errand into the South African Wilderness." [30] Etherington applied his extensive knowledge of South African mission history to show how American Board efforts to evangelize the Zulus in the 1830s were an attempt to reproduce "the American experience among the primitive peoples of Africa" (62). An important example of viewing American missions as quintessentially American was the essay by Scottish professor Andrew Walls, "The American Dimension in the History of the Missionary Movement." [31] Walls is probably the most profound analyst of global Protestant mission history today, and his article analyzed the particularities of both American thought and culture as evident in Protestant missions.

The history of Protestant mission theory in its fullness is just coming into its own; increasingly, secular scholars are realizing that they cannot generalize about missionaries but must take into account the ideological tradition out of which they operated, not to mention their social location. The historical study of Protestant mission theory has its limitations, however. For one thing, as essentially an exercise in intellectual history, it faces the same problems of sources as nationalist mission history. Another problem is its tendency not to be grounded in study of actual missionary practice. Until studies of mission theory can be cross-checked with how such theories played themselves out in different mission fields, and in comparison with non-American missiologies, the full implications of mission thought are unknowable. Lacking also have been historical examinations of mission theory in the broader context of American theology. Like nationalist mission theory, for historians the study of Protestant mission theory so far has been the most helpful in understanding American identity.

Protestant Missions and Pluralism

One fruitful by-product of the collapse of consensus over American identity in the 1960s and 1970s was the unshackling of foreign missions from national purpose. Historians began to realize that foreign missions were not an activity confined to male New England Congregationalists in the early nineteenth century, but were intrinsic even to apparently marginal Protestant groups, ethnic minorities, and women. By the 1980s, pluralistic mission history became possible, with the relationship of various groups to nationalism only one of the questions asked of the data. Ethnic and gender analysis, the techniques of social and cultural history, and increased historical awareness by denominations ranging from Mennonites to Southern Baptists to Nazarenes to Assemblies of God produced a range of new studies, although it must be said that most of the denominational literature has been ignored by the academy.

Missions and Ethnicity

In 1982, three books appeared on the mission history of African Americans. Despite its coverage of a narrow time period, the best overview of the subject was Walter Williams's exploration of the way in which missions in various denominations stimulated interest in Africa among African Americans and thus prepared the way for pan-Africanism.[32] Sylvia Jacobs edited a volume that included articles on African American missionaries, motivations, and missionary ideology.[33] The third important book on African Americans that appeared in 1982 was by David W. Wills and Richard Newman.[34] Their edited volume contained valuable essays on prominent antebellum missionaries, such as Daniel Coker, Francis Burns, Alexander Crummell, and Lott Carey. Wills and Albert Raboteau are coediting "African-American Religion: A Documentary History Project" that will contain considerable information on African American contact with Africa, including foreign missions.

Although brief overviews exist in broader denominational histories, book-length treatments of African-American missions by denomination are rare. An exception was Sandy D. Martin's history of black Baptist missions to Africa.[35] In 1989, James T. Campbell wrote a dissertation on the relationship between black Americans and South Africans, the role of the AME in educating South Africans, and debates over "industrial education" for blacks.[36] Biographies of important black denominational mission leaders that have appeared recently are of James Theodore Holly, founder of the Episcopal Church in Haiti; Lott Carey, first African American missionary to Liberia; Alexander Crummell, Episcopal missionary; Henry McNeal Turner, African Methodist Episcopal bishop and pan-Africanist; and William Sheppard, Presbyterian missionary to the Congo.[37]

Many ethnic Protestant denominations such as Lutherans, Mennonites, and Moravians have received more attention for their work with immigrants or their substantial work with Native Americans than for overseas missions.[38] With overseas mission work organized relatively late, the historiography of traditionally ethnic denominations is not as well-developed as that of the Protestant mainstream. Nevertheless, a number of fairly recent full-length accounts appeared in the 1970s and 1980s.[39] Articles on particular aspects of these missions are occasionally found in denominational periodicals and newsletters.[40]

Missions and Evangelicalism

One of the most important directions in the pluralization of Protestant mission history has been recent study of twentieth-century evangelicals. Although evangelicals have been the most active proponents of foreign missions since 1945, until 1990 there was virtually no examination of evangelical missions as a whole. The reason for such neglect was probably that most critically trained church historians were biased toward church unity and saw twentieth-century evangelicals to be fissiparous and on the margins of American history. The first attempt at a general interpretation appeared as the result of a conference sponsored by the Institute for the Study of American Evangelicals, published in 1990 under the title *Earthen Vessels: American Evangelicals and Foreign Missions, 1880–1980*. The volume contained valuable essays on conservative evangelical mission theory and on evangelical missionaries in several parts of the world, and an important essay on fundamentalist missions by Joel Carpenter.[41] Probably the greatest contribution of *Earthen Vessels* was that it opened the way for further studies on the topic of evangelicalism and missions. It also included an article by Grant Wacker that explored the views of liberal Protestants toward other religions.[42]

There have been several good studies of twentieth-century evangelicals in actual mission situations, although what exists is only a drop in the bucket of what is possible.[43] The most detailed analysis of an evangelical/ fundamentalist mission in relation to the indigenous culture in which it worked was David Sandgren's study of the Africa Inland Mission in Kenya.[44] Sandgren's research was remarkable in its use of oral interviews obtained from indigenous converts, but its use of missionary documentation was narrow. The area in which the study of evangelical missions has excelled is in-house denominational or parachurch institutional histories. Although the in-house materials are of varying quality and are usually pioneer attempts to chart the basic parameters of the missionary work, some of them contain real critical insight.[45]

In 1993, the Wesleyan/Holiness Studies Center at Asbury Theological Seminary held a conference on "Mission in the Wesleyan/Holiness Traditions," which should result in a volume on the Holiness movement in American missions, to be edited by David Bundy. When Pentecostalism emerged from the Holiness movement, it carried with it the Holiness movement's commitment to missions. At present, no survey of Pentecostal mission history exists, although the fine work of Gary McGee on the Assemblies of God must be mentioned.[46] An in-house periodical that contains frequent high-quality articles on Pentecostal mission history is *Assemblies of God Heritage*, edited by archivist Wayne Warner. Finally, reference must be made to the *Dictionary of Pentecostal and Charismatic Movements*, which contains valuable entries on Pentecostal missionaries, mission organizations, and mission theory.[47]

The surge of interest in evangelical history in general has stimulated a number of works on the "home base," the context out of which twentieth-century conservative Protestant missions emerged. Bible schools provided most of the training for evangelical missionaries, and Virginia Lieson Brereton explored their history in 1990.[48] Timothy Weber examined the ideological developments that produced the turn-of-the-century fundamentalist missionary movement, including missions to the Jews.[49] My doctoral dissertation on mission theorist Arthur T. Pierson, published in Korean in 1988, looked at the transition from denominational missions to faith missions during the same time period.[50]

Evangelical and Pentecostal mission history from many angles will continue to increase in importance as interpreters gain historical distance from the topic, and it becomes self-evident that the future of world Protestantism belongs more to Pentecostalism than to the old "mainline." The story of how Pentecostalism impacted missionary activity and emerging indigenous Christianity is just beginning to be told.[51] Topics in the greatest need of future research include evangelical missionary attitudes toward other cultures and religions, the relationship between American and non-western evangelicals, and studies of evangelical work "in the field." The most serious barriers to evangelical mission history are the tendency toward hagiography among evangelicals for whom missionary biography is primarily a source of spiritual inspiration, and the activistic orientation that provides power for missions but considers historical analysis to be a waste of time. An important exception to the biography as hagiography tendency with a focus on evangelicals was Ruth Tucker's biographical history of missions published in 1983.[52]

The biggest problem in writing twentieth-century evangelical history is that of sources. Activistic evangelicals are notoriously poor at keeping records, especially when their theology predisposes them to look toward an imminent second coming of Christ. The age of the telephone and e-mail has also preempted traditional source material such as letters, personal journals, and regular mission correspondence. Fortunately, places like the Billy Graham Center Archives at Wheaton College and the Assemblies of God Archives are collecting oral histories of evangelical and Pentecostal missionaries. Another important resource is the Ida Grace McRuer Missions Resource Centre, sponsored by missiologist Jon Bonk at Providence College and Seminary in Otterburne, Manitoba. The center collects ephemeral material such as fund-raising literature and prayer letters sent free of charge by nearly six hundred evangelical mission organizations.

Missions and Women

Aside from work on evangelicals, the greatest amount of recent historical work on a subgroup in Protestant missions has been on women. Since the late nineteenth century, women have constituted a numerical majority in the mission field, and in all denominational traditions they have dominated educational and social work, as well as mission support in local churches. In terms of the transmission of American culture abroad, the role of missionary women has been paramount. Although the early twentieth century saw a massive amount written by women on women and missions, little of this penetrated the male-dominated history profession. The bias toward intellectual history also kept the contributions of missionary women hidden from view because women tended to produce "popular" writing.

Once again missiologist R. Pierce Beaver pioneered the way for historians when he wrote *All Loves Excelling: American Protestant Women in World Mission.*[53] An institutional history of the woman's missionary movement, Beaver's book reflected his bias toward Christian unity and therefore concentrated on women in the mainline churches and the movement toward ecumenism. Consequently, there was no reference to twentieth-century evangelical or Pentecostal women in the first edition. A revised edition issued in 1980 claimed that the women's missionary movement was "the first feminist movement in North America" but failed to define feminism or put the material into the context of women's history. Beaver's volume is still useful as an institutional overview of nineteenth- and early-twentieth-century mainline women in mission.

By the late 1970s feminist historians had begun to appreciate the importance of studying missionary women for understanding gender relations in America. As a popular movement involving millions of women, the women's missionary movement became a filter through which women historians could analyze the roles of Protestant women in America. Barbara Welter opened the topic with her essay "She Hath Done What She Could: Protestant Women's Missionary Careers in Nineteenth-Century America."[54] Welter argued that although women's careers as missionaries were varied and fulfilling, mission careers for women typified the phenomenon whereby men abandoned an occupation to women when they lost interest in it. In 1980, Joan Jacobs Brumberg issued a study of the Judson family, Adoniram and his three wives Ann, Sarah, and Emily. Adoniram and Ann Judson were the pioneer missionaries of the Congregationalists and later the Baptists.[55] Although Brumberg's group biography was an important social study of evangelicalism, its chief importance was in showing how missionary wives as role models contributed to the self-understanding of American Protestant women.

In 1984, Jane Hunter forcefully demonstrated the value of examining women missionaries as representatives of American female culture in a doctoral dissertation-turned-book.[56] Relying on the correspondence and journals of mainline China missionaries, Hunter uncovered how female missionaries were representative of the struggle of middle-class Protestant women between public outreach and private home life. Women missionaries were "the most successful emissaries" of American culture abroad (xiv). Continuing the exploration of missionary women as "civilizers," or promoters of western culture and social change, Leslie A. Flemming in 1989 edited a volume on women missionaries and social change in Asia.[57]

The largest contingent of American Protestant women abroad in the early nineteenth century were the Congregational missionary women in Hawaii. The Hawaii women were in a unique position to reproduce New England female culture in a controlled setting where it could be studied, and ample documentation through correspondence exists. Studies of these women began to appear in the 1980s. Char Miller discussed the impact of domestic responsibilities on their missionary work in "Domesticity Abroad: Work and Family in the Sandwich Island Mission, 1820–1840."[58] A book-length examination of the stresses and strains of missionary life, particularly of enforced domesticity and gender discrimination, appeared in 1989 by Patricia Grimshaw.[59] The most recent and well-nuanced examination of the Hawaiian missionary wives, particularly sensitive to their religious motivations, was Mary Zwiep's 1991 study of the first group of Congregational missionary women.[60]

Consideration of the home base of the woman's missionary movement began with the publication of a book by Patricia Hill, the first in-depth analysis of the mainline women's missionary movement at its height.[61] Hill argued that the success of the women's missionary movement was based on its gender-based ideology, and the collapse of the movement occurred when professionalization and secularization undercut its distinctive rationale. The most important inter-Protestant women's organization at the height of the missionary movement was undoubtedly the Young Women's Christian Association. The history of the missionary wing of the YWCA was ably chronicled by Nancy Boyd.[62]

Gender analysis from a conservative evangelical perspective first appeared in 1988 when Ruth Tucker produced a biographical history of woman's missions.[63] Although *Guardians of the Great Commission* was anecdotal rather than systematic, it contained helpful observations on domesticity, gender relations, and mission theory scattered throughout the biographical sketches. The greatest significance of Tucker's book was that it was the first book on women in mission to cover twentieth-century evangelical women.

Denominational historians have produced material of quality on women and missions in their own tradition. Noteworthy among these are studies of missionary women in the Southern Baptist, Episcopal, Presbyterian, United Methodist, Congregational, and Canadian Methodist denominations.[64] A number of denominational women's organizations have issued popular books containing biographical sketches of prominent missionaries or home base leaders.[65] One of the most illuminating biographical studies of women leaders at the home base is Louise A. Cattan's treatment of Helen Barrett Montgomery and Lucy Waterbury Peabody. The two American Baptist women were important American leaders of the ecumenical women's missionary movement in the twentieth century.[66]

The discovery of women missionaries by feminist historians has been a valuable contribution to American history. Analysis of women missionaries permits study in a microcosm of self-conscious, articulate groups of women who either deliberately or despite themselves were bearers of American culture to other groups. Feminist history of the woman's missionary movement has been outstanding in its sensitivity to cultural issues, even though the explanatory category of separate male and female "spheres" has probably been overemphasized. Missionary women represented Protestant Christianity both at its most self-denying and at its most culturally imperialistic. The weakness of the feminist history approach toward missionary women, however, parallels the weakness of nationalist mission history. Religious piety has sometimes been treated as a screen for domesticity or for social control of nonwestern women, as cultural imperialism rather than being taken seriously on its own terms, thus reflecting a bias against considering religiosity as a category separate from race, class, or gender. Feminist analysis of women missionaries has concentrated on American gender identity and ideology, much as nationalist history focused on American identity. Unsurprisingly, feminist historians have studied almost exclusively mainline Protestant women during the height of the imperialist era. Except for self-avowed evangelical historians, the twentieth-century conservative evangelical woman has been relegated to marginality, as retrograde in the development of the woman's movement.

A recent theme in women's missionary history is to move away from preoccupation with how missionaries did or did not reflect the domestic women's movement and social change, toward examination of women's motivations, piety, and mission theory both in their own right and in relation to the total missionary enterprise. Although written in different styles and for different audiences, Mary Zwiep's and Ruth Tucker's aforementioned works are examples of this approach. Emphasizing a comparative approach so as to analyze how social context affected the development of women's mission thought, I have written several articles in preparation for a forthcoming history of American women's mission theory.[67]

The examination of American women's mission history by nonwesterners is another new development that promises to help historians evaluate American culture and theology from the so-called receiving end. The December 1986 issue of *Indian Church History Review* focused on the roles of women missionaries in India.[68] Kwok Pui-lan's recently published study of Chinese women and their appropriation of Christianity is a model of how western missionary women's materials need to be used to evaluate the missionary movement from broader perspectives than those defined by American agendas.[69]

Missions and Denominationalism

Finally, in the discussion of the pluralization of Protestant missionary history, it is important to revisit the idea of mainline denominational history. Now that the hold of nationalist interpretations of mainline mission history has been broken, the time has come to look at the mission work of Methodists, Presbyterians, American Baptists, Congregationalists, Disciples, and others with new eyes. How did denominational mission movements not only reflect American identity and create church unity, but change over time in connection with the wider debates in American Christianity? How have missions transmitted knowledge of other cultures back to American Protestants? How have the social reform agendas of the mainline been evaluated by indigenous historians? Rather than seeing Protestant mission as a monolith, were there differences among denominations that led to differing relationships with non-Christian cultures and religions? How has the drastic change in mission thought and the decline of the mainline missionary force since the 1950s affected the vitality and self-understanding of American Protestantism? From the perspective of the twenty-first century, how should historians evaluate the record of mainline missions in the twentieth century, the most productive century in mission history thus far? Rare is the denominational mission history that integrates the contributions of men and women into a balanced whole, or that considers missions as essentially a relationship between different cultures rather than implicitly an imposition by one on another.

The rewriting of mainline denominational mission history is one of the key tasks for mission history in the 1990s. Beginnings have been made, but much more needs to be done. The interest in taking a new look at mainline mission history was exemplified by a recent volume of reprinted essays edited by church historian Martin E. Marty.[70] In 1992, Ian Douglas completed a dissertation on Episcopal mission structures and theology covering the mid–twentieth century.[71] Also in 1992 appeared Gerald De Jong's study of the Reformed Church in China.[72] James Cogswell, former associate general secretary for overseas ministries of the National Council of Churches, is writing a comprehensive history of Presbyterian missions. Both Presbyterian and Mennonite mission historians hope to meet with colleagues in the Third World to stimulate the collaborative writing of mission history from both sides.

The advent of denominational oral history projects in the 1980s has pulled together some of the resources necessary for fresh evaluations of twentieth-century denominational history. The Evangelical Lutheran Church of America, for example, has been engaged in an oral history project on women in mission. Denominational church history magazines have frequently published articles on particular aspects or fields of American mission history and are one of the best sources for local studies.[73]

The role of American denominations in specialized forms of mission is another area needing research.[74]

A subsidiary focus of the emerging interest in denominational history is the renewed appreciation for missionary biography. From the time of David Brainerd's diary in the eighteenth century, to Harriet Newell's journal in the nineteenth, to the numerous biographies of Ann and Adoniram Judson in the nineteenth and twentieth, missionary biography has inspired Protestants to become missionaries. Evangelical Christians continue to read missionary biographies of twentieth-century heroes.[75] Historians are realizing, however, that missionary biography is not necessarily hagiography: critically done, it can illuminate aspects of American identity, cross-cultural relations, and theological development. A case in point is Char Miller's biography of the Bingham family of Hawaii over multiple generations.[76] Where, we might ask, is the study of the Dulles family, which began with Myron and Harriet Winslow in Ceylon in 1819, and continued into India, culminating in John Foster Dulles as secretary of state under President Dwight D. Eisenhower? Where is the critical study of the Samuel Moffetts or the Horace Underwoods, whose families have spent a century in Korea?

In addition to the missionary dynasties, the lives of "ordinary" missionaries should be mined for the perspective they provide on American history. Privately printed and limited-edition missionary journals are sometimes issued by family members. Important missionaries sometimes write their autobiographies.[77] These first-person accounts are the primary sources of twentieth-century missions and should be collected by libraries interested in mission history, but frequently are not considered of sufficient interest to justify the expense. Some missionary biographies are published by university presses with an interest in particular geographic areas. Probably the part of the world that has generated the largest number of mainline missionary biographies is China.[78] Edwin Mellen Press publishes a mission series that includes scholarly missionary biographies and collections of writings.[79] Autobiographies and biographies of leading "home base" leaders and ecumenists have also found a market.[80] Among missionary biography, denominational history magazines, and archival projects, there is reason to hope that mainline mission history is at the beginning of a much-needed renaissance.

Protestant Missionary History in International Perspective

The study of Protestant foreign missions has been important to American history because it has shown how commitment to the spread of Christian faith, myth, and ritual has helped to shape American identity, both in religious and secular realms. The continued importance of mission history, however, lies not only in what it will reveal about changing American self-perceptions, but in its function as a bridge to understanding the

United States in relation to the rest of the world. The triumphalistic tendency to see the world as the playground of "Yankees" is being left in the past; new world realities demonstrate that American Protestantism's importance for the future might not lie so much in its own destiny, but in the role it has played in the rise of Christianity in the nonwestern world. Even as Protestantism struggles to hold its own in the west, the growth of the church in Africa, Asia, and Latin America are shifting the dynamic center of Christianity to the southern hemisphere. Future considerations of American Protestant foreign missions must take into account that the old Rome is giving way to the new; Boston and Nashville are yielding to Seoul and Nairobi.

Increasingly, the significance of missions for American history lies in international relationships. Scholars should no longer study missionaries without recognizing how they were affected by indigenous peoples, or how the cultures in which they worked shaped their mission theories. Historians should study how the interaction of Christianity with other religions has shaped its message in different settings. Since American Protestantism resides in a global village, it must be studied in relation to European, African, Asian, and Latin American Christianity.

Indigenous historians of Christianity bring their own agendas to the source material and can thereby enrich with new perspectives American self-understanding. One theme that international scholars have isolated from their study of American Protestant missions is the role played by missions among the larger forces of modernization in nonwestern cultures: American missions were frequently an important path to westernization and/or nationalism.[81] Ethicist Masao Takenaka examined how American missionaries contributed to the transition from feudalism during the Meiji Restoration in Japan.[82] In 1967, historian Sushil Madhava Pathak studied the interplay between Hinduism and Protestant missionary thinking, including the social modernization and Hindu renaissance stimulated by Christianity.[83] Sociologist Chung Chai-sik has written on how progressive Koreans in the late nineteenth century deliberately accepted American missionaries as agents of modernization.[84] H. K. Barpujari developed an important study of Baptist missionaries among the Assamese. He showed how through their mission work, translation work, and study of the people's culture, missionaries played a vital role in the identity formation and rejuvenation of the Assamese in Northeast India.[85] Studies of missionaries by indigenous scholars demonstrate convincingly how the values and practices offered by missionaries were used by converts for their own ends: converts were not passive victims of a monolithic American imperialism.[86]

The influence of American missionaries on indigenous evangelism and church-planting in nonwestern cultures is another topic addressed by indigenous church historians. To take the influence of American Protestant missions on South African churches as but one example, two works by South Africans have traced the influence of conservative American faith missionaries on the founders of black Zionist churches.[87] A Rhodes University dissertation dealing with the American sources of Indian Pentecostalism in South Africa was written by Gerald John Pillay.[88] In 1992, the influence of American Methodism on black Methodism in South Africa was explored in an article by South African missiologist Daryl M. Balia. Balia showed how the famous revivals of American Methodist William Taylor were in fact dependent on the indigenous preacher Charles Pamla.[89] Increasingly, works on church-planting written by indigenous historians show that American missionaries interacted with and were dependent on indigenous Christians for their success in evangelism. The "lone ranger" western missionary capable of single-handedly evangelizing thousands of people was a rare or nonexistent phenomenon.

The new era of world Christianity demands that American mission history be considered as part of a whole, as part of the dynamic interplay of cultures and religions that characterizes our world today. The global nature of Christianity in many ways gives a greater urgency to the study of Protestant mission history than it has had previously. There is a greater legitimacy in the academy to studying American foreign missions today than there was twenty-five years ago, a factor perhaps of the dawning realization that Christianity is global, and that mission history can provide an entree into the larger reality.

Increasingly, Protestant foreign missions are being studied by international teams of scholars who bring with them the expertise in various languages and histories that American historians lack. One example of the team-based approach is the North Atlantic Missiology Project, a series of conferences held on both sides of the Atlantic to develop and compare British and North American themes in mission history. The project seeks to examine how Christian mission interacted with other religions, and how other religions shaped Christianity at points of initial contact. Missiologists Andrew Walls of the Centre for the Study of Christianity in the Non-Western World (University of Edinburgh) and Lamin Sanneh of Yale Divinity School have held a series of consultations bringing together American with European mission historians, along with secular historians in related fields. Sinologist Daniel Bays of the University of Kansas is heading a project funded by The Pew Charitable Trusts to create a data base of pre-1949 Christianity in China. Chinese and American scholars are working collaboratively to make the data base possible, which when completed will be a valuable addition to what exists in western mission archives. In another major Pew-funded, team-based project, Indologist Robert Frykenberg of the University of Wisconsin is coordinating research into Christianity in South India, including transcultural interactions between Indian and Western Christians. Although American Protestant foreign missions constitute only one aspect of the projects listed here, they will be analyzed in broader contexts and by people from the so-called "receiving" as well as the "sending" end of missionary activity.

In the nineteenth century, foreign missions captured the imagination of American Protestants and turned their eyes toward the rest of the world. In the twentieth century, North American Protestantism became one of the most powerful forces for world mission in the history of Christianity. In the twenty-first century, American Protestant foreign missions must take their place as part of a larger world that they helped to create, but that they can neither organize nor control.

Directions for Further Research

The journey from "mission" to "beyond missions," from unitary interpretation of the American missionary enterprise toward decentralized and pluralistic interpretations, has been a welcome trend in the historiography of American Protestant missions since the Second World War. A rebirth of mission historiography that includes denominational missions but is more inclusive than the old formulae has the potential to reimage the history of American Protestantism. The essence of American Protestantism, a crucial source of its vitality, has lain in what William Hutchison and others have called its "activism," and at many times in American history, Protestant activism and missions were coterminous. Even in periods of relatively reduced missionary activity, foreign missions represented the cutting edge of theological application, international relations, and conscious cultural interaction on the part of American Protestants.

In addition to what it shows about American Protestantism, mission history can be used as a prism through which to illuminate many aspects of American culture. Freed from its prison as a subject of interest only in theological seminaries and Bible colleges, the history of Protestant missions needs to be taken in new directions, some of which have already been suggested by the scholarship reviewed above. In international perspective, to move from mission to beyond missions is to use the study of American foreign missions as a bridge to Asia, Africa, and Latin America. Just as transatlantic dialogue with Europe in the eighteenth and nineteenth centuries mediated cultural change and provided a mirror for American self-understanding, so has traffic with Asia, Africa, and Latin America increasingly defined North America in the twentieth century. Missionaries have not only carried American culture abroad, but they have been the chief interpreters of nonwestern culture in churches and small towns throughout the heartland of America. There is urgent need to study missionaries as messengers of nonwestern culture, critics of American foreign policy, and mirrors reflecting American identity for the "folks back home."

In significant ways, foreign missionaries have created America's image of the rest of the world in the twentieth century. The number of missionary children who have become seminary professors, shapers of American foreign policy, or leaders in international business has often been noted but seldom studied. As multicultural elites, foreign missionaries have

382 PROTESTANTISM AND THE MAINSTREAM

played a major role out of proportion to their actual numbers in the conduct of the United States abroad. The American obsession with communism in the 1950s, for example, needs to be studied in relation to the missionary mediators who were critics of anti-Christian or Marxist political systems. The influence of anticommunist former China missionaries should be balanced against that of missionaries who supported the nationalist struggles of indigenous peoples, such as the efforts of Ho Chi Minh. The "missionary factor" in mid-twentieth-century foreign policy is but one area that needs critical scholarly analysis.

The development of international ethical movements around such issues as world peace and human rights cannot be understood apart from missionary influence. Another neglected area of research in mission history is the role played by foreign missions in the pacifism and focus on world friendship that emerged between the two world wars. The extensive dialogue between Protestant women in the United States and Japan prior to World War II is but one small example of an important but unstudied contribution of foreign missions to internationalism. The full story of missions and refugee relief has never been told. Missions have been frequently analyzed in relation to American nationalism. Unexamined but equally important is the contribution made by missions to internationalism and America's ability to transcend its own narrow self interest.

In the theological arena, the nexus among mission theory, missionary thought, and American understanding of non-Christian religions has been seriously neglected. Changing American attitudes to non-Christian religions could be charted by reviewing missionary literature of the past century. Although formal interfaith dialogue would not exist without the centuries of missionary effort that have gone before, theologians, philosophers, and comparativists seldom acknowledge that the groundwork for their study was laid by the very missionaries they sometimes denigrate.[90] Sound historical scholarship on the relationship of missions to interfaith understanding is needed to correct the unidimensional portrait that now exists.

Study of mission institutions in their social contexts is another area desperately needing research. In the early twentieth century, American mainline Protestants supported seven interdenominational women's institutions of higher learning in China, Japan, and India, as well as thousands of lower-level schools. Western medical practice was mediated to the rest of the world by missionaries, and mission discoveries in the "field" helped to change the western understanding of disease and treatment. The impact of missionary institutions on their social, economic, and cultural contexts on both sides of the water has yet to be analyzed, although a beginning is being made in current doctoral-level research. Missionary institutions are an unexplored source of important transcultural interactions and social change.

As areas of further research into American Protestant foreign missions are mapped out, and the complex and diverse picture of American Protestant missions takes shape, the historiographic task will of necessity revolve around interpretation. Taken in its fullness, what has the mission impulse meant for American Protestantism and for American culture, society, and theology? How has the mission experience, broadly defined, affected the larger course of American history and of world history? In 1964, R. Pierce Beaver unrealistically prophesied in *From Missions to Mission* a future for Protestant missions that flowed from ecumenical unity and confidence. But despite his failure as a prophet, his assessment of missionary historiography made in 1968 still stands today. Writing for a study called *Reinterpretation in American Church History*, Beaver noted of American mission history that interpretation needed to take place before reinterpretation could occur.[91]

A generation after R. Pierce Beaver, the tools for interpretation are being shaped and honed. The historiographic task began with denominational missions, and from there proceeded to mission. Following a narrowing of historical interest in mission, mission studies collapsed in the late 1960s. The last decade has seen a revival of mission history with the growing realization that it has the potential to enliven numerous other fields of inquiry and to provide an entrée into nonwestern Christianity. At last the historiography of Protestant foreign mission is maturing, growing through adolescence into adulthood, through and beyond missions to perspectives that may reveal the global historical significance of American Protestant foreign missions for the first time.

NOTES

1. Even Yale professor Kenneth Scott Latourette's magisterial seven-volume history of world missions was largely a compilation of denominal activity in the course of Christianity's propagation throughout the world. Kenneth Scott Latourette, *A History of the Expansion of Christianity*, 7 vols. (New York: Harper and Brothers, 1937–1945).

2. Ralph Henry Gabriel, *The Course of American Democratic Thought: An Intellectual History Since 1815* (New York: Ronald Press, 1940).

3. Miller's essay was reprinted in Perry Miller, *Errand Into the Wilderness* (Cambridge, Mass.: Belknap Press of Harvard University Press, 1956).

4. See R. Pierce Beaver, *Ecumenical Beginnings in Protestant World Mission: A History of Comity* (New York: Thomas Nelson & Son, 1962); William Richey Hogg, *Ecumenical Foundations: A History of the International Missionary Council and its Nineteenth Century Background* (New York: Harper, 1952); Robert T. Handy, *We Witness Together: A History of Cooperative Home Missions* (New York: Friendship Press, 1956).

5. Robert Handy, *A Christian America: Protestant Hopes and Historical Realities* (New York: Oxford University Press, 1971).

6. Paul H. Varg, *Missionaries, Chinese and Diplomats: The American Protestant Missionary Movement in China, 1890–1952* (Princeton, N.J.: Princeton University Press, 1958).

7. Kenneth MacKenzie, *The Robe and the Sword: The Methodist Church and the Rise of American Imperialism* (Washington, D.C.: Public Affairs Press, 1961).

8. John A. Andrew III, *Rebuilding the Christian Commonwealth: New England Congregationalists and Foreign Missions, 1800–1830* (Lexington, Ky.: University Press of Kentucky, 1976).

9. Joseph L. Grabill, *Protestant Diplomacy and the Near East: Missionary Influence on American Policy, 1810–1927* (Minneapolis: University of Minnesota Press, 1971).

10. Rosa del Carmen Bruno-Jofre, *Methodist Education in Peru: Social Gospel, Politics, and American Ideological and Economic Penetration, 1888–1930* (Waterloo, Ontario: Wilfrid Laurier University Press, 1988).

11. Kenton Clymer, *Protestant Missionaries in the Philippines, 1898–1916: An Inquiry into the American Colonial Mentality* (Urbana, Ill.: University of Illinois Press, 1986).

12. Arthur Schlesinger, Jr., "The Missionary Enterprise and Theories of Imperialism," in *The Missionary Enterprise in China and America*, ed. John K. Fairbank (Cambridge, Mass.: Harvard University Press, 1974), 336–73.

13. William R. Hutchison, "A Moral Equivalent for Imperialism: Americans and the Promotion of 'Christian Civilization,' 1880–1910," in *Missionary Ideologies in the Imperialist Era: 1880–1920*, ed. Hutchison and Torben Christensen (Aarhus, Denmark: Christensens Bogtrykkeri, 1982), 167–78 (174).

14. Among secular historians, sinologists have made the greatest use of American missionary documentation to illuminate their field of research and thus represent an exception to the academic neglect of missions. Some of the best scholarly studies of American missionaries both collectively and individually are by sinologists. In particular, the research of Harvard professor John King Fairbank and of his students and followers represents the finest body of work that analyzes the role of missions in relation to foreign policy, American nationalism, internationalism, and cultural interaction. Fairbank's interest in the "missionary factor" transformed the history of United States–China relations. For valuable studies of American Protestant missions in China, see for example Paul A. Cohen, *China and Christianity: The Missionary Movement and the Growth of Chinese Antiforeignism, 1860–1870* (Cambridge, Mass.: Harvard University Press, 1963); Kwang-Ching Liu, ed., *American Missionaries in China: Papers from Harvard Seminars* (Cambridge, Mass.: East Asian Research Center Harvard University, 1966); James C. Thomson, *While China Faced West: American Reformers in Nationalist China, 1928–1937* (Cambridge, Mass.: Harvard University Press, 1969); Shirley S. Garrett, *Social Reformers in Urban China: The Chinese Y.M.C.A., 1895–1926* (Cambridge, Mass.: Harvard University Press, 1970); Sidney A. Forsythe, *An American Missionary Community in China, 1895–1905* (Cambridge, Mass.: Harvard University Press, 1971); Jessie Gregory Lutz, *China and the Christian Colleges, 1850–1950* (Ithaca: Cornell University Press, 1971); John K. Fairbank, ed., *The Missionary Enterprise in China and America* (Cambridge, Mass.: Harvard University Press, 1974); Ellsworth C. Carlson, *The Foochow Missionaries, 1847–1880* (Cambridge, Mass.: Harvard University Press, 1974); Philip West, *Yenching University and Sino-Western Relations, 1916–1952* (Cambridge, Mass.: Harvard University Press, 1976); James Reed, *The Missionary Mind and American East Asia Policy, 1911–1915* (Cambridge, Mass.: Harvard University Press, 1983); Suzanne Wilson Barnett and John King Fairbank,

eds., *Christianity in China: Early Protestant Missionary Writings* (Cambridge, Mass.: Committee on American-East Asian Relations of the Department of History with the Council on East Asian Studies Harvard University, 1985); Jessie Gregory Lutz, *Chinese Politics and Christian Missions: The Anti-Christian Movements of 1920–28* (Notre Dame, Ind.: Cross Cultural Publications, 1988).

15. See Clifton Phillips, "The Student Volunteer Movement and Its Role in China Missions, 1886–1920," in *The Missionary Enterprise in China and America,* ed. John K. Fairbank (Cambridge, Mass.: Harvard University Press, 1974), 91–109; Valentin H. Rabe, *The Home Base of American China Missions, 1880–1920* (Cambridge, Mass.: Harvard University Press, 1978).

16. R. Pierce Beaver, "North American Thought on the Fundamental Principles of Missions During the Twentieth Century, *Church History* 21 (4) (1952): 3–22; "Eschatology in American Missions," in *Basileia. Walter Freytag zum 60. Geburtstag,* ed. J. Hermelink and H. J. Margull (Stuttgart: Evang. Missionsverlag, 1959), 60–75.

17. R. Pierce Beaver, ed., *To Advance the Gospel: Selections from the Writings of Rufus Anderson* (Grand Rapids, Mich.: Eerdmans, 1967).

18. R. Pierce Beaver, ed., *Pioneers in Mission: The Early Missionary Ordination Sermons, Charges, and Instructions* (Grand Rapids, Mich.: Eerdmans, 1966).

19. R. Pierce Beaver, "Missionary Motivation Through Three Centuries," in *Reinterpretation in American Church History,* ed. Jerald Brauer (Chicago: University of Chicago Press, 1968), 113–51.

20. R. Pierce Beaver, *Church, State, and the American Indians* (St. Louis, Mo.: Concordia, 1966); "Methods in American Missions to the Indians in the Seventeenth and Eighteenth Centuries," *Journal of Presbyterian History* 47 (2) (1969): 124–48; and "The Churches and the Indians: Consequences of 350 Years of Missions," in R. Pearce Beaver, ed., *American Missions in Bicentennial Perspective* (Pasadena, Calif.: William Carey Library, 1977), 275–331.

21. J. A. DeJong, *As the Waters Cover the Sea: Millennial Expectations in the Rise of Anglo-American Missions, 1640–1810* (Kampen: Kok, 1970).

22. Charles Chaney, *The Birth of Missions in America* (South Pasadena, Calif.: William Carey Library, 1976).

23. Charles Forman, "A History of Foreign Mission Theory," in Beaver, ed., *American Missions in Bicentennial Perspective,*69–140.

24. Roger Bassham, *Mission Theology, 1948–1975: Years of Worldwide Creative Tension: Ecumenical, Evangelical, Roman Catholic* (Pasadena, Calif.: William Carey Library, 1979).

25. Gerald Anderson, "The Theology of Missions: 1928–1958" (Ph.D. dissertation, Boston University, 1960).

26. For example, see Dana L. Robert "The Origin of the Student Volunteer Watchword," *International Bulletin of Missionary Research* 10 (4) (1986): 146–49; Nathan D. Showalter, "Crusade or Catastrophe? The Student Missions Movement and the First World War," *International Bulletin of Missionary Research* 17 (1) (1993): 13–17. Anderson collected many of the articles on the mission thought of outstanding nineteenth and twentieth century mission leaders into Gerald H. Anderson, Robert T. Coote, Norman A. Horner, James M. Phillips, eds., *Mission Legacies: Biographical Studies of Leaders of the Modern Missionary Movement* (Maryknoll: Orbis, 1994).

27. Gerald Anderson, "American Protestants in Pursuit of Mission: 1886–1986," in *A Century of Church History: The Legacy of Philip Schaff,* ed. Henry Warner Bowden (Carbondale, Ill.: Southern Illinois University Press, 1988), 168–215. Reprinted in the *International Bulletin of Missionary Research* 12 (3) (1988): 98–118.

28. Gerald Anderson, "Mission Research, Writing, and Publishing: 1971–1991," *International Bulletin of Missionary Research* 15 (4) (1991): 165–72.

29. William R. Hutchison, *Errand to the World: American Protestant Thought and Foreign Missions* (Chicago: University of Chicago Press, 1987).

30. Norman Etherington, "An American Errand into the South African Wilderness," *Church History* 39 (1) (1970): 62–71. See also Etherington's full study, *Preachers Peasants and Politics in Southeast Africa, 1835–1880* (London: Royal Historical Society, 1978).

31. Andrew Walls, "The American Dimension in the History of the Missionary Movement," in *Earthen Vessels: American Evangelicals and Foreign Missions, 1880–1980,* ed. Joel Carpenter and Wilbert Shenk (Grand Rapids, Mich.: Eerdmans, 1990), 1–25.

32. Walter Williams, *Black Americans and the Evangelization of Africa, 1877–1900* (Madison, Wis.: University of Wisconsin Press, 1982).

33. Sylvia Jacobs, ed., *Black Americans and the Missionary Movement in Africa* (Madison, Wis.: University of Wisconsin Press, 1982). Jacobs has written articles on the missiological contributions of African American women, including "Three Afro-American Women: Missionaries in Africa, 1882–1904," in Rosemary Keller, Louise Queen, and Hilah Thomas, eds., *Women in New Worlds: Historical Perspectives on the Wesleyan Tradition,* vol. 2 (Nashville, Tenn.: Abingdon, 1982), 268–280; and "Their 'Special Mission': Afro-American Women as Missionaries to the Congo, 1894–1937," in Jacobs, 155–176.

34. David W. Wills and Richard Newman, eds., *Black Apostles at Home and Abroad: Afro-Americans and the Christian Mission from the Revolution to Reconstruction* (Boston: G. K. Hall, 1982).

35. Sandy D. Martin, *Black Baptists and African Missions: The Origins of a Movement, 1880–1915* (Macon, Ga.: Mercer, 1989).

36. James T. Campbell, "Our Fathers, Our Children: The African Methodist Episcopal Church in the United States and South Africa" (Ph.D. dissertation, Stanford University, 1989). Campbell's revised dissertation was published as *Songs of Zion: The American Methodist Episcopal Church in the United States and South Africa* (New York: Oxford University Press, 1995). See also the earlier dissertation by Josephus R. Coan, "The Expansion of the Missions of the African Methodist Episcopal Church in South Africa, 1896–1908" (Ph.D. dissertation, Hartford Seminary, 1961).

37. David M. Dean, *Defender of the Race: James Theodore Holly, Black Nationalist Bishop* (Boston: Lambeth Press, 1979); Leroy Fitts, *Lott Carey: First Black Missionary to Africa* (Valley Forge, Pa.: Judson Press, 1978); Wilson Jeremiah Moses, *Alexander Crummell: A Study of Civilization and Discontent* (New York: Oxford University Press, 1989); John R. Oldfield, *Alexander Crummell (1819–1898) and the Creation of an African-American Church in Liberia* (Lewiston, N.Y.: E. Mellen Press, 1990); Stephen Ward Angell, *Bishop Henry McNeal Turner and African-American Religion in the South* (Knoxville, Tenn.: University of Tennessee Press, 1992); William E. Phipps, *The Sheppards and Lapsley: Pio-*

neer Presbyterians in the Congo (Louisville, Ky.: Presbyterian Church, USA, 1991).

38. For example see Ann Fienup-Riordan, The Real People and the Children of Thunder: The Yup'ik Eskimo Encounter with Moravian Missionaries John and Edith Kilbuck (Norman, Okla.: University of Oklahoma Press, 1991); Earl P. Olmstead, Blackcoats among the Delaware: David Zeisberger on the Ohio Frontier (Kent, Ohio: Kent State University Press, 1991).

39. See G. W. Peters, Foundations of Mennonite Brethren Missions (Hillsboro, Kans.: Kindred Press, 1984); Elaine Rich, Mennonite Women: A Story of God's Faithfulness, 1683–1983 (Scottdale, Pa.: Herald Press, 1983); Theron Schlabach, Gospel Versus Gospel: Mission and the Mennonite Church, 1863–1944 (Scottdale, Pa.: Herald Press, 1980); George F. Hall, The Missionary Spirit in the Augustana Church (Rock Island, Ill.: Augustana Historical Society, Augustana College, 1984); Albert T. Ronk, History of Brethren Missionary Movements (Ashland, Ohio: Brethren Church, 1971); and James C. Juhnke, A People of Mission: History of General Conference Mennonite Overseas Missions (Newton, Kans.: Faith and Life Press, 1979).

40. For example, see Martin Schrag, "Societies Influencing the Brethren in Christ Toward Missionary Work," Notes and Queries in Brethren in Christ History 8 (January 1967): 1–12.

41. Joel Carpenter, "Propagating the Faith Once Delivered: The Fundamentalist Missionary Enterprise, 1920–1945," in Carpenter and Wilbert Shenk eds., Earthen Vessels (Grand Rapids, Mich.: Eerdmans, 1990), 92–132.

42. Grant Wacker, "Second Thoughts on the Great Commission: Liberal Protestants and Foreign Missions, 1890–1940," 281–300. Wacker is continuing to work on the theme of liberalism and missions and presented a paper on missionary Pearl S. Buck at the December 1993 meeting of the American Society of Church History.

43. See for example Allen V. Koop, American Evangelical Missionaries in France, 1945–1975 (Lanham, Md.: University Press of America, 1986). Ralph Covell's Mission Impossible: The Unreached Nosu on China's Frontier (Pasadena, Calif.: Hope, 1990) reflected one aspect of the work of Conservative Baptists in the 1940s.

44. David Sandgren, Christianity and the Kikuyu: Religious Divisions and Social Conflict (New York: P. Lang, 1989).

45. The following is a list of some of the better histories of evangelical mission agencies: Baker J. Cauthen et al., Advance: A History of Southern Baptist Foreign Missions (Nashville: Broadman Press, 1970); Robert L. Niklaus, John S. Sawin, and Samuel J. Stoesz, All for Jesus: God at Work in the Christian and Missionary Alliance Over One Hundred Years (Camp Hill, Pa.: Christian Publications, 1986); Robert Wood, In These Mortal Hands: The Story of the Oriental Missionary Society, the First Fifty Years (Greenwood, Ind.: OMS International, 1983); J. Fred Parker, Mission to the World: A History of Missions in the Church of the Nazarene through 1985 (Kansas City, Mo.: Nazarene, 1988); Gary B. McGee, This Gospel Shall Be Preached: A History and Theology of Assemblies of God Foreign Missions, 2 vols. (Springfield, Mo.: Gospel, 1986, 1989); Edwin L. Frizen, Jr., 75 Years of IFMA, 1917–1992 (Pasadena, Calif.: William Carey Library, 1992); Lester A. Crose, Passport for a Reformation: A History of the Church of God Reformation Movement's Missionary Endeavors Outside N.

America (Anderson, Ind.: Warner Press, 1981); A. J. Broomhall's six-volume history of the China Inland Mission, *Hudson Taylor and China's Open Century* (London: Hodder & Stoughton and the Overseas Missionary Fellowship, 1981–); H. Wilbert Norton, *To Stir the Church: A Brief History of the Student Foreign Missions Fellowships, 1936–1986* (Madison, Wis: Student Foreign Missions Fellowship, 1986); David M. Howard, *The Dream That Would Not Die: The Birth and Growth of the World Evangelical Fellowship, 1846–1986* (Exeter, England: Paternoster Press; and Grand Rapids: Baker Book House, 1986); William R. Estep, *Whole Gospel—Whole World: The Foreign Mission Board of the Southern Baptist Convention, 1845–1995* (Nashville: Broadman & Holman, 1994).

46. See McGee, *This Gospel . . . Shall be Preached*. Articles of interest by McGee include "The Azusa Street Revival and Twentieth-Century Missions," *International Bulletin of Missionary Research* 12 (2) (1988): 58–61; and "Assemblies of God Mission Theology: A Historical Perspective," *International Bulletin of Missionary Research* 10 (4) (1986): 166–170.

47. Stanley M. Burgess, Gary B. McGee, and Patrick H. Alexander, *Dictionary of Pentecostal and Charismatic Movements* (Grand Rapids: Regency Reference Library, 1988).

48. Virginia Lieson Brereton, *Training God's Army: The American Bible School, 1880–1940* (Bloomington, Ind.: Indiana University Press, 1990).

49. Timothy Weber, *Living in the Shadow of the Second Coming: American Premillennialism 1875–1925* (New York: Oxford University Press, 1979).

50. Dana L. Robert, "Arthur Tappan Pierson and Forward Movements of Late-Nineteenth-Century American Evangelicalism" (Ph.D. dissertation, Yale University, 1984); published in Korean by Yangsuh Publishing Company, 1988. An earlier dissertation on the origin of faith missions was Marybeth Rupert, "The Emergence of the Independent Missionary Agency as an American Institution, 1860–1917" (Ph.D. dissertation, Yale University, 1974).

51. See, for example, the unpublished paper by Daniel H. Bays, "The Impact of Early Pentecostalism on Established American Missions in China," written for a conference on "Pentecostal Currents in the American Church" held in March of 1994.

52. Ruth Tucker, *From Jerusalem to Irian Jaya: A Biographical History of Christian Missions* (Grand Rapids, Mich.: Zondervan, 1983).

53. R. Pierce Beaver, *All Loves Excelling: American Protestant Women in World Mission* (Grand Rapids, Mich.: Eerdmans, 1968). Republished as *American Protestant Women in World Mission: History of the First Feminist Movement in North America* (Grand Rapids, Mich.: Eerdmans, 1980).

54. Barbara Welter, "She Hath Done What She Could: Protestant Women's Missionary Careers in Nineteenth-Century America," *American Quarterly* 30 (Winter 1978): 624–38.

55. Joan Jacobs Brumberg, *Mission for Life: The story of the family of Adoniram Judson, the dramatic events of the first American foreign mission, and the course of evangelical religion in the nineteenth century* (New York: The Free Press, 1980).

56. Jane Hunter, *The Gospel of Gentility: American Women Missionaries in Turn-of-the-Century China* (New Haven: Yale University Press, 1984).

57. Leslie A. Flemming, *Women's Work for Women: Missionaries and Social Change in Asia* (Boulder, Colo.: Westview, 1989). Of particular importance to

the question of women's missions and social change were the articles by Flemming, "New Models, New Roles: U.S. Presbyterian Women Missionaries and Social Change in North India, 1870–1910"; and Marjorie King, "Exporting Femininity, Not Feminism: Nineteenth-Century U.S. Missionary Women's Efforts to Emancipate Chinese Women." Women and social change was also the focus of Alison R. Drucker's article, "The Influence of Western Women on the Anti-Footbinding Movement, 1840–1911," in Richard W. Guisso and Stanley Johannesen, eds., *Women in China: Current Directions in Historical Scholarship* (New York: E. Mellen Press, 1981), 179–99.

58. Char Miller, "Domesticity Abroad: Work and Family in the Sandwich Island Mission, 1820–1840," in Miller, ed., *Missions and Missionaries in the Pacific* (New York: E. Mellen Press, 1985), 65–90.

59. Patricia Grimshaw, *Paths of Duty: American Missionary Wives in Nineteenth-Century Hawaii* (Honolulu: University of Hawaii Press, 1989). See also her earlier article, "Christian Woman, Pious Wife, Faithful Mother, Devoted Missionary: Conflicts in Roles of American Missionary Women in Nineteenth-Century Hawaii," *Feminist Studies* 9 (3) (1983): 489–521.

60. Mary Zwiep, *Pilgrim Path: The First Company of Women Missionaries to Hawaii* (Madison: University of Wisconsin Press, 1991).

61. Patricia Hill, *The World Their Household: The American Woman's Foreign Mission Movement and Cultural Transformation, 1870–1920* (Ann Arbor, Mich.: University of Michigan Press, 1985).

62. Nancy Boyd, *Emissaries: The Overseas Work of the American YWCA, 1895–1970* (New York: Woman's Press, 1986).

63. Ruth Tucker, *Guardians of the Great Commission: The Story of Women in Modern Missions* (Grand Rapids, Mich.: Academie Books, 1988).

64. See Catherine B. Allen, *A Century to Celebrate: History of Woman's Missionary Union* (Birmingham, Ala.: Woman's Missionary Union, 1987), a history of the powerful women's auxiliary of the Southern Baptist Convention. Allen also wrote an excellent biography of Lottie Moon, "patron saint" of Southern Baptist missions, *The New Lottie Moon Story* (Nashville: Broadman Press, 1980). Episcopal missionary women received treatment in Mary Sudman Donovan's *A Different Call: A History of Women's Ministries in the Episcopal Church, 1850–1920* (Wilton, Conn.: Morehouse, 1986). Lois A. Boyd and R. Douglas Brackenridge produced the insightful *Presbyterian Women in America: Two Centuries of a Quest for Status* (Westport, Conn.: Greenwood Press, 1983) which explored the role of women's missions in the Presbyterian context. Of predecessor denominations to the United Methodist Church, Audrie Reber wrote *Women United for Mission: A History of the Women's Society of World Service of the Evangelical United Brethren Church, 1946–1968* (Dayton, Ohio: Board of Missions of the United Methodist Church, 1969); and Ethel Born wrote *By My Spirit: The Story of Methodist Protestant Women in Mission, 1879–1939* (Cincinnati: Women's Division of the General Board of Global Ministries, 1990). Barbara Brown Zikmund, ed. *Hidden Histories in the United Church of Christ* (New York: United Church Press, 1984), contained an article by Zikmund and Sally A. Dries entitled "Women's Work and Woman's Boards." An important recent book on Canadian Methodists was Rosemary R. Gagan's *A Sensitive Independence: Canadian Methodist Women Missionaries in Canada and the Orient, 1881–1925* (Montreal: McGill-Queen's University Press, 1992).

65. These include Catherine Allen, *Laborers Together with God: 22 Great Women in Baptist Life* (Birmingham, Ala.: Woman's Missionary Union, 1987); Octavia W. Dandridge, *A History of the Women's Missionary Society of the African Methodist Church 1874–1987* (New York: Women's Missionary Society, 1987); and *They Went Out Not Knowing: An Encyclopedia of 100 Women in Mission* (NY: The Division; Cincinatti: General Board of Global Ministries, United Methodist Church, 1986). *Heroes of the Faith* (Springfield, Mo.: Assemblies of God Division of Foreign Missions, 1990), stories of Assemblies of God missionaries, is an example of a book that contains information on both men and women.

66. Louise A. Cattan, *Lamps are for Lighting: The Story of Helen Barrett Montgomery and Lucy Waterbury Peabody* (Grand Rapids, Mich.: Eerdmans, 1972). Between them, Montgomery and Peabody attended the Edinburgh 1910 conference, began publication of Christian literature for women around the world, wrote study materials for women's mission groups, and acted as leaders of the combined women's mission boards. Peabody founded a faith mission, and Montgomery was first woman moderator of the American Baptist Convention. See also William H. Brackney, "The Legacy of Helen B. Montgomery and Lucy W. Peabody," *International Bulletin of Missionary Research* 15 (4) (1991): 174–78.

67. Dana Robert, "Evangelist or Homemaker: The Mission Strategies of Early Nineteenth-Century Missionary Wives in Burma and Hawaii," *International Bulletin of Missionary Research* 17 (1) (1993): 4–12. A recent article published in the journal of the South African Missiological Society, "Mount Holyoke Women and the Dutch Reformed Missionary Movement, 1874–1904," *Missionalia* 21 (August 1993): 103–23, explored how American women's mission theory, piety, and culture influenced the missionary culture of white South Africans. My forthcoming book is the first overview of women's mission thought and treats mainline Protestant, evangelical, and Catholic women missionaries. Dana L. Robert, *American Women in Mission: A Social History of Mission Theory* (Macon, Georgia: Mercer University Press, forthcoming).

68. It included articles by Indian scholars such as S. Immanuel David, "A Mission of Gentility: The Role of Women Missionaries in the American Arcot Mission, 1839–1938," 143–52. A study of the interaction between Indian and American missionary women was the dissertation by American Charlotte Staelin, "The Influence of Missions on Women's Education in India: The American Marathi Mission in Ahmadnagar, 1830–1930" (Ph.D. dissertation, University of Michigan, 1977).

69. See Pui-lan Kwok, *Chinese Women and Christianity, 1860–1927* (Atlanta: Scholars Press, 1992).

70. Martin E. Marty, ed., *Missions and Ecumenical Expressions* (New York: K. G. Saur, 1993). Unfortunately the articles in Marty's volume are mostly concerned with the "old" issues of American identity and imperialism.

71. Ian Douglas, "Fling Out the Banner: The National Church Ideal and the Foreign Mission of the Episcopal Church" (Ph.D. dissertation, Boston University, 1992). See his related article " 'A Light to the Nations': Episcopal Foreign Missions in Historical Perspective," *Anglican and Episcopal History* 61 (4) (1992): 449–81.

72. Gerald DeJong, *The Reformed Church in China, 1842–1951* (Grand Rapids, Mich.: Eerdmans, 1992).

73. See for example Mark Douglas Norbeck, "False Start: The First Three Years of Episcopal Missionary Endeavor in the Philippine Islands, 1898–1901," *Anglican and Episcopal History* 62 (June 1993): 215–36; Dana L. Robert, "Methodist Episcopal Church, South, Missions to Russians in Manchuria, 1920–1927," *Methodist History* 62 (January 1988): 66–83; "The United Presbyterian Church in Mission: An Historical Overview," *Journal of Presbyterian History* 57 (Fall 1979, full issue); "Whom Shall I Send?" *American Baptist Quarterly* (September 1993, full issue); Peggy Brase Siegel, "Moral Champions and Public Pathfinders: Antebellum Quaker Women in East Central India," 81 *Quaker History* (Fall 1992): 87–106; Dennis C. Dickerson, "Bishop Henry M. Turner and Black Latinos: The Mission to Cuba and Mexico," *The A.M.E. Church Review* (January–March 1993): 51–55.

74. A large recent history of missions to seamen includes a section on American activity in this field. Roald Kverndal, *Seamen's Missions: Their Origin and Early Growth* (Pasadena, Calif.: William Carey Library, 1986).

75. See for example, Elizabeth Elliot, *Shadow of the Almighty: The Life and Testament of Jim Elliot* (New York: Harper Collins, 1989); Olive Fleming Liefeld, *Unfolding Destinies: The Untold Story of Peter Fleming and the Auca Mission* (Grand Rapids, Mich.: Zondervan, 1990); Mary H. Wallace, compiler, *Profiles of Pentecostal Missionaries* (Hazelwood, Mo.: World Aflame Press, 1986); Anna Marie Dahlquist, *Burgess of Guatemala* (Langley, B.C.: Cedar Books, 1985); Andres Kung, *Bruce Olson, Missionary or Colonizer?* (Chappaqua, N.Y.: Christian Herald Books, 1981); John Dekker, *Torches of Joy* (Westchester, Ill.: Crossway Books, 1985).

76. Char Miller, *Fathers and Sons, The Bingham Family and the American Mission* (Philadelphia: Temple University Press, 1982).

77. See, for example, John Leighton Stuart, *Fifty Years in China* (New York: Random House, 1954); Ralph E. Dodge, *The Revolutionary Bishop Who Saw God at Work in Africa: An Autobiography* (Pasadena, Calif.: William Carey Library, 1986); Don Richardson, *Peace Child* (Ventura, Calif.: Regal Books, 1974); Loren Cunningham, *Is that Really You, God?* (Seattle: Chosen Books/Baker Books, 1984).

78. A few that have been published in recent years include E. G. Ruoff, ed., *Death Throes of a Dynasty: Letters and Diaries of Charles and Bessie Ewing, Missionaries to China* (Kent, Ohio: Kent State University Press, 1990); Elsie Landstrom, ed., *Hyla Doc: Surgeon in China Through War and Revolution, 1924–1949* (Fort Bragg, Calif.: Q.E.D. Press, 1991); Ralph Covell, *W. A. P. Martin: Pioneer of Progress in China* (Washington D.C.: Christian University Press, 1978); Edward V. Gulick, *Peter Parker and the Opening of China* (Cambridge, Mass.: Harvard University Press, 1973); Adrian A. Bennett, *Missionary Journalist in China: Young J. Allen and His Magazines, 1860–1883* (Athens, Ga.: University of Georgia Press, 1983); Stephen Endicott, *James G. Endicott: Rebel Out of China* (Toronto: University of Toronto Press, 1980); Irwin T. Hyatt, Jr., *Our Ordered Lives Confess: Three Nineteenth-Century American Missionaries in East Shantung* (Cambridge, Mass.: Harvard University Press, 1976).

79. See for example Daniel M. Davies, *The Life and Thought of Henry Gerhard Appenzeller (1858–1902): Missionary to Korea* (Lewiston, N.Y.: E. Mellen Press, 1988); Char Miller, ed. *Selected Writings of Hiram Bingham—Missionary to the Hawaiian Islands, 1814–1869: To Raise the Lord's Banner* (Lewiston, N.Y.: E. Mellen Press, 1988). Mellen Press also plans to publish Appenzeller's collected writings.

80. See for example C. Howard Hopkins, *John R. Mott, 1865–1955* (Grand Rapids, Mich.: Eerdmans, 1979); John Coventry Smith, *From Colonialism to World Community: The Church's Pilgrimage* (Philadelphia: Geneva Press, 1982): and Marilee Pierce Dunker, *Days of Glory, Seasons of Night* (Grand Rapids Mich.: Zondervan, 1984).

81. American historians who are fluent in languages other than English are also beginning to evaluate the influence of American missionaries in disseminating modern ideas that affected larger issues in nonwestern cultures. For example, historian Richard Elphick is working on a manuscript that analyzes how missionaries inserted liberal ideas into twentieth-century South African political discourse.

A critical usage of mission sources can also reveal how indigenous Christians opposed mission policy and learned from the unwitting missionaries ways to promote their own independent agendas. See the case study by Myra Dinnerstein, "The American Zulu Mission in the Nineteenth Century: Clash over Customs," *Church History* 45 (2) (1976): 235–46; Dana L. Robert, "The Methodist Struggle Over Higher Education in Fuzhou, China, 1877–1883," *Methodist History* 34 (April 1996): 173–89.

82. Masao Takenaka, *Reconciliation and Renewal in Japan* (New York: Friendship Press, 1957).

83. Sushil Madhava Pathak, *American Missionaries and Hinduism: A Study of their Contacts from 1813 to 1910* (Delhi: Munshiram Manoharlal, 1967).

84. Chai-sik Chung, "Tradition and Ideology: Korea's Initial Response to Christianity from a Religious and Sociological Perspective." *Asia Munhwa* 4 (1988): 115–46. Another article by Chung on the themes of missions, westernization, and interfaith relationships is "Confucian–Protestant Encounter in Korea: Two Cases of Westernization and De-Westernization," in Peter K. H. Lee, ed., *Confucian–Christian Encounters in Historical and Contemporary Perspective* (Lewiston, N.Y.: E. Mellen Press, 1991), 399–433.

85. H. K. Barpujari, *The American Missionaries and North-East India, 1836–1900* (Delhi: Spectrum Publishers, 1986).

86. Unlike mission history that sought to show "results," critical studies by indigenous historians familiar with American and indigenous sources sometimes demonstrate that the influence of decades of mission work was modest. In her study of American Board missionaries among the Bulgarians, for example, Tatyana Nestorova shows that Bulgarians took from the missionaries what would promote their national interest and ignored what else the missionaries had to offer. Tatyana Nestorova, *American Missionaries Among the Bulgarians: 1858–1912* (Boulder, Colo.: East European Quarterly, 1987).

87. Christiaan Rudolph De Wet, "The Apostolic Faith Mission in Africa: 1908–1980. A Case Study in Church Growth in a Segregated Society" (Ph.D. dissertation, University of Cape Town, 1989); G. C. Oosthuizen, *The Birth of Christian Zionism in South Africa* (KwaDlangezwa, South Africa: University of Zululand, 1987).

88. Gerald John Pillay, "A Historico-Theological Study of Pentecostalism as a Phenomenon within a South African Community," (Ph.D. dissertation, Rhodes University, 1983).

89. Daryl M. Balia, "Bridge Over Troubled Waters: Charles Pamla and the Taylor Revival in South Africa," *Methodist History* 30 (January 1992): 78–90. For an analysis of how the Taylor Revival fit into the African social context, see

the earlier article by Wallace G. Mills, "The Taylor Revival of 1866 and the Roots of African Nationalism in the Cape Colony," *Journal of Religion in Africa* 8 (2) (1976): 105–122.

90. Negative use of missionary history is sometimes taken as the starting point for reflection by theological pluralists. See for example John Hick, "The Non-Absoluteness of Christianity," in *The Myth of Christian Uniqueness: Toward a Pluralistic Theology of Religions,* ed. Hick and Paul F. Knitter (Maryknoll, N.Y.: Orbis Books, 1987), 16–36. Ideological use of mission history fails to acknowledge that a source of the western pluralistic theological enterprise was the mission experience itself.

91. R. Pierce Beaver, "Missionary Motivation through Three Centuries," in Jerald C. Brauer, ed., *Reinterpretation in American Church History* (Chicago: University of Chicago Press, 1968), 113–51 (113).

13

EXPERIENCE AND EXPLANATION IN TWENTIETH-CENTURY AMERICAN RELIGIOUS HISTORY

❖ ❖ ❖

Richard Wightman Fox

I REMEMBER MY DISMAY a decade ago when a colleague, a historian of early modern Europe, gruffly remarked that all twentieth-century American historiography was "journalism." It was nothing but the reporting of "current events," he said. Having learned to take fright at the mere term "journalistic," academia's favored term of execration, I leapt to the defense of my field and rattled off the names of excellent books on the twentieth century. I confidently rebutted his comment, but all the while the thought gnawed away inside me that the greatest historians of our day did seem to work in earlier periods. The history of early twentieth-century Progressivism or the New Deal had attracted many leading historians in the 1950s, but by the 1960s and 1970s the most interesting work seemed to be on such topics as Puritanism, slavery, or nineteenth-century women, immigrants, or laborers.

In recent years I have come to see the justice of my colleague's point. Historians of the twentieth century, it seems to me, have not typically felt their period as "past" in the same way that historians of earlier periods do. Their period really is "current"; it comprises events and institutions that form part of their own (at least imagined) lived experience. Of course historians of earlier periods can imagine their way into their own distant worlds. Edmund Morgan once told me he knew nothing about contemporary society because he lived in the eighteenth century. But I sense historians of the twentieth century have often been drawn to that period because they want to understand, and perhaps influence, the workings of power in their own society. They want history to serve the present instrumentally. They have a vested interest in fashioning a past continuous with the present—distinct from the present in the sense that the past had its own discrete events and institutions, but identical with the present in the sense that it comprised the very same sort of events and institutions. Past and present, subject to the same kinds of forces, occupying the same causal grid, can be knit together into a tapestry of readily comprehensible patterns. This is a familiarizing history. It may revere past accomplishments, or it may bewail past injustices. Either way it offers direct access to a past that can be of immediate service in present struggles or celebrations. Whether Arthur Schlesinger, Jr., is writing about JFK or FDR, he is celebrating the power of great leaders to inspire the people and to reform America by mastering political obstacles that would defeat lesser men.

Twentieth-century historiography is the last bastion within the academic historical profession of event- and institution-centered history. A new cultural history has made huge inroads in the historiography of earlier periods, and it is a history that often looks askance at the recounting of public events and the rise and fall of institutions. There are many ways to summarize what the new cultural history is about, since it is a rubric that includes many different and often contradictory tendencies. It includes, for example, a post-structuralist wing devoted to the analysis of language and discourse in their relation to knowledge and culture, and a narrative wing devoted to telling fine-grained stories that evoke the lived experience of the past. Narrative cultural history is often "essentialist," offering, for example, stories about the inexpungeable vitality or indelible identity of a particular individual or group. Language-centered cultural history, by contrast, is often anti-essentialist, nominalist; it challenges the conceptual foundations and linguistic conventions of essentialism by spotlighting the constructedness of such categories as "self," "identity," "race," or "nationality." What unifies the new cultural history, essentialist or not, is its interest in discerning "meanings" in the private as well as the public experience of the past, its turning away from the tracing of causes and effects in the public happenings of the past. It is about letting the past be alien to us, savoring our distance from it (a distance that may nevertheless serve present purposes by contrastively illuminating the "meaning" of our own time). It is not about seeing how we are connected to the past in a linear succession of events that stand in relation to one another as an occurrence stands to its consequences. It is not about explanation as much as it is about description, not about grasping the historian's traditional "change over time" as much as it is about experiencing our "difference" from other cultures.[1]

I am a big fan of much of the new cultural history, and increasingly I try to be a practitioner as well as a reader of it. Whatever we may think of it, however, there is no denying its growing power, even in twentieth-century historiography. It seems to correspond to the postprogressive temper of the times, in which the future is a very cloudy notion and the idea of "progress" toward it evokes yawns at best and outright fear at the worst—as in the expectation of ecological disaster that, along with the now somewhat displaced prediction of nuclear annihilation, has since the 1970s been perhaps the key animating myth (in the nonpejorative sense) on the progressive left. When it is the conservatives (such as the free-marketeers of the American Enterprise Institute) who sing of progress through economic development and the liberals who preach limits, a major break in the cultural episteme is underway. The liberals and leftists who predominate (by default, I think, not by conspiracy) in the academic humanities are increasingly wedded to a postmodern, antiprogressivist sensibility that promotes cultural history at the expense of political, diplomatic, and even social history. Cultural anthropology, which centers itself on the problem of translating one culture to another, has increasingly replaced empirical and theoretical sociology (the patient assembling of facts in the interest of explanatory precision) as the neighboring discipline that historians most revere as a model of inquiry.

Of course there are not only ideological reasons but much simpler chronological and demographic ones for the spread of culturalist assumptions to twentieth-century historiography. More of the twentieth century has been slipping into the past, and more and more historians of the twentieth century have lived all of their lives in the last half of the century. Most of our present graduate students have lived theirs entirely in the last third of the century; their parents' earliest memories are now often of the 1950s. An approach to history that stresses the distance between the historians' own world and their subject of inquiry is bound to make sense to the younger generation of historians of the twentieth-century United States.

A fine example of the new cultural history in the field of twentieth-century American religion is Robert Orsi's *Madonna of 115th Street*. This is an anthropological history, in which readers are invited to confront a culture alien to their experience. In this book Orsi's style of cultural history is more-or-less essentialist: he is giving us the "real" Italian and Italian-American experience, uncovering the deep source of spiritual bonds in the Italian "domus," welcoming us to a warmer, rooted world and encouraging us to look for and cultivate such roots in our own traditions. He is not as self-conscious about method, language, or cultural constructedness as poststructuralist cultural historians are. Orsi defamiliarizes only to reach for a deeper, fuller familiarity; distance between past and present is both preserved (the Italian-American community remains cut off from the mainstream culture of the present) and overcome (if we care to enter the living world of the domus, the past can come to life for us, enrich our experience in the present; we can live imaginately in a connected world).[2]

To take the measure of the vast gap that separates Orsi's approach from traditional work in twentieth-century American religious history, it is helpful to contrast it to the most up-to-date version of the traditional perspective, the ongoing series of volumes on *Modern American Religion* by Martin Marty. Marty's work is quintessentially the history of events and leading personalities. It is a chronicle of public developments with the implicitly upbeat message that we may be perplexed, but not unto despair: with faith in the future we will survive, and perhaps even flourish, as we confront events and rebuild structures just as our forbears did. Like the work of Arthur M. Schlesinger, Jr., in political history, this is familiarizing history, history that opens doors and allows us to walk briskly into the past, where we can rub shoulders and converse with the leading personalities of the day. And it improves on the institutional history of the previous generation by its resourceful quest for inclusivity: there is now attention to women and blacks, Jews and Catholics. The same can be said of William R. Hutchison's Protestant establishment project: no book on that theme conceived a generation earlier would have thought of including essays on women and religious outsiders. Marty narrates public events and personalities, the Hutchison project analyzes public institutions, but both are driven by the controlling sense that the twentieth century is our world and our responsibility: if we are equal to the task we can learn from its history and help mold its future.[3]

Marty's *Modern American Religion* is an especially pivotal contemporary document because its liberal openness to diversity and pluralism gives an ironic boost to the cultural approach to religion that Marty himself eschews. His own Protestant liberalism—a conviction that all viewpoints deserve a hearing, that a free exchange of ideas will ultimately serve the cause of justice and equality, that religion has nothing to fear from secularity but in fact is best served by regular infusions of secular distrust of religious pomposity—remains an unexamined ("privileged," in the current academic phrase) starting point and controlling sentiment. In his analysis pluralism is not pushed to the point of relativizing liberalism—seeing it as one perspective among others—but is appropriated, in a subtle apologetic gesture (in the sense of Christian apologetics), as a feather in the liberal cap. Yet Marty's fundamental openness unlocks a door he does not himself pass through: the door to a culturalist perspective that approaches liberalism, like all other faiths, as one pathway to truth that can claim no special exemption from historical relativity.

From the standpoint of scholarly consumption, Orsi's style of essentialist cultural history in *Madonna of 115th Street* offers two distinct advantages: first, that of retaining the affirmative, inspirational, and celebratory impulse embedded in Marty's progressive-minded church history, and second, that of embracing the new-fangled, anthropological defamiliarization of cultural history (a defamiliarizing circumscribed in Orsi's

Madonna by the containment chamber of essentialism). The historical profession as a whole will continue to encourage work like Orsi's, I suspect, because cultural religious history has a much less sectarian aroma about it. An Orsi-style religious history, focused on the life of a single ethnic neighborhood, may seem more particularist and therefore marginal than a Marty-style history, which stresses large-scale public events occurring on the boundary of the religious and secular, but it seems to me the reverse is true. Orsi's defamiliarizing gesture, his (at least initial) standpoint of distance from his subject, makes his work, and work like his, much more persuasive to secularists who already feel a normative distance from religion. Religion seen as a force in the world of political events and social institutions (Marty) can seem intrusive, uppity; religion interpreted as a nonconventional experience can be safely exoticized, while still being probed and exploited for its revealing disclosures about "culture."[4]

It may be that religious history of *any* sort will be unable for a long time to come to mount the main waves of twentieth-century historiography. Most historians may continue to consider religion to have been unimportant in twentieth-century America, may indeed keep wanting it to have been unimportant. How else can we explain, for example, the absence of work by intellectual or cultural historians on such figures as Paul Tillich or Aimee Semple McPherson, or by mainstream (as opposed to divinity school–based) institutional historians on, say, the Student Volunteer Movement or the Rockefeller Foundation's Institute for Social and Religious Research? Twentieth-century religious history may appear to junior professors and graduate students in history departments to be just about as marketable as the history of sports or agriculture.[5] For the time being we may have to rely on journalists, religionists, and anthropologists for probing analyses of the culture of twentieth-century American religion, and on theologians for studies of twentieth-century American religious ideas.[6]

Yet the culturalist turn among mainstream secular historians offers an opportunity for religious history to push toward the center of the historical enterprise, and Robert Orsi's work on twentieth-century Catholics is beginning to find its Protestant equivalents. Leigh Eric Schmidt's *Consumer Rites,* a study of "the buying and selling of American holidays," is an exemplary case in point. A version of one of the book's chapters, "The Easter Parade: Piety, Fashion, and Display," was published in the journal *Religion and American Culture,* the founding of which in 1990 marked an important opening for a relativizing, nonapologetic, anthropological culturalism in twentieth-century religious history.

Schmidt's essay on Easter brilliantly illuminates the complex commingling of religious and secular habits in the lived experience of the late nineteenth- and early twentieth-century northern Protestant middle class. Like Orsi, Schmidt invites us to enter a world we thought we knew—

since we assumed it was rather like our world—and shows us its particular texture, indeed its particular odor, since this was a culture zealously devoted to its flowers. Schmidt defamiliarizes twentieth-century culture by tying it closely to Victorianism, letting his analysis flow back and forth across the barrier of 1900. He shows us, rather than merely telling us, that gender was at the heart of the middle-class experience: Easter was a women's festival, a holiday that permitted Protestant women to do what Catholic women had long been doing, namely, adorning themselves and their places of worship. Moreover, he makes clear that the commercialization of Easter derived from its ritualization as a Protestant festival; retailing the festival took on a life of its own, but economic interests succeeded in selling Easter only because it was so deeply rooted in popular piety.[7]

The strength of Schmidt's account is its thick description of Victorian Protestant life; its weakness is its evasion of explanation. Schmidt does not push his analysis toward posing and answering the fundamental question that would tie the experiences of his Victorian flower arrangers and paraders to our own: What is the character and course of secularization in modern American culture? Is it possible in the end even to distinguish secular from religious experience? If it is not possible to do so today, or in Victorian America, when was it ever possible to do so? Schmidt's analysis makes plain that in Victorian America secularity did not simply replace religiosity but drew its strength and its particular character from it. That finding raises the critical problem of how to explain the development of secularity in American history. The challenge for cultural historians such as Schmidt will be to continue probing and portraying the experience of earlier generations while also attempting to explain how their experiences turned into ours.

In my own work I am trying to meet this challenge by examining the development of liberal Protestant culture in the nineteenth and twentieth centuries. I am endeavoring to shed light on the lived experience of religion while also addressing the key question that has driven the traditional historiography of twentieth-century American Protestantism in recent years. It is the same question that has bedeviled liberal Protestant churchpeople over the last generation: what happened over the course of the century to liberal Protestant religious and cultural hegemony? What is the meaning of the rise of evangelicalism in general and of the Christian right in particular? Sometimes this scholarship is driven by institutional, confessional, and personal soul-searching (how do we explain "our" loss, how do we get back our bearings or our influence?), but it is also frequently driven by a broader unsettling and disbelief at what can still seem to many of us a very sudden turn of events. A quarter-century ago it seemed obvious to most observers that Reinhold Niebuhr and Paul Tillich were by general cultural acclamation the uncontested religious authorities, and Billy Graham was (as Niebuhr regarded him during Graham's 1957 New York revival) fundamentally unserious, a hick and a huckster whose prime aspiration was to graze with presidents on lush fairways.

Liberalism was taken for granted as the political faith of any reasonable educated person. One might prefer Kennedy to Johnson, or (Eugene) McCarthy to any Kennedy, but Goldwater was sinister as well as laughable; he would eagerly drop hydrogen bombs on children clutching daisies, as a Johnson political advertisement implied. The ideological world that many of us assumed was well cemented only a few short decades ago has crumbled before our eyes. It is natural that we would devote considerable scholarly resources and existential energy to trying to explain what happened to liberalism in general, and to liberal Protestantism in particular, and to account for and assess the meaning of the new wave of evangelicalism.

Explaining the decline of liberal Protestantism and the rise of evangelicalism is a very complicated task, and rather than attempt a full explanation here, I will make a few comments about this question and then try to make a case for a particular research approach to the question that combines the traditional interest in explanatory history with the narrative, literary, and descriptive inclinations of the new cultural history. The whole question of "decline," first of all, must continue to be problematized. There is no denying the steep drop in membership suffered by the liberal mainstream churches since the 1970s, and no gainsaying the monumental fact that sometime in the twenty-first century—despite the explosive growth of evangelical Protestant groups—Protestantism will become for the first time a minority religion in the United States. But percentage decline in church membership does not automatically signify a corresponding loss in cultural power or prestige. Conservatives fighting a "culture war" today against liberal forces in the university, the press, public agencies, and foundations are not tilting at imaginary targets. I suspect they are right that liberal, and liberal Protestant, values are entrenched in those powerful places no matter how severe liberal losses may be in the pews. Indeed, a key paradox of liberal Protestantism—one that must be a cornerstone of any history of liberal Protestantism—is that its goal has always been, in part, to sanctify the secular, to bring forth out of the natural and human worlds the divine potential contained within them. Secularization can be seen, in some of its forms, as a sign of success for liberal Protestantism, not a marker of defeat.[8]

My sense, furthermore, is that the "decline" of liberal Protestantism should be traced to the 1920s at least, even though Reinhold Niebuhr, Paul Tillich, John Bennett, and others were still to come. I believe that Niebuhr and Tillich effected a Great Confirmation of the secularizing tendency that raced through liberal Protestantism after World War I. With their extraordinary dialectical skills they could manage to keep the two faces of the liberal Protestant coin—one secular/natural, the other religious/divine—in play simultaneously. But because many of their listeners were not equally skilled at or tolerant of paradoxical thinking, and because their own versions of Christianity tended toward pluralism (as in Niebuhr's opposition to evangelization among the Jews) and rationalism (for all Niebuhr's correct insistence that he was also a biblicist), they helped erode the already weakened link between liberalism and evangelicalism, a link that had given liberal Protestantism its culture-shaping power up through the early twentieth century.

Niebuhr underwent a poignant experience of soul-searching in the 1920s that can stand as a compelling microcosmic marker for the cultural fissure between liberalism and evangelicalism. This split was both a biographical event in individual lives—one can find it happening in many instances in the nineteenth century, just as one can see it in the late twentieth century, as in Randall Balmer's televised self-disclosure in *Mine Eyes Have Seen the Glory*—but in the 1920s it seems to have been a culture-wide happening with a special impact on public consciousness. Sherwood Eddy, a paradigmatic liberal evangelical, tried in 1924 to recruit Niebuhr to join a team of evangelists who would tour the colleges (Henry Van Dusen, fresh out of Union Seminary, was another vaunted recruit). Eddy knew that Niebuhr was unmatched at moving crowds, but he wondered if Niebuhr was committed enough to "personal work," to the saving of souls. A weekend retreat in New York with Eddy, Van Dusen, and the others brought Niebuhr to the realization that although personal work was admirable, it was neither where his talent lay nor the most pressing task that faced the church. Niebuhr determined to embrace the "social field," "to study," as he wrote to Eddy, "some of the implications of liberalism and see whether spiritual power cannot be developed squarely upon the basis of modernism." Personal piety was one thing, Niebuhr sensed, spiritual power another. If culture-wide spiritual power was still attainable at all, it would have to be grounded in modernism.[9]

This sequestering of liberalism from evangelism, followed by the choice of liberalism *over* evangelism, strikes me as a pivotal event in Niebuhr's life and in the life of the broader culture. (Anyone who knows Niebuhr must even be tempted momentarily by the now-heretical Great Man theory of history: whichever way Niebuhr goes, there goes the culture.) In the previous generation the leading liberals had not thought the choice necessary. Walter Rauschenbusch, for example, preached a gospel that, from a Niebuhrian standpoint, seems implausibly personal *and* social. He thought personal piety was central to the Christian life, but so was the "scientific" reform of society. For him "personality" was a concept whose reach was always both individual and collective; it expressed the highest ideal and the most powerful tool of the good life in every arena, from the smallest circle of family and friends to the largest field of fellowship. Indeed, there was no transformation of society that did not also entail a transformation of individual personality—a perception that harkened back to the antebellum revivalism of Charles Grandison Finney and that sparked the "secular" (but Protestant in origin and inspiration) liberalism of such progressives as Jane Addams, Randolph Bourne, and John Dewey from the 1890s through World War I (and in Dewey's case long beyond).[10]

The vision of Walter Rauschenbusch, who died in 1918, was emblematic of liberal evangelicalism at its peak. His commitment to reconstructing the personal as well as the social life, and his devotion to the Bible, to prayer, to evangelism (he was a great admirer of Dwight Moody), to the spread of love through all human relationships (he was blessed with an especially congenial companionate marriage, which may have promoted his rosiest reflections about the possibilities for communal fellowship), was combined with a radical critique of social injustice. His progressivism was closely akin to Debsian socialism in its emphasis on the needs and promise of the working class, its focus on the empowerment as opposed to the containment or disciplining of the masses. Other religious progressives could hold very different ideas about society and about reform—Washington Gladden or Richard T. Ely tended toward top-down managerialism, Josiah Strong tended toward nativist exclusionism—but their very significant differences could dissolve in the solvent of scientifically informed evangelism and keep them all together in the liberal movement. They could all assume that expertise and professionalism tied to Protestant moral vision would supply the energy and competence for social reconstruction.

Until World War I, that is. The war did not put an end to scientific professionalism—if anything the war gave it a boost by creating a national state hungry for innovative institutional controls—but it had a devastating impact on the belief that liberal ideals could be successfully preached by traditional evangelism, however closely tied it might be to scientific expertise. Reinhold Niebuhr has almost nothing in common with H. L. Mencken, but there is one important point of contact: the brash assault on sentimentality and conventional piety. Niebuhr, for all his rejection of Mencken's curmudgeonly cynicism, was at one with Mencken in bewailing the self-delusion of those who expected fine professions of love and good will to change the world. Each was seeking a tauter, tougher standpoint in a world beyond innocence. Of course Niebuhr did not abandon evangelism in the sense of ceasing to preach God's judgment upon society, but he did abandon Rauschenbusch's generation's fixation on the transformation of personality. And in the wake of Woodrow Wilson's performance at Versailles, he had no inclination to see the United States as a carrier of democratic virtue to the rest of the world—or to see American Christianity as a plausible carrier of the Christian gospel to the heathen. He thought it more likely that Christians from the rest of the world would some day bring the judgment of the Gospel upon a morally profligate and politically inept United States.

Liberal evangelism did not die a sudden death in 1920. It lingered on even into the 1930s and beyond in the work of Harry Emerson Fosdick and others, and it reemerged powerfully in the black churches during the civil rights movement. But in the white churches after World War I it was increasingly subject not only to the blistering assault of the Niebuhrian critics but to the equally telling, if much quieter, withdrawal of liberals who abandoned the churches altogether to work in secular pursuits. Robert Lynd, who got his B. D. from Union Theological Seminary and then marched out the church door into the profession of sociology (after a detour through advertising and free-lance social research), and Norman Thomas (who left the Presbyterian ministry to join and lead the Socialist Party) were among the most visible of thousands of other "apostates." They left the church, but it is an open question whether they left liberal Protestantism. By carrying liberal, moral reformism into the secular worlds of academia and politics, they were still decidedly about their father's business, as understood by the liberal Protestant tradition.

After 1920 liberalism increasingly meant secular liberalism, and liberal Protestantism increasingly dissolved into the surrounding liberal culture. Liberal Protestants tended to cede to conservatives a whole range of beliefs and practices: miracles, prayer, piety, hell, the devil, God as transcendent judge, missionary work (of the "soul-saving" kind). What they kept, in one way or another, was Jesus, and that is what ultimately separated them from secular liberals. It was clever of traditionalist J. Gresham Machen to suggest in 1923 that, since liberal Christianity was a new religion, liberal Protestants ought to found a new church rather than keep trying to take over the old one. But he admitted that liberal Christians were devoted to Jesus—much as their reduction of Jesus (in his view) to "the sage of Nazareth" struck him as a "cruel mockery." [11]

Garry Wills has recently pointed out that the Scopes Trial of 1925 is best understood not as a battle between liberalism and fundamentalism— the view that has come down to us from Mencken and *Inherit the Wind*—but a conflict between liberal modernism and liberal evangelism. The real loser in Tennessee was not fundamentalism (or, more precisely, traditionalist evangelicalism), which merely went underground to right itself after the lambasting it received from the enlightened northern press. The real loser was liberal evangelism. It was so completely defeated that it was expunged from liberal memory. Today nearly no one remembers that William Jennings Bryan was not a conservative fundamentalist but a liberal evangelical. "The Scopes trial," Wills writes, "comic in its circus aspect, left behind it something tragic: it sealed off from each other, in mutual incomprehension, forces that had hitherto worked together in American history. Bryan's career had been a sign of the possible integration of progressive politics and evangelical moralism." [12]

A satisfactory explanation for the "decline" of liberal Protestantism over the course of the twentieth century must concentrate in more depth than we have yet mustered on the split between liberalism and evangelicalism. As long as secular liberalism could persuasively occupy the cultural position of morally legitimizing public faith—as it did from the mid-1930s to the mid-1960s—the decline of liberal Protestantism could be ignored or discounted. Its rising numbers of adherents in the 1950s (at a time of general religious resurgence) could produce complacency even though evangelical denominations were growing faster. It was so obvious to educated people that only a science-friendly, secular-inclining liberal faith could retain plausibility in the modern world that there was no need for concern: Billy Graham could be safely snickered at. Vietnam, the war embraced and transformed by liberal, reformist expertise, brought secular liberalism—considered as a moral foundation for the good society—crashing to the ground. The resulting "public theological" vacuum would have to be filled either by a skeptical, antifoundational, pragmatic liberalism or by some kind of conservative faith—the secularized faith in western truth-statements of a William Bennett, Lynne Cheney, or Allan Bloom, or the Christian intellectualism or revivalism of the new fundamentalists or Pentecostals. Masses of Americans were not done yearning for miracles and wonders, even if children of the Enlightenment (including Bennett, Cheney, and Bloom) could do without them. In the 1970s and 1980s they flocked into old evangelical churches such as the southern Baptists, new community megachurches, independent Pentecostal temples, and such extra-Protestant Christian groups as the Mormons, Seventh-Day Adventists, and Jehovah's Witnesses.

In the remainder of this essay, I want to suggest that a cultural history of liberal Protestantism can contribute importantly to conceptualizing and explaining the "decline" of liberal Protestantism in the twentieth century. Remembering that liberal Protestantism can decline as a mass faith while retaining preponderant cultural power, and that liberal Protestantism "succeeds" as much as it "fails" when it declines as a mass faith (since one of its prime goals is to encourage the embrace of the secular and the natural worlds), we can still seek to explain why it should have declined as a mass faith. My sense is that it declined for two reasons. Many Christians, first of all, took its validation of secularism seriously and became secularists *tout court*. Many others were drawn away by faiths that persisted in seeing the divine–human encounter as a site of the miraculous.

One of the most significant aspects of Reinhold Niebuhr's work lies in its validation of secularism. He understood the appeal of secularism from the inside, and undertook to argue as a Christian apologist that a Judeo-Christian perspective was superior to pure secularism because it offered what was best about secularism—its critical-minded suspicion of all pious claptrap, all groundless idealism—in an even purer form. Even secularism was too sentimental, too contaminated by dreamy complacency. A stringent and uncompromising tough-mindedness led one inexorably, Niebuhr imagined, to the trustingness of Job and the expectancy of the early Christians. But Niebuhr's apologetic was in the end pluralistic, if not quite relativistic: all faiths were not equally valid in his view (only Christianity insisted on original sin, for example, a doctrine the truth of which was verified daily, he believed, in human experience), but the acquisition of faith was a process filled with historical and cultural contingencies. Just as a good Jew like Will Herberg should be encouraged to become a better Jew, not a Christian, so a good secular humanist like his Detroit mentor Fred Butzel should be venerated as a secular saint. The ultimate paradox and "scandal" of Christianity (God dying on the cross) might carry Niebuhr further in the spirit than any other faith, but that conviction had deep roots in his own experience, as another person's faith would be similarly rooted in a different experience. By depicting and validating Christianity as a no-nonsense realism, Niebuhr erected no-nonsense realism as a standard of ultimate judgment, and by that standard many of the most educated, cosmopolitan Americans found liberal Protestantism, by the early or mid-twentieth century, woefully wanting.

The second reason liberal Protestantism declined as a mass faith is that many people (for the most part many *other* people, less cosmopolitan, less highly educated) missed the aura of the transcendent and the miraculous, and the accompanying forms of piety, which evangelicalism stressed. For many decades of the late nineteenth and early twentieth century, I hypothesize, liberal churches would have continued, sometimes without knowing it, to appeal to the miraculous, to preserve evangelical sentiments, even as they touted the natural, the secular, the scientific, the social. The process of transition would have been halting in some places, precipitous in others. The full paradox of the transition, I sense, would lie here: many liberals would initially be able to give up the miraculous in one sphere (e.g., downgrade the New Testament miracles to symbolic stories) only by keeping the miraculous in (or extending it to) another sphere. Social science would be seen as capable of performing miracles. Preaching itself would be seen as miracle-working; the encounter between preacher and hearers would be singled out as sacramental.

Here is where a cultural history of liberal Protestantism can help answer the long-standing question of why liberal Protestantism declined. A cultural history can give us access not just to what people said they were doing but to what they may actually have been doing, sometimes in spite of themselves. My suspicion is that liberal Protestants surrendered the miraculous to traditionalist evangelicals not all at once, but in stages. The liberals always preserved their attachment to Jesus, but their "Jesus" may have evolved decisively from one stage to another. An earlier Jesus may have been much more the miracle-worker (even after his own New Testament miracles were discounted) than was a later Jesus, and the inspired preaching of the liberal pulpit may have supplied instances of miracle-working long after Jesus had, for liberals, lost much of his power to inspire social transformation or to effect miracles in the individual prayer life. When inspired preaching in the liberal pulpit declined in the middle third of the twentieth century, liberal Protestantism may have had no miracles left. There were certainly still inspired voices in the liberal ministry, but the cultural supports for great religious *or* secular oratory may have eroded to such a degree that orators of great power (William

Sloane Coffin, Jr., is a prime example) could no longer be heard. The most intellectually inclined audiences, trained by the early twentieth century to appreciate the critical-minded, scholarly truth-seeking of the universities, may have learned to distrust the wide-ranging amateurism of clerical truth-tellers. It was no longer possible to be a great learned preacher in the Henry Ward Beecher mode: knowing a little about an endless range of topics and presenting that knowledge in a language rich in classical and Shakespearean cadences and expressions. Or perhaps, still more simply, twentieth-century audiences increasingly lost the capacity to attend to challenging oral discourse of any sort.

In his 1956 autobiography, Harry Emerson Fosdick makes a very suggestive comment, one that points us in the right direction for investigating the actual lived experience of liberal Protestantism over the nineteenth and twentieth centuries. "What present-day critics of liberalism often fail to see," he writes, with obvious reference to his quarter-century-long standoff with Reinhold Niebuhr, "is its absolute necessity to multitudes of us who would not have been Christians at all unless we could thus have escaped the bondage of the then reigning [i.e., turn-of-the-century] orthodoxy." As a youth, Fosdick tells us, he was "morbidly conscientious, . . . weeping at night for fear of going to hell. . . . In those early days the iron entered my soul and the scene was set for rebellion against the puerility and debasement of a legalistic and terrifying religion." Liberalism offered Fosdick deliverance from arbitrary and tyrannical authority, as it had generations of secular and religious Europeans and Americans—who resisted not only the unpredictable Calvinist God, but the unjust infringements of kings and queens, metaphysical abstractions, and cultural proscriptions on unconventional behavior. The companionate God revealed in Jesus was Fosdick's personal savior. If Fosdick's experience was typical, as he asserts it was by using the first-person plural to describe those who resisted the "then-reigning orthodoxy," then the liberals of his generation not only *kept* Jesus when they abandoned orthodoxy, but kept a Jesus whom they met in prayer and who brought them to a new life. For these liberals personal piety was not to be surrendered to traditionalists; devotion to Jesus was not a matter of debate but of survival.[13]

My sense is that whether or not Fosdick's experience was typical in 1900 (conservative orthodoxy was scarcely unbroken in 1900), it probably was typical of first-generation migrants from orthodoxy to liberalism throughout the nineteenth and twentieth centuries. Thinking chronologically leads us astray here. Liberalism was not like a single wave that gathered over the nineteenth century and then broke at some distinct point in the nineteenth or twentieth. It was a current that flowed continuously and broke through different individual and institutional levees at different times. For that matter, it was and is a current that also sometimes *stopped* flowing in particular places. Moreover, traditionalism is not just a stationary (dark) terrain that either is or is not flooded (with light) by liberalism; traditionalism is a contending current in its own right. We need to know more about conversions from liberalism to traditionalism within Protestantism, although there may have been more of them from liberalism to Catholicism.

Fosdick, born in 1878, may have had more in common with a liberal like Henry Ward Beecher, born in 1818, than he did with a liberal like Washington Gladden, born in 1836, or Reinhold Niebuhr, born in 1892. Beecher was another first-generation migrant to liberalism. He needed deliverance from his father Lyman's evangelical orthodoxy, and like Fosdick he preserved an attitude of personal piety toward Jesus, his savior. (He also kept an open mind about Jesus's miracles.) Gladden and Niebuhr, by contrast, deemphasized personal piety and venerated Jesus not as a personal savior but as a model of social concern (Gladden) or as the "God-man" who gave to Christianity its ultimate paradox, its scandal of particularity (Niebuhr). Neither Gladden nor Niebuhr had a crisis of faith as a youth; their liberalism came to them as an inheritance. They had no need for a Jesus who performed miracles because they had no need for miracles, no need for rescue from the young Fosdick's "terrifying religion." They needed a Jesus who could spark people to unprecedented feats of sacrifice for social reconstruction, or a Jesus who could stand for the impossible possibility of the reign of love.

Gladden's *Reminiscences* (1909) tells the story of a liberal upbringing. Religion was never "thrust" upon him; "my personality was respected, perhaps too carefully." As a result he never had a religious experience, though he was steeped in the Bible: as a child he heard it read through four or five times in its entirety at evening readings in his home. Gladden knows that something was lost when religion became less "intense," "fervid," and "self-centered"—less preoccupied with personal salvation—but in 1909 he considers it unwise to attempt to restore it. Like Niebuhr in his encounter with Sherwood Eddy in 1924, Gladden turned away from "individual pietism" and toward "a religion that laid hold upon life with both hands, and proposed, first and foremost, to realize the Kingdom of God in this world." For a devotee of social salvation like Gladden, Jesus became an indispensable personal model for a particular kind of career.[14]

It was not just that Jesus provided ethical and ideological inspiration for the reform enterprise by preaching love as the rule of all of life, individual and social. It was also that Jesus showed how one could personally love all humanity, however "high" or "low." What may have been distinctive to Gladden's generation of religious progressives, what may demarcate their era from Niebuhr's, was their overweening desire to make contact with the working class (while avoiding contamination by it). The ever-more-immigrant, Catholic, and Jewish working class was increasingly regarded by native-born Protestants as an alien bacterium in the body politic. The driving goal of a progressive like Gladden was to show—as Jesus had shown in associating with prostitutes and other outcasts—that we are all children of God and to show, by extension, that we are all one American people. His autobiography is unself-consciously self-congratulatory when he describes actually being *listened to* by working-class members of a Cleveland audience in 1886 when he addressed them on the labor question. It is a scene that is repeated perfectly in Charles Sheldon's *In His Steps* (1896), where the Rev. Henry Maxwell becomes a mediator par excellence after overcoming his terror at entering the foul working-class district and is transformed there into an oratorical hero. It is a ritual, liminal moment that appears to be common in early twentieth-century clerical autobiography.[15]

Sheldon's pastor, like Gladden, needs Jesus as a model of courage in the face of social division and social isolation (his own personally depressing isolation from the working class, which mirrors the socially dangerous isolation of the working class from the rest of society). But unlike Gladden, Maxwell discovers a life of prayer, piety, and intense religious experience as he tries to quell his anxiety about preaching to the hoi polloi. He becomes an evangelical *as well as* a liberal Christian: he achieves a (politically liberal) critical standpoint on the world around him *and* undergoes a personal (evangelical) transformation in the encounter with Jesus. Paul Boyer has rightly noted that Sheldon lacks much of a social vision; he keeps posing the question "What would Jesus do?" but offers no coherent answer. Sheldon hedges by having the Rev. Maxwell tell his parishioners that following Jesus means deciding for oneself, in conscience, what Jesus would do. Each individual, Maxwell concedes, will of necessity answer the question differently. Boyer correctly observes that in the end Sheldon's outlook of pained concern about social division amounts to a sanctification of bourgeois individualism. Yet I think Boyer underestimates the importance of Sheldon's reassertion of evangelicalism. It is in prayer and sacrifice, according to Sheldon, that Maxwell overcomes his routinized, dessicated existence. Jesus is indispensable not because his law of love can be readily applied to all social situations, supplying the outline of a social program, but because he makes miracles happen: a mediocre preacher like Maxwell is transformed into a prophet of justice and reconciliation.[16]

By the early twentieth century, most liberals probably regarded Sheldon's liberal evangelicalism as quaint, unserious because insufficiently scientific. By the 1920s, if not well before, the liberal vanguard was in Reinhold Niebuhr's modernism—a place from which the faith of a Sherwood Eddy or a Henry Maxwell looked spiritually sappy. But even at this point Jesus remained for most liberals crucial as a personal model, and not just as an ideological (ethical and political) ancestor who put love over law, not even just as the great advocate of "personality" over impersonality in human relations (though this is what was most often said about Jesus by liberal modernists). If we look at the rash of liberal writing about Jesus in this period, we discover that Jesus also offered a model of the exemplary life course. Even if his own New Testament miracles were suspect, even if he was not so likely any more to meet a person in prayer and there bring a person to new life, he presented a picture of how to live one's life. This modeling might for the most part be social, as Gladden and Maxwell had grasped it: Jesus was a pure democrat in all his relations and could inspire modern activists to resist social exclusions as well as their own lethargy in the face of social injustice. But it could also be personal. Jesus took his own life choices so seriously, was so earnest about the question how best to realize himself, that critical-minded modernists could be inspired in making their own difficult moves through adulthood.

At least since the publication of Adolf Harnack's *Das Wesen des Christentums* in 1900 (the English translation was published as *What is Christianity?* in 1901), liberal Christians had combined a critical–historical analysis of Gospel narratives with a veneration of Jesus as prototype of the modern man. Still reverencing Jesus as the indispensable foundation of the faith, they imagined him not only as the peerless embodiment of the ideal of personality (the move of an earlier generation of liberals eager to safeguard his divinity while stressing his humanity) but as the model of the self-conscious, earnest individual taking charge of his life. This modernizing of Jesus passed unnoticed in liberal circles because liberal writers were so busy upbraiding popularizers (such as Bruce Barton in *The Man Nobody Knows* [1925]) for *their* modernizing of Jesus. But Barton's sincere if comical effusions—if Jesus said he was about his father's "business," that meant he was a "businessmen"—let liberal critics off easy, since they got to focus on the splinter in a Barton's eye rather than the two-by-four in their own.

As Henry Cadbury pointed out in *The Peril of Modernizing Jesus* (1937), even such a careful scholar as Shirley Jackson Case fell victim to the fallacy of anachronism by unintentionally inducting Jesus into the ranks of the modern. Case thought he was resisting the liberal, Harnackian tendency to lift Jesus out of his concrete ancient Jewish culture, but he was in fact all the while persisting in a very basic liberal gesture. Liberals regarded the modern world, at its best, as a universal culture, unbesmirched by local, parochial allegiances. It was the product of long centuries of progress, during which one superstition after another was supplanted by enlightened thought and action. Jesus, to be God or the Son of God, must be enlightened too, not in his humanity just a premodern Near Eastern Jewish peasant. The scandal of particularity had its limits: God could be crucified on a cross or allow his Son to be sacrificed on the cross, but he could not be culturally circumscribed by the mentality of first-century primitives. Case's rejection of the modern appropriation of Jesus stopped just short of its announced goal. He supplied a dense cultural context for Jesus' life, but could not escape the bedrock liberal need to have Jesus endorse a modern universalism. So he presented a Jesus who, for all the premodern content of his beliefs and practices, was a reasoned deliberator about his major life choices. Jesus was calmly detached as he made his way through adulthood, not rash or impulsive; he weighed his choices carefully (rather than, say, submitting his will to that of his Father). Case gave Jesus much of the ancient Near Eastern *content* of his life, but framed that life in modern *form*.[17]

Much further work needs to be done on the changing motifs of the liberal Protestant encounter with Jesus over the course of the last century. That cultural as well as theological inquiry will help answer the question of why in the twentieth century liberal Protestantism has ebbed as a social institution even as it has retained substantial ideological clout. So will further investigation of other cultural practices, such as the liberal experience of oratory. As the scholarly wheel of fashion (and fortune) turns toward the descriptive evocation of past culture and experience, we can hope that long-standing issues of historical explanation will still receive new illumination.

NOTES

1. A similar analysis is developed at greater length in the "Introduction" to Richard Wightman Fox and T. J. Jackson Lears, eds., *The Power of Culture: Critical Essays in American History, 1820–1980* (Chicago, 1993). On the reemergence of "description" as a respectable form of historical writing alongside "explanation," see Alan Megill, "Recounting the Past: 'Description,' Explanation, and Narrative in Historiography," *American Historical Review* 94 (June 1989): 627–53.

2. Orsi, *The Madonna of 115th Street* (New Haven, 1988). Other recent books on the cultural history of twentieth-century American religion include Paul Boyer's *When Time Shall Be No More: Prophecy Belief and Modern American Culture* (Cambridge, 1992) and Robert Gambone's *Art and Popular Religion in Evangelical America, 1915–1940* (Knoxville, 1989). Neither is framed, however, in Orsi's anthropological mode, and neither, therefore, exemplifies the "new" cultural history. Thomas Cole's *The Journey of Life: A Cultural History of Aging in America* (New York, 1992) is a hybrid of new cultural history (in its superb opening examination of "meanings" in the history of aging) and conventional historical research and argument; it includes extended treatment of religion in relation to aging. A book only partially about religion which comes much closer to the new cultural history is (journalist!) A. G. Mojtabai's *Blessed Assurance: At Home with the Bomb in Amarillo, Texas* (Boston, 1986). Orsi's recent book *Thank You, St. Jude: Women's Devotion to the Patron Saint of Hopeless Causes* (New Haven, 1996) appeared too late for consideration in this essay. It marks a new departure in American religious history because of the care with which Orsi listens to the voices of his subjects, and because of his self-consciousness about his own standpoint. See my review essay "Speak of the Devil: Popular Religion in American Culture," *American Literary History*, forthcoming.

3. Martin E. Marty, *Modern American Religion, Volume I: The Irony of It All, 1893–1919* (Chicago, 1986), *Volume II: The Noise of Conflict, 1919–1941* (Chicago, 1991) and *Volume III: Under God, Indivisible, 1941–1960* (Chicago, 1996); William R. Hutchison, ed., *Between the Times: The Travail of the Protestant Establishment in America, 1900–1960* (Cambridge, 1989).

4. The enthusiastic response garnered among secular historians by Ramón Gutiérrez, *When Jesus Came, the Corn Mothers Went Away* (Stanford, 1991), may offer support for my contention, since he approaches the religion of the Indians and the Spanish colonists the way an anthropologist would. On the other hand, Gutiérrez's book may have proved palatable (and prize-winning) in the profession as a whole because it is really two books in one: a bold anthropological reconstruction of gendered *mentalités,* and a highly conventional, empirical, history of political events and social institutions. For many historians, the latter "book" (perhaps the original dissertation) may have compensated for the former one; or to choose a religious metaphor, the fact-gathering second book may have been Gutiérrez's penance for the transgressive constructivism of the first one.

5. Can it be accidental that the authors of recent books on McPherson (Daniel Mark Epstein, *Sister Aimee: The Life of Aimee Semple McPherson* [New York, 1993]) and Billy Sunday (Robert A. Bruns, *Preacher: Billy Sunday and Big-Time American Evangelism* [New York, 1992]), along with Robert Gambone *(Art and Popular Religion),* all work outside of academia? If the dust jackets of their books are still accurate, Epstein is a playwright and poet, Bruns a public historian at the National Archives, and Gambone an archivist for the Catholic archdiocese of St. Paul, Minnesota.

6. Samuel G. Freedman, *Upon This Rock: The Miracles of a Black Church* (New York, 1992); Carol J. Greenhouse, *Praying for Justice: Faith, Order, and Community in an American Town* (Ithaca, 1986); Robert L. Hall and Carol B. Stack, eds., *Holding on to the Land and the Lord: Kinship, Ritual, Land Tenure, and Social Policy in the Rural South* (Athens, Ga., 1982); Karen McCarthy Brown, *Mama Lola: A Vodou Priestess in Brooklyn* (Berkeley, 1991); Elmer S. Miller, *Nurturing Doubt: From Mennonite Missionary to Anthropologist in the Argentine Chaco* (Urbana, Ill., 1995); Wilhelm and Marion Pauck, *Paul Tillich: His Life and Thought* (New York, 1976).

7. Leigh Eric Schmidt, *Consumer Rites: The Buying and Selling of American Holidays* (Princeton, 1995), and "The Easter Parade: Piety, Fashion, and Display," *Religion and Culture* 4 (Summer 1994): 135–164. For a good example of a self-labeled "cultural" analysis that invokes the primacy of gender as an explanatory concept but stops short of showing the actual experience of it, see Gail Bederman, " 'The Women Have Had Charge of the Church Long Enough': The Men and Religion Forward Movement of 1911–1912 and the Masculinization of Middle-Class Protestantism," *American Quarterly* 41 (September 1989): 432–65. Bederman's interest in explaining why the centuries-long predominance of women among churchgoers suddenly became a problem in the early twentieth century— a question she answers schematically and tautologically by asserting that "feminized religion, tailored for laissez-faire capitalism, no longer answered the needs of the new modern [corporate] society" (437)—and leads her to deemphasize the question of whether the Men and Religion Movement Forword can tell us anything about the actual masculine experience of religion. An important article offering an alternative viewpoint to Bederman's is Margaret Marsh, "Suburban Men and Masculine Domesticity, 1870–1915," *American Quarterly* 39 (March 1988): 165–86. Marsh is not writing about religion, but her insights into the male experience of domestication can contribute a great deal to the debate over the feminization of American Protestantism.

8. Essential recent works on the fate of liberal Protestantism in the twentieth century, in addition to the already cited volumes by Marty and Hutchison, in-

clude Robert Wuthnow, *The Restructuring of American Religion: Society and Faith Since World War II* (Princeton, 1990), Wade Clark Roof and William McKinney, *American Mainline Religion: Its Changing Shape and Future* (New Brunswick, N.J., 1987), Robert Handy, *Undermined Establishment: Church-State Relations in America, 1890–1920* (Princeton, 1991), and James W. Lewis, *The Protestant Experience in Gary, Indiana, 1906–1975: At Home in the City* (Knoxville, 1992). On the rise of evangelicalism—fundamentalist and Pentecostal—a sampling of the best work can be found in George M. Marsden, *Fundamentalism and American Culture: The Shaping of Twentieth-Century Evangelicalism, 1870–1925* (New York, 1980) and *Reforming Fundamentalism: Fuller Seminary and the New Evangelicalism* (Grand Rapids, Mich., 1987); James Davison Hunter, *Evangelicalism: The Coming Generation* (Chicago, 1987); Grant Wacker, "Pentecostalism," in Charles H. Lippy and Peter W. Williams, *Encyclopedia of the American Religious Experience,* vol. 2 (New York, 1989); and Nancy T. Ammerman, "North American Protestant Fundamentalism," in Martin E. Marty and R. Scott Appleby, eds., *Fundamentalism Observed* (Chicago, 1991).

9. Richard Fox, *Reinhold Niebuhr: A Biography* (New York, 1985), 82; Randall Balmer, *Mine Eyes Have Seen the Glory: A Journey into the Evangelical Subculture in America* (New York, 1989). Balmer narrated this very personal story of a former evangelical's encounter with evangelical religion in a several-part public television documentary in 1992.

10. I undertake a fuller analysis of "personality" in liberal Protestantism in "The Culture of Liberal Protestant Progressivism, 1875–1925," *Journal of Interdisciplinary History* 23 (Winter 1993), 639–60.

11. J. Gresham Machen, *Christianity and Liberalism* (New York, 1923), 103.

12. Garry Wills, *Under God: Religion and American Politics* (New York, 1991), 106.

13. Harry Emerson Fosdick, *The Living of These Days* (New York, 1956), 35–36, 48, 66.

14. Washington Gladden, *Reminiscences* (Boston, 1909), 33, 36, 38–39, 63.

15. Gladden, *Reminiscences,* 300–03. Another example of clerical euphoria at overcoming the rift between social classes is William Jewett Tucker's description, in *My Generation: An Autobiographical Interpretation* (Boston, 1919), 70, of his success at getting his parishioners in Manchester, New Hampshire, to stop segregating themselves by status groups, the more affluent in front, the less affluent in back. He got several well-heeled families "to leave their pews below and colonize the [usually empty upstairs] galleries," which quickly produced "one homogeneous congregation."

16. Paul Boyer, "*In His Steps:* A Reappraisal," *American Quarterly* 23 (1971): 60–78. Boyer makes the excellent point that Sheldon's working class is both a threatening contaminant and a mysteriously vital entity; the middle-class is enticed by it even while abhorring it.

17. Henry J. Cadbury, *The Peril of Modernizing Jesus* (New York, 1937), 132. Case's *Jesus, A New Biography* (Chicago, 1927) is a classic of liberal Protestant scholarship. It is an important precursor of such contemporary studies as John Dominic Crossan's *The Historical Jesus: The Life of a Mediterranean Jewish Peasant* (New York, 1991) because it insists on the fullness of Jesus's immersion in his own (to us alien) mental universe. Case's "The Life of Jesus," in Gerald Birney Smith, ed., *Religious Thought of the Last Quarter Century* (New York, 1927), 26–41, is a very illuminating survey of liberal scholarship. It points out

that "every shade of modern activity which has behind it the inspiration of a religious impulse depicts Jesus in accordance with its own immediate interests and ideals. He is made the authoritative teacher for a modern social order, or even an exemplary social reformer himself. Some interpreters have made him the ideal pacifist, while others would see in him the ideal belligerent. At other times he becomes an ideal for the man of affairs, or the model for a Y.M.C.A. worker" (31–32).

PART V

PROTESTANTS
AND OUTSIDERS

14

ON JORDAN'S STORMY BANKS

Margins, Center, and Bridges in African American Religious History

Judith Weisenfeld

THE CHICAGO WORLD'S Columbian Exposition of 1893 was an event rife with difficult meanings for African Americans. Thirty years out of slavery and on the cusp of a new century, many African Americans were contemplating their place in history, searching the Bible for a key to their destiny, and looking to the future with an unmitigated faith in progress and in the "uplift of the race." At this exposition, a moment for the nation to evaluate the status of the world since Columbus and to consider the future, however, the organizers of this public self-examination vigorously excluded African American representation in the exhibits. Ida B. Wells and Frederick Douglass[1] embarked on a campaign to raise money at Chicago's black churches and to solicit donations from visitors to the fair in order to expose this injustice. From the Haitian exhibit, Wells distributed 10,000 copies of *The Reason Why the Colored American Is Not in the World's Columbian Exposition,* in which she, Douglass, Ferdinand Barnett, and others called into question the American claim to true democracy. Paradoxically, at the same time that Wells was protesting African American exclusion from the exhibits, other African American women were participating as speakers at various congresses taking place at the fair. Fannie Barrier Williams, part of the Chicago's growing black elite, addressed the World's Parliament of Religions at the fair, emphasizing to her audience that "it should be the province of religion to unite, and not to separate, men and women according to the superficial differences of race lines."[2]

The figure of Fannie Barrier Williams before the World's Parliament of Religions makes clear the difficulties of attempting to speak of a normative African American religious experience. Williams embodied many of the complexities of African American religious history. Her status as a woman, born in the north and educated in the public schools of the north, marks her as atypical of African Americans at the turn of the century. Through her career as an educator in the Reconstruction South and an activist in Chicago, however, Williams marked herself as an African American, and while she recognized and even insisted upon class distinctions among black Americans, she also lamented and celebrated commonalities of experience. Region, time period, denomination, class, gender, sexuality, color, education, and other factors have combined to ensure that there is no univalent African American religious experience. Williams's religious experience and history is *as* African American as the religious experience of a southern, poor, unschooled African American farmer or of any individual at any point on the spectrum of experience. With the reality of such variety within African American religious experience confronting us, where do we begin a systematic overview?

In reflecting on developments in the study of African American religious history and in attempting to chart new courses, it is useful to begin by placing these questions in the context of two broad themes. The first is marginality—experiences of literal or metaphorical distance from a constructed center or centers. Racial stratification has profoundly shaped the religious experience of all Americans, but most especially those whom the dominant caste view as inferior. Perhaps the most obvious example of the interplay of race and religion in African American experience is the tradition of religious justifications of slavery. That this repugnant institution could be seen by so many Americans of European descent as sanctioned by Christian teaching meant for most African Americans that this Christianity as understood and practiced by many whites was, at the very least, deeply skewed and even bankrupt. In the American context, the meaning of Christianity for blacks and whites could not be anything but disparate. Distanced from the exercise of power in the American system, the dominant African American interpretations of Christianity as liberative in this life were likewise distanced from the triumphalism of the white American moral drama. For African Americans in the context of slavery, this America bore within it no possibility of becoming God's new Israel, but loomed, surely, as Egypt the enslaver. The chasm in meaning is broad and deep. In this sense, then, marginality emerges as a forceful theme in any discussion of the experiences of black Protestants in America.[3]

Centrality, the second theme that frames this discussion, initially seems incompatible with our first theme, but a revisioning of both terms will make their congruence in this context clear. African American experiences are central to American religious history in that this larger story necessarily turns on the fluidity of cultures. Whereas we may not view white Protestant cultures as wholly discrete and unmediated across time and space, it is equally impossible to describe African American cultures as developing in isolation from other cultural streams in America. As a narrative of interactions, every element deserves its place at the center of the unfolding drama.[4] It is possible to view African American religious history as simultaneously "marginal" and "central" to the larger story of Protestantism in America. To exist on the periphery of white Protestantism and of the master narrative of American religious history implies disempowerment in some ways, but a profound empowerment in others. The margin has functioned as a space in which African Americans have been able to resist racial domination, to find a voice, and to create religious meaning from an African American perspective.[5] Yet from this space black Protestants have always been entwined with other Protestants and engaged religious and social questions central to the development of the nation, thus participating in and at times occupying the center. Moreover, whether or not African Americans were physically present at the "center" of the story at any given time or place, white Americans have often made black bodies and "blackness" present as a trope and put them to various uses. For white Protestant cultures, black Americans have always been available to represent "heathenism," unbridled sexuality, aggression, and a host of other imagined dangers to the Christian West. As the shadow of white Protestants, then, African Americans occupy the center in yet another symbolically charged way.[6]

To see African Americans as traversing this distance between margin and center in their religious lives and as being creative agents in both arenas illuminates aspects of both stories—African American and "American." To do this calls into question a narrative of American religious history that draws a narrow center and places impermeable boundaries around it. This kind of revisioning of "margin" and "center" with respect to the story of African American religious history functions to help us see black Protestants as full agents in their religious lives and in the larger religious history of the United States. Since it is far beyond the scope of this essay to examine developments in all areas of the study of African American religious history, I will limit discussion to five topics that raise significant questions for the field and that illustrate the larger themes of marginality and centrality: continuities with the African past(s), "the" black church, gender, religious culture, and bridges between black and white Protestants.

Continuities

The transmission and transformation of African traditions to African American traditions, religious and otherwise, is perhaps the most compelling question to consider in the field of African American religious history and, predictably, has prompted a heated scholarly debate over the years. How could enslaved Africans from so many different cultural backgrounds hold on to their traditions and perpetuate them under the hard lash of American slavery? To what extent can we see echoes of this past in the religious practices of black Protestants?

Two polarized critical camps developed early in the debate, with one side, exemplified by sociologist E. Franklin Frazier, contending that Africans could not have transferred their cultures intact because of the trauma of the middle passage, demographics in the Atlantic world, and the forcible separation on plantations of Africans from the same or related ethnic groups. From this point of view, African American cultural developments are uniquely American and lacking any African nuances. The other pole in the debate, represented forcefully by anthropologist Melville Herskovits, argues that Africans were indeed able to reestablish significant aspects of their cultural traditions in the Atlantic world, particularly in settings like Bahia, Brazil, and the Caribbean.[7] But where does this leave British North America and later African American Protestants?

It seems clear that a scholarly consensus has been reached on this question to the degree that the literature now embraces Herskovits's assertion that there are, indeed, some African influences in African American religious thought and practice. In part, the process of reaching a consensus on this issue required that the image of African religious traditions be "redeemed" as well and viewed by American scholars as *religion*. As progress was made on this front, scholars could also begin to see the African background as an important factor in the uniqueness of African American religious life. African Americans, in converting to Christianity, made that life their own and made the margin a productive arena for fashioning a religious life connecting the African past(s) and their American present(s). The critical consensus becomes less firm, however, as historians trace that influence and its weight in the black Protestant story. Here considerations of time and space become crucial factors in advancing the discussion.

What was the time frame for the development of African American religious cultures? At what point in the development of North America did the journey back and forth between margin and center begin for people of African descent? As Albert J. Raboteau and others have shown, large-scale conversions by African Americans to Christianity came with the revivals of the late eighteenth century.[8] But of what did the spirituality of enslaved African peoples in North American consist prior to the revivals if, as Raboteau asserts, African institutions were not transferred to the North American context intact? Here we find a range of answers. Raboteau sees a subdued African ethos as the grounding for African American Protestant experiences, an ethos manifest in folk belief and practice and in cultural forms like music. For Raboteau this African past plays a small, albeit not insignificant role, but he places much greater emphasis on the import of evangelical Christianity in the development of African American cultures.

Robert Farris Thompson insists upon strong connections between West African cultures and the Atlantic world cultures that develop in the age of slavery. He looks neither to formal rituals nor to institutions to trace this influence in North America, but to African aesthetic and philo-sophical principles manifested in folk practice. He finds features such as burial practices in the southern states, as well as in the Caribbean, that show a marked continuity with Kongo–Angola practices. These graves, covered with objects the deceased used last, decorated with shells, or situated under or adjacent to trees, conform to Kongo–Angola beliefs about the proper way to direct the spirit of the dead to the next world. The specific burial rite may no longer exist in the social and institutional context that it did in West Africa, but the aesthetic manifestation and the meaning of the burial practice are African in origin. Thompson's lively and creative study emphasizes that we must not be bound by written text or by institution in the endeavor of discerning continuities. While the bulk of Thompson's work centers on West African and Caribbean art and philosophy, he points the way to uncovering an enduring influence of African cultures in North America, and his work moves us beyond the search for individual items of culture and seeks, instead, to identify the boundaries of an African ethos.[9]

Sterling Stuckey's work directs us to other possibilities as he traces threads of African cultural traditions through black nationalist thought in America. Like Thompson and others, Stuckey emphasizes the strong influence of Kongo–Angola culture in the developing African American cultures in North America.[10] But Stuckey sees this influence as taking shape in spheres in addition to those of folk belief and practice. Arguing for a period in which the elements of the West African backgrounds of enslaved Africans in America fused to become an African American cul-ture, Stuckey asserts that, rather than destroying the African cultural background, slavery provided a context in which a coherent pan-African culture had in fact developed. Through an analysis of folk tales, sacred dance, music, quilts, slave rebellions, and other elements of "the circle of culture," African and American, Stuckey examines the ways in which African ethnic groups overcame differences of language and culture to embrace commonalities under the heavy burden of American slavery. Ac-cording to Stuckey, this new common culture—a pan-African, black na-tionalist one—provides a powerful connection between African American cultures and the African past. Moreover, the common culture binds to-gether varied forms of black nationalist thought in the American context.

Here he points to such figures as David Walker, Henry Highland Garnet, W. E. B. DuBois, and Paul Robeson, broadening our vision of black nationalism and showing the connections between nationalist thought and religion and culture. Stuckey's work thus renders the margin as the most productive site, indeed the only possible site, for the development of an oppositional religiously grounded black nationalist thought, both in slavery and freedom.

Mechal Sobel's two studies of American culture under slavery stand somewhere between Raboteau and Stuckey with respect to the process of formation of an African American sacred world. Sobel posits a period of gestation in which a commonly shared, generalized West African sacred cosmos is transformed into a quasi-African worldview. For Sobel, the failure of Anglican missionaries to make headway among African Americans provided a context in which a quasi-African worldview could develop. She emphasizes, in contrast to Stuckey, that this quasi-African worldview was not necessarily a coherent one. Because this developing worldview had to overcome the cultural barriers separating African peoples brought to North America, as well as suffer the brutality of developing white American cultures directed against people of African descent, the path could not be uncomplicated. Nevertheless, it is this quasi-African grounding that encountered the white American Baptist experience, through which African Americans generated a unique Afro-Baptist sacred cosmos.[11]

Sobel gives African Americans full agency in developing an African-based worldview in the American context, but she also moves the discussion forward by giving African Americans agency at the *center* of the story of religion in America. She insists, for example, that the issue of African American attraction to Baptist and Methodist revivals is far more complex than one of reactive emotionality and expressivity in the conversion experience. Instead, she maintains that African Americans participated in the southern revivals from very early on and, thus, significantly shaped the character and tenor of those revivals. Certainly, part of the attraction of the revivals themselves lay in the opportunity they provided for African Americans to contribute at such a significant juncture in American religious history. In her study of black and white culture in eighteenth century Virginia, Sobel examines attitudes towards time and work, space and the natural world, and understandings of causality and purpose. While in both works Sobel often relies too heavily on a generalized conception of an "African" or "European" worldview, her work nevertheless points to new ways to discuss both an enduring presence of African "values," and one pivotal place to seek them—southern white cultures. In this way, Sobel proposes, African Americans occupy the center as well. Sobel's work is especially valuable in its refusal to compartmentalize cultural developments and influences. Her perspective warrants further critical attention.[12]

The one North American context about which there has been little dispute concerning African influences in religion is provided by the Gullah people of the Sea Islands. Margaret Washington Creel's study of religion and culture among the Gullahs yields a stellar example of the many issues this particular context reveals. Washington Creel traces the continued influence of West African sacred/political secret societies of Poro (for men) and Sande (for women) and, importantly, does not argue for mere "survivals" but rather shows the dynamic and creative nature of Gullah cultural development. Throughout the strong discussion of Gullah attitudes toward death and the supernatural, Washington Creel demonstrates the multiple ways in which African-derived attitudes melded with Christian beliefs. This study may be considered, in many ways, to be a deepening of previous work by Raboteau, Thompson, and Lawrence Levine.[13]

Time and geography matter deeply here. Sobel's study of eighteenth-century Virginia and Creel's study of the Gullahs make this abundantly clear and demonstrate that, in order to advance our understanding of the question of continuities with the African cultural pasts of African American cultures, we must delve deeply into examining local contexts in smaller slices of time. These works highlight an additional direction for consideration in that they point to the possibility of viewing the constructed nature of race through the analytical lens of religion. Recent works have evaluated the fashioning of categories of race and the interaction of race and gender, race and class, and race and sexuality. The construction of race in America in the context of slavery and beyond reveals this process as something carried out upon black people in America, with boundaries and categories changing over time: that is, that Americans of European descent were prompted by the very nature of the slave system and subsequent segregation in North America to form a hierarchy on the basis of "race." The body of work that explores the continuities between African religious traditions and African American traditions invites us to reconsider the way in which religion might have served to mediate the process for African Americans. What role might commonalities from the African religious pasts of enslaved African Americans have played in the process through which African Americans established racialized identities? A consideration of these issues also affords African Americans agency in the process of constructing race. The critical examination of the connections between religious identity and the social construction of race blurs the line between margin and center in the story of the development of ideas of race in America.

"The" Black Church

Institutional manifestations of black Protestantism must loom largely in any recounting of African American history. The classic studies of these institutions as "the black church"[14] have emphasized two broad ways of viewing the role of the churches in African American history. E. Franklin Frazier, for one, saw the black church as serving a compensatory function as an institution to which African Americans looked as a means of escaping the brutal realities of life in America. The church promised certain hope of justice for all of God's people in the future time of God's kingdom. Through this renunciation of agency in earthly history, the churches functioned to divert the people's attention from seizing social and political rights in the present. Frazier's work on the black church argues that "on the whole, the Negro's church was not a threat to white domination and aided the Negro to become accommodated to an inferior status." Whereas Frazier does not deny that the black church served as an arena for developing leadership skills and for affirming humanity in order to resist racism psychologically, for him, the church developed only as a "second best" alternative.[15]

From another perspective, Carter G. Woodson, Joseph Washington, and Gayraud Wilmore focus on the positive political functions of the church. According to this view, the black church tradition embraced the role of historical agent and provided the only possible arena for political action given the restrictions of a racist society. Joseph Washington maintains that the fantasy that Christianity among African Americans was "otherworldly" derives from the desire of white Americans who "extoll[ed] the virtues of the next world" in looking to subdue and pacify black Americans. African Americans who heard such preaching, however, listened and nodded, and in their own secret camp meetings spoke of other things.[16] Gayraud Wilmore writes of the slave church as a well of underground resistance but, nonetheless, recognizes the constraints placed on slave preachers with regard to the fomenting of open rebellion. Elements of "otherworldliness" in slave preaching were, for Wilmore, nothing more than an interim strategy. He insists, however, that for these preachers to have adopted this interim strategy and to have thereby provided some relief for the flock does not mean that they abrogated their commitment to the dignity of the community or of individuals in that community. And, certainly, slave religion and armed resistance sometimes supported each other as the cases of Gabriel and Nancy Prosser, Nat Turner, and Denmark Vesey illustrate.[17]

Other scholars of the black church have added a layer to functionalist analyses of the institutional life of black Protestants through an exploration of the theological and ethical formulations of the black churches. Peter Paris's discussion of the social ethics of black Baptist churches and of the African Methodist Episcopal church furnishes an admirable example of this kind of work. Paris argues that the sociological reality of the independent black church tradition, namely that it arose in the context of oppression based on race, necessitated that the church be *both* pastoral and prophetic, caring for the present material and social needs of its people and directing them towards change, both historical and eschatological. The concern for community is inclusive in the tradition because its bedrock is the absolute assertion that humanity is one and equal under God. For Paris, the institution of the church manifests this principle in history. He further emphasizes that, because the institution of the black church is authorized by the principle of "the parenthood of God and the kinship of all peoples," it is impossible to draw fast distinctions between religious practice and sociopolitical issues. "Whenever religion, politics, and morality are isolated from one another, the tradition itself is severely threatened." The essential connection between these elements, Paris argues, has led the principles of the black church to become normative for the community as a whole.[18]

Two other models addressing the role of the black church endeavor to complicate the notion that the church functioned *either* as a revolutionary arena *or* as a facilitator of accommodation. C. Eric Lincoln and Lawrence H. Mamiya's approach this problem by proposing a dialectic model that "holds polar opposites in tension, constantly shifting between the polarities in historical time. There is no Hegelian synthesis or ultimate resolution of the dialectic."[19] They see the black church as vacillating between six poles: priestly/prophetic, otherworldly/this-worldly, universal/particular, communal/private, charismatic/bureaucratic, and resistant/accommodating. The key innovation of this model is that it allows for a great deal of change over time and according to circumstance, refusing to fix the black church as an entity with a stance for all time.

Evelyn Brooks Higginbotham presents a further sophisticated model of the black church that seeks to move beyond the polarized view of otherworldly versus secular/political. In providing "a gendered perspective" on the black church, Higginbotham employs a modified version of Jürgen Habermas's concept of the "public sphere." In distinguishing the public sphere from concepts like Robert Bellah's "civil religion" and John F. Wilson's "public religion," Higginbotham portrays the black church as a structure that both mediates between the black community and the government and itself encompasses the public life of the community. Most important, she denies that the public sphere of the black church contains one single discursive thread or, as Lincoln and Mamiya assert, contains polarities that interact in a dialectic mode of conflict. Higginbotham asserts, instead, that, as public sphere, the black church should be viewed as dialogic arena in which participants create meaning that at times binds them or separates them. "The black church constitutes a complex body of shifting cultural, ideological, and political significations. . . . Such multiplicity transcends polarity—thus tending to blur the spiritual and secular, the eschatological and political, and the private and the public."[20]

While much of the more recent literature on the nature and place of the black church tradition overlaps at points and is in conflict at others, it all represents a significant move away from the long-standing emphasis on a radical dichotomy between a "this-worldly" or an "otherworldly" function of the church. It is only through moving beyond this false dichotomy that the broader field of American religious history can take full measure of the impact of the black church tradition on American Protestant life.

Beyond this, however, what is urgently needed in the field is sustained attention to denominational history. The broad studies of "the" black church are useful, particularly from a functional perspective, but they also work to create a false monolith of a unified institutional history. The denominations that constitute the black church are brought together by common experiences in a racially stratified society, but assuredly have particular histories that must be recovered and applied to a rethinking of the larger view of the black church tradition. A number of exemplary studies can guide this process. James M. Washington's work on black Baptist history provides an indispensable grounding as he presents a nuanced discussion of the interplay between theological developments and issues of social power. Evelyn Brooks Higginbotham's work complements Washington's as she examines similar issues in the women's movement among black Baptists and furnishes an interpretation that takes full account of the role of gender in denominational history. For the African Methodist Episcopal Church, Clarence Walker and Katherine Dvorak examine the Civil War and Reconstruction periods.[21] As our view becomes broadened by a full appreciation of denominational specificity, the importance of geography must be underscored as well. What shape did these denominations take as they developed in the western United States, for example, and how did African American churches interact with the American frontier? An additional important component of the recovery of the particularity of denominational history in African American Protestantism is the revival of the stories of particular figures, both those who had enduring and public impact and those whose lives serve to illustrate some aspect of the larger picture. Studies of well-known figures such as Henry McNeal Turner and Thomas Andrew Dorsey and the less-acclaimed Jane Edna Hunter and Theophilus Gould Steward have begun the process of fleshing out the biographical resources for work in African American religious history.[22]

The growing importance of Holiness and Pentecostal churches for African Americans emerges as another area that requires careful consideration. The available literature examines the interracial origins of Pentecostalism and the relative importance of central white and black figures, Charles Fox Parham, William J. Seymour, and Charles H. Mason.[23] In addition, there are pressing questions of theory at stake in the study of African American Pentecostals. Is the attraction of African Americans to such revitalization movements solely due to some psychological, emotional, and material deprivation relative to white America? Or, as other evidence indicates, is the issue far more complex? What is the interplay of religious revitalization and political protest in the context of these theologically conservative movements? How do gender issues play out?

As the body of literature on black Holiness and Pentecostal groups continues to take on these questions, the larger picture of the shape of the black church tradition will necessarily be modified by the answers.[24]

Although almost 90% of African American Christians belong to predominantly black denominations, the current and historical relationship between these black church denominations and predominantly white denominations must also be recognized and explored. A prudent consideration of this aspect of African American religious history will assist in the process of complicating the notion of a normative experience for African Americans. Moreover, making progress at this task would be one useful avenue for the investigation of class issues for African American Protestants. Given the relationship between church/denomination affiliation and social status, and the old elite affiliation with predominantly white churches, a probing analysis of the history of African Americans in white churches could begin to unravel the complex webs of color, class, education, and religion.[25] In what ways have African Americans in predominantly white churches and in traditionally black churches dealt with changing constructions of race in America? In what form, separately or in communion, did they participate in fixing boundaries of race and "community"? Or, perhaps, have African Americans in white churches resisted the construction of those boundaries in favor of others such as class or, perhaps, none at all?

Finally, to reassemble these pieces would provide a new vision of black churches, unified at some points—on theological, political, social issues—and divided along these same lines at other points. This readjusted broad image would appreciate denominational uniqueness, region, class, historical moment, and gender. We need to view the history of the institutions of black Protestantism as evolving in a dynamic process that embraces the range of issues affecting African Americans within those institutions and outside of them, rather than envision them as a reified monolith. Recognizing the inaccuracy of viewing black Protestant institutions as a unified monolith serves to dislocate the rigid center *within* African American religious experiences and create room for exchange between internal margins and centers.

Gender

Without question, the proliferation of literature over the past ten years on the role of gender in African American religious experience has revolutionized the field on two primary fronts. First, with regard to the issue of reclaiming women's roles in this history, feminist scholars have mined the archives and used this material to demonstrate the centrality and value of women's presence and participation in Protestant churches. What has bolstered this work, especially, has been the recovery of the first-person experience in such crucial sources as spiritual narratives.[26] Second, feminist scholars in this field, as in so many other fields, have explored the gendered nature of life in the African American religious tradition, as well as the gendered nature of political/religious discussions in the churches. Like the best gender studies, such work tells us not only about women's lives but also about the construction of meaning for the lives of both black men and women.

The work of three scholars in particular has been pivotal in breaking methodological ground for speaking about African American women's religious experiences. An important overview of the possibilities for research in this field came with Jualynne Dodson and Cheryl Townsend Gilkes's chapter for Rosemary Radford Ruether and Rosemary Skinner Keller's volume on women and religion in twentieth-century America. Dodson and Gilkes review the range of experiences of black Christian women, primarily Protestant, in the black church tradition, and they discuss the growing importance of the sanctified church. They also emphasize the importance of music ministry for women across denominations, with examples like Mattie Moss Clark in the Church of God in Christ, Lucie E. Campbell in the National Baptist Convention, and Mother Willie Mae Ford Smith and Sallie Martin, key figures in the National Convention of Gospel Choirs and Choruses. Dodson and Gilkes highlight a particular perspective for recovering and discussing the experiences of African American women in the churches that gives these women full agency. They indicate that, "If anything characterizes the role of black women in religion in America, it is the successful extension of their individual sense of regeneration, release, redemption, and spiritual liberation to a collective ethos of struggle for and with the black community." The literature on black women's religious experiences in specific contexts bears out this assertion that the struggle is one that is grounded in a collective vision for African Americans' spiritual and material progress.[27]

Jualynne Dodson's work on women in the African Methodist Episcopal Church has, first, laid the historical groundwork by piecing together a narrative line describing the lives and work of nineteenth-century preaching women like Jarena Lee, Zilpha Elaw, and Julia Foote.[28] In addition, Dodson's work demonstrates the support for (as well as the opposition to) these extraordinary women among their sisters who did not experience a call to preach. Dodson's work goes much farther, however, in examining the response of the church hierarchy to the demands of preaching women for access to formal positions of leadership. The church hierarchy responded to these periodic onslaughts by creating roles, like those of stewardess and deaconess, that in many ways institutionalized subordination and contained these women's protest. In this sense, AME women suffered successive defeats.

But Dodson demonstrates, through reshaping the definition of power, that AME women in the nineteenth century exercised a great deal of agency within the confines of the structure. Following other sociologists, Dodson emphasizes that a view that power rests alone in positions of authority necessarily excludes conventionally disenfranchised people in any context. By looking at power as interactional, rather than static, she insists, we find other kinds of power that intersect with that type of power which rests in authority positions. According to Dodson's model, women in the AME church had the ability to put into play their majority numbers, their organizations, and their resources in order to exercise power in the life of the AME church. Consider, for example, the case of the Daughters of Conference groups dating back to the early nineteenth century. These women's voluntary associations supported the male hierarchy financially and spiritually to such a degree that successful Daughters of Conference groups imparted great status to their conferences, causing ministers to vie for appointments. Dodson found that AME Bishops often conferred with the Daughters of Conference before making appointments because experience had shown that the withdrawal of the support of these groups could result in great financial or other losses to the Conference.[29] Her conclusions in this small study point to what she terms a pattern of surrogate leadership in which the formal structures of the church often permitted women decision-making power or were forced to acknowledge women's authority through this interactive mechanism. Her related argument that the AME church in the nineteenth century took this approach, rather than ordaining women, in order to retain the support of white Americans is not necessarily borne out by her evidence or evidence outside her study. This work, however, has shed a great deal of light on the lives of black women in the AME church, as should Dodson's forthcoming monograph on the subject.

Cheryl Townsend Gilkes makes suggestive use of the model of dual-sex political systems in West African societies as influential in the development of an arena for African American women to exercise leadership, particularly through the role of the church and community mother. She argues that the parallel sex-specific structures found in community or church work among African Americans is not a mere reproduction of Euro-American traditions of sexism, but evidences strong influences of this West African structure. For Gilkes, church and community mothers, as emblems of wisdom and experience, represent to the community its past and provide continuity through their leadership. This focus on the local community mothers also demonstrates the important interplay between national and local structures for black women's work, between women like Mary Church Terrell and Ida B. Wells, and women in smaller contexts whose names have been forgotten by most. Gilkes' work on church mothers touches on Baptist and Methodist women but examines in greater detail the roles of these women in the Holiness and Pentecostal churches. These are women, she emphasizes, who may be known as spouses of men in formal leadership positions, but who are sometimes themselves founders of churches or important institutional leaders. Like Dodson's work on AME women, Gilkes's work shows African American women adopting a stance in which they oppose the male hierarchical structure through demonstrating their leadership abilities in a variety of arenas.[30] Dodson, Gilkes, and Evelyn Brooks Higginbotham all oppose the approach taken by Lincoln and Mamiya in their work on *The Black Church in the African American Experience*. Where Lincoln and Mamiya place the entire burden of the role of black women in the churches on the question of ordination, these feminist scholars emphasize a more complex view of the issue. The view of black women in the churches as concerned with ordination *as well as* with other ways of utilizing their leadership potential and expressing their religiosity also has implications for the study of women in all areas of religion in America.

Without question, the best available monograph in the field now is Evelyn Brooks Higginbotham's on black Baptist women.[31] Higginbotham's work is especially strong because she so carefully balances issues facing African American men, African American women and the community as a whole. It is impossible, her work persuades us, to speak of black women's lives and work in black Baptist churches without understanding how they related to men's work. In addition, Higginbotham makes it abundantly clear that, although this period sees strong African American "separatist leanings," the cooperation and involvement of white (mostly Northern) Baptist women was important to the development of black (mostly Southern) Baptist women's work.

Higginbotham's chapters on "Feminist Theology, 1880–1900" and "The Politics of Respectability" are central ones to the project of moving forward our understanding of African American women's religious and secular work. Through her examination of the theology of Baptist women like Mary Cook, Virginia Broughton, and Lucy Wilmot Smith, we see that black Baptist women in this period took a very different approach to their challenge to the church than did AME preaching women of an earlier era. These women looked to the Bible for support from the mothers of Isaac, Samson, Moses, and Jesus. They wielded the Bible as an "iconoclastic weapon" to deny men the power to subordinate women and to argue for leadership roles for women. This oppositional stance participated as well in the prevailing notion that women's religiosity was inherent and necessary to the uplift of the race. As Higginbotham cogently argues here and elsewhere, African American women were also enmeshed in a complex of the American tradition of constructing gender through the lens of race. African American women in the black Baptist women's movement and in other social movements walked the tightropes of race, class, and gender lines in which the work and ideological positions necessary to make progress along one line sometimes impeded progress on the others. As a result, Higginbotham shows us, black Baptist women emphasized "respectability" to counter and combat rampant negative images of African American women and African Americans in general. Higginbotham asserts that, "Notwithstanding the sincerity of the Baptist women's appeals to respectable behavior, such appeals were also explicit rejections of Social Darwinist explanations of blacks' biological inferiority to whites. Respectability was perceived as a weapon against such assumptions, since it was used to expose race relations as socially constructed rather than derived by evolutionary law or divine judgment."[32] At the same time, this "politics of respectability," for the most part, embraced the overarching social norms of white American society and sometimes engendered classism and class conflict among African Americans.

A new analytical perspective of some significance with regard to addressing gender issues in African American religious history lies in the developing field of womanist theology.[33] Womanist theology seeks to provide a perspective for expressing black women's religious experience that takes full account of the interlocking nature of both experience and oppression. The womanist perspective refuses to prioritize race, class, gender, or sexuality in its analysis of black women's lives, thus differentiating it from other theologies of the oppressed. Womanist theologians see this perspective as an organic one, one that is faithful to the community because it grows out of the experiences of African American women. In this sense, then, it does not represent an innovation, but rather the naming of a tradition of black women's resistance and celebration of themselves, of community, and of their relationship with the divine.

Scholars in the field of African American religious history must take note of this emerging field because of the concern that womanist theologians demonstrate for recovering and interpreting African American women's history. Embedded within the writings of these theologians is a great deal of material of use to historians. In order to formulate womanist theology and womanist ethics, Delores Williams, Katie Geneva Cannon, Cheryl Townsend Gilkes, and others argue, we must first grasp the complexity of black women's lives throughout American history. Womanist theologians emphasize that nothing produced or experienced by African American women is to be excluded as an invalid tool for constructing this theology. Because of this approach, womanists weave together black women's literature, art, music, and testimonies of suffering and loving to build this theological perspective. Among the notable works in this field are Emilie Townes' work on Ida B. Wells and Katie Cannon's analysis of Zora Neale Hurston as a womanist figure.[34]

Higginbotham, Gilkes, Dodson, and others are providing the grounding so that we may begin to ask questions concerning the gendering of black religious life. We can no longer assume that African American women addressed the pressing questions of their religious experiences in the same way that African American men did. This literature has begun to demonstrate the ways in which African American women's negotiation of their positioning vis-à-vis margin and center differ from the approach of African American men. This demonstration not only calls upon us to reevaluate the notion of a normative religious experience based on gender and to press on to uncover yet more information of African American women, but also to reevaluate our understanding of African American men's experiences as equally gendered experiences.

Religious Culture

Any discussion of institutional Protestant life among African Americans must be balanced by attention to religious culture outside the realm of the formal power structures of the churches. A growing body of literature has emerged to help trace the shape of black religious culture and, in so doing, has asserted forcefully that the religious lives of African Americans have also been mediated by entities and experiences other than church hierarchies. Music occupies a central position in this consideration of religious culture. From spirituals to gospel music, the black sacred musical tradition has represented an arena in which to experience the divine, to transcend material circumstances, and to create community cohesion. The study of African American religious music also provides an opportunity to consider the constructed boundary between sacred and secular. Black musical traditions constitute a complex network of cross-influences that are difficult to separate. The relationship between spirituals, blues, and gospel is just one example of the transformation of black musical traditions through secular and sacred forms. [35]

Another opportunity for considering the interplay of sacred and secular forms of culture lies in the almost completely unexplored area of black film. A number of known instances of individuals using the essentially secular medium of film to impart religious information and help shape African American Protestant identities in the early twentieth century should encourage scholars to give extant black religious films a place in African American religious culture and to seek out other such films for study. [36] Other areas of the arts have also proved to be fruitful arenas for exploring black religious culture. Robert Farris Thompson's work and that of other scholars moves us to consider approaches to the use of folk art and material culture as sources for studying African American religious history. [37]

Another area of black religious culture that calls out for sustained attention is that of folk practice. While it is difficult to identify a discrete category that is "folk" as opposed to other forms of religious practice, we should not allow the study of the institutional life of black Protestants to overwhelm the field. In order to avoid such an imbalance, our attention to folk practices must extend beyond the antebellum period and trace them into the twentieth century and to locations outside the south. [38] We also need to know more about the relationship between the persistence of folk practice and institutional opposition to it—beyond the well-known AME church hierarchy polemics against "heathenish" practices. Broad perspectives on styles of African American worship can bring together music, preaching, the arts, and material culture in a productive move that crosses disciplinary boundaries. It is essential that scholars addressing African American religious history work against compartmentalizing religious thought and religious culture and/or the institutional and the folk aspects of this history while cultivating a perspective that weaves together both of these elements.[39]

Bridges

The theme of the negotiation of margin and center abounds in African American religious history, but it must be underscored that these are renovated versions of margin and center. African American religious experience has rendered the margin a site of power and of creativity, an activity that necessarily alters the character of the center. And while the story of black Protestants in America may be one of navigating the divide between margin and center, it is also one of the deliberate and conscious building of bridges. We cannot view the experiences of African American Protestants in isolation from other African American religious groups or from white Protestant groups in America. Because of the interaction among all these groups, bridges of a variety of sorts figure significantly in African American religious history.

Although the majority of African Americans affiliated with a religious group are Protestant, the presence of black Catholics, Jews, Muslims, and members of new religious groups cannot be discounted.[40] Little work has been done on the history of black Catholics, and even less on the interactions between African American Catholics and Protestants. Cyprian Davis's overview provides a solid grounding, but we need a more nuanced understanding of time and place in order to address productively the multitude of questions that arise in approaching black Catholic history. We need to know, for example, in what ways the experience of being doubly or triply a religious outsider (black/Catholic/woman) has shaped the approach of African Americans to issues of race, power, and religion in America. The struggles of black Catholic men to be ordained and of black Catholic women in religious orders, as well as a sense of the experiences of lay people, must be retrieved first before we can begin to discuss interactions with Protestants.[41]

Another area that has yet to be thoroughly explored is the connection between the urban "sects" and "cults" and African American Protestant traditions. Groups like Father Divine's Peace Mission Movement, Daddy Grace's United House of Prayer for All People, W. D. Fard and Elijah Muhammad's Nation of Islam, the Black Hebrew Israelite Nation, and other groups have received some attention.[42] While the recent literature takes these movements as religious options for African Americans seriously, most tend to downplay or eradicate the connections between the theologies of these options and the traditions of black Protestants. Randall Burkett's study of the religious component of Marcus Garvey's Universal Negro Improvement Association (UNIA) and Hans Baer's and Merrill Singer's work on black religion in the twentieth century both point to alternative approaches, however. Burkett understands the uniqueness of Marcus Garvey's use of religiopolitical symbolism in the UNIA movement, but significantly refuses to allow this religious ethos to be placed entirely outside the black Christian tradition. African American ministers, in their support of Garvey and in their role in developing the UNIA's religious ethos contributed significantly to Garvey's success in creating a powerful mass movement. Baer and Singer trace the themes of protest and accommodation through African American religious traditions in the twentieth century and successfully weave together the stories of margin and center internal to black religious life through attention to black denominations, African Americans in white churches, messianic–nationalist sects, conversionist sects, and thaumaturgical sects. Both works provide models for rethinking the relationship between the center (Baptist and Methodist) and the margins in African American religious history and bridging the gap.[43]

The ongoing relationship of black Americans to Africa forms another bridge in our story. An understanding of the relationship of black Americans to Africa has been one component of African American quests for individual and communal identities throughout American history. The activities of black Protestant missionaries have served in part to define this relationship. Sandy Dwayne Martin's and Sylvia Jacobs's studies of African American missionaries in Africa provide a solid foundation for future scholarship.[44] It is also essential that we take note of the importance of African-derived traditions on the American scene. Both Santería and Vodou are becoming increasingly visible with growing numbers of practitioners in urban contexts, particularly with the 1993 Supreme Court decision protecting animal sacrifice in Santería. African-derived religions as well as African traditional religions are attractive to African Americans who seek an alternative to Christianity or a return to a more "authentic" religious tradition for people of African descent. While there is little hard data on the conversions of black Protestants to these traditions, it is an area that merits further attention, as does the issue of the relationship between black Protestant churches and African and African-derived religions in the United States.[45]

Arenas of conflict and cooperation between African American and white Protestants on issues of spiritual life, politics and racial justice should be investigated. The Social Gospel, the Civil Rights Movement, the YMCA, the YWCA, the Fellowship of Southern Churchmen, and other such ecumenical movements and organizations provide fertile ground for exploring the role of religion in addressing these crucial questions in African American life.[46] The case of the Harlem YWCA is highly suggestive of the research possibilities in an examination of the bridges that African American Protestants built to work with white Protestants in the twentieth century.

The Harlem YWCA was founded in 1905 when a small group of African American women gathered to consider ways of addressing issues facing black New Yorkers, particularly young women. As a result of the meeting the women formed a Young Women's Christian Association in and of the African American community. This YWCA emerged as one of the central institutions created by African American women in New York City in the early twentieth century and, perhaps, the most visible and developed of all African American YWCAs in the country.[47] Women like Cecelia Cabaniss Saunders, Emma Ransom, and Virginia Scott, principal guiding figures for the institution, sought to create a membership organization that would provide a Christian family atmosphere for young African American women in the context of a city with many "temptations." In addition, the leadership thought that attention to both the spiritual needs of young women (through Bible study) and to their material needs (through vocational education) would prove essential to the social and moral uplift of the entire black community. The organization met its earliest goals with ease, anchoring a group of Protestant African American women in the difficult city of New York. What began as a small Bible and prayer group meeting in rented rooms was moved, by increasing migration into the city and a growing number of religious and secular "temptations," to shift its emphasis and provide services for a population less and less interested in finding only a Christian family at the Harlem YWCA. The growing population and shifting issues challenged the women of the Harlem YWCA to find ways to remain relevant to the community in the first half of the twentieth century.

The Harlem YWCA provided an impressive array of services that included job training for domestic workers and seamstresses, vocational guidance and training for potentially new employment arenas for black women, a summer camp for children, a residence, recreational facilities, social events, adult education courses, and the staple Bible study and vesper services. The women who volunteered at the Harlem YWCA, as well as those who were paid staff, came from the large black Protestant congregations in the city and forged strong bonds between New York's African American churches and the YWCA. In the face of the attraction of new religious movements, the women of the Harlem YWCA made a strong statement concerning what they considered to be "respectable" and "appropriate" religious affiliations for their members.

All of the institution's work came under the Harlem YWCA's umbrella of the combined mission of "bringing about the Kingdom of God among young women," and helping them to live "the more abundant life." The leaders of the Harlem YWCA, like other African American women who were drawn to the YWCA movement, saw the possibility of combining the club tradition and church work in unique ways to benefit the community. Like the National Association of Colored Women and its local and regional affiliates, the Harlem YWCA identified and addressed a range of practical issues facing African American women and their families. And, as did women's groups within the churches, the women who worked at the Harlem YWCA grounded their activism in Christian community. The combination of these concerns in the YWCA, a nondenominational membership organization, made cross-class, interdenominational cooperation possible in new ways that proved important for the increasingly urban African American population in the twentieth century.

As the structure through which to combine church and club concerns in twentieth-century black New York, the YWCA was not without its difficulties. The National Board of the YWCA pursued a policy of segregated work until the adoption of the "Interracial Charter" in 1946. Under this segregated arrangement, African American city associations were required to become branches of white associations and could only receive recognition as YWCAs at the national level through these white branches. This policy was meant to provide a system of stewardship for African American women, whom white women felt needed particular guidance in their work, as well as to placate white women who found the presence of African American women in the organization objectionable. In practice, this system allowed southern white YWCAs to deny access to the movement to black women and northern white YWCAs to severely restrict access. In New York City's YWCA, the white leadership continually questioned the ability of the Harlem YWCA's leadership to guide and govern the institution. In addition, the white women who led the New York City YWCA attempted to consign the Harlem YWCA to the margins by denying its directors an equal voice in the affairs of the citywide organization. Emma Ransom, Cecelia Cabaniss Saunders, Dorothy Height, and other leaders of the Harlem YWCA challenged the New York City YWCA and the National Board of the YWCA to renounce the notion that Christian work could be carried out through a segregated institution. Their work and the activism of other African American leaders in the YWCA in this area were instrumental in moving the National Board to reconsider and revise the policy in 1946.

Despite the persistence of segregation in the national YWCA, the women who founded and built the Harlem YWCA into a thriving community institution believed that the YWCA structure allowed them to pursue their goals in unique ways. Scholarship on African American women's work in clubs and in churches provides a grounding for understanding the attraction of the YWCA movement for African American women. As literature on the club movement has demonstrated, African American women's clubs did not just mirror or merely react to white women's work. The black women's club movement had an internal dynamic, generated by African American women's concerns, hopes, and desires.[48] Similarly, this work and others on black women in the YWCA emphasizes that African American women's use of the YWCA structure was not a blind adoption of the model set by white women.[49] In fact, one of the struggles that the women of the Harlem YWCA engaged in with the white women of the New York City YWCA stemmed from the Harlem YWCA's insistence that its membership and leaders must define the nature of their work based on the needs of New York's African American women. The YWCA was a means for African American women to pursue religious goals held in common with white Protestant women—"the bringing in of the Kingdom of God among young women"— *and* to pursue their own community's sociopolitical goals. The case of the Harlem YWCA aptly illustrates the complex and interwoven nature of African American religious history and the salience of margins, centers, and bridges as metaphors for the complexities in African American religious history. In developing the institution, its leadership used the margin as a productive site for resisting the onslaught of daily racism in twentieth-century America and for affirming the uniqueness of African American history and culture. At the same time, they interacted with and built bridges to work with white Protestant women in the YWCA movement and sought to address as Christian women issues of concern to all Americans.

The 1893 World's Columbian Exposition as a national and international event consciously stood at the crossroad from which Americans looked backward and projected their hopes into the future. Frederick Douglass, Ida B. Wells, and Fannie Barrier Williams arrived at that crossroad from quite different directions—Douglass from slavery to freedom and international renown, Wells fleeing the wrath and terrorism of the southern white lynchers she continually exposed, Williams from the upper class of African American society in the north. All three moved forward on different, yet complementary paths directed toward achieving justice for African Americans. As guides to the twentieth century through the portal of the Columbian Exposition, Williams, Wells, and Douglass point to images of margins, centers, and bridges time and again. Their lives were dedicated to both engaging the center in conflict and cooperation and to rendering the margins spaces that affirm the full humanity of African American people. As we continue the process of fashioning new interpretive frameworks for understanding American religious history, we should continue to let their examples guide us.

The opportunity to reflect on the literature on African American religious experiences occasions a discussion of the broader implications of this history for charting new directions for the study of religion in America. Recognizing the negotiation of margins and centers that has characterized much of African American religious history illuminates *both* the margins and centers. Such an interpretive strategy negates any attempts to view the history of black Protestants or African Americans in other religious traditions as a monolith and underscores the complexity and variety contained within the story. Moreover, it continually calls on those scholars who present the history of white Protestants in America to recognize that the center, as those Protestants have constructed and reconstructed it, has never been fixed or bounded by impregnable walls, but has been a process that involved many groups, including African Americans. The religious bridges that black, white, and other American Protestants built to connect communities carry information, insights, and ideas in both directions, something we must not ignore as we move forward. In addition, the creative revisioning of margins, bridges, and centers in African American religious history can provide insights for other religious groups that have been constructed and placed on the margins of American society and struggle to make it a productive and creative arena in their own lives. Models from African American history cannot be adopted as the appropriate model for understanding Latino or Native American religious experiences, for example, or for telling the particular stories of women, gays, and lesbians in American religious history, but the themes, theories, and approaches in African American studies can be useful for such studies nonetheless. Reshaping the way we tell the stories of all Americans in relation to margins, centers, and bridges will ensure that we may begin fully to value the true complexities inherent in our collective narrative.

NOTES

1. Douglass was a participant in the fair as the supervisor of the Republic of Haiti exhibit.

2. Jean M. Weimann, *The Fair Women* (Chicago: Academy Chicago, 1981); Ida B. Wells, *Crusade for Justice* (Chicago: University of Chicago Press, 1970); John Henry Barrows, ed., *The World's Parliament of Religions* (1893). Other black women who participated in the exposition were Anna Julia Cooper, Hallie Quinn Brown, Frances Ellen Watkins Harper, Fanny Jackson Coppin, and Sarah Jane Early.

3. See David W. Wills, "An Enduring Distance: Black Americans and the Establishment," in William R. Hutchison, ed., *Between the Times: The Travail of the Protestant Establishment in America, 1900–1960* (New York: Cambridge University Press, 1989), 168–92; David W. Wills, "The Central Themes of American Religious History: Pluralism, Puritanism, and the Encounter of Black and White," *Religion and Intellectual Life* 5 (Fall 1987): 30–41; Albert J. Raboteau, "Afro-Americans, Exodus, and the American Israel," (unpublished essay); Jon Butler, "Enlarging the Bonds of Christ: Slavery, Evangelism, and the Christianization of the White South, 1690–1790," in Leonard I. Sweet, ed., *The Evangelical Tradition in America* (Macon, Ga.: Mercer University Press, 1984), 87–112. On the question of destiny in the late nineteenth century, see Albert J. Raboteau, " 'Ethiopia Shall Soon Stretch Forth Her Hands': Black Destiny in Nineteenth Century America," University Lecture in Religion at Arizona State University, 1983; Timothy E. Fulop, " 'The Future Golden Day of the Race': Millennialism and Black Americans in the Nadir, 1877–1901," *Harvard Theological Review* 84 (1991): 75–99.

4. For one such presentation, see R. Laurence Moore, *Religious Outsiders and the Making of America* (New York: Oxford University Press, 1986).

5. bell hooks, "Choosing the Margin as a Space of Radical Openness," in *Yearning: Race, Gender and Cultural Politics* (Boston: Beacon Press, 1990), 145–53.

6. See, for example, Ruth Frankenberg, *White Women, Race Matters: The Social Construction of Whiteness* (Minneapolis: University of Minnesota Press, 1993); Toni Morrison, *Playing in the Dark: Whiteness and the Literary Imagi-*

nation (New York: Pantheon Books, 1992); Evelyn Brooks Higginbotham, "African-American Women's History and the Metalanguage of Race," *Signs* 17 (Winter 1992): 251–274; Winthrop Jordan, *White Over Black: American Attitudes Towards the Negro, 1550–1812* (Chapel Hill: University of North Carolina Press, 1968).

7. See, for example, E. Franklin Frazier, *The Negro Church in America* (1963; reprint, New York: Schocken Books, 1974), and *The Negro Family in the United States* (Chicago: University of Chicago Press, 1966); Melville Herskovits, *The Myth of the Negro Past* (1941; reprint, Boston: Beacon Press, 1990).

8. Albert J. Raboteau, "The Black Experience in American Evangelicalism: The Meaning of Slavery," in Sweet, ed., *The Evangelical Tradition*, 181–97; Albert J. Raboteau, *Slave Religion: The "Invisible Institution" in the Antebellum South* (New York: Oxford University Press, 1978).

9. Robert Farris Thompson, *Flash of the Spirit: African and Afro-American Art and Philosophy* (New York: Vintage Books, 1983).

10. Sterling Stuckey, *Slave Culture: Nationalist Theory and the Foundations of Black America* (New York: Oxford University Press, 1987). For more on Kongo–Angola influence, see Joseph E. Holloway, "The Origins of African-American Culture," in Joseph E. Holloway, ed., *Africanisms in American Culture* (Bloomington: Indiana University Press, 1990), 1–18; Sidney W. Mintz and Richard Price, *The Birth of African-American Culture* (Boston: Beacon Press, 1992).

11. Mechal Sobel, *Trabelin' On: The Slave Journey to an Afro-Baptist Faith* (Princeton: Princeton University Press, 1988).

12. Mechal Sobel, *The World They Made Together: Black and White Values in Eighteenth Century Virginia* (Princeton: Princeton University Press, 1987).

13. Margaret Washington Creel, *"A Peculiar People:" Slave Religion and Community Culture Among the Gullahs* (New York: New York University Press, 1988). See also Lawrence Levine, *Black Culture and Black Consciousness: Afro-American Folk Thought From Slavery to Freedom* (New York: Oxford University Press, 1977); Charles W. Joyner, *Down By the Riverside: A South Carolina Slave Community* (Urbana: University of Illinois Press, 1984). Two recent works in the arts deal quite effectively with Gullah culture and are particularly useful as teaching tools—Gloria Naylor, *Mama Day* (New York: Vintage Books, 1989), and Julie Dash, *Daughters of the Dust* (A Geechee Girls Production, 1991; released by Kino International Corporation).

14. The black church is composed of the following denominations: African Methodist Episcopal; African Methodist Episcopal Zion; Christian (Colored) Methodist Episcopal; National Baptist Convention, U.S.A., Inc.; National Baptist Convention of America, Unincorporated; Progressive National Baptist Convention; and Church of God in Christ. Lincoln and Mamiya define the black church as "those independent, historic, and totally black controlled denominations which were founded after the Free African Society of 1787 and which constitute the core of black Christians." C. Eric Lincoln and Lawrence H. Mamiya, *The Black Church in the African American Experience* (Durham: Duke University Press, 1990), 1.

15. Frazier, *The Negro Church in America,* 51. See Adolph Reed, *The Jesse Jackson Phenomenon* (New Haven: Yale University Press, 1986), for an examination of the implications of the black church as an antipolitical arena. Reed argues that the black church accepted second class citizenship for African Americans and grew as a sphere that became a substitute for political participation in

America. He views Jackson's 1984 campaign as a resurgence of the role of the church in politics. Reed argues that the function of the church as the arena that authenticates political leadership is redundant given the existence of an established political leadership that is authenticated through electoral politics.

16. Joseph R. Washington, Jr., *Black Religion: The Negro and Christianity in the United States* (1964; reprint, Lanham, Md.: University Press of America, 1984), 33.

17. Gayraud Wilmore, *Black Religion and Black Radicalism: An Interpretation of the Religious History of Afro-American People* (Maryknoll, N.Y.: Orbis Books, 1983).

18. Peter Paris, *The Social Teaching of the Black Churches* (Philadelphia: Fortress Press, 1985), 12; On this issue, see C. Eric Lincoln, *The Black Church Since Frazier* (New York: Schocken Books, 1974), and Cornel West, *Prophesy Deliverance! An Afro-American Revolutionary Christianity* (Philadelphia: Westminster Press, 1982). West asserts for a union of this prophetic black Christian tradition and progressive Marxism, two traditions dedicated to individuality and democracy and that affirm humanity and value community.

19. Lincoln and Mamiya 11.

20. Evelyn Brooks Higginbotham, *Righteous Discontent: The Women's Movement in the Black Baptist Church, 1880–1920* (Cambridge: Harvard University Press, 1993), 16. In *Uplifting the Race: The Black Minister in the New South, 1865–1902* (Lanham, Md.: University Press of America, 1986), Edward Wheeler takes a similar approach through an examination of the philosophy of "racial uplift." Wheeler challenges the notion that the post–Civil War black church embraced accommodation and white American standards and he provides an enlightening picture of the "ironic" relationship between black southern ministers and the philosophy of "uplift," which incorporated both a degree of accommodation to the American reality and a commitment to alternatives.

21. James Melvin Washington, *Frustrated Fellowship: The Black Baptist Quest for Social Power* (Macon, Ga.: Mercer University Press, 1986); Clarence Walker, *A Rock in a Weary Land: The African Methodist Episcopal Church During the Civil War and Reconstruction* (Baton Rouge: Louisiana State University Press, 1980); Katherine Dvorak, *An African-American Exodus: The Segregation of the Southern Churches* (Brooklyn, N.Y.: Carlson Publishing, 1990). Also, Leroy Fitts, *A History of Black Baptists* (Nashville: Broadman Press, 1985).

22. Among the growing body of biographies and collections of figures are Stephen Ward Angell, *Bishop Henry McNeal Turner and African-American Religion in the South* (Knoxville: University of Tennessee Press, 1992); Michael W. Harris, *The Rise of the Gospel Blues: The Music of Thomas Andrew Dorsey in the Urban Church* (New York: Oxford University Press 1992); Calvin S. Morris, *Reverdy C. Ransom: Black Advocate of the Social Gospel* (Lanham, Md.: University Press of America, 1991); William Seraile, *Voice of Dissent: Theophilus Gould Steward and Black America* (Brooklyn: Carlson Publishing, 1991); Adrienne Lash Jones, *Jane Edna Hunter: A Case Study of Black Leadership, 1910–1950* (Brooklyn: Carlson Publishing, 1990); Richard Newman, ed., *Black Preacher to White America: The Collected Writings of Lemuel Haynes, 1774–1833* (Brooklyn: Carlson Publishing, 1990); Jacqueline A. Rouse, *Lugenia Burns Hope: Black Southern Reformer* (Athens, Ga.: University of Georgia Press, 1989); Philip S. Foner, ed., *Black Socialist Preacher: The Teachings of Reverend George Washington Woodbey and His Disciple, Reverend G.W. Slater, Fr.* (San Francisco: Synthesis Press, 1983).

23. Cf., L. Grant McClung, Jr., ed., *Azusa Street and Beyond: Pentecostal Missions and Church Growth in the Twentieth Century* (South Plainfield, NJ: Bridge Publishing, 1986); Vinson Synan, *The Holiness–Pentecostal Movement in the United States* (Grand Rapids, Mich.: Eerdmans, 1971); Leonard Lovett, "Black Origins of the Pentecostal Movement," in Vinson Synan, ed., *Aspects of Pentecostal–Charismatic Origins* (Plainfield, N.J.: Logos International, 1975), 123–41; James Tinney, "William J. Seymour: Father of Modern-Day Pentecostalism," in Randall Burkett and Richard Newman, eds., *Black Apostles: Afro-American Clergy in the 20th Century* (Boston: G. K. Hall, 1978), 213–25.

24. See, for example, Peter Goldsmith, *When I Rise Cryin' Holy: African-American Denominationalism on the Georgia Coast* (New York: AMS, 1989); Arthur Paris, *Black Pentecostalism: Southern Religion in an Urban World* (Amherst: University of Massachusetts Press, 1982); Robert Mapes Anderson, *Vision of the Disinherited: The Making of American Pentecostalism* (New York: Oxford University Press, 1972); Luther P. Gerlach, "Pentecostalism: Revolution or Counter-Revolution?" in Irving I. Zaretsky and Mark P. Leone, eds., *Religious Movements in Contemporary America* (Princeton: Princeton University Press, 1974), 669–99; Luther P. Gerlach and Virginia H. Hine, *People, Power and Change: Movements of Social Transformation* (Indianapolis: The Bobbs-Merrill Company, 1970).

25. For a discussion of class and church affiliation in the late nineteenth and early twentieth centuries, see Willard B. Gatewood, *Aristocrats of Color: The Black Elite, 1880–1920* (Indianapolis: University of Indiana Press, 1990). On African Americans in predominantly white churches, see William B. McClain, *Black People in the Methodist Church: Wither Thou Goest?* (Cambridge, Mass.: Schenkman, 1984); Mark D. Morrison-Reed, *Black Pioneers in a White Denomination* (Boston: Beacon Press, 1984); Gayraud S. Wilmore, *Black and Presbyterian: The Heritage and the Hope* (Philadelphia: Geneva Press, 1983); Alfred K. Stanley, *The Children Is Crying: Congregationalism Among Black People* (New York: Pilgrim Press, 1979); Robert Bennett, "Black Episcopalians: A History from the Colonial Period to the Present," *History Magazine of the Protestant Episcopal Church* 43 (1974): 231–36.

26. See, for example, William Andrews, ed., *Sisters of the Spirit: Three Black Women's Autobiographies of the Nineteenth Century* (Indianapolis: University of Indiana Press, 1986); Henry Louis Gates, Jr., ed., *Spiritual Narratives* (New York: Oxford University Press, 1988); Jean Humez, ed., *Gifts of Power: The Writings of Rebecca Jackson, Black Visionary, Shaker Eldress* (Amherst: University of Massachusetts Press, 1981).

27. Jualynne E. Dodson and Cheryl Townsend Gilkes, "Something Within: Social Change and Collective Endurance in the Sacred World of Black Christian Women," in Rosemary Radford Ruether and Rosemary Skinner Keller, *Women and Religion in America. Vol. 3. 1900–1968* (San Francisco: Harper and Row, 1986), 80–130.

28. Jualynne E. Dodson, "Nineteenth-Century A.M.E. Preaching Women," in Hilah F. Thomas and Rosemary Skinner Keller, eds., *Women in New Worlds: Historical Perspectives on the Wesleyan Tradition* (Nashville: Abingdon, 1981), 276–89. A forthcoming work by Nellie Y. McKay will take a literary criticism approach to these narratives.

29. Jualynne E. Dodson, "Power and Surrogate Leadership: Black Women and Organized Religion," *Sage* 5(2) (Fall 1988): 39. See also David W. Wills,

"Womanhood and Domesticity in the AME Tradition: The Influence of Daniel Alexander Payne," in David W. Wills and Richard Newman, *Black Apostles at Home and Abroad: Afro-Americans and the Christian Missions From Revolution to Reconstruction* (Boston: G. K. Hall, 1982), 133–46; Stephen W. Angell, "The Controversy Over Women's Ministry in the AME Church, 1881–1888: The Case of Sarah Ann Hughes," in Judith Weisenfeld and Richard Newman, eds., *This Far By Faith: Readings in African-American Women's Religious Biography* (New York: Routledge, 1996), 94–109.

30. Cheryl Townsend Gilkes, "The Roles of Church and Community Mothers: Ambivalent American Sexism or Fragmented American Familyhood?" *Journal of Feminist Studies in Religion* 2 (Spring 1986): 41–59, and "Together in Harness: Women's Traditions in the Sanctified Church," *Signs* 10 (1985): 678–99.

31. Higginbotham, *Righteous Discontent.*

32. Higginbotham, *Righteous Discontent*, 192.

33. The term "womanist" was coined by Alice Walker and defined in *In Search of Our Mothers' Gardens: Womanist Prose* (San Diego: Harcourt, Brace, Jovanovich, 1983). In part, her definition reads: "1. From *womanish* . . . (Opp. of 'girlish,' i.e., frivolous, irresponsible, not serious.) A black feminist or feminist of color. From the black folk expression of mothers to female children, 'You acting womanish,' i.e., like a woman. Usually referring to outrageous, audacious, courageous or willful behavior. Wanting to know more and in greater depth that is considered 'good' for one . . . Responsible. In charge. *Serious.* 2. Loves music. Loves dance. Loves the moon. Loves the Spirit. Loves love and food and roundness. Loves struggle. *Loves* the Folk. Loves herself. *Regardless.*"

34. Emilie M. Townes, *Womanist Justice, Womanist Hope* (Atlanta: Scholars Press, 1993); Katie Geneva Cannon, *Black Womanist Ethics* (Atlanta: Scholars Press, 1988). See also Delores Williams, *Sisters in the Wilderness* (Maryknoll, N.Y.: Orbis Books, 1993); Cheryl Sanders, Katie G. Cannon, Emilie M. Townes, M. Shawn Copeland, bell hooks, and Cheryl Townsend Gilkes, "Roundtable Discussion," *Journal of Feminist Studies in Religion* 5 (1989): 83–112; Delores Williams, "The Color of Feminism: Or Speaking the Black Woman's Tongue," *Christianity and Crisis* 45 (April 25, 1985): 164–65.

35. The classic introductory text is Eileen Southern, *The Music of Black Americans: A History,* 2nd ed. (New York: Norton, 1983). Also see Jon Michael Spencer, *Black Hymnody: A Hymnological History of the African-American Church* (Knoxville: University of Tennessee Press, 1992), and *Protest and Praise: Sacred Music of Black Religion* (Minneapolis Fortress Press, 1990); Joan R. Hillsman, *Gospel Music: An African-American Art Form* (Washington, D.C.: Middle Atlantic Regional Press, 1990); Paul Oliver, *Songsters and Saints: Vocal Traditions on Race Records* (New York: Oxford University Press, 1989); Irene V. Jackson, *Afro-American Religious Music: A Bibliography and a Catalogue of Gospel Music* (Westport, Conn.: Greenwood Press, 1979); Eileen Southern, *African American Traditions in Song, Sermon, Tale, Dance, 1600s–1920: An Annotated Bibliography of Literature, Collections, and Artworks* (New York: Greenwood Press, 1990). "Say Amen, Somebody" (Pacific Arts Video Records, 1982) is an excellent teaching tool.

36. See, for example, G. William Jones, *Black Cinema Treasures Lost and Found* (Denton, Tex.: University of North Texas Press, 1991); Thomas Cripps, *Black Film as Genre* (New York: Oxford University Press, 1978).

37. Gladys-Marie Fry, "Harriet Powers: Portrait of a Black Quilter," *Sage* 4

(Spring 1987): 11–16; Michelle Cliff, " 'I Found God in Myself and I Loved Her / I Loved Her Fiercely.' More Thoughts on the Work of Black Women Artists," *Journal of Feminist Studies in Religion* 2 (Spring 1986): 7–39; Freida High W. Tesfagiorgis, "In Search of a Discourse and Critique/s That Center the Art of Black Women Artists," in Stanlie M. James and Abena P. A. Busia, eds., *Theorizing Black Feminisms: The Visionary Pragmatism of Black Women* (London: Routledge Press, 1993), 228–66; bell hooks, "Aesthetic Inheritances: History Worked by Hand," in *Yearning*, 115–22.

38. Martia Graham Goodson, "Medical–Botanical Contributions of African Slave Women to American Medicine," *The Western Journal of Black Studies* 11(4) (1987): 198–203; Albert J. Raboteau, "The Afro-American Traditions," in Ronald L. Numbers and Darell W. Amundsen, eds., *Caring and Curing: Health and Medicine in the Western Religious Traditions* (New York: Macmillan, 1986), 539–62; Onnie Lee Logan, *Motherwit: An Alabama Midwife's Story* (New York: Dutton, 1989); Lewis V. Baldwin, " 'A Home in Dat Rock': Afro-American Folk Sources and Slave Visions of Heaven and Hell," *Journal of Religious Thought* 41 (Spring/Summer 1984): 38–57; Hans Baer, "Toward a Systematic Typology of Black Folk Healers," *Phylon* 43 (Winter 1982): 327–43; Morton Marks, " 'You Can't Sing Unless You're Saved': Reliving the Call in Gospel Music," in Simon Ottenberg, ed., *African Religious Groups and Beliefs: Papers in Honor of William R. Bascom* (Cupertino, Ca.: Folklore Institute, 1982), 305–31. *Daughters of the Dust* (Geechee Girls, 1991) directed by Julie Dash and *To Sleep With Anger* (Samuel Goldwyn, 1990) directed by Charles Burnett are two films that use black folk religious beliefs and practices as central themes.

39. On black preaching traditions, see Jon Michael Spencer, *Sacred Symphony: The Chanted Sermon of the Black Preacher* (Westport, Conn.: Greenwood Press, 1987). Sterling Stuckey's *Going Through the Storm: The Influence of African-American Art in History* (New York: Oxford University Press, 1994), a collection of essays, old and new, is a strong example of the kind of benefits that such an approach yields.

40. For information on religious affiliations of African Americans, see Wardell J. Payne, ed., *Directory of African-American Religious Bodies* (Washington, D.C.: Howard University Press, 1991).

41. Cyprian Davis, *A History of Black Catholics in the United States* (New York: Crossroad Press, 1990); Stephen J. Ochs, *Desegregating the Altar: The Josephites and the Struggle for Black Priests, 1871–1960* (Baton Rouge: Louisiana State University Press, 1990); Sister M. Reginald Gerdes, O.S.P., "To Educate and Evangelize: Black Catholic Schools of the Oblate Sisters of Providence (1828–1880) *U.S. Catholic Historian* 7 (Spring/Summer 1988): 183–99; Albert J. Raboteau, "Black Catholics: A Capsule History," *Catholic Digest* (June 1983): 32–38.

42. See, for example, Arthur Huff Fauset, *Black Gods of the Metropolis* (Philadelphia: University of Pennsylvania Press, 1944); Howard Brotz, *The Black Jews of Harlem: Negro Nationalism and the Dilemma of Negro Leadership* (New York: Schocken Books, 1970); Jill Watt, *God, Harlem, USA* (Berkeley: University of California Press, 1992); Robert Weisbrot, *Father Divine and the Struggle for Racial Equality* (Urbana: University of Illinois Press, 1983).

43. Randall K. Burkett, *Garveyism as a Religious Movement: the Institutionalization of a Black Civil Religion* (Metuchen, N.J.: Scarecrow, 1978), and *Black Redemption: Churchmen Speak for the Garvey Movement* (Philadelphia: Temple University Press, 1978); Hans A. Baer and Merrill Singer, *African-American Reli-*

gion in the Twentieth Century: Varieties of Protest and Accommodation (Knox-ville: University of Tennessee Press, 1992).

44. Sandy Dwayne Martin, *Black Baptists and African Missions: The Origins of a Movement, 1880–1915* (Macon, Ga.: Mercer University Press, 1989); Sylvia Jacobs, "Afro-American Women Missionaries Confront the African Way of Life," in Rosalyn Terborg-Penn, ed., *Women in Africa and the African Diaspora* (Washington, D.C.: Howard University Press, 1988), 121–33; Sylvia Jacobs, " 'Say Africa When You Pray': The Activities of Early Black Baptist Women Missionaries Among Liberian Women and Children," *Sage* 3 (1986): 16–21; Sylvia Jacobs, ed., *Black Americans and the Missionary Movement in Africa* (Westport, Conn.: Greenwood Press, 1980). See also Elliot P. Skinner, *African Americans and U.S. Policy Toward Africa, 1850–1924* (Washington, D.C.: Howard University Press, 1992).

45. Joseph M. Murphy, *Working the Spirit: Ceremonies of the African Dias-pora* (Boston: Beacon Press, 1994) and *Santería: An African Religion in America* (Boston: Beacon Press, 1988); Raul Canizares, *Walking With the Night: The Afro-Cuban World of Santería* (Rochester, Vt.: Destiny Books, 1993); George Brandon, *The Dead Sell Memories: Santería From Africa to the New World* (Indi-anapolis: University of Indiana Press, 1993); Karen McCarthy Brown, *Mama Lola: A Vodou Priestess in Brooklyn* (Berkeley: University of California Press, 1990); Leslie G. Desmangles, *The Faces of the Gods: Vodou and Roman Catholi-cism in Haiti* (Chapel Hill: University of North Carolina Press, 1992). An espe-cially useful teaching tool is Karen Kramer's film, *Legacy of the Spirits* (New York, 1985) on Vodou in New York.

46. The following works demonstrate the benefits of such research: Ralph Luker, *The Social Gospel in Black and White: American Racial Reform, 1885–1912* (Chapel Hill: University of North Carolina Press, 1991); Ronald C. White, *Liberty and Justice For All: Racial Reform and the Social Gospel, 1877–1925* (San Francisco: Harper and Row 1990); Susan Lynn, *Progressive Women in Conserva-tive Times: Racial Justice, Peace and Feminism, 1945–1960's* (New Brunswick, NJ: Rutgers University Press, 1992); Anne Firor Scott, *Natural Allies: Women's Associ-ations in American History* (Urbana, Ill.: University of Illinois Press, 1991).

47. After spending many years in rented quarters, the Harlem YWCA's newly constructed facilities at 137th Street and Lenox Avenue opened in 1921. The basement housed the cafeteria and its kitchen, with a capacity of one hundred. The main floor had reception rooms, meeting rooms, classrooms, offices, and the information desk. The third floor had locker rooms, showers, and a laundry, as well as gymnasium rooms. The fourth floor housed the pool. An annex was built a number of years later to provide additional classroom space. The Harlem YWCA also constructed an adjacent building which housed the residence. See Judith Weisenfeld, "The More Abundant Life: The Harlem Branch of the New York City Young Women's Christian Association, 1905–1945" (Ph.D. disserta-tion, Princeton University, 1992).

48. Among these works on clubs are Paula Giddings, *Where and When I Enter: The Impact of Black Women on Race and Sex in America* (New York: Bantam Books, 1984); Dorothy Salem, *To Better Our World: Black Women in Organized Reform, 1890–1920* (Brooklyn: Carlson, 1990); Stephanie J. Shaw, "Black Club Women and the Creation of the National Association of Colored Women," *Journal of Women's History* 3(2) (1991), 10–25.

49. See, for example, Adrienne Lash Jones, *Jane Edna Hunter: A Case Study of Black Leadership, 1910–1950* (Brooklyn: Carlson, 1990).

15

RECENT AMERICAN CATHOLIC HISTORIOGRAPHY

New Directions in Religious History

▦ ▦ ▦

Patrick Carey

SINCE AT LEAST THE late nineteenth century the major histories of American Catholicism and Protestantism have been influenced by many of the same historiographical canons and methodologies.[1] My reflections here on the recent (post-1970) historiography of American Catholicism are governed by the convictions that historians of Catholic and Protestant traditions share similar diverse historical methods and goals, and that the subjects of their historical examinations have social and religious identities that are inextricably and historically tied together. Both convictions mean that what I say here and the questions I raise about the historiography of American Catholicism apply *mutatis mutandis* to the historiography of American Protestantism.

In the last twenty years historical studies of American Catholicism have increased in quantity, deepened in quality, and burgeoned in a variety of new directions. I have reviewed that literature in another place.[2] Here I will not examine the multiple new directions of that historiography, but instead will point to some benefits and limits of the New Social History, indicate topics that I believe need more comparative historical analyses, and suggest some areas in American Catholic intellectual history, my own field of interest and study, that require examination.

Historians of American Catholicism, like historians in other fields, have been particularly influenced since the 1960s by the New Social History. They have been receptive to the dynamics of social history not only because it came to prominence in the general field of history but also because of the paradigmatic theological shift fostered by the Second Vatican Council. The shift in ecclesiological orientations from a perception of the church primarily as an institution that preserved and fostered unity and continuity to a concept of the church as "People of God," as Jay P. Dolan explicitly acknowledged in his social history of *The American Catholic Experience,*[3] had major consequences for the topics and objects that commanded the attention of the post-1960s historians.[4]

Unlike John Tracy Ellis and Thomas McAvoy, consensus historians of the 1950s and early 1960s, who emphasized the institutional and social–political unity of the Catholic tradition,[5] New Social Historians of Catholicism like Jay P. Dolan emphasize the diverse social forces within the tradition, the extra- and para-institutional dimensions, the roles of the laity in general and women in particular, the dynamics of ethnicity and race, the internal conflict of competing social and ethnically based religious traditions, and the differences between the religious and moral prescriptions of the institutional church and the actual practices of the family, local parish, voluntary group, or individual Catholic. The major section of Dolan's general history, for example, covers a period from about 1830 to 1930 and is called "The Immigrant Church," a phrase that defines the church primarily in social rather than theological or institutional categories.[6]

Because the immigrant experience was such a major part of American history, Dolan suggested in another work, it should become a "major theme or organizing principle" in the study of American religion and not just of Catholicism. This historical focus, he argued, could be as important as Puritanism, evangelicalism, and fundamentalism in providing coherence and synthesis for understanding an interdenominational social dimension of religion in the United States.[7] The attempt to discover the religious mentality of the immigrant laity, moreover, had the benefit of expanding the scope of historical interests from the intellectual elites to the Christian masses. Dolan's advocacy of immigration as a topic of investigation in religious history is consistent with the concerns of other social historians that religious history be more inclusive than in the past.

Other historians of American Catholicism have called for a broader examination of the ways in which Catholicism has been a common as well as a distinct part of American cultural and religious history. David O'Brien demonstrated convincingly in 1972 that historians of American religion had neglected the story of American Catholicism in their general histories and offered as one of the reasons for that development the failure of historians of American Catholicism to present Catholicism as part of American cultural history. So much previous history had focused almost exclusively upon the institutional Catholic church as a separatist denomination that it was almost impossible for the general historian to perceive the relevance of Catholicism to American history.[8]

Although general histories of American culture have failed to incorporate new studies of American Catholicism in their works, recent general histories of religion in America, from Sydney Ahlstrom's *A Religious History of the American People* (1975) to Mark Noll's *A History of Christianity in the United States and Canada* (1992), have given much greater attention to the Catholic experience than previous histories. Historians of American Catholicism, moreover, have increasingly followed suggestions made by Dolan, O'Brien, and others, giving greater attention to those dimensions of Catholicism that fit into the history of American culture and that resonate with the social–historical interests of other historians of religion.

Since the late 1960s, social history, with its emphases upon the study of particular units of society and broad demographic and quantitative trends, has influenced the historical studies of American Catholicism in a number of different directions and has caused historians to highlight the stories of people generally left out of the early histories. Recent historical monographs have focused on African American Catholics, Hispanic Catholics, American Catholic women, religious women in particular, local and regional parish histories, new diocesan histories that reflect the social as well as institutional dimensions of the tradition in different geographical areas, and forms of popular Catholic spirituality.[9]

One of the most creative recent attempts to understand popular Catholic spirituality has been that of Robert Orsi, who has combined the methodologies of social history and religious studies to uncover the religious mentality of Italian Catholics at Mount Carmel parish in East Harlem, New York, between 1880 and 1950.[10] Centering his examination on the annual *festa* of the Madonna, Orsi has reconstructed the religious world of the people of the parish by examining the inner meaning the *festa* had for them. Analyzing recorded interviews of the 1920s and 1930s, his own oral interviews with surviving participants, local parish documents and family records, and the actual ritual practices associated with the *festa,* he shows how urban Italian-Americans related their faith to their understanding of gender, family, and community under the sacred canopy of their annual ritual celebration. Orsi argues that their religion was "deeply Catholic" even though it differed from Americanized institutional forms of Catholicism and was periodically criticized by the religious establishment as superstitious or pagan. By popular religion Orsi means the integration of religious drama (as expressed in the people's sacred rituals, practices, symbols, prayers, and faith) and the inner meaning of ultimacy that the participants found in their actions.

In addition to revealing the presence and voices of people missing from the former American Catholic historical narratives, the great benefit of the social historian's study of Catholicism has been the unveiling of multiple levels of diversity and conflict that have existed within the tradition, the varying degrees of alliance to the institutional church, the effectiveness of ethnically based social relations and institutions in the transmission and preservation of the faith, the roles of laity and women in particular in the communication of Catholic life and thought, and the religious mentalities of the immigrants and others.

Social history has made, is making, and will continue to make valuable contributions to our understanding of Catholicism. But the shift to social history raises at least three issues for me. The first issue is really the lack of a sufficient number of detailed social histories and monographs that could provide sufficient ground for the writing of a generally representative social history of American Catholicism. There is nothing comparable to the French *Annales* school among scholars of American Catholicism—at least not in terms of the number of detailed social histories of parishes and regions, the number of historians involved, and the methodological sophistication. There are just too many areas of American Catholic life and thought that are unexamined by historians— whether they are social historians or not. Social histories of parishes, dioceses, geographical regions, religious orders, clergy, bishops, and various voluntary movements within American Catholicism, to name a few areas, still need historians.

Second, the question of what is truly representative of Catholicism comes to the fore. The present state of historical scholarship, with its emphases on various ethnic and social groups within the tradition, makes it difficult to distinguish what is central and what is peripheral to Catholicism. The focus of social historians upon what is statistically representative raises the issue of representation even more pointedly. Is what counts as representative what is numerically representative or what is historically representative in the church's tradition and historic documents of self-understanding? Has one represented Catholicism when one has described what the Catholic masses think, believe, and do when they think, believe, and do it in relation to what they consider divine? Does the historian square the social description of what is representative with the normative descriptions that emerge from representative traditional documents? The problem becomes even more compounded in view of the fact that Catholic self-understandings, even in the normative documents, develop and are conditioned by historic social, political, and psychological factors. Does all this simply mean that what is representative of Catholicism is historically relative and pluralistic? The same question could be raised in reference to the study of various Protestant traditions.

The question is difficult. First, I agree with Yves Congar's view that "knowledge of history makes possible a healthy relativism, which is quite different from scepticism."[11] A "healthy relativism" makes it possible to attribute absoluteness only to what is really absolute. Relativism helps one avoid the mistake of identifying as "tradition," for example, that which is only recent or American and which has been altered more than once in the course of time. Second, a healthy relativism need not deny the permanent and the transcendent, even though the historical method may not be able to locate or identify it. A healthy relativism, moreover, need not deny that there is such a thing as the Catholic Tradition, which has a continuous as well as a developing and decaying dimension to it.

Third, and closely related to the second, is the issue of the implicit or explicit definitions of Catholicism that are found in the social descriptions of Catholicism. The shift from the institutional or even theological definition of Catholicism to the social definition was significant because the shift carried with it certain assumptions about the nature of church as a social reality, and because of that historians tended to favor some forms of evidence (e.g., statistics, polls, forms of popular religion) over others (e.g., ecclesiastical statements, literature of the clerical and theological elites) and some forms of behavior (e.g., conflicts with ecclesiastical authority, folk religious expressions) over others (e.g., joint episcopal conciliar actions and statements, ecclesiastical laws) as the primary subjects of historical investigation. The very "form" of social historical narratives of Catholicism, moreover, carried with it a "content"—if I might borrow and adapt an approach of Hayden White. Like other kinds of historical narratives, the social historical narratives of Catholic Christianity involve "ontological and epistemic choices" with distinct theological, ideological, and political implications.[12]

Few historians today have any illusions about objective history or completely detached historians even when, like Philip Gleason, they argue for a "common-sense realism" in affirming that historical statements can have a knowable objective referent and that there is a "truth" about the past that is the fundamental premise of all historical investigation, understanding, and interpretation (although that "truth" may not be fully reached because of the inadequacy of the sources and the individual and social subjective conditions and values of the historian).[13] Like other historians, social historians of Catholicism have made definite epistemic choices that are not theologically neutral or (entirely) scientifically objective. Their preoccupations with what is general or popular or folk or statistically representative tend to identify Catholicism itself with the social description found in the narratives.

The problem that emerges from this tendency in the social narrative, if I am correct about it, is not only the reader's inability to distinguish what is central from what is peripheral in the tradition but also the historian's inability to make decisions about genuine developments or aberrations within a tradition. To identify a development or a decay implies a standard by which such a judgment can be made. What criteria does the historian use to judge an historic development, abuse, or aberration in the institutional church or among the people of a religious tradition? What enables the historian to distinguish traditions from the Tradition in Catholicism?[14] What, too, are the norms for judging success or failure in a religious tradition? These are all normative questions, but they seem to me to be inherently involved in any descriptive narrative of historical change and continuity. Is it not incumbent upon the historian to make clear to the reader the criteria that are consciously operative in the historian's work? Analogous questions might be raised in regard to developments in American Protestantism.

Another issue that affects both Protestant and Catholic traditions is the persistence of denominational identities. I am unaware, however, of any comparative historical examinations of the reasons for denominational persistence. Many recent religious historians have desired to transcend the celebratory denominational histories of the past because they were considered sectarian and unrelated to cultural developments in American society. Major transdenominational phenomena like Puritanism, evangelicalism, fundamentalism, and immigrant religion, to name a few of the twentieth-century interests, have captured the attention of historians who are inclined to discover the patterns that unite peoples or that transcend parochial interests. There is a need, however, to explain the obvious persistence of denominationalism, however weakened it might be.

Some contemporary commentators and social analysts of religion in the United States have pointed to the decline of denominationalism since World War II,[15] and historians have frequently acknowledged that denominational affiliation in United States has generally been fluid and tenuous. Historians, too, have been aware of the transdenominational nature of much religious activity in the United States and of the cross- and intradenominational nature of liberal, conservative, and fundamentalist movements. Most studies of American religion and most general histories of religion among the American people, moreover, focus more upon the commonalities than upon the distinctives of American religious traditions; even when they point to major religious differences that exist they show how these differences are intradenominational as well as transdenominational.

These judgments on the decline or weakness of denominationalism have the support of historical evidence, but they leave unanswered a major question about the equally obvious persistence of denominationalism. How is it that some liberals or fundamentalists remain Baptists? What is there in the Baptist tradition that holds them together—even if in uneasy alliance? What is there in the passing on of the tradition, in the structures of socialization, and in the organizational operation that preserves the denominational alignment? Current official ecumenical dialogues between theologians and ecclesiastical leaders, as well as sociological studies and opinion polls, demonstrate very clearly that denominationalism still exists, even though somewhat attenuated by the ecumenical spirit among some religious peoples. Denominationalism, too, is pervasive not only among church elites but also among rank and file membership, even though many within the rank and file may not be able to give cogent reasons for their denominational distinctives and their own denominational affiliation. What is it in the specific traditions that effectively passes on and preserves a sense of denominational identity?

I raise the question because I think historians, not just social scientists, need to think about the long-term implications of denominationalism and what makes it work over the long haul—because it certainly functions in the United States at the national as well as at the local level through denominational church bodies. Paying closer historical attention to denominational structures and specific traditions or forms of religious socialization may also help us to understand more clearly how and why some denominations have continued to increase and some have experienced severe decline over the last two centuries—forces that social scientists have not explained.[16] Tradition (understood here as a process of handing on the faith) operates very specifically in Protestantism as well as in Catholicism and Eastern Orthodoxy, and it needs more historical reflection on how it operates within the Protestant denominations, even those that are almost confessionally and traditionally antitraditional.

Another area that needs closer historical attention is the comparative study of American Protestantism and Catholicism. Sociologists have been much more active in such comparative studies than have historians of religion in the United States. As far as I am aware, there are few comparative historical studies of how these two traditions function in American society and almost none on their comparative intellectual histories.

A comparative historical study of conservative twentieth-century American Protestantism with Catholicism, for example, may prove fruitful in revealing how a large proportion of the religious population has functioned in American society. The critical and yet sympathetic recent studies of evangelicalism, conservative Protestantism, fundamentalism, Pentecostalism, and Holiness movements by Joel Carpenter, Wilbert Shenk, Nathan Hatch, George Marsden, Mark Noll, Ernest Sandeen, Leonard Sweet, Grant Wacker, and a host of others offer an arena for numerous comparisons to developments in nineteenth- and twentieth-century American Catholicism.[17]

These historians have revealed the theological mindset, mentality, and religious sensibilities of a very large segment of the Protestant population in this country and have helped to put in historical context the evangelical rise to political and social influence in the last third of the twentieth century. More significantly, especially for someone like myself, who was not exposed to the history of conservative American Protestantism in graduate school, these studies have tended to change understandings of what is dominant (at least numerically) in twentieth-century American Protestantism. It is no longer possible to believe, as I once did, that liberal and neo-orthodox Protestants were representative of the Protestant mainstream simply because they had control over most of the major centers of intellectual culture.

Although there were numerous and significant differences between Catholicism and conservative evangelicalism in ecclesiastical structures, theology, sacramentalism, and general religious sensibilities, there were a number of parallel experiences, especially in the twentieth century prior to the Second Vatican Council, that flowed from their mutual isolation and alienation from the sources of cultural power and their gradual emergence as major players in the political and social arena in the last third of the twentieth century. Historians of American Catholicism would do well to examine the analogous experiences for the light they might throw on both traditions and upon the role of conservative religious traditions in American society.

Historians could also analyze and compare pre–Vatican II twentieth-century American Catholic and conservative Protestant religious thought. Although isolated from the centers of intellectual and cultural power and prestige throughout much of the twentieth century, both traditions developed intellectual positions that in different ways challenged many presuppositions and conclusions of their liberal and neo-orthodox fellow Christians who resided in the mainline universities and seminaries. An examination of these intellectual traditions would present a more complete picture of the various Christian intellectual options in American society than is normally presented in intellectual histories that focus almost exclusively on the thought of the neo-orthodox and liberal Christian cultural elites.

Prior to the mid 1960s, Catholics and conservative evangelicals shared a view that America was being captured by a growing secularism (i.e., as the American Catholic bishops jointly defined it in 1947: a progressive exclusion of God and the supernatural from education, politics and law, marriage, literature and movies, and economics[18]), that a militant religious opposition was the remedy, and that the church needed to focus its attention on building effective institutional organs for the transmission of the faith, for the protection of its integrity, and for the preservation of a moral and religious lifestyle at odds with an increasing secularism. Neither the conservative evangelicals nor the Catholics, moreover, were monolithic in their approaches to culture, to institutional arrangements, or to ecumenical affairs. After World War II, numerous internal disagreements erupted in both traditions, most notably over the issues of separationism and militancy in the public forum.[19]

What is needed, it seems to me, are long-term comparative historical studies that draw attention to these parallels from the perspective of their mutual social location outside the realms of cultural power. These two groups in particular represent a significant portion of the Christian presence in the United States in the twentieth century, and we cannot adequately understand the religious texture of the United States without the light of more comparative analyses. Currently, most studies of these two groups are done pretty much in isolation. References to Catholicism in studies of conservative evangelicalism as well as references to evangelicalism in studies of Catholicism lack the specificity that would provide for a fuller understanding of the respective roles of each.

The history of American religious thought provides other areas in which a comparative study might prove insightful. Most histories leave out of the picture almost completely the Catholic side of the intellectual debates. References to Catholicism, if there are any, are so generalized that they leave the impression that Catholics had nothing to say about the particular religious issues. One gets the impression also that there was a Protestant monolithic view of Catholicism and that that view was unaffected by particular intellectual developments and/or specific historical events within the American Catholic community. The defect lies not with those scholars who have examined the development of Protestant thought in the United States but with historians of American Catholicism who have failed to examine the Catholic reactions to major intellectual developments within European Catholicism and American Protestantism.

Intellectual history is one area of study that escaped the concerns of major pre- and immediate post–Vatican II historians of American Catholicism, presumably because there was no history there to uncover.[20] Pre-1960 historians of American Catholicism paid little attention to ideological elements.[21] Catholics had few centers of vibrant intellectual activity in the nineteenth century and produced only a few creative intellectual contributions in the first half of the twentieth century. Periodically through their newspapers, journals, and apologetical tracts, however, they engaged in the intellectual and especially theological or polemical discussions of their day.

Since 1970 more attention has been given to the intellectual development of the American Catholic tradition. Numerous recent dissertations, articles, and monographs have focused on various aspects of the evolution of American Catholic intellectual life,[22] but until 1989 only one major comprehensive work exclusively devoted to that development had been published.[23] Philip Gleason's works have been perhaps the most insightful and most enlightening for placing twentieth-century American Catholic ideological developments in the broad context of American intellectual history. His seminal articles on the semantic and intellectual history of twentieth-century concepts like Americanization, assimiliation, consensus, cultural pluralism, identity, and neo-Thomism have brought conceptual clarity to the field.[24]

Although there have been some overtures in the direction of intellectual history, historians of American Catholicism have rarely examined in detail the actual interaction that took place between Protestant and Catholic scholars in the nineteenth and twentieth centuries over religious issues, or the Catholic understanding of major developments in American Protestant thought.

To be more concrete, let me outline a few areas of intellectual history where the Catholic perspective needs to be represented, not only because it existed but because it tells us much about what was common as well as distinctive in American religious thought. The rise of Unitarianism, for example, created a few significant reactions in the American Catholic community that have never been acknowledged. The Jesuit Anthony Kohlmann, president of Georgetown College, wrote a two-volume attack upon Unitarianism in 1820–21, revealing a Cartesian and Gallican-influenced theology that was typical of many American Catholic clergy.[25] Siding with Moses Stuart and other opponents of Unitarianism, Kohlmann demonstrated what he perceived to be the Unitarian threat to Protestant as well as Catholic Christianity. Historians have never examined his arguments nor, more importantly, the whole Gallican–Cartesian connection and intellectual milieu of many of the Catholic clergy who served and taught in the antebellum period. Historians of American Catholic thought, following the example of historians of American Protestantism, need to examine more fully the transatlantic intellectual environment in which most American Catholic thinkers lived in both the nineteenth and twentieth centuries. Rarely have historians studied the European, particularly the influential French, context and origins of much nineteenth-century Catholic thought, its reception and transformation in the American social setting, and its development in interaction with specific American issues and discussions.[26]

After the 1840s, Unitarianism was for some Catholics a symbol of Protestant decline but simultaneously an attractive alternative to a Calvinism they believed had denigrated reason and human nature. Orestes Brownson and Isaac Hecker, both before and after their movement into Catholicism, were preoccupied with the meaning of Unitarianism for the United States. After his entrance into Catholicism, Brownson repeatedly in the late 1850s and 1860s returned to examine Unitarian principles from the perspective of French traditionalism and Italian ontologism, which by then had greatly influenced his religious epistemology and his view of church and society. Brownson's arguments from his Catholic period have not been a part of the major intellectual histories of American religious thought, even though his traditionalist and ontologist perspective represented a religious intellectual option for major thinkers in France, Belgium, and Italy, and for a number of European-educated American Catholic clergy during the 1850s and 1860s.

The religious battles over Transcendentalism, moreover, also had Catholic dimensions to them. Although historians are well aware of the role Brownson played in the debates while a member of the Transcendentalist movement, they seldom follow his later reactions as a Catholic when he came under the influence of traditionalism and ontologism. Brownson's intuitive religious epistemology and his ontologism, moreover, came into play in his reactions to Horace Bushnell's and John Williamson Nevin's approaches, providing a Catholic Romantic alternative to their thought as well as to that of Ralph Waldo Emerson and Theodore Parker. Yet one does not usually find mention of this option in histories of American religious thought.

Histories of nineteenth-century evangelicalism, too, leave out the Catholic reactions to the movement or simply indicate in very general terms the anti-Catholicism that drove some in the evangelical empire.[27] Beneath the Catholic and evangelical polemics of the 1830s and 1840s, however, were some significant and very specific issues that need more than a cursory nod. Behind some of the Catholic newspaper slurs on the evangelical "saints," for example, were issues of religious liberty and separation of church and state, which some Catholics like John England saw threatened in the evangelical attempts to Christianize America.[28] Bringing the early nineteenth-century Catholic understandings of these issues into more general histories would do much to correct the mistaken impression that American Catholics began to articulate a sympathetic and systematic view of religious liberty only with John Courtney Murray, S.J., in the middle of the twentieth century.

A number of attempts have been made in recent years to relate late-nineteenth- and early-twentieth-century Americanism and modernism to developments in the liberal Protestant evangelical tradition,[29] but few efforts have been focused upon a specifically Catholic progressivism during the early twentieth century, especially as it relates to Protestant progressivism.[30] Although there have been a number of perceptive works on the early twentieth century rise of neo-Thomism in recent years,[31] there are few studies of the neo-Thomists' reactions to William James's pragmatism, John Dewey's humanism, neo-orthodoxy, fundamentalism, or neo-evangelicalism. No doubt the reactions were generally negative, but those reactions are worth examining to help understand the twentieth-century intellectual tradition that did develop within a huge segment of the American religious population. The generality of my comments here indicates the lack of specific studies in these areas.[32]

We would have a wider picture of what intellectual religious options were available in the United States if we bring Catholic perspectives into our intellectual history. It seems to me that this is particularly imperative for historians who write for Catholic as well as Protestant students and other public audiences who no longer know, if they ever did, what was at stake in the religious issues discussed in the nineteenth and twentieth centuries. American religious issues were not exclusively Protestant affairs. Catholics were periodically involved. And, Catholics had their own particular internal intellectual debates that also need careful historical analysis.

In a culture that was predominantly Protestant and republican, how did American Catholic elites make intellectually credible a tradition that most in the culture considered alien to reason and the biblical tradition? Certainly, Catholic bishops and others from the nineteenth century onward were well aware of the task before them, and they worked assiduously in formulating a sense of Catholic identity that was not merely a matter of authoritarian control. The intellectual and polemical dynamics involved in this experience need more careful examination than has been given in the past.

Intellectual historians, moreover, need to examine the shared presuppositions within the Catholic communities during particular periods, to penetrate the implied major premises, and to explain the changes that took place from age to age among the elites and the general membership. The Catholic emphases upon organic community and hierarchical authority became a significant part of the American experience—one, however, that is largely overlooked by those who define religious America largely in terms of individualism or voluntarism. What is needed is a history of the American Catholic mentality akin to studies of Puritanism, evangelicalism, liberalism, and fundamentalism. What is it that constitutes the overriding sense of Catholicism from age to age, and precisely where and how do the shifts in self-understanding take place?

The current advocacy of more social history of American Catholicism, which I support, should not obscure the need for intellectual history, an area that is wide open for new historians. In American Catholicism there is not, as there is in American Protestantism, a tradition of intellectual history that new historians need to revise. New historians must create it. These new intellectual historians, however, would be well advised to incorporate the insights and findings of the social historians, pay attention to the broad issue of religious mentalities, and be more circumspect than some previous intellectual historians in making claims for representation where the evidence is not available. They might also seek to discover how the theological thought of the clerical and lay elites came to be diffused to the Catholic masses. How much of what major systematic theologians wrote was changed and modified by episcopal, clerical, and lay communicators in order to have a collective impact upon the people? How did complex theological issues become simplified and rendered more or less flexible, rigorous or rigid in popular formulas for purposes of popular consumption? In response to these and other questions, the intellectual historian will establish a dialectic between what is "given" by the elites and what is "received" and "lived" by the general Catholic population. There is also a need, however, to examine how the experience of the general Catholic population influenced the thought of the elites.

The historiography of American Catholicism is not entirely unlike the historiography of American Protestantism, as I said above. Historians of both traditions are concerned with describing what was continuous and what was going forward in the various self-identities of the communities over time. For most of the last four centuries, there was a sense of what constituted Protestant and Catholic identity that was inextricably reciprocal. Much of Protestant self-understanding evolved in distinction to what was perceived to be Catholic self-awareness, and vice versa. My call for more comparative analysis here is predicated upon the belief that historians of both traditions need to pay closer attention to the interactive presuppositions, sensibilities, and collective imaginations that contribute to the formations of individual and communal identities in the past. These identities came out most clearly when religious groups defined themselves in opposition to other groups, even when they shared much more than they explicitly admitted (and historians need to pay more attention to the historic unadmitted religious commonalities underlying Protestant and Catholic differences). Faithful Unitarians, liberals, conservatives, and fundamentalists know they are Protestant, and they know in knowing this that they are not Catholic or Eastern Orthodox. Describing Protestant identity in America should take into account the intellectual and cultural interaction with Catholicism (as a Protestant-constructed mental image and as a concrete historical reality). Drawing Catholicism into the history of Protestantism is not ultimately just a matter of fair representation but a matter of defining social and religious identities.

NOTES

1. For a good comparative examination of this historiography, see Henry Warner Bowden, *Church History in the Age of Science: Historiographical Patterns in the United States, 1876–1918* (Chapel Hill: University of North Carolina Press, 1971); idem, *Church History in an Age of Uncertainty: Historiographical Patterns in the United States, 1906–1990* (Carbondale: Southern Illinois University Press, 1991). For particular studies limited to the historiography in American Catholicism, see J. Douglas Thomas, "Interpretations of American Catholic Church History: A Comparative Analysis of Representative Catholic Historians, 1875–1975" (Ph.D. dissertation, Baylor University, 1976); idem, "A Century of American Catholic History," *U.S. Catholic Historian* 6 (Winter 1987): 25–49; James Hennesey, "Church History and the Theologians," *U.S. Catholic Historian* 6 (Winter 1987): 1–12; Martin E. Marty, "Is There a *Mentalité* in the American Catholic House?" *U.S. Catholic Historian* 6 (Winter 1987): 13–23; David O'Brien, "American Catholic Historiography: A Post-Conciliar Evaluation," *Church History* 37 (March 1968): 80–94; idem, "American Catholicism and American Religion," *Journal of the American Academy of Religion* 40 (March 1972): 36–53; Jay P. Dolan, "The Immigrants and Their Gods: A New Perspective in American Religious History," *Church History* 57 (March 1988): 61–72; idem, "New Directions in American Catholic History," in Jay P. Dolan and James P. Wind, eds., *New Dimensions in American Religious History* (Grand Rapids, Mich.: Eerdmans, 1993): 152–74; and Philip Gleason, "The New Americanism in Catholic Historiography," *U.S. Catholic Historian* 11 (Summer 1993): 1–18.

2. See my "Bibliographic Essay" of post-1980 works on American Catholic history in my *Roman Catholics*, No. 6 of *Denominations in America*, ed. by Henry Warner Bowden (Westport, Conn.: Greenwood Press, 1993), 353–63.

3. Jay P. Dolan, *The American Catholic Experience: A History from Colonial Times to the Present* (Garden City, N.Y.: Doubleday, 1985), 9.

4. This is not the place to pursue the topic of the theological influence upon religious history, but I believe a good case could be made to show that historians of American religion, even those who have deliberately tried to abandon the tutelage of theology in their work, have been influenced either explicitly or implicitly by some theological orientation in their selection of the topics they believed needed historical reflection or study, the methodologies they employed, and in the written narratives or scientific presentations that were the results of their work.

5. John Tracy Ellis, *American Catholicism* 2nd ed., rev. (Chicago: University of Chicago Press, 1969); Thomas T. McAvoy, *A History of the Catholic Church in the United States* (Notre Dame, Ind.: University of Notre Dame Press, 1969).

6. For a positive assessment of the new directions in the social history of Catholicism, see Leslie Woodcock Tentler, "On the Margins: The State of American Catholic History," *American Quarterly* 45 (March 1993): 104–27. For a more critical analysis of recent social history of American Catholicism, particularly as practiced by Dolan, see George Weigel, "Capturing the Story Line: The New Historiography of American Catholicism," in his *Freedom and Its Discontents: Catholicism Confronts Modernity* (Washington, D.C.: Ethics and Public Policy Center, 1991), 129–49.

7. "Immigrants and Their Gods," 66.

8. "American Catholicism and American Religion" 36–53. Twenty years after O'Brien's complaint, Leslie Woodcock Tentler, "On the Margins," did not see much change in the general historians' awareness and use of new studies in American Catholicism. Twenty years of new historical analyses of Catholics and Catholicism are still, she charged in 1993, either ignored or at best of a marginal interest to the general historians of American culture.

9. Cyprian Davis, *The History of Black Catholics in the United States* (New York: Crossroad, 1990); Moises Sandoval, *Fronteras: A History of the Latin American Church in the USA Since 1513* (San Antonio, Tex.: Mexican American Cultural Center, 1983); idem, *On the Move: A History of the Hispanic Church in the United States* (Maryknoll, N.Y.: Orbis Books, 1990); James J. Kenneally, *The History of American Catholic Women* (New York: Crossroad, 1990); Karen Kennelly, ed., *American Catholic Women: A Historical Exploration* (New York: Macmillan, 1989); Margaret Susan Thompson, "Discovering Foremothers: Sisters, Society, and the American Catholic Experience," *U.S. Catholic Historian* 5 (1986): 273–90; idem, "Women, Feminism, and the New Religious History: Catholic Sisters as a Case Study," in Philip VanderMeer and Robert Swierenga, eds., *Belief and Behavior: Essays in the New Religious History* (New Brunswick, N.J.: Rutgers University Press, 1991), 136–63; idem, "Sisterhood and Power: Class, Culture, and Ethnicity in the American Convent," *Colby Library Quarterly* 25 (September 1989): 149–75; Barbara Misner, *Highly Respectable and Accomplished Ladies: Catholic Women in America, 1790–1850* (New York: Garland, 1988); idem, "Women Religious: Historical Explorations," *U.S. Catholic Historian* 10 (1992): 1–118; Jay P. Dolan, ed., *The American Catholic Parish: A History from 1850 to the Present*, 2 vols. (New York: Paulist Press, 1987); Thomas Spalding, *The Premier See: A History of the Archdiocese of Baltimore, 1789–1989* (Baltimore: Johns Hopkins University Press, 1989); Clyde F. Crews, *An American Holy Land: A History of the Archdiocese of Louisville* (Wilmington, Del.: Michael Glazier, 1984); Leslie Tentler, *Seasons of Grace: A History of the Catholic Archdiocese of Detroit* (Detroit: Wayne State University Press, 1990); Jay P. Dolan, *Catholic Revivalism: The American Experience, 1830–1900* (Notre Dame, Ind.: University of Notre Dame Press, 1978); Ann Taves, *The Household of Faith: Roman Catholic Devotions in Mid-Nineteenth Century America* (Notre Dame, Ind.: University of Notre Dame Press, 1986); Joseph P. Chinnici, *Living Stones: The History and Structure of Catholic Spiritual Life in the United States* (New York: Macmillan, 1989).

10. *The Madonna of 115th Street: Faith and Community in Italian Harlem, 1880–1950* (New Haven: Yale University Press, 1985). Orsi has also initiated a

major study of the popular devotion to St. Jude Thaddeus, the patron saint of hopeless cases. See his " 'He Keeps Me Going': Women's Devotion to Saint Jude Thaddeus and the Dialectics of Gender in American Catholicism, 1929–1965," in *Belief in History: Innovative Approaches to European and American Religion,* ed. Thomas Kselman (Notre Dame, Ind.: University of Notre Dame Press, 1991), 137–69.

11. Yves Congar, "Church History as a Branch of Theology," in *Church History in Future Perspective,* ed. Roger Aubert, vol. 57 of *Concilium* (New York: Herder and Herder, 1970), 88.

12. *The Content of the Form: Narrative Discourse and Historical Representation* (Baltimore: Johns Hopkins University Press, 1987), ix.

13. *Keeping the Faith: American Catholicism Past and Present* (Notre Dame, Ind.: University of Notre Dame Press, 1987), 217.

14. The distinction between traditions and Tradition, I take from Yves Congar, *Tradition and Traditions: An Historical and a Theological Essay,* trans. Michael Naseby and Thomas Rainborough (London: Burns & Oates, 1966).

15. See, for example, Robert Wuthnow, *The Restructuring of American Religion* (Princeton, N.J.: Princeton University Press, 1988), 71–99.

16. One attempt to explain the phenomenon of persistence, growth, and decline is that of Roger Finke and Rodney Stark, *The Churching of America, 1776–1990: Winners and Losers in Our Religious Economy* (New Brunswick, NJ: Rutgers University Press, 1992). Historians need to examine, more thoroughly than Finke and Stark do, the multiple historical motivating factors for the rise and decline of specific denominations. I am not convinced by their view that secularization or a transformation from sect to church was the reason for specific declines, nor that effective marketing and the promise of supernatural rewards was sufficient to explain growth. The explanation seems too one-dimensional for such a complex phenomenon.

17. Among numerous sources that could be cited, see Joel Carpenter, "A Shelter in the Time of Storm: Fundamentalist Institutions and the Rise of Evangelical Protestantism, 1929–1942," *Church History* 49 (March 1980): 62–75; idem and Wilbert R. Shenk, eds., *Earthen Vessels: American Evangelicals and Foreign Missions, 1880–1980* (Grand Rapids, Mich.: Eerdmans, 1990); Nathan O. Hatch, *The Democratization of American Christianity* (New Haven: Yale University Press, 1989); George M. Marsden, *Fundamentalism and American Culture: The Shaping of Twentieth Century Evangelicalism, 1870–1925* (New York: Oxford University Press, 1980); Mark A. Noll, *Between Faith and Criticism: Evangelicals, Scholarship, and the Bible in America,* 2nd ed. (Grand Rapids, Mich.: Baker Book House, 1991); Ernest R. Sandeen, *The Origins of Fundamentalism: Toward a Historical Interpretation* (Philadelphia: Fortress Press, 1968); Leonard I. Sweet, ed., *The Evangelical Tradition in America* (Macon, Ga.: Mercer University Press, 1984); Grant Wacker, *Augustus Strong and the Dilemma of Historical Consciousness* (Macon, Ga.: Mercer University Press, 1985).

18. "Statement on Secularism," in *Pastoral Letters of the United States Catholic Bishops,* ed. Hugh J. Nolan, vol. 2 (Washington, D.C.: National Conference of Catholic Bishops/United States Catholic Conference, 1984): 74–81.

19. For the Catholic side of these developments, see my "Cold War Catholicism: 1945–1965," in *The Roman Catholics,* 93–114. For one history of the evangelical side, see George M. Marsden, *Reforming Fundamentalism: Fuller Seminary and the New Evangelicalism* (Grand Rapids, Mich.: Eerdmans, 1987).

20. James Hennesey, "Papacy and Episcopacy in Eighteenth and Nineteenth Century American Catholic Thought," *Records of the American Catholic Historical Society* 77 (September 1966): 175–89.

21. There are of course exceptions here, as is evident in the works of Aaron Abell on American Catholic social thought. See, for example, Abell's *American Catholicism and Social Action: A Search for Social Justice, 1865–1950* (Garden City, N.Y.: Hanover, 1960).

22. R. Scott Appleby, *"Church and Age Unite!" The Modernist Impulse in American Catholicism* (Notre Dame, Ind.: University of Notre Dame Press, 1992); Gerald P. Fogarty, *American Catholic Biblical Scholarship: A History from the Early Republic to Vatican II* (San Francisco: Harper and Row, 1989); Arnold Sparr, *To Promote, Defend, and Redeem: The Catholic Literary Revival and the Cultural Transformation of American Catholicism, 1920–1960* (New York: Greenwood Press, 1990); Patrick W. Carey, ed., *American Catholic Religious Thought: The Shaping of a Theological and Social Tradition* (New York: Paulist Press, 1987), 3–70; idem, "Catholic Religious Thought in the U.S.A.," in *Perspectives on the American Catholic Church, 1789–1989,* ed. Stephen J. Vicchio and Virginia Geiger (Westminster, Md.: Christian Classics, 1989), 143–66; David J. O'Brien, *Public Catholicism* (New York: Macmillan, 1989); Joseph P. Chinnici, *Living Stones;* Christopher J. Kauffman, *Tradition and Transformation in Catholic Culture: The Priests of Saint Sulpice in the United States from 1791 to the Present* (New York: Macmillan, 1988); William M. Halsey, *The Survival of American Innocence: Catholicism in an Era of Disillusionment, 1920–1940* (Notre Dame, Ind.: University of Notre Dame Press, 1980); Thomas E. Wangler, "The Ecclesiology of Archbishop John Ireland: Its Nature, Development and Influence" (Ph.D. dissertation, Marquette University, 1968); Margaret Mary Reher, "The Church and the Kingdom of God in America: The Ecclesiology of the Americanists" (Ph.D. dissertation, Fordham University, 1972).

23. Margaret Mary Reher, *Catholic Intellectual Life in America: A Historical Study of Persons and Movements* (New York: Macmillan, 1989).

24. Philip Gleason, *Keeping the Faith;* idem, *Speaking of Diversity: Language and Ethnicity in Twentieth-Century America* (Baltimore: Johns Hopkins University Press, 1992); idem, "American Identity and Americanization," in *Harvard Encyclopedia of American Ethnic Groups,* ed. Stephan Thernstrom, Ann Orlov, and Oscar Handlin (Cambridge, Mass.: Belknap Press, 1980), 31–58.

25. Anthony Kohlmann, *Unitarianism Philosophically and Theologically Examined: In a Series of Periodical Numbers; Comprising A Complete Refutation of the Leading Principles of The Unitarian System,* 2 vols. (Washington City: Henry Guegan, 1821–22).

26. An exception here is Christopher Kauffman's excellent *Tradition and Transformation.*

27. See, for example, Leonard I. Sweet, ed., *The Evangelical Tradition in America* (Macon, Ga.: Mercer University Press, 1984).

28. See, for example, England's "The Republic in Danger," in Ignatius A. Reynolds, ed., *The Works of the Right Rev. John England, First Bishop of Charleston* 5 vols. (Baltimore: John Murphy & Co., 1849), 4: 13–68.

29. William Portier, "Isaac Hecker and *Testem Benevolentiae:* A Study in Theological Pluralism," in *Hecker Studies* ed. John Farina (New York: Paulist Press, 1983); Gerald P. Fogarty, *American Catholic Biblical Scholarship;* idem, *The Vatican and the Americanist Crisis: Denis J. O'Connell, American Agent in*

Rome, 1885–1903 (Rome: Universita Gregoriana, 1974); R. Scott Appleby, *"Church and Age Unite!"*.

30. There are a few exceptions to this, especially Joseph McShane, *"Sufficiently Radical": Catholicism, Progressivism, and the Bishops' Program of 1919* (Washington, D.C.: Catholic University of America Press, 1986).

31. Philip Gleason, "In Search of Unity: American Catholic Thought, 1920–1960," *Catholic Historical Review* 65 (April 1979): 185–205; William M. Halsey, *The Survival of American Innocence*; Arnold Sparr, *To Promote, Defend, and Redeem*; Gerald A. McCool, *Nineteenth-Century Scholasticism: The Search for a Unitary Method* (New York: Seabury Press, 1977); and idem, *From Unity to Pluralism: The Internal Evolution of Thomism* (New York: Fordham University Press, 1989).

32. I am aware of only two exceptions: Noel Shuell, "American Catholic Responses to the Religious Philosophy of William James: The Neo-Traditionist Responses" (Ph.D. dissertation Marquette University, 1985); and John W. Cooper, *The Theology of Freedom: The Legacy of Jacques Maritain and Reinhold Niebuhr* (Macon, Ga.: Mercer University Press, 1985).

16

JEWISH INTELLECTUALS AND THE DE-CHRISTIANIZATION OF AMERICAN PUBLIC CULTURE IN THE TWENTIETH CENTURY

🀫 🀫 🀫

David Hollinger

"ANY LARGE NUMBER OF free-thinking Jews" is "undesirable" if one wants to maintain or develop a society in which a Christian tradition can flourish, said T. S. Eliot in 1934. He was right. At least he was right if the standard for a flourishing Christian tradition is the one Eliot took for granted. This conception of an ideal, racially and religiously homogeneous society Eliot illustrated with his ancestral New England and with the Virginia whose self-image he flattered by respectfully invoking, in the presence of his Charlottesville audience, the agrarian manifesto *I'll Take My Stand*. It was an inauspicious time for a sophisticated and internationally minded intellectual to send off to the press a suggestion that there might be any context at all in which Jews should be declared undesirable; a full year had passed since Hitler had begun his notorious purge of Jews from German universities.[1] Amid the dismay now routinely registered about Eliot's anti-Semitism, we risk losing touch with two insights embedded in this, his most lamented public utterance. Eliot was right to suggest that community building and maintenance involves at least some drawing of social boundaries. And he was correct to single out Jews, especially freethinking Jews, as a unique threat in the 1930s to the realization in the United States of a Christian community of the sort in which Eliot—and not Eliot alone—would have preferred to live.

Religious and nonreligious Jews were far from the only agents and referent points in the story of American Protestantism's encounter with diversity and the consequent attraction of Protestantism's leaders to "pluralism." But this story will not be accurately told until the role of Jews is explored more extensively than it has been in previous tellings.[2] Although Catholics had long been a more numerous non-Protestant presence in the United States, and a more formidable threat to Protestant religious leaders, these Catholics were, after all, Christians. The challenge they presented to Protestant hegemony was less absolute than the one presented by an entirely non-Christian demographic bloc, even if this non-Christian bloc was made up of "People of the Book." Despite the existence of the American Jewish Committee and the several councils of rabbis, Jews were not so easily categorized as a single religious entity. Jews threw themselves more directly into American cultural life and embraced the public schools with enthusiasm, while Catholics developed their own comprehensive educational system supervised by a single network of organizations ultimately responsible to the Vatican. Moreover, substantial segments of the Jewish population were in possession of greater capital holdings, higher class position, and stronger technical skills than were the bulk of their Catholic counterparts. Although Catholics developed effective political bases in some urban localities, the political visibility of Jews within the circles of the nation's old Protestant elite was signaled by the appointment of Louis Brandeis to the United States Supreme Court in 1916. This Jewish presence was also concentrated to a large extent in the most conspicuous of places: New York City, the closest thing to an American cultural capital. By 1920, nearly one-third of the population of New York was Jewish.

In addition, there arose from within the Jewish population an articulate and energetic minority of intellectuals—the "free-thinking Jews" of Eliot's most pointed concern—who took little interest in Judaism but did not become Christians, and who, even more portentously, brought a skeptical disposition into the American discussions of national and world issues that had been the virtually exclusive domain of Protestants and ex-Protestants. To these freethinking Jews there was virtually no Catholic equivalent.[3] Even if Protestants managed to mentally shoehorn religious Jews into the categories of religious particularism—another peculiar "denomination" like the Mormons or the Seventh Day Adventists—the cosmopolitan, Enlightenment-inspired Jews refused to stay put. It was not adherence to some un-American "tribal" faith that created a problem here; rather, what made these intellectuals special was their manifest failure to be Jewish parochials. This applied to many of the Zionist as well as the non-Zionist intellectuals in the group. This transcending of conventional religious categories rendered them a problem for Protestants quite distinct from the challenge presented by Orthodox, Conservative, and Reform Jews.[4] Like their European prototypes Marx, Freud, and Durkheim, these emancipated Jews engaged the same "universal" discourses which American professors and authors had reproduced in terms more distinctly Protestant than would be widely acknowledged until later. This Protestant matrix was cast into bold relief first by Jews, then by Catholics who had long resented it but did not confront it very directly until the era of John Courtney Murray and Vatican II,[5] and eventually by a third, very different set of critics: the multiculturalists of our own time, for some of whom the exposure of the parochially Anglo-Protestant character of earlier American intellectual life has become an almost sacred calling. Before the role of Jews in this process can be properly assessed, however, it is important to clarify the question to which American Jews are part of a satisfactory answer.

No one doubts that the public culture of the United States was more decisively Protestant at the beginning of the twentieth century than it is today. The point is not simply that the overwhelming majority of religiously affiliated Americans had always been identified with one or the other of a host of Protestant denominations. Nor is it that American ecclesiastical institutions were dominated in the early and middle decades of this century by a loose "Protestant Establishment" consisting of the recognized leaders of the most socially prominent of these denominations (especially Congregationalists, Baptists, Methodists, Presbyterians, Disciples, Episcopalians, and Lutherans). The question is not thus situated in "religious history," narrowly conceived.[6] The starting point for the inquiry lies instead in the larger history of the United States itself, and in the influence there of a generic Protestantism for which the ecclesiastical "Protestant Establishment" was assumed to be a reliable voice. This generic, transdenominational Protestantism had come by the end of the nineteenth century to be taken for granted by nearly all of the Americans in a position to influence the character of the nation's major institutions, including those controlling public education, politics, the law, literature, the arts, scholarship, and even science.[7] This confident spiritual proprietorship lay behind the continued currency well into the century of the idea that the United States was a "Christian nation." In recent decades Protestants, increasingly aware that the old, generic Protestantism is taken for granted by fewer and fewer of the people running the relevant institutions, have tended to acknowledge that the religious character of the nation is contested. They have been inclined to describe themselves as but one of a variety of parties to a "pluralism" that accepts the legitimacy within the American nation not only of Catholics and Jews, but, more recently, of a vast expanse of cultural units defined by ethnoracial as well as religious principles.[8] What accounts for this transition from "Protestant culture" to the acceptance, however gradual and in some cases grudging, of a pluralism in which Christianity is acknowledged to be but one of several legitimate religious persuasions in America? This is the question.

The place to begin is with a recognition that this question should be nested within another one, beyond the scope of this essay. Why is there so much Christianity in the United States in the twentieth century? What most needs to be explained is surely not the decline of Protestant cultural hegemony in one of the most socially diverse and highly literate of the industrialized nations of the North Atlantic West, but rather its persistence in such a setting. It would be implausible to expect the generic Protestantism of 1900 to be able to maintain its authority for long against the aggressive expansion of scientific culture, against the pluralizing force of massive migrations of Catholics and Jews down to 1924, and against the particularizing pressures of social diversity within the ranks of American Protestants.[9] The relative slowness and limited extent of de-Christianization in modern American history even down to the present is an event of the same order as the failure of the American Left to develop social democratic movements comparable to those of Great Britain, France, and Germany. The historiography of twentieth-century America has wrought many variations on the classic question, "Why is there no socialism in the United States?" but this relative "failure of the Left" has a less widely addressed counterpart in the relative "failure of secularization." Why, indeed, is there so much Christianity in America today?

We do have a literature on this question,[10] although it is not always cast in these terms. The parallel to the Sombartian interrogative beloved of political historians has not, to my knowledge, been made explicit.[11] Treatments of the persistence of Christianity under implausible circumstances fall into some of the same patterns as do interpretations of the failure of the Left. It is often said, for example, that what appears superficially to be Christianity really is not—Harold Bloom's recent book on American "post-Christianity" is a convenient example[12]—just as a range of ostensibly nonsocialist protest movements are revealed by close study to have had sufficient anticapitalist content to render them American equivalents of social democracy. What shall count as "real" socialism and "real" Christianity is, of course, at issue in all of these studies. Yet the question of Christianity's persistence in twentieth-century America has not been as much in the foreground of inquiry as a world-historical perspective demands. The historiography of American religion since 1900 is more caught up in a master narrative of declension within an isolated national tradition than in a narrative of persistence informed by a comparative perspective on the destiny of Christianity in other highly literate, industrialized societies.

This is not the place to attempt an answer to the question, "Why is there so much Christianity in the United States?"[13] *But awareness of some of the historic conditions that make this question compelling can help guide an examination of the transition from Protestant culture to pluralism.* The most salient of these historic conditions are part cognitive and part demographic.

Cognitively, refinement of the critical tradition of the Enlightenment created structures of credibility within which many of Christianity's truth-claims looked highly suspect. This sharpening of Enlightenment-inspired critique was visible in the historical study of the Bible, in the Darwinian revolution in natural history, in the development of materialist analyses of the human self and of society, and in a multitude of efforts to substitute "science" for other authorities in a variety of specific contexts. Throughout the nineteenth century most of the Americans who welcomed and helped to advance the Enlightenment in these respects were, of course, Christians, many of whose descendants were in turn able to retain or to reconstitute their faith in relation to the increased cultural authority of science. But some were not. By the turn of the century, many of the leading intellectuals whose professional work was most associated with the defense of a religious sensibility—Josiah Royce and William James are convenient examples[14]—knew better than to count biblical evidence as among the reasons for accepting a given idea as true. Careers like those of Margaret Mead, David Riesman, and Daniel Bell indicate the extent to which social scientists replaced the clergy as the most authoritative public moralists for educated Americans. The simple notion that the Enlightenment diminished the place of Christianity in the West may be banal, but it is also true.[15] It applies in an arena stretching far beyond twentieth-century America, but it applies there too, and formidably so.

Demographically, the immigration to the United States between about 1880 and 1924 and again after 1965 brought directly into the polity large numbers of people who were not only non-Protestants, but who also lacked the Protestant past that churchgoers shared with those who, like John Dewey, rejected or drifted away from the faith. Although a majority of the non-Protestants in both of these historic migrations were Catholic—from Europe in the first instance, from Latin America and the Philippines in the second—there were of course many Jews in the earlier one and many Muslims, Hindus, and Buddhists in the more recent one. Multiplicity as a social condition does not always produce pluralism as an ideological persuasion, but it often generates some effort in that direction. It did in both of these cases, although the pluralism inspired by the 1880–1924 migration—the pluralism of Brandeis, Randolph Bourne, and Horace Kallen—was aborted.[16] Indeed, old Protestant establishment's influence persisted until the 1960s[17] in large measure because of the Immigration Act of 1924: had massive immigration of Catholics and Jews continued at pre-1924 levels, the course of American history would have been different in many ways, including, one may reasonably speculate, a more rapid diminution of Protestant cultural hegemony. Immigration restriction gave that hegemony a new lease on life.

Demographic diversification put pressure on Protestant predominance in some contexts without much reference to cognitive demystification, and vice versa. The challenge presented by Catholic immigrants from Italy, Poland, and elsewhere in Europe entailed very little Enlightenment resonance; on the contrary, Protestants generally felt that Catholics were not enlightened enough. But as prejudice diminished and as Protestant leaders worried more about secularism, one cohort after another of Protestant leaders came around to recognizing in their Catholic coreligionists a force that could be mobilized against religious indifference and even against the de-Christianizing influence of secular intellectuals and, some felt, Hollywood. The same alliance was extended, with some theological adjustments, to religious Jews through the popularization of the idea of a "Judeo-Christian Tradition." [18] In the meantime, the secular modes of thought descending from the Enlightenment found constituencies among the sons and daughters of the old Protestant establishment, even when sheltered from social diversity. Cognitive demystification was a comprehensively western and ultimately a global movement; secular inquiry could feel liberating in Peoria as well as in Paris, in Baltimore as well as in Berlin.

Yet the cognitive and demographic pressures on Protestant hegemony were not altogether unconnected. One leitmotif of Enlightenment commentaries on Christianity, after all, had been the diversity of the world's religions, and the extent to which some of the most esoteric of these actually contained myths similar to those basic to Judaism and Christianity. This diversity of credible religious witnesses was a staple of nineteenth-century free thought driven home to American Protestants by Col. Robert Ingersoll's scandalous public lectures during the Gilded Age, and reinforced in a more benign voice by William James's prodigious *Varieties of Religious Experience.* The difficulty of establishing Christianity's superiority to other religions—once they were really scrutinized with a modicum of honest sympathy—bedeviled many in the wake of the 1893 World's Parliament of Religions. And foreign missionary experience, too, sometimes had the effect of undermining a confidence more easily maintained within the confines of a small town in rural America.[19] Moreover, it was the secular intellect's claim to be able to handle any experience that came along that most distinguished it from its apparently more parochial rivals. All methods of "fixing belief" other than science will eventually fail, Charles Peirce explained in the pages of *Popular Science Monthly,* because of the social world's diversity: the tenaciously faithful may try to hide from the diversity of human testimony about the world, but they will be unable to ignore it forever.[20] "The scientific method is cosmopolitan," insisted a representative ideologue of science at the turn of the century, because it is truly "world-wide" and tries to take everyone's reports into account.[21] Immigration brought to the United States a tiny fraction of the world that the ideologues of science believed they could eventually encompass, but in bringing home even this measure of demographic diversity immigration joined science as a force for the destabilization of a public culture grounded in Protestantism.

For the history of the nation's academic and literary elites, however, the most relevant connection between demographic diversification and cognitive demystification is highly specific. Jews who managed to find a place for themselves in the public intellectual life of the nation—rather than speaking to a distinctly Jewish constituency—reinforced the most de-Christianized of the perspectives already current among the Anglo-Protestants. If lapsed Congregationalists like Dewey did not need immigrants to inspire them to press against the boundaries of even the most liberal of Protestant sensibilities, Dewey's kind were resoundingly encouraged in that direction by the Jewish intellectuals they encountered in urban academic and literary communities. Franz Boas was among the earliest of these Jewish intellectuals to achieve prominence. He founded a tradition of relativist anthropology that exercised enormous deprovincializing influence through both Gentile (Margaret Mead, Ruth Benedict) and Jewish (Edward Sapir, Melville Herskovitz) followers.[22] Boas himself was the only prestigious American scientist to campaign actively against the ostensibly scientific racism used to justify the immigration exclusion act of 1924.[23] The biologist Jacques Loeb also became a celebrity well before World War I. Loeb was a forthright atheist whose rejection by New York's Century Association led the Columbia psychologist J. McKeen Cattell to mount a public protest.[24] Loeb became a symbol for the ethical austerity of science, and served as a model for Max Gottlieb, the Jewish scientist–hero Sinclair Lewis contrasted to the priggishly moralistic Reverend Ira Hinkey in Lewis's most acclaimed novel, *Arrowsmith*.[25] A third academic Jew who became an animating presence in the second decade of the century was the literary critic Joel Spingarn. He proclaimed a radical aestheticism that violated the prevailing literary culture of moral uplift. After speaking in defense of a colleague being fired when love letters to a secretary were made public, Spingarn himself was dismissed from Columbia University in 1911 by the authoritarian President Nicholas Murray Butler. Spingarn is most remembered today for having helped to found the National Association for the Advancement of Colored People, and for having served for many years as chair of its board.[26]

Boas, Loeb, and Spingarn were all based primarily in New York, as was the editor and novelist Abraham Cahan.[27] Gentiles in the New York of this era produced a number of testimonies to the cosmopolitan influence of Jewish intellectuals.[28] The most famous of these testimonials is "The Intellectual Preeminence of Jews in Modern Europe," written by Thorstein Veblen shortly after his 1918 arrival in New York. Veblen treated Jewish intellectuals—with whom the "rootless" and "marginal" Veblen, a son of Norwegian immigrants, clearly identified—as "the vanguard of modern inquiry."[29] But if Veblen's essay on the pains as well as the benefits of marginality was in part the product of his Chicago years and of his energetic reading, Randolph Bourne's more romantic "Transnational America" and "The Jew and Transnational America"[30] were full of New York, and were openly grounded in Bourne's personal experiences at Columbia and in Greenwich Village. Bourne named Justice Brandeis as an obvious example of a Jewish presence serving to undercut the old Anglo-Protestant provincialism, but he also mentioned four men of Bourne's own generation: Felix Frankfurter, Horace M. Kallen, Morris R. Cohen, and Walter Lippmann.[31] It is a mark of Bourne's astonishing prescience that he was able, on the basis of their very earliest work, to identify these four as the major agents of cultural change that each in fact, became.

One of Bourne's four young Jewish intellectuals, Cohen, wrote with special eloquence then and later about the passion with which Jewish youth on the Lower East Side were determined to absorb all of the benefits of "the Age of Reason" and to commit themselves fully to its exploration and development.[32] The frustrations men like Cohen experienced while trying to act on these ambitions affected the character of their gradual impact on the old Protestant culture. The obstacles faced by Jews trying to obtain first-rate educations and to make academic careers are well known. Although Harvard's president emeritus Charles W. Eliot and some other liberals within the establishment opposed the quotas that capped Jewish enrollment in the early 1920s at a number of prominent eastern schools, these quotas did operate, and were deeply resented by their victims.[33] Equally enraging was the shunning of prospective Jewish faculty, evidence of which is known to anyone who has read academic correspondence from the period 1910–1945.[34]

At issue was more than religion. Jews were suspect in academia partly because many Anglo-Protestants thought them socially crude and aggressive, and politically radical. But religion was a large part of it, as is revealed by patterns in the location and intensity of suspicion of a Jewish presence. The barriers to Jews in business, engineering, medicine, and law—where technical skills rather than responsibility for constituting and transferring culture were central—were not as high, nor as entrenched. Intellectually ambitious Jewish undergraduates of the teens, twenties, and thirties were routinely counselled to give up on the idea of becoming philosophers or historians and were encouraged to pursue, instead, a career in one of the service professions. Economics, in keeping with the prevailing stereotypes, was the one academic field Jews were regularly encouraged to enter. Psychology, too, was understood to be potentially appropriate for Jews, especially when psychology was viewed as a branch of medicine or of physiology. The social snobbery that victimized Jews was thus the most potent when allied with the defense of a generic, if theologically inconspicuous, Protestantism. As late as 1929, there were in New York City alone twenty-eight "home missions" designed to convert Jews to the Christian faith.[35]

These aspects of the American scene help give meaning to the specific ways in which the Jewish intellectuals began to make a difference, even while still held largely at bay during the quarter-century prior to World

War II. An example is Jewish leadership of the movement to make Oliver Wendell Holmes, Jr., into an iconic representative of the American spirit.[36] Holmes's greatness was hailed by American intellectuals of a variety of backgrounds, but Jews did the most to establish Holmes in the public mind as more than just a great judge and scholar.[37] Responsibility for effectively promoting Holmes as a cultural hero is often assigned above all to Frankfurter and Harold J. Laski. Grant Gilmore has argued that these two "concocted the picture of the tolerant aristocrat, the great liberal, the eloquent defender of our liberties, the Yankee from Olympus."[38] From his strategic position at the Harvard Law School, Frankfurter affirmed his reverence for Holmes repeatedly, declaring in 1927 that Holmes had "built himself into the structure of our national life" and "written himself into the slender volume of the literature of all time."[39] It was Frankfurter's recruit to the Harvard faculty, Laski, who took responsibility for putting together Holmes's *Collected Legal Papers* in 1920. The representation of Holmes as the Complete American Liberal was carried on by Cohen,[40] and later by Jerome Frank[41] and Max Lerner. In Lerner's 1943 rendition, Holmes was "perhaps the most complete personality in the history of American thought." Holmes had always stood by "faith in social reason and in the competition of ideas" and to a "belief in the steady, if slow march of social progress." Holmes "was a great man," emphasized Lerner, "regardless of whether he was a great justice."[42]

Holmes was a good choice. His influence promised to help release American culture from a Christian bias that most Jewish intellectuals found provincial at best, and at worst a basis for continued discrimination against Jews and other non-Christians. The old Brahmin was about as "American" as it was possible to get, but he had put great distance between himself and exactly those parts of Protestant culture most oppressive to Jews. Holmes was aloof from Anglo-Saxon nativism and from the genteel tradition in literature for which his father remained an enduring symbol. Moreover, the Olympian Holmes had actually befriended Frankfurter, Laski, and Cohen at a time when Jews felt deeply the sting of social and professional rejection by most men and women of Holmes's milieu.[43] Holmes was not noticeably Christian, and what echoes of heroic Calvinism he carried were easily detached from quotas for Jews at Harvard and Columbia. Jewish intellectuals had a real enemy to fight, and they knew Holmes was no part of it. Hence it is not surprising that of the various specific projects moving the public culture of the United States more decisively in a secular, cosmopolitan direction, the particular project of managing the reputation of Holmes should become one in which Jewish intellectuals took the lead. The making of the agnostic Holmes into an emblem for American life was one step in the construction of a secular vision of American culture—a vision deemphasizing that culture's historically Protestant components. And this secular vision became a common possession of the American academic and literary intelligentsia during the middle decades of the century.[44]

The men and women who made up this intelligentsia were cultural products of a process of accommodation that left both Jews and Gentiles different from what they would have been had they not interacted with one another. To refer to certain of these intellectuals as Jews, or as Anglo-Protestants, need not imply an ethnic essentialism according to which each party to this historical engagement brought to it a static and monolithic inventory of traits and dispositions. On the contrary, individuals identified ethnically as Jews or as Anglo-Protestants displayed a great range of characteristics, yielding a sometimes anxious discourse over assimilation (were Jews becoming too "anglicized"?) and liberalization (were Anglo-Protestants of this or that particular persuasion giving up a precious heritage in order to participate in a polyglot and secular modernity?).

By the midcentury mark, intellectuals of Jewish origin were no longer systematically excluded from even the teaching of English and philosophy. It is not easy to separate cause from effect in the ethnodemographic transformation of American academia during the midcentury decades. Did Jews find their way into this sector of American life because of a prior de-Christianization well advanced among intellectuals of Anglo-Protestant origin, or because these Jews, themselves, had helped by their very presence and by their pressure against the old exclusionary system to de-Christianize the space they were gradually entering? Both were surely true, but there was an additional factor, more easily isolated.

Hitler was a major agent of this transformation in two respects. His example—horrifying to many Americans even before the full dimensions of the "Final Solution" became known—rendered anti-Semitism of even the genteel sort more difficult to defend. If this helped American Jews beginning careers in the late 1940s and early 1950s, a second of Hitler's acts made a more dramatic and immediate impact: he pushed from Central Europe to a relatively welcoming[45] America a distinctive cohort of Jewish scholars, scientists, and artists that attracted extensive notice within the American academic and literary worlds. This cohort included not only Albert Einstein and a substantial percentage of the physicists who built the atomic bomb, but a galaxy of distinguished humanists and social scientists.[46] The fame and prestige of some of these men and women enabled this migration to have a symbolic impact far beyond the specific, local communities into which these refugee intellectuals were absorbed.[47]

American academia expanded rapidly in the postwar era, and a larger and larger portion of faculties turned out to be Jews, the descendants, in most cases, of the East European Jewish immigration of 1880–1924. In the process, the critical debates conducted in the *Partisan Review*—since the 1930s the central organ of the largely Jewish group known as "the

New York intellectuals"—was absorbed into academic departments of English and comparative literature.[48] As this ethno-demographic transformation of several major academic disciplines proceeded during the 1950s and 1960s, the argument was not that these disciplines needed "a Jewish perspective"; these faculty appointments were made on the basis of prevailing professional standards as understood by the disciplines' leaders. As with Cohen and Spingarn a half-century before, but now on a huge scale, Jews were entering communities of discourse on the "universal" terms proclaimed by these communities themselves. By the early 1960s the large number of Jews in sociology led to faculty-club banter to the effect that sociology had become a Jewish discipline. In the literary world the triumphs of Norman Mailer, Saul Bellow, and J. D. Salinger led Leslie Fiedler to hail "the great take-over by Jewish-American writers" of a task "inherited from certain Gentile predecessors, urban Anglo-Saxons and midwestern provincials of North European origin"—the task of "dreaming aloud the dreams of the whole American people."[49]

The de-Christianization that accompanied these changes in the ethno-demographic base of American intellectual life was indirect but not necessarily trivial. Gentiles could take pride in the creation of a collegial environment in which Jewish colleagues would not feel marginalized. Religion was increasingly private, and public discussion was increasingly secular. It is worth considering, in juxtaposition to one another, two widespread perceptions concerning the elite college and university faculties of the last quarter-century. One perception is that the prevailing culture of these faculties is more secular than is the rest of the society and even the rest of the American academy, and that within these faculties the open profession of Christian belief in the course of one's professional work is uniquely discouraged. Most investigators trying to answer the question, "Why is there so much Christianity in the United States?" would squander little time interviewing the citizens of Cambridge, New Haven, Ann Arbor, Hyde Park, Madison, and Berkeley.[50] The second perception is that these same faculties are disproportionately Jewish. The first of these two perceptions may be impressionistic in foundation, but the second has been confirmed by a report of the Carnegie Commission on Higher Education. This 1969 study found that while Jews constituted only about 3% of the American population, they accounted for 17% of the combined faculties of the seventeen most highly ranked universities.[51]

No doubt the culture of elite universities would be more secular than it used to be even had there been no change in their ethnodemographic composition. But I hope it is not unwarranted to suggest that we get some insight into the weakening of the old Protestant cultural hegemony if we attend closely to the settings in which it was once the strongest and was then weakened the most decisively. Such a setting was the elite university. This major American institution was created by people who were, among their other vital identities, Protestants—that fact is surely indisputable, and applies even to the era's nonpareil theologian-baiter, Andrew Dickson White—who gradually yielded control of it to people who were either less public about their Protestantism, less fully Protestant, or not Protestant at all, indeed, not even Christian. An informal alliance among liberal Protestants, ex-Protestants, religious Jews, and freethinking Jews did much to bring about this transformation. The role of Jews in the story has rarely been addressed as directly I address it here.[52] Perhaps this dimension has been avoided because many who have thought about the transition from Protestant culture to religious pluralism have continued to honor an old suspicion that America would be better off today were it somehow more Christian than it is. Given this presumption, any account of how Jews contributed to the diminution of Christianity's influence could be construed as a criticism of Jews, and as grist for the mill of T. S. Eliot's ideological descendants. But this historiographical inhibition disappears if we believe, instead, that whatever may be wrong with American universities, and with America, it is not that they are insufficiently Christian.

This decisive removal from our historiographical presuppositions of the ideal of a Christian America can also have a liberating effect on our treatments of the historical significance of liberal Protestantism in modern United States history. That liberal Protestantism is still much maligned in many circles reflects, I believe, an uncritical acceptance of the most popularly disseminated and polemical of the constructions of Reinhold Niebuhr.[53] What secular followers of Niebuhr sometimes fail to understand is the extent to which Niebuhr's constructions of liberal Protestantism derived from his own affirmations of Christianity: Niebuhr thought the liberals had sold out. Hence many of the "atheists for Niebuhr"[54] disparaged and even effaced the liberal Protestants who facilitated the de-Christianized discursive space they, themselves, were delighted to inhabit. The religious "integrity" the liberals were said to have abandoned was easy to admire from the safe distance the secularists owed, in part, to the liberals who presided over the decline of Protestant hegemony. Efforts to develop a more fair-minded and nuanced interpretation of liberal Protestantism have been advanced within the circle of "church historians,"[55] but in the larger profession of American historians these have attracted little notice. A promising turn is the recent work of Niebuhr's most convincing interpreter, Richard Fox.[56]

The widespread acceptance of "pluralism" has left a matter for ongoing debate the exact character and implications of this idea for American religious life. Among the unresolved issues is the relation between religious pluralism and the various ideas put forth in the name of "multiculturalism." Although we have been awash in discussions of multiculturalism for several years now, a persistent deficiency in the multiculturalist debate is the relative silence of almost all of its major participants concerning the place of religious affiliation amid other kinds of affiliation. The building and maintaining of communities does involve the drawing of boundaries, and even a measure of exclusion, but where and how to draw the lines that enclose and exclude, and how to assign different weights and roles to the national community as opposed to ethnoracial, religious, and other communities remains a matter of persistent confusion and contention. Some of the ingredients and tensions within the multiculturalist controversy are displayed in figure 1. Here, a Bible-carrying and cross-wearing family of presumably evangelical Protestants is positioned alongside an orthodox Jewish family and in front of a Muslim couple. Religious categories are thus at the center of this multicultural scene, but the cartoonist understandably situates religious identity within a panorama of dress-coded identities defined by race, sexual orientation, and "life-styles" ranging from straights and yuppies through Dead-heads and bikers.

This is not the place to try to provide a sketch of the multiculturalist controversy,[57] but by way of epilogue I do want to identify and comment briefly upon three closely related initiatives in this ongoing discussion as it regards religious pluralism. I select these three because they indicate the dynamism of the struggle to clarify the implications of pluralism, reveal the resentments that some Protestants continue to feel over the loss of their hegemonic position, and raise issues that I believe should concern anyone committed to building or maintaining communities in which both non-Christians and Christians can function in an atmosphere of mutual respect.

One such initiative is to resist the trend toward the "privatization" of religion that has accompanied the transition from Protestant culture to pluralism. Is not religious commitment trivialized, some ask, by the understanding that one should voice these commitments primarily within one's community of faith and not abroad? This query may carry specifically evangelical notions of religious authenticity that are uniquely threatened by the transition from Protestant culture to pluralism. Another model of religious authenticity is that of Judaism, as practiced, for example, by the many Jewish politicians and Jewish professors who display very little eagerness to project their own particular religion into American law or into the classrooms of American universities. It may be that a corollary of the recognition that the United States is not a Christian Israel, Christians will eventually come to accept a model for religious authenticity that owes less to Saint Paul than to the Judaism of the diaspora.

A second initiative visible in these same, searching discussions concerns the status of science. The salient move is to diminish the cultural authority of science by construing it as but one of many parties to a pluralism the implicit rules of which can then bring science's cognitive reach to a size manageable by those threatened by it. The enhancing of religion's claims through delimitation of science's scope is a venerable strategy, employed with some skill by Poincaré and Eddington, and advanced in our time in settings ranging from the theology of the Yale School to the creationism of local school boards. Gadamerian, Kuhnian,

FIGURE 16.1 Reprinted by permission of the *Colorado Springs Gazette Telegraph*

and Foucaultian critiques of "the myth of objectivity" have been invoked in the cause. This initiative, too, seems to bespeak a residual resistance to the historic fact that the Enlightenment has essentially won in the cognitive realm, as Schleiermacher sensed it would, and as neither Gadamer, Kuhn, nor Foucault have actually doubted. This initiative also risks treating "science" as an all-or-nothing proposition, silencing, in the manner of many of today's self-styled postmodernists, the hermeneutically self-aware variations on "objectivity" developed by varieties of pragmatists and realists. It will be a challenge for defenders of Christianity to direct the more radically postmodernist theories of knowledge and of the human self against the authority of science without, at the same time, undercutting the authority of Christianity, about which Nietzsche, the fountainhead of postmodernist theory, had a lot to say.

A third initiative is to present Christians as victims, to appropriate for Christianity—in its newly adopted role as a beleaguered minority—the arguments developed by feminists, gays, and ethnoracial minorities seeking full participation in the society and the polity. The complaint of Christians as "the newest minority" insists that Christians are discriminated against, and that their opinions are not taken seriously. Everyone but traditional Christians, it seems, gets to say their piece. The attitude to which I refer is neatly encapsuled in a remark recently quoted by George Marsden. "Christians," said Mark R. Schwehn, "are now treated in a manner rather like women were treated in the pre-feminist era. Women could be hired, promoted, and retained, so long as their feminism did not figure prominently in their research interests, their scholarly perspectives, and their manner of life generally."[58] Such sentiments invite curiosity as to whether Christianity is generating a number of exciting new research programs, as feminism has proved able to do. Feminism gets attention in the academy partly because its voice is relatively new, and the questions it asks often redirect old discourses in novel and fruitful directions. Women, moreover, have been truly excluded from public and academic life, and are now being included on a large scale for the first time. Hence the appropriation by Christians of the moral standing of a constituency so long victimized invites the suspicion that some of these Protestant appropriators are slow to shed the expectations and psychological habits of hegemony. The universities are, after all, among the few locations in American society in which ideas identified as Christian are not uncritically accepted, and in which feminism is actively encouraged as an intellectual program. Obviously, Christians should not be denied the basic rights owed to any member of the society or of the academy, and the history of Christianity needs to be taught like any other aspect of the American past, no matter what some of us today may think of Christianity's substantive merit.[59] But if some auditors withdraw when religious testimony begins, it may be less a violation of a Christian speaker's rights than an expression of the feeling that this particular message has been heard before and has already contributed most of what it has to offer. If any party to the conversation has had an abundance of opportunities to be heard, it is surely Christianity.

Christianity marched into the modern era as the strongest, most institutionally endowed cultural program in the western world. The people in charge of this program tried through a variety of methods, some more coercive than others, to implant Christian doctrines and practices in as much of the globe as they could. Yet, as the centuries went forward, this extraordinary empire of power/knowledge lost some of the ground it had once held. Christianity at the end of the twentieth century—the "Christian Century," prophesied by the Protestant hegemonists at its start—is less triumphant in the North Atlantic west than it was in 1500 or 1700 or 1900. Whether what has happened in this part of the world amounts to "secularization" or, as Hans Blumenberg insists, "reoccupation," something has certainly changed.[60] Whether or not other agencies have become vehicles for values that Christianity carried, plenty of other chariots are at hand. The story of the fate of Protestant culture in the United States in the twentieth century is but a fragment of this larger drama of the transformation of the North Atlantic west from a society heavily invested in the cultural program of Christianity to a society in which Christianity found it harder and harder to retain the spiritual capital of its most thoughtful and learned members. If Christianity's continuing adherents include some of the most thoughtful and learned men and women in the world—as I believe they do—the trend is nonetheless real, and the historian's obligation to understand it is no less compelling.

NOTES

1. Eliot signed the preface to *After Strange Gods: A Primer of Modern Heresy* (London, 1934) in January of the year in which it was published. The text was composed of lectures Eliot had delivered in 1933 at the University of Virginia. See especially pages 14–21. It should be pointed out that this book, so often maligned and dismissed as an anomaly in the Eliot canon, is distinguished by many of the same virtues that helped make Eliot one of the finest critical essayists of the twentieth century. Hence his construction in these pages of an ideal society is all the more important a document of its time and place. The manifesto of the "Nashville Agrarians," *I'll Take My Stand* (New York, 1930), was not overtly anti-Semitic, but, of course displayed a commitment to particularity of people and place that Eliot endorsed.

2. Hence this essay seeks to build upon, and to supplement, existing accounts of this important event in modern American history. Of these accounts, I want especially to acknowledge the relevant portions of three very recent books: William R. Hutchison, ed., *Between the Times: The Travail of the Protestant Establishment in America, 1900–1960* (New York, 1989); George M. Marsden and Bradley J. Longfield, eds., *The Secularization of the Academy* (New York, 1992); and Martin Marty, *Modern American Religion*, vol. 2, *The Noise of Conflict 1919–1941* (Chicago, 1991), although Marty has put much of his telling of this particular story aside in order to focus more directly on it in the third, and forthcoming, volume of this trilogy. An earlier, classic study is Robert T. Handy, *A Christian America: Protestant Hopes and Historical Realities* (New York, 1971).

3. Some historians would say that there did emerge, by the midcentury decades, a small cohort of dissenting Catholic and ex-Catholic intellectuals who constituted an distinctive, radical presence in American intellectual life. Among these were Dorothy Day, Mary McCarthy, C. Wright Mills, and Jack Kerouac. A beginning in the study of this phenomenon has been made by James T. Fisher, *The Catholic Counterculture in America, 1933–1962* (Chapel Hill, 1989).

4. Yet when historians of Christianity address the role of Jews in American society, they almost always do so within the fairly narrow frame of "religious history," thus confining their attention to religious Jews. See, for example, Gordon Tucker's "A Half-Century of Jewish–Christian Relations," in *Altered Landscapes: Christianity in America, 1935–1985,* ed. David W. Lotz (Grand Rapids, Mich., 1989), 140–154.

5. For an excellent study of this change in the role of Catholics in American intellectual life, and for a compelling interpretation of Murray, see Patrick Allitt, *Catholic Intellectuals and Conservative Politics in America: 1950–1985* (Ithaca, N. Y., 1993). See also the informative and discerning essay by Philip Gleason, "American Catholic Higher Education, 1940–1990: The Ideological Context," in Marsden and Longfield, *Secularization of the Academy,* 234–258.

6. What accounts for the decline, *within American Protestantism,* of the relative influence of the old Protestant Establishment's classical denominations, and the simultaneous growth in the relative influence of groups distinguished by evan-

gelical, fundamentalist, and Pentecostal tendencies largely avoided by the "main-line" churches? This more narrowly situated question does need to be distinguished from the major concern of this essay.

7. For a vivid invocation of the taken-for-granted status of Protestantism in 1900, see the opening pages of Robert T. Handy, *Undermined Establishment: Church–State Relations in America, 1880–1920* (Princeton, N.J., 1991), esp. 7–8. For a broader account of the generically Protestant public culture of the United States in this era, see the ethnographic portrait of America in 1912 presented in part 1 of Henry F. May, *The End of American Innocence: A Study of the First Years of Our Own Time* (New York, 1959), 3–117.

8. A major occasion for, and indicator of, this acceptance of religious "pluralism" was the enormously favorable reception Protestant leaders gave to Will Herberg's *Protestant–Catholic–Jew* (New York, 1955). This book took specific issue with attacks on pluralism found even within liberal journals such as the *Christian Century* as late as 1950. As the acceptance of pluralism was more and more widely articulated during the 1960s, in the wake of the election of the Catholic John F. Kennedy as president, it became clear that some had in mind a pluralism flourishing within a broadly conceived Judeo-Christian tradition, while others were willing to accept as legitimate a greater variety of religious persuasions, including principled unbelief. An example of the former, Protestant–Catholic–Jew perspective is Franklin Hamlin Littell, *From State Church to Pluralism: A Protestant Interpretation of Religion in American History* (New York, 1962); while an example of the latter, more cosmopolitan vision is Harvey Cox, *The Secular City: Secularization and Urbanization in Theological Perspective* (New York, 1965). By the 1990s the acceptance of the idea of pluralism—however much its exact meaning remained a matter for debate—had reached the point that even some evangelically-committed voices were urging that Christians "recognize that they are part of an unpopular sect" in a society populated by a vast diversity of voices on religious issues; see George Marsden, "The Soul of the American University: A Historical Overview," in Marsden and Longfield, *Secularization of the Academy*, 41.

9. That these conditions would militate against the perpetuation of the American religious status quo of 1900 is an implication of the bulk of our sociological and historical literature on "secularization." For a recent sampling and critical reconsideration of this formidable literature, see Steve Bruce, ed., *Religion and Modernization: Sociologists and Historians Debate the Secularization Thesis* (Oxford, 1992), especially the judicious concluding remarks of Bryan R. Wilson, "Reflections on a Many Sided Controversy," 195–210.

10. A recent, controversial example is Roger Finke and Rodney Stark, *The Churching of America, 1776–1990: Winners and Losers in Our Religious Economy* (New Brunswick, N.J., 1992).

11. The closest approach to this parallel I have seen is Leo Ribuffo's reference to "American exceptionalism" at the end of "God and Contemporary Politics," *Journal of American History* 79 (1993): 1533. This perspicacious essay is the best summary treatment of the historiography of politics and religion in the twentieth-century United States.

12. Harold Bloom, *The American Religion: The Emergence of the Post-Christian Nation* (New York, 1992). For a discerning critique of this book, see Henry F. May's review in *Reviews in American History* 21 (June 1993): 185–189.

13. I believe that a sound answer to this question would emphasize the absence of a formal ecclesiastical establishment in the American constitutional order and the consequent availability of voluntary religious affiliation as a device for the formation and maintenance of communities that mediate between the individual and the apparatus of the modern state. In this view, the flourishing of religious groups is largely an "ethnic" phenomenon responsive to a need for social solidarity in units of manageable size authorized by cultural symbols endowed with spiritual authority by accessible traditions. Being "religious" can thus be a way of being "American" in an America understood to be constituted by a dispersal of subgroup identities compatible with American national identity itself. This understanding renders explicable the tendency of immigrants from Mexico and other Latin American countries to become more Catholic as part of their engagement with American society. One work highly relevant to this line of analysis, sadly underexploited by both "church historians" and the larger historical profession, is R. Laurence Moore, *Religious Outsiders and the Making of Americans* (New York, 1986).

14. Consider Royce's *The Religious Aspect of Philosophy* (New York, 1885) and *The Problem of Christianity* (New York, 1913), and James's *The Will to Believe* (New York, 1897).

15. James Turner, *Without God, Without Creed: The Origins of Unbelief in America* (Baltimore, Md., 1985), helps us understand the complexity of this process by revealing the precise nature of the decisions made along the way by Protestant intellectuals, but it does not render less real the historical forces with which Turner's cast of characters were obliged to deal. Historians enthusiastic about Turner's provocative claim that "religion caused unbelief" (xii) have sometimes paid insufficient attention to the vital qualifiers Turner attached to his argument—for example, "Unbelievers appeared most often in intellectual locations exposed to science, economic locations shaped by new means of production and distribution, geographic locations unsettled by industrialization and urbanization" (260).

16. Indeed, a striking fact about the multiculturalism of our own time is the relative lack of awareness its earliest adherents displayed of the "cultural pluralism" of Kallen's generation. Kallen himself lost interest in cultural pluralism shortly after he gave this doctrine its name in 1924. So lost from sight was Kallen's cultural pluralism even by 1955 that Herberg made no reference to Kallen when discussing pluralism; when Herberg did cite Kallen, it was in the latter's capacity as a commentator on secular religiosity. Finally in the 1990s Kallen became a major reference point in the multiculturalist debates; see, for example, Michael Walzer, "What Does it Mean to be an American?" *Social Research* 57 (1990), 591–614.

17. It was in the 1960s, most students of the old Protestant establishment's history seem to agree, that the public authority of the combined leadership of the "mainstream" denominations finally collapsed; see, e.g., Robert S. Michaelsen and Wade Clark Roof, eds., *Liberal Protestantism: Realities and Possibilities* (New York, 1986), esp. 6; Wade Clark Roof and William McKinney, *American Mainline Religion: Its Changing Shape and Future* (New Brunswick, N. J., 1987), esp. 10–39; and the essays collected in Hutchison, *Travail*.

18. On the popularization of this concept in the midcentury decades, see Mark Silk, "Notes on the Judeo-Christian Tradition in America," *American Quarterly* 36 (1984): 65–85.

19. Typically," Grant Wacker tells us, "the missionaries' perceptions moved from abhorrence to grudging admiration to varying degrees of approval of the ethical and religious ideals of the peoples among whom they worked." Grant Wacker, "A Plural World: The Protestant Awakening to World Religions," in Hutchison, *Travail*, 256. Concerning the cognitive security of small towns, however, one of the finest novels ever written about small-town Protestant culture is organized around the diversifying forces present even in the Burned-Over District at the end of the century: Harold Frederic, *The Damnation of Theron Ware* (New York, 1896). Theron Ware's experiences with the freethinking Dr. Ledsmar, the urbane priest Father Forbes, the aesthete Celia Madden, and the realistic, diversity-accepting Sister Soulsby prefigure much of the next century's transition from Protestant culture to pluralism.

20. Charles Peirce, "The Fixation of Belief," *Popular Science Monthly* 12 (1877): 1–15.

21. Conway MacMillan, "The Scientific Method and Modern Intellectual Life," *Science* n.s. I (1895): 541.

22. Boas and his students and their collective impact on American culture have been the subject of a number of studies, perhaps the most pointed of which is Richard Handler, "Boasian Anthropology and the Critique of American Culture," *American Quarterly* 42 (1990): 252–273.

23. The singularity of Boas's leadership in this respect is emphasized in Kenneth M. Ludmerer, *Genetics and American Society: An Historical Appraisal* (Baltimore, 1972), esp. 25.

24. This episode is described in Philip Pauly, *Controlling Life: Jacques Loeb and the Engineering Ideal in Biology* (New York, 1987), 142–44.

25. Sinclair Lewis, *Arrowsmith* (New York, 1925).

26. For an overview of Spingarn's career in the specific context of the academy's response to Jewish intellectuals, see Susanne Klingenstein, *Jews in the American Academy, 1900–1940: The Dynamics of Intellectual Assimilation* (New Haven, 1991), 104–111. This is a helpful, if sketchy introduction to the topic of its title, but Klingenstein speaks only about professors of philosophy and literature. An adequate treatment of the topic, even for the period Klingenstein addresses, would be obliged to deal extensively with natural scientists (e.g., Samuel Goudsmidt, J. Robert Oppenheimer) and social scientists (e.g., E. R. A. Seligman, Simon Kuznets).

27. Although Cahan edited the leading Yiddish-language newspaper in New York, the *Forward*, he was widely appreciated by Anglophone intellectuals well before the publication of his *The Rise of David Levinsky* in 1917.

28. And not only in New York. When the New York Jew Emma Goldman lectured in St. Louis, the young Roger Baldwin—soon to be the founder of the American Civil Liberties Union—found his life transformed. This incident is discussed in Candace Serena Falk, *Love, Anarchy, and Emma Goldman* (New Brunswick, N.J., 1984), 9–10.

29. Thorstein Veblen, "The Intellectual Preeminence of Jews in Modern Europe," *Political Science Quarterly* 39 (1919): 33–42.

30. Both of these essays of 1916 are reprinted in Randolph Bourne, *War and the Intellectuals: Collected Essays, 1915–1919*, ed. Carl Resek (New York, 1964), 107–133. For additional examples of Anglo-Protestant declarations concerning the culturally liberating effect of contact with immigrant Jews, see the cases cited in my essay, "Ethnic Diversity, Cosmopolitanism, and the Emergence

of the American Liberal Intelligentsia," reprinted in *In the American Province: Studies in the History and Historiography of Ideas* (Bloomington, Ind., 1985), esp. 39–40.

31. Bourne, "Jew and Transnational America," 132.

32. Morris R. Cohen, "The East Side," *Alliance Review* 2 (1902), 451–54; Morris R. Cohen, *A Dreamer's Journey* (New York, 1949), esp. 98. For another memoir of Jewish–Protestant interaction from the Jewish side in early-twentieth-century New York City, see Joseph Freeman, *An American Testament* (New York, 1936).

33. See e.g., Marcia Graham Synott, *The Half-Open Door: Discrimination and Admissions at Harvard, Yale, and Princeton, 1900–1970* (Westport, Conn., 1979).

34. The difficulties faced by Jewish historians in the historical profession, for example, have recently been documented by Peter Novick, *That Noble Dream: The "Objectivity Question" and the American Historical Association* (New York, 1988), esp. 172–173.

35. See Benny Kraut, "A Wary Collaboration: Jews, Catholics, and the Protestant Goodwill Movement," in Hutchison, *Travail,* 207. Kraut reports that over half of these missions were operated by the established, "mainline" denominations. See also Egal Feldman, *Dual Destinies: The Jewish Encounter with Protestant America* (Urbana, Ill., 1990), which concludes that Protestant efforts to "witness to Jews" were "unrelenting" until the middle of the twentieth century (243).

36. In this paragraph and the next, I draw upon my own study of this episode, "The 'Tough-Minded' Justice Holmes, Jewish Intellectuals, and the Making of an American Icon," ed. Robert W. Gordon, *The Legacy of Oliver Wendell Holmes, Jr.* (Stanford, Calif., 1992), 216–28, 307–13.

37. This ethnodemographic fact is rendered all the more striking by another one: among the earliest and loudest voices to express puzzlement at the liberal's adulation of Holmes was H. L. Mencken, perhaps the era's most vociferous opponent of the established culture of Protestantism, but one without any Jewish connections (and not lacking anti-Semitic prejudices of his own). Mencken understood the antiliberal strains in Holmes that now dominate studies of the jurist but seems not to have grasped Holmes's utility for Mencken's Jewish allies in the fight against the genteel tradition. See Mencken's discussions in *American Mercury* in 1930 and 1932, reprinted in *The Vintage Mencken* ed. Alastair Cooke, (New York, 1955), 189.

38. Grant Gilmore, *The Ages of American Law* (New Haven, Conn., 1977), 48.

39. Felix Frankfurter, *Mr. Justice Holmes and the Constitution* (Cambridge, Mass., 1927), 44.

40. Cohen's *New Republic* essay on the occasion of Holmes's death in 1935 was reprinted in Morris R. Cohen, *Faith of a Liberal* (New York, 1946); see esp. 30.

41. Jerome Frank, *Law and the Modern Mind* (1930; reprint, New York, 1963), 270–77.

42. See Lerner's extensive introduction in *The Mind and Faith of Justice Holmes,* ed. Max Lerner (Boston, 1943), esp. vii, xix, xlvii, xlix–l.

43. This was true even in the century's second decade, but it was more dramatically manifest in 1934, when, just at the moment Eliot was warning against freethinking Jews, the ninety-three-year-old, freethinking Holmes represented

himself to Cohen as being of partly Jewish ancestry. See Leonora Cohen Rosenfield, *Portrait of a Philosopher: Morris R. Cohen in Life and Letters* (New York, 1962), 443.

44. See, for example, Henry Steele Commager, *The American Mind: An Interpretation of American Thought and Culture Since the 1880s* (New Haven, Conn., 1950), 385–90, which includes a lyric appreciation of Holmes, climaxing with the application to Holmes of Stephen Spender's "I Think Continually of Those Who Were Truly Great."

45. Although America became a permanent or temporary home for refugees from Hitler's Europe possessed of strong connections in the United States and of international reputations in the arts, science, or scholarship, it cannot be repeated often enough that American authorities rejected multiple opportunities to receive or to otherwise save Jews who looked to the United States for help. From 1933 to 1945, the United States accepted 132,000 refugees from the Third Reich, scarcely more than the equivalent of the 1940 population of Spokane, Washington. The overwhelming majority of these, moreover, were able to enter the United States only after *Kristallnacht* (November 9–10, 1938). For a helpful demographic and political overview of the migration, see Herbert A. Strauss, "The Movement of People in a Time of Crisis," in *The Muses Flee Hitler: Cultural Transfer and Adaptation, 1930–1945* (Washington, D. C., 1983), 45–59.

46. In order that we be reminded of the scope and character of this influx of Jewish intellectuals, it may be well to list here the names of some of them: Hannah Arendt, Leo Strauss, Erik Erikson, Bruno Bettelheim, Eric Fromm, Kurt Lewin, Kurt Gödel, Paul Lazarsfeld, Leo Lowenthal, Theodore Adorno, Alexander Gerschenkrohn, Albert O. Hirschman, Erwin Panofsky, Ludwig von Mises, Herbert Marcuse, and Eric Auerbach. The deprovincializing effect of Gentile intellectuals from Central Europe was also strong; these ranged from principled atheists like the logical positivist Rudolf Carnap to theologians like Paul Tillich and Jacques Maritain. Their numbers also included Ernst Cassirer, Vladimir Nabokov, and Werner Jaeger.

47. This episode in American intellectual history surely deserves more rigorous study than it has received. Of the studies that have been completed, an especially readable and informative one is H. Stuart Hughes, *Sea Change: The Migration of Social Thought, 1930–1965* (New York, 1975). Hughes points out (18–19, e.g.) that the particular segment of European intellectual life that came to the United States was the most abrasively critical, skeptical, and cosmopolitan within German-speaking Europe.

48. Of the many studies of the *Partisan Review* and its circle, the most detailed, comprehensive, and convincing is Terry A. Cooney, *The Rise of the New York Intellectuals: Partisan Review and Its Circle, 1934–1945* (Madison, Wis., 1986). See also Fred Matthews, "Role Models? The Continuing Relevance of the 'New York Intellectuals,' " *Canadian Review of American Studies* 11 (1988): 69–88.

49. Leslie Fiedler, "Master of Dreams: The Jew in the Gentile World," *Partisan Review* 34 (1967): 347.

50. As one of the most respected and well-informed commentators on the contemporary American religious scene has summarized the situation in regard to the scientific and social scientific segments of these faculties, "Evidence suggests that rationality, natural science, and the social sciences have all exercised a negative effect on traditional religious beliefs and practices. Not only do scientists—and espe-

cially social scientists—demonstrate radically low levels of religious commitment, but scientific and social scientific meaning systems also appear to operate as functional alternatives to traditional theistic ideas for a number of people." See Robert Wuthnow, *The Restructuring of American Religion: Society and Faith Since World War II* (Princeton, N.J., 1988), 301–02. Wuthnow also notes, concerning the society as a whole, that "The United States may well be an exception among industrialized countries in the extent of its religious activities" (309).

51. Stephen Steinberg, *The Academic Melting Pot: Catholics and Jews in American Higher Education* (New York, 1974), 103. I have not been able to locate comparable figures for the leadership of the American Civil Liberties Union, and for other groups often said to have played a large role in construing the constitutional church–state separation in terms that have diminished the public space in which Christian belief was once proclaimed with explicit or tacit support of governments. A useful study of the tradition of Jewish devotion to "separationism" is Naomi W. Cohen, *Jews in Contemporary America: The Pursuit of Religious Equality* (New York, 1992).

52. Only the slightest notice of this aspect of the story is taken even by the ultraliberal Harvey Cox; see *Secular City*, 99. The new evangelical historians have also been remarkably silent in this regard, even down to the present; see, for example, the scant treatment of Jews in George Marsden, *The Soul of the American University* (New York, 1994), one of the most comprehensive analyses ever written of the "secularization" of American academic life. For an affectionate but mildly skeptical portrait of Marsden and other newly prominent, evangelically committed historians, see Leonard I. Sweet, "Wise as Serpents, Innocent as Doves: The New Evangelical Historiography," *Journal of the American Academy of Religion* 56 (1988): 397–416. Sweet is especially sensitive in describing how these historians have dealt with their own awareness that many of their fundamentalist forbears were "on the tracks of their souls," as Sweet puts it "creeps" (402).

53. Responsibility for this uncritical acceptance within the historical profession rests largely, I believe, with Perry Miller.

54. This phrase was coined and popularized by Morton White, especially in *Social Thought in America: The Revolt Against Formalism* 2d. ed. (New York, 1957), 257.

55. I have in mind especially the many contributions of Martin A. Marty and William R. Hutchison and some of their students. See, for example, Hutchison's "Past Imperfect: History and the Prospect for Liberalism," in Michaelsen and Roof, *Liberal Protestantism*, 65–82.

56. See Fox's "The Culture of Liberal Protestant Progressivism, 1875–1925," *Journal of Interdisciplinary History* 23 (1993): 639–60. esp. the two central paragraphs on 640.

57. I have addressed the multiculturalist debate in my "How Wide the Circle of the We? American Intellectuals and the Problem of the Ethnos Since World War II," *American Historical Review* 98 (1993): 317–37, and in my *Postethnic America: Beyond Multiculturalism* (New York, 1995).

58. Mark R. Schwehn to George M. Marsden, June 4, 1990, quoted in Marsden, "The Soul of the American University," in Marsden and Longfield, *Secularization*, 45.

59. I share Leo Ribuffo's lament that the "editors of the standard volumes surveying historiographical trends" do not "consider religious history worthy of

much mention, let alone a separate essay." See Ribuffo, "God and Contemporary Politics," 1533.

60. For my understanding of the character and import of Hans Blumenberg's *The Legitimacy of the Modern Age*, brought out in an English translation in 1983, I am largely indebted to Martin Jay, "Blumenberg and Modernism," in Jay's *Fin-de-Siècle Socialism* (New York, 1988), 149–64. I prefer "de-Christianization" to "secularization" partly because the former specifies the decline of a particular cultural program, while the latter has become more deeply mired in contentious disputes over its meaning in relation to what is and is not "religious." A lucid survey of the problem, although couched in the terms of one major thinker's agendas, is Thomas Luckmann, "Shrinking Transcendence, Expanding Religion?" *Sociological Analysis* 30 (1990): 127–36. For a more detailed study of an episode in the Protestant culture–to–pluralism story that is informed by an understanding of these semantical ambiguities, see Henry C. Johnson, Jr., " 'Down from the Mountain': Secularization and the Higher Learning in America," *Review of Politics* 54 (1992), 551–88.

AFTERWORD

17

LATER STAGES OF THE RECOVERY
OF AMERICAN RELIGIOUS HISTORY

▦ ▦ ▦

Anne C. Loveland

THE TITLE OF THIS essay refers to Henry May's now-famous essay, "The Recovery of American Religious History," first published in 1964,[1] in which he points to a combination of historical and historiographical developments that promoted the "recovery" of American religious history. According to May, the turn to neo-orthodoxy in the 1930s and 40s, followed by the religious revival of the post–World War II period generated interest in religion on the part of intellectuals and academics. Those developments, along with changes in the field of American literature, intellectual history, and sociology and social theory, produced the generation of historians now regarded as the founders of modern American religious history—Perry Miller, Sidney Mead, Timothy Smith, Sydney Ahlstrom, and Edwin Gaustad.

I propose to update May's observations by discussing the historical and historiographical developments of the last three decades that influenced the writing of American religious history. The original insight as to the relationship belongs to him; I am simply extending it to later decades.

Sydney Ahlstrom described the period bracketed by the election of John F. Kennedy and the resignation of Richard M. Nixon as "tumultuous, troubled, and traumatic"—all the more so by virtue of its contrast with the "serene" 1950s.[2] American society seemed to be "coming apart."[3] The civil rights revolution, the anti–Vietnam War movement, the new feminism, the "resurgence of ethnicity"[4]—all signaled the emergence of a "discontented society."[5]

The era of protest and discontent ushered in what Ahlstrom termed a "moral and theological transformation" in the United States. The confident nationalism and religious revivalism of the 1950s sputtered out, and Americans experienced "a *crise de conscience* of unprecedented depth," he wrote in A *Religious History of the American People*.[6] The crisis gave rise to a new "secular theology" which taught that the task of the church and believers lay within the secular world and in the midst of its problems. The new theology propelled a "New Breed" of politically active clergy into "the freedom revolution"—marching for civil rights in Selma, joining striking grape pickers in California, organizing welfare unions and tenants' councils in Buffalo and Chicago, protesting against the Vietnam War.[7] Interestingly, this emphasis on secularization did not slow the recovery of religious history May described. The discipline continued to develop and expand, discovering new subject matter and utilizing new approaches along the way.

The discipline of United States history also registered the impact of these turbulent years. A host of revisionist historians challenged the prevailing interpretations of consensus historiography. Instead of unity, they depicted division; instead of compromise, they stressed conflict. Instead of liberalism, they celebrated radicalism; instead of assimilation, ethnicity. Social and economic conflict became the major theme of American historiography. At the same time, so-called New Left historians joined with "New Social Historians" in insisting that history should be written "from the bottom up," a perspective intended to reflect the concerns, not of the elite, but of the common people, minority groups, the inarticulate masses.

As a result of this kind of thinking the profession confronted an "explosion"[8] of works focusing on social groups heretofore "invisible" in American history—such as African Americans, women, native Americans, workers, immigrants, and "ethnics"—the very groups that were becoming highly visible through the protest and consciousness-raising movements they organized. The books and articles the "new breed" of scholars produced not only grew out of such movements. They were often written so as to be directly relevant to their objectives. They were, many of them, a kind of advocacy history.

The "new breed" of historians who emerged in the 1960s and 70s developed new interpretations of their subject matter. In the area of black history, for example, historians put aside the earlier preoccupation with race relations or individual black leaders. Instead, they focused on the "internal black world" and on black people's development of a distinctive culture. Also, the new black history generally regarded blacks not as passive victims of white oppression but as a people who responded creatively and constructively to enslavement, racism, and discrimination by developing a cooperative ethos and communal social structure that fortified them against oppression.[9]

Similarly, the new women's history that emerged in the 1960s and 70s focused on a segment of American society who had generally been neglected in accounts of the nation's past. As a result, much of the new scholarship, particularly in its early phases, was what Gerda Lerner called "compensatory" and "contribution history."[10] It aimed at adding women to American history—as Linda Gordon has noted, "like painting additional figures into the spaces of an already completed canvas." Also like the new black history, the new women's history gradually moved away from emphasizing women's victimization and oppression. By the late 1980s, according to Gordon, most historians of women agreed on "a balanced portrayal of the interaction of women's oppression and women's power."[11] Peter Novick has suggested that the shift away from emphasizing women's oppression contributed to the development of a "particularist" view of women's history. Just as the new black history focused on the "internal black world" and the distinctive black culture it produced, Novick argues that the new women's history, particularly that done by feminist historians, celebrated "an at least semiautonomous separate cultural realm, with distinctive values and institutions." According to Gerda Lerner, "the 'true' history of women was the story of 'their ongoing functioning in that male-defined world *on their own terms.*' "[12]

But there is also at least one important difference between the new black history and the new women's history. Whereas the new black history, at least until recently, tended to be separatist, focusing on the "internal black world," some practitioners of the new women's history adopted an approach that emphasized the reconstruction of the whole of American history using gender as a category of analysis—"repainting the earlier pictures," to continue Linda Gordon's analogy, "because some of what was previously on the canvas was inaccurate and more of it misleading."[13]

The turbulent 60s and early 70s and the new approaches to historical writing they inspired had a significant impact on the field of religious history, which, as Leo Ribuffo points out, "paralleled and borrowed from" the new histories of blacks, women, workers, and immigrants. Like their counterparts in the area of "secular" history, Ribuffo notes, the new religious historians broke with consensus theory by emphasizing religious pluralism; they "examined beliefs and behavior from the bottom up rather than from the denominational top down, and paid sustained attention to African Americans, Hispanics, and women."[14]

The continued vitality of the new approach to the history of religion that developed during the 1960s and 70s is registered in Martin Marty's recently published bibliography of American religious history in the 1980s. Marty noted a significant increase compared with previous decades in the notice given women in American religion during the 1980s, but expressed surprise at the relatively small number of titles produced, observing, rather pointedly, that their story was "just beginning to be told." Native Americans, African Americans, and (mostly Catholic) immigrants also continued to receive attention in the 1980s, but treatment of the religious life of Hispanic Americans, the largest non-English-speaking group in the United States, remained "sadly deficient." Marty listed no books treating the religious life of another important ethnic group, Asian Americans.[15]

While the concerns sparked by the 1960s and early 70s continued to influence the religious history written in later decades, historical and historiographical developments of the late 1970s and 1980s seem to be taking the discipline in a somewhat different direction. In 1976, for example, the American media discovered what *Newsweek* called "the most significant—and overlooked—religious phenomenon of the 70's: the emergence of evangelical Christianity into a position of respect and power."[16] During the "year of the evangelicals," as it was labeled, evangelical religion attained unprecedented national recognition and influence, culminating in the election of a professed born-again Christian, Jimmy Carter, to the presidency of the United States. That was only the beginning of an ascendancy that continued into the 1980s and 1990s. During the next fifteen years public opinion polls, news magazines, and evangelicals themselves reported ever-larger percentages of Americans identifying themselves as evangelicals.[17] Presidents Ronald Reagan and George Bush and other politicians found increasing favor with voters by adopting the rhetoric and supporting the political and social agenda of evangelical religion.[18] A phalanx of parachurch groups contributed to the expansion of evangelistic, missionary, and social and political activities.[19] And in the 1980s the New Christian Right put its distinctive ideological stamp on the decade's political campaigns.[20]

Because the media paid somewhat less attention to them, Americans hardly noticed other, equally important developments in American religion during the 1970s and 80s. In April 1984, a *New York Times Magazine* article proclaimed "a return to religion" on the part of intellectuals (philosophers, writers, artists, and political activists) and American college and university students. Author Fran Shumer cited overflow enrollments in religious studies classes and quoted such notables as Harvey Cox, the Rev. Andrew Greeley, Robert Coles, Alan Dershowitz, and Ted Solotaroff on intellectuals' revived interest in traditional religion.[21] Other commentators on the religious scene of the 1970s and 80s pointed to an increasing "privatization of religious commitment"—defined by Wade Clark Roof as "the trend toward greater individualism in religious choice and practice."[22] A 1985 Gallup survey of religion in the United States reported "a retreat from activism to individualism and a concentration on personal spirituality."[23] Paradoxically, in September 1984, Kenneth Briggs of the *New York Times* discovered increasing political activism on the part of liberal Protestants as well as conservative Christians, both "grappl[ing] for a firmer foothold in public affairs." Alongside the well-known activities of the conservative Moral Majority, Briggs cited the less publicized efforts of the National Council of Churches to gain a hearing in shaping public policy. "Over the past four years," he pointed out, that body had "become a growing voice of dissent from Reagan Administration policies on a host of issues from the nation's involvement in Central America to cuts in social welfare programs."[24]

These religious developments of the late 70s and 80s exploded the secularization theory that had mesmerized so many social scientists, historians, and journalists for several decades. As Robert Wuthnow put it in *The Restructuring of American Religion* (1988), "religion simply has not beat a humiliating retreat in the face of secularization."[25] Even Harvey Cox, whose 1965 book *The Secular City* heralded a "world of declining religion," admitted that his predictions had proved incorrect. In *Religion in the Secular City*, published nineteen years later in 1984, he noted that the 1980s were turning out to be not an era of "rampant secularization and religious decline," but "more of an era of religious revival and the return of the sacral."[26]

Besides exploding the secularization theory, the new religious developments of the 70s and 80s provoked growing interest in the role of religion in American public life. Evangelicals, especially those involved in the New Christian Right, gained a good deal of media attention by virtue of their crusade "to reintroduce religious values into American political life."[27] In the mid-1980s thinkers identified with the mainline churches, such as the neoconservative Richard John Neuhaus and the neoliberal Robert Bellah, also spoke out in favor of a place for religion in American public life.[28] In *The Naked Public Square* (1984), Neuhaus lamented the exclusion of "religion and religiously grounded values from the conduct of public business." Like it or not, he declared, religion and politics mix. "The question is whether we can devise forms for that interaction which can revive rather than destroy the liberal democracy that is required by a society that would be pluralistic and free." His book may be seen as an attempt to steal the thunder of the religious New Right by offering a different interpretation of "the public meaning of the gospel."[29] In *Habits of the Heart*, published the following year, Bellah and his coauthors advanced the idea of a "public church" (inspired by Martin Marty's notion of the same) that would "bring the concerns of biblical religion into the common discussion about the nature and future of our society."[30] A few years later, in *The Good Society*, Bellah and company reiterated the same view: "Now more than ever the churches can, and must, engage the larger public and the state in moral argument and education."[31]

On the eve of the bicentennial of the United States Constitution an ecumenical group made up of leading religious liberals, evangelicals, Catholics, and Jews signed the Williamsburg Charter pledging to "work for a consensus on the place of religion in public life."[32] The introduction to the Charter described it as "a call to a vision of public life that will allow conflict to lead to consensus, religious commitment to reinforce political civility."[33] More recently, the general secretaries of the United States Catholic Conference, the National Council of Churches, and the Synagogue Council of America issued a document entitled "The Common Good: Old Idea, New Urgency" in which they urged "a holistic approach to social welfare as a matter of human rights as well as human need" and grounded in "the values inherent within our faiths . . . ." Proclaiming the biblical basis of the proposed policy, the signers declared, "Making common appeal to the biblical foundation of creation, covenant, and community, we offer a provisional public theology of the common good, whose moral core is social justice, human dignity, and human rights."[34]

As the issuance of "The Common Good" suggests, interest in the role of religion in the public realm remained high in the early 1990s. Pat Buchanan's and other speeches at the 1992 Republican National Convention provided evidence that the New Christian Right was still thinking about it.[35] In 1993 Neuhaus began publishing a new journal of opinion, *First Things*, described as "a monthly journal of religion and public life."[36] One of its contributors was Os Guinness, a drafter of the Williamsburg Charter and author of a recently published book entitled *The American Hour: A Time of Reckoning and the Once and Future Role of Faith*. Part history, part jeremiad, it reviewed the ongoing controversy over religion and public life and offered Guinness's own "vision" (to use the word on the dust jacket) of the proper relationship. The time has come, he said, "to recognize that the United States today is passing through a period of reckoning, when the deepest national issues have a critical religious component and the deepest religious issues have critical national consequences. Few things are therefore more in the public interest now than to understand the present significance of faiths in America and to assess their social, national, and international consequences." Like Neuhaus, Guinness offered a brief for "reforging" a religiously based "public philosophy for a civil public square." He dismissed "the double-headed drive to privatize religion and secularize public life" as "constitutionally unwarranted, historically unprecedented, and—at least for the biblical family of faiths, including Judaism, the Christian faith, and Islam—theologically without excuse."[37] Also in 1993, Yale law professor Stephen L. Carter, writing from the liberal camp (he is a church-going Episcopalian), sounded a similar note in *The Culture of Disbelief: How American Law and Politics Trivialize Religious Devotion*. Its criticism of the exclusion of religion from the public square received considerable attention in the national media.[38]

Notwithstanding their different party affiliation, the new occupants of the White House in the mid-1990s were almost as conscientious about articulating their concern for religious values as Presidents Reagan and Bush had been. In the summer of 1993, the media spotlighted First Lady

Hillary Rodham Clinton's proselytizing of a "politics of meaning" based, at least in part, on religion.[39] The president's efforts received less coverage in the national media but more in denominational newsletters and the religious press. At an interfaith breakfast in the White House in August 1993, Clinton, a Baptist, commended Stephen Carter's book and indicated his agreement with its thesis. "Sometimes I think the environment in which we operate is entirely too secular," he commented. "The fact that we have freedom *of* religion doesn't mean we need to try to have freedom *from* religion. It doesn't mean that those of us who have faith shouldn't frankly admit that we are animated by that faith." According to Fred Barnes of *The New Republic,* "Clinton ostentatiously left a copy of Carter's book on his Oval Office desk for weeks."[40] Then in November 1993, he spoke more pointedly about the need to inject religion into discussions of public policy. The occasion was the signing of the Religious Freedom Restoration Act into law. In extemporaneous remarks following the ceremony Clinton declared that Americans "are a people of faith" who "have enshrined in our Constitution protection for people who profess no faith. And good for us for doing so. . . . But let us never believe that the freedom of religion imposes on any of us some responsibility to run from our convictions. Let us instead respect one another's faiths, fight to the death to preserve the right of every American to practice whatever convictions he or she has, but bring our values back to the table of American discourse to heal our troubled land."[41]

Just as Henry May noted the influence of developments of the 1940s and 50s on the writing of American religious history, I would suggest that the preoccupation with religion in the public square has already made an impact on the discipline of American religious history and will likely continue to do so.[42] The proof is in the growing number of books and articles in the discipline treating the role played by religion during the second half of the twentieth century in what is variously termed "the public realm," "American public life," "the public arena," or, to use the currently fashionable term, "the public sphere."[43]

Significantly, a variety of public policy, research, and academic institutes—which constitute a growing presence in the public sphere—have encouraged scholarship on the role of religion in American public life. Richard John Neuhaus and Peter Berger steered the American Enterprise Institute and the Institute on Religion and Democracy in that direction.[44] Organizations such as the Institute for the Study of American Evangelicals, the Ethics and Public Policy Center, and the Brookings Institution have published books on the subject.[45] In 1984, at a Conference on Religion and the Campaign for Public Office jointly sponsored by the Harvard Divinity School and the John F. Kennedy School of Government, Harvey Cox urged making room for religiously based values "in the arena of public discourse" to halt "the progressive enfeeblement and impoverishment" of political language in the United States.[46] Also in the 1980s, the Kenyon Public Affairs Conference Center at Kenyon College sponsored a conference on religion and politics, aided by the Alfred P. Sloan and Exxon Foundations, among others, and the Institute for the Advanced Study of Religion at the University of Chicago Divinity School, assisted by a grant from the Henry R. Luce Foundation, sponsored a conference on "Religion and the Future of American Public Life."[47] In the 1990s The Center for the Study of Religion and American Culture, aided by grants from the Lilly Endowment, held conferences on "Public Religious Discourse in America's Pluralistic Society" and the "Public Expressions of Religion."[48]

Many of the books and articles produced by these conferences treat the relationship between religion and political culture in the second half of the twentieth century. This is an area that historians have only begun to explore. So far, much of the work has been done by public opinion pollsters, political scientists and sociologists, concentrating on the recent presidential elections and the impact of the televangelists and their constituency.[49] There are, however, a growing number of historical studies of the church–state relationship.[50] The nineteenth-century "ethnocultural" or "ethnoreligious" studies done by historians such as Paul Kleppner, Richard J. Jensen, Ronald P. Formisano, and Daniel Walker Howe may provide a model for historians seeking a broader perspective on religion and politics in the post–World War II period.[51]

What Robert Wuthnow calls "special purpose religious groups" constitute an important dimension of religion in the public sphere.[52] A number of studies have appeared on the way church-affiliated groups, as well as voluntary religious associations, have sought to shape public discourse regarding national policy. James C. Hefley, Edward E. Plowman, and Allen D. Hertzke have treated the influence church lobbying groups exert in the political arena.[53] Other pathbreaking works include Mitchell Hall's book on Clergy and Laymen Concerned About Vietnam (CALCAV),[54] Donald L. Davidson's study of the American churches' positions on nuclear weapons as well as my own book discussing American evangelicals' views of national defense policy,[55] and Andrew Michael Manis's and James Findlay's monographs on the civil rights movement.[56] Robert Booth Fowler's recent examination of Protestant environmentalism and Stephen Bates' journalistic account of fundamentalist efforts to rid the public schools of secular humanism point to other issues that have drawn religious groups into the public sphere.[57] *The Cutting Edge: How Churches Speak on Social Issues* by Mark Ellingsen provides a useful compilation of recent church declarations on racism, economic development, ecology, nuclear armaments, marriage, abortion, genetic engineering, social justice, and sociopolitical ideologies.[58] Much remains to be done, however. Besides special purpose groups, the influence of church colleges, seminaries, denominational publishing houses, and the religious media needs to be examined.[59]

Among the more useful general studies of religion in the public sphere are two by Robert Booth Fowler: *A New Engagement: Evangelical Politi-*

cal Thought, 1966–1976 and *Unconventional Partners: Religion and Liberal Culture in the United States.*[60] Mark Silk's *Spiritual Politics*[61] and James Davison Hunter's *Culture Wars* also treat the impact of religion on American public discourse.[62] Erling Jorstad provides a brief but useful survey of the "social outreach ministry" of the mainline churches in the 1980s, involving a variety of so-called peace and justice issues such as racial and gender equality, poverty, hunger, and the environment.[63] Many of the essays in *The Political Role of Religion in the United States,* edited by Stephen D. Johnson and Joseph B. Tamney, are enlightening, as are those in *Religion and American Public Life,* edited by Robin W. Lovin.[64] Some of the essays in the series on *The Bible in American Culture,* edited by Edwin S. Gaustad and Walter Harrelson, discuss the way certain religiously motivated groups in the United States have appealed to the Bible in their efforts to shape the formation of public policy or law.[65] A recently published festschrift to Martin Marty, featuring, significantly, "new *dimensions*" in religious history, offers several essays dealing with religion in the public sphere.[66] And Richard P. McBrien combines a theoretical discussion of the role of religion in public life with analyses of such issues as abortion, religion in the public schools, and publicly supported Nativity scenes in *Caesar's Coin: Religion and Politics in America.*[67]

The larger significance of religion's presence in the public sphere has yet to be analyzed in depth. One thing seems certain—the public square in post–World War II America was never as "naked" as Richard Neuhaus asserted. Religion contributed, and continues to contribute, to public discourse in many ways. The question is whether its concern with public policy is a reassertion of an older, even an inherent, proclivity of American religion, or something new, arising out of the postwar context. On the one hand, Garry Wills and Richard Neuhaus suggest that the current involvement of religion in the public sphere is part of a long tradition of such concern. In *Under God,* for example, Wills asserts "the centrality" of religion in American public life. "The first nation to disestablish religion has been a marvel of religiosity, for good or ill," he writes. "Religion has been at the center of our major political crises, which are always moral crises—the supporting and opposing of wars, of slavery, of corporate power, of civil rights, of sexual codes, of 'the West,' of American separatism and claims to empire. If we neglect the religious element in all those struggles, we cannot understand our own corporate past. . . ."[68] Neuhaus makes a similar point in noting "the incorrigible religiousness of the American people"[69] and the "inescapability of moral judgment," shaped by religious convictions, in matters of public policy.[70] On the other hand, Robert Wuthnow speculates that the current involvement of religion in American public life is an outgrowth of a "deepening polarization between religious liberals and conservatives" that began in the 1960s. He also mentions two other factors: the postwar domestic political upheaval precipitated by events such as the civil rights revolution, the

Vietnam War, and the Supreme Court abortion decision; and "a broader reorientation in public life toward bringing values back in" which began in the early 1970s. At the same time, however, Wuthnow notes the traditional this-worldly orientation of American religion, which "encourages the faithful, individually and through their churches, to be interested in public affairs"—which seems to lend credence to Wills's and Neuhaus's assumption of continuity.[71]

The attention historians are giving to the role of religion in the public sphere constitutes an important recovery of a somewhat neglected area of American religious history. Moreover, it would appear to have encouraged, and will likely continue to encourage, religious historians to look beyond the boundaries of religion per se to its entangling relations with political, social, cultural, and economic developments. Indeed, the introduction to a book of essays on "the new religious history" indicates that part of its newness stems from a new appreciation of the role of religion in American social, economic, and political life.[72]

Significantly, the integrating impulse within the discipline of American religious history parallels a similar impulse—or at least desire—among American historians generally. In the mid- and late 1980s, historians such as Herbert Gutman, Peter Novick, and Thomas Bender decried the fragmentation of the American historical profession and the resulting loss of "the vision of a convergent past."[73] Novick's prognosis for the discipline of American history was generally pessimistic. Thomas Bender, on the other hand, prescribed a cure similar to the tonic historians of American religion were beginning to urge on their colleagues. Just as practitioners of the latest new religious history recommended integrating religion into general American history by focusing on its influence in the public sphere, Bender urged historians to "go beyond partial analysis," to "reclaim the public realm, where groups interact to make a national politics and culture, as the central territory of history." This was to be done, he observed, "without sacrificing the rich harvest—as well as the cultural and political point—of recent studies of particular groups."[74]

What all this suggests is that in the early 1990s historians of "secular" and religious history are moving in the same direction. Their eventual meeting in the public square not only promises the recovery of the public realm, of "public life,"[75] and the recovery, in a different sense, of the discipline of American history from the debilitating influences of the 1960s and 70s.[76] It also signals yet another stage in the recovery of American religious history, by facilitating the integration of religion and general American history.

NOTES

1. Henry May, "The Recovery of American Religious History," in *Ideas, Faiths, and Feelings: Essays on American Intellectual and Religious History*

1952–1982 (New York: Oxford University Press, 1983), 67–86. The essay origi- nally appeared in the *American Historical Review* in 1964.

2. Sydney Ahlstrom, "The Traumatic Years: American Religion and Culture in the 60s and 70s," *Theology Today* 36 (1980): 511.

3. William L. O'Neill, *Coming Apart: An Informal History of America in the 1960's* (Chicago: Quadrangle Books, 1971).

4. "Resurgence of ethnicity" is Timothy L. Smith's phrase in "Religion and Ethnicity in America," *American Historical Review* 83 (December 1978): 1157.

5. LeRoy Ashby and Bruce M. Stave, eds., *The Discontented Society: Inter- pretations of Twentieth-Century American Protest* (Chicago: Rand McNally & Company, 1972).

6. Sydney E. Ahlstrom, *A Religious History of the American People* (New Haven: Yale University Press, 1972), 1091, 1081.

7. On the new "secular" or "radical theology" and the "New Breed" of clergy, see Langdon Gilkey, "Social and Intellectual Sources of Contemporary Protestant Theology in America," and Harvey G. Cox, "The 'New Breed' in American Churches: Sources of Social Activism in American Religion," *Daedalus* 96 (Winter 1967): 69–98, 135–50.

8. Historians writing about the historiography of the 1960s use terms like "explosion" and "flood" to suggest the volume of articles and books treating the newly discovered social groups. See, for example, "Women in History: Main- stream or Minority?" and "Black History Since 1865: Representative or Racist?" in *Interpretations of American History: Patterns and Perspectives,* ed. Gerald N. Grob and George Athan Billias (6th ed.; New York: Free Press, 1992), 2: 68, 76, 131; Alice Kessler-Harris, "Social History," and Thomas C. Holt, "African- American History" in *The New American History,* ed. Eric Foner (Philadelphia: Temple University Press, 1990), 163, 212.

9. Holt, "African-American History," 211–31. The quote is on 229.

10. Gerda Lerner, "Placing Women in History: A 1975 Perspective," in Bere- nice A. Carroll, *Liberating Women's History: Theoretical and Critical Essays* (Ur- bana, Ill.: University of Illinois Press, 1976), 357–58.

11. Linda Gordon, "U.S. Women's History," in Foner, *New American His- tory,* 185, 187.

12. Peter Novick, *That Noble Dream: The "Objectivity Question" and the American Historical Profession* (Cambridge: Cambridge University Press, 1988), 470, 497, 499–500, 510; Lerner quoted on 500.

13. Gordon, "U.S. Women's History," 186–87.

14. Leo Ribuffo, "God and Contemporary Politics," *Journal of American History* 79 (March, 1993), 1523. See also David W. Lotz, "A Changing Histori- ography: From Church History to Religious History," in *Altered Landscapes: Christianity in America, 1935–1985,* ed. Lotz with Donald W. Shriver, Jr., and John F. Wilson (Grand Rapids, Mich.: Eerdmans, 1989), 332–36.

15. Martin E. Marty, "American Religious History in the Eighties: A Decade of Achievement," *Church History* 62 (September, 1993): 336, 343–44, 351–53, 355, 357, 358, 361–64, 374.

16. "Born Again! The Year of the Evangelicals," *Newsweek,* October 25, 1976, 68.

17. See, for example, George Gallup, Jr., and Jim Castelli, *The People's Reli- gion: American Faith in the 90's* (New York: Macmillan, 1989), 13, 16–17, 93; Phillip E. Hammond, "Another Great Awakening?" in *The New Christian Right:*

Mobilization and Legitimation, ed. Robert C. Liebman, Robert Wuthnow (NY: Aldine Publishing Company, 1983), 207; David Edwin Harrell, Jr., *Pat Robertson: A Personal, Religious, and Political Portrait* (San Francisco: Harper & Row, Publishers, 1987), 138–39; Kenneth A. Briggs, "Evangelicals Turning to Politics Fear Moral Slide Imperils Nation," *New York Times,* August 19, 1980, D17.

18. See, for example, Richard G. Hutcheson, Jr., *God in the White House: How Religion Has Changed the Presidency* (New York: Macmillan, 1988); Richard V. Pierard, "Cacophony on Capitol Hill: Evangelical Voices in Politics," in *The Political Role of Religion in the United States,* ed. Stephen D. Johnson and Joseph B. Tamney (Boulder: Westview Press, 1986), 71–96.

19. Richard G. Hutcheson, *Mainline Churches and the Evangelicals: A Challenging Crisis?* (Atlanta: John Knox Press, 1981), 63, 66–67, 73; Liebman and Wuthnow, *The New Christian Right.*

20. For a good overview of the New Christian Right, see Michael Lienesch, *Redeeming America: Piety and Politics in the New Christian Right* (Chapel Hill: University of North Carolina Press, 1993); William Martin, *With God on Our Side: The Rise of the Religious Right in America* (New York: Bantam Doubleday Dell, 1996).

21. Fran Schumer, "A Return to Religion," *New York Times Magazine,* April 15, 1984, 90–94, 98.

22. Wade Clark Roof, "America's Voluntary Establishment: Mainline Religion in Transition," in *Religion and America: Spiritual Life in a Secular Age,* ed. Mary Douglas and Steven Tipton (Boston: Beacon Press, 1982), 131.

23. George Gallup, Jr., "50 Years of Gallup Surveys on Religion," *Gallup Report* 186 (May 1985): 4, 10, 13, 14. See also Erling Jorstad, *Holding Fast/ Pressing On: Religion in America in the 1980s* (New York: Praeger, 1990), part 3.

24. Kenneth A. Briggs, "Political Activism Reflects Churches' Search for a Role in Secular Society," *New York Times,* September 9, 1984, 17.

25. Robert Wuthnow, *The Restructuring of American Religion: Society and Faith Since World War II* (Princeton, N.J.: Princeton University Press, 1988), 4. Skepticism regarding the secularization theory began to develop as early as the 1960s, as Martin E. Marty shows in "Religion in America Since Mid-Century," in *Religion and America: Spiritual Life in a Secular Age,* Douglas and Tipton, 273–87.

26. Cox quoted in John A. Coleman, "The Revival of God" [review of Harvey Cox, *Religion in the Secular City: Toward a Postmodern Theology* (New York: Simon & Schuster, 1984)], *New York Times Book Review,* March 4, 1984, 1.

27. Lienesch, *Redeeming America,* 139. See also Pierard, "Cacophony on Capitol Hill," 71–96.

28. Mark Silk, *Spiritual Politics: Religion and America Since World War II* (New York: Simon and Schuster, 1988), 174–75.

29. Richard John Neuhaus, *The Naked Public Square: Religion and Democracy in America* (Grand Rapids, Mich.: Eerdmans, 1984), vii, 9, 18–19. See also, for an early statement of this theme, Richard John Neuhaus, "Calling a Halt to Retreat," in *Against the World For the World: The Hartford Appeal and the Future of American Religion,* ed. Peter L. Berger and Neuhaus (New York: Seabury Press), 161–62; and for later statements, Richard John Neuhaus, "From Providence to Privacy: Religion and the Redefinition of America," in *Unsecular America,* ed. Neuhaus (Grand Rapids, Mich.: Eerdmans, 1986); Richard John

Neuhaus, "Politics and the Best Thing In the World," in *America Against Itself: Moral Vision and the Public Order* (Notre Dame, Ind.: Notre Dame Press, 1992), 25–51.

30. Robert N. Bellah, Richard Madsen, William M. Sullivan, Ann Swidler, and Steven M. Tipton, *Habits of the Heart: Individualism and Commitment in American Life* (New York: Harper & Row, Publishers, 1985), 239, 246.

31. Robert N. Bellah, Richard Madsen, William M. Sullivan, Ann Swidler, and Steven M. Tipton, *The Good Society* (New York: Alfred A. Knopf, 1991), 216.

32. "Poll Says Religion Belongs in Public Life," *Christianity Today* 32 (March 4, 1988): 38, 40.

33. Os Guinness, *The American Hour: A Time of Reckoning and the Once and Future Role of Faith* (New York: Free Press, 1993), 255; see also 20–21.

34. Quoted by Richard John Neuhaus in "The Public Square: A Continuing Survey of Religion and Public Life," *First Things* (November 1993): 44–45.

35. E. J. Dionne, Jr., "Buchanan Heaps Scorn on Democrats," *Washington Post*, August 18, 1992, A18.

36. Richard John Neuhaus, editor-in-chief, to Dear Reader [September, 1993], advertisement by mail to me.

37. Guinness, *The American Hour*, part 2 (for the discussion of the controversy) and 19–20, 261 (for the quotes).

38. For three reviews of the book, see Peter L. Berger, "Who's Afraid of Religious Values?" *New York Times Book Review*, September 19, 1993, 15; Kenneth L. Woodward, "Making Room for Religion," *Newsweek*, September 20, 1993, 55, 57; Phillip E. Johnson, "The Swedish Syndrome," *First Things* (December 1993), 48–50.

39. Michael Kelly, "Saint Hillary," *New York Times Magazine*, May 23, 1993, 22, 24–25, 63–66.

40. Fred Barnes, "Rev. Bill," *New Republic*, January 3, 1994, 10–11.

41. Quoted by Robert P. Dugan, Jr., editor, *NAE Washington Insight* 16 (January 1994).

42. The impact is not limited to studies of American Protestantism. See, for example, David G. Dalin, ed., *American Jews and the Separationist Faith: The New Debate on Religion in Public Life* (Washington, D.C.: Ethics and Public Policy Center, 1993); Naomi Cohen, *Jews in Christian America: The Pursuit of Religious Equality* (New York: Oxford University Press, 1992); David O'Brien, *Public Catholicism* (New York: Macmillan, 1989); William A. Au, *The Cross, the Flag and the Bomb: American Catholics Debate War and Peace, 1960–1983* (Westport, Conn.: Greenwood Press, 1985); George Weigel and Robert Royal, eds., *Building the Free Society: Democracy, Capitalism, and Catholic Social Teaching* (Grand Rapids, Mich.: Eerdmans, 1993); Robert P. Hunt and Kenneth L. Grasso, eds., *John Courtney Murray and the American Civil Conversation* (Grand Rapids, Mich.: Eerdmans, 1992); Jay P. Dolan, "New Directions in American Catholic History," in *New Dimensions in American Religious History: Essays in Honor of Martin E. Marty*, ed. Dolan and James P. Wind (Grand Rapids, Michigan: Eerdmans Publishing Company, 1993), esp. 162–67; Patrick Allitt, *Catholic Intellectuals and Conservative Politics in America, 1950–1985* (Ithaca: Cornell University Press, 1993).

43. "The public sphere" is Jürgen Habermas's term, meaning an arena in which private citizens come together as equals to engage in "rational–critical dis-

course" regarding issues involving state authority. On Habermas, see Craig Calhoun, "Introduction: Habermas and the Public Sphere," in *Habermas and the Public Sphere*, ed. Calhoun (Cambridge, Mass.: MIT Press, 1992), 1–48. On the various terms employed by historians of religion ("the public sphere," "the public realm," "public life," "the public arena," "public church," and "public religion"), see Michael Yale Simon, "Religion and the Public Good: A Plurality of Silences," *Evangelical Studies Bulletin* 7 (Spring, 1990): 1–4; Richard J. Bernstein, "The Meaning of Public Life," in *Religion and American Public Life: Interpretations and Explorations*, ed. Robin W. Lovin (New York: Paulist Press, 1986), 29–52; Robert Wuthnow, *Christianity in the Twenty-first Century: Reflections on the Challenges Ahead* (New York: Oxford University Press, 1993), 170–71; W. L. Sachs, "Public Religion and the Crisis of American Protestantism in Japan, 1923–1940," in *New Dimensions in American Religious History*, 28.

44. A. James Reichley, *Religion in American Public Life* (Washington, D.C.: The Brookings Institution, 1985), 333–34, 336.

45. See, for example, Mark A. Noll, ed., *Religion and American Politics: From the Colonial Period to the 1980s* (New York: Oxford University Press, 1990); Richard John Neuhaus and Michael Cromartie, eds., *Piety and Politics: Evangelicals and Fundamentalists Confront the World* (Washington, D.C.: Ethics and Public Policy Center, 1987); David G. Dalin, ed., *American Jews and the Separationist Faith;* Reichley, *Religion in American Public Life;* Michael Cromartie, ed., *No Longer Exiles: The Religious New Right in American Politics* (Washington, D.C.: Ethics and Public Policy Center, 1993); Michael Cromartie, ed., *Disciples and Democracy: Religious Conservatives and the Future of American Politics* (Washington, D.C.: Ethics and Public Policy Center, 1994).

46. Harvey G. Cox, "Religious Pluralism," in *Religion in Politics,* ed. Richard McMunn (Milwaukee, Wisc.: Catholic League for Religious and Civil Rights, 1985), 101, 105.

47. Fred E. Baumann and Kenneth M. Jensen, eds., *Religion and Politics* (Charlottesville: University Press of Virginia, 1989); Reichley, *Religion in American Public Life.*

48. "Lilly Awards Grant to Study Public Expressions of Religion," *Evangelical Studies Bulletin* 8 (Fall, 1991): 5; "The Public Expression of Religion in the American Arts, April 4th–9th[,] 1994" (brochure issued by Center for the Study of Religion and American Culture, Indianapolis, January, 1994).

49. See, for example, George Gallup, Jr., "Divining the Devout: The Polls and Religious Belief," *Public Opinion* (April/May, 1981) 20, 41; Gallup, Castelli, *The People's Religion;* Liebman and Wuthnow, *The New Christian Right;* Pierard, "Cacophony on Capitol Hill," 71–96; Allen D. Hertzke, *Echoes of Discontent: Jesse Jackson, Pat Robertson, and the Resurgence of Populism* (Washington, D.C.: CQ Press, 1992); Lienesch, *Redeeming America;* Erling Jorstad, *The Politics of Moralism: The New Christian Right in American Life* (Minneapolis: Augsburg, 1981); Ted G. Jelen, ed., *Religion and Political Behavior in the United States* (New York: Praeger, 1989); Jeffrey K. Hadden and Anson Shupe, *Televangelism: Power and Politics on God's Frontier* (New York: Henry Holt and Company, 1988); Mark J. Rozell and Clyde Wilcox, eds., *God at the Grass Roots: The Christian Right in the 1994 Elections* (Lanham, Maryland: Rowan and Littlefield Publishers, Inc., 1995); Robert Booth Fowler and Allen D. Hertzke, *Religion and Politics in America: Faith, Culture, and Strategic Choices* (Boulder, Colo.: Westview Press, 1996).

50. See, for example, the books cited by Marty, "American Religious History in the Eighties," 369–70.

51. Philip R. Vandermeer and Robert P. Swierenga, eds., *Belief and Behavior: Essays in the New Religious History* (New Brunswick, NJ: Rutgers University Press, 1991), 3–4, 6. See also Robert P. Swierenga, "Ethnoreligious Political Behavior in the Mid–Nineteenth Century: Voting, Values, Cultures," in Noll, *Religion and American Politics*, 146–71.

52. Wuthnow, *Restructuring of American Religion*, 113, 114, 117.

53. James C. Hefley and Edward E. Plowman, *Washington: Christians in the Corridors of Power* (Wheaton: Tyndale House, 1975); Allen D. Hertzke, *Representing God in Washington: The Role of Religious Lobbies in the American Polity* (Knoxville: University of Tennessee Press, 1988); Allen D. Hertzke, "Faith and Access: Religious Constituencies and the Washington Elites," in Jelen, *Religion and Political Behavior in the United States.*

54. Mitchell K. Hall, *Because of Their Faith: CALCAV and Religious Opposition to the Vietnam War* (New York: Columbia University Press, 1990).

55. Donald L. Davidson, *Nuclear Weapons and the American Churches: Ethical Positions on Modern Warfare* (Boulder, Colo.: Westview Press, 1983); Anne C. Loveland, *American Evangelicals and the U.S. Military, 1942–1993* (Baton Rouge: Louisiana State University Press, 1996).

56. Andrew Michael Manis, *Southern Civil Religion in Conflict: Black and White Baptists and Civil Rights, 1947–1957* (Athens, Ga.: University of Georgia Press, 1987); James F. Findlay, Jr., *Church People in the Struggle: The National Council of Churches and the Black Freedom Movement, 1950–1970* (New York: Oxford University Press, 1993).

57. Robert Booth Fowler, *The Greening of Protestant Thought* (Chapel Hill: University of North Carolina Press, 1995); Stephen Bates, *Battleground: One Mother's Crusade, the Religious Right, and the Struggle for Control of Our Classrooms* (New York: Poseidon Press, 1993).

58. Mark Ellingsen, *The Cutting Edge: How Churches Speak on Social Issues* (Grand Rapids, Mich.: Eerdmans, 1993).

59. Wuthnow, *Christianity in the Twenty-first Century*, 179.

60. Robert Booth Fowler, *A New Engagement: Evangelical Political Thought, 1966–1976* (Grand Rapids, Mich.: Eerdmans, 1982); Robert Booth Fowler, *Unconventional Partners: Religion and Liberal Culture in the United States,* (Grand Rapids, Mich.: Eerdmans, 1989).

61. Mark Silk, *Spiritual Politics: Religion and America Since World War II* (New York: Simon & Schuster, 1988).

62. James Davison Hunter, *Culture Wars: The Struggle to Define America* (New York: Basic Books, 1991).

63. Jorstad, *Holding Fast/Pressing On*, chap. 3.

64. Johnson and Tamney, *The Political Role of Religion in the United States;* Lovin, *Religion and American Public Life.*

65. Published by Fortress Press for the Society of Biblical Literature. See, e.g., James Turner Johnson, ed., *The Bible in American Law, Politics, and Political Rhetoric* (Philadelphia, Pa.: Fortress Press, 1985).

66. Sally M. Promey, " 'Triumphant Religion' in Public Places: John Singer Sargent and the Boston Public Library Murals"; Mark G. Toulouse, "*The Christian Century* and American Public Life: The Crucial Years, 1956–1968"; and James P. Wind, "Religion and the Great American Argument about Health," in

Dolan and Wind, *New Dimensions in American Religious History*, 3–27, 44–82, 103–27.

67. Richard P. McBrien, *Caesar's Coin: Religion and Politics in America* (New York: Macmillan, 1987).

68. Garry Wills, *Under God: Religion and American Politics* (New York: Simon & Schuster, 1990), 89, 25.

69. Richard John Neuhaus, "The Public Square: A Continuing Survey of Religion and Public Life," *First Things* (December 1993), 66.

70. Neuhaus, "The Public Square" (December 1993), 66–67.

71. Wuthnow, *Christianity in the Twenty-first Century*, 140, 142, 144, 153, 155, 160, 178.

72. Vandermeer and Swierenga, *Belief and Behavior*, 3, 6.

73. Peter Novick, *That Noble Dream*, 510, 573, 584, 590, 592, quote from 573; Thomas Bender, "Making History Whole Again," *New York Times Book Review*, October 6, 1985, 1, 42, 43; Thomas Bender, "The Need for Synthesis in American History," *Journal of American History* 73 (June 1986): 120–36.

74. Bender, "Making History Whole Again," 43; see also 42.

75. Bender, "Making History Whole Again, 43.

76. Bender, "Making History Whole Again," 43, refers to the reclaiming of the public realm as an "act of recovery."